Superb. David Pogue, The Mac Street Journal

Excellent. Step-by-Step Electronic Design

Rating: A. Computer Book Review

Wonderful. Gail McGovern, MacNexus

A must-have. Sylvia Hanna, V.I.S.T.A.

Indispensable. Patrick Dewey, Booklist

Rating: 95 out of 100. Doug Miles, MacGuide

Great work! Keep it up. Jim Eason, KGO radio

The best Mac advice around. Jay Bail, The Book Reader

Witty and fascinating. A real bargain.
Macintosh Video News

A good example of a complete product.
Guy Kawasaki, The Macintosh Way

Pertinent, pithy, to-the-point. A bargain.
A-E-C Automation Newsletter

We _love_ this book and highly recommend it.
Wendy Woods, NewsBytes

Well done. Contains a lot of things I didn't know.
Andy Hertzfeld, Macintosh programming legend

It may be the only book on the Mac you'll ever need.
PD Mac Update

I loved the book! Everyone who owns a Mac should have it.
                                    Bob LeVitus, The MACazine

Interesting, amusing and enlightening. Filled with insights....Entertaining enough to read for its own sake.... [The Third Edition] is better than ever.
                                    Marion Delahan, Slightly Used Review

You come away with something useful every time you open the Bible. The book covers an amazing range of subjects, in Naiman's amusing, un-nerdy style. Just may be the resource you've prayed for.
                                    In House Graphics

Well organized and well written. If you're new to the Mac, The Macintosh Bible is an excellent reference to own.
                                    Gordon Firestein, Bay Area Mac Classifieds

Known for its opinions, trivia and amusing asides, but it's nevertheless crammed full of information. There's probably no other way to get so much information on so many Mac software packages in one place.
                                    Information Center

[An] enormous amount of information that is lucidly explained. Any school that uses Macintosh computers or any library where there will be an interest should seriously consider this book.   Kliatt Young Adult Paperback Book Guide

For readers' comments, see pages 1108–1115.
For reviews, see the back cover and the front and back of the book.

the
Macintosh
Bible
Third Edition

thousands of basic and advanced
tips, tricks and shortcuts,
logically organized and fully indexed

Sharon Zardetto Aker et al.

edited by
Arthur Naiman

Goldstein & Blair
Box 7635
Berkeley, California 94707

Additional copies of *The Macintosh Bible* are available from Goldstein & Blair, Box 7635, Berkeley CA 94707, 510/524-4000. Single copies cost $28 + $4 for shipping and tax (if any) to US addresses. (For information on other products, and shipping rates to foreign addresses, see the order pages in the back of the book.)

We offer quantity discounts to computer stores, other retailers and wholesalers (except bookstores and book wholesalers), user groups, businesses, schools and individuals. Distribution to the book trade is through Publishers Group West, Box 8843, Emeryville CA 94662, 510/658-3453 (toll-free: 800/788-3123).

Goldstein & Blair donates at least 10% of its pretax profits to organizations working for social justice.

Technical editing—Rich Wolfson, Byron Brown, John Kadyk, Chris Allen, Susan McCallister, Paul Snively, Cliff Joyce, Marty Sobin, Eric Alderman

Copy-editing and proofreading—Susan McCallister, John Kadyk, Karen Faria, Ty Koontz

Appendix B—Sherry-Ann, Women's Empowerment Project

Index—Ty Koontz

Margin icons—Thomas & Joel Friesch, Esther Travis, WetPaint, Arthur Naiman, Ken Millman

Illustrations—WetPaint, Esther Travis, Gerald Clement, Adobe, Steve Price, Byron Brown

Cover design and art—Charles Fuhrman

Inside design and cover concept—Arthur Naiman

Page layout (using PageMaker 4)—Byron Brown, Connie Torii, Chris Molé, Arthur Naiman

Fonts—text, Benguiat; tables, Optima; headers, Zapf Chancery; scripts, Courier (all from Adobe)

Printing—Michelle Selby, Consolidated Printers, Berkeley, California

Names, addresses and phone numbers are in Appendix B (if people wanted them to be).

Library of Congress Cataloging-in-Publication Data

The Macintosh bible : thousands of basic and advanced tips, tricks and shortcuts, logically organized and fully indexed / Sharon Zardetto Aker, et al. ; edited by Arthur Naiman. -- 3rd ed.
    p.   cm.
Rev. ed. of: The Macintosh bible / Dale Coleman & Arthur Naiman. c1987.
Includes index.
ISBN 0-940235-11-0 : $28.00
1. Macintosh (Computer) I. Aker, Sharon Zardetto. II. Naiman, Arthur. III. Coleman, Dale, 1951–   The Macintosh bible.
QA76.8.M3M325   1991   90-3849
005.265--dc20   CIP Rev.

Printed in the United States of America   printing #   7 8 9

This edition of The Macintosh Bible

is dedicated

with love and gratitude,

to Steven and Cheryl Blazar,

because I wrote this one sitting up

—Sharon

and to

Davida Coady, Blase Bonpane, Fred Ross

and all the other lovers of justice

who are working to prevent

the murder of innocent people.

—Arthur

Contents

*Each chapter also has a more detailed
table of contents of its own.*

Trademark notice

Because a major purpose of this book is to describe and comment on various hardware and software products, many such products are identified by their tradenames. In most—if not all—cases, these designations are claimed as legally protected trademarks by the companies that make the products. It is not our intent to use any of these names generically, and the reader is cautioned to investigate a claimed trademark before using it for any purpose except to refer to the product to which it is attached.

In particular: *Apple* and *Macintosh* are registered trademarks of Apple Computer, Inc. *The Macintosh Bible* is a trademark of Goldstein & Blair, which is not affiliated with Apple Computer, Inc.

Disclaimer

We've got to make a disclaimer that common sense requires: Although we've tried to check all the tips, tricks and shortcuts described in this book to make sure they work as described, we can't guarantee that they do. Don't try anything except on a backup file. Satisfy yourself that the technique you're trying works before using it on your valuable files.

We can't be—and aren't—responsible for any damage or loss to your data or your equipment that results directly or indirectly from your use of this book. We make no warranty, express or implied, about the contents of this book, its merchantability or its fitness for any particular purpose. The exclusion of implied warranties is not permitted by some states. The above exclusion may not apply to you. This warranty provides you specific legal rights. There may be other rights that you may have which vary from state to state.

Preface *(AN)*

Most computer books are out-of-date a few months after they're published. But not this one. To keep the information in it current, we include *free* quarterly updates in the price of the book. To get them, all you have to do is send us your name and address (it's easiest if you use the card in the back of the book, just inside the back cover).

The Macintosh Bible contains thousands of basic and advanced tips, tricks, shortcuts and product evaluations that help you get the most from your Mac. The information is logically organized and fully indexed, so it's easy to find what you're looking for.

This third edition has been *completely* revised and updated, and contains many hundreds of pages of new material. In fact, you'd have to look long and hard to find a book being published for the first time that has more completely new material in it than there is in this new edition.

The Macintosh Bible is a reference book and isn't meant to be read from beginning to end—although we keep getting letters from readers that say, "once you start reading it, you can't put it down," "as good as curling up with a good novel" and "I've read it from cover to cover—twice!"

Naturally, we'll be delighted if you have the same reaction; if not, use the table of contents and the index to dip into the book wherever you want. But first read the *Introduction* (pp. 13–15) and the section called *How to use this book* (pp. 16–19).

If you want to try out some of the best shareware and public-domain programs mentioned in the book, as well as a few things of our own devising, check out *The Macintosh Bible Software Disks, Third Edition,* described on pp. 908–11.

Acknowledgments (SZA)

The reason this book is finished with my sanity more or less intact (or at least no more in question than it was before I started) is because of all the help I received from my friends, especially at the last minute when I needed it the most:

Rich Wolfson (well, it's *Dr.* Wolfson, but he's shy about his Ph.D.)—network consultant, tech reader and general listening post at all hours; Jim Matthews, of the Kiewit Computation Center at Dartmouth—network consultant (the fact that I needed two of those is a reflection on me, not on either of them); Jerry Szubin—editorial assistant, virtuoso at two kinds of keyboards, and, lately, dance partner; Marty Sobin—Excel whiz and proud new papa; Paul Snively of Apple Computer—tech reader who even returned my calls while I was at Disney World; and Cliff Joyce of Dubl-Click Software—tech reader for the font chapter despite his own busy schedule.

Acknowledgments (AN)

The book wouldn't exist without the incredible efforts expended by Sharon Zardetto Aker on the third edition and by Dale Coleman on the first. Eric Alderman, Julie Bennett, Tom Bennett, Brad Bunnin, Allen Glazer, Paul Hoffman, Dennis Klatzkin, Don McCunn, Roxie Lum McCunn, Steve Michel, Carol Pladsen, Steve Rosenthal, Charlie Rubin and Harry Sadler offered advice whose brilliance was only surpassed by the generosity with which it was given.

I'm very grateful to all the reviewers who were kind enough to take the time to look at and comment on the book. I want to express special gratitude to the first two of those, Peter Lewis and Andy Hertzfeld, who helped get the *Mac Bible* off to a flying start (Pete Lewis interrupted his Christmas vacation to review the first edition of this book—and all just to help a struggling new publisher he'd never even met).

At Publishers Group West, Anne Brooks, Randy Fleming, Bill Hurst, Mark Ouimet, Gary Todoroff, Charlie Winton and Susan Wright keep astounding me with their monthly sales reports (a tradition I sincerely hope they'll continue). It's a real pleasure to work with people this bright. I'd also like to thank Joanna (who does the job I thought no one could—including her), Bonnie Beren, Mike Winton, Tim Powala, Paul Rooney and Paul Wiley.

The people who work (or worked) at Goldstein & Blair—Teresa Reitinger, Susan McCallister, Sherry-Ann Nichols, Sheila Sugrue, Robin Chin, Rob Corry, Natalie Lee, Michael Hengl, Moneca Neary, Karen Gilbert, Karen Faria, Judith Gibbens, John Kadyk, John Grimes, Jeremy Carrico, Jan Brenner, Diana Damonte and Allen Lau (in reverse alphabetical order by first name, for a change)—contributed to this book just as surely as the people who helped write it (not to mention the fact that several of them *did* help write it). They keep astounding me with their sales reports too.

Byron Brown did his usual terrific job of pouring the book into PageMaker and, when he had to leave for vacation, taught Connie Torii and Chris Molé to follow in his footsteps. Ty Koontz did an even more obsessively detailed index than I would have done; I consider it one of the great features of the book. Michelle Selby is the printer's rep of my dreams—knowledgeable, reliable and patient—and Jim Puzey and Howard Samarin are a pleasure to work with as well.

Bonnie Edwards and Linda Spangler listened to my endless litany of complaints with equanimity and, when appropriate, with amusement (or, in the case of Bonnie, when not appropriate).

Now for my favorite part of the acknowledgments—the exotic names club! (Who says acknowledgments have to be dull? You just have to know people with interesting names.) Nevin Pfaltzgraff showed the kind of perfectionistic attention to detail that I love. Ann Jauregui did her job with a skill that kept surprising me. Tanta Rivoli (née Rebele) provided unfailing support, as she has since time immemorial. The talented and glamorous Gloria Zarifa was a continual inspiration.

I want to tell you how all of us here at Goldstein & Blair enjoy hearing from readers. We wish we had time to answer each note personally—and not only because it would be a lot more fun than what we otherwise spend our time doing. But since there are thousands of letters, and since we seem to be in a chronic state of catastrophic overload, please accept our thanks here and believe me when I say, we *really love* your cards and letters.

I'd like to thank the following people for acts of kindness too various to specify, but which were greatly appreciated in every case: Larry Abel, Judy, Stew and Jessica Albert, Carole Alden, Jeffry Anderson (and Lisa), Eric Angress, Ray Biase, Simone Biase, Dave Brast, Hermann Bühlmann, Nenelle Bunnin, John Boeschen, Tony Bove, Margery Cantor, Michael Castleman, Raines Cohen, Steve Costa, Tom Cottingham, Lila Dargahi, Brian Davis, Rachelle DeStephens (of the Lima, Ohio DeStephens), Dan Doernberg, Ellie Dolganos, Francis Dreher, Fokko Du Cloux, Derek and Richard Dunsay, Dan Farber, Sherrin Farley, Caitlin and Vic Fisher, Matt Foley, Steve Friedman, Ruth Gendler, George at Computerland of Oakland, David Goldman, Cynthia Harriman, Larry Harrison (and Donna), Brent Heslop, Larry Jacobs, Judith Jantz, Reese Jones, David Jouris, Judy July, Chris Kafitz, Nate Kaufman, Diana Kehlmann, Ed Kelly, Art Kleiner, Chris Korich, Nancy Krompotich, Scott Kronick, Sunny Kwon, Renee Larson, Lyon Leifer, Ron Lichty, Bevin Lindell, Xenia Lisanevich, Yvette Manson, Malcolm Margolin, Court and Marling Mast, Harvey Mayes, Chuck Meyer at CJS Systems, Ken Miller, Albert and Nettie Naiman, Dave Nee of Another Change of Hobbit, Cheryl Nichols, Nick of Cody's (someday I'll learn his last name), Sandy Niemann, Guy Orcutt, Alan Orso, Harold Patterson, Marianne Petrillo, Gloria Polanski, Larry Press, Susan Quinn, Kal Rabinowitz, Phil Reese, Cheryl Rhodes, Richard at the Swiss National Tourist Office in San Francisco, Mark Richardson, Ira Rosenberg, Ed Rosenthal, Phil Russell, Tom Santos, Chris Schelling, Marty Schiffenbauer, Scott Schwartz, Moin Shaikh of Hunza Graphics, Nancy Shine, Gar Smith, Denny Smithson, David Socholitzky, Joani Spadaro, Martha Steffen, Jack Stich, Jean-Luc Szpakowski, Levi Thomas, Paul Towner, Mark Tucker, Sandy and Marcia Van Broek, Jan and Lisette van Vliet, Anne Walzer, Esther Wanning, Joe Waxman, Roy Webb, Ruth Weisberg, Malka Weitman, Barbara Wientjes and Neil Wilkinson.

As always, I'd like conclude by thanking my ophthalmologist, Rod Cohen (yes, it's a joke).

Introduction (AN)

It's a common saying that the best source of tips is the manual that comes with a product. To this is often added a mild reproach: "if only people would take the trouble to read it."

Of course manuals contain a lot of good tips. There are also a lot of needles in that haystack over there. The trick is to *find* them.

The typical manual buries its useful information beneath tons of idiotic over-simplification ("Lift your hand into the air, using your arm and shoulder muscles, and lower it onto the mouse, palm down"), ridiculous warnings ("Do NOT grasp the back of the picture tube with the power on and jump into a bathtub full of water") and unintelligible computerese (*"Guess* is an optional argument that specifies the starting value of the iteration"—this last, as you may have guessed, is a quote from a real manual).

You have better things to do with your time than read hundreds of pages of this sort of stuff every time you want to use a new product. So we've tried to do some gleaning for you.

Needless to say, this book can't cover the ground it does and still do a comprehensive job in each area (although the size of the book shows you we tried). It's inevitable that some areas will be covered more thoroughly than others. Still, within each area, we've tried to be selective and concentrate on the most useful stuff.

Product evaluations are an important part of the book but you have to take them with a grain of salt, if for no other reason than that they may be out-of-date by the time you read them. (That's what the updates are for, so be sure to send for your free copies.)

A certain amount of subjectivity is bound to creep into product evaluations; in an attempt to combat that, I've sometimes had more than one person review (or comment on) a product.

As always, it was a real crunch getting the book to the printer on time. I decided that the least important thing to put time into was getting new art to filling blank pages (and parts of pages) at the end of chapters. As a result, you'll note that some of the art is recycled from the last edition. Fortunately, it's all beautiful stuff. I'm not tired of it yet, so why should you be?

We recommend what we think are the best products, but we give you tips on the most popular, whether we like them or not. For example, I can't stand Word, but a lot of people use it, so we devote many pages to helping you get the most out of it.

Some of you who bought earlier editions of the book didn't get your updates as quickly as you should have (or at all). We really try to do a good job of that and we're always trying to do a better one (unlike the post office, which doubtless deserves at least some of the blame—since we don't have the same problem with orders, which go by UPS). Anyway, please let us know if you send in the card at the back of the book but don't get your updates.

We try to ship orders within 24 hours, and usually succeed (there's an order form in the back of the book). If you have any problem with anything you order from us, or simply don't like it, please take advantage of our money-back guarantee (just return the product in resellable condition within 30 days). We want you to be totally satisfied in your dealings with us.

Throughout this book, I have some rather uncomplimentary things to say about the user-sadistic, brain-dead interface of MS DOS and of most PC programs. Please understand that I don't mean to be denigrating PC's (which are usually better values than Macs) or PC users (who often do the sensible thing by working on PC's instead of Macs).

I'm simply against the primitiveness of the typical PC user interface (and even that's been fixed, to some extent, by Windows 3). I'm just trying to promote computers that are really fun to use, not side with one computer manufacturer (or user) against another.

Far be it from me to complain about success. But there's a (small but significant) downside to having a book as successful as *The Macintosh Bible,* and part of that is the knock-off artists it attracts. One Japanese publisher was going to call a completely unrelated book *The Macintosh Bible,* to compete with the actual *Macintosh Bible,* which was being translated at the same time by another

Japanese publisher (as they well knew, since we'd offered the translation rights to them too).

I sent them a draft of a proposed press release that began with the words: *Although the Macintosh community is, for the most part, mercifully free of sleazeballs,* and they suddenly decided that it might be in their best interests to call their book something else. The Japanese translation of the (real) *Macintosh Bible* came out and is now a best-seller there, having gone through five printings in less than a year.

Will that technique work on Americans? Probably not. The largest religious publisher in the United States, Zondervan (owned by Harper & Row, which is owned in turn by Rupert Murdoch) has for a long time offered the Holy Bible on disk. Their original name for the product was quite clever, I thought—they called it *The WORD Processor.*

But that name apparently lacked something in Zondervan's eyes, so they changed it to *The PerfectWORD.* Word Perfect Corporation naturally thought there was a problem there; their lawyers told Zondervan to cut it out, and Zondervan did, changing the name of the Mac version of the product to—you can see it coming, can't you?—*macBible.*

Although everyone, including ourselves, refers to the book you're reading familiarly as "the Mac Bible," and although it occasionally gets shelved in the religious section of bookstores, Zondervan's lawyer tells us there's no danger of confusion. Why? Well, for one thing, we capitalize *Macintosh* and they don't capitalize *mac.*

Can you believe this? I'm bringing out a new soft drink called *koka kola.* No danger of confusion there—not only did I use lowercase letters, I changed the *c*'s to *k*'s. I'm not even using a hyphen. I'm going to have Zondervan's lawyer represent me when Coca-Cola brings suit.

Anyway, it looks like Zondervan won't change the name unless we sue them. Isn't it ironic? I just wish these guys spent more time *reading* the Bible and less time *marketing* it.

How to use this book (AN)

This book covers a wide range of subjects and a wide range of Mac experience. No matter how much or how little you know, there will be stuff in here that's either too easy or too hard for you. So just skip over the stuff that obviously isn't meant for you—there'll be plenty that is.

Margin icons are one way we help you find items you're likely to be interested in. There are eleven of them:

esp. for beginners

If you're new to the Mac, it might make sense for you to check out all of these entries first. (They're listed in the index.) Unlike other icons, this one usually refers to a whole page or entry, rather than just to a single paragraph.

esp. for power users

At the other extreme, these entries are for people who eat RAM chips for breakfast.

very hot tip

All our tips are hot, but these are particularly hot.

shortcut

Isn't that a beautiful icon? It comes from the WetPaint clip art collection.

very good feature

We're critical enough when that's what's called for, so we like to also give credit where credit is due.

very bad feature

These two icons are a subtle plug for left-handers.

Bugs are mistakes, or unexpected occurrences, as opposed to things that are intentional (they get the previous icon).

bug

We use this icon to indicate particularly good values.

bargain

This icon is pretty self-explanatory.

important warning

Nobody can predict the future, but we try.

things to come

This icon is for stuff that's more interesting than useful. Look for it when you need a break.

gossip/ trivia

The table of contents at the start of the book tells you the general area each chapter covers; in addition, each chapter has a more detailed table of contents of its own, facing the first page of text.

The index was compiled by master indexer Ty Koontz. It's 90 pages long, in two columns (and that's reducing the type one point from the rest of the book; if we'd used the same size type, it would have been well over 100 pages). That's all by way of saying that it's a *real* index, not one of those imitation ones that's there just so the publisher can say the book has one. You can really *find* things in our index.

Appendix A is a 68-page glossary of Macintosh terms. Don't say, "Oh, yeah, a glossary, OK." We worked *very* hard to make it as useful and complete as possible. If you run across a term you're not sure of, that's the place to look it up (although we try to define terms in context as well).

Appendix B lists addresses and phone numbers for the products, companies and Mac experts mentioned in the book (or who contributed to it one way or the other—except those who didn't want to be listed).

Except for the first chapter and the appendices, the book is made up of *entries* whose titles look like this: **⌘ *entry title*.** They're grouped into sections, whose titles look like the one at the top of page 16.

A single entry may contain several tips, or just background information. In general, entries are meant to stand on their own—although I've grouped them into subject areas within the sections, and have also put them into logical order wherever possible. I've tried to place the more basic entries toward the start of each section, but sometimes grouping by topic made this difficult.

The name or initials of whoever wrote the initial draft for each entry appears in parentheses after its title (for who's who, see *Notes on contributors* on pp. 20–22). All unsigned entries were written by Sharon Zardetto Aker (occasionally her entries are signed too, when that helps make things clearer).

When I add a comment to someone else's entry, it's in italics, enclosed in square brackets and signed *AN.* Comments by Sharon (or by other contributors) follow the same format.

Regardless of who wrote the original drafts, I rewrote them with a very heavy hand, to try to make the whole book speak with one voice (mine—for better or worse). So if something's incorrect (and isn't a typo), it's the fault of the person whose name or initials follow the entry title (myself included). But if something's *unclear,* it's my fault, regardless of whose name or initials appear there. Naturally except but other than whether not it be—oh my God, I'm doing it already. (If the jokes aren't funny, that's my fault too.)

When we refer to a key combination like ⌘W , we usually use the capital letter—which is how the keys are labeled on the keyboard. But you don't actually need to press the Shift key unless we specifically indicate that you do: Shift ⌘ W. (Sometimes we show a key with both the shifted and unshifted characters on it:)₀. We do that to make sure you know we're referring to, say, the zero key (as in this case) and not the letter *O*.)

We use those symbols throughout the book to make it easier for you to enter key combinations. When doing that, we always list them in the order shown above (which is how the keys are arranged on Apple's standard ADB keyboard)—so you don't sometimes see Option ⌘ A and sometimes ⌘ Option A (except when a contributor prepared a diagram the other way). This also makes it easier for you to put your fingers down on the keys left to right as you read a command.

One other note about keys: the ⌘ key, which was originally called things like *cloverleaf* and *pretzel*, is now always called by its official name, the *command* key. Some third-party keyboards simply label the command key with the word *command* and don't even put the ⌘ symbol on it. *O tempora! O mores!* (Who says computer books can't be literate?)

Since it isn't our job to sell the stock of computer companies, we usually refer to programs the way people do when talking—as *Word* instead of *Microsoft Word*, for example. And we generally leave version numbers off—*FileMaker*, for example, instead of *FileMaker II* (except when we're referring to a specific version)—since that's also what people do when talking.

Prices, when shown, are just to give you a *very* general idea of what things cost, at list. Prices change rapidly and discounts are almost always available, so don't rely on the prices we quote. Since this book is written for people with IQs in *three* figures, all prices are rounded up ("Oh, it's only $995? What a relief! I thought I was going to have spend at least a thousand dollars.").

Notes on contributors (AN)

Three of us wrote enough of this book that repeating our names at the beginning of each of our entries would quickly have become tedious. Instead, we've used our initials, as indicated below. Notes on other significant contributors follow. You'll find contact info (for those who want to be contacted) in Appendix B.

SZA—Sharon Zardetto Aker is the principal author of this edition of *The Macintosh Bible;* all unsigned entries were written by her. Depending on when you read this, she's either working on, has just finished, or has retired on the royalties from her eighth book, *The Macintosh Bible Guide to SuperPaint.*

DC—Dale Coleman is Editor-at-Large at *MacWEEK* and is currently working on a book about an unannounced word processing program. He was the principal author of the first edition of *The Macintosh Bible.*

AN—Arthur Naiman has edited, published and contributed to all three editions of *The Macintosh Bible.* His twelve books—eleven of which are about personal computers—have sold almost a million copies.

Carol Aiton claims to be living proof that a Macintosh computer can make even a "Mac mouse" like her into a character in the Bible.

Eric Alderman is a senior partner with the HyperMedia Group, a custom hypermedia software development company in Emeryville, California. He's the author of several computer books, and of numerous articles and columns.

Chris Allen is president of Consensus Development, a software development and consulting firm. He's also forum leader of the Mac Developers Forum on America Online and a freelance writer for Macintosh publications.

Michael Bradley has been a technical writer since 1982. Before that he was everything from a carpenter to a video producer. He's also active in the National Writer's Union.

Byron Brown is a freelance desktop publisher who's been typesetting from his various Macs since 1985. He did the page layout for the last two editions of *The Macintosh Bible*, as well as other books, magazines, brochures and manuals.

Brad Bunnin is an attorney who restricts his practice to literary law. He's the principal author of *The Writer's Legal Companion.*

Karen Faria had her first Mac attack at Goldstein & Blair in 1988. She's been working with Macs ever since, focussing on using them effectively in business.

Paul Hoffman is the author of many popular computer books, including *Microsoft Word Made Easy—Macintosh Edition*. He's also News Editor at *MicroTimes*.

John Kadyk is the *nom de plume* of Jean-Christophe, le duc de Cadique, the internationally known steel drummer, bicyclist and sometime Mac manager at Goldstein & Blair.

Susan McCallister taught reading, writing and math to adults for fifteen years, using Macintoshes for the last five. She now works at Goldstein & Blair and has lost count of how many hats she wears there.

Steve Michel is the author of *HyperCard: The Complete Reference, IBM PC and Macintosh Networking* and *Steve Michel's Super-Card Handbook*. He writes the StackWEEK column in MacWEEK.

Larry Pina is a software developer and technical writer living in Westport, Massachusetts. He's the author of *Macintosh Repair and Upgrade Secrets* and *Macintosh Printer Secrets.*

Charles Rubin, an Oakland-based writer and consultant, is the author of nine books, the most recent of which is *The Macintosh Bible "What Do I Do Now?" Book.*

Dr. **Steven Schwartz** is a computer-industry writer and gaming consultant. He currently writes for *Macworld* and is the author of a series of Nintendo books.

Marty Sobin provides Excel training and consulting when he isn't studying the stock market, playing squash or looking for collectible cookie jars.

Rich Wolfson pilots a plane, races go-karts, skydives, skin-dives and flies stunt kites. He's also a college professor, which is what gives him time for everything else.

C.J. Weigand is editor and publisher of *The Weigand Report: The Working Newsletter for Macintosh Professionals.* He's an independent Macintosh consultant and a popular speaker at trade shows.

Chapter 1

General principles

The Ten Commandments (AN)

I. This is the Mac. It's *supposed* to be fun.

For years, most businesspeople treated the Mac as a toy, while those of us who'd already had a bellyful of the deranged command structure of more primitive computers romped happily in the fields of Macintosh. Now that the Mac has gotten some corporate acceptance, there seems to be a campaign on to make it as dull as the IBM PC. What a great idea!

The rigid dichotomy between work and fun—and the acceptance of that dichotomy as inevitable and necessary—is, to quote Dr. "Happy" Harry Cox, "Old Age thinking." More clearly than any other computer, the Mac demonstrates that aesthetics enhance, rather than detract from, efficient work.

So don't let them turn the Mac into an expensive version of the PC. Demand fun as your birthright!

II. Easy is hard.

There's a macho attitude among some computer jocks (although certainly not among the best of them) that the harder something is to deal with, the more advanced it is. That's what usually lies behind the absurd idea that the PC is a more powerful machine than the Mac.

Actually, of course, it's very hard to make things easy. The more work you put into something, the less work the person who uses it has to do.

So if you find yourself beating your head against a wall erected by someone's laziness (or greed), look around for a different wall that someone else took the trouble to put a door in. And if anybody mocks what you're using as a toy, just smile and say, "Easy is powerful. Hard is primitive."

III. It's not your fault you're confused.

Over the years, manuals have gotten better and programs are designed more sensibly than they used to be, but that's a little like saying how much nicer Himmler has been since his lobotomy. The standard is still abysmally low.

very hot tip

Often the problem is expertosis (the inability of experts in a given field to remember what it's like not to be an expert). Sometimes it's simple money-grubbing. In any case, the thing to remember is this: If you're confused, it's not because you're stupid—it's because the people who designed that product, or wrote that manual, or rushed their employees so they couldn't do a good job, are stupid. Just make sure they, not you, pay for it.

IV. You can't do it all.

Some experienced Mac users can make you feel like a loser because you're not up on the new products and techniques they're always discovering. But it's really just that you have different interests. Theirs is exploring the Mac and yours (if you're like most people) is simply using it.

Each approach has its virtues and neither is inherently superior to the other. So feel free to restrict yourself to a small number of Mac programs that you master and use intensively.

Remember—you can't do it all and, unless you're a Mac fanatic, you shouldn't even try.

𝔙. 𝔐ake the 𝔐ac your own.

There's never been a computer you could, as Omar put it, mold *"nearer to the heart's desire." So give yourself time to customize it. Find the software you like best. Spend hours rearranging the Desktop or the files on your disks. The more the Mac feels like your own creation, the more efficient and enjoyable your work on it will be.*

Think of the Mac as your home. You wouldn't try to move every different piece of furniture in the world into it, just because you could. You have furniture you feel comfortable with, appliances you need and use, decorations and toys that amuse you. Treat your Mac the same way.

𝔙𝔍. 𝔄 file saved is a file saved.

What shall it profit you if you create the greatest piece of work in the world but lose it because you forgot to save?

important warning

Despite how wonderfully easy it is to use, the Mac has as many traps and pitfalls as any other computer—maybe more. These don't have to be a problem, if you save your work! Of course it's a pain and interrupts the flow of your thoughts, but that's nothing compared to what it feels like to lose work.

People are always telling you to save, as if it mattered to them. It's too bad saving has acquired this taint of moralism. Saving your work isn't something you should do because some authority tells you to. The appeal here is pure pleasure principle—you'll be a lot happier if you get in the habit.

VII. Two, three, many backups.

important warning

Saving is only half the battle. Disks crash all the time. If you don't make regular backups, you may as well not save your work at all.

VIII. Combat the tragedy of the commons.

In English villages, the "commons" was (or is) a piece of land on which everyone can graze livestock. (That's what the Boston Commons originally was.)

It's clearly in each villager's individual interest to graze as many head of, say, sheep on the commons as he or she can. And yet if all the villagers follow their own best interest, the common gets grazed bare and all the sheep starve. This is called "the tragedy of the commons."

The solution, of course, is simple: limit the number of sheep each villager can graze (hopefully in some sort of equitable way). But that can be hard to enforce since, even when a quota exists, it's <u>still</u> in each villager's individual interest to graze as many sheep as possible on the commons. It requires some social and environmental consciousness on the part of all the villagers, some long-range, unselfish thinking, to avoid the ecological tragedy.

Just the same thing is true on the Mac. It's no big deal if one person doesn't pay for a shareware program, but if a lot of people don't, good shareware stops getting written. It's no big deal if one person copies a commercial program and uses it for free, but if a lot of people do that, software developers have trouble making money and start cutting corners. In both cases, slowly but surely, the commons becomes a barren patch of dirt.

IX. Allow for Murphy's Law (since you can't avoid it).

Here's a piece of trivia few people know—the origin of Murphy's Law. In 1949, Captain Ed Murphy was an engineer working at Edwards Air Force Base in California. When a technician working in his lab miswired something, Murphy said, "If there's any way to do it wrong, he will." A co-worker of his, George E. Nichols, dubbed this Murphy's Law.

Murphy's Law has evolved into, "If anything can go wrong, it will," but it's interesting to note that it originally referred to incompetence, not to some sort of impersonal malevolence on the part of the cosmos.

gossip/ trivia

Here's the clincher—that anecdote itself is an example of Murphy's Law. After I published it in the last edition, I got a letter from Duane Olesen of Houston, who wrote:

"Your story about Captain Ed Murphy may be accurate, but it was not the first use of the expression. Way back in 1946... the term was already in use. As a matter of fact, we had a kid in my class [in the Navy] who had the misfortune to have the name Murphy. Whenever something went wrong, he was automatically blamed....

"Later, in 1948, when I started college, the Dean of Engineering asked a group of us freshmen if we had heard of Murphy's Law. Most us that had been in the service knew about it."

You know, maybe <u>any</u> explanation of the origins of Murphy's Law is bound to be wrong, just by the nature of what it's explaining. We could call this Murphy's Meta-Law.

In any case, things certainly do go wrong with distressing regularity. This happens less on the Mac than elsewhere, thanks to the care and dedication of its original designers. In fact, the

Mac's ease of use can lull you into the dangerous delusion that Murphy's Law has been banished from its realm.

important warning

No sooner do you assume this than reality disabuses you of the notion—usually more abruptly than you'd like. It works sort of like the Greek concept of hubris: Pride—or, in this case, complaisance—goeth before a fall.

X. That goes double for Sturgeon's Law.

In the late 50's, Theodore Sturgeon (1918–85) wrote a book-review column for a magazine called Venture Science Fiction. It was there he first enunciated Sturgeon's Law. "It's well known," he wrote (I'm paraphrasing), "that 90% of all science-fiction writing is crap. But then, 90% of underlineeverything is crap."

When I first started writing about computers, I wasted a lot of time railing at some of the more wretched products popular back then, and at the brain-damaged ways they went about things. Today, you hardly ever hear their names. (In Bach's day, Hasse's music was more popular than Bach's. You remember Hasse, right?)

Natural selection is going on at a blinding pace in this field, so just find some good stuff, use it until something better comes along and forget about the rest.

The trick, of course, is finding the good stuff. That's one of the things this book is designed to help you do. So stop browsing and buy it already. (This is the famous Lost Eleventh Commandment.)

Hardware buying tips (AN)

The extent to which computers are sold like cars never ceases to amaze me. But then, the extent to which cars are sold like cologne never ceases to amaze me.

Hard disk manufacturers advertise access times as if a millisecond or two is going to make a difference to the average user (not to mention the fact that access time is seldom the main determinant of how fast a hard disk is). It's like choosing a car because it has a top speed of 125 instead of 120.

The three most important things to look for in a piece of computer hardware, as with a car, are whether it can do what you want it to, how reliable it is and (with a nod to Commandment IX above) how easy it is to get it fixed.

One way to maximize your chances of getting a reliable (and repairable) piece of hardware is to buy from a company with a commitment to quality. Granted, that commitment can evaporate like the morning dew—and has, many times—but you *still* stand a better chance from a company that's had it in the past than one that hasn't.

It's astounding how little some companies care about their customers. I could give you several examples of this, but it doesn't seem fair to single out just a few companies when there are so many bad ones.

If you do get screwed, don't waste a lot of time writing long letters. If people don't treat you decently, it's usually because they *aren't* decent, and your heart-wrenching appeals are going to fall on deaf ears and hearts of stone.

*very
hot
tip*

Make a few, good-faith efforts to get them to do what they're supposed to, then go *directly* to Small Claims Court. (*DO NOT PASS GO. DO COLLECT $200+.*) Marshals seizing their office equipment—that's the kind of thing these companies understand. (For how to do it, see *Everybody's Guide to Small Claims Court* from Nolo Press.)

On the bright side, there are a lot of excellent, caring, moral manufacturers out there, but if I were to start listing them, I'd be sure to leave some out, and some of the ones I did list would be sure to go sour before the next edition of the book (as happened last time, when I did name specific companies). I can, however, give you some general guidelines:

First, look for a good long warranty. Apple finally gave in and went from its embarrassing 90-day warranty to one year. A year is the shortest warranty you should consider for any product you buy; there are lots of companies that offer two-year, or even five-year, warranties. (Of course these companies may not be around in five years, or even two, and that's definitely something else to consider.)

Another important consideration is good support. You want to buy from a vendor that will answer any questions and deal with any problems that come up, and that will make you feel like a colleague, not an annoying pest, while doing so.

bargain

We've had great experiences at Goldstein & Blair with Alliance Peripheral Systems of Independence, Missouri. Because their prices are usually the lowest around, we've bought several Quantum hard drives from them.

very good feature

One drive we reshipped to an employee who works in an outlying office. Although the drive worked at our office, it was broken when it got to her. She called APS and was immediately impressed by their competence on the phone. She was even more impressed with their service: in spite of the fact that we had reshipped the drive, they sent her a replacement drive *overnight, at no cost.* The morning after she called, she had the new drive.

APS didn't even ask her to return the old drive until she got the new one. (I should mention that the people she dealt with at APS had no idea who we were or that they could get some good publicity out of this. They thought we were just another customer.)

MacConnection keeps blowing people's socks off with the speed with which they ship orders. ComputerWare has a reputation for being very knowledgeable and great to deal with.

very good feature

We know there are a lot of other great sources for products out there. If you'll send us your experiences about them, good or bad, to the attention of Karen Faria, we'll try to incorporate them into the next edition.

Last—but not, needless to say, least—is price. How important it is depends on your budget, of course, but let me say this: Don't underestimate the Mac's importance in your life. This is not some trivial plaything—this is a very powerful tool for personal expression.

If you *want* something—a laser printer instead of a dot-matrix printer, say, or a Mac II instead of an SE—you'll usually be happier if you figure out some way to justify having it. I've seldom if ever heard anyone say, "I really shouldn't have bought this *(expensive piece of computer equipment)*. I really could have gotten by with *(something simpler and less expensive)*." But I can't count the number of times I've heard people who've gotten some powerful new piece of hardware say, "How did I live without this?"

On the other hand, don't buy something you plan to grow into; by the time you grow into it, you'll be able to buy something better for less. There's one exception to this rule: If you're about to buy your first hard disk, get twice as much capacity as you think you'll need. You'll fill it up before you know it.

very hot tip

(Since I first wrote that, I've discovered that there's an exception to the exception. After struggling with hard disk whose capacity was a mere 144 megs, having to constantly clean up the disk to make room for more files—the chapters of this book in PageMaker take up a *lot* of room— I bought a 300-meg hard disk. I've owned it a year and I've still filled up less than 170 megs of it—and I've hardly deleted any files (who needs to?). So once you get into the stratosphere, it is possible to actually get more hard disk than you need. But it ain't easy.)

Because computer technology is still on the steep upslope of its growth curve, technological advances that provide more power for less money have—so far—always greatly outstripped increasing material and labor costs. Sometimes prices go down a lot and sometimes they go down a little, but they almost always go down.

Because of that, people will sometimes advise you to wait and buy later, when whatever you're buying will cost you less. This advice doesn't always make sense. For one thing, if you followed it faithfully, you'd never buy anything. For another, it fails to consider the value of owning and using the equipment, which, in my experience, has almost always outweighed whatever money I might have saved waiting for tomorrow's lower price.

So, if you have a use for something right now, and you *want* it, do without the new car—the Mac is more fun.

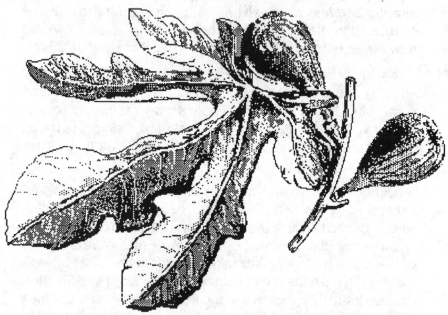

Software buying tips *(AN)*

This book is filled with specific evaluations and comparisons of Mac programs. What follows here are some general guidelines on what to look for and avoid.

Ease of use

Most software—with its impenetrable manuals, commands reminiscent of Shriners' initiation rites and what Michael Ward calls "unpleasant surprises"—isn't worth the trouble it takes to learn it.

One of the major reasons people buy the Mac is to avoid all that intimidating, user-hostile gobbledygook. Fortunately, most companies that publish software for the Mac seem to realize that. But not all. Some let their programmers' bizarre thinking mold the final product and others let dollar-crazed marketing executives make the decisions.

You shouldn't have to put up with any of that, so *don't*— not even for a second. The Mac is an inherently easy-to-use machine. If you find yourself having *any trouble at all* learning how to use a program for the Mac, stop wasting your time and find another program that doesn't give you the same trouble.

very
hot
tip

Logical hierarchy of commands

For software to be easy to use, it should be hierarchically organized. This means that most basic operations are simple and central to how the program works and the more advanced operations are off to the side, so you don't even know about them until you need them.

Mac software should be Mac-like

Aside from being easy-to-use, the Mac's interface has another major virtue: you don't have to learn a new set of commands and procedures for each program. At least you *shouldn't* have to.

very good
feature

Fortunately, most Mac programs have all the standard Mac features: pop-down menus, icons, windows, a mouse-controlled pointer, dialog boxes and buttons, scroll bars, cut-and-paste, etc. Some also have an *Undo* command (and the more circumstances it works in, and the more steps it can take you backward, the better). But other programs have simply been converted slap-dash from a version that runs on inferior computers like the PC and these should be avoided.

There is a third category, however—programs that take advantage of the Mac's features but do so in a nonstandard way. Whether you like one of these programs or not depends on whether you find the features it offers spiffy enough to justify switching gears between it and other Mac programs (and hitting a lot of wrong keys in the process).

You won't get consistency, so settle for customizability

Although the commands in Mac software are much more standardized between programs than those on the PC, they're still nowhere near as standardized as they should be. One thing that really irks me is the lack of consistency around the commands for boldface, italics and plain text.

very bad feature

On most programs (including the ones I learned on), you get italics with [⌘][I] and boldface with [⌘][B]. But in Word and PageMaker, you have to hit [⌘][Shift][I] and [⌘][Shift][B]. Even worse is the command for plain text (that is, stripping out italics, boldface and all other type styles). In the original MacWrite, it was [⌘][P]; in MacWrite II, it's [⌘][T]; in Works I, it was [⌘][N]; in Word, it's [⌘][Shift][Z]; and in PageMaker, it's [⌘][Shift][Spacebar].

Does this lead to frustrating typing mistakes? Is the Pope Catholic? Do presidents tell lies?

very good feature

Since there are lots of people who are now very used to lots of different commands, true Macintosh consistency is a lost cause. What you can get instead (and which is almost as good) is the ability to change a program's commands to what you want them to be. Now that I've done that with Word, I can actually use the program without screaming every five minutes.

Unfortunately, one program I use isn't customizable— PageMaker. If that damned Indents/Tabs dialog box pops up just one more time when I hit ⌘ I to get italics, I'll go berserk. (Wait a minute—I'm *already* berserk. Hmmmm....)

very bad feature

If you can, deal with the best

The best program isn't always the most expensive, although it usually isn't the cheapest (if it is, jump on it). And, of course, it often isn't easy to know which program is the best. But if you have a pretty good idea, don't tell yourself, "Well, I really can't afford that," or "I can get by with less."

This is almost always a false economy, as we all know from our experience of buying junky products that soon fall apart. You end up not only having to pay to replace the defective product (or program), but you also lose the time you've invested installing (or learning to use) the first one. So bite the bullet and get the best to start with—if you can figure out which it is.

If there's a standard program, you probably want it

In certain areas, one piece of software has more or less become the standard. When this happens, it makes sense to get that program. But watch out for false, or premature, standards. Don't be lured into getting a program until it's clearly a standard (or is just what you want anyway).

Make sure there are plenty of doors and windows

Here's something a two-year-old could figure out. When you buy a program, you don't know if you're going to want to use it always for everything. Even if you do, you're going to need to convert files created in other programs.

So the most elementary logic tells you that if you hope to succeed selling a Mac program, it needs to *import* documents from other Mac programs and *export* documents to them. And this is particularly true if you're hoping to break into a market dominated by a competing product.

If there was ever a category of software dominated by one product, it was (and is) Mac spreadsheets. Excel had 85–90% of the market when a slick new spreadsheet called Wingz tried to challenge it. Wingz' publisher lavished (what looked like) millions of dollars promoting the product before it came out.

very bad feature

I couldn't wait to see what Wingz' powerful graphics capabilities could do for my tired old Excel spreadsheets. So as soon as I got Wingz, I tore open the package, flipped the manual open to the index and looked up *import* (or *importing,* or *importing data).* No entry. So I looked up *data, importing.* No entry. So I looked up *Excel.* No entry. So I looked up *foreign files.* No entry. So I looked up to the sky, shook my head, thought about how many Excel spreadsheets I use in an ongoing way and am not about to redo, and tossed Wingz back into the box.

(By the way, it wasn't just the index. Wingz had no way to directly import Excel files.)

This would be pathetic if it were the story of one publisher. But it's the story of dozens. They act as if their product is the only one around, the only one their potential customers have ever—or will ever—come in contact with. Connecting with other software seems like some sort of treason to them. It's almost like xenophobia, but what I really think it is, is stupidophilia.

Speed

As many people have learned to their sorrow, ease of use isn't everything. How fast a program runs can be even more important. Unfortunately, that's seldom mentioned in ads or by salesclerks and it's one of the hardest things to evaluate in an in-store tryout.

But delays of even a few seconds can be very annoying if you keep running into them. Because of that, speed is one of the prime things to look for in a program. Many computer novices tend to ignore this consideration—since doing something on a computer is always so much faster than doing it by hand. But, believe me now or believe me later, if you buy a slow program, you'll live to regret it. (Steve Michel says no one *ever* realizes this; they just go for the power.)

very
hot
tip

You want a great manual you don't need

No matter how great a program is, it doesn't do you any good unless you know how to use it. Mac software should be so clear, its menu commands so understandable, that you don't even need a manual. If you *do* need a manual, at least it should be a good one.

Ironically (but predictably), the easiest programs to learn tend to have the best manuals and the hardest programs to learn tend to have the worst manuals.

A manual should have an index, not an imitation of one

I don't know about you, but I'd rather have all my teeth removed without anesthetic than follow the tutorial in most manuals. They're the equivalent of being strapped into a chair and forced to listen to scales for three months, then *Three Blind Mice*, then *Twinkle, Twinkle, Little Star*, then Lawrence Welk—all under the guise of teaching you music appreciation.

very bad
feature

All I want from a manual is a good index, so I can look up what I need to and get out of there. Unfortunately, the only purpose most indexes serve is to allow the company whose manual it is to say, "Look! An index!" And it's true—they do *look* like indexes. Why should I spoil the illusion by pointing out that you can never *find* anything in them?

Take reviews (including ours) with a grain of salt

One problem with reviews is that most reviewers aren't like most users. They tend to have much more experience

important
warning

with Mac programs and to be much more interested in exploring the Mac as an activity in itself. (I call this tendency *expertosis;* it also causes a problem with manuals.)

Another problem is that reviewers seldom have enough time to really get to know the ins and outs of the software they're evaluating. Lots of programs are complicated enough that you don't really get a feeling for their strengths and weaknesses until you've used them fairly heavily for a couple of months.

A third problem is that magazines are supported by advertising revenues, and while I'm always surprised by how tough they're willing to be in spite of that fact, no magazine's reviews are going to be, on the average, 75% or even 50% negative.

Still, reviews are a great place to learn about products. Just don't treat them as the holy gospel—even when they appear in the Bible. (In fact, especially when they appear in the Bible. Magazines can afford to do a much more comprehensive and thorough job of evaluating whole classes of products. All we can do is give you the opinions of an expert or two, or—at best—what the general consensus is among the Mac experts we know.)

Shareware is worth trying

esp. for beginners

To be absolutely sure you're going to want a program before you buy it, you need to use it for some reasonable period of time. The best way to do that is *shareware*— software you're allowed to copy freely and only pay for if you like it and continue to use it. As you'll discover from reading this book, some of the best Mac programs are shareware.

bargain

In order to encourage this proconsumer approach to software distribution, always give shareware a try before spending money for a commercial program that does the same thing, and *always* pay for any shareware you end up keeping and using.

If you don't, the people who write it will have to find some other way to make a living and will no longer be able to update their programs or create new ones. In the short run, you'll save a little money; in the long run, you'll lose a lot, as you end up paying more for programs you're not even sure you'll use, because no good shareware alternatives are available.

important
warning

Public-domain software

Lots of programs are available absolutely free, thanks to the generosity of their authors. You can get this software from good computer stores (if you've done business with them), user groups or bulletin boards. You often have to put up with skimpy documentation, or none at all, and early versions of most programs have bugs. But there's a lot of terrific public-domain software, some of it better than commercial programs.

bargain

(You can get a sampling of great Mac shareware and public-domain software on *The Macintosh Bible Software Disks,* which have a money-back guarantee. See the last chapter for details.)

In-store tryouts

Any decent computer store will let you sit and play with software for hours at a time, as long as no one else wants to use the machine (unfortunately, someone almost always will). Trying a program in a store will often (but not always) give you enough of a feeling for it to decide if you want to buy it.

Money-back guarantees

If you're buying a program mail order and sight unseen, try to get a money-back guarantee. Remember—a lot of software isn't worth using, no matter how good it sounds.

important
warning

Support, support, support

There's a saying in real estate that the three most important things to consider when buying property are

very hot tip

location, location and location. Likewise, the three most important things to consider when buying a computer product are *support, support and support.* (Support is the availability of someone to answer your questions, usually on the phone, and to fix things if they go wrong.)

Support is the reason it often makes sense to pay a little more to buy from a vendor whose staff knows something (whether it's a local store or a mail-order distributor). Don't imagine you can depend on the publisher's telephone support line. Although there are some exceptions, most of them are so understaffed that you might as well just play a tape recording of a busy signal and not tie up your phone.

Claris's telephone support is the best we've ever encountered from a large, established company (and that was true even when they didn't realize that we review Mac products). Other people we've talked to have had the same good experience with Claris. The only problem we found with their support was having to wait too long on the phone before someone could take our call, but once we got through, they were very helpful.

Don't use a bazooka to kill a fly

very hot tip

You should use a computer to do things you can't do more easily in some other way (with pencil and paper, for example). The Mac can't make you organized or creative (although it can certainly help you organize and create).

Thou shalt not steal

In the case of some programs, there are more illegal copies in existence than legal ones. (Not that this is always bad for the publisher. WordStar became an industry-standard word processing program at least partly because so many people had bootleg copies of it.)

Most of the problem is that people give copies to their friends; few computer hackers are despicable enough to steal someone else's work and then *sell* it. Still, the average program represents many person-years of labor, and you can't blame a publisher for wanting to protect that investment.

As a result, most Mac software used to be *copy-protected.* (There are many ways to make it difficult to copy a disk and no way to make it impossible, so it becomes a question of percentages: "How many hackers can we outsmart.")

important warning

Copy-protection was a real drag and virtually all Mac software publishers have stopped doing it. This puts the burden on us. If people can't make money developing software because everyone is stealing their software instead of buying it, soon there won't be any good programs at all. (I know I'm repeating myself. This bears repeating.)

Beware of vaporware

So much software has been promised that never saw the light of day (or saw it on a day many months after it was supposed to) that there's even a name for it—*vaporware.*

important warning

So when some salesclerk (or ad, or friend) tells you that a new product will be along "real soon now," don't depend on it. Few computer products come out on time, and lots of software ends up being nothing more than vaporware.

Don't pay to be a beta tester

When software publishers get a product to a certain stage, they hand out copies to people on the outside and ask them to test it. This work, called *beta testing,* is almost always unpaid; the testers are motivated by the advantage (or prestige) of being the first to know about something.

esp. for beginners

That's all fine, but don't *pay* to beta-test a product that's already been released. Vaporware is bad enough, but it's much worse to spend your good money on a product that's full of bugs.

So wait a while when a new product comes out. Go to a user group meeting or two and see if anyone's having problems with it. If you telecommunicate, ask about it on a

important warning

bulletin board. Remember: feeling impatient is a lot less painful than feeling victimized.

Trust good publishers

Since movie reviewers spend most of their time telling you the plot (and usually can't even do that with any accuracy), one of the best ways to decide if a movie is worth seeing is to find out who directed it. Similarly, one of the best ways to tell if a program is worth buying is to judge by the company that publishes it.

Avoid companies with growth disease

important warning

In certain companies that are lousy with MBAs, talking about what consumers *need* will get you snickered at. (Talking about what consumers *want* is usually tolerated, because that's related to what they're willing to spend money on.) These companies are out to conquer the world (quite openly—that's the way they talk) and they can't see any farther than their bottom line.

Needless to say, companies with growth disease should be avoided like the plague (unfortunately, their hypertrophied legal departments prevent me from mentioning any by name).

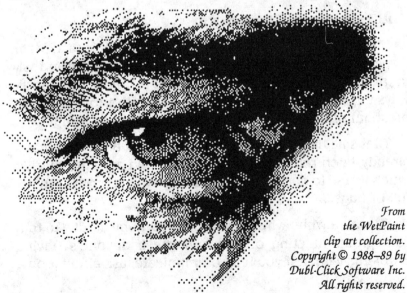

*From
the WetPaint
clip art collection.
Copyright © 1988–89 by
Dubl-Click Software Inc.
All rights reserved.*

Why don't they all...? (SZA)

Some software publishers introduce such nice additions to the standard Mac interface that all programs should copy them. For example, Microsoft programs let you doubleclick on a window's title bar to make the window fill the screen (and/or to toggle it back to the original size)—and they did that long before Apple introduced the zoom box.

very good feature

Even now, Microsoft's is the better approach, because the zoom box is often off the right edge of the screen when you're shuffling windows around—and, even when it's not, it's still always going to be harder to get to and click on than simply doubleclicking anywhere on the title bar.

I like symbols in a menu that indicate when Shift is needed in addition to ⌘ to execute a menu command from the keyboard. Popup menus in dialog boxes are another good idea. The first time I saw either of these features was in PageMaker.

Here are some other features Arthur and I wish were standard on all Mac programs. We'll mention the program(s) we first saw each feature in, but be aware that that's not necessarily all the programs that have it.

If there are features you wish were part of the standard Mac interface, please tell us about them. We'll publish a compiled list in the next edition(s) of the book and mention your name if you're the first person to suggest the idea.

- Word has what I call "smart windows." You don't have to close the Untitled document that's on the screen when you start the program; if you open an existing document, it goes away by itself.

shortcut

- Works avoids the annoying "nothing screen." When you close the last open document, the Open dialog box automatically appears. *[This is obviously the way all Mac software should work. The "nothing screen" is confusing to many beginners (it certainly was to me) and it's completely useless to boot—after all, if you*

shortcut

didn't intend to open another document, you'd quit the program rather than simply close the last document. Yet, so far as Sharon or I know, Works is the only program that does this.—AN]

- Works also lets you create a new document or even quit while the Open dialog box is on the screen, so you're not stuck there if you don't want to open something.

very good feature

[This is another great feature. Instead of blindly locking out all the menus while a dialog box is open, Works let you access the ones that make <u>sense</u>. Not only can you quit the program while the Open dialog box is on the screen, you can also access the Font and Style menus while the Page Setup dialog box is open—so you can format the headers and footers you type in the dialog box.

Here again, all Mac software should clearly work this way, and yet only Works does. (Of course, Works' basic method of handling headers and footers is totally ridiculous—as is Excel's, which is the same—but that's another subject.)—AN]

very good feature

- If you've edited a document but haven't saved the changes, More II lets you know that by underlining the filename in the Window menu. (Utilities like AutoSave periodically save documents, but if you're working on several at once, it's hit or miss which ones will be open when the Save command gets executed. It's very easy to forget to save one or more of the files as often as you should.)

very good feature

- Nisus has a built-in save function that lets you save every so-many keystrokes (you choose the number).

very good feature

- When you drag a tab to place it on Nisus's ruler, a line extends from the tab all the way down the page. This eliminates annoying guesswork about exactly where to put the tab.

very good feature

- Both Word and Nisus automatically make backup copies, so you always have the last *two* versions of your file on disk. (You can disable this feature if you don't want it.)

- Nisus and Word let you change page margins by dragging them in the page preview display, so you can see the exact effect of your changes. As you move the margins, the measurements are indicated on the screen.

- Both Nisus and Word make it very easy to add, remove or change the keystroke equivalents (using ⌘ and ⌘ Shift or menu commands.) When you do that, the new commands show up on the menus.

very good feature

- When you're in the Save or Open dialog box, DiskTools II lists the names of the disks you have mounted, so you can go directly to the one you want instead of having to cycle through them with the Drive button. This is especially handy in a network situation where you're likely to have several volumes mounted at a time.

shortcut

- DiskTools also remembers what folder you were in—when you move back to a disk that you've used before, you're not back at its top level. *[DiskTop will do the same thing if you ask it to.—AN]*

- Many programs (Acta, Word, More, PageMaker, etc.) give you the "smart quotes" option; that is, you can have straight quotes and apostrophes automatically replaced with curly ones.

- I haven't seen this feature except in my imagination, but, instead of a single, crowded menu bar, I'd like a double menu bar with general system menus—the menu and menus for DA's, inits and MultiFinder—on top and application-specific menus on the bottom.

- *[I haven't seen this anywhere, but I'd like a word processor with a horizontal lock, so you don't find yourself always scrolling sideways when you don't want to. I have a big screen and I don't <u>ever</u> need to move sideways in a window. It's an annoyance every time it happens.—AN]*

- *[Word 4 has a nice feature that should be universal. When the I-beam ( ) pointer enters text that's formatted as italic, it bends over to the right (so does the insertion*

very good feature

point, if you click to lay one down there). This makes it much easier to see what you're doing and banishes the old annoyance of selecting the wrong character because you can't figure out which one the pointer is on.

This feature avoids another old annoyance as well. Since there's no way to tell how a space is formatted just by looking at it, it's a common experience to place the insertion point in a space and have the text you begin typing come out in italics (so you have to go back, select it and change it to plain text). With Word's approach, however, you know immediately when you move the I-beam to a space whether it's formatted italic or not, because if it is, the I-beam will bend to the right (as will the insertion point when you place it).—AN]

A guide for beginners (AN/SZA)

The Mac is the most intuitive computer ever sold, but that's not saying much. There are still things about it that confuse beginning users, and Apple's manuals, while better than most, tend to make you wade through a lot of stuff you already know—or that's obvious—to get to the useful information.

esp. for
beginners

Here's a brief introduction to the Mac that's designed to get a beginning user started off on the right foot and to guide you around some of the more common pitfalls. You can supplement it with Apple's manuals to get more details on various points, but it should get you up and running a lot faster than they will.

One word of caution: Apple is always updating and changing the Mac's basic software, so what appears on your screen may not exactly match the screen shots printed in this book. Don't let that throw you—the basic principles will be the same (until System 7, that is; that's a whole new ballade).

The pointer

The Mac's way of communicating with people is the *pointing interface,* sometimes also referred to as the *graphical interface* (for you fans of 19th-century diction) or the *visual interface* (as if all computer screens weren't visual). As its name implies, the pointing interface lets you control a computer by pointing at *icons* (little pictures) or at clear, simple, English words, instead of forcing you to memorize a bunch of abbreviated commands.

Icons represent *files* (collections of computer data), of which there two basic kinds: *programs,* or *applications* (instructions that tell the Mac what to do) and *documents* (what you create with a program—a letter, say, or a drawing). Each different kind of file has a different-looking icon.

You do your pointing on the Mac with an on-screen symbol called, with simple elegance, the *pointer*. Although it can take many shapes, its basic one is a left-leaning arrow ( ). When you're dealing with text, it takes the shape of an *I-beam* ( ). Graphics programs like MacPaint have a whole slew of specialized pointers; for example, , , , and .

Each pointer has a *hot spot*—the spot that "counts." On the arrow pointer, for example, the tip is the hot spot. If just the tip of the arrow is inside something, then you're pointing to it (as in the illustration below); if all the arrow *except* the tip is inside, then you're not pointing to it.

You typically control the pointer with a *mouse*—a small box with a ball on the bottom and a button on the top. When you roll the mouse around, the pointer moves in the same direction on the screen (although not normally the same distance). You get so used to it after a while, it begins to feel as if you're moving the pointer directly with your hand.

The desktop

A basic Apple program called the Finder creates a gray area that covers the screen. Because most of the kind of work that's done on a Mac is otherwise done at a desk, this gray area is called the *desktop*.

The things you point to are arranged on the desktop. Just as on a real desktop, you can open folders and files and read what's in them, throw things in the wastebasket and so on (except, of course, in the real world, the wastebasket is next to the desk, not on top of it). The top of the next page shows you what a (very empty) desktop looks like.

Menus

The only thing on the desktop that clearly doesn't follow this real-world analogy is the line of words across the top.

This is called the *menu bar* and the words on it are called *menu titles*. If you put the pointer on a menu title and hold down the mouse button, a menu pops down over the desktop.

(As you probably know, a *menu* is a list of commands available to you at a particular time. *Commands*, of course, are things you can tell the computer to do.)

Apple insists on calling these *pull-down menus*—presumably on the theory that, in real life, things pop *up* (like toast) but *pull* down (like window shades). Well, first of all, that isn't always the case; for example, those oxygen masks stewardesses demonstrate before a flight pop *down* from overhead if the air pressure in the cabin drops (at least you hope they do.)

But even if nothing in the real world ever popped down, that's *still* what the Mac's menus do. You don't grab the menu title and pull the menu down over the desktop; you

esp. for beginners

touch the menu title with the pointer, press the mouse button and the menu *pops* down over the desktop. The pointer stays up at the menu title, not down at the bottom of the menu, which is where it would have to be if you were pulling it.

Arthur could go on for days about this important point, but it's probably easiest simply to say *menus* instead of *pop-down menus* and to save the adjectives for describing other sorts of specialized menus (we'll be talking about some in a moment). Anyway, here's what a standard, pop-down menu looks like:

This is called the *Apple menu* (since so few people can pronounce). The first command on it always tells you about the software you're using—what version it is, who wrote it, etc. Sometimes you also get other information—it depends on the program you're using.

To select a command on this or any other menu, you slide the pointer down it, keeping your finger on the mouse button. As you pass each command, it *highlights*—that is, instead of appearing as black letters on a white background, it appears as white letters on a black background. When the command you want is highlighted (as *About the Finder...* is above), you just release the mouse button and the command executes.

All the other items on the menu are for *desk accessories*—programs you can use without having to exit whatever software you're working with at the time.

At the top of the next page is the next menu on the menu bar. As you can see, some of the commands on this menu are *dimmed* (or *grayed*). This means you can't use them at the present time—if you slide the pointer past them, they won't highlight. For example, *Print* is dimmed because we haven't picked a document to print.

Some commands have *keyboard equivalents* listed next to them on the menu—like ⌘ O for *Open.* (That cloverleaf symbol appears on a special key on the Mac keyboard that's called the *command* key.) A keyboard equivalent means that instead of moving the pointer up to the File menu, pressing the mouse button to make the menu pop down, going down the menu to the *Open* command and then releasing the mouse button, you can simply hold down the ⌘ key, hit the O key and get the same result.

Sometimes a menu has more commands in it than can fit on your screen. When that happens, you'll see a downward-pointing triangle at the bottom of the menu. Sliding the pointer to (or past) the bottom of the menu will make additional menu items *scroll* up (roll past you as if on a scroll, like the end credits of a movie).

When you see the command you want, you just slide the pointer to it to select it (actually, menu scrolling tends to really zip along, so you'll probably wind up sliding the pointer back *up* the menu to catch the item you want).

Some items on menus are followed by a right-pointing triangle. If you highlight one of these, a *submenu* pops out to the right of it (unless there's no more room on the right, in which case it pops out on the left). You then slide the pointer onto the submenu to select the command you want.

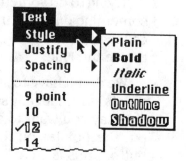

Icons

*esp. for
beginners*

Look back at the illustration of the desktop shown on page 51. The icon in the upper right corner, labelled *SEmore*, represents the hard disk that Arthur was running off of on the SE where these screen shots were made. (It wasn't called SEmore when it was bought, but you can change the names of most things on the Mac and make them whatever you want.)

In the lower right corner of the desktop on page 51 is another icon, the *Trash;* this is where you put things when you don't want them any more. There are various desktops on the Mac, but the way to tell that you're at the basic one, the one created by the Finder, is to look for that Trash can in the lower right corner. Only the Finder's desktop has it.

The Trash icon is white with black lines and lettering—which is the normal way for icons to look. But the SEmore disk icon is black with white lines and lettering. As with a command on a menu, that means it's *selected.*

Selecting, clicking and dragging

Selecting is the single most important concept for understanding how Mac software works. The basic two principles are:

1. You always have to select something before you can do anything with it. (Apple calls this the "noun, then verb" or "hey, you—do this" approach. Another way to remember it is "select, then affect.")

2. *Selecting, in and of itself, never alters anything.*

Trying to do something when nothing is selected, or with something different from what you think is selected, is the cause of 90% of the confusion people have when learning to use the Mac.

We didn't have to select the *SEmore* icon because a hard disk is automatically selected when you start up from it. But let's say you want to select the Trash. To do that, you just put the pointer on it, then press and release the mouse button (this is called *clicking*).

Unselected   *Selected*

You can also move icons around the desktop. To do that, put the pointer on an icon, then press and hold the mouse button as you move the mouse. A "ghost" of the icon will stick to the pointer until you release the mouse button, at which point the icon will appear in the new location. This is called *dragging*.

 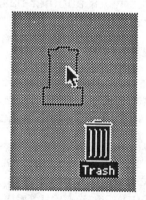 

When you click on an icon, the previously selected icon automatically becomes deselected (turns from black to white). You can, however, select more than one icon at a time, by holding down the [Shift] key while clicking on them. This is called *shift-clicking*.

Another way to select more than one icon at a time is to drag a *selection rectangle* around them. To do that, you point to one corner of an imaginary rectangular area that will surround all the icons, hold the mouse button down, drag the pointer to the diagonally opposite corner, and release the mouse button. (See the illustration at the top of the next page.)

You can also rename icons by typing the new name while the icon is selected. You can use any character but the colon (:) in an icon name, including spaces. (More primitive computers like the IBM PC don't let you use spaces in file names.)

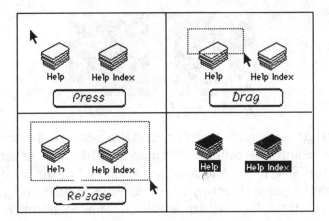

Now you're ready for another basic concept: *Icons can (and often do) contain things.*

Windows

To see what's in an icon, you *open* it. To open an icon, you point to it and click the mouse button twice in rapid succession. This is called *doubleclicking.*

(You can also click once on the icon, go up to the File menu and choose the *Open* command, but that's a whole lot more trouble than doubleclicking. There's even a third possibility. If you look at the *Open* command on the File menu above, you'll see that ⌘ O follows it. So you can also click on an icon and hit ⌘ O to open it.)

Doubleclicking on the Trash icon (or using either of the other two techniques just described) produces this:

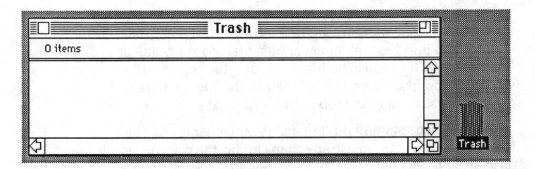

This is called a *window*. It's empty, because nothing has been thrown into Trash since we began working.

When you put an icon into the Trash, it's kept there for a while in case you change your mind. If you do, you just open the Trash window and retrieve it. You can drag out the icon manually, or select it by clicking on it and then choose Put Away from the File menu; the icon zips back to wherever it came from.

When there's something in the Trash, it bulges to let you know it's not empty any more. When you want to actually get rid of whatever's in the Trash, use the *Empty Trash* command in the Special menu. (The Trash is also emptied automatically under certain conditions, which we describe in an entry called *flushing the Trash* in Chapter 6.)

In order to do anything with—or to—a window, it has to be *active* (selected). When it is, you'll see six horizontal lines in the *title bar* (which runs across the top of the window with the title in the middle).

A window is always active when it first opens (this is only logical, since you have to select its icon to open it). To select a different window—that is, to make a different window the active one—all you have to do is click anywhere in it. (The first click just activates the window; to select something in the window, you have to click again.)

The active window is always on top of other windows as shown at the top of the next page.

A window must also be active for you to close it. You do that by clicking in the little *close box* at the left end of the title bar or choosing the *Close* command from the File menu.

To move a window, you drag it by its *title bar*. To change its size, you drag the *size box*. The *zoom box* makes the window fill the screen; the next time you click the zoom box, the window goes back to its original size.

When the active window has gray scroll bars on its bottom and right sides, that means there are items in it that aren't

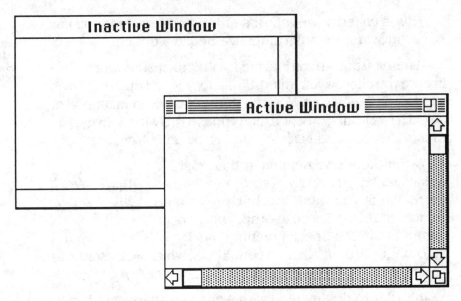

showing. When the scroll bars are white, that means everything is already displayed in the window (or that the window
is inactive). Sometimes one scroll bar is gray and the other is
white; it depends on where the missing information is
located.

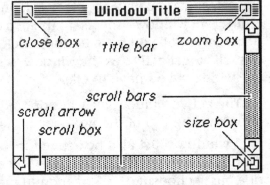

To bring missing
information into view,
you can use the scroll
box, the scroll arrows
or the gray area of
the scroll bar itself.
It's fairly tedious to
explain in words ex-
actly what each does
(since they work in
right-brained, Mac-like ways), but if you experiment with
them, it will quickly become obvious.

The scroll controls seem at first to work backwards. Click
in an up arrow and things scroll down; click in a left arrow
and things move to the right. You have to picture the
contents of the window as being stationary and the window
as moving over them. As you move it to the right, the
contents shift to the left—relatively speaking.

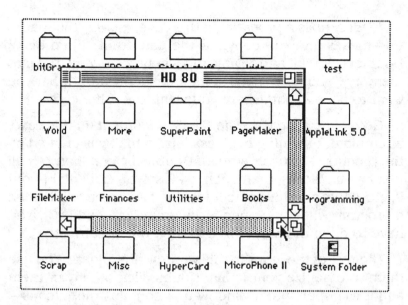

Here's another way to think of it: if you want to see what's towards the bottom of the window, you press the down arrow. If you want to see the items off to the right, you use the right arrow.

Programs, documents and folders

Now let's talk about what the icons in a window *mean*. To do that, lets go back to our old friend *SEmore,* the hard disk icon, and doubleclick on it. That produces this:

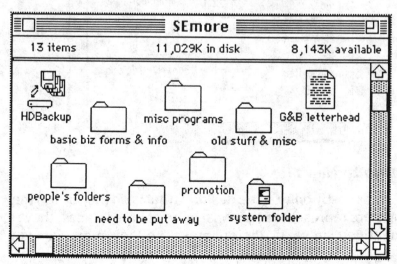

**esp. for
beginners**

HDBackup is a *program* (in this case, a *utility* that backs up—makes an extra copy of—the data from a hard disk). Doubleclick on it and HDBackup will be *launched* (put into memory). You'll be asked some questions about what you want to backup and where you want to put the copy.

G&B letterhead is a *data file* or *document* (in this case, a template for writing business letters that was created by the program Microsoft Works). Doubleclick on it and it will first launch Works, then open itself so you can edit it, print it, etc. (More primitive machines won't automatically launch a program when you open a document created by it. You have to open the program first, then the document.)

The rest of the icons in this window are *folders.* You use them to organize your icons. Doubleclick on any of them and it will open into a window that contains more icons— like the one below. You can put folders within folders to your heart's content—whatever you need to organize your work and make it easy to find.

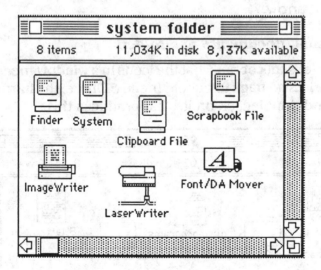

Ways to view files

It's mostly only on the desktop (that is, in the Finder) that files are represented by icons; in most other places, they're identified simply by their names. The View menu lets you display documents by names instead of icons on the desktop as well.

As you can see, you can list or display them:

- *by Small Icon* —the same as *by Icon* except that the icons are smaller

- *by Name*—in alphabetical order

- *by Date*—in order of when you last changed them, with the most recent one first

- *by Size*—from biggest to smallest

```
View
  by Small Icon
✓ by Icon
  by Name
  by Date
  by Size
  by Kind
  by Color
```

- *by Kind*—with all the documents of a particular sort (applications, folders, MacWrite documents, MacPaint documents, etc.) grouped together

- *by Color*—according to the order of the colors in the Color menu (this, of course, is only available on color monitors)

The system folder

The *system folder* is treated specially by the Mac. It's where the Mac looks for the basic software that tells it how to operate: the System file, the Finder, MultiFinder, the *drivers* that tell it how to control various kinds of printers, etc. (By the way, this tutorial assumes that you're running the Finder, not MultiFinder, which is definitely what you should do when you're a beginner.)

The system folder is so special that it gets a special icon on the desktop:

Apple updates the System and Finder frequently, and changes to these two programs may make some of the screen shots and information in this section out-of-date.

You can modify certain aspects of the System yourself, by adding or removing fonts or desk accessories (see the chapters on these topics for more details).

Cut, Copy, Paste and the Clipboard

*esp. for
beginners*

One of the most elegant and useful concepts of Mac computing is that of the *Clipboard*—a temporary holding place for material that you *cut* or *copy* from one place so you can *paste* it in another. It's temporary for two reasons:

- when you put something on the Clipboard, its current contents are replaced (that is, it can only hold one thing at a time)

- when you shut off the computer, the Clipboard's contents disappear.

To *cut* something, you select it (how you do that varies with the program you're using), then pick the *Cut* command from the Edit menu—or just hit ⌘X. Whatever you've selected disappears from its original location and is stored in Clipboard. (Many programs let you check the contents of Clipboard by choosing *Show Clipboard* from the Edit menu.)

Copy (⌘C) works the same way as *Cut*, except that the selected material stays in the original location in addition to moving to the Clipboard.

To *paste* what you've cut or copied, you just indicate where you want it and hit ⌘V —or select *Paste* from the Edit menu. (How you indicate the spot to paste depends on the application you're in.)

You can cut and paste both within and between most Mac programs. The amount of material you can transfer is virtually unlimited since, although the Clipboard is usually held in memory, it can also use disk space when it needs more room.

Remember that the Clipboard will hold only one selection at a time, so each time you cut or copy something new, the previous material disappears. On the other hand, since things stay in the Clipboard until you flush them, you can paste the same thing many different places—as long as you remember not to cut or copy anything else in the interim.

If you simply want to get rid of something, you can just cut it and never paste it; it will disappear the next time you cut or copy. Or you can just hit the [Delete] key after it's selected and it will disappear without even passing through the Clipboard.

The Scrapbook

While the Clipboard is a temporary holding area for cut or copied material, the *Scrapbook* is a permanent file that you access with a command on the menu. What you put in the Scrapbook stays there not only when you add more stuff but also when you turn the machine off. (You can, of course, remove things from the Scrapbook whenever you want.)

Since you use *Cut, Copy* and *Paste* to get things into and out of the Scrapbook, they all pass through the Clipboard on the way. If you're just transferring a few things, it's easier to move them one at a time with the Clipboard—that is, to simply Cut and Paste them. If you have several things to transfer at one time, or if you want them to be available for pasting for more than one work session, the Scrapbook is more convenient.

Dialog boxes and alerts

Choosing a command with a trailing ellipsis (like *Open...* or *Print...*) opens a *dialog box* (called that because the Mac is telling you something and asking for a response). Here's an example of a print dialog box. (They vary depending on what printer, and also what version of the printer driver software you're using.)

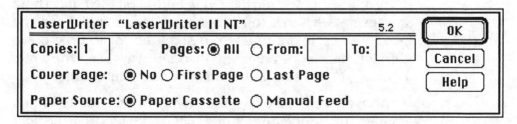

The circular and oval areas are *buttons.* You click on them to tell the Mac what you want. The three rectangles are

esp. for beginners

called *text boxes;* you type information into them (numbers, in this case, but some text boxes ask for words).

Dialog boxes can get more complex than this. For example, if you choose the *Open* command from the File menu while inside Microsoft Works, you'll get one that looks like this:

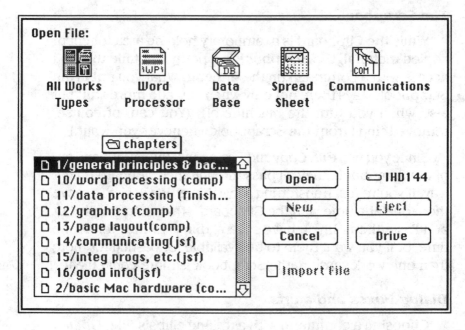

Although this Open dialog box from Works is not the standard Open dialog box, many of its elements are the same.

As with all Open dialog boxes, this one contains a smaller *list box* (in its lower left corner). You can scroll through the documents listed in it and open one, either by doubleclicking on its name or by using the *Open* button on the right. There are several ways to scroll through the document names; the two most basic are to use the scroll bar or to drag down through the list of names. (For other ways, see the entry titled *keyboard shortcuts in dialog boxes* in Chapter 6.)

Above the list box is the name of the folder which contains these documents (it's called *chapters).* On the right is the name of the disk on which the *chapters* folder is located *(IHD144).* Clicking on the *Drive* button switches you between disks. When the disk or folder changes, so do the names in the list box.

Here is another busy dialog box, from PageMaker:

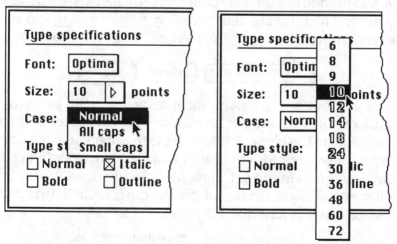

The squares at the bottom of the box are another kind of button. The rectangles with drop shadows are called *popup menus*, because they pop up out of the dialog box. The rectangles with the hollow triangles to their right are a combination of the standard text box that you type information in and a popup menu that you use to enter the information in the text box automatically:

As you can see, dialog boxes can be quite complex in sophisticated applications. But the basics are always reassuringly the same.

esp. for beginners

Similar to a dialog box is the *alert box* (or simply *alert*). In this case, there's no dialog between you and the Mac; an alert either warns you or gives you some information, and your sole role is to acknowledge that by clicking on an OK button. (Sometimes there's also a Cancel button to get you out of a place you didn't really want to be.) Here's an example of an alert box:

Buttons

There are three kinds of buttons in dialog boxes—*push buttons, radio buttons* and *checkboxes.*

Push buttons are rounded rectangles with commands inside them. When you "push" the button (click on it), the command inside the button is executed. This is analogous to selecting a command from a menu. When a push button is also framed in a thicker rounded rectangle, it's the *default* button, which means that pressing Return or Enter on the keyboard has the same effect as clicking on the button.

Radio buttons are used for lists of mutually exclusive choices. They're little circles with labels next to them; when you click on the circle, it fills in. As with the presets on a car radio, only one radio button in a set *can* be selected at a time, and one in the set *must* be selected at all times. So when you click on a radio button, the other radio button that was selected is automatically deselected.

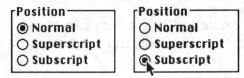

Checkboxes (squares with labels next to them) are used for lists of options that aren't mutually exclusive. Clicking in a checkbox alternately turns it on and off, by putting an X in it and blanking it again. (When the same action does and undoes something like that, we call it a toggle.)

```
┌Style──────────┐
│ ⊠ Bold        │
│ ⊠ Italic      │
│ ☐ Outline     │
│ ☐ Shadow      │
│ ☐ Strikethru  │
│ ⊠ Small Caps  │
│ ☐ All Caps    │
│ ☐ Hidden      │
└───────────────┘
```

Closing, quitting and the "nothing screen"

When you're done working on a document, the File menu of the program you're using gives you two choices—*Close* or *Quit. Quitting* takes you out of the program and back to the Finder (that is, to the desktop). *Closing* leaves you in the program, so you can open another document.

In many programs, closing a document (or the last document, if several were open) leaves you with a blank screen with no icons on it. Arthur calls this the *nothing screen* (although nobody else does); it's a place where people learning the Mac often get lost—especially if they're in MultiFinder.

The thing to remember is that no desktop is completely blank—there's always the menu bar across the top. If you pop down various menus, you'll see that there are lots of things you can do. So here's the last basic principle: *When in doubt, explore the menu bar.*

Shutting Down

When you're done working and want to turn off the Mac, the first thing to do is to get back to the desktop (to the Finder, in other words). Then choose *Shut Down* from the Special menu. In a second or so, the Mac will tell you it's OK to turn off your machine.

It's very important to shut down properly, and not simply turn the computer off. Shutting down gives the Mac time to do a little housekeeping and make sure everything you think is stored on the disk really is stored there.

Summary

esp. for beginners

Here's a recap of the most important principles to keep in mind when using the Mac:

- You have to select something before you can do something.

- By itself, selecting never alters anything.

- To open icons, doubleclick on them.

- When in doubt, explore the menu bar.

(For a discussion of the theory and principles behind the Mac's user interface, a good book is *Human Interface Guidelines: The Apple Desktop Interface,* written by people at Apple and published by Addison-Wesley. Although it's primarily aimed at programmers, it's quite accessible and very interesting.)

Chapter 2

Basic
Mac
hardware

Models of the Mac

❖ *the Mac family* (SZA/AN)

There are now three basic kinds of Macintosh computers:

- *Compacts.* With built-in monitors, these are the size and shape of the original Mac. The SE and the SE/30 are the compact Macs currently in production; the Plus, the 512, the 512e and the original 128K Mac are no longer in production.

- *Modulars.* These are component systems, like stereos—the monitor isn't part of the CPU. So far, all modular Macs have been in the Mac II family, so throughout this book, we simply refer to modular Macs as Mac II's. In addition to the original Mac II (which is no longer being made), there's the IIx, IIcx, IIci and IIfx (the last three of which are usually referred to without the *II* in front of their names).

- *Portables.* So far there's only one, called—straight forwardly enough—the Macintosh Portable.

All the models of the Mac are described below in entries of their own, but we've provided a chart in this entry that shows how they compare in four important areas: the size of their ROMs, the maximum amount of RAM they can handle, the processor chip they're built around (and the coprocessor, if any) and their clock speed.

Before we get to the chart, let's discuss each of these areas in turn:

ROM stands for *read-only memory*. It's the information that's built into the computer and doesn't need to be loaded in from disk. An increase in ROM size (from 256K to 512K, say) makes the Mac smarter and capable of doing more things. It can also add convenience; for example, by the time the SE was introduced, system fonts like Chicago and Geneva were built into the ROM.

esp. for beginners

(Like many words, *ROM* can be used to refer to either stuff or things. When you say, *How much ROM does it have?*, you're referring to the total amount of read-only memory, considered as undifferentiated stuff; when you say, *It has the new 512K ROMs*, you're referring to things—the chips themselves.)

RAM stands for *random-access memory* but it would be more accurate to call it *read/write memory*—memory you can both write data into and read data out of. A computer's RAM is the working space in which you create and modify documents and do other work. All applications load at least partially into RAM, as do system files, inits, etc.

Manufacturers keep cramming more and more RAM onto memory chips; this changes how much memory a given Mac model will take. The figures in the chart are for the densest chips commonly available as of mid-1990 and are for memory installed inside the case, on the Mac's regular motherboard, not on an expansion chassis or an add-on board.

Memory chips usually come packaged in SIMMs, *single in-line memory modules*. The SIMM protects the actual memory circuits and contains the little prongs with which the chips plug into the computer.

The *processor* is the brains of the computer, where the actual processing of information is done. It's also called the *processing chip*, the *CPU (central processing unit)* or simply the *chip*. (*CPU* is sometimes also used to refer to the Mac itself, as distinct from the keyboard, mouse, external monitor, etc.) Macs use Motorola processors from the 68000 series; in general, the higher the number, the more advanced the chip's capabilities.

A *coprocessor* is a second processing chip that specializes in math, graphics or some other specific kind of computation. When the main processor is handed the kind of job the coprocessor specializes in, it hands off the job to the coprocessor, which takes care of it faster than the processor could and then hands back the answer. The most common coprocessor chips used in Macs so far (the 68881 and 68882) both specialize in mathematical computation.

esp. for
beginners

The operations of a computer are synchronized to a quartz crystal that pulses millions of times each second. These pulses determine things like how often the screen is redrawn and how often the central processing unit accesses RAM or a hard disk. The frequency of these pulses is called the computer's *clock speed* or *clock rate* and is measured in *megahertz*—millions of cycles per second— which is abbreviated *MHz.*

On the chart below, we give the clock speed in round numbers. That's the normal practice, but be aware that 8 MHz, for example, is actually 7.83 MHz.

Also be aware that clock speed alone won't tell you how fast a computer is. The 68020 and 68030 chips not only think faster than the 68000, they also move twice as much data at a time as the 68000 chip (in 32-bit chunks instead of 16-bit chunks). That's one reason why the Portable, with its 68000 chip, is slower than other 16-MHz Macs. The 68030 also has a memory-management coprocessor (the 68851 PMMU chip) built right into the chip, and that speeds things up too.

The models are listed in chronological order. Those shown in italics are no longer in production.

Mac model	ROM (in K)	maximum RAM	processor (coprocessor)	speed (in MHz)
128	*64*	*128K*	*68000*	*8*
512	*64*	*512K*	*68000*	*8*
512e	*128*	*512K*	*68000*	*8*
Plus	*128*	*4MB*	*68000*	*8*
SE	256	4MB	68000	8

II	256	8MB	68020 (68881)	16
SE/30	256	8MB	68030 (68882)	16
IIx	256	8MB	68030 (68882)	16
IIcx	256	8MB	68030 (68882)	16
IIci	512	8MB*	68030 (68882)	25
Portable	256	2MB	68000	16
IIfx	512	8MB*	68030 (68882)	40

*Under System 7, these machines will be able to accommodate more RAM than 8MB.

Here are a couple of points the table makes obvious:

• Despite its late introduction, the Portable is sort of a throwback, since it uses the same 68000 processor as the earliest Macs (although it runs much faster than they did).

• In a certain way, the Mac II is the black sheep of the family—the only Mac with a 68020 processor. (For more on why this is a technological dead end, see the entry on the Mac II below.)

The diagram on the next page *[another one of Sharon's brilliant illustrations—AN]* gives you a more visual way of looking at the history of the Mac. In general, as you go up and to the right, the machines get more powerful—so the least powerful Mac, the original 128K model, is in the lower left corner, and the most powerful (so far), the IIfx, is in the upper right corner.

⌘ what's in a name?

Now that there's a whole family of Macs, here's how to keep track of what their names mean. Words, letters and roman numerals refer to the basic model: *Plus, SE, Mac II, IIx,* etc. Arabic numerals less than 10 indicate megabytes of RAM, while arabic numerals over 10 indicate how many megs are on the hard disk. Thus the Mac IIcx 4/80 has four megs of RAM and an 80-meg hard disk.

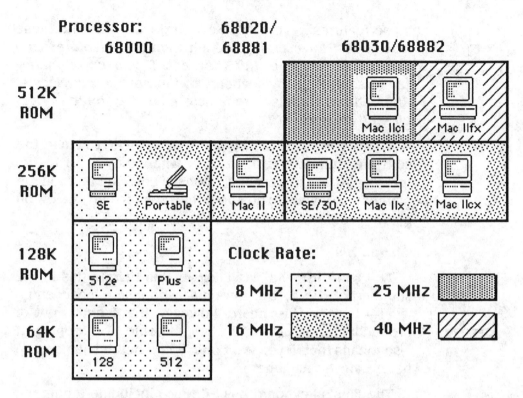

The SE/30 violates these naming conventions, because the *30* in its name refers to the 68030 chip the machine is built around, rather than a 30-meg hard disk. Apple usually uses an *x* to indicate the 68030 chip—as in IIx, IIcx and IIfx—but they apparently didn't think we could handle a machine called the *Macintosh SEx*.

gossip/ trivia

⚫ *the classic Macs*

Isn't *classic* a nicer word than *obsolete* to refer to the first three models of the Mac—the original 128K, the 512 and the 512e? The number in each name tells you how much RAM the machine has. The 128 and 512 have 64K ROMs and single-sided (400K) floppy-disk drives. The 512e (for *enhanced*) has the 128K ROMs and double-sided (800K) drives.

The keyboards that came with these models didn't have numeric keypads or arrow keys—although, if you want

very good feature

those features, a Mac Plus keyboard will work with these machines. *(However, if you don't want those features, and the space-wasting clutter they entail, you unfortunately can't use these early keyboards with more recent Macs.— AN)* All three models were fanless *(allowing you to work in blessed silence—AN)*.

While the classic Macs still work fine if you use the software that was current back when they were made, there's virtually no recent versions of software that will run on them. (For what to do about that, see the entry below on upgrading.)

❤ *the Plus*

esp. for beginners

At $1800 list, the Mac Plus was, as I wrote this in the summer of 1990, the low-end—whoops, I mean entry-level—Mac. I've just heard, however, that it's now out of production. This means the price should be dropping. It also means that, if you want one, you'd better snap one up before they're all gone.

The Plus's keyboard has 78 keys, including a numeric keypad and arrow keys. It was the last Mac to use the old-style mouse, and the last not to have a fan. Its battery is easy to replace—you just snap it in and out.

The Plus comes with one meg of RAM which can be expanded to a total of four megs. The Plus wasn't designed to allow for things to be added inside—an internal hard disk, say, or a video card for an external monitor. That's not to say it *can't* be expanded—Radius had its full-page display up and running on Pluses before the SE was born.

With a hard disk and an extra meg of memory (which only costs about $80), the Mac Plus remains a viable system for serious work. *(I agree that the extra meg is a good investment. But if the software you're using isn't a memory hog, you can do serious work on a Plus with just one meg. I've written several books using that configuration, or less powerful ones.—AN)*

☀ *the SE* (SZA/AN)

The original SE, like the Plus, came with an 800K drive, but now it comes with a 1.4-meg SuperDrive. The SE introduced the 256K ROMs and was the first Mac to have a fan.

Since the SE has ADB connectors, you can get it with either of Apple's ADB keyboards—the 81-key standard or the 105-key extended. (This is true of all the models below.) The SE's battery is soldered in, so you can't replace it yourself (but they say it will last seven years). There's one slot for expansion cards.

You can soup up an SE in lots of different ways, but Apple currently sells three configurations (each includes a mouse and, of course, the screen, but the keyboard is extra). With a meg of RAM and two internal SuperDrives, it currently lists for about $2600; with a 20-meg hard disk instead of one of the SuperDrives, it lists for about $3000; with two megs of RAM and a 40-meg hard disk, $3400. You can expand the RAM on any of these systems to four megs.

☀ *the SE/30* (SZA/AN)

The SE/30 is similar to the SE, but it's built around a 68030 processor chip running at sixteen megahertz, aided by a 68882 math coprocessor chip. This combo makes it about four times faster than the SE overall.

The SE/30 is also the only compact Mac to offer advanced sound capabilities and stereo output. Another important, often over-looked feature of the SE/30 is that it has color QuickDraw in its ROM, which means that with the correct video card, it will produce color output.

The cards that go in the SE/30's *Direct Slot* expansion slot aren't compatible with those that go in Mac II's or with those that go in the regular SE's slot.

An SE/30 with a meg of RAM and a SuperDrive currently lists for about $3900; with a 40-meg hard disk, for about

$4400; with four megs of RAM and an 80-meg hard disk, for about $5600. You can expand the RAM on any of these systems to eight megs.

🍎 *the Mac II* (SZA/AN)

things to come

The Mac II has been out of production for quite a while now. Since it's the only Mac with a 68020 processor chip, it's destined to become something of an orphan. Future software is either going to be written to run on all Macs (including those with 68000 chips), in which case it won't take advantage of the 68020's added power, or it's going to be written for the 68030 chip and thus won't run on the Mac II at all.

Buying a used Mac II is a little like buying a Lisa used to be—it may be worth doing if you get a *great* deal on it, but be aware that you're probably going to want to upgrade at some time in the not-too-distant future.

🍎 *the IIx* (SZA/AN)

Like the SE/30, the IIx is built around a 68030 processor chip running at sixteen MHz and a 68882 coprocessor. It uses the 256K ROMs and will take up to eight megs of RAM. It has six slots and stereo sound output, but (for some reason) no port for an external floppy drive.

A IIx with just a single floppy drive currently lists for about $5300. With a 40-meg internal hard disk, it lists for about $6000; with an 80-meg drive and four megs of RAM, for about $7200; and with a 160-meg drive and four megs of RAM, for about $8300.

🍎 *the IIcx* (SZA/AN)

The IIcx is the same as the IIx except for three things: it's smaller, it has only three slots instead of six and it has a port for an external floppy disk drive (which can be useful if you're doing extensive floppy-to-floppy copying).

With a floppy drive and a meg of RAM, it currently lists for about $4700; with four megs of RAM and a 40-meg hard disk, for about $5400; with four megs of RAM and an 80-meg hard disk, for about $6600. In other words, each system costs about $600 less (at list) than a comparable IIx.

᭑ *the IIci* (AN)

Based on a 25MHz 68030 microprocessor, the ci really rips along. You can speed it up even more with a third-party memory-cache card, like the Fast Cache from DayStar. The ci's speed comes in handy if you work with large databases or spreadsheets, or complex graphics. I love it for how quickly it moves me between two-page spreads in PageMaker.

esp. for power users

The ci's footprint is the same as the cx's (approximately 12" by 14") and, like the cx, it has three slots. In a way, the ci has four slots, because its built-in video capabilities let you use monitors (up to 640 x 870 pixels) without having to install a separate video card. But be aware that running a grey-scale or color monitor off the built-in video chip slows things down a lot; for those monitors, you really should get a separate video card.

Finally, the ci has some advanced capabilities (32-bit addressing, and 32-bit QuickDraw built-in) that give it some real advantages under System 7.

The ci currently lists for about $6300 with one meg of RAM and no hard disk. With a 40-meg hard disk, it lists for about $7000 and with an 80-meg hard disk and four megs of RAM for about $8700.

᭑ *the Portable* (AN)

Expensive (about $5800 list, or about $7150 with a hard disk and two megs of RAM) and heavy (over 20 lbs for the hard-disk model in the case, with the power supply), this is nevertheless a high-powered and well-designed Mac you can take anywhere. And when you get there, you've got a *Mac* to use, not some odious stripped-down PC. That's something Mac lovers have been anxiously awaiting for a long time.

The Portable has a nice crisp screen that's fast enough to show you the pointer as it moves, even when you move it quickly. The screen is easy to read in bright light, but it has a weird double image in dim light.

Although the screen is physically smaller than those on compact Macs, it has 640 pixels across and 400 from top to bottom, compared to the compact Macs' 512 x 342. This means it can display 46% more information (the whole width of a letter-sized page, for example). It does that by using smaller pixels (dots). I don't consider that a disadvantage; to my eye, the compact Macs' 72-to-the-inch pixels are too big—horsy, as a designer might say.

The sophisticated power-management system and special low-power RAM chips maximize battery life; together, they make it possible to get 6–12 hours out of each battery. What's more, the batteries are rechargeable (or they will be, if Apple *ever* ships the recharger—I've been waiting *nine months* for mine).

The Portable's memory is only expandable to two megabytes (until eight-meg SIMMs start being made). The extra memory is handy, but the special chips used in the Portable are much more expensive than normal ones. Apple charges $650 (list) for the one-meg upgrade, compared to an Apple list price of $300 (and a street price of about $80) for a meg of regular memory chips.

You can plug the Portable into the wall without an adaptor virtually anywhere in the world, since it automatically handles 85–270 volts and 48–62 Hz (cycles per second). (The US uses 110 volts and 60Hz, but many foreign countries use 220 volts, 50Hz or both.)

If you (like most people) don't like using a trackball, you can plug a mouse into the Portable. There's even a nice compartment for it in the case. The built-in keyboard seems fine to me, but if you don't like it, you can also plug in any ADB keyboard.

All in all, the Portable is a slick machine. It's a pain to lug around but a joy to use. If you have strong arms, good credit and a need for it, I doubt you'll be disappointed with it.

🍎 *the Portable* (SZA)

Despite Arthur's closing remark, I was very disappointed with the Portable. After lugging it around four airports on a trip, I was very grateful that I had borrowed it, not bought it. *(Maybe Apple should rethink its marketing for the Portable and target brawny, he-man computer nerds, guys who do a hundred curls each morning with an ImageWriter in each hand.—AN)* And why did Apple emblazon its name and logo on the carrying case? To cry out *Hi! Steal me!* in airports?

very bad feature

On my next working vacation, I'm just going to ship my cx ahead to meet me there. (Or if I splurge and get a second computer, I'll buy a compact Mac to ship around.)

🍎 *the IIfx* (AN)

In Ken Kesey's fabulous novel, *One Flew Over the Cuckoo's Nest*, Randall McMurphy describes himself as "the bull-goose loony." Well, the fx is the bull-goose Mac. As the brochure says, it's "for people who need the ultimate in Macintosh responsiveness."

esp. for power users

Using an fx for most common Mac tasks is like shooting at a fly with a bazooka (except it's easier on your walls). But for high-end jobs like manipulating 24-bit color images or computation-intensive operations, it's the only way to go.

The fx's 68030 chip runs at 40 MHz—five times faster than an SE or a Plus—but the speed improvement is even greater than that, thanks to sophisticated hardware en- hancements like a 32K static RAM cache. Access to SCSI devices like hard disks is also speeded up.

The fx comes in the larger, six-slotted case, like the IIx and the II, but it has a variable-speed fan and the case doesn't make that hideous cracking sound when you open it.

The fx's speed and power don't come cheap (although they do come cheaper than on comparable workstations made by most other companies). The current list price for the base model, which comes with a floppy drive and four megs of RAM, is about $9000. With a built-in 80-meg hard disk, it lists for about $10,000, and with a built-in 160-meg hard disk, for about $11,000.

⬤ *comparing pairs* (SZA/AN)

When shopping for a Mac, most people narrow down their choice pretty quickly but then wonder if—for a little more money, or a little less—they should get the model above or below the one they thought they'd decided on. To facilitate that kind of decision-making, here's a list of Macs compared by pairs:

Plus vs. SE: You can put an internal hard disk in the SE, and its expansion slot lets you add an accelerator board or a card for another monitor. (It's possible to add an external monitor to a Plus, but it wasn't designed for that.) The SE has more ROM than the Plus, but from the user's point of view that doesn't make that much difference—without a higher clock rate, the speed of the computer isn't changed much.

SE vs. SE/30: The difference is speed, speed, speed and speed. (Okay, and total memory capacity—the SE/30 can be expanded to eight megs of memory, while the SE only goes to four.) With its faster CPU and higher clock rate, the SE/30 is four times faster than the SE.

You don't necessarily need to go to the SE/30 to get more speed; many third-party vendors sell 16-MHz accelerator cards for about $400–$500 that really light a fire under the SE. But they still don't make it as fast as an SE/30.

The SE/30 has another advantage: because it has the current 68030 processor, it won't be outdated as soon as the SE will be. (SE's made prior to about August, 1989 can't read 1.4-meg floppies, but current models can.)

SE/30 vs. IIx or IIcx: Portability is the main issue here— and the fact that if you want a large screen, you'll have two screens with the SE/30 but just one with a IIx or cx. (It probably won't even cost you more, bought from a third party.) Still, if you don't need portability, you do get two extra slots in the cx and five extra slots in the IIx.

IIx vs. IIcx: The IIx offers six expansion slots and the cx three; but the IIx takes up more room. Three slots are plenty for most people, but the difference (at current list prices) is only about $600, so if the extra three slots are worth $200 apiece to you, go for the IIx.

IIcx vs. IIci: One main difference is speed. Out of the box, the ci is about 56% faster than the cx, thanks to its 25 MHz clock speed. And with a third-party memory card in the ci's cache connector slot, you can speed things up another 20–30%.

The ci also comes with a built-in video card, so factor that in when you're comparing prices for a total system built around either of these models. But remember, the ci's built-in video card should be used only with a black-and-white monitor; with a gray-scale or color monitor, it slows the machine down too much.

Finally, the ci has some advanced capabilities that would be boring to explain but which will mean greater speed and power under System 7 (and beyond).

IIci vs. IIfx: Here again, the difference is speed, but it's a rare Mac user who *needs* any more speed than the ci can provide. Those of you who do, know who you are and certainly don't need advice from mere mortals like us.

esp. for power users

❦ upgrading your Mac

You can't turn a sow's ear into a silk purse, but you can turn a 512 Mac into a Plus—or perform other minor and major upgrades from one model to another. Upgrading involves a number of elements—the ROM, the clock speed, the internal drive, amount of RAM—and can be done with Apple's upgrade kits or ones from other vendors. (We're not covering RAM upgrades here; see Chapter 3 for info about adding memory to your computer.)

Whether or not an upgrade is cost-efficient is another story. You may find it more worth your while to, say, sell a Mac Plus and put the money towards the purchase of a new SE, rather than to upgrade the Plus.

**gossip/
trivia**

Personally, I've always used the trickle-down theory instead of upgrading. I buy a new model and give my current one to the kids. The one *they've* been using gets sold. That worked fine for the 128, 512e and Plus— although I ripped out the extra memory from the Plus before I gave it to them—but they're not getting my cx when I move on from it! *[I bet they will. By that time, you'll probably think of it as an old, slow machine.—AN]*

I'll want something faster, but I'm not giving a cx to two kids whose ages added together don't make them an adult. Readers can tune in to future editions to see what really happens.

Here are some basic upgrade paths:

From a classic Mac: The original 128K Mac, Mac 512 and 512e can all be upgraded to a Mac Plus. For the 128 and 512 models, you need the *Macintosh Plus Disk Drive Kit,* which includes the 800K drive and 128K ROMs and which lists for about $300. (The 512e already has those parts.)

You also need the *Macintosh Plus Logic Board Kit,* which lists for about $650. This brings you up to one megabyte of memory and gives you a SCSI port—as well as a new rear panel for the case to accommodate the SCSI port.

That's $950 so far, not counting a new keyboard if you want a built-in numeric keypad and arrow keys. Some careful shopping can probably find you a *new* Mac Plus for not much more than that—and you can certainly find a used one for less than that.

Clearly, upgrading a classic along Apple's path isn't worth the money. But keep in mind that dealers get rebates for the parts that they turn in when the upgrade's done; that gives you bargaining room and you might be able to get both upgrade components for about $750.

From a Plus: There's no way to turn a Plus into an SE— you can't exchange its 128K ROMs for the 256K ones and the 1.4-meg floppy drive isn't available for the Plus. But you can boost the Plus's speed even beyond the SE's by installing an accelerator board like the one from Radius (list price, about $800).

From an SE: First, if you have an old SE with an 800K drive, you can get Apple's SuperDrive replacement (the *Macintosh SE FDHD Upgrade Kit)* for about $600.

You can also turn an SE into an SE/30 with Apple's *Macintosh SE/30 Logic Board Upgrade Kit.* This kit, which costs about $1700, gives you the SE/30 main board and the SuperDrive, as well as a replacement for part of the case to accommodate the SE/30's different expansion slot.

From a II to a IIx: Apple's upgrade kit to change your II into a IIx is about $2200. For that price, you get to swap your existing innards for new ones, giving you the IIx logic board and the SuperDrive kit. Or you can get just the drive kit ($600) and get the 68851 PMMU chip you need to put on the logic board from another company, for about $300.

From a IIx or IIcx: You can speed the performance of either of these models into the IIci range by getting an accelerator board. The IIci logic board replacement (for the IIcx only) is about $2400.

From a II or IIx to an fx: Believe it or not, the price is the same whether you're going from the II or IIx: $3000. As with other board-swap upgrades, the dealer gets a credit, and so might be open to some bargaining. (You naturally can't upgrade from a cx or ci to an fx, since the cases are different sizes.)

Two places you can get non-Apple upgrade kits are Computer Care and MacProducts USA—you'll find them both in Appendix B.

General hardware tips

✎ *Macintosh slots*

Macintosh slots come in four confusing varieties:

- the SE Expansion Bus, available only on the SE
- the Direct Slot, available only on the SE/30
- the NuBus slots used in the Mac II line
- the special slots in the Portable.

Apple's NuBus structure is almost unique in the computer world, because the cards don't have to fight for priorities (who gets to go first). The Mac's main board handles all the traffic (the signals to and from the installed boards).

important
warning

Be aware that cards made to work in one kind of slot won't work in another. Fortunately, you won't really have to remember the type of slot you have—just make sure you get a card that's made for your computer and not for some other model.

✎ *replacing the battery*

Batteries in Mac models up to and including the Plus eventually need to be replaced, although they'll last for two or even three years. They're easy to get at—just remove the battery cover, snap out the old battery and snap in the new. It's the same size as an ordinary AA battery, but it's not—it's a 4.5-volt alkaline, Everready 523 or equivalent.

In SE's, Mac II's and IIx's, the special lithium battery is soldered to the main board and can only be replaced by a dealer. (The II and the IIx have *two* batteries soldered in.) We were all told originally that these batteries had a seven-year life, but it seems that maybe that's the *shelf* life. In talking to a few repair services, I've found that they're getting Mac II's in for repair because of dead batteries—and they're barely three years old.

very bad
feature

The battery in the IIcx, ci and fx is on the main board, but it's easy to remove it from the socket and replace it.

When do you know you need a new battery? When you lose Control Panel settings—time and date, for instance—when you shut off the machine. Your Mac, of course, will work whether or not you give it a fresh battery but you'll get tired of resetting all your Control Panel options.

⚫ *clearing parameter RAM*

The Mac's battery provides power to a special area of memory called *parameter RAM,* or *PRAM* (usually pronounced *pram* but techies prefer *PEE-ram* so that's probably the more correct pronunciation). In addition to keeping track of the date, time and various Control Panel settings, parameter RAM also remembers what's connected to the printer and modem ports on the back of the Mac.

If the information in parameter RAM ever becomes corrupted, you can reset it to the original defaults. On any Mac up to the Plus, you can do that by removing the battery for ten minutes. On later models, you have to *zap the PRAM.* (You can do this on the earlier models too, if you prefer.)

To zap the PRAM, restart from a floppy that has the Control Panel desk accessory on it. Open the ⚫ menu and select *Control Panel* while holding down 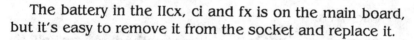 . You'll get a dialog box that looks like this:

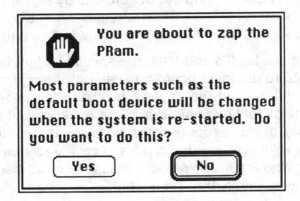

Click *Yes.*

Clearing the PRAM by either method returns all the Control Panel settings to their defaults, so you'll have some resetting to do. Conveniently, though, it doesn't change the time or date.

Tips on Mac II's

⌘ *opening the case* (AN/SZA)

Mac II's provide expansion slots, and to get at them, you're going to have to open the case. There are two basic kinds—the larger, six-slotted box used for the Mac II, IIx and fx and the smaller, three-slotted box used for the cx and ci.

very hot tip

On both boxes, you have to begin by removing a single screw at the center back of the case. (If you like, you can just leave the screw out of the back altogether, so you don't have to worry about finding a screwdriver every time you want to open the case.)

very bad feature

On the larger case, you then have to push in the two latches on either side of the top (at the back) and tilt the cover forward. A hideous cracking noise ensues (except on the fx, which has an improved case). It sounds like you're breaking something, but that's how it was designed; yes, believe it or not, it's really *supposed* to sound like that.

Make sure you haven't accidentally left an ejected (but not removed) floppy in the disk drive. If you did, you won't be able to get the top off, and trying to will pry the disk up inside the drive.

important warning

When you put the cover back on, you have to take some care to line up the front of the cover with the front of the case. After a while you'll see what goes where, but it's not terribly obvious. Sometimes the cover catches in the back but not the front; when that happens you can usually just push down on the front and snap it into place (even after you've reattached the little screw in the back).

The smaller case for the IIcx and ci has different—and more convenient—latches at the back. You're spared the terrible cracking sound, but the procedure is about the same.

🍎 *the opening chord* (AN)

When you turn a Mac II on—by pushing the button at the center top of the basic ADB keyboard or the upper right corner of the extended keyboard—it strikes a chord (C major, in case you're wondering). This tells you that all is right with the machine—or at least that certain basic things are right.

If something's wrong, the notes sound separately rather than together. The harsh, broken chord (or arpeggio) means one of your memory chips is bad or, more usually, that a SIMM is simply not seated firmly in its socket. At worst it means you'll have to replace the main board of your computer.

Apple trains service personnel to be able to recognize what's wrong with your computer by which particular broken chord it plays on startup.

⌘ *the programmer's switch* (AN/SZA)

The *programmer's switch* is that little piece of plastic you didn't know what to do with when you got your Mac. Despite its name, it's not just for programmers—it's for anyone whose Mac crashes occasionally (and that's all of us).

On the Mac II, IIx and IIfx, you install the programmer's switch in the rearmost vents on the right side of the case, with the loose ends of the buttons facing up. It snaps into place; you don't have to open the case. On the Mac IIcx and IIci, you do open the case and install the switch on the front of the machine, on the left side (the pictures in the manual make the procedure very clear). Putting the switch on the front of the machine wasn't a great idea, because it's much more likely to get accidentally hit by a book or something than when it's on the side.

The switch actually has two buttons—*reset* and *interrupt.* On some Macs, each of the buttons is labelled; on others, they're marked by symbols (a left-facing arrow for reset, a circle for interrupt). In any case, when the switch is on the side of the Mac, the reset button is the one nearer the front of the machine; when the switch is on the front of the machine, the reset button is on the left.

The interrupt button is pretty much just for programmers; the reset button is for the rest of us. If your Mac crashes (and you don't have a dialog box that provides a Restart button on the screen), don't switch the power off and on again—press the reset button instead. This avoids the electrical power surge the Mac experiences each time you switch it on.

⌘ *locking the power switch*

The power switch on the back of a Mac IIcx and ci can be locked in the *on* position, so that the computer automatically restarts after a power interruption (which is useful if you're using it as a file server). To lock the switch, simply rotate it—with a paper clip or some other handy tool—so that the notch is vertical.

the II's fans (AN)

Before I got a Mac II, I was afraid the fan was going to drive me crazy (the one on the original SE certainly did). But I've found the fans on all the II's I've used (a II, cx and ci) to be a lot better—not nearly as nice as silence, you understand, but quite bearable.

That's because they put out white noise (sounds at all frequencies) or something pretty close to it. White noise drowns out other noises and is even considered soothing by some. I wouldn't go that far, but you can actually work in front of a Mac II.

keeping them quiet (SZA)

If the fan in your Mac II gets noisier as you work, make sure there's enough space around the vents. If there isn't, the Mac will heat up and the temperature-controlled fan will work harder.

very
hot
tip

Also, if you don't need to use all the expansion slots (and who does?), skip the one closest to the power supply. The heat generated by a card in that slot can also make the fan run faster.

the startup battery on the II and IIx

Mac II's and IIx's have two batteries. The one toward the front powers up the Mac when you hit the *on* key on the keyboard. The other powers the *parameter RAM* (the time, date and Control Panel settings; for more on that, see the entry called *clearing parameter RAM* on page 87).

The startup battery dies more quickly because of the repeated strain on it, and when it dies you won't be able to start your computer. (This less-than-brilliant design has been changed from the cx on.) Don't let anyone tell you your Mac's logic board is dead and needs replacing until they've determined that it's not just a dead battery.

**important
warning**

The smart thing to do, however, is to replace the battery *before* it dies. It's a four-volt battery. If it reads 3.3 volts or below on a battery tester, it's time to replace it. Three volts is dead for startup purposes.

⚫ the II's missing hard disk icon

bug

Early versions of the Mac II had a bug that messed up parameter RAM when an application crashed, and other things can confuse PRAM as well. One result can be that your Mac will lose track of an internal hard disk; its icon won't show up on the screen. You can often recover from this dilemma by "zapping" the PRAM —that is, making it revert to its default settings. (For more on this, see the entry *clearing parameter RAM* on page 87.)

The next time you restart the machine, the icon for your internal hard disk should reappear (unless there's something seriously wrong with the disk) and most—but usually not all—of the settings in parameter RAM will revert to their default values (time and date are never affected).

⚫ don't double-up on disks (AN)

important
warning

It's a lot less obvious when there's a disk in a Mac II's floppy drive than it is on an SE or a Plus. Several times I've tried to stick a second disk in and once or twice I've actually succeeded (the second disk slides in over the first at an angle).

I've always been able to get the second disk out, but this can't be good for the drive, so pay special attention to whether that drive slot is occupied before you blithely shove a disk into it.

⚫ the Mac IIci and Apple's CD-ROM player

bug

After the IIci's intro, Apple found (to its embarrassment, we assume) that it didn't work with the CD-ROM drive. Version 3.01 of the CD-ROM driver (software) solves this problem. You can get it free from your Apple dealer.

Tips on compact Macs

🍎 *opening the case* (SZA)

The compact Macs weren't designed to be opened by anybody but a certified technician—and even then only for repairs. Nobody at Apple imagined that users would want to install more memory, a fan, an internal hard disk or anything else. (I guess we weren't supposed to be able to improve upon perfection.)

As a result, you need special tools and special techniques to open the case. The following information is provided because it's common knowledge and very useful—but we can't officially recommend it. Why? Well, for one thing, opening the case voids your warranty with Apple. There must be some way they can tell. *(You bet your boots there is,* says one of our tech editors who works at Apple.)

For another thing, the Mac contains high-voltage components, as well as capacitors that can hold those high charges for 30–60 minutes after you turn the Mac off. *If you don't know what's going on in there and what precautions to take, you shouldn't be messing around inside your computer.*

important
warning

The first tool you need is a Torx T-15 screwdriver with a long shaft—at least 8 inches. The early Macs, up to and including the Plus, have five screws—two deep inside the handle (that's why you need the long shaft), two just above the row of ports at the bottom of the back and one inside the battery compartment. Since SE's don't have battery compartments, they only have four screws.

To open the case, put a towel down on a level surface (to protect the screen) and place the Mac face down on top of it. Remove the battery cover and battery (unless you're working on an SE) and unscrew all the screws. Don't worry about actually removing the screws—just leave them in their holes in the case. (If the programmer's switch is installed, remove it before proceeding.)

Now you need another special tool—variously referred to as a *cracker* or a *splitter*. The two pieces of the compact Mac case are *very* firmly snapped together and you need to wedge something in the seam between the pieces to pry them apart. Apple sells a case cracker to its dealers and technicians but they're not available to the rest of us. An architect's three-sided ruler works pretty well.

I saw another wonderful substitute tool at a friend's office—but he's an orthopedic surgeon and the tool was designed to crack open fiberglass casts and costs several hundred dollars. Another friend of mine made a splitter tool in a school metal shop. It's a simple door hinge with the edges filed thin enough to fit in the crack in the Mac's case. Attach handles to each side of the hinge so that they extend beyond it and are about half an inch apart when the hinge is closed. When you squeeze the handles together, the hinge pries the case apart.

Once you crack the case—using whatever tool—slowly and carefully lift the back piece off. If you've left the screws in their holes, you'll want to keep it level as you find a place to put it down.

Compact Macs have an *RF shield* that covers the area around the ports at the bottom of the back. On early models, it's shiny metallic; on later models, it looks more like cardboard.

🍎 *installing the programmer's switch* (AN)

If you don't know what the programmer's switch is, see the entry on it in the previous section. To install it on compact Macs, you snap it into place in the rearmost vents on the left side of the Mac, with the loose end of the buttons facing down (you don't have to open the case).

🍎 *quieting the original SE* (SZA/AN)

Early SE's had cheap, noisy, squirrel-cage fans that were eventually replaced by better ones. Early SE's also had some very annoying screen jitters. Apple's policy for the screen jitter problem, though not advertised, is to replace the main board for free. Guess what the fan's attached to?

If you tell your dealer you've got a noisy fan, he'll sell you a new fan. If you tell him you've got screen flicker, he'll replace the board for free. (If the dealer tells you he doesn't know about that replacement policy, tell him to check with the home office in Cupertino.)

bargain

If you feel funny about taking that approach, Apple will sell you a new fan for about $90 (part number 076-0311). But why do that when you can get the $50 SE Silencer from Mobius, a bladed fan that runs slower than the original and has a two-year warranty?

Installing the Mobius fan is relatively simple and shouldn't take more than about fifteen or twenty minutes. But be careful not to zap any chips with static electricity, watch out for high voltage around the picture tube and make sure you don't break the neck off the tube (as one friend of Arthur's—who shall, to his great relief, remain nameless (don't worry, Eric)—did *twice*). Also be aware that once you open the SE, its warranty is voided.

⚫ *adjusting the voltage* (Rich Wolfson)

Early Mac Pluses were notorious for their failing power supplies. (Sharon went through three in less than two years and Arthur went through four in less than a year.) This problem has been fixed in more recent Pluses, but if you have an old one, you can keep the unit from overheating— if you know some basics and have the right tools—by making sure the voltage is set to exactly five volts.

very bad feature

Open the case and use a volt meter to check the voltage between pins 1 and 2 of the mouse port. Using a plastic screwdriver or a TV alignment tool, adjust the potentiometer at the side of the machine to five volts. The voltage changes as the unit heats up, so leave it on for five to ten minutes and check that it's still at five volts.

esp. for power users

Most Mac Pluses come set to anywhere from 4.8 to 5.1 volts despite Apple's recommendation that they be set to exactly 5.0 volts. In one of our campus computer labs of more than a dozen Mac Pluses, there wasn't one that was set to the correct voltage. We had one power supply problem early on, but none after we set the voltages correctly. (And the Macs have been in use for three years now.)

⌘ *keeping it cool* (Rich Wolfson)

Another way to avoid potential problems in a Mac Plus is to install a fan to keep it from overheating. A piezoelectric fan is small, inexpensive and makes very little noise. (For more on this, see the chapter on hardware accessories.)

⌘ *fixing the power supply* (Rich Wolfson)

esp. for power users

When the power supply in a Plus fails, you don't have to replace the whole thing—it's almost always just the flyback transformer and its related parts that are causing the problem. One company that sells flyback-transformer parts kits is Soft Solutions. Their prices and service are good, their tech support is great and their parts are heavy-duty— exceeding the Mac's minimum requirements.

Tips on the Mac Portable

⌘ *opening it up* (AN)

important warning

If you're not careful to fully release both catches when opening the Portable's screen, you can unintentionally lift up the whole computer in the process, only to drop the bottom part of it back down on the table with a resounding crash when the screen finally opens. (An adroit, graceful person like myself would never do anything like this. No way. But you may not be as agile as I am, so read on.)

To open the Portable, push in *firmly* with your thumbs at the *ends* of the handle to release the catches. Then lift the screen from either side with your fingers, making sure you're not also lifting the bottom part of the computer. The hinge on the Portable's screen is quite stiff, so it may take you a while to get used to the amount of effort required, which is more than you expect (although well within the capabilities of most world-class triathletes).

🍎 *lighting the screen* (AN)

The people who designed the screen on the Mac Portable came to a very sensible conclusion—few people are going to be using their computers in absolute darkness. So rather than figuring out how to light the image on the screen to make it visible, they concentrated on making the image easily readable in the light that's already in the room, being used by you to avoid bumping into furniture.

This means the Portable is hard to use when your task lighting is poor. But it also means that all you have to do to make the screen a delight to read is to get adequate task lighting—which is something you should do anyway.

In order not to be victimized by 40-watt bulbs in hotel rooms (usually installed in 300-lb table lamps placed in the least convenient place in the room), I carry a small fluorescent table lamp and an extension cord with me when I travel with my Portable. The lamp weighs less than a pound but it lights up the screen like a movie marquee, with plenty of light left over for my notes.

very
hot
tip

I set the lamp up on a box on the back of the Mac, so the gooseneck extends the fluorescent tube over the screen (but several inches above it). The light shines directly down on the screen. (It sounds horrible but it works pretty well. The only problem is finding a box or something to use to get the lamp high enough over the screen.)

🍎 *real bugs in the screen* (AN)

As I write this—on a working vacation in a warm climate—small insects, attracted by the dazzlingly bright light

bug

shining on my Portable's screen (see previous entry), are landing on the screen and sliding down into the little slot at the bottom. God only knows what happens to them down in there, but if it causes any problem, you'll be the first to kn*FRIZZ...SPREEAKK...BRIZZZAT!!!*

🍎 *you don't have to use it just because it's there* (AN)

As mentioned above, you can plug a mouse into the Portable. There's also a trackball built into the keyboard, which is handy in case your mouse gets run over by a truck. Otherwise, using the trackball is a little like living off the emergency supplies in your bomb shelter—you can do it, but what's the point? (Well, some people like them.)

No, of course I don't really have a bomb shelter.

Monitors

🍎 *bit-mapping and QuickDraw* (AN)

very good feature

One of the Mac's greatest features, and one that Mac users tend to take for granted, is how quickly all the graphic elements on its screen can be manipulated— created, redrawn, moved around. For example, windows can be shrunk, stretched, squeezed, overlapped and moved around with amazing rapidity, especially given how much detail there is in them.

This is possible because the Mac's screen is *bit-mapped*— that is, for every little dot on the screen (called a *pixel),* there's a little switch in memory that controls it. Since you can control the screen directly, you can change it quickly.

But it takes more than hardware to get a screen image as responsive and fast as the Mac's. Software is the key, and in this case the software is QuickDraw, which is built into the Mac's ROM. Developed by Apple programming genius Bill Atkinson (also the creator of HyperCard), QuickDraw is certainly a milestone in the history of personal computers. It makes your life more pleasant every time you touch the mouse.

⚫ black-and-white *(AN)*

The Mac displays black letters on a white background, thank God. I've never been able to understand the supposed advantage of all these green (or amber) screens. It's not natural, or any good for your eyes, to look at one color all the time.

very good
feature

People suggest putting some red object near a green screen to compensate, but why bother with all that? A white surface reflects all colors, black contains all colors, and black on white is what we're used to looking at on paper.

⚫ black-on-gray *(AN)*

One problem with black-on-white is that, because of the large white area on the screen, it increases the amount of flicker (see the entry on refresh rate below); that makes it harder to look at the screen for a long time. This is particularly troublesome on very large monitors, where it would be a relief to be able to switch to white-on-black, at least some of the time.

One thing you can and should do to make the screen easier on your eyes is turn the brightness down. A bright white background is very hard to look at—you want black on *gray*, not black on white. Most people keep their computer screens too bright, which puts a real strain on their eyes.

very
hot
tip

Another important step is to keep your room as dark as possible, and to eliminate reflections on the screen. If daylight does seep in, or if there are lights you can't turn off, turn the brightness up to compensate. But a dimly lit room and a black-on-gray screen are ideal.

very
hot
tip

⚫ refresh rate *(AN)*

One of the most important characteristics in a monitor is its *refresh rate*—how often it redraws the image on its screen. The refresh rate is measured in *hertz* (times per second)—abbreviated *Hz.*

If the refresh rate is too slow, you get *flicker* (also called *strobe).* Regular house current alternates at 60 Hz (here in the US); if you can see the flicker in fluorescent lights, a refresh rate of 60 Hz is probably too slow for you. 60 Hz is the refresh rate on compact Macs, but because the screen is only 9", most people find that acceptable.

Peripheral vision is particularly sensitive to flicker, so if you're in doubt about a screen, turn away from it and see how it looks out of the side of your eye. Another good way to accentuate flicker is to wave your hand in front of the screen.

The larger a monitor is, the more critical the refresh rate is. Apple uses 67 Hz on its 12" and 13" monitors for Mac II's, and other companies go up to 72 Hz and beyond on their larger monitors.

🍎 *big-screen basics* (AN)

I was never one who thought the 9" screen on compact Macs was too small. I loved its crisp, readable image and recognized that *resolution*—the number of pixels, or dots, per square inch—was just as important as the physical size of the screen. (To realize that, all you need to do is walk up close to a big-screen color TV—one of those room-filling monsters, I mean—and watch the snarling, boiling lines wrestle each other. It's a real 20th-century nightmare image.)

Still, it was annoying only to be able to see about a third of a standard 8-1/2 x 11 page at a time—especially when doing layouts for this book. So I got a Mac II and a Radius Two-Page Display. After about a day, I could no longer work on a compact Mac without having to constantly repress the urge to grab the edges of the screen and pull them farther apart. After about a week, I couldn't look at a compact Mac without feeling there was something *wrong* with it: *How come the pixels are so big? How come there's so little information on the screen?* I don't think I've ever been more quickly spoiled by anything in my life.

Larger external monitors are required with Mac II's, and you can also buy them for SE's, Pluses and other Macs. But if you get one, be aware that there's no turning back—working with a compact Mac's 9" screen will quickly become uncomfortable, then almost unbearable. (Oddly enough, I don't feel that way about the Portable's screen, which only displays 46% more information than the standard 9" screen.)

important
warning

Like TVs, the size of monitors is given in diagonal inches—the distance from one corner of the tube to another. Since not all tubes are the same shape, however, two 19" screens can be very different. The basic distinction is between tall and wide screens—or *portrait* and *landscape*, as they're sometimes called.

The wide screens are better for layout work involving facing pages and for graphics, design and engineering work in general; they're also good for large spreadsheets, and for running multiple applications in MultiFinder. If you primarily do word processing, or lay out single pages, a tall screen will be more economical.

So your first consideration, when buying a screen, is which shape you prefer. The next consideration is how much data you need to display.

You'll actually know more about a screen if you measure its width and height rather than simply rely on its advertised (diagonal) size. But even the width and height won't tell you what you want to know about a screen's capacity, because the size of the pixels—and therefore the number of them—also varies from monitor to monitor. In other words, they have different *resolutions*—different numbers of *dots per inch (dpi)*.

So let's say you know a monitor's resolution and the height and width of its screen. You still need to know how wide a border it leaves around the image (it can be half an inch or more). So my advice is to leave your measuring tape at home and think in terms of pixels.

The original Mac screen (used on the 128K, 512K, Mac Plus and SE) has 512 pixels across and 342 down, and displays them at 72 dpi. Simple division tells you, therefore, that it will display an image 7.1 inches wide and 4.8 inches high. Just think of it as 7 x 5.

(4.8 inches is actually about 44% of the 11-inch length of a standard sheet of paper, not a third. But by the time you allow for the menu bar, the horizontal scroll bar and so on, it takes just about three screenfuls to display a page.)

What size the 7 x 5 image on the original Mac screen ends up actually being on paper is a complex matter and depends both on what software and what printer you're using. But, in general, the screen image corresponds fairly closely in both size and shape to the printed copy.

The best measure of a screen's capacity is the total number of pixels it displays. The original 9" screen on compact Macs has a total of just over 175,000 pixels. Monitors available as of this writing are capable of displaying up to two million pixels—more than fourteen times the capacity of the original Mac screen—although they usually do it at more dots per inch than 72.

(I personally think 72 dpi is too large. Once you get used to 82 dpi or 92 dpi, 72 dpi looks ridiculously big and clunky. But of course it was chosen because type has always been measured in *points,* and there are 72 points to the inch.)

very hot tip

When comparing the price of monitors, forget about screen size (unless you have some particular reason for caring about it). Instead, calculate how many pixels you get per dollar. Just multiply the number of pixels across by the number of pixels down, then divide the price of the monitor into that. The bigger the resulting number, the better (everything else being equal—which, of course, it seldom is).

very hot tip

Pixels per dollar can vary quite widely. But this measure should only be the beginning of your comparison. Monitors are a lot like speakers—you can look at technical specs all day long, but the only way to buy speakers is to listen to them, and the only way to buy monitors is to look at them, ideally side-by-side.

What you're looking for is a crisp, high-contrast, rock-solid image—one that isn't washed-out, that doesn't waver or flicker, and that isn't distorted around the edges. Getting that is more important than any other consideration, and worth paying more for. Remember that you're going to be staring at the screen for hours on end; anything less than a great image will really begin to bother you.

monochrome, gray-scale, color

Monochrome monitors are the crisp black-and-white of the original Macintosh screen. What looks like gray—the Desktop, for example—is actually an arrangement of alternating black and white dots.

Each dot on a *gray-scale* monitor can be black, white or any of a number of shades of gray. With real grays available, instead of just alternating black and white dots, screen images can be of photographic quality. (Of course the grays on a gray-scale monitor are *also* composed of black and white dots, but the dots are much smaller.)

Color monitors—well, you know what *they* are. Each pixel on the screen (there are 80 per inch on Apple's color monitors) is composed of three tiny splotches of color—red, green and blue—that your eyes merge into a single, colored dot.

color video cards

To use a color monitor, you need a color video card. (A *video card* plugs into a slot on your Mac and controls the display of information on an external monitor. The more information on the screen, the more memory you need on the video card.)

On a monochrome monitor, every *pixel* (dot on the screen) is controlled by one *bit* of memory (a bit can either be a zero or a one, and thus can represent either a black or a white dot). It takes about 22K of memory to keep track of the standard Mac 9″ screen.

If you allow two bits of memory per pixel, you can have any of four colors (or shades of gray) per dot, because two bits can represent four different numbers (in the binary notation computers use, 00, 01, 10 and 11). You don't see two-bit color on the Mac much. What you do see is *four-bit color*—four bits of memory per pixel, which can represent sixteen different colors.

Eight-bit color—eight bits of memory per pixel—lets you display 256 colors on the screen. Even that's not enough for some purposes. For photographic-quality color, you need *24-bit color*, which lets you display more than sixteen million colors *at one time*—or as many as will fit on the screen.

♣ color into gray scale

If you have a color monitor, you also have a gray-scale monitor. To turn it into one, go to the Monitors icon in the Control Panel and click the *Black & White/Grays* button instead of *Color*. Then choose a number from the little list box on the right—16 if you have a four-bit color card, 256 if you have an eight-bit card. (Of course, once you click *Black & White* instead of *Color*, these numbers indicate not colors, but shades of gray.)

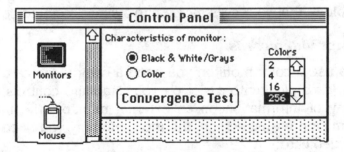

♣ faster refreshes on color monitors

Redrawing the screen of a color monitor—especially a large one—can take significantly longer than on a black-and-white monitor. If you're not working in color and want to speed things up, open the Control Panel, click on the Monitors icon and choose *Black & White/Grays* and *2* in the Colors list box.

⬤ *do you need color?*

Well, you probably *want* it, but do you *need* it? No, probably not—very few people do. Unless you're in the graphic arts industry, your output, in all likelihood, is going to be black-and-white, so you don't need color on the screen.

Keep in mind that a black-and-white screen doesn't mean you can't *assign* colors to certain elements of your document—you can, for instance, apply spot colors in PageMaker even when working in black and white. You just won't be able to see them on the screen.

If you can afford the luxury, though, there are benefits to a color monitor, even when your output's going to be black-and-white. You can organize your Desktop differently—and more efficiently, one hopes—by using colored icons. Programs like More let you outline in colors as well as fonts and styles, adding to the hierarchy of visual clues you can use to organize your thoughts. In programs like PageMaker, you can more easily distinguish between margins and rules because they're different colors. And then there's always the basic pleasure of looking at color.

⬤ *Radius monitors* (AN)

Radius makes the crispest and most contrasty Mac monitors I've seen; next to them, other big screens tend to look washed out. In addition, you get tear-off menus in all applications, a built-in screen saver you can set for five seconds or in one-minute increments up to 59 minutes, screen dumps you can crop, and menus in larger-than-normal type (the one feature I don't use).

very good feature

I bought a Radius Two-Page Display (aka *TPD)* for myself, and later bought the equivalent Apple monitor for use at Goldstein & Blair's office. I was knocked out by how much more contrast there was on the Radius screen.

The TPD displays 1152 x 882 pixels on its 19″ screen (1,016,064 pixels total—5.8 times the compact Mac screen's). This gives you an effective display area 10.75″ high by 14″

wide. This isn't quite enough for two 8-1/2 x 11 pages—unless you don't care about seeing the margins. (Don't forget that many publications are smaller than 8-1/2 x 11. Of course some are larger too.)

There are 82 dots to the inch (better than the normal 72 dpi, I think) and the refresh rate is a refreshing (sorry) 72 Hz—which is pretty good, although not the highest available.

The 19″ black-and-white Two-Page Display currently lists for $2000 (including the video card), which gives you about 508 pixels per dollar. There's also a gray-scale version (current list, $3300, with video card). The 21″ versions list for $400 more, but I don't recommend them. For one thing, they don't display any more pixels, just bigger ones; for another, that much screen is simply overkill unless you plan to sit *at least* 2–3 feet away from the monitor. (Sharon also says there's distortion around the edge of her 21″ monitor; see the next entry for details.)

Radius also makes a very slick single-page display that *pivots* from horizontal to vertical to accommodate different tasks. When you move from, say, a letter to a spreadsheet, you just tip the monitor over onto its side. It takes just a moment for the image to reform in the new configuration.

Called, logically enough, the Pivot, it currently lists for $1700 with video card. This sounds great until you realize that for a mere $300 more (at list), you can get a big, luxurious Two-Page Display that you don't *have* to tip.

Radius monitors (SZA)

very good feature

Radius was the first company to make a full-page display (called the *FPD*) for the Mac, back when the Plus was the top-of-the-line Mac. You can still get the FPD for the Plus; its ROMs have been upgraded as necessary and they're easy to get from Radius—and reasonably priced. We've had two FPD's in a Mac lab for three years at the college where I teach. They get heavy use, but there's never been a moment's problem with either of them.

The FPD (which has now been pretty much replaced by the Pivot—see the previous entry) has less distortion at the edges and corners than any monitor I've ever seen—there's so little that you don't even notice it unless you're really looking for it.

very good feature

I'm using Radius's 21″ gray-scale TPD (two-page display) now. It's a little overwhelming, but for laying out side-by-side pages in PageMaker, you can't beat something this size. Still, it's a little disappointing. Unlike the FPD, this 21″ monitor has a definite distortion for the lower third of the monitor. *[I've never noticed that on my 19″ TPD.—AN]*

It's not so terrible that it interferes with the work you're doing in the document but you can definitely see it when you keep a window open to the edges of the screen—the edges seem to curve inward towards the bottom. Despite this, I still prefer this large screen to others I've seen of its size.

E-Machines' two-page monitor has more distortion and a less crisp picture; RasterOps has less distortion around the edges but the overall picture is not as clear. (For more on both these monitors, see the next two entries.) I'll bear with the Radius's curving edges to get the clear, crisp picture.

Radius' tear-off menus are a neat trick but they clash with some inits and applications. Running the newest version of AutoSave (1.1) and tear-off menus at the same time crashes the machine. The tear-offs clash with On Cue too. And in Word, they hang up the whole system. This is no reason not to get a Radius, however, since you can always turn off the tear-off option. *[Tear-off menus work just fine in Word on my system, and with version 1.01 of AutoSave. There must be some specific configurations that cause the problem.—AN]*

important warning

Radius tech support is hard to get to—but if you hold the line long enough, you'll be given a chance to leave a message so they can call you back. And they always do. Once you get the tech people, they know what they're doing—most of the time they even know what *you're* doing.

[The head of Radius tech support called to say they've doubled their staff and now have an average wait of about a minute, with no wait in the previous two weeks exceeding 2.5 minutes. But one of our contributors recently had a problem getting some fairly simple help from them.—AN]

Mobius monitors *(AN)*

bargain

A small company, whose only previous claims to fame were Macintosh accessories like a quiet fan for early models of the SE (see the entry called *quieting the original SE* above), has come out with a one-page monitor that looks just about as good as Radius's but only costs $800.

Mobius says that both monitors are made by the same OEM *(original equipment manufacturer—*the actual producer of the basic equipment) and are identical. Radius, however, has told me that they do some advanced technical witchcraft to make the picture sharper, and certainly I've never seen better contrast on any monitors than on theirs, regardless of who the OEM was.

But even if the Mobius monitor isn't quite as good as Radius's, and doesn't have the slick software, it costs *less than half* as much, so it's certainly worth checking out. The monitor works with SE's (whose speed it claims to double) and II's. Mobius promises a free 48-hour replacement on monitors returned for warranty repairs.

gossip/ trivia

In related trivia, the company is named after the German mathematician August Möbius (1790–1868) whose one-sided surface, the *Möbius strip*, gives us the symbol for infinity (∞). Failing, for some unaccountable reason, to follow in the gold-paved footsteps of Mötley Crüe, this company neglects to use the umlaut (¨) in its name—even though, unlike Mötley Crüe, it has every right to it.

monitors for the Plus *(AN)*

If the main thing you don't like about your Plus is its small screen, at least two companies, MegaGraphics and Radius, make external monitors for the Plus—although we've heard that external monitors can overload the Plus's already marginal (and non-fan-cooled) power supply.

important warning

♦ *Moniterm's Viking monitors* (AN)

If you really want a lot of information on your screen, try the Viking 2 from Moniterm, a 19" monochrome monitor that works with SE's or II's. It displays 1280 by 960 pixels, for a total of 1,228,800—more than seven times the regular Mac screen. This is more than enough to show two full 8-1/2 x 11 pages; in fact, when you ask whatever software you're using to fit both pages on the screen instead of showing them actual size, they *expand!*

very good feature

Pixels are displayed at 92 dots per inch, which means the characters on the screen are about 70% the size they'll end up on paper. So 12-point type appears as 8.5-point, 10-point as 7-point and 9-point as 6.5-point. In general, type down to about 6-point is readable (that's even true of small fonts like Times; big fonts like Helvetica and Benguiat are readable even smaller). *Greeking* (indicating the type rather than showing the actual letters) isn't the end of the world for type below 9-point, so I don't see any problem with 92 dpi.

At its current list price of $2000, the Viking 2 gives you about 615 pixels per dollar. There's a gray-scale version that lists for $3100 and a 24" monochrome version that lists for $2600. It has the same number of pixels (who'd need more?) but they're at the regular 72 dpi instead of the Viking 2's 92 dpi. I'd think twice about getting a monitor that enormous.

I haven't had a chance to look at the Viking 2, but the image on an earlier version, the Viking 1, wasn't as crisp and contrasty as on the Radius TPD. Still, it was adequate for most applications, and Moniterm says they've improved the picture on the Viking 2. The refresh rate is 66 Hz, which is on the low end of what you want in a monitor this size.

Viking monitors are made by Moniterm itself, which also supplies them to many other monitor companies (without that name on them, of course). They seem to be well-made and Moniterm is a very well-run company, adequately

very good feature

staffed by competent people; I always get right through to the knowledgeable tech support staff, and the one time I didn't (it was before or after hours), the receptionist knew the answer to my question).

✎ *Apple monitors* (AN)

The two, small, "high-resolution" monitors (a 13" color and a 12" monochrome) don't give you a lot of pixels—just 640 x 480, not even twice as many as on the compact Macs' 9" screen. At least they now give you decent value (at their original pricing, they didn't). Based on its current list price of $600 (including the video card), the mono-chrome monitor provides 512 pixels per dollar.

Apple's two-page display isn't as good a deal. It currently lists for $2700 (with the video card), while Radius's (su-perior) TPD lists for $700 less. Apple's Portrait (single-page) Display is somewhat more competitive; it currently lists for $1700 (with the card). But still, for just $300 more (at list—less at street prices), you can have a Radius TPD! And let me tell you—staring at it at this very moment, as I have for two years—it's really a terrific monitor.

✎ *the thin gray line*

very bad feature

The thin line that appears across the width of Apple's 13" monitor about three-quarters of the way down is, they claim, a feature, not a bug. (That means you can't do anything about it; it's not a mistake—it was *designed* that way.)

The Sony Trinitron monitor Apple uses has a grid of vertical wires behind the screen that keeps the electron gun from shooting at the wrong-color phosphors. The gray line you see is the shadow cast by a stabilizing wire that keeps this grid in place—it's blocking the electrons from hitting anything on that part of the screen.

Apple says this problem is inherent in the technology that is otherwise the best available. And it's true—aside from the line, it's a good, high-quality monitor.

✦ L-View monitors *(AN)*

This 19", two-page monochrome display for the SE and the II has a fairly crisp picture (but not as crisp as the Radius's). The refresh rate is only 60 Hz, so you may have a problem with flicker.

The software lets you choose between two resolutions—832 x 600 (about 500,000 pixels; 2.85 times the normal Mac screen) or 1664 x 1200 (about 2,000,000 pixels; more than *eleven* times the regular Mac screen). That's a lot of pixels, but they're awfully small; at high resolution, things can get awfully hard to read.

At current list prices of $2400 for the SE and $2500 for the II, the L-View offers about 200 big pixels, or 800 tiny pixels, per dollar.

✦ E-Machines *(Rich Wolfson)*

I purchased two of the original E-Machine large-screen displays for the Mac Plus for our college lab and had significant problems with them right from the beginning. Despite the replacement of a bad clip (the one that connected the screen to the Mac's motherboard) and various software upgrades, the terrible wave *(raster)* traveling down the screen (caused by electromagnetic emissions from the Mac itself) made the monitor very hard to work with. Even ignoring the raster problem, the screen image wasn't ever sharp enough.

very bad feature

bug

Although E-Machine's tech support people were friendly and knowledgeable, there wasn't anything they could do. At one of the early Expos, I saw a perfectly clear E-Machine on display and was told the "fix" hadn't yet been approved by the FCC. I was told that at the next Expo, too. I've given up—the E-Machines are in boxes in a closet now.

✦ Raster Ops *(Carol Aiton)*

The RasterOps 19" color display that I use has been quite a disappointment—enough so that I'm getting a

bug

very bad feature

different monitor as soon as I can afford one. The main problem is that no matter how you adjust the convergence, only one area of the screen is sharp at any one time; at least a third of the screen is always out of focus.

Another problem is that the color is set entirely too high—a bright yellow comes out orange. Since there are no external adjustments for this, I've learned to live with it, but I haven't learned to like it.

✎ *Stepping Out* (AN)

For another approach to stretching the Mac's screen, see the entry on this program in the utilities chapter.

✎ *protecting the phosphor* (AN)

important warning

The phosphor that's painted on the inside of your screen and glows when the electron beam hits it can become exhausted from too much use, leaving dark spots on your screen. For that reason, it's a good idea not to leave an image visible on your screen except when you're actually using the computer. But you also don't want to be constantly turning the Mac on and off, because that's hard on the electronics.

That's where programs called *screen blankers,* or *screen savers,* come in. They keep track of how long it's been since you hit a key or the mouse button and black out your screen automatically after a certain amount of time— which you select—has passed. They can also create some sort of moving pattern on the screen (fireworks, stars, a clock that moves around) so you know the Mac is on. Hitting any key or the mouse brings back the image.

The bigger the screen is, the more important a screen blanker is. Fortunately, most big monitors come with their own built-in.

If you telecommunicate, make sure any screen blanker you use checks the modem port for activity. If it doesn't, and you're sending or receiving a file when it goes into action, the connection will be lost and you'll have to start the file transfer all over again.

If you don't want to use a screen blanker, you can simply turn the brightness down when you get up from the Mac. On all Macs through the SE's, the brightness control is on the front of the machine, to the left, just underneath the Apple logo (⌘).

esp. for beginners

Now don't feel that I'm patronizing you by telling you something as basic as that. I was once at the house of a very intelligent writer friend who uses her Mac extensively (and who has thanked me several times for not identifying her more specifically than this, for reasons which will immediately become obvious).

gossip/ trivia

I saw an image on her Mac's screen, so I casually walked over and turned the brightness down to black. She had no idea what had happened and totally freaked out. I showed her how to adjust the brightness, but she wouldn't calm down until I turned it back up and left it there. Even then she had the sneaking suspicion that I'd done some sort of subtle but irreparable damage to her machine.

External monitors almost always have brightness controls as well, although they're sometimes not as conveniently located. But screen blankers are really the way to go. (They're discussed in the utilities chapter.)

⌘ *Test Pattern Generator* (AN)

If you really want to compare monitors, you need this nifty piece of software written by Macintosh Bible contributor Larry Pina. In addition to testing color monitors every way you can imagine (and several you can't), it also lets you measure the speed of printers.

This piece of shareware is very well done. You can get it in all the regular places (bulletin boards, user groups, etc.) and it also comes bundled with Larry's book, *Macintosh Repair & Upgrade Secrets*.

bargain

An even more powerful version, Color Test Pattern Generator, does a wealth of color-specific tests and also a whole bunch of non-monitor-related tests that troubleshoot and pin down what's wrong with your computer. You can get it by sending $10 to Larry at 47 Meadow Road, Westport MA 02790.

❡ *multiple screens* (AN)

If you have two or more monitors connected to a Mac, icons for them will show up in the Monitor section of the Control Panel. To get more control over them (for example, to tell the Mac which one is on the right and which is one the left), hold down the [Option] key when you click on the Monitor icon.

Make sure you keep the happy-face icon on the same screen as the menu bar. To move both screen icons together, hold down the [Option] key.

Keyboards

❡ *evolution of a keyboard*

As the Mac has grown, so has its keyboard (much to Arthur's dismay, as will become obvious). The original keyboard had the basic necessities—according to Steve Jobs, who didn't view arrow keys as necessities. *(Of course not! That's what the <u>mouse</u> is for.—AN)*

~	1	2	3	4	5	6	7	8	9	0	-	=	bkspc
tab	Q	W	E	R	T	Y	U	I	O	P	{	}	\
caps lock	A	S	D	F	G	H	J	K	L	:	"	return
shift	Z	X	C	V	B	N	M	<	>	?	shift
opt	⌘								⌘	opt

The Mac Plus keyboard introduced arrow keys and also included a numeric keypad, which up until then had been available only as a separate device. *(Only?! That's how it <u>should</u> be available.—AN)* The [Return] key was enlarged and a few other keys were shifted around:

~	1	2	3	4	5	6	7	8	9	0	-	=	bkspc		=	/	*
tab	Q	W	E	R	T	Y	U	I	O	P	{	}			7	8	9	-
caps lock	A	S	D	F	G	H	J	K	L	:	"	return		4	5	6	+
shift		Z	X	C	V	B	N	M	<	>	?	shift	↑	1	2	3	
option		⌘							\	←	→	↓		0		.	ent

When the SE was introduced, two *ADB* keyboards, the standard and the extended, became available (see the next entry for more on ADB). Since you now had a choice of keyboards, you had to pay for them separately from the computer.

On the ADB keyboards, the ⌈Backspace⌉ key became ⌈Delete⌉, a special key (⌈◁⌉) was added that lets you turn on any of the Mac II family from the keyboard, the ⌈Esc⌉ and ⌈Ctrl⌉ keys appeared *[so you can run DOS software on your Mac, should you take leave of your senses and wish to do that— AN]* and the entire look and feel of the keyboard (to coin a phrase) was re-engineered. Here's how the keys are laid out on the standard ADB keyboard (current list price, $130):

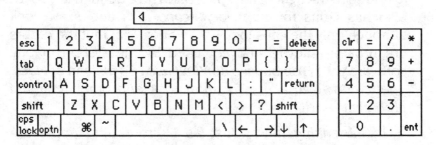

Here's the extended keyboard layout (its current list price is $230):

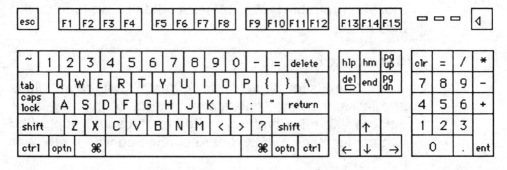

What's the hundred-dollar difference?

First, as you can see, the extended keyboard has a bunch of extra keys. They come in two groupings. The first is a row of fifteen function keys (F1 , F2 and so on) across the top of the keyboard. The first four are labeled *Undo, Cut, Copy* and *Paste;* if you're running System 6.0 or later, they perform those functions. The remaining function keys can serve any purpose you assign them with a macro program.

The second group of keys is something I call—since no one has a name for it—the *command cluster*. It includes Home , End , PgUp , PgDn , Help and ⌦ (forward delete). The first four help you move around quickly in a document. The Help key works in almost every application that has on-line help, and the forward delete key is handy (it deletes to the *right* of the insertion point instead of to the left).

The other extra you're paying for on the extended keyboard is the more conveniently-placed and logically arranged cluster of arrow keys and the extra ⌘ , Option and Ctrl keys to the right of the spacebar. The extended keyboard also has lights for *num lock, caps lock* and *scroll lock* although only the caps lock light works. (Not that the others are broken—they're just not used by the system or any software yet.) *(Too bad we don't all use PCs instead of Macs. Then we'd have a use for num lock and other technoid gibberish.—AN)*

Late-breaking news: Just as I wrote this, Apple announced the Extended Keyboard II. It costs the same and looks pretty much the same as the original extended keyboard, but you can adjust the angle from 6° to 14° for more comfortable typing. (At least I didn't have to re-do the illustration!)

🍎 *ADB* (SZA/AN)

ADB stands for *Apple Desktop Bus*. With its round plugs and jacks, it's now Apple's standard for connecting input devices like mice and keyboards to Macs and Apple II's. (On earlier Macs, the keyboard connected with a modular plug like the one on telephone cords and the mouse used a trapezoidal plug.)

ADB keyboards have an jack on either end, so you can plug the mouse into whichever side is more convenient and use the other jack for connecting to the computer.

ADB lets you chain up to sixteen devices together. This can be helpful if you want to use a trackball or digitizing tablet for some jobs and a mouse for others, if you're comparing different input devices, or if you're training people and want them all to have keyboards and mice of their own.

✦ wanted: a non-Star-Trek, non-IBM-obsequious keyboard (AN)

very bad feature

In line with the classic American belief that bigger is better, keyboard manufacturers, Apple included, keep going for larger and jazzier-looking keyboards. They seem to assume that Mac users would rather feel like they're commanding the Starship Enterprise than be able to reach the mouse without dislocating their shoulders.

Personally, I miss the tiny keyboard that came with my original 128K Mac (and that still comes with Pluses). I like my mouse *in front of me,* not six miles east of me (I probably wouldn't feel that way if I were a gibbon, but it's just my bad luck to have been born a human being) and if I preferred arrow keys and function keys to the mouse, I'd use a PC instead of a Mac and save lots of money.

very bad feature

All the current Mac keyboards share this slavish pandering to the world of IBM. On the regular ADB keyboard, for example, the Ctrl key (which virtually no Mac programs use) is more than *twice* the size of the Option key (which gets used all the time). An Esc key, four arrow keys and a numeric keypad waste further space.

I have nothing against people who need those keys for compatibility with PC software. And it's fine with me if some people prefer these yard-wide keyboards with their bewildering arrays of keys. I'm not suggesting making them *illegal.*

things to come

But why won't some far-sighted manufacturer *also* make an ADB-compatible keyboard that's as small and efficient as the one for Pluses? No numeric keypad, no arrow keys, no IBM-obsequious features like [Ctrl] and [Esc]—just a 6" x 13" little beauty that makes sense for a Mac and a mouse, rather than for an interstellar journey to the planet of the IBM drones.

● *wanted: a Star-Trek keyboard*

I don't believe that bigger is always better, but better is always better. And better is often in the eye of the beholder.

I like the larger keyboard. I use the mouse for large-scale editing and moving and the arrow keys for fine work. They're great for moving graphics a pixel at a time (in software that supports that feature) and they're also handy for moving around in lists like the ones in Open dialog boxes.

I love the [Ctrl] key—it gives me so many more options for assigning macros. The function keys at the top of the keyboard also expand macro possibilities. And now that I'm in the habit of using it, I love the forward-delete key, [⌦], which deletes the character to the *right* of the insertion point instead of to the left of it.

No one's desktop real estate could be more precious than mine has been the last few years, but the extra width of the keyboard has been worth every inch.

● *found: a non-Star-Trek keyboard* (Rich Wolfson)

If you want a few extra keys ([←][→][↑][↓], [Ctrl] and [Esc]) *without* the extra size, try the keyboard Apple makes for the Apple IIGS. It's only 4" x 15" and works with any Mac II or SE . [*Nice try, Rich, but no cigar. It's the width that's the problem, and 15" is almost as wide as the standard ADB keyboard (16.5"). I want a keyboard <u>without</u> a numeric keypad. Is that so much to ask?—AN*]

● *a longer ADB cable*

My keyboard is four feet away from the jack it plugs into on the back of my cx. Even though the coiled cable that came with the keyboard stretches to a reasonable length, it's often not long enough for that. Fortunately, Kensington, Monster Cable and several other companies make 6-foot ADB cables.

🍎 *don't use telephone cords* (DC/AN)

Just because the cables that connect pre-ADB keyboards *look like* telephone cords doesn't mean you can substitute telephone cords for them. The wires in a telephone cord twist from one end to the other, while in the pre-ADB keyboard cable they connect straight through. So if you want a longer keyboard cable, you can't simply substitute a phone cord. (But you can buy a longer cable for these keyboards from most of the Mac cable companies mentioned in the miscellaneous hardware chapter.)

important warning

🍎 *keyboard mapping* (AN)

The keys on computer keyboards aren't *hard-wired*—for example, the *x* key doesn't have to always transmit an *x* just because that's the letter on top of the key. The keys are *mapped* by software—that is, a program tells the computer what character to put on the screen when you hit a given key on the keyboard.

This means you can change the key layout to Dvorak, say, (that's a much more efficient arrangement of the keys than the standard *qwerty)* simply by modifying the keyboard driver software. (You could pry the key caps off and put them back down where they belong in a Dvorak layout if you wanted, but it's not necessary—regardless of what the key says, it will generate the character the driver software has mapped for it.)

QuicKeys is a utility program that lets you remap as many (or as few keys) as you want. For example, the way I have my keyboard set up, the ⌜,⌟ and ⌜.⌟ keys generate commas and periods even when the ⌜Shift⌟ key is held down, the ⌜'⌟ key gives me a curly apostrophe, the ⌜"⌟ and ⌜"⌟ keys give me curly quote marks, etc. When I need the usual

very good feature

characters back, I just turn QuicKeys off with a simple keyboard command. (For more on this program, see the utilities chapter.)

✇ *DataDesk Mac 101 keyboard* (AN)

This third-party ADB keyboard was one of the first that, for less than the price of Apple's extended keyboard, let you create custom command keys by assigning macros to them. But I had some problems with it when I tested it.

bug

I use a lot of em dashes—these words are surrounded by them, in case you don't know what they look like—so I'm always hitting the [Shift], [Option] and hyphen keys simultaneously to generate them. But on the MAC-101, you have to hold down [Shift] and [Option] first, *then* hit the hyphen key (I assume the same problem occurs with all [Shift][Option] characters). That doesn't sound like much of a problem, but when a certain procedure is totally ingrained, it's really maddening to have it changed on you.

Cables attach to the back of the MAC-101 (an inconvenient place) and go in upside down (the opposite of how they go into a regular Apple keyboard).

bug

Finally, the keyboard is very sensitive to being plugged in when the power is on. Doing that is never a good idea, and isn't recommended, but I've never heard of an Apple keyboard being harmed by it.

✇ *the MacPro keyboard*

The MacPro ADB keyboard from Keytronic has basically the same layout as the Apple's extended keyboard—the only differences being that the L shape of the [Return] key faces in the opposite direction and, as a result of that, the [\] key is to the right of the right [Shift] key (the domino effect makes that [Shift] key a little shorter too).

The feel of a keyboard is always a very personal thing. The MacPro is a little spongy for my taste, but the touch is adjustable (although to do that, you have to remove the keys with a special tool and replace the little rubber domes underneath them).

I don't like the way MacPro arranges its cables and connectors. First, the cable that connects it to the computer is hard-wired into the keyboard, which means you can't replace it with a longer one. It emerges from the back of the keyboard on the right—is your CPU on your left?

very bad feature

Then there's the connection for the mouse cable. At least it doesn't cater to right- or left-handers. It's smack in the middle of the back of the keyboard, so no matter which side your mouse is on, the cable has to snake around the keyboard to get to it. This also shortens the mouse cord and therefore limits the mouse's range of action. And because the cable connects in the back instead of in the side, I can't push the keyboard against the back of my desk to move it out of the way.

very bad feature

Mice and mouse substitutes

Apple's ADB mouse (AN/SZA)

The ADB mouse (standard on SE's and II's) is a joy to use. (If you don't know what ADB is, see the beginning of the keyboard section above.) Smaller and with a much lighter and more delicate touch, it's a great improvement over the original Macintosh mouse (used on the Plus and earlier Macs) which is too big, clunky and stiff.

very good feature

The ADB mouse also moves more easily, thanks to its Teflon bearings and the Teflon strip on its bottom, and it uses a heavier ball, which gives it more stability. (Since that was written, the mouse and the ball have both gotten lighter, in an unannounced equipment change from Apple. The new mouse still seems to function just fine.)

To make an old-style mouse move more smoothly, you can add Teflon to its bottom too. MouseEase from Teclind Design is a kit of four small disks of Teflon designed for that purpose.

◉ *plugging in an ADB mouse*

If you plug in a mouse after you start up, the Mac won't know it's there, because it only checks for ADB devices when it starts up. However, you can *change* your mouse while the Mac is running without any problem—at least I have done it often without any problem, and so have many people I know. But be aware that Apple recommends you shut down your system before adding or removing any ADB device.

◉ *Lester leaps in* (AN)

I've often found the cord on my mouse getting in my way as I made the big, sweeping arm movements so typical of people with my particular constellation of neurological defects. Perhaps you have the same problem. If so, you'll want to check out Lester, the cordless mouse from Light-wave Technologies. Lester works off an infrared beam, picks up mouse movements over a suitably large area and comes with a *five-year* warranty.

I plugged in Lester and a regular Apple (ADB) mouse and switched between them to compare them. Lester feels pretty similar to the Apple mouse, but the ball sometimes seems to get stuck, which means you either see no movement, or jerky movement, from the pointer. This may be a problem in software rather than hardware, but in any case, it's annoying. That's too bad, because a cordless mouse is a great idea and, as an implementation of that idea, Lester is almost there.

(Karen Faria at the G&B office tried out Lester and didn't have the same experience as I did. She writes, "I did have a problem getting used to the movement, but now I'm comfortable with it and it doesn't seem jerky at all. It's comparable to the mouse I was using before, but it's easier because it doesn't have a cord.")

◉ *trackballs*

A trackball is sort of like an upside-down mouse. A ball that's many times larger than the one on a mouse is exposed at the top of the unit, where you can roll it with your fingers or the palm of your hand. Many people swear by trackballs (I actually know one of them) and others can't stand them. They certainly take a lot of getting used to.

Kensington produced a trackball for the early Macs and now has an ADB version for later models. It has two buttons. One functions just like the button on a mouse and hitting the other locks the mouse button down until you hit it again. This is pretty convenient for keeping menus open till you decide which command you want, and it's also neat to leave the pointer in a window's scroll arrow and lock the button— *look Ma, no hands* and the window keeps scrolling.

You can set the trackball's DIP switches so that either button serves as the regular or lockdown button, and you can choose one of eight basic commands (*Undo, Save, Print* and so on) that will be executed if you hit both buttons simultaneously.

Kensington rather optimistically assumes that you'll just hang up your mouse—and so they provide a free mouse pocket with their trackballs. What you'll probably do instead is plug your mouse into the ADB connector on the trackball so you can use whichever device you're more comfortable with for the job at hand.

Like all of Kensington's products, the TurboMouse is nicely designed and very well made (I know, I dropped it down the stairs; I'd like to say it was a test, but it was an accident).

very good feature

RollerMouse from CH Products is another nicely-designed trackball. I didn't drop it down the stairs, but it looks as though it would keep on ticking if I did.

On each side of the ball, there are the two "mouse" buttons—one serves as the basic clicking button and the other as the lockdown button. As on the Kensington model, the design makes it easy enough to click any one of them comfortably. There are also four, smaller, programmable buttons; you can assign them any of eight basic commands

very good feature

(*Undo, Quit, Save*, etc.) by flipping tiny switches on the bottom of the unit. In the same way, you can choose which mouse button performs which function.

RollerMouse has more buttons than Kensington's, but that's not enough to make it a clear winner here. And I don't want to use either one of them long enough to decide which might feel better. I like my keyboard, but when my fingers have to leave it, I want a mouse waiting.

🍎 *cleanlimouse is next to smoothly mouse*

very hot tip

Cleaning your mouse occasionally will keep it gliding smoothly. The procedure is basically the same whether you have the ADB mouse or the earlier one.

Turn the ring at the bottom of the mouse to remove it and drop the ball out into your palm. Clean the three little rollers inside the mouse with a Q-Tip dipped in alcohol. Rub the ball clean with a cloth before replacing it.

very good feature

If you want to give the rollers a more thorough cleaning, Ergotron has a mouse cleaning kit that's the epitome of simple yet elegant design. You insert a velcro-covered ball into the mouse (where the regular ball normally goes), then roll the mouse around on a velcro pad that's been moistened with the cleaning fluid.

A comfortable place to work

🍎 *the importance of comfort* (AN)

The reason this section is here in the basic hardware chapter, instead of in the chapter on miscellaneous hardware and accessories, is that the importance of a comfortable place to work can't be overemphasized. Working on a computer is an *intensely* unnatural act for an animal that originally evolved to swing from tree to tree. And yet people usually pay less attention to making their workplace comfortable than they do to other, less important (although still significant) issues like which disk drive to buy.

If you're going to sit still in front of a screen for hours and hours, tapping on a keyboard and moving a mouse around, make sure you can do that with the least possible discomfort. The following entries tell you how.

⚫ basic ergonomics (AN)

If you put a compact Mac (SE, Plus, etc.) and its keyboard on the same surface, either the screen will be too low or the keyboard too high. This is less true of modular Macs, where the monitor is separate, but sometimes even putting the screen on top of the CPU doesn't get it high enough.

For comfortable typing, your wrists should never be higher than your elbows. Depending on your height and the height of your chair, this means the keyboard should be on a surface 24–27 inches from the floor.

very
hot
tip

You can also simply raise your chair, but that can cause a problem if your legs are dangling. On the other hand, dangling legs can be good for your lower back. In any case, whatever height your chair is, the critical relationship is between you and the keyboard, not between the keyboard and the floor. And the main point is, your wrists should *never* be higher than your elbows when you type (it's worth repeating).

The bottom of the screen should be 4–8 inches higher than the surface the keyboard is on, so that you can look at it comfortably without having to bend your head. And don't strain your eyes by putting it too close—allow at least a foot between the back of the keyboard and the front of the Mac.

very
hot
tip

However comfortable your workspace is, it's important to periodically change your position. Chris Allen says there's a highly rated ergonomic chair that slowly changes its position over the course of the day—automatically! It probably costs a fortune, but getting up and walking around every couple of hours (at least) is free—and very helpful.

Here's another tidbit from Chris: Just moving from the keyboard to the mouse can help prevent *carpal tunnel syndrome*, the painful wrist ailment caused by too much typing.

very
hot
tip

It's the keyboard-only users who get it the worst (and I'm willing to bet that flexed wrists are a major factor in it).

Another vital issue is eliminating reflections from your screen. (Usually they're called *glare,* which is a misleading term.) You don't want any lights or windows behind the computer; in fact, it's much better to put a computer directly in front of a window than opposite one.

**very
hot
tip**

The best place for a light is on the ceiling (or bouncing off the ceiling) somewhere between you and the screen. I use one of those $10 swing-arm drafting lamps clamped to the shelf of a bookcase. The shade is turned to the ceiling and is about six inches in front of and three feet above my left ear. When I'm working on the computer, that's the only light in the room (except, of course, for the light from the screen). There are *no* reflections on the screen.

To block the light from the windows, I have solid wooden shutters on the windows (built especially for that purpose). It's not hard to do; just get pieces of wood or particle board the right size (plywood warps) and use door hinges to attach them. If that's too much of a project for you, go to a photographic supply store and get some of the blackout cloth used to light-seal darkrooms. It's easy to install it with duct tape or push pins, but a pain to take down when you want to let some daylight into the room.

⚫ *cheap but effective computer furniture* (AN)

bargain

One way to put together a comfortable workstation is to put two tables together—a low typing table (24–27") in front for the keyboard, and a table of normal height (29–30") in the back for the monitor. A swivel can help raise the monitor (built-in or not) to where it should be, or just put it on a thick book or a sturdy box.

bargain

Another inexpensive approach is to find an old desk that has a typing well. Secure the well in the open position and use it for the keyboard, then build a higher platform behind it (using the edge of the opened typing well cover for a support) for the Mac or monitor to rest on. (The platform doesn't have to be anything fancy; just a piece of plywood will do.)

🍎 Sharon's solution *(AN/SZA)*

SZA: For comfortable mouse-reaching, I pull out the writing board of my desk and put the mouse pad there. With the keyboard's main keys centered in front of me and its numeric keypad off to the right, the mouse is too far to the right to be comfortable if it's on the same surface. Kept on the writing board, however, the mouse is to *my* right instead of the keyboard's, and it's a little lower too—very comfortable.

AN: You *bet* the mouse is too far to the right to be comfortable with those gigantic keyboards you favor— that's just the problem with them. (For more on this debate, see the keyboard section above.) But putting the mouse on a writing board hardly solves the problem. (For those of you who don't know what a writing board is, it's a slab of wood that slides out to provide a writing surface on some older desks.)

For one thing, most desks don't have writing boards. For another, those that do almost always have them on the right side—which makes them useless for most left-handers. Third, the surface of a normal desk is way too high for a keyboard—your wrists are bound to be higher than your elbows. *(But I adjust my chair, so it's fine.—SZA)*

But the main problem with what you propose is that it's hideously uncomfortable for most people. You talk about the mouse being to your right instead of the keyboard's, as if that were an advantage. But reaching back for the mouse is obviously going to put a strain on your shoulder. It certainly put a strain on *my* shoulder (I have a desk with a writing board and have tried this approach). *(Listen, if it works for me, with my orthopedic history, it's gotta work for others.—SZA)*

Amazingly (given the biomechanics of it), some people do find this approach comfortable; in addition to you, there's a woman in my office who likes it. *(Maybe there's something in the Y chromosome...—SZA)* There's certainly no harm in somebody trying it if they already have a desk with a writing board *and* a typing well (to get the keyboard low enough). But certainly no one should go out and buy such a desk, imagining that this is going to be some sort of panacea, unless they've spent a significant amount of time trying it out.

🍎 *MacTable* (AN)

Several people I know love a work table designed specially for the Mac called MacTable. Made of beechwood and plastic laminate, it's attractive and sturdily made.

very good feature

The MacTable comes with two shelves, one of which is made up of three parts. Either shelf can be put in the front or back of the table to accommodate various kinds of Macs and can be tilted 15° to minimize screen glare or to make for easier typing (the tilt also means you don't have to raise the screen as much). You can also adjust the height of whichever shelf is in the front from 26″ to 28.5″.

Made by a ScanCo, a small company in Seattle, MacTables are reasonably priced, and one friend who has one raves about their customer service.

🍎 *Ergotron monitor stands* (AN)

As I mentioned above, a computer's screen should be 4–8″ higher than the surface the keyboard rests on, so you can look at it comfortably without having to bend your head. Some people also like to be able to change the viewing angle during long sessions.

For that you need a tilt/swivel and I favor Ergotron's very heavy-duty line of them. (They also make a bunch of related accessories.) For example, MacTilt is an ergonomic stand for a compact Mac that both raises it 4″ and lets you position it just about any way you can imagine. It tilts 15° forward and 15° back, and rotates 360°. You can adjust the Mac with the touch of a finger, and it stays where you put it.

MacTilt is built so tough you can stand on it. That kind of construction doesn't come cheap but I think you save money in the long run by getting something this well made.

very good feature

⚫ *Apple's monitor stand*

Apple makes a terrific swivel-tilt monitor stand that you can get for about $65 from mail-order houses like MacConnection. It's beautifully and sturdily designed.

very good feature

⚫ *Kensington's stands*

Kensington's tilt/swivel stand for Pluses and SE's is like most of Kensington's accessories—terrific. On the other hand, its stand for the Mac II monitors is badly designed and much too lightweight. It's called a *universal monitor stand* and, like so many other one-size-fits-all items, it's really one-size-fits-none-right.

From the WetPaint clip-art collection.
Copyright © 1988–89 by Dubl-Click Software Inc.
All rights reserved.

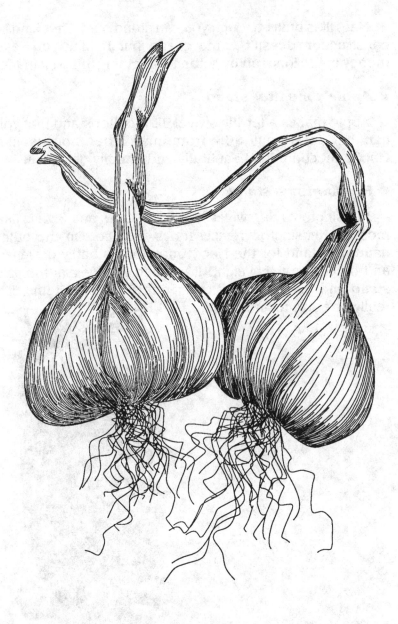

Chapter 3

Storage and memory

The basics

⚫ *storage vs. memory* *(AN/SZA/Chris Allen)*

Even experienced Mac users are often confused about the difference between *storage* and *memory*. Sharon has lost count of the number of people who've said to her, "But why am I getting out-of-memory messages? My hard disk is only half full!"

Well, there's a reason for this confusion. Storage and memory are both ways of storing information, and they're both measured in the same units—*bytes, kilobytes, megabytes,* etc. The difference is in *how* they store the information—memory does it *electronically,* on chips, and storage does it either *magnetically,* on disks or tapes, or *optically,* on CD-ROMs and optical drives.

esp. for beginners

This isn't as theoretical a distinction as it may seem; there are dramatic practical differences between the two methods.

The most common type of memory is *RAM,* which is where your Mac temporarily keeps information that you're working on. (The letters stand for *random-access memory,* because the information can be accessed in any order.) RAM is fast but it's also volatile: its contents last only as long as power is being supplied to it. If you turn your Mac off without *saving* your work, what was in memory during your work session disappears.

That's where storage comes in. It takes much longer to *write* information (store it) or *read* it (retrieve it) from magnetic or optical storage *media* (the stuff the information is put on), but once the information is in storage, it's there permanently—or at least for a long time, assuming you take reasonable care of your disks and tapes.

So—memory is like your own memory (it's fast to put things in and out of, but when you die, everything in it is gone) and storage is like books, films, tapes, letters, notes,

**esp. for
beginners**

etc. (it takes more time to get information in and out of them, but they outlive you). That's the basic distinction, and it's a good, clear, useful one. Unfortunately, there are some exceptions to it.

ROM *(read-only memory)* is information built into the computer that tells it things like what to do when the computer is switched on. Although it's stored on chips, like RAM, ROM retains its information permanently, and the information can't be changed (at least by mere mortals like you and us—there are machines that can change the data on certain kinds of ROM chips). Information is *stored* in ROM permanently, but ROM is *memory;* no wonder so many people are confused.

There are also ways to put aside some of your memory and treat it like a disk *(RAM disk),* and ways to put aside part of your disk and treat it like memory *(virtual memory).* These concepts are covered in the last section of this chapter, *memory allocation.*

The analogy Chris Allen uses for all of this is interesting and may help clarify things. He says RAM is like the top of your desk and disks are like filing cabinets nearby. (To make the analogy more precise, imagine that the overzealous people who clean your office at night throw everything they find on top of your desk into the trash.)

If you have a small desk (little RAM), you have to constantly run back and forth between it and your filing cabinets, because not many things will fit on top of the desk at one time. If you have a large desk (a lot of RAM), you have the luxury of not running over to the filing cabinets as often.

RAM disks are like drawers in your desk—smaller than filing cabinets, but convenient for some purposes because they're close at hand. ROM is like having some information permanently etched on your desk's surface so that you will never forget it.

♠ *bits, bytes, K, megs and gigs* (SZA/AN)

A *bit* is the smallest possible unit of information. It can represent one of only two things—on or off, yes or no, zero or one. Bits are the basic unit of measure for computers because computers are made up of tiny electronic switches, each of which is either on or off at any given time.

esp. for beginners

Storage media like disks are composed of tiny, magnetically charged particles of metal that point either north or south. Since there are again only two choices, the information on disks is also made up of bits.

(Working with bits means using a base-2, or *binary*, numbering system, as opposed to our everyday base-10, *decimal* system. And, in fact, *bit* is short for *binary digit*. But you don't have to know anything about binary numbers to use a computer; they're transparent to you as a user.)

A *byte* is made up of eight bits, and thus lets you represent 256 different pieces of information (00000000, 00000010, 00000100 etc., on up to 11111111). Bytes are typically used to represent single characters (letters, numbers, punctuation marks and other symbols) in text.

Hard-core computer people aren't humorless. Half a byte—four bits—is known as a *nibble* (sometimes spelled *nybble)*. Two bytes aren't a called a *gulp*, however, but a *word*. (This is pretty confusing, since in the real world, words are made up of, on average, six characters—*six* bytes—not two.)

The next commonly used unit is quite a jump from a byte. A *kilobyte*, known familiarly as a *K*, is 1024 bytes (or, if you're into math, 2^{10} bytes). Since the prefix *kilo-* means *thousand*, why 1024 bytes?, you ask. Because computers are binary and normally increase their capacities in multiples of two: 2, 4, 8, 16, 32, 64, 128, 256, 512, 1024 (a very familiar series of numbers if you've been around computers for a while).

(Despite the fact that the industry standard for a K is 1024 bytes and always has been, some companies treat a K as 1000 bytes. This is particularly true when it's in their economic interest to do so, by making their products appear to have greater capacities than they actually do. I call these shortchanged K mini-K.—AN)

The window that appears when you use the *Get Info* command on an icon gives the size both in bytes and the nearest whole K (or mini-K—since here, as everywhere, Apple counts 1000 bytes to a K, not the standard 1024):

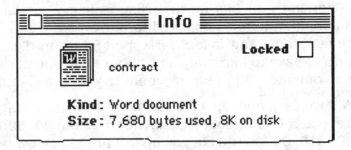

The next unit is a *megabyte* or *meg* (often abbreviated *MB*). This equals 1024 kilobytes or 1,048,576 bytes (2^{20} bytes). Here again, megabytes are sometimes rounded down to a million bytes, which we call *minimegs*.

As storage devices get more and more humungous, you'll hear the next unit of measure used more frequently: *gigabyte,* or *gig,* which is 1024 megs (2^{30} bytes). That's more than a million K and more than a billion (1,073,741,824) bytes. (We confidently expect that, marketing being what it is, gigs will be treated as an even billion bytes instead of as their true value—which, as you can see, is more than 7% higher.)

Gigabyte and *gig* are both pronounced with hard g's (as in *go*). We mention this because *gigawatt* (a billion watts) is often pronounced with a soft g (like the *j* in *jig*)—as it is, for example, in the movie *Back to the Future*. (You may remember the moment when Doc Brown, in 1955, staggers into his living room, grabs a framed picture of Thomas Edison and yelps at it: "1.21 gigawatts! Tom! How am I going to generate that kind of power?"—followed, a moment later, by: "Marty, I'm sorry, but the only power source capable of generating 1.21 gigawatts of electricity is a bolt of lightning....Unfortunately, you never know when or where it's going to strike.") Like a gigawatt, a gigabyte represents *a lot* of power.

gossip/ trivia

Here's a summary:

8 bits = 1 byte

1024 bytes = 1 K (1000 bytes = 1 mini-K)

1024 K = 1 meg (1000K = 1 minimeg)

1024 megs = 1 gig (1000 megs = 1 minigig)

In practical terms, one K equals about 170 words (1024 characters divided by the six characters in the average word)—assuming, of course, you're dealing with a text file. A bunch of text files totaling one meg would contain about 175,000 words—equivalent to three or four average-sized books.

Be aware that most Mac documents also take up a certain amount of extra space for *overhead* (things like the size, shape and location of the window in which the document appears on the screen, the fonts used, other formatting information, etc.). For example, Sharon knew that one of her Word files contained about a thousand characters, but when she checked the size of the file on disk, it was 2.5K. Overhead accounted for the additional 1.5K.

￼ what disks are made of (AN)

All computer disks consist of an iron-oxide coating on a *substrate.* In the case of floppy disks, the substrate is a flexible plastic similar to recording tape. Inside the rectangular, hard-plastic case, it's doughnut-shaped—round with a hole in the center. *(Floppies* get their name from the flexibility of their substrate.)

On hard disks, the substrate is less...floppy. It's usually made of aluminum and is called a *platter*. Typically, there's more than one platter in a hard disk drive (so calling it a hard *disk* isn't really accurate).

⚫ *how disks work* (AN/SZA)

Read/write heads put magnetic charges into the iron-oxide coating (when writing to disks) and check to see what these charges are (when reading from disks). As the disk spins, the read/write head, which is mounted on an arm, moves in toward the center of the disk and out toward the edge to find the information it wants.

Single-sided floppy drives have a single read/write head; double-sided drives have two, one on the top side of the disk and another on the bottom, as do hard disk drives.

Since iron oxide is what rust is made of, you can think of the contents of computer disks as stories written in rust with a magnet.

⚫ *initializing disks* (SZA/AN/Chris Allen)

All disks, hard or floppy, have to be *initialized* before you can use them. Initializing (also called *formatting*) divides the disk into *tracks* (concentric circles running around the disk) and *sectors* (sections of those tracks).

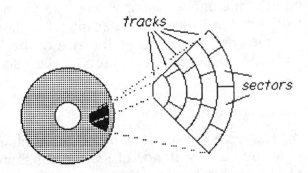

Here again, Chris Allen has an analogy that may prove helpful. He says a new disk is like a huge, blank sheet of paper. What formatting does is draw a numbered grid (like graph paper) that gives you boxes to put information in. Since disks aren't square, we can't use columns and rows for the grid; instead we have tracks (rings around the disk) and sectors (divisions within a track).

You can double the amount of information on a piece of paper by using both sides, so double-sided floppies have twice the storage of a single-sided floppies. The finer you can make the grid, the more little squares there are to put information in, so high-density disks can contain more information in the same space.

This grid takes up room on your paper, so you have less room on a formatted disk than on an unformatted one. When comparing hard disks, be aware that a 105MB hard drive from one company may have the same amount of storage as a 100MB hard drive from another company, if the first company is advertising unformatted capacity and the second formatted capacity.

Initializing is easy. When you insert a new, unused floppy into a Mac, you get a dialog box that tells you *This disk is unreadable* and asks *Do you want to initialize it?* Simply click the *Initialize* button. (To abort the process, click the *Eject* button.)

the directory and desktop files (SZA/AN)

Initializing reserves part of a disk for special files like the *directory*. Like the directory in an office building, which tells you which companies are in which offices, the directory on a disk keeps track of which files are in which sectors. Every time you save a file to disk, its location is recorded in the directory. If it weren't, you'd have to know the actual track and sector locations to find a file again; the name of the file wouldn't do you any good at all.

Another important file for which room is reserved on the disk during initialization is the *desktop file.* It stores the size and location of open windows, how the contents of windows are viewed (by Icon, Name or whatever), what each application's icons look like, the Get Info information for every file, etc. While the directory keeps track of where files are stored on disk, the desktop file keeps track of how their icons and windows are displayed on the screen.

Both the directory and desktop files are normally invisible—that is, they don't show up on the desktop. But you can get to them with programs like DiskTop or most of the other file-handling software described in the utilities chapter.

The more windows and different kinds of icons you have, and the more often you've moved things around, the larger the desktop file will get; periodically, you'll need to *rebuild* it. (For how to do that, see the entry called *rebuilding the desktop* in the hard disk section below.)

The directory and desktop files are some of the reason why the figures for *K in disk* and *K available* that appear at the top of a disk's window (when Viewed by Icon) never add up to the full capacity of the disk.

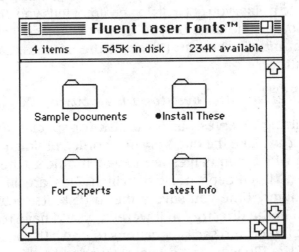

In the illustration above, which is the window for an 800K disk, the figures add up to 779K. The disk space that's unaccounted for is occupied by the directory, desktop file and similar housekeeping files (boot blocks, etc.—

you don't want to know about them). Sharon recently took an admittedly unscientific survey of her friends and found that, although these files vary in size, they consistently take up about 3% of a floppy disk's total capacity.

The desktop file, directory and other housekeeping files are found on all Mac disks, hard and floppy. The space they take up increases with the size of the disk (naturally, since the larger a disk is, the more there is to keep track of). Here's the window for Sharon's 80-meg hard disk:

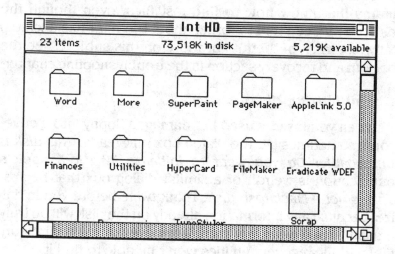

Since the actual capacity of this disk is 81,920K (mini-K, since this is a report from the Mac's desktop and Apple uses the 1000-byte K), there's 3183K dedicated to the directory, desktop files, etc. In Sharon's little survey, the percentage of space used for this purpose varied with the brand of hard disk—ranging from about 3% to 8%.

Now you might think that difference wasn't the brand of disk but rather how many files Sharon's friends had on their disks and how they were arranged—that is, how big their desktop files and directories happened to be. But hard disks reserve a certain area for these files regardless of how big or small they happen to be at any particular time. If you have one file on a hard disk or a thousand, that area remains the same.

❤ deleting and recovering files *(SZA/AN)*

When you delete a file from a disk, whether by dragging it into the Trash or by using a *Delete* command, the information isn't actually removed; the directory is simply told that the sectors previously occupied by that file are now available for storing new files. The deleted file still exists on the disk, until new information is put into the sectors in which it was stored and overwrites it.

That's what makes file recovery possible—utility programs that know how to find lost files, even though the directory's been told to forget about them (or has accidentally lost track of them). For more on this subject, see the backup and recovery section in the troubleshooting chapter.

❤ reinitializing disks *(SZA/AN)*

**important
warning**

When you insert a used but damaged floppy into a drive, you'll sometimes get the dialog box that reads, *This disk is unreadable: Do you want to initialize it? (God,* Apple's punctuation is weird!) or a similar dialog box that begins, *This is not a Macintosh disk.* Think twice before you initialize, because any information already on the disk will be truly erased (wiped clean, not merely removed from the directory file) and file-recovery utilities won't be able to find it.

If you want to reinitialize a disk that already has information on it, use the *Erase Disk* command on the Finder's Special menu; it does the same thing to a disk that initializing does.

❤ backup and recovery

For information on this important topic, see the section with that title in the troubleshooting chapter.

Floppy disks

⚜ Mac floppy disks and drives

The Mac uses three types of floppy disks, each capable of holding a different amount of information: 400K *single-sided* disks use only one side of the disk; 800K *double-sided* disks use both sides of the disk; 1.4MB *high-density* disks use both sides and pack in the information more tightly.

esp. for beginners

How can you tell these different types of disks apart? 400K and 800K disks look basically the same, but most of the latter are marked *800K* or *Double-sided* on the metal shutter or in faint print on the back.

High-density disks are easy to identify. In addition to the hole in the upper right corner that all Mac disks have (see the entry below on locking disks), there's another hole in the upper *left* corner. Unlike the locking hole, this left-hand hole has no sliding tab.

Apple makes three different floppy drives to match the three different types of disks. The high-density drive is usually called the *SuperDrive* but is also known as the *FDHD* (for *floppy drive high density*). The 400K and 800K drives are called simply that.

400K drives are no longer being made and are obsolete; unless you're running a very primitive, bare-bones, live-off-the-land Mac system, you shouldn't even buy a cheap 400K drive used. (A friend of mine was offered 20 of them *free* and said no thanks.) 800K drives, however, are far from obsolete; all the Mac Pluses still have them, and lots of other Macs as well.

important warning

The SuperDrive not only handles 1.4MB floppies but it can also read DOS-formatted 3.5-inch disks (when used with file translation software). Every current Mac model except the Plus comes with one or more SuperDrives built-in (although SE's and Mac II's didn't have them until in August, 1989).

Each of these drives can read disks up to its own capacity—so 400K drives read only 400K disks, 800K drives read 400K and 800K disks and SuperDrives read 400K and 800K and 1.4MB disks. (For an exception to this, see the entry below titled *high-density disks initialized as 800K.*)

❡ *how many K on an 800K disk?* (SZA/AN)

gossip/
trivia

And who's buried in Grant's tomb? *[This classic Groucho Marx question isn't as easy as it seems. In fact, no one is buried in Grant's tomb. The remains of General Grant and his wife are in sarcophagi (stone coffins) <u>above ground</u>.—AN]*

Once initialized, 800K floppy disks have a total capacity, for both visible files and invisible ones like the directory and desktop, of 819,200 bytes, or *exactly* 800K. The 1.4-meg floppies have a total capacity of 1,474,560 bytes, or 1.41 megs.

❡ *caring for your disks*

important
warning

Taking care of a disk protects the data that's stored on it. Here are a few basic cautions:

• Avoid opening the metal shutter; it lets dust in.

• If you do open the metal shutter, keep your fingers off the medium.

• Don't use a disk (or a drive) that has just come in from the cold or that's been sitting in the sun; wait for them to reach room temperature before using them.

• Keep disks away from magnets and magnetic fields. (For more on this, see the next entry.)

❡ *disks melt before paper burns* (AN)

Paper burns at 451° Fahrenheit (whence the title of Ray Bradbury's book). Floppy disks melt at about 160° F (the disk itself, that is—the part that actually holds the data). So a normal fireproof safe won't protect the data on your disks.

There *are* safes that are designed to keep their contents below 160° but they cost an arm and a leg.

I have another approach, which is to put a fireproof storage box inside a fireproof safe. I don't know if this will work but it ought to (if my house burns down, I'll let you know the results). It certainly costs less, since both fireproof safes and fireproof storage boxes (the regular ones, designed for paper) are relatively inexpensive.

bargain

¢ *floppy disks and magnets* (SZA/DC/Chris Allen)

Because information is stored on disks magnetically, magnets placed near disks can hopelessly scramble that information. Halogen lamps and electric motors generate magnetic fields. There are even magnets in some paper-clip dispensers.

Anything with a speaker has a magnet in it; this includes your phone as well as your stereo. Usually this isn't a problem, but can be if the floppy is exposed for a long period of time, or if it's an old AT&T phone. They have very strong electromagnets in them to make the bell ring. Since the bottom of the phone case is metal, the entire phone becomes an electromagnet. So it's not a great idea to set one of these phones down on top of a floppy disk.

important warning

The ImageWriter I has a magnet underneath the left side of the cover, so put your disks there at your own risk. The cover of the ImageWriter II has a much smaller magnet on the right side, but since the surface is slanted at an angle, disks will probably slide off if you try to put them there.

Then of course, there's always the magnet you can't anticipate. Sharon's sister's friend stored seldom-used disks in the bottom drawer of a metal desk. After only a few months of storage, they became unreadable, although disks stored for only a few weeks were fine. It turned out that the heavy-duty vacuum cleaner used by the office cleaning staff had a very large magnet in its head to pick up paper clips from the carpet. Weeks of that vacuum head coming in contact with the metal desk magnetized the disks.

⑤ airport X-ray machines

I've never met anyone who's lost a disk to airport security—floppies or hard disks. But keep in mind that while the X-rays themselves are harmless, the motors that drive them have magnetic fields strong enough to damage a disk. So, as with film, the prudent thing is to keep your disks out of the X-ray machine and have them checked by hand.

⑤ disks are tougher than you think

All the above advice notwithstanding, disks can take most of what you dish out. When I got my first Mac, my younger son was two years old. While I worked, he often amused himself with disks—stacking them, knocking them over and even giving them an occasional Frisbee toss. I never had a problem with any of the disks—except, perhaps, for *finding* them when they wound up under the couch.

Even as I write this, I have a stack of floppies right next to the telephone—sometimes there's one on or under the phone. I've never had a problem from that either. I guess I'd rather be sloppy than safe, but my official advice is that it's better to be safe than sorry.

⑤ the yellow plastic disk

**important
warning**

The yellow plastic disk that comes with 800K floppy drives keeps the drive heads from cracking against each other or going out of alignment when you transport the drive. If you misplace the disk and can't find it when you move the Mac, insert a floppy disk in the drive instead; it won't provide as much protection as the yellow plastic disk, but it's better than nothing. Use a disk you don't need, however, since disks can be ruined when left in an inactive drive, especially during transport.

The SuperDrive, though double-sided, doesn't need a disk during transport because when you Shut Down the Mac, the heads automatically *park*—that is, they lock securely apart so they can't bang together. Although everything I've read recommends that you *don't* use the yellow plastic disk for the SuperDrive, Apple inserts it when it ships new machines with SuperDrives and fines its dealers for improper packing if the yellow plastic disk isn't in a SuperDrive when it's returned.

❡ *when to buy an external SuperDrive*

If you have an internal SuperDrive, you'll never need a second, external one—especially since you can buy a 40-meg hard disk for just $50 more!

If you don't have an internal SuperDrive, you should only buy an external one if you need to read Macintosh high-density disks (which aren't a standard and won't be for a while) or the 3.5-inch disks used on IBM PCs or compatibles. (For more information about reading non-Mac disks, see the communications chapter.)

❡ *where to put an external floppy drive* (SZA/DC)

A floppy drive can be placed flat or on its side, but *where* you put it is also important. Keep it to the right of an SE, Mac Plus or earlier Mac. The power supply on the left side of these models sometimes interferes with reading from and writing to the disk.

Did you ever notice how short the cable is that comes with the external drive? That's to remind you not to put the drive on the top of your Mac. It's too hot up there, and such an arrangement could damage your disks or even the Mac itself, if you block its air vents.

**important
warning**

❡ *re-using floppies*

When you want to re-use a floppy, use the Special menu's *Erase Disk* command, even though that takes longer than just dragging the disk's contents to the Trash. Erasing the disk reinitializes it and causes the Mac to check that the entire disk is in good working order. (When it's not, you get the *initialization failed* report.)

❡ 400K disks reinitialized as 800K

The difference between 800K (double-sided) and 400K (single-sided) disks is that one side of a 400K disk either failed the manufacturer's quality control tests or wasn't tested at all. In spite of this, most new 400K disks can be formatted as 800K—but I don't recommend it. If they were good enough to sell as double-sided, wouldn't the manufacturer have done that and made more money on them? 800K disks don't cost much more than 400K ones, so why take a chance?

**important
warning**

400K disks that have already been used in single-sided drives are extremely difficult to reformat as double-sided. That's because the unused side of the disk has been pressed—and usually damaged—by the single-sided drive's pressure arm. I took 25 old 400K disks and tried to reinitialize them as 800K disks; all but five failed, and I wouldn't trust those five either.

❡ high-density disks initialized as 800K *(SZA/Chris Allen)*

High-density (1.4MB) floppies use a finer iron oxide dust than regular floppies, and SuperDrives use lower magnetic power to read and write to them. This makes them less reliable than 800K floppies.

800K drives can't detect when a high-density floppy has been inserted and will format it as an 800K floppy. The disk will work fine…in other 800K drives. But if you put it in a SuperDrive, the Mac won't recognize the formatting and you'll get a *This disk is improperly formatted for use in this drive. Do you want to initialize it?* dialog box. (This comes as an unpleasant surprise to those of us who were used to 400K disks being read in the 800K drives without any problem.)

**very
hot
tip**

If you need the information from a disk that's been formatted in this way and there's no 800K drive available, you can fool the drive by using tape to block the hole in the upper left corner of the disk. Consider this a temporary fix only—the tape's bound to come off sooner or later, and Murphy says it will come off in the drive.

You can try to reformat the disk as 1.4-megs, but since 800K drives use more magnetic power, a SuperDrive won't be able to thoroughly erase the disk and it's likely to be *much* less reliable. So—*don't* mix 800K and high-density floppies.

important warning

⚫ *using 800K disks as high-density*

A few friends of mine have drilled holes in the cases of a few 800K disks and initialized them as high-density disks, with fair-to-middling success.

I don't recommend this procedure for two reasons. First, it's extremely difficult, if not impossible, to make a hole in the case without leaving some tiny speck of plastic loose inside the case, which can eventually work its way onto the actual disk and wreak havoc.

Second, as mentioned in the last entry, the magnetic particles on a high-density disk are smaller (that's how they pack more information into the same amount of space). The read/write head on a SuperDrive can't always align the coarser magnetic particles on an 800K disk properly. Even though it might work one time, it might not the next, and you can wind up with all the data on the disk being ruined.

important warning

⚫ *the paper-clip trick*

The tiny round hole next to the floppy drive slot is for manually ejecting disks. It's sized exactly for a straightened-out paper clip. Put the clip into the hole and push firmly to eject the disk. This is the only way to get a disk out when the computer's off, and it works in *emergency* situations while your computer's on.

esp. for beginners

⚫ *disks that bomb when you insert them*

If you get a bomb as soon as you insert a disk, either the disk is bad or you have a corrupted desktop file. If there's information you want to recover from the disk, see the *Backup and recovery* section in the troubleshooting chapter. If there isn't, try the methods below to get your disk back into working order.

Insert the disk while holding down ⌘ and Option. You'll get a dialog box asking if you want to rebuild the desktop; click the *Yes* button. Rebuilding the desktop creates a new desktop file. You'll lose any Get Info comments you've put in your files, but everything else will be fine. (In early system versions, rebuilding meant losing all your folder names, too. In System 7, rebuilding shouldn't even affect the Get Info comments since they're stored in a different file.)

If that doesn't work, hold down Tab, Option and ⌘ while you insert the disk. If you accomplish this minor gymnastic feat, you should see the *This is not a Macintosh disk. Do you want to initialize it?* dialog box. Click the *OK* button.

very hot tip

If *that* doesn't work, insert another (blank or dispensable) disk into the drive. Select it and choose *Erase Disk* from the Special menu. While the confirmation dialog box (*Are you sure you want to erase...*) is on the screen, use the paper-clip trick described in the entry above to eject the disk. Then insert the damaged disk and click the *OK* button, allowing the initializing to proceed. The Mac won't know you switched disks.

If none of these methods works, or if the initialization fails, your disk is really trashed and you should recycle it as a high-tech coaster.

❖ *disks stuck in drives*

important warning

If a disk is *really* stuck in a drive, don't force it. (I know someone who tried to get one out with needle-nosed pliers.) Whether it's a problem with the disk label or the drive's read/write heads, forcing a disk out is likely to ruin the drive.

A stubbornly stuck disk requires that the drive be taken apart. Your dealer can do it, and probably should, but a knowledgeable and intrepid friend can also come in handy. *(Remember—intrepid alone isn't enough. Free help can turn out to be expensive, if you end up having to buy a new drive.—AN)*

✦ disk ejection at startup

If you're starting your Mac and there's a startup disk in the drive that you don't want read, hold the mouse button down while you start the machine, and keep it down until the disk ejects. You'll probably only need to do this if you crash with a disk in the drive. At most other times, you won't have a disk in a drive when you start up, because the Mac normally ejects all disks when you shut down (and you won't have put one in after the Mac shut down because it's not a good idea to store disks in a machine when it's off).

You only have to do this manual ejection with startup disks—other disks get spit out automatically when you start the Mac.

✦ protecting confidential data (DC/AN)

If you work with confidential data on disk, keep in mind that deleting a file doesn't actually remove the data (see *deleting and recovering files* in the basics section above). The information stays on the disk and anyone can recover your secrets using any one of several utility programs. Writing another file to the disk may remove the old file; reinitializing the disk certainly will. (For other approaches, see the *complete delete* entry in the utilities chapter and the entries on security software in the troubleshooting chapter.)

✦ locking disks

To lock a disk so that nothing can be changed on it, and so it can't be erased accidentally, simply slide the little tab in the upper right corner so that the square hole is open. (It's always bothered me that the disk is *locked* when the hole is open and *unlocked* when it's closed.) It's a good idea to lock all your master disks.

A disk that's locked shows a lock (what else?) in the upper left corner of its window:

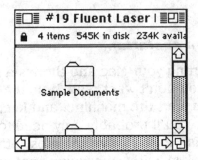

❖ removing old disk labels *(C.J. Weigand/Chris Allen)*

CJ: Ordinary lighter fluid will quickly remove old, stubborn labels from your disks without causing damage. (Even if it seeps inside, it just evaporates. I've even used lighter fluid to clean fingerprints and sticky, dried soft drink off the actual floppy-disk surface itself.)

Saturate the label for a few seconds, then gently remove it with an inexpensive razor-blade scraper (you can get one in any hardware store). The label should lift off pretty much in one piece. You can then use a cloth moistened with lighter fluid to scrub off any leftover residue.

CA: Most lighter fluids are impure; they don't evaporate completely and leave a film. A better approach is to use "stickum" removers available from most art-supply houses that are specifically designed for removing labels and other sticky paper. With these you don't even have to use a razor blade.

SCSI devices

❖SCSI basics

SCSI (which is short for *small computer system interface* and is pronounced *scuzzy*) is a standard way to connect computers to hard disks and other devices so information can pass between them. (Anything that connects to the Mac through a SCSI port is called a *SCSI device*; this includes most hard disks, scanners, CD-ROM readers and non-PostScript laser printers.)

esp. for beginners

Apple introduced a SCSI port on the Mac Plus; all Mac models since then have had at least one external SCSI port plus an internal SCSI connection for a hard disk. Those of us who were thrilled by how much faster than floppies the first Mac hard disk was were bowled over by the first SCSI hard disk.

Another benefit is the ability to connect one SCSI device to another, creating a chain of linked devices any one of which the Mac can access. (This is sometimes also called the SCSI *bus.)*

❖ SCSI ID numbers (Michael Bradley/SZA/Chris Allen)

A SCSI chain can contain seven devices plus the Mac. Each device on the chain gets its own SCSI ID number (also known as an *address),* from 0 to 6. The Mac itself (which isn't technically a SCSI device) is always assigned ID number 7 and the internal hard disk (if there is one) always gets number 0.

If you don't have a particular drive set as the startup device in the Control Panel (and you can't do that on a Plus), the Mac will look first to SCSI ID number 0 (typically the internal hard drive), then try to start from ID number 6, then 5, and on down to 1. Thus an external hard disk you want the Mac to start from should be given a higher ID number than SCSI devices that you don't want to start up from.

very bad feature

Some hard disks allow you to set their SCSI ID numbers with software. This isn't a good idea, because if any two SCSI devices in a chain have the same ID number, your system will crash; you may even wipe out data on one or more hard disks. (It doesn't matter whether you've changed the numbers or they came that way.)

If you disconnect all of the devices except one, you still won't be able to change its ID number because it will be "in use by the System" (since you started from it). Even if you start from another SCSI disk, and put the device whose number you want to change behind it in the chain, you may get that message when you try to change the ID number of the nonstartup disk (it shouldn't happen, but sometimes it does).

This isn't a problem if the ID numbers are set with actual physical switches on the hardware. If there's an ID number conflict, your system will crash just the same but you'll be able to turn the device off, reset one of the switches and then restart. (The best kind of SCSI number switches are dials, because buttons can easily get bumped and change the number of a SCSI device while in use.)

⚝ *terminators* (SZA/AN)

This has nothing to do with Arnold Schwarzenegger. A *terminator* is a little piece of hardware that looks like the plug at the end of a SCSI cable, except there's no cable attached to it. Terminators keep signals from echoing back and forth along the SCSI cabling, which can cause errors. The faster a machine is, and the more peripherals are attached to it, the more important termination is.

Every SCSI chain needs one or two terminators. Internal hard disks always come already terminated, so if that's all you have, you're set. If you have more than one SCSI device, you need a terminator on the first and the last device in the chain (not counting the Mac, of course) and no terminators in between. (This means the first and last devices *in the actual, physical chain*—the one nearest the Mac and the one farthest away—not the ones with the highest and lowest SCSI ID numbers.)

Since virtually all external SCSI devices have two SCSI jacks on the outside of the case, and since all the devices in the middle of the chain will have both jacks filled, the simple rule is: if a jack doesn't have a terminator in it, plug one in.

The problem with that simple rule is that some devices—many hard disks, for example—come with termination already built in. The manual should tell you whether or not that's the case, but given how wretched most manuals are, it probably won't. If it doesn't, give the company a call to find out. Apple now recommends that manufacturers not use internal termination.

Some devices also have a little termination switch on the outside that let you turn termination on and off (depending on whether the device is at the end of the chain or not). This should be standard equipment on all SCSI devices.

The IIfx is particularly fussy about termination. You *must* use Apple's special black external terminator at the end of the fx's SCSI chain, and no device in the chain, including the last one, can be internally terminated.

important warning

✎ *chaining SCSI devices* (C.J. Weigand)

Chain more than a few SCSI devices together and you're bound to run into problems. The types of devices installed, the way they're terminated, the order in which they're hooked up, the SCSI addresses assigned to each device and the total length of the interconnecting cables all play a role in determining whether or not the system will function properly. (For a supposedly standard interface, SCSI needs a lot of work.)

bug

Some devices won't work correctly if installed together on the same bus. For example, if you use a tape drive for periodic backups, don't also try to hook up a removable hard disk drive. Apple, in its infinite wisdom, designed SCSI with only one backup channel and both types of drives are considered backup devices. If you connect

important warning

both, only one will work. They may both appear to work, but you'll discover, probably too late (as I did), that one of them really isn't doing the job:

bug

I thought I'd backed up my hard disk successfully on tape, but found when trying to restore information from the tape to the disk that no files were visible or accessible, even via MacTools. Then I tried a different arrangement of the drives. The result? Only half a backup was made before the tape froze in the drive. A third arrangement resulted in the removable-media drive not even appearing on the desktop.

bug

Contrary to expectations, some SCSI devices function properly only if connected in a certain order; at least one tape drive manufacturer requires their unit to be at the other end of the chain from the Mac. So you may have to experiment a bit to hit upon a satisfactorily working combination. If all else fails, sometimes changing a SCSI address to a higher or lower number can get a balky drive working again. Make sure no two devices are assigned the same number, though, or you might wipe the contents of both disks.

important warning

Some SCSI devices come terminated but, as mentioned above, only the first and last in the chain should remain so. If you want to use an internally terminated device in the middle of a chain, you'll have to remove the termination.

esp. for power users

Generally, you have to open the case and lift out the internal mechanism to get at a device's terminating resistor, a job best reserved for a qualified technician. If you're fearless enough to try it yourself, however, you should know that terminating resistors are usually burnt yellow or robin's-egg blue. Most are socketed and snap out easily, although you'll occasionally find some that are permanently soldered in place.

important warning

If you use too much cable, you'll experience the same kind of problems improper termination can cause. The total cable length, from the back of your computer to the last device in a SCSI chain, shouldn't exceed eighteen feet (to be extra safe, fifteen feet).

Officially, the standard is seven meters (about 23 feet), but that's a dream. The fail length seems to vary slightly according to the type of cables, connectors and devices used. In my experience (I generally have all SCSI addresses in use with a variety of devices), it usually turns out to be about eighteen feet, but I lost the chain once with as little as fifteen feet.

When experimenting with different SCSI arrangements, be sure to turn off all power before you connect or disconnect cables. If you do it with the power on, you can get transient voltage spikes that can damage the equipment.

important warning

⬥ *SCSI cables* *(AN/SZA)*

There are two kinds of SCSI connectors—25-pin and 50-pin—and thus many possible kinds of SCSI cables (25-pin male to 25-pin male, 25-pin male to 25-pin female, 25-pin male to 50-pin male, etc.—not to mention all the various lengths).

The industry standard is the 50-pin connector, and most SCSI manufacturers keep to it, which means you can use one standard kind of cable to chain them together. But, to save room, Apple went with a 25-pin connector on the back of the Mac. (They do use the 50-pin connector for their internal hard disks, but even here, their implementation of the interface isn't standard.)

Most hard drives come with a 25-pin to 50-pin cable (called the *system cable)* for hooking up to the Mac directly; if not, you'll need to buy one. The standard 50-pin to 50-pin SCSI cable is sometimes called the *peripheral cable.* (For the best peripheral cable to get, see the entry on Liberty hard drives in the hard disks section below.)

Most SCSI cables are about three feet long; you can get longer ones, or use expanders on the basic ones, to get noisy drives out of earshot. But remember not to go over eighteen feet (less is better).

❝ *when SCSI devices won't boot*

If you start your system and one or more of the SCSI devices you have hooked up doesn't appear on the desktop, it's usually due to one of these problems:

- one (or more) of the SCSI devices in the chain isn't turned on (for more on this, see the next entry)

- two (or more) of the devices share the same SCSI ID number

- the chain is improperly terminated

- the total cabling is too long

- something's broken—a SCSI device, a cable or a terminator

Utility programs like SCSI Probe or SCSI Tools (described in the *SCSI utilities* entry below) can sometimes help you *mount* devices (get the Mac to realize that they're there).

bug

If your chain includes an Apple scanner, there are some special considerations—not the least of which is that you may need new ROM for the scanner. See the miscellaneous hardware chapter for more details.

very
hot
tip

The inits used with many SCSI devices can also cause problems. If your system runs too low on memory or if the inits clash with one another, that can prevent a SCSI device from mounting (getting the Mac's attention) For more on how to manage inits, see the utilities chapter.

❝ *all SCSI devices must be on...probably* (SZA/AN)

In general, every device that's connected in a SCSI chain must be turned on or the whole chain won't boot. But there *are* some circumstances when you can leave a device off.

Sharon experimented with a SCSI chain of a Mac IIcx, an Apple internal hard disk, an Apple CD-ROM reader, a DaynaDrive and an Apple scanner—in that order. With the scanner off, everything else still worked. With the DaynaDrive off, she couldn't access the scanner but the CD-ROM still worked. With the CD-ROM off, she couldn't access the DaynaDrive or the scanner.

That led her to assume that you simply can't access anything on the chain beyond the turned-off device...but then she reconfigured the chain as follows: IIcx, internal hard disk, DaynaDrive, CD-ROM and Apple scanner. Now she could access the other devices even when the DaynaDrive was off.

Chris Allen says that if a SCSI device is properly designed, you should be able to turn it off without it interfering with the other devices on the chain. In any case, the simple approach is just to hook up all your SCSI devices to one surge suppressor and always turn them on together.

✝ *SCSI utilities*

Here are three utility programs that are helpful when you're using SCSI devices:

SCSI Probe (a shareware program written by Robert Polic) tells you what's assigned to each SCSI number (if anything), who manufactured the device and even what version it is. It also lets you mount and unmount devices (that is, bring them to the Mac's attention and make the Mac forget they're there).

very good feature

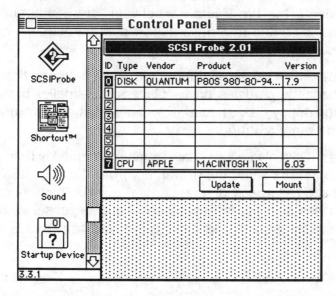

(I use this program—it's neat. We would have put it on The Macintosh Bible Software Disks, but we couldn't find Robert Polic to get permission from him. Too bad.—AN)

Like SCSI Probe, SCSI Tools (shareware by Paul Mercer) lets you see which ID numbers are assigned to which devices in a chain, and lets you mount and unmount devices.

SCSI Evaluator ($20 shareware by William Long) does a lot of pretty technical things, like check the performance of your SCSI drive and bus. When you pay your shareware fee, you receive a 100-page manual for the program.

Hard disks

❖ hard disks and hard drives

Unlike floppies, where the disk and its drive are two separate things, a *hard disk* and *hard drive* are two names for the same thing: a rigid, usually nonremovable disk (usually several disks, or *platters*, stacked one on top of the other) and the case that houses them.

There's space between the platters and each has its own set of read/write heads (top and bottom). In floppy drives, the read/write heads actually touch the disk; in hard drives, they don't, but the tolerance between the heads and the platters is so fine that the smallest dust particle can get in the way. That's why hard disks are sealed.

A hard disk stores a lot more data than a floppy. Because the magnetic particles on its platters are smaller than the ones on floppy disks, a hard disk can pack more information into the same amount of space.

Hard disks also access data much more quickly than floppies (open the same file from a floppy and a hard disk and you'll see the speed difference right away). That's because hard disks spin faster than floppies and because, with the information packed more closely, the read/write heads don't have to travel as far. Also, since the hard disk is always spinning, there's no waiting for it to come up to speed. (One final reason hard disks are faster: you don't have to spend time looking for, inserting and ejecting all those floppies.)

the advantage of hard disks

The speed of hard disks varies, with two main determinants being *fragmentation* and *interleave*. For more on this, see the entries on those topics below.

A third advantage of hard disks is convenience—you have all your applications and desk accessories in one place. I still remember what a thrill it was to get my first hard disk and not have to wonder, as I did when I used several different system floppies, *which* Scrapbook, Note Pad or Calendar information would come up.

Before a hard disk can be used, it must be initialized. Some manufacturers make you do the initializing yourself, but usually the disk is already initialized when you buy it.

❡ *you need a hard disk* (AN)

Hard disks used to be seen as luxuries, something lusted after by the great masses of computer users (myself among them) but owned by few. Now they're pretty much standard equipment. A Mac running off floppies isn't useless but it's hard to do any kind of serious work without a hard disk. So if there's any way you can afford one, get one. Once you have it, you won't know how you lived without it.

⬢ *internal vs. external hard disks* (AN)

The advantage of an internal hard disk (one that's mounted inside the Mac itself) is that you don't have to lug a separate hard disk around when you're moving your Mac. Internal hard disks also tend to be somewhat cheaper than an equivalent external hard disk and of course they take up no desk space.

There are several disadvantages to internal hard disks, however. A Mac with an internal hard disk is both more fragile and heavier than a normal Mac. If the disk needs to be repaired, you'll be without your Mac for the interim (unless you want to pull the internal hard disk out). If you want to diagnose whether the hard disk or something else in the Mac is causing the problem, it's a lot easier to disconnect an external hard disk and plug in a different one than it is to remove an internal hard disk.

So, I think that, everything else being equal, an external hard disk is usually a smarter move.

(You'll certainly want an external drive if you use a Mac at work and another at home. It's great to be able to take just the drive back and forth.—SZA)

⬢ *$/meg* (AN)

*very
hot
tip*

The first things to look for in a hard disk are reliability, support and length of warranty. Then you want to think about price, and the best way to evaluate that is dollars per megabyte of capacity. Just take the cost and divide it by the number of megs the drive holds (but don't rely on the advertised capacity—see the next entry for more on that). The lower the number, the better.

The final consideration is speed. I put this last because all hard disks are pretty fast by now, and also because advertised speeds don't always have a lot to do with how fast a hard disk actually is when you're using it. Even if they did, it's a little like getting a car with a top speed of 150 instead of 130—what practical advantage is there?

🍎 *untruth in labelling* (AN)

With very rare exceptions, the number of megabytes a manufacturer says you get is a lot more than the actual capacity of the drive. It's really a disgrace how completely unprincipled this has become.

very bad feature

First they all treat a *megabyte* as a million characters (it's actually 1,048,576 characters—almost 5% more). If you don't think that's significant, I'll be happy to take a 5% commission on everything you buy. But even using these *minimegs* (as I like to call them), they lie.

I own one "144MB" hard disk that holds 133.5 megs (136.7 minimegs) and a "45MB" hard disk that holds 41.7 megs (42.7 minimegs). I'd tell you the brands but it wouldn't be fair to them, because virtually everyone does the same thing.

Another way drive manufacturers cheat is by advertising the unformatted instead of the formatted capacity. So— ignore a drive's advertised capacity in megs. Get its actual, *formatted* capacity in bytes, divide by 1,048,576, and use that in your $/meg calculations. Don't think for a moment that you can compare the prices of two "80MB" or "150MB" drives until you've determined what each one *really* holds.

very hot tip

🍎 *which brand to buy* (AN)

We're not big enough to set up a comprehensive program of hard disk testing, so what we'll give you here are just some rules of thumb. Still, like most rules of thumb, they're based on a lot of experience, mine and other people's, and they should serve you well.

*very
hot
tip*

The first and most important rule of thumb is: *The manufacturer of the disk itself is more important than whose name is on the case.* (It is true that it's the name on the case, not the maker of the actual drive mechanism, that's going to provide the support. But even the best company isn't going to be able to provide good support if all their drive mechanisms start going bad, and if the drive mechanisms don't fail, you won't *need* support.)

*very good
feature*

In our opinion, the best maker of actual drive mechanisms (platters, read/write heads, etc.) is Control Data Corporation. Their CDC Wren mechanisms are famous for continuing to run while being shot from cannons, but they only come in larger sizes—about 100 megs on up.

*very good
feature*

Most people we know seem to think that the best mechanism for smaller drives is made by Quantum (despite some problems that developed with the Quantum drives installed in Macs). We use several of these, and have been quite happy with them.

*very bad
feature*

In our experience, the worst maker of drive mechanisms is Rodime. At the office we had Rodime mechanisms in three different makes of drive and had problems with every single one of them.

*very good
feature*

Since the drive mechanism is the heart of a hard drive (virtually all you have to add is a power supply and a case), some mail-order houses are putting them together themselves. For example, one company we've had very good service from, APS, packages 40-meg Quantum drives and sells them at a very good price. I suppose they have some sort of name on the case, but we just think of them as Quantums.

Since you won't always know which drive mechanism a manufacturer uses (they sometimes switch, or even use several suppliers at the same time), a second rule of thumb is: *Get the longest warranty you can.*

Since manufacturers' warranties don't do you any good if a company collapses (as those of us with Jasmine drives discovered), a third rule of thumb is: *Buy from a vendor you know and trust (and hope they don't change).*

The fourth and final rule of thumb is: *Talk to people who've had good, hands-on experience, and get the same kind of drives they have.* Unfortunately, drive manufacturers come and go, and the quality of their products sometimes seems to wax and wane with the phases of the moon. So the fact that a friend has had good luck with a particular brand is no guarantee that you will too, months or years later.

Still, your friend's experience is likely to be more current than ours can be, given time lag inherent in publishing a book. That said, the entries that follow describe our experience with various brands of hard disk.

❤ *Magic drives* (AN)

I've been using a Magic 300 drive from MacProducts USA for almost a year and I haven't had a bit of trouble with it. This isn't surprising, since the drive mechanism is a CDC Wren (see the previous entry).

very good feature

300 megs may be more than you need to handle your Christmas card list and one-page letters, so you'll be happy to know that there's also a Magic 150 (for $1500, or around $10–$11/meg, depending on what its actual capacity is). But if you can afford $2150, consider the Magic 300; it's really a luxury to never have to even *think* about how much disk space you have left, and with a capacity of 290,295K (283.5 real megs), the cost per meg is only $7.58.

bargain

❤ *Liberty hard disks* (Chris Allen)

Liberty Systems is a small hard-disk manufacturer that makes small hard disks. In fact, their drives are the smallest on the market—only two inches wide, five inches tall and seven inches deep (just a little larger than floppy disk drives). Yet they contain from 40 to 205 megs of data!

very good feature

**very good
feature**

Everything is included in the attractive gray metal case; there's no external power supply, just a standard power cable to the wall. (There's also no fan, so these drives are virtually silent.) You can easily fit a Liberty drive into a briefcase, with plenty of room left over. For transporting large amounts of data, only SyQuest cartridges are smaller, but they require an expensive drive at both locations.

The actual mechanism in the three smallest Liberty drives is made by Quantum and comes with a two-year warranty. As of this writing, the 40-meg Liberty drive lists for $700, the 80-meg for $950 and the 105-meg for $1050. They also make a 210-meg drive with a Rodime mechanism *(I wouldn't trust it.—AN)* for $1600.

You only get the most basic software with these drives, but at least it's reliable. Their manual isn't great but their telephone support is adequate. Liberty only sells direct to consumers. When you order a drive, there are a couple of other things you should get.

**very good
feature**

One is a nice grey padded carrying case with a shoulder strap ($30). The strap is overkill for such a small drive, but the case is nice and worth the small expense. The other is a cable for connecting SCSI peripherals. Instead of the usual stiff, bulky affair, it's a three-inch ribbon cable—perfect for anyone whose drives have so many SCSI cables behind them they can't get pushed against the wall. And it only costs $20.

Ehman hard disks

bargain

Ehman Engineering has a line of internal and external hard disks. We bought the 20-meg external for our user group because it was the lowest-priced unit around ($400 at the time). It worked well, it was quiet and it survived a lot of travel but...well, there's no way to put this kindly—it was ugly (or at least very homely). And its awkward size—about three inches wider than the standard Mac—kept it from fitting in a Mac carrying case.

The cases have since been redesigned—not only are they prettier but they now match the standard Mac footprint and thus will fit in carrying cases. If you have one of the ugly ones, for $80 Ehman will put the innards in a new case and ship it back to you. (I just broke down and bought a 20-meg hard drive for the kids' machine—and I bought an Ehman, because I trust it and nobody could beat the price.)

Jasmine (AN)

We praised Jasmine in the last edition of this book and we were right to—*then*. But in late 1989, the quality of their drives—and of their service—dropped off a cliff. This may have been caused in part by bad components being shipped them, but whatever the reason, Jasmine went into Chapter 11 bankruptcy in the spring of 1990 and, by the time you read this, will probably have been purchased by another company.

important
warning

If this happens, they'll have the cash to buy the parts to fix all the drives sitting on their shelves. So don't give up hope; you still may see that Jasmine drive you sent in for a warranty repair nine months ago (you haven't needed it in the meantime anyway, right?).

things
to come

DataFrame hard disks (SZA)

We used a DataFrame 40 as a File Server at the college where I teach, with no problems during nearly three years of continuous use (it was never turned off). (*Unfortunately, I've had less success with DataFrames.—AN*) I used the same one in my home office for a while and the noise drove me crazy. In a large office, the noise may not matter.

DataFrame hard disks (AN)

This is a classic example of how the financial fortunes of a hard drive company affect their products. When SuperMac (the maker of DataFrames) was doing well, at the beginning of their life, their products were superior. But when they started to concentrate on video monitors, the quality went down.

things to come

When they were bought out by another company, the quality and service dropped even further. When the company bought itself back from its parent, quality and service improved. Today they appear to be on an upswing, but rumor has it that SuperMac wants to sell their hard drive arm so that they can concentrate on video products, so who knows what the quality will be like in the future.

♠ MacinStor hard disks

The MacinStor drives from Storage Dimensions come in sizes from 60 to 660 megabytes. The footprint is the same as the SE and it's a nicely-designed unit although, at a little more than three inches high, it's not as sleek as I'd like. It has good partitioning software and comes with PC Tools for the Mac.

The noise level of the unit I tested, however, was unacceptable—at least for a home office. Storage Dimensions says (I have no reason to doubt it, but I haven't heard it for myself, either) that their new units are quieter.

♠ SyQuest cartridges *(Chris Allen)*

One of the most popular kinds of hard disk today is the 45-megabyte removable cartridge manufactured by SyQuest. Yet you rarely hear SyQuest's name mentioned, because other manufacturers package SyQuest's drive with their own case, power supply and custom software and sell it under their own names.

All these drives function the same. The 45MB cartridges are interchangeable among all of them, and even the software from one company can be often used on another company's drive (although this isn't recommended.)

bargain

While SyQuest drives typically cost twice as much as regular hard drives of about the same size, additional SyQuest cartridges are cheap, usually around $120. Obviously, the ability to pick up another 45MB of storage for $120 is very attractive and, in fact, most SyQuest drive owners find they've accumulated five or ten cartridges in no time at all.

Unlike Bernoulli drives (a competitive removable-cartridge system), SyQuest drives are as fast as ordinary hard drives—in fact, with an access time of about 25 milliseconds, they're faster than most of Apple's drives. They are louder, however, so they're more often used for secondary purposes like backup and archiving, rather than as primary units.

shortcut

[These drives use some impressive technology. The platter is made from a nickel-cadmium slurry, which is very hard stuff, and is coated with a fluorocarbon that's many times more slippery than Teflon. To get dust and other junk off it, the disk spins up to 4200 rpm when you turn it on, then back down to its operating speed of 3260 rpm.—AN]

SyQuest drives are good for people who do project or client work. You can put each project or each client's data on a separate cartridge, leaving your applications and personal files on your primary hard drive. SyQuest drives are also useful for desktop publishers—many typesetting bureaus now have them, so that customers with large documents or complex color images to print can bring in a cartridge instead of a raft of floppies.

The press has generally given the SyQuest technology good reviews, but some people have claimed that the cartridges are not reliable. I personally believe that the cartridges are just as reliable as any hard drive on the market—it's just that most people don't treat them with the same care they accord their regular hard drives. In my experience, if you treat each SyQuest cartridge as well as you would a more expensive regular hard drive, you won't encounter reliability problems. For example, a car can get hot when parked in the sun, so you shouldn't leave cartridges in your briefcase in the back seat.

Several companies sell SyQuest drives, including Mass Micro (DataPak drives), PLI (Infinity 40 Turbo), MicroTech (R45 drives) and AIC (Slimline).

Mass Micro's drives come in three shapes. One is for putting under compact Macs like the Plus and SE, and it has a slight tilt to position the Mac screen for better viewing. The second fits perfectly on top of a Mac II, IIx or IIfx; its styling is coordinated and it has room for two SyQuest drives or a SyQuest drive and an ordinary hard drive. The third is sized and styled for the Mac IIcx and IIci. Mass Micro's drive software is somewhat inelegant and utilitarian, but it does the job.

The Infinity 40 Turbo from PLI (reported to be the most reliable) comes in a one-drive and two-drive configuration. Both are designed to fit under a compact Mac; if you're using them with a II, you can stand them on their sides. PLI's case has a unique rounded style you either like or dislike. Their drive software is among the best—elegant and full-featured. The drive comes with Symantec's SUM and is filled with public-domain files, shareware, clip art and software demonstrations.

bargain

MicroTech's R45 is newer and only comes in one shape—a traditional rounded-corner box that looks like hard drives from other manufacturers and fits under a Mac Plus or SE. MicroTech's drive software is almost as good as PLI's. The drives come with a copy of Norton Macintosh Utilities and Total Recall, a backup application. At $1100 list, the R45 is also one of the least expensive of the name-brand SyQuest drives.

things to come

MicroTech is reportedly coming out with a new hard drive that uses a Ricoh 50MB removable cartridge. I'm unfamiliar with this cartridge, and I don't know if MicroTech will discontinue production of SyQuest drives.

(We've used SyQuest drives from AIC (Advanced Information Concepts) for years and have been impressed with the service we've gotten from the company. Many of the people who work at AIC came from Custom Memory Systems, the very first company to sell SyQuest drives for Macintoshes, so they have as much experience with this technology as anybody—if not more.—AN)

Many other SyQuest hard drives are available on the market, including some "generic" brands that have no label on the case. Be sure to check out the drive software with a dealer or a friend before purchasing a no-name brand of SyQuest hard drive (actually, this is good advice before purchasing any no-name hard drive).

🍎 *care and feeding of hard disks* (DC/AM)

Hard disks are remarkably tough, but cruel and unusual punishment can damage them. The most important rule is not to move a hard disk when it's turned on. And when you move it, pick it up—never scoot it across the desk surface.

important warning

Another thing to avoid is rapid temperature changes. Don't carry a hard disk around in your trunk all day in the dead of winter, bring it inside and start it up; give it a couple of hours to warm to room temperature.

When you transport a hard disk, make sure its heads are *parked*. Some hard disks automatically park the heads each time you shut down (the right way to do it); others require that you specifically tell them to park the heads.

🍎 *starting and turning off hard disks* (AM)

In general, you should turn on your hard disk(s) first, wait until it's up to speed and then turn on the Mac. If both are connected to a surge suppressor or a power strip, it's fine to turn them on simultaneously (although the larger your hard disk is, the more likely you are to have trouble with this).

esp. for beginners

When shutting off the Mac, you should follow exactly the opposite procedure—first shut off the Mac (by choosing Shut Down from the Finder's Special menu), then shut off your hard disk(s).

🍎 *accidentally shutting off a hard disk*

If you accidentally turn off your hard disk during a work session, as I once did—don't panic. Just turn it back on. Usually, your Mac won't know the difference. There are two times when it will. If you were in the middle of opening a file, you'll have to try opening it again. If you were in the

very hot tip

middle of saving a file, you probably won't be able to get at it unless you know how to recover damaged files.

🍎 *organizing a hard disk* (AN)

The general principles of good organization apply to hard disks as much as they do to anything else. Prime among these, of course, is *apfeaeiip*. By an incredible co-incidence, the letters that make up this word (which, as you undoubtedly know, means *good housekeeping* in Fijian) are also the initials of the English phrase *a place for everything and everything in its place*.

Apfeaeiip is, of course, an unattainable ideal. That's why you need a wrong-place box. I came upon this concept when living with four roommates. We'd take turns straightening up but that was an impossible task when all kinds of stuff, of indeterminate ownership and importance, lay randomly about the house.

So we got a big cardboard box and put it in a central location. Then we had a meeting and agreed where things belonged. From that point on, if anything wasn't in its place, whoever was straightening up put it in the wrong-place box. If you couldn't find something where you left it, you just looked there. (This sounds sort of fascistic, but it was actually a very simple and easy way to deal with the problem.)

If you share your hard disk (and maybe even if you don't), you need a wrong-place box—a folder called *need to be put away, left in the wrong place* or the like. You just pop things in there when they're in the way and then periodically, when you don't have anything more pressing to do, you open that folder and figure out where all the stuff in it really belongs.

There are two basic ways to organize folders on a hard disk—by type of application (graphics, word processing, databases, etc.) and by type of work (Project A, Project B, budget, personal, etc.). In general, it makes sense to use both kinds of folders, even though you'll sometimes forget whether a given document is filed away under a work category or under the kind of application that created it.

Don't lay down a rigid organizational scheme and then be afraid to break out of it. For example, if you use a particular program frequently, it's fine to put its icon by itself out in the disk window (also known as the *root directory)* even if all the related programs and documents are in a folder.

very
hot
tip

By the same token, if you use one particular document most of the time you use a given application, put its icon, rather than the application's icon, somewhere easy to get to—not where related programs and documents are kept. (You may prefer to use one of the utilities that let you get at applications and documents without having to go through folders; they're described in the utilities chapter.)

I like to view folders and programs by name and documents by date (so the ones you worked on most recently rise to the top of the list). Viewing by name or date also gives you nice, small icons that don't take up a lot of room. Combining that with careful positioning and "staircasing" of nested windows allows the maximum amount of data to be viewed.

One last general rule: *it's your desktop.* You can do whatever you want with it. There's no right or wrong way to organize things. In particular, remember that you can name your folders whatever you want. (I have one called *dealing with psychopaths*—which, unfortunately, is chock full of stuff.) Feel free to reorganize and rename folders and files often—a good desktop is constantly evolving.

very
hot
tip

🍎 *putting hard disks where you can't hear them* (AN)

Hard disks are great, but even the ones without fans make a fair amount of noise. If you're sensitive to noise and love the fact that all Macs through the Plus were virtually silent, a hard disk is likely to bother you.

Fortunately, the solution is simple. Just attach a long cable to your hard disk and put it in a closet or some other place where you can't hear it (for a long time I kept them on a shelf outside—and above—the door to my workroom).

As mentioned in the SCSI section above, SCSI drives are designed to accept cables up to seven meters, or 21 feet (seven meters is almost 23 feet, not 21, but don't blame us—we're just quoting from the box Apple's cables come in). Hardware pundit C. J. Weigand says you shouldn't go more than 15–18 feet.

Since it seems unlikely that you can physically harm a drive by putting it on a long cable, it makes sense to at least experiment with one; if you do have problems, you'll only be out the price of the cable. I think long cables may somewhat increase the number of crashes you experience, but since you always back up your work every fifteen minutes or half hour (right?), you won't lose much data.

✿ *a fleet is only as fast...* (DC)

If you have more than one hard disk connected to your Mac, you'll find that returning to the desktop from an application will only be as fast as the slowest drive connected. You can speed things up somewhat by keeping all the windows on the slower drive(s) closed.

✿ *rebuilding the desktop* (SZA/AN)

**very
hot
tip**

The desktop file keeps track of deleted files as well as current ones, which means it just keeps getting bigger. Since the file has to be read each time the desktop is displayed, starting up and returning to the Finder can get pretty sluggish. The solution is to rebuild the desktop (file), which flushes out all the obsolete information.

To rebuild the desktop file on the startup disk, hold down ⌘ Option while starting the computer or while inserting the disk. Another way to do it is to delete the current desktop file, using one of the utilities, like DiskTop or Disk Tools, that lets you work with invisible files. When you return to the Finder, a new desktop file will be created.

If you try to rebuild a hard disk's desktop file while running MultiFinder, you may get a message that there's not enough memory to complete the operation. Switching out of MultiFinder and starting again with ⌘ Option down usually takes care of that problem.

🍎 *fragmentation*

Each sector on any Macintosh disk holds 512 bytes, or half a K, of information. Since most files are bigger than 512 bytes, they occupy several sectors, and large files may take up several tracks.

When a disk is relatively empty, a file is stored on it in contiguous sectors, one after the other; this makes for fast saves, and for fast reads when you want to open the file later. But here's what happens after you've been using your disk for a while:

Let's say you start by saving three files to disk: A (which takes up ten sectors) B (five sectors) and C (fifteen sectors). Your disk will now look something like this (for the purpose of saving me hours of extra work on these illustrations, please ignore the fact that, on a disk, sectors are arranged in concentric circles, not in a grid):

A	A	A	A	A	A	A	A	A	A
B	B	B	B	B	C	C	C	C	C
C	C	C	C	C	C	C	C	C	C

Now you erase file B; this frees up five sectors. You create a new file, D, and save it to the disk, where it requires eight sectors. The first five go where B was and the last three are put after file C. Now your disk looks like this:

A	A	A	A	A	A	A	A	A	A
D	D	D	D	D	C	C	C	C	C
C	C	C	C	C	C	C	C	C	C
D	D	D							

Then you edit file C and save it again—oops, it needs more than fifteen sectors now, so the overflow is put after the second part of file D. Now your disk looks like this:

A	A	A	A	A	A	A	A	A	A
D	D	D	D	D	C	C	C	C	C
C	C	C	C	C	C	C	C	C	C
D	D	D	C	C	C	C	C	C	C
C	C	C	C						

And so on. As your disk gets fragmented (actually, it's the *files* that are fragmented, but the phrase everyone uses is *disk* fragmentation), both reading from it and writing to it really slow down.

Fragmentation occurs on all disks that get a lot of use, but floppies are so small and so slow anyway that it's really only a concern on hard disks. For what to do about fragmentation, see the next entry.

® *defragmenting hard disks* (AN/SZA)

shortcut

Once a disk is fragmented, you're not stuck with it that way—all you have to do is *defragment* it. This involves using a program like DiskExpress or PowerUP to rewrite all the files to your disk so they occupy contiguous portions of the disk. SUM from Symantec also includes a defragmentation utility.

important
warning

Always back up your work before you defragment. If the computer crashes or the electricity goes off, you risk losing the files that are temporarily in memory while they're transferred from one part of the disk to another.

Don't think that defragmenting is a minor housekeeping chore to do at the end of the day. It took Sharon about three hours to defragment a 20-meg drive; larger drives would of course take longer.

You can also defragment manually (that is, without the help of a defragmentation utility). Simply back up all your files, reinitialize the drive and then copy the files back onto it from the backups. This approach obviously gets less and less practical the larger your hard disk gets.

❡ *interleave ratio and disk speed*

The *interleave ratio* controls how the sectors are organized on each track of the disk. A ratio of 1:1 means that the sectors are in straight numerical order—1, 2, 3, etc. A ratio of 2:1 means that numbers skip to every *other* sector—1 is the first sector, 2 is the third sector, 3 is the fifth sector, and so on (which numbers are on the intervening sectors depends on how many sectors there are all together).

Here's what those two interleave ratios look like (except, of course, there are actually hundreds of sectors in a track):

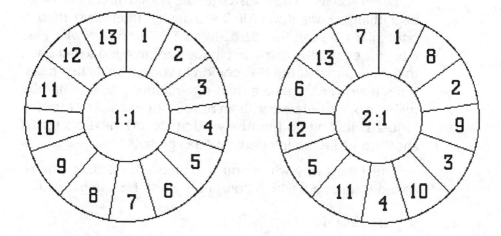

A 3:1 ratio means that sequential numbers are on every third physical sector:

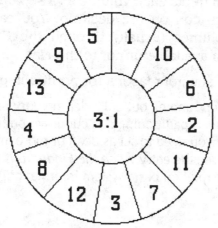

A 1:1 interleave allows information to be read the most quickly, since the Mac can read all the sectors in just one revolution of the disk. But some Macs just can't read that fast. They'd still be digesting the information from sector 1 while sector 2 whizzed by and then they'd have to wait another revolution of the platter till sector 2 showed up again—and then they'd miss sector 3.

Mac II's and SE/30s can process data fast enough to use the 1:1 ratio on their drives. Regular SE's need the 2:1 interleave. The Plus is a slow reader—it needs the 3:1 ratio.

When you use a hard disk with the wrong interleave ratio, everything slows down. If it's a faster interleave than a particular Mac can handle (using a 1:1 interleave with Mac Plus, for example), extra revolutions are needed to get back to the sectors that the Mac couldn't process on its first pass. If it's a slower interleave than a particular Mac can handle (using a 3:1 interleave with an SE/30, for example), the Mac is just twiddling its thumbs waiting for the next sector to show up while the interleaved ones go by.

And *that's* why when you initialize a hard disk, you're asked to indicate which computer you'll be using it with.

● *partitioning*

Most hard disks come with *partitioning* software that lets you divide the disk into smaller segments called *volumes*. The Mac then treats each volume as a separate disk, giving each its own icon on the desktop. You can *mount* and *unmount* volumes (usually through the Control Panel), making them available or not to the Mac.

There are several reasons for partitioning a disk:

• If you keep running out of Finder memory under MultiFinder, partitioning can cut down on how much memory you need to set aside. (For more information on that, see the entry *when the Finder runs out of room* in the chapter on basic system information.)

- With fewer megs of information to read through on startup, the Mac gets to the desktop faster and also returns to it more quickly when you quit an application.

- When you back up your work, you only have to back up the volumes you've worked with instead of the entire drive.

- Since the system folder and application files don't usually get changed that much, keeping them in their own partition means you won't have to defragment that section very often.

- Some partitioning programs can be used as security systems by not letting you mount a volume without the right password. Even without password protection, partitioning can provide low-level security because if someone doesn't know there's another volume, or how to mount it, the information on it remains private.

Here are some examples of the sort of things you might want to partition:

- I keep all my finance and tax stuff in one volume; I don't need it except once a month when I do the checkbook, and four times a year for estimated tax. I don't want to keep all that stuff on floppies, but I don't need it hanging around every day on my desktop either.

- Fonts and clip art that I use on-and-off stays off till I need it, but I don't have to get up for a floppy when I do.

- I have friends with megabytes of info on specific clients (graphic design stuff, newsletters) that's only needed when they're working on particular projects.

- Every two or three months I find time to get back to programming, but I don't need that stuff around in the meantime.

(I've never partitioned a disk and have never felt the need to, but I think Sharon makes some interesting arguments for it here.—AN)

❡ *another reason to partition* (Chris Allen)

There's a limit to how many different applications and documents can exist in a single volume. The first thing to run out will be icons, and you'll see generic icons on many documents and applications. You can actually get to a point where the Finder loses track of a file and it "disappears" from view, although it's really there.

This is the reason why there's a limit to how many files can be put on a public-domain CD-ROM. BMUG recently had to split theirs into two separate disks even though there was room on the CD for more stuff. This problem will always occur as you exceed a certain number of files, or 600 megs or so, but can occur much sooner if you have many different types of files (as many of us do who collect public-domain software.)

The only solutions to this problem are partitioning or using the Desktop Manager file from the AppleShare disks (Apple's networking software). Desktop Manager creates multiple desktop files rather than just one, and thus lets you have lots more files in a volume. It also brings the desktop up much faster.

things to come

Although Apple doesn't endorse using Desktop Manager except with AppleShare, I know many people who do. Desktop Manager will be incorporated into System 7 to solve the problem of too many files in a volume.

❡ *what to look for in partitioning software*

There are two major kinds of partitioning software—the real thing and something called file partitions. These are simply giant files on the same disk, rather than a separate, mountable and dismountable volumes.

File partitions are extremely difficult to recover, since they're a combination of all sorts of file types, so if something happens to one of them, everything you've stored in it will probably be lost. So it's best to stick with true partitioning software.

Here are some considerations to help you choose among partitioning programs:

- Once you choose a size for a partition, can you change it later?

- How easy is it to mount and unmount the volumes? Most volumes are manipulated through the Control Panel, but you should also be able to simply drag a volume to the Trash to unmount it.

- Is password protection available for any or all partitions?

- Can specific partitions be automatically mounted when you start your Mac?

- How will the partitioning affect any backups you've already made, and how will it interact with backup and defragmenting software?

Memory upgrades

⬥ *how much memory do you need?* (AN)

One meg is enough to use most word processors, simple graphics programs, spreadsheets and the like, one at a time. If you're running MultiFinder, you'll need at least two megs to do anything useful, and you'll probably be happier with four or five megs. The same is true if you want to use PageMaker or other heavy-duty page layout, graphics or CAD programs.

⬥ *memory upgrade basics* (Larry Pina/SZA/AN)

When reading about memory chips, keep in mind that they're sized in *kilobits* (1024 *bits*). Unfortunately, kilobits are abbreviated *K*, just like *kilobytes* (1024 *bytes*)— the eight-bit units used to measure the computer's total memory. Likewise, both mega*bits* and mega*bytes* are commonly called simply *megs*. Since there are eight bits to a byte, you need *eight* one-mega*bit* RAM chips to get a mega*byte* of RAM.

The original 128K Mac contained sixteen 64-kilobit RAM chips—for what, at the time, seemed a whopping amount of memory. A year later, Apple substituted 256K chips and was able to produce essentially the same machine with four times as much memory (512K). In both cases, the chips were soldered (not socketed) to the *motherboard* (the main printed circuit board in the Mac).

Rather than having to desolder and resolder 256 connections (sixteen pins times sixteen chips), dealers took your old board in trade (it went back to the factory to become someone else's upgrade) and sold you a new one. This is called a *board swap.*

To upgrade the 512K Mac, you need a *daughter board* (so called because it mounts on top of the motherboard). Some daughter boards snap into place without soldering, but they only work with absolutely perfect motherboards; if there's been any previous upgrade or repair work, the snaps may not line up properly.

An important consideration when buying a daughter board is whether the extra memory is socketed or soldered—socketed is always easier to deal with but soldered is more reliable.

Beginning with the Mac Plus, Apple started supplying RAM chips on tiny boards called SIMMs (*single in-line memory modules).* Each SIMM has eight memory chips on it (some also have a ninth parity chip as well). When each of the eight chips is 256 kilo*bits,* you have a 256 kilo*byte* SIMM. (Unlike individual memory chips, SIMMs are measured in kilo*bytes* and mega*bytes.)* When each chip is 1024 kilobits (one megabit), you have a 1024K (one-meg) SIMM.

By replacing the SIMMs that come with the computer with higher-density ones (that is, ones that have more memory on each chip), you can increase the memory in your computer. The Plus and the SE have four slots for SIMMs; the SE/30 and all the II's have eight.

❖ DRAM vs. static RAM

Most memory chips are DRAMs (*DEE-ram,* for *dynamic RAM).* DRAMs need to be constantly powered with electricity to remember what's been stored in them. (That's why you lose the contents of memory when you shut down your computer.)

Static RAM, the kind of memory used in the Mac Portable, doesn't need to be constantly supplied with electricity, but its cost is phenomenal compared to DRAM.

❖ all about SIMMs

When you buy SIMMs to upgrade your memory, there are a number of things to consider: size, RAM amount, profile, parity and speed.

The overall size of SIMMs depends on where they're going—into your Mac, the LaserWriter or wherever—but, in general, they're about 1" x 4". Be aware that SIMMs for LaserWriters and SIMMs for Macs aren't interchangeable.

Two kinds of SIMMs are currently available—256K and one-meg. (Denser SIMMs are on the way.) Few people buy the 256K SIMMs when they upgrade—they get the one-meg chips. How many chips you need depends on the model of Mac you have and its maximum amount of RAM (as well as how much RAM you *want* or can afford to add). For details, see the entries below on upgrading different types of Macs.

**things
to come**

The *profile* of a SIMM is something else you need to know about when you add memory. Depending on how the DRAM chips are installed on the SIMM, it's known as *high profile* (also called a *DIP SIMM)* or *low profile* (also called *surface mount).* Be sure to get low-profile SIMMs if you're upgrading an SE—high-profiles are hard to get into the sockets, and even if they go in, they might interfere with the installation of an accelerator (or other) board.

**important
warning**

Some SIMMs have a ninth chip that's used for *parity-checking* (don't worry about what that is). Since the government sometimes requires this ability in the machines it buys, Apple has made it an optional feature on the newest Macs. You can use parity SIMMs in any machine, and the ninth chip will just be ignored if you don't need the parity—but they cost more, so it's normally not a good idea

SIMMs also vary in speed, which is measured in *nanoseconds* (billionths of a second, abbreviated *ns*). SIMMs currently come in speeds of 60ns, 80ns, 100ns, 120ns and 150ns. (In this case, the *lower* the number, the faster the chip—since we're measuring how long it takes the Mac to access the memory.)

The Mac Plus and SE were designed for 150ns SIMMs, the SE/30, II, IIx and IIcx require 120ns SIMMs and the ci and fx use 80ns SIMMs. You can always put a faster SIMM into a machine (an 80ns into a cx, for example), but you won't gain any speed by it and will probably cost you more. You can also mix SIMMs of different speeds, as long as the slowest isn't slower than your machine needs.

If you don't know what speed your SIMMs are, look for some numbers in fine print; *-10, -20* and *-15* stand for 100, 120 and 150 nanoseconds, respectively.

⚫ *upgrading Pluses and SE's*

The Plus and SE each have four slots for SIMMs, and each *pair* you put in must be the same size. So there are only three possible combinations:

SIMMs installed	total RAM
four 256K SIMMs	1MB
two 256K SIMMs + two 1MB SIMMs	2.5MB
four 1MB SIMMs	4MB

important warning

One pair of SIMMs goes in the first two slots and the other in the back two slots. (If all four are the same size, you don't have worry about this. If you're mixing sizes, however, you can't put one pair in the first and fourth slots and the other pair in the middle slots.)

In the Plus and early SE's, the pair of larger SIMMs goes into the first two slots and the smaller pair into the back slots. On later SE's, it's reversed: the larger pair goes into sockets 3 and 4.

For the Plus and the SE to make use of the extra memory, certain resistors—or, in the later SE's, a jumper cable—also need to be cut. Let an experienced person do this for you.

● *upgrading SE/30s and Mac II's*

The SE/30 and most Mac II's have eight slots for SIMMs, arranged in two *banks* of four. All four SIMMs in each bank must be the same size. You can fill all four slots with 256K SIMMs (unless you have an fx) or with 1MB SIMMs, or you can leave all four empty, but you can't fill fewer than four slots in a bank. So there are five possible combinations:

SIMMs in bank A	SIMMs in bank B	total RAM
256K	empty	1MB
256K	256K	2MB
1MB	empty	4MB
1MB	256K	5MB
1MB	1MB	8MB

Installing SIMMs in a cx, ci or fx is a cinch—just take off the cover and carefully plug them in. In the II, IIx or IIfx, you have to take off the cover, detach the floppy drive cables and remove the hard disk to get at the SIMM sockets. The SE/30, of course, has to have its case cracked open and its logic board removed (by someone who knows what he or she is doing) for the slots to be reached.

● *never use a 2MB or 4MB machine*

This entry title isn't quite accurate, but it caught your eye, didn't it? The real title is *never upgrade a Plus or SE to two megs of RAM and never upgrade an SE/30 or any Mac II model to four megs.* Here's why:

The Plus and the SE come with four 256K SIMMs (one meg total). If you buy two 1MB SIMMs, simply replace two of the smaller SIMMs and leave the other two in place; this gives you 2.5MB of memory instead of just 2MB.

The same general rule applies to SE/30's or II's that come with four 256K SIMMs. Buy 1MB SIMMs for the four slots that are empty and leave the 256K SIMMs in the other bank of slots; this takes you up to 5MB.

If you fill all your slots with 1MB SIMMs (giving you four megs of total RAM on a Plus or SE and eight megs on an SE/30 or any of the Mac II's), you're likely to have 256K SIMMs left over. You won't be alone. There are so many 256K chips around, you can probably get some for free. At the college where I teach, they're being turned into key rings. I have four of them somewhere amid the clutter of my desk.

✎ do use a 2MB machine (AN)

Exactly because 256K SIMM's are so readily available, for little or no money, it makes sense for a lot of people to upgrade a 1MB Mac II, IIx, cx or ci to 2MB. Just put 256K SIMMs in the empty four slots. (This will also work to upgrade an fx, which comes with 4MB, to 5MB.)

Two megs are plenty if you don't use MultiFinder, PageMaker or other memory hogs. If you decide it's worth the extra $300+ to go to 5MB (or 8MB on an fx), you're only out what those 256K chips cost you—which shouldn't have been very much, if anything at all.

Memory allocation

✎ checking memory amount

To see how much memory your Mac has...well, you probably already know how much memory *your* Mac has. To check how much memory someone *else's* Mac has, choose *About the Finder* from the ✎ menu when you're on the desktop and look at the *Total Memory* figure.

```
┌────────────────────────────────────────────────────────┐
│ ▤□▤▤▤▤▤ About the Macintosh™ Finder ▤▤▤▤▤▤            │
├────────────────────────────────────────────────────────┤
│  Finder:   6.1         Larry, John, Steve, and Bruce    │
│  System:   6.0.3       © Apple Computer, Inc. 1983–88   │
│                                                          │
│  Total Memory:    8,192K  Largest Unused Block: 4,915K  │
│  ─────────────────────────────────────────────────────  │
│  ◆ Word          1,500K  ▓▓▓▓▓▓▓▓▓░░░░░░               │
│  ▤ Finder          160K  ▓                              │
│  ▤ System        1,617K  ▓▓▓▓▓▓▓▓▓▓░░░                 │
└────────────────────────────────────────────────────────┘
```

☙ *unexpected* out of memory *messages*

When I graduated to five megs of memory, I never expected to see an *out of memory* message again—but I did. I haven't yet seen one with my new eight megs of memory, but no doubt I will eventually.

Here are some of the situations that can give you *out of memory* messages even when you think you have more than enough:

- Inits in your System take up memory. Each one alone usually doesn't take up much, but together they can add up.

- The more things your System is expected to handle, the more breathing room it needs (see the *System heap* entry below).

- The RAM cache in the Control Panel can be configured to use varying amounts of RAM, but you may not even know that it's on. (See the entry on RAM caches below.)

- Using a special facet of a program, like Word's spelling checker, uses up RAM that would otherwise be available for the program or document.

very hot tip

- Opened desk accessories use up memory.

Potential memory-usage problems that are specific to MultiFinder are covered in detail in the chapter on system basics, but here's a brief list:

- Partitions for applications may be set too small. Applications can't take advantage of extra memory unless you set them up to do so.

- Memory can get fragmented, so that while you have enough total memory, it's broken up into unusable bits and pieces.

- When you're using large storage devices, there might not be enough memory allocated to the Finder.

♣ *the System heap*

Without getting too technical, the *heap* is a portion of memory set aside for a special purpose. There are the *System heap* and *application heaps.* You shouldn't ever have to worry about application heaps, but the System heap is something you need to pay attention to if you're running MultiFinder with more than a few basic inits and/or applications (the *number* of applications is the problem, not the amount of memory you give each one).

When you choose *About the Finder* from the ♣ menu on the desktop, you'll see a bar that indicates how much memory is allocated to the System; the dark part shows how much of that allocation is in use. To provide enough breathing room for your System when several applications are open, about a third of the bar should be light when none are open:

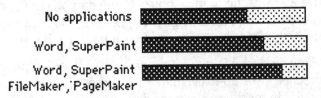

The easiest way to adjust the System heap allocation is with a utility like CE Software's HeapFixer. It comes with most of CE's products, and is also available on bulletin boards and electronic information services.

⚫ the RAM cache

A *RAM cache* is a portion of memory set aside to hold information about the operations you perform frequently on your computer. When the cache is on, each thing you do that requires disk access is stored there, so the next time you do it, the information is retrieved from RAM (*very* quickly) instead of from the disk (a lot more slowly). Here are some of the things you can speed up with a RAM cache:

- *Opening and quitting applications or desk accessories.* Immediately after starting my computer, it took nine seconds for my Control Panel to open. The second time I opened it, it took only four seconds (because all the Control Panel info was in the RAM cache).

- *Operations within an application.* Large applications don't reside entirely in memory. When you do something beyond the basics (print preview, say, or checking the spelling), the information on how to do it is loaded into memory from the disk. Using a RAM cache leaves these segments of the program in memory so you'll get them faster the next time you want to do the same thing.

- *Switching between applications in MultiFinder.* Parts of each application remain in memory even when you switch to another application, so when you switch back to it, less stuff has to be pulled off the disk.

You can't *assign* things to a RAM cache; whatever you do is stored there until you need it again (unless it's been flushed out to make room for other things you've done since).

You set the RAM cache size—and turn it on and off—using the General icon in the Control Panel. (See the figure at the top of the next page.)

As with many Control Panel devices, the settings you choose will not be activated until the next time you start your Mac.

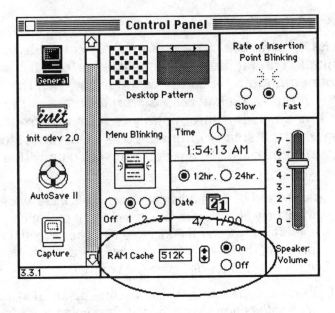

✦ RAM cache settings

Apple recommends the following RAM cache settings:

- when running under MultiFinder, 32K for each meg of RAM

- when not running under MultiFinder, 25% of your total RAM

If you want more RAM cache than this, keep in mind that the maximum you can use while in MultiFinder is 348K for each meg of memory you have. If you set the cache higher, it's automatically reset to 348K per meg. Here's a summary of the recommended amounts and the maximums:

total megs of RAM	rec. without MultiFinder	rec. with MultiFinder	max. with MultiFinder
1	256K	32K	348K
2	512K	64K	696K
2.5	640K	80K	870K
4	1024K	128K	1392K
5	1280K	160K	1740K
8	2048K	256K	2784K

▲ RAM disks

A *RAM disk* is a portion of memory that's set aside to act as a temporary disk. You use a utility program to create the RAM disk, which then appears as an icon on your desktop. You use the disk as you would any other disk, except that when you shut off your computer, everything in the RAM disk disappears.

So what good is it? Well, what's stored on a RAM disk can be retrieved a lot faster than what's stored on a disk. Put an application there and you'll notice that virtually all its operations speed up. Put your System and Finder there and all the things they do will speed up.

shortcut

So where do you get a RAM disk utility? None are sold commercially, but you can get them from user groups, bulletin boards, commercial information services and on *The Macintosh Bible Software Disks,* described in the last chapter of the book.

▲ virtual memory

Virtual memory is sort of the opposite of a RAM disk—it's a technique that lets the computer use part of a hard disk as if it were RAM. This is extremely useful for large graphics, long animations, complex sounds, lots of scanning, or keeping a lot of files open at the same time.

Things get swapped from RAM to the virtual memory section of the disk and back again based on when (and where) they're needed. If things work as they should, the swapping is transparent to the user, with no slowing of operations for disk access. The main advantage of virtual memory is that disk space is much cheaper than RAM.

System 7 allows virtual memory—*if* you have at least two megs of RAM and a Mac based on the 68030 chip (or a Mac II with a PMMU—*paged memory management unit—* added to it.) Although you can run System 7 with two megs of RAM, you really need about four megs for virtual memory to run smoothly and efficiently—to make the memory swaps really transparent.

Virtual 2.0 (Chris Allen)

If you can't wait for System 7, virtual memory capabilities are available in a product called Virtual 2.0. The program requires two megs of real RAM. On an SE/30, Virtual turns that into fourteen megs of virtual memory; on the various models of Mac II, you get fourteen megs minus one meg for each card you have installed. If you have more than two megs of RAM, things speed up but don't get any more virtual memory.

Virtual 2.0 costs $200 for the software alone, which is all you need on an SE/30, IIx, cx, ci or fx. To run on a Mac II, you also need the PMMU chip; Connectix, Virtual's publisher, will sell you that, along with the software, for $275. The program won't run on an SE or any earlier Mac.

by
Byron Brown
1989

Chapter 4

Printing

Printers that work with Macs

⚫ *types of printers* (AN)

Three types of printers are commonly used with Macs—dot-matrix, laser and ink-jet. You can also output from a Mac directly to an *imagesetter*.

esp. for beginners

Dot-matrix printers form characters out of a pattern of dots, the way the Mac forms images on the screen. Typically, each dot is made by a separate pin pushing a ribbon against the paper, although there are other ways of producing the image. ImageWriter is the name Apple gives to its line of dot-matrix printers.

Laser printers create images by drawing them on a metal drum with a beam of laser light. The image is then made visible by electrostatically attracting dry ink powder to it, as in a photocopying machine. LaserWriter is the name Apple gives to its line of laser printers.

Like dot-matrix printers, *ink-jet printers* form characters out of little dots, but because the dots are formed by tiny jets of ink, they're more like splotches. They blend together much more than the dots produced by dot-matrix printers. Both Kodak's Diconix and Hewlett-Packard's DeskWriter are ink-jet printers that are compatible with the Mac.

Imagesetters are digital typesetters that can produce graphics as well as text. These high-end machines output onto film like the kind used for photostats, rather than onto paper.

⚫ *relative resolutions of various printers* (AN)

In a normal ImageWriter text printout (from a word processing program, say), there are 80 dots per inch across and 72 down (5760 dots per square inch). If you choose *Tall Adjusted*, there are 72 dots per inch in both directions (5184 dpsi).

The LaserWriter's resolution is 300 dpi, which amounts to 90,000 dpsi—about 16 to 17 times the ImageWriter's. But 90,000 dpsi is nothing compared to what an imagesetter can do. For example, the 1270-dpi Linotronic 100 can produce 1.6 million dpsi—about 18 times the resolution of a LaserWriter and almost 300 times that of an ImageWriter.

esp. for power users

The 1690-dpi Linotronic 500 can produce 2.85 million dpsi—almost 32 times the LaserWriter's and about 520 times the ImageWriter's. The 2540-dpi Linotronic 300 can produce 6.45 million dpsi—more than 70 times the LaserWriter's and well over 1000 times the ImageWriter's.

⬥ *letter-quality* (AN)

Letter-quality was a name commonly given to formed-character printers and their output back in the Dark Ages of the early 1980s. Now it's more often used to refer to the output of high-resolution dot-matrix printers like the ImageWriter LQ.

What, you ask, is a formed-character printer? It's one that produces images the same way typewriters do—by pushing something the shape of a character against an inked ribbon and then into the paper. The something they push is a daisywheel or thimble containing all the available characters—sort of like the type ball used by IBM's Selectric typewriters.

Because formed-character printers work like typewriters, they're able to produce pages that look like they were typed on a typewriter. The question is: why would any computer user want to imitate a machine as primitive as a typewriter?

If you ever hear someone say that only a (formed-character) letter-quality printer will do for their work, imagine you're back in the 1800s. You've just suggested to the president of your company that he invest in a typewriter. His response: "What!? Send out a letter that isn't hand-written? Never!"

In fairness, early dot-matrix printouts did look crummy. But today, even a regular ImageWriter can produce documents that are much more pleasant to look at than those from a typewriter or formed-character printer; laser printers, ink-jet printers and high-resolution dot-matrix printers simply leave typewriters and formed-character printers in the dust. Fortunately, most people have by now come to realize this. In fact, thanks mostly to the Mac, expectations about the visual quality of documents have risen markedly.

⌘ *models of the ImageWriter* (AN/SZA)

The first model of the ImageWriter spelled its name with a lowercase *w* and was never called "the ImageWriter I," but by now that's the name everyone uses, so we'll use it too. It's easy to tell an ImageWriter I from an ImageWriter II: the I is beige and rectangular while the II is light gray—what Apple calls "platinum"—and looks sort of like a flattened version of R2D2 doing pushups.

esp. for beginners

The ImageWriter II has fewer problems with paper feed than the I, and it also prints more clearly (the same number of dots are used, but since the II's pins are smaller, so are the dots they create). The II prints faster than the I and has a slot for a card that lets you use it on a network (i.e., hooked up to more than one Mac).

It's hard to find any ImageWriter I's around anymore, but some people swear by them. They're very cheap and very rugged. If you're on a limited budget and want low-tech reliability, it may make sense to look for one. But you'd probably be better off with one of the ImageWriter substitutes described in the next entry.

bargain

In this book, when we refer to the ImageWriter, we mean the ImageWriter II, unless we specifically say otherwise. Of course, many of the tips in the ImageWriter section of this chapter apply to both models.

There's also a 27-pin version of the ImageWriter called the LQ, for "letter-quality" (the ImageWriter I and II are

*very
hot
tip*

9-pin printers). There've been a lot of problems with the LQ, and we don't know anyone who uses one. For the price, you're much better off with a non-PostScript laser printer or an ink-jet printer. And for a *third* the price (or less), you can get a printer that's functionally superior (see the end of the next entry).

ImageWriter substitutes *(Larry Pina)*

The ImageWriter II is the best-selling printer in the world but it's hardly the best bargain. Not only is its $625 list price high for its capabilities, but discounts on it are usually a lot shallower than on third-party competitors, which often sell for 40–50% off. So here are some substitutes for it (read this entry through, because the best deal is at the end).

bargain

The least expensive ImageWriter substitute (at well under $200 by mail order) is the Seikosha SP-1000AP. Built by the makers of Seiko watches and Epson printers, it's very reliable; unlike my ImageWriters, this unit's never jammed on me and I use it almost every day. Another advantage: If you need a ribbon at 8 o'clock at night or on a Sunday, you'll be happy to know that the SP-1000AP uses the same (inexpensive) ribbons as Radio Shack's DMP-130 printer.

The SP-1000AP's paper separator rotates 45° and doubles as a sheet feeder, and it's refreshingly quiet (less than 55 db). So what's wrong with it? Well, it's slow. Draft-quality printing is only 75 characters per second (compared to the ImageWriter II's 250 cps) and near-letter-quality is really slow, only 15 cps (compared to the ImageWriter II's 45 cps).

The flip side of this is that the 1000AP's slow printout is much straighter than the ImageWriter's. And when you stop to think that you can buy two, possibly three, Seikoshas for less than the price of a single ImageWriter, even the speed difference becomes negligible. The slow, reliable Seikosha SP-1000AP is hard to beat for value per dollar and it may be all the printer you need.

A little faster and a little more expensive ($370 list, street prices around $250) is the Olympia NP30APL. In performance, this printer is more or less equivalent to an ImageWriter I and slightly faster than the Seikosha (150 cps draft, 26 cps near-letter-quality).

Because it works just as well connected to a PC as a Mac, the NP30APL is an excellent choice for office environments with mixed equipment. Parallel and serial ports are standard; so are a push-type tractor feed and semi-automatic sheet feeding. A pull-type tractor feed ($50) and a true sheet feeder ($170) are available as options. It uses inexpensive Epson LX80 ribbons that you can get anywhere, even at stationery stores.

The printer is guaranteed for a year, and after that you can order individual parts and service manuals directly from Olympia. They've sold typewriters and office machines since 1904, and they still do business the old-fashioned way—they won't make you buy a $200 board when all you really need is a $2 part.

very good feature

As far as the Mac is concerned, having either of these printers at the end of the cable is just like having an ImageWriter there, with one exception—they handle the top margin differently. Unless you adjust for the difference, the first line of whatever you print will always be two lines too low.

One solution is to waste the first page and manually wind the second page back until its top is just even with the printhead (as you have to do with dot-matrix printers that work with the PC). A better solution is to reset the margins in your software to .67" (four lines) for the top and 1.33" (eight lines) for the bottom, instead of the Mac standard of 1" (six lines) top and bottom.

The next notch higher than the NP30APL is occupied by a whole slew of printers that are functionally superior to the ImageWriter LQ, Apple's expensive ($1430 list), noisy, trouble-prone, letter-quality printer. Amazingly, these 24-pin printers cost well under $300 mail-order, which is much less than an ImageWriter II!

very hot tip

very good feature

You can connect a Mac to any Epson LQ or compatible printer that has a serial port (which may be an optional feature); all you need is the Epson LQ printer driver software and the cable used to connect a Mac with an ImageWriter I. You copy the new printer driver software to your hard disk (or to every floppy you use as a startup disk), select the new software in the Chooser and you're ready to go.

very good feature

The package I like best is the PrintLink Collection from GDT Softworks. On the disk is a set of Macintosh printer drivers that lets you connect to *hundreds* of 24-pin and 9-pin printers, including ones made by Okidata, NEC, Epson, Diconix and Panasonic. Also included is the cable you need to connect to a Mac and a great manual.

bargain

You can get the PrintLink Collection for well under $100, which means that the whole thing—printer, serial port, cable and software—should cost you less than $350. That's for a *24-pin* printer that's light-years beyond an ImageWriter II in both quality and speed. There's really no other way to go.

🍎 *PostScript and non-PostScript printers* (AN)

esp. for beginners

There are two basic kinds of laser printers—those that use PostScript (Adobe's page-description programming language) and those that don't. PostScript devices let more than one machine share the printer, give you access to PostScript outline fonts (described in the font chapter) and let you print PostScript-encoded graphics like the ones that Illustrator and Freehand produce.

Most Macintosh laser printers that don't use PostScript, like General Computer's Personal Laser Printer and Apple's LaserWriter IISC, rely on QuickDraw, the Mac's built-in imaging software, to scale bit-mapped fonts like those used on the Mac's screen.

The output looks great but there are two problems: because they can't connect to LocalTalk, only one Mac at a time can use these non-PostScript printers, and because they use the Mac to do their calculations, they're usually much slower than PostScript printers. (They also sometimes run out of memory in the Mac for doing their calculations, and require you to jump through some hoops to print.)

As mentioned above, there are also PostScript image-setters that print at high resolution on film rather than paper, like the Varityper and the Linotronic.

● *the LaserWriter I's* (AN/SZA)

The first laser printers Apple sold were the LaserWriter and the LaserWriter Plus. Although neither was ever called the "LaserWriter I," that's the name commonly given them, to distinguish them from the models described in the next entry.

Both LaserWriter I's were built around the Canon's CX *marking engine* (the part of the printer that actually makes the image). The CX works fine for most things but, unlike the more advanced marking engine used in the LaserWriter II line, it can't produce a solid black area (it ends up gray or streaked).

The main difference between the original LaserWriter and the LaserWriter Plus is the number of built-in fonts. The original LaserWriter had Helvetica, Times, Courier and Symbol. The LaserWriter Plus came with:

Avant Garde Gothic (regular, demi, oblique and demi oblique)

Bookman Light (light, light italic, demi and demi italic)

Courier (regular, bold, oblique and bold oblique)

Helvetica (plain, bold, oblique and bold oblique)

Helvetica Narrow (plain, bold, oblique and bold oblique)

New Century Schoolbook (roman, bold, italic and bold italic)

Palatino (roman, bold, italic and bold italic)

Symbol

Times (roman, bold, italic and bold italic)

Zapf Chancery (medium italic)

Zapf Dingbats

There were actually two models of the LaserWriter Plus, but the second, which had a ROM upgrade to version 47 of PostScript, wasn't given a separate name.

very bad feature

All LaserWriter I models were hamstrung by just 1.5 megabytes of RAM, which greatly (and very annoyingly) limited the number of fonts you could use in a document.

the printer with three brains *(AN)*

gossip/ trivia

I could have combined this entry and the one above but then I wouldn't have been able to use that title. It refers, of course, to a wonderful Steve Martin movie called *The Man with Two Brains,* which is worth seeing just to hear Kathleen Turner hiss at her rich husband (who she's trying to give a heart attack so she can inherit his money): "You just hate me because I'm so young and *hot!"*

Anyway, the LaserWriter II comes in three models. All are built around Canon's second-generation marking engine, the SX, which produces much solider and darker blacks (in fact, sometimes they're too dark), but each has a different logic board (or brain, in my tortured analogy).

The lowest-priced LaserWriter II ($2800 as of this writing) is the SC, so called because it connects to the Mac through the SCSI port, like a hard disk. The SC's brain is built around a 68000 chip like the one in the SE, the Plus and earlier Macs.

The SC can be accessed by only one Mac; it's not a PostScript device and uses bit-mapped fonts (although they look great on a laser printer). It has only one meg of RAM, but since it isn't using PostScript fonts, this isn't much of a disadvantage.

The intermediate model in the LaserWriter II line is the NT (for *new technology).* Like the SC, the NT's brain (also known as a *controller card)* is built around a 68000 chip, but one that runs at 12 MHz (as opposed to the SC's 7.45 MHz). The NT is a PostScript device, so it can be shared by several Macs, and it comes with the same eleven built-in

Adobe font families as the LaserWriter Plus (see the previous entry). The current list price is $4600.

The high-end LaserWriter II ($6600 list) is the NTX (the *x* stands for *expandable).* Its brain is built around the 68020 and like the NT, it comes with two megs of RAM standard (as opposed to the SC's one meg). But the NTX also lets you expand RAM up to twelve megs just by popping in some SIMMs.

esp. for power users

The NTX comes with the same eleven built-in Adobe font families as the NT. You can connect a SCSI hard disk (for storing additional fonts) directly to an NTX, but if you do, make sure you get one that's compatible with this use (some won't work).

You can upgrade an SC to an NT or an NTX, and an NT to an NTX. You just buy new brains.

All LaserWriter models to date (the original, both Pluses, the SC, NT and NTX) print out eight pages a minute, but that doesn't take into account the time the printer (and/or your Mac) spends figuring out what to put on the page. To speed that up, you need a faster chip and more memory.

That's what the LaserWriter IINT and particularly the IINTX give you, and believe me, the NTX is a *lot* faster than the original LaserWriter (I know, because I moved directly from one to the other).

✦ which LaserWriter to get

There are four basic differences between the NT and NTX, but they all add up to one thing: *speed.* First, the NTX is inherently faster because it's built around a different processor (the 68020 instead of the 68000). Second, it runs at a faster clock rate (16 MHz instead of 12 MHz).

Third, the NTX's expandable memory lets you download more fonts and keep them downloaded—so you don't waste time with repeated downloading. Finally, the NTX's SCSI port lets you attach a hard disk full of printer fonts—another time-saver, especially since it frees up your computer sooner than if you were downloading from it.

very good feature

The expandability of the NTX (both in memory and in hard disk hookup) has another benefit besides speed. There are some complicated documents that just can't be printed on a lesser LaserWriter because too many fonts are used or the graphics on the page take too much memory and just can't be processed. So the NTX can sometimes make a formerly impossible print job possible.

[Both times we bought a new laser printer, we opted for an NTX instead of an NT. The extra benefits always seemed worth the extra money.—AN]

Up till now, lack of PostScript capability has kept me from recommending the SC. Now I say, wait (if you can) and see. With the release of System 7 and Apple's outline font technology, you should be able to get the quality of PostScript fonts without a PostScript printer.

The SC will be perfect for those new fonts. But it still won't print PostScript graphics (EPS files) or be able to use PostScript fonts. And it's too soon to tell if 1MB of RAM will be enough to handle the new outline fonts.

very hot tip

[If you don't need PostScript, printer whiz Larry Pina recommends getting an HP LaserJet and the JetLink Express software package. For details, see the entry below titled the DeskJet Plus is even better.*—AN]*

⚫ telling LaserWriters apart

It's easy to distinguish LaserWriter I's and II's, because the styling of the machines is so different (that's the II on the right).

But if you're shopping in the "previously-owned" category, how can you tell the difference between the original LaserWriter and the two versions of the LaserWriter Plus (which weren't given separate names)? Here's how: print a startup sheet. (If someone has turned the startup page off, see the LaserWriter tips section below for how to turn it back on.) If the name of the printer hasn't been changed, the startup sheet will say *LaserWriter* or *LaserWriter Plus*.

very
hot
tip

Of course this won't work if the printer has been re-named, and it won't distinguish the two different LaserWriter Pluses. To do that, look at the number on the line graph that appears on the startup sheet. It will be either 1.0 (original LaserWriter), 2.0 (first version of the LaserWriter Plus) or 3.0 (second version of the LaserWriter Plus).

From the outside, all LaserWriter II's look alike; again, it's the test sheet that identifies just which printer you have. You can also use a utility like LaserStatus to check what's in the printer—which fonts and how much memory—and figure out from there which printer you've got, but the startup sheet is usually easier.

⚫ *buying a used LaserWriter* (Chris Allen)

very
hot
tip

One of the first things you do when buying a used car is check the odometer. So one of the first things you should do when buying a used LaserWriter is check out the startup page to see how many copies it's printed. I have a friend who found a used LaserWriter with only 6000 pages on it; another one she looked at had over 90,000!

⚫ *the Diconix M150 Plus* (AN)

This is a tiny (2" x 6.5" x 11") ink-jet printer made by Kodak that's great for taking with you when you travel. At $700 list, it doesn't really compare to the printers in the previous entry for use on your desk (unless ultraquiet op-eration is important to you), but at 3.75 pounds including batteries, or 3.1 pounds without, it's a great companion for a Mac Portable.

With twelve ink jets producing 192 dots per inch, the print quality is about on the level of a fax—better than an ImageWriter but not as good as a laser printer. In a speed test we ran, it took about a minute to print out one page from MacWrite II in draft mode, about 2:40 in near-letter-quality mode and about 3:25 in quality mode.

The Diconix comes with Adobe Type Manager and thirteen outline fonts. It uses a disposable printhead with a self-contained ink supply that's good for about 500 pages of standard text.

Unfortunately, the Diconix's tractor-feed mechanism lacks a lock, which makes it annoying to use, but you can also feed single sheets into it. The margins must be at least 7/10 of an inch, which may cut off text in some documents.

⚫ *the DeskWriter ink-jet printer* (Chris Allen)

bargain

Hewlett-Packard's DeskWriter is small, quiet, well designed, sturdy and reliable. Because it prints at 300 dpi (with *50* jets of ink!), its output is similar to a laser printer's; in fact, some people think it's superior, because the blacks are blacker. Yet the DeskWriter is commonly available for less than $1000.

The DeskWriter doesn't use PostScript outline fonts, but comes with its own set of outline fonts (Helvetica, Courier, Times and Symbol). For about $200, you can get a disk that contains an equivalent font set to the one included with a LaserWriter IINT or NTX. You can also use Adobe's Type Manager to print PostScript fonts. About the only programs the DeskWriter can't print from are those that use PostScript directly, like Illustrator and FreeHand, or those than incorporate EPS (encapsulated PostScript) graphics, like PageMaker.

very good
feature

A number of well-designed features make the DeskWriter very space-efficient. For one thing, it only takes up about two square feet on your desk, so you don't need another table to put it on. To clear even more space, there's a recessed well for cables in the back, so you can slide the DeskWriter all the way up against a wall. You can put both letter and legal paper in its paper tray, and there's a small slot for feeding business-size envelopes.

Because the DeskWriter uses an ink jet, it's slower than most laser printers, typically producing two to four pages a minute (depending on the number of fonts on the page, and the complexity of any graphics). But the ink jet has other advantages—it's so quiet you can barely hear it, and replacement cartridges are inexpensive. One minor problem is that the current ink is water-soluble, and thus prone to smearing if the page gets wet. But HP has announced that an indelible ink cartridge will be available soon.

important warning

Although the DeskWriter's manual recommends printing on higher-quality paper, ordinary paper has worked fine for me. I have run into a problem printing on label paper that seems to be too thick and stiff to wrap around the roller without slipping. I don't recommend printing a lot of labels on the DeskWriter, although the envelope feature is superb.

Until recently, you had to disconnect from AppleTalk to use the DeskWriter. But now there's an AppleTalk version of the DeskWriter, so several Macintoshes can share it. It costs the same as the original DeskWriter, and current DeskWriter owners can get upgraded to the new version fairly cheaply. This is an example of HP's good support.

🍎 *the DeskJet Plus is even better* (Larry Pina)

The DeskWriter is basically an HP DeskJet Plus that's been adapted to work with Macs. You can save some money (and gain some flexibility) by doing the job yourself. Buy a regular, generic DeskJet Plus (which usually sells for less than $600, not counting periodic rebates from HP), then get GDT Softwork's JetLink Express, which lists for $130.

bargain

The JetLink Express disk contains software that supports both DeskJets, all LaserJets and compatibles, as well as the DeskWriter, bit-mapped fonts and font cartridges. You also get the cable you need to connect with the Mac, and the same set of outline fonts that come with the DeskWriter.

very good feature

Basic printing tips

♠ printer drivers

**esp. for
beginners**

Printer drivers are programs that tell the application programs you use on your computer how to communicate with your printer. Without drivers, each application would have to contain information about every type of printer you might use. Instead, applications simply send the data to the printer driver you've selected and the driver tells the printer what to do.

The ImageWriter and LaserWriter icons in your system folder are printer drivers. Without them, you can't print. (The original MacPaint could print its documents without a driver, but I'm not aware of any current software that can do it.)

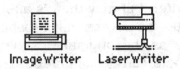

ImageWriter   LaserWriter

You may not need a separate driver for each type of printer you use; sometimes a single driver works for several related printers. For example, Apple's LaserWriter driver works for all five kinds of LaserWriters (but PageMaker has a separate driver for each).

Apple's basic printer drivers get updated along with other System software, so make sure you replace them when you upgrade your System. You can find the version number of the currently selected printer driver software in the Page Setup or Print dialog box, just to the left of the OK button. Or you can simply Get Info on any printer driver icon from the desktop.

Make sure the printer drivers are in your system folder or else they won't show up in the Chooser dialog box (see the next entry for more on that).

✦ *using Chooser*

Whenever you have more than one printer to choose from—whether multiple printers on a network or an Image-Writer and LaserWriter both hooked up directly to your Mac—you have to tell the Mac which one you want it to print to when you choose the *Print...* command. To do that, you select *Chooser* from the ✦ menu and click on the icon of the printer you want to use.

**esp. for
beginners**

If you click on the ImageWriter icon, Chooser will ask you to tell it what port the ImageWriter is connected to.

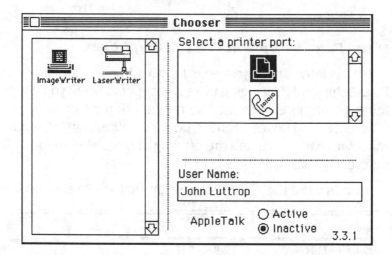

If you click on the LaserWriter icon, a list of available LaserWriters will appear in the list box at the right (even if there's only one). Just click on the printer you want to use. (See the figure at the top of the next page.)

If you use Chooser to switch to a different *type* of printer—that is, not just from one LaserWriter to another but from a LaserWriter to an ImageWriter or vice-versa—there's something else you need to do. But it's important enough to merit its own entry (see *changing printers* below).

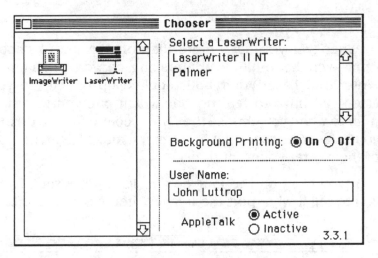

 the Page Setup and Print dialog boxes

*esp. for
beginners*

The printer driver you select with Chooser generates the Page Setup and Print dialog boxes that appear when you choose those commands from the File menu. Different printers need different dialog boxes because printing options differ from one machine to the next, and the printing options also change with different *versions* of the same driver.

Here's what the basic Page Setup dialog boxes look like:

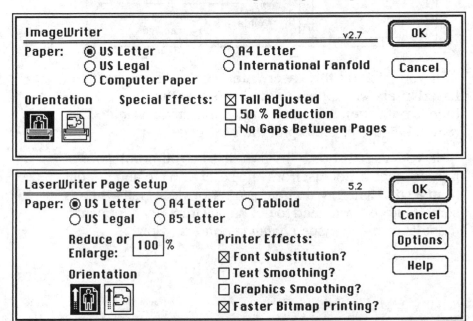

And here are the basic Print dialog boxes:

```
┌─────────────────────────────────────────────────────────────┐
│ ImageWriter                              v2.3      ╭─ OK ─╮   │
│ Quality:      ○ Best      ⦿ Faster    ○ Draft      ╰──────╯   │
│ Page Range:   ⦿ All       ○ From: │  To: │         ┌ Cancel ┐ │
│ Copies:       │ 1 │                                └────────┘ │
│ Paper Feed:   ⦿ Automatic   ○ Hand Feed                      │
└─────────────────────────────────────────────────────────────┘
```

```
┌─────────────────────────────────────────────────────────────┐
│ LaserWriter  "LaserWriter II NT"          5.2     ╭─ OK ─╮    │
│ Copies: 1          Pages: ⦿ All ○ From: │ To: │   ╰──────╯    │
│ Cover Page:    ⦿ No ○ First Page ○ Last Page     ┌ Cancel ┐   │
│                                                  └────────┘   │
│ Paper Source: ⦿ Paper Cassette ○ Manual Feed     ┌ Help ┐     │
│                                                  └──────┘     │
└─────────────────────────────────────────────────────────────┘
```

Many applications substitute their own dialog boxes for these basic ones to give you even more printing options to choose from.

⚫ *changing printers* (AN)

If you use more than one type of printer on a Mac (say, an ImageWriter and a LaserWriter), be sure to choose *Page Setup...* when you switch between them. The ImageWriter and the LaserWriter use different print areas on the page, so applications need to be told, via Page Setup, that you've switched.

esp. for beginners

A dialog box will remind you of this when you switch printers:

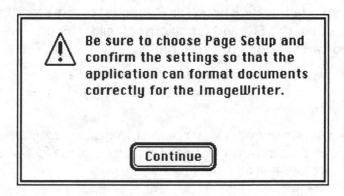

Be sure to choose Page Setup and confirm the settings so that the application can format documents correctly for the ImageWriter.

Continue

You don't have to *do* anything in the Page Setup dialog box—just open and then close it again.

You should also choose *Page Setup...* the first time you print from an application after installing a new version of a printer driver. Here again, you only need to enter and exit Page Setup—you don't have to change any settings—to activate the new driver.

important warning

Because changing printer drivers can have drastic effects on line breaks, page breaks and the like, don't expect to be able to proof a document on an ImageWriter and go straight to final output on a LaserWriter. You'll almost certainly have to proof each page that comes off the LaserWriter as well.

🍎 *which fonts for which printer*

esp. for beginners

For an ImageWriter (including the LQ), LaserWriter SC or other non-PostScript printer, you need bit-mapped fonts—and you need them in a variety of sizes. The most important size is the one you're using to display the font on the screen, but the printer needs a larger size to produce high-quality printouts.

For best results, ImageWriters I and II require a font that's twice the size of the one you're using—in other words, for a good-looking 12-point printout, you need the 24-point font installed in your system.

The ImageWriter LQ needs a triple-size font—36-point to print 12-point well. The LaserWriter SC needs a quadruple-size font—48 point for 12-point. For any LaserWriters other than the SC, and for all other PostScript printers, you need two versions of each font:

• the *screen font* installed in your System file (so the font will appear in menus and can be displayed on your screen)

• the *printer font* in your system folder (so the Mac can tell printers how to form the characters of the font when you use it in a printout

In the following situations, however, you don't need a printer font:

- when you're using a font that's already built into the printer (that is, the printer came with the font included)

- when the printer font is on a hard disk attached to a LaserWriter NTX (or another printer that uses hard disks this way)

- when you're on a network that's set up to share printer fonts stored on the file server

- when you're preparing a document that will be printed using a different system folder (on a friend's Mac, at a service bureau, at the office or wherever)

- when you're using a bit-mapped font that doesn't *have* a printer font (the printout won't look as good, but it may be worth it to you to get just the font you want)

One size of the screen font is all any PostScript printer needs (actually, the *printer* doesn't need a screen font at all; *you* need one to see the font on the screen and on the font menu).

For more information on screen and printer fonts, see the font chapter.

✎ *cancelling printing*

No matter what kind of printer you're using, a dialog box appears on the screen letting you know that printing is in progress.

esp. for
beginners

> **Printing in progress.**
>
> **Document: Facing Chapter 5 page**
>
> [Cancel]   [Pause]   [Continue]

It usually has a Cancel button so you can stop the printing. But whether there's one or not, almost every program lets you cancel the program with ⌘ . . The key also works in many programs as a general cancel command, as does the accent grave (`).

Don't expect instant compliance with your cancel command. The ImageWriter receives sections of the page (called *bands)* from the Mac at a time, and it's going to finish printing the band it's on before it pays any attention to the Mac.

important
warning

The LaserWriter processes a full page at a time, so you'll still get the page it's working on when you cancelled. This means that if you've asked for 100 copies of a document, cancelling the print job won't stop the LaserWriter from spewing out 100 copies of the page it's working on. The only way you can stop it is by shutting it off.

In either case, the printing dialog box should disappear from the Mac screen while the printer goes merrily on its way. Sometimes this won't be instantaneous either, if the Mac is busy processing something to send to the printer and can't stop in the middle. Your ⌘ . sequence is stored until the Mac is ready for keyboard input, so you don't have to keep pressing it to make your point—although repeated pressings won't have any harmful effect.

If you're using any sort of print spooler (see the entry called *print spoolers and buffers* below), you'll have to cancel the printing by whatever method the spooler requires.

very
hot
tip

Whatever the situation, remember: the printer has an off switch and using it in the middle of printing isn't going to hurt anything. At worst, the LaserWriter will have a half-fed sheet of paper inside; if it does, just open the case and pull it out.

❤ how much longer?

As soon as I see a printing-in-progress dialog box, I feel like a kid in the back seat of a car on a family trip, whining *"Are we there yet?"*

It's frustrating to have to walk over to the printer and see where you are in a print job. Word tells you what page is currently being printed, but unless you remember the total number of pages you're printing, that only tells the kid in the back seat how far she is from home, not how close she is to DisneyWorld.

Backgrounder, WriteNow, Nisus and PageMaker all take the right approach—they let you know how many more pages there are to be printed. All applications should do this.

✎ *printing the screen* (AN/SZA)

Printing the image currently on your Mac's screen is easy—if you want to print it to an ImageWriter. All you have to do is hit [Caps Lock] [Shift] [⌘] [4]. [Shift] [⌘] [4] prints the current *window* instead of the whole screen. (In spreadsheets, the current window is simply the entry bar—the little text box that shows the contents of the selected cell; so if you press [Shift] [⌘] [4] in a spreadsheet, that's all you'll get.)

There are two ways to print a screen to a laser printer. One is to get any one of the public-domain, shareware or commercial utilities that let you do that. The other is to save the screen image as a graphic, then print it from disk.

[Shift] [⌘] [3] puts an image of the screen onto your disk, but only if you're using a compact Mac (i.e., an SE, Plus, etc., with a 9″ screen). If you need a *screen dump* (as pictures of the screen are called) on a larger screen, use one of the screen capture programs described in the utilities chapter.

✎ *printing from the desktop*

You can print almost any document from the desktop by selecting it and then choosing *Print* from the File menu. The program that created the document will open, print the document and then close both itself and the document, returning you to the desktop. (The program has to be either on the startup disk or the same disk as the document.)

esp. for beginners

But don't select Print and then walk away from the computer, expecting your printout to be ready when you get back. Most programs will go only as far as opening the document and putting the Print dialog box on the screen for you to select the number of copies, the page range and so on. You'll still need to click OK to get the printing started.

🍎 *printing multiple files*

esp. for beginners

A few programs support the printing of more than one document at a time; for example, SuperPaint has a command that prints all the opened documents and Word (among other programs) lets you chain documents so they'll be printed one after another.

But, for most programs, if you want to print more than one document at a time, you have to select them all on the desktop and choose *Print* from the File menu. You'll usually only have to deal with the Print dialog box once—the same settings (number of copies and so on) will be applied to all the documents you're printing.

After each document is printed, it will be closed and the next one will be opened and printed. When they're all printed, the program will close itself and return you to the desktop.

🍎 *printing multiple copies* (AN)

esp. for beginners

Because most programs take a long time to figure out a page but not very long after that to print it, it's usually much faster to ask for multiple copies of a document than to reprint it several times. Of course, you also have to consider how long it will take you to collate the sheets into separate sets.

So if your document is in a word processor that really spits out the pages, it may make more sense to print out single copies and avoid collating. But if your document is in PageMaker, say, printing multiple copies and collating (or printing one copy and photocopying that) can save you a lot of time.

❡ *print spoolers*

Macs can send out information to printers much faster than printers can receive and process it, so the computer is tied up in the printing process much longer than is really necessary.

A *print spooler* is a program that lets you create a special print file on the disk which then gets fed out to the printer in chunks—at a rate the printer can handle. Since the Mac creates this print file on disk quite quickly, you can get back to work and leave the computer and the printer to talk to each other in the background. *(Spool* is an acronym for *simultaneous print operations on-line.)*

A decent laser-printer spooler comes with Apple's system software (see the entry on Backgrounder and Print Monitor in the LaserWriter tips section below). If you're shopping for a print spooler for your ImageWriter, be careful: most spool only plain text (no fonts, type styles, etc.) and print only in draft quality. Sometimes that's good enough— you can print out a draft while you keep working.

Print spoolers can be terrific but they're not miracle-workers. The Mac still needs to tend to the printer to some extent, feeding out information from the print file when necessary, and that interrupts your work.

I gave up with spoolers on the Mac Plus because the slowdown was too much—I found it less frustrating to just take a break during printing than to deal with a computer that ignored me for up to a full minute out of every three or four. I use Backgrounder only occasionally with my IIcx— the slowdown is acceptable for brief work periods, but when I'm printing a document of more than twenty or so pages, I prefer just to take a break.

(Byron Brown likes SuperLaserSpool from SuperMac, which works with PageMaker (not all spoolers do). To give you an idea of how much more quickly a spooler gives you back the use of your Mac, Byron did a test run. He found that it took Super-LaserSpool two minutes to read a 27-page PageMaker file onto

shortcut

the disk, and another twenty minutes to actually print the file out. The eighteen-minute difference is time you get to work on the Mac that you otherwise wouldn't have.—AN)

⚫ printer buffers

Printer buffers do the same thing as spoolers, but with hardware rather than software. That is, they provide extra memory in which to store a print file. Printer buffers never really caught on in the Mac world—they need too much memory to handle all the Mac's fonts and graphics, and thus are too expensive.

ImageWriter tips

⚫ print modes

esp. for beginners

The ImageWriter offers three print modes. *Best quality* is achieved by a double pass of the printhead, with the second set of dots slightly offset. In addition, the Mac prepares the file differently for a Best-quality printout—it creates a map that's twice the size of what the printer needs and then shrinks it by 50%.

This double-it-then-halve-it approach requires a font that's twice the size of the one you want (24 point when you want 12, for example). If the double-size font isn't installed in your system folder, the Mac looks for one that's four times the size.

Faster printing is, of course, faster; the trade-off is lower quality. Only a single pass is made to print the document so there aren't any offset dots to smooth curves. But Faster is perfect for proof-reading and fine for all sorts of informal situations—especially with a newer ribbon that smears the dots ever-so-slightly.

Draft mode is pretty ugly but it serves a purpose. It won't print graphics, it doesn't know about fonts and it can only give you basic type styles like boldface. What's more, to make sure your line and page breaks will be the same as when you print out at higher quality, Draft mode puts ugly gaps between words.

🍎 *faster Draft* (Paul Hoffman)

According to its manual, the ImageWriter II will print at 250 cps. Needless to say, that's only in Draft mode, and even then you need to know a couple of tricks to get that kind of speed out of it.

*very
hot
tip*

The first trick concerns fonts. The font the ImageWriter uses in Draft mode is Monaco 10. If your document is in any other font, the ImageWriter will try to adjust the spacing between the letters and the words to make them match how the text looks on the screen. It will fail, miserably, but it will try, and the trying takes time.

If you put your document into Monaco 10 before printing it, you will be spared that exercise in futility. (You can also write and edit your documents in Monaco 10, but it's ugly and hard to read on the screen.)

Here's the other trick: for the fastest speed, you not only have to select Draft mode in the Print dialog box, but you also have to select it on the print quality switches on the ImageWriter itself. (These switches only have an effect when you're printing in Draft mode).

By doing those two things, you'll get printouts in the shortest time possible.

🍎 *faster Faster*

You can speed up Faster mode further by making the ImageWriter print *bidirectionally*—both on the forward and backward pass of the print head. Press [Caps Lock] [Shift] [Option] while you click the OK button in the Print dialog box.

*very
hot
tip*

This setting survives turning off the computer and the printer (it's stored in the printer driver). To revert to normal printing, press [Caps Lock] [Shift] [⌘] while clicking the OK button in the dialog box. (But why do that? As far as I know, there's no disadvantage to leaving the ImageWriter in bidirectional mode all the time.)

¢ ImageWriter bands

[Can you imagine how terrible they'd sound?—AN]

When your ImageWriter pauses after a few lines and then starts again there's nothing wrong; it's just getting information from the Mac. The ImageWriter has very little memory—so little that an entire page can't be transferred from the Mac to the printer in one shot. Instead, the page is sent in *bands* (horizontal chunks).

You'll notice many more pauses in Best mode than in Faster mode, since there's so much more information going to the printer for the higher-quality printout.

¢ high-quality graphic printing

To print a high-resolution graphic on the ImageWriter, shrink it in your application to 50% of its original size and then print it at Best quality. (Of course this dictates how big the graphic will be.)

¢ using the Tall Adjusted option

esp. for beginners

Since the ImageWriter's normal printouts (called *Tall* in the Page Setup dialog box) don't match the 72 x 72 resolution of the Mac screen, graphics are distorted (circles become ovals, for example). To avoid that, just choose the Tall Adjusted option in the Page Setup dialog box; this tells the ImageWriter to print at 72 dpi both horizontally and vertically.

Be aware that this will increase the overall width of your document by about 11% and that can cause problems with text or graphics near the left and right margins.

¢ printer gibberish

Occasionally, your ImageWriter will do a "hex dump"—printing strings of hexadecimal numbers—instead of printing normally. This usually happens when you've reset the Mac but not the printer.

(You can even hear it happen. Since hex dumps are rows and columns of four-digit numbers, the firing of the pins in the print head is so regular—compared to the usual non-rhythmic firing for different-length words and para-graphs—that you'll know right away that something's wrong.)

To fix the problem, simply turn the ImageWriter off and back on again. To avoid it, turn your ImageWriter on *after* you turn the Mac on and reset it each time you reset the computer.

● *stocking up on and storing ribbons*

Unless you run into a fabulous once-in-a-lifetime sale (and maybe not even then), don't stock up on ImageWriter ribbons, because the ink dries up. If you have ribbons that aren't going to be used for a while, store them in a closed plastic bag to help keep the ink fresh.

important warning

● *re-inking ribbons*

Re-inking ribbons is, as far as I'm concerned, more trouble than it's worth. Unless you use just the right amount of ink—and it's *so* difficult not to overdo it—the smear factor when you're done ruins printouts for a long time (until a lot of the ink is used or dried up).

Another concern with re-inking is that if you overuse a ribbon, the pins on the printhead will eventually wear it down or even wear holes through it. Tiny fibrous pieces from the ribbon can then get stuck on the pins, and that can lead to a hundred-dollar repair job.

If you *are* going to re-ink your ribbons (with one of those clever little machines that wind the ribbon around ink-soaked felt rollers) make sure you buy ink specifically in-tended for dot-matrix printer ribbons. It contains a lubri-cant that the pins on the printhead need.

important warning

● *alternative ribbons* (DC)

From time to time your local supplier may run out of ImageWriter ribbons. This will probably happen late Satur-day afternoon, just before you plan to begin a marathon weekend of printing to meet Monday morning's deadline. If you can't find any ImageWriter ribbons, don't panic—you can substitute ribbons for the C. Itoh 8510, the NEC 8023 and DEC LA50 printers. (If you can't find them either, *then* you can panic.)

❤ *used ribbons are better*

very
hot
tip

What? Yes, for high-quality printing, a moderately-used ribbon is much better than a new one. The double-strike method used by the ImageWriter to achieve high-quality output tends to smear the ink from a new, or newly-inked, ribbon.

On the other hand, a new ribbon works best with draft-quality output; in that case, the extra smear fills in all those spaces between the dots.

So keep at least two ribbons around—a new one and a used one—and swap them in and out of the ImageWriter depending on the print job. When a new ribbon is a little worn out (worn in?), you can promote it from draft to high-quality jobs.

❤ *sheet feeders* (DC/AN)

Using fan-fold paper is a lot of trouble. It often gets jammed (particularly on the ImageWriter II, whose tractor feed isn't very good) and when the job is done, you're faced with the task of removing the perforated edges with the holes in them, separating the individual pages and collating them.

A sheet feeder frees you from all that. You can use virtually any kind of paper you please and change it as often as you want. When the printing is finished, the pages of your document are not only separated but also collated. One final advantage: regular 8-1/2 by 11 paper is less expensive than fan-fold paper.

So why doesn't everyone use sheet feeders? Because they're usually expensive and not very reliable. Although the sheet feeder Apple sells for the ImageWriter II isn't terribly expensive (it lists for $225), we've found it to be not very reliable. If you need a sheet feeder, it may still be worth buying; just make sure you take out an AppleCare extended warranty on it.

⚫ *laser perf paper*

If you use tractor-feed paper, the best kind is something known as *laser cut* or *laser perf* or some variant of that phrase. What it means is that instead of the normal perforations between pages and along the sides, the cuts are very fine (I don't know if they're *really* cut by lasers). As a result, the final papers have very clean edges and don't look tractor-fed at all.

⚫ *perfory*

I read someplace, years ago, of a contest to name those paper strips with the holes in them that you tear off fan-fold paper. I don't know whether it was the winner or not, but the best name submitted was *perfory*.

gossip/ trivia

Does anybody have any use for this stuff? Before I switched to laser printing, I always had piles and added them to the regular kindling in the wood stove during the winter. *[Well, Sharon, <u>there's</u> a use for them. Send all your used perfory to Sharon Aker, 20 Courtland Drive, Sussex NJ 07461. The postage won't be much, and think of the joy you'll get from knowing that you're keeping the wolf—or frostbite, anyway—from Sharon's door.—AN]*

⚫ *printing envelopes* (Brad Bunnin)

Printing envelopes on an ImageWriter can be a troublesome process. They tend to jam and minimum margin settings make it difficult to print a return address in its usual location in the upper left corner. There are more complicated ways around this problem, but here's the simplest: just feed the envelope into the printer with the flap open and compensate by adding as much length as you need to the top margin.

very hot tip

My return address is already printed on my envelopes, so all I need to print is the recipient's address. I set my top margin by measuring down from the top of the closed envelope to the first line of the address (1.75" on my envelopes) and adding another inch for the flap (for a setting of 2.75").

If you need to print your return address, just measure how far you want its top line to come below the top edge of the envelope and add an inch to that figure—or whatever distance works for the flaps on your envelopes. (I think the response of the ImageWriter's paper sensor depends on where the edge of the flap meets the sensor.)

The natural curl of the envelope flap can cause the envelope to wrap around the platen. To avoid that, just bend the tip of the flap back a little before you feed it.

(You can also buy form-fed envelopes to run through the printer and then tear them apart—along the dotted lines, of course—after they're printed.—SZA)

🍎 *mimeo stencils* (Michael Bradley)

If you use an ImageWriter to cut mimeograph stencils, you may run into trouble: with some brands, the wax backing gums up the pins in the ImageWriter's print head. Try leaving an old, faint, fabric ribbon in the printer, to shield the print head from the stencil wax. *(You can also sometimes buy "blank" ribbons that are meant to be inked in the color of your choice.—SZA)* Some stencils are made especially for computer printers—A.B. Dick's part #2060, for example.

When you make drawings for mimeo stencils, use dotted lines instead of solid ones. Solid lines can tear the stencil and/or smear the image, especially if they're closely spaced.

When you fill an image, use a light pattern instead of a dark one. Areas filled with dark or solid black patterns can smear the drum of the mimeo printer with ink. This also means being careful about using symbols that are solid images, like 🍎.

❤ squished lines on the LQ

When you have trouble with squished lines on your printout—especially on multipart forms or other thicker-than-regular-paper stock—use the bottom feed slot and the pull tractor and keep the fanfolds of paper at least 12" below the printer. This keeps the paper wrapped tightly around the platen.

❤ two LQ problems

Here are a couple of documented ImageWriter LQ problems (which means Apple admits them):

LQ's made between February and April of 1989 (serial numbers lower than 183181813) sometimes stop or unexpectedly reset when on a network. You need a new logic board for the printer, which Apple provides for free.

bug

Early LQ's had problems with the print head sticking; those with serial numbers lower than 180700530 are most prone to this problem. Apple provides a free fix through its dealers; ask for the *Home Position Switch Kit.* Better yet, see the next entry.

bug

❤ free ImageWriter LQ exchange (SZA/AN)

If you purchased your ImageWriter LQ before March, 1989, any authorized Apple dealer will exchange it for a factory-refurbished one that makes less noise and has fewer output problems. But hurry, because this offer is scheduled to expire sometime in the fall of 1990. (Sorry if you've already missed it; we wanted to leave this tip in for people who bought the book early.)

things
to come

LaserWriter tips

A lot of the information in the following sections doesn't apply to non-PostScript laser printers like the LaserWriter SC. It would be tedious for us to disclaim each such tip, so please just use your judgement. Stuff on maintenance, cartridges, paper and other aspects of the physical machines, or on basic software, applies to all laser printers, but anything to do with PostScript obviously only applies to PostScript printers.

🍎 the LaserPrep file

When you're using a LaserWriter, you need not only the LaserWriter driver but also the LaserPrep file in your system folder. (They must have compatible version numbers, so make sure you get the Prep file from the same place you get your driver.)

The LaserPrep file is a sort of dictionary of special PostScript terms that the Mac needs to communicate with the printer. It bridges some of the differences between PostScript (the language the printer uses) and QuickDraw (the language the Mac uses to draw its screen images). It also interprets the special PostScript files that the Mac sends to the printer, which aren't quite standard but are optimized for speedy transmission over AppleTalk networks. (When your Mac is connected to a LaserWriter, that's considered an AppleTalk network.)

🍎 naming your printer

esp. for beginners

The Apple utility Namer lets you name your LaserWriter anything you like. The name appears in the Chooser desk accessory when you select the LaserWriter driver icon.

Renaming LaserWriters (they start out named *LaserWriter Plus* or *LaserWriter IINT,* or whatever) is possible at any time, but it's absolutely necessary on a network that has more than one LaserWriter. Otherwise, your printout might end up in another room, on another floor or even in another building.

🍎 LaserWriter page-setup options (AN/SZA)

esp. for beginners

The LaserWriter driver gives you a number of useful features in the Page Setup dialog box. One of these is Faster Bitmap Printing, which preprocesses bit-mapped images before they're sent to the LaserWriter. Apple states that "in rare cases, some documents may not print with this option turned on," but this has never happened to me. If it happens to you, just turn the option off and try again.

The *graphics smoothing* or *smoothing bitmap* option removes some of the jagged look bit-mapped graphics might otherwise have—the stair-step effect around curves, for example, turns into a slightly squiggly line. This option is only for Apple's LaserWriters, not for other brands of PostScript printers. Programs like PageMaker have smoothing routines of their own that work on all PostScript printers.

There's a button in the Page Setup dialog box called Options. Clicking on it gives you several additional choices. You can flip the entire image on your page either vertically or horizontally, or "invert" it (print a negative of it, changing whites to blacks and blacks to whites).

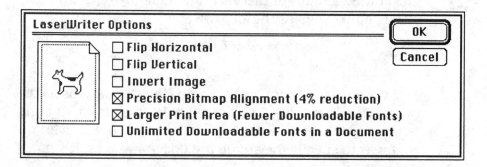

Precision Bitmap Alignment improves bit-mapped graphics by reducing the entire image on the page to 96% of its normal size. This gets around the incompatibility between the 72 dots per inch of the Mac's screen and the 300 dots per inch of the LaserWriter's output (300 divided by 72 is 4.1666, but 96% of 300 is 288, into which 72 goes exactly 4 times).

Chris Allen has a neat trick that avoids having to reduce the whole document—just enlarge the graphic to 104% of its original size (of course this only works in documents that give you that precision). Neither this approach or Precision

very hot tip

Bitmap Alignment will work if the graphic has been reduced or enlarged from its original size.

Larger Print Area lets you cover slightly more of the page—but only if the application you're using lets you. Doing this limits the number of fonts you can use, which may or may not be a problem, depending on how much RAM your printer has.

A dog of indeterminate breed helps you see the effect of all these options by acting them out for you as you select them.

✦ the amazing dogcow

gossip/ trivia

The animal that appears in many print option dialog boxes is not only, as Arthur puts it in the last entry, "of indeterminate breed," it's of indeterminate species. In acknowledgement of this fact, it's regularly referred to by Apple employees as the *dogcow.*

I was so used to seeing it as a dog that seeing it as a cow was difficult at first—but not after hearing my two sons argue about what it was. Apple's technical notes even go so far as to specify the sound the dogcow makes: it's *moof* (of course).

If this Thurberesque dogcow appeals to your sense of whimsy, make it your own. Just choose Cairo from the font menu and hit ⌤ .

✦ back-to-front printing

very bad feature

LaserWriter I's output sheets face up, so the second page ends up on top of the first page, the third on top of the second and so on. In a marked improvement, the LaserWriter II line puts the pages upside down when they come out—so the second page is *beneath* the first when you take the papers out and look at their printed sides.

To keep from shuffling LaserWriter I printouts around, use the *Back to Front* option you'll sometimes find in Print dialog boxes. It begins printing at the last page of the document, so the final pile of printed papers is in the right order.

very good feature

๔ *laser printer hangups* (AN)

Laser printers sometimes get confused and hung up (just like the rest of us). When this happens, reset the printer (with LaserStatus or some other utility program). If that doesn't help, restart your Mac (with the *Restart* command on the Special Menu).

If there's still a problem, turn both the Mac and the printer off and wait five minutes before turning them back on (check all the cable connections while they're both off). If even that doesn't help, replace your printer drivers. If *that* doesn't help, reinstall the System and Finder files from the disk you got from Apple (or a copy thereof).

If you're *still* having a problem, it may actually be in the hardware.

๔ *feeding single sheets on the LaserWriter II* (AN)

The LaserWriter II will pull a sheet from the single-sheet feed on the top of the paper tray whether you tell it to or not. So all you have to do is put a sheet of paper in the slot; you don't gain anything by clicking the Manual Feed button in the Print dialog box.

๔ *suppressing the LaserWriter's startup page* (AN/SZA)

Every time you turn on the LaserWriter, it spits out a rather attractive test page that tells you how many copies have ever been printed on the machine. While it's possible to get into this constantly mounting total as a measure of your productivity (and therefore your general worth as a human being: *I've printed 3217 pages on my LaserWriter—I must be doing something useful with my life*), it does cost you about 3¢ in toner, some fraction of a cent in paper and some hard-to-figure but probably significant amount of wear-and-tear on the machine.

So it's sometimes nice to be able to turn off the startup page, at least for a while. The easiest way to do that is to use Widgets, which comes as part of DiskTop (reviewed in Chapter 8). Century Software also has a pair of programs called Start-up On and Start-Up Off that...well, we're sure you can figure it out.

Here's another approach to suppressing the startup page. Just type out the short PostScript program below, save it as a text-only file (with a name that's easy to remember) and send it to the LaserWriter with one of the downloading programs that comes on disks of outline fonts.

```
serverdict begin 0 exitserver statusdict
begin false setdostartpage
```

This program stays in the LaserWriter even when you turn it off, so you only have to send it once. (That's a good thing; otherwise you'd have to send the program to the LaserWriter after you turned it on, at which point it would have already printed the startup page.)

When you want to turn the startup page back on—to recheck your worth as a human being or for some other reason—use the same program but replace the word *false* with the word *true*.

Neale Hall wrote from Alexander Hill, Australia to suggest yet another (very simple) way to suppress the startup page—but, unlike the approaches above, you have to do it each time you turn the printer on, which makes it somewhat tedious. You just pull out the paper tray before you turn the LaserWriter on each time and don't push it in again until the LaserWriter's warmed up.

♦ ready and waiting

One function of the startup page is to tell you exactly when the LaserWriter is ready to begin printing. If you turn off the startup page, how do you know when the printer's ready?

When you turn the LaserWriter on, it tests itself; while it's doing that, the green light blinks (on the LaserWriter II, some other lights come on first, but just ignore them). When the green light stops blinking, wait a few seconds and the machine is ready to use.

In a cold room, this warmup and test procedure may take about a minute—or longer, if you have a lot of memory in your printer. If you've used the machine recently and/or the room is warm and/or your printer has a brain the size of a pea, it may take much less time than that.

✎ *flashing messages and lights* (AN)

When a Mac is collaborating with a LaserWriter to figure out how to print a document, a message appears on the Mac's screen that lists its *status* as *processing job*. With certain combinations of hardware and software, this message may flicker off and on again every five seconds or so. *Do not panic* (as I, of course, did). The periodic flashing doesn't mean that the power pole outside your house is about to fall over, or that enemy aliens from Saturn are trying to destroy your Mac by sending power surges through the house wiring. It's perfectly normal, just a way of reminding you that the Mac is thinking.

The LaserWriter I lets you know it's thinking by flashing its yellow light every two seconds. (Double-flashing indicates a *wait* state, which usually doesn't last more than 30 seconds.) The LaserWriter II has a green light for the same purpose.

When the Mac's role in the printing collaboration is done, the status message will disappear from the screen, but a page still may not have emerged from the LaserWriter. *Do not panic* (as I, of course, did). The LaserWriter is still thinking on its own about how exactly to print the document; you know that because the yellow light is still flashing.

You're free to continue editing the document, to close it, to quit the application or whatever. The LaserWriter will print the document eventually, all in its own good time.

⚫ *Backgrounder and PrintMonitor*

Backgrounder is a perfectly adequate print spooler that Apple provides for its LaserWriters (and I don't mean to condemn it with faint praise). To use it, you need *both* the Backgrounder and the PrintMonitor files in your system folder. Then select the LaserWriter icon in the Chooser desk accessory to activate the *Background Printing* buttons and turn the spooler on or off.

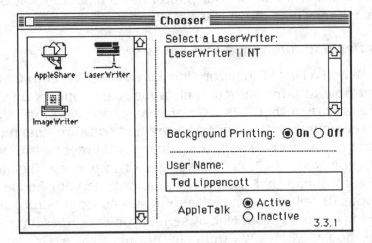

Keep in mind that Backgrounder, like all spoolers, saves a *print file* to the disk to be fed out to the printer. You need enough room on your disk to hold the print file—which will be at least the size of the document—and your work on the Mac will be periodically interrupted for the feeding of the printer. The frequency and duration of the interruptions depends on the Mac model you're using. Whether the interruptions are worth the background printing capabilities depends on your personality. (Type A's need not even apply.)

PrintMonitor is a desk accessory that lets you keep track of what's going on in the printer—what document's being printed, how many pages are left to go, what documents are waiting to be printed, etc. On a network, it will also tell you *whose* document is being printed and what other documents are in line to be printed.

There's one other nice feature: when the printer needs attention (because it's out of paper, say), PrintMonitor flashes the in the upper left corner of the screen, alternating it with the PrintMonitor icon.

one spooler is enough (Chris Allen)

One of the most common problems I've seen with spoolers is that people will have *both* a third-party print spooler *and* Backgrounder running at the same time! Amazingly enough, this will work, but it costs you time, since everything is done twice.

important
warning

let us now praise a clearly written manual (AN)

The LaserWriter manual has an excellent section on all aspects of setting up and maintaining the printer; it's clearly written and full of helpful illustrations.

very good
feature

printing custom stationery and envelopes (AN)

Access to a LaserWriter can not only save you the expense of buying stationery, it can allow you to modify your stationery as often you like. You can change the text, the fonts, the graphics or the paper you print it on. (On the LaserWriter, it's just as economical to produce a batch of five sheets of letterhead with matching envelopes as it is to produce a batch of five hundred.) Custom stationery makes a wonderful present, particularly if you use fancy paper and spend some time making the stationery match the recipient's personality.

esp. for
beginners

There's no special trick to doing letterhead on the LaserWriter. (There are some general tips on the subject in the general word processing tips section of Chapter 10). But envelopes can be tricky. You have to hand-feed them into the LaserWriter, face up and against the back edge of the manual feed guide. Certain kinds of envelopes don't feed very well—like ones made from "parchment"-type or "laid" paper. (They also don't take toner well.)

If you print your name and return address along the length of the envelope—that is, in the same direction as the name and address of the person you're sending it to—you'll only have to run the envelope through the LaserWriter once. If you want your name and address to run across the end of the envelope—which looks snazzier—you'll either have to run the envelopes through a second time, print labels and stick them on, or address the envelopes by hand.

very hot tip

Whichever direction you use for your address, you may find yourself frustrated by the LaserWriter's inability to print closer than a quarter of an inch to the edge of the envelope. But a reader named Mike Chan wrote in with a cunning trick. He uses Post-It notes to trip the paper guide (he sticks them on the envelope with about a quarter of an inch protruding). He says he's only had to open the LaserWriter two or three times to retrieve Post-Its that have fallen off inside.

Mike also said that a toner cartridge recharging company told him that running envelopes through the LaserWriter will do in the drum in the cartridge (I assume from glue melting off the flap) and that they didn't recommend recharging cartridges if envelopes have been run through them. (For more on this, see the entry on labels and envelopes in the laser-printer supplies section below.)

♠ *hard disks attached to NTX's*

If you attach a hard disk to an NTX for storing fonts, you only get to use some of it for the printer files. The rest of the disk is used as an extension of the printer's *font cache*—where the currently used fonts are stored. Without a hard disk attached, the printer purges fonts from memory to make room for the latest one that's downloaded, but with the hard disk attached, the purged font is temporarily stored for easy and quick retrieval.

♠ *maximum image areas on LaserWriter I's* (AN)

The maximum area a LaserWriter I will print on a standard US letter-size (8.5 x 11) sheet of paper is 8 by 10.92

inches, centered on the page. The width limitation is the most significant; it means you must always have a margin of at least a quarter inch on each side. (The required .04-inch border top and bottom is, of course, trivial.) What's more, many programs can't even fill that the entire area.

The image-size restriction is even more dramatic on legal-size paper (8.5 x 14). There the LaserWriter can only fill an area 6.72 inches wide by 13 inches deep, thus requiring margins of more than 7/8″ on each side and 1/2″ borders top and bottom. (There are similar restrictions for the common European paper sizes, A4 and B5.)

The reason for these limitations is the LaserWriter I's memory. A meg and a half is only enough to image between 87 and 88 square inches of page (which is what both 8″ x 10.92″ and 6.72″ x 13″ amount to). To really process a page adequately with PostScript, a printer should have at least two megs of memory. Many other PostScript printers and imagesetters do have that much memory (the LaserWriter IINT and NTX among them).

very bad feature

One time it's important to remember these size limitations is when you're proofing something on the ImageWriter that will ultimately be printed out on the LaserWriter. Because the ImageWriter can print wider than the LaserWriter, be sure to leave adequate margins; otherwise your image will get cropped on the edges when you put it on the LaserWriter. (This is just one of the problems with switching printers for an existing document.)

◆ *how to get rich, deep blacks* (DC/AN)

Buy a LaserWriter II or some other laser printer built around Canon's SX marking engine. The LaserWriter I's (and other laser printers built around Canon's CX marking engine) simply can't do it. Black areas of any significant size will contain small white splotches or streaks, regardless of where you put the print density dial.

very hot tip

This is only a problem with areas of black, not regular text—which tends to look good no matter how low you set the print density dial. And it's also only a problem if the printer's output is used as the final product. The film used by printers will almost always fill the black areas in and you can even get the same result from a photocopy machine (usually). In any case, don't bother turning the dial all the way to high—you'll just be wasting toner for no purpose.

basic LaserWriter care *(Rich Wolfson)*

very good feature

LaserWriters are extremely durable machines. We have some here at Montclair State College that have printed more than 100,000 copies and haven't given a single moment of trouble—and this is in open-access labs where they get heavy use from novice users.

The basic maintenance for LaserWriters is simple and really amounts to little more than careful cleaning. Each time you replace a cartridge (or anytime you notice vertical light streaks or very fine white lines on your printouts), you should remove excess toner from the inside of the LaserWriter. Wipe it off surfaces—especially the rollers—with cotton balls or a lint-free cloth; use Q-Tips for the hard-to-reach places.

Sometimes the corona wire gets a white crusty buildup (it's composed of heated toner particles). This too needs to be cleaned off since it causes white streaks on the printout.

The corona wire stretches across the width of the printer, and is so thin you can hardly see it. What you'll be able to see more easily is another wire that's wrapped around the area the corona wire passes through, at about one-inch intervals. This wire should be cleaned, too, but it's only there to prevent a paper from curling down against the corona wire.

important warning

Use a Q-Tip to reach past the protective wire to clean the corona wire. Be very careful wiping down the corona wire—it's easy to break and hard to fix. Alcohol or cleaning fluid isn't necessary; a plain wiping will do.

Another spot you might miss is the covering over the laser diodes. To find them, open the printer, remove the cartridge and look up underneath the lid (they're in the lid). In LaserWriter I's, the covering is a red strip running almost the width of the lid. In the II's, the covering is overlaid by a metal piece so it shows as a series of red rectangles. (You can't see it if you don't take out the cartridge.)

In extreme cases you may need to vacuum out the insides of the LaserWriter. If you do, use a vacuum specifically made for electronic equipment. 3M makes one that has a conductive and grounded nozzle so there's no static buildup, but it costs about $250.

A regular dust buster, like any other regular vacuum, is going to be moving dry air across a piece of plastic and thus will build up a static charge, like the one that builds up on a plastic comb when you run it through dry hair. Static charges can zap electronic circuits, in which case you'll be left with a dead LaserWriter. (This warning goes double for vacuuming the inside of your computer.)

important warning

▲ *where to put your laser printer* (AN)

Most laser printers make a fair amount of noise. They're nothing like the average PC, which sounds like a commercial jet testing its engines, but they still can be pretty annoying. (This is particularly true if you're lucky enough to have a quiet place to work; in the typical office environment, you may barely be able to hear a laser printer.)

[LaserWriter II's aren't so noisy; mine's five feet from my desk and it doesn't bother me. But then there are usually a few kids within twenty feet of my desk and I've learned to ignore them too. Another reason not to have any laser printer too close to where you're working is the sometimes noxious odor of the toner.—SZA]

One way around this problem is to put the laser printer in a closet. Since it's connected on LocalTalk, there's no problem with the cables not reaching, and most closets are large enough. I've kept two different models of LaserWriters

very hot tip

in a closet with just 8" to the front, 7" to the rear and a couple of feet to each side of the printer, and have had no problems with insufficient ventilation or heat buildup. (Because closets usually have no windows and often have no external walls, the temperature tends to vary less than it does in regular rooms.)

If you're really worried about heat buildup, hang a thermometer on the closet wall and check it regularly. I did that and mine never registered above 80°—even on days when it was hotter than that outside and when the LaserWriter had been on for many hours (although, admittedly, it never gets really hot where I live—the average high temperature during the hottest month is just 72°).

The LaserWriter's manual says the temperature of the air around the printer shouldn't get over 90°, which means that if you live in New Orleans or some other place where the sidewalks melt in the summer, you're going to need air conditioning to stay within their specs (which also call for humidity of 80% or less). But if you live in a place like that, a laser printer in your closet isn't going to be the only reason you need an air conditioner.

There is, of course, one major disadvantage to putting your laser printer in a closet—you have to get up and walk over to it each time you want to look at the output. I don't find this bothersome; in fact, I enjoy the break and exercise (if walking ten feet can be called exercise). But it could get annoying, particularly if you're doing a lot of trial-and-error futzing with a document.

gossip/ trivia

Update: On a trip to Damascus, a vision appeared to me in the road. I fell to my knees. The vision spoke: "Closets are for *clothes,* you shmendrick!" I immediately grasped the implications—I could take all those clothes I had no room for in my bedroom closet and put them in the closet in my study. What a revelation!

But where would I put my LaserWriter? In the basement, of course, where the toner smell would never be a problem.

This new arrangement is a little strange sometimes—like when I'm printing many different versions of a one-page document (the constant tromping up and down the stairs makes me feel like I'm in an amateur production of _Arsenic and Old Lace)_—but at least I get some exercise.

You have no basement, you say? Try to see the _general_ point: _You can put a laser printer just about anywhere you want. There's no law that says it has to sit next to your Mac._

Fonts on laser printers

♦ _downloadable fonts_ (AN)

PostScript laser printers almost always come with some outline fonts built into their ROMs. If you want other outline fonts, you have to buy them on disk and _download_ (send) them to the printer.

esp. for
beginners

Downloadable fonts have several advantages over fonts in ROM. The main thing is that there's a much greater selection of them (see the font chapter for a sampling of just a few of the thousands that are available). And they're much easier for the publisher to enhance, upgrade or update.

The only disadvantages of downloadable fonts are that they take longer to print and use up some of the printer's RAM, which is in short supply on LaserWriter I's. Still, downloadable fonts are where it's at. Don't restrict yourself to what some printer manufacturer thinks you need.

♦ _two ways to download fonts_ (AN)

Outline fonts that reside on disk rather than in ROM can be sent to the printer two ways. You can "manually" download them to the LaserWriter before printing or you can have them downloaded automatically during printing (you just use the screen fonts in your document and the Mac sends the fonts' printer files to the LaserWriter as it runs across them). Most applications support automatic downloading.

esp. for
beginners

(Apple and Adobe refer to manual downloading as *permanent* downloading, which is pretty confusing, since the fonts stay in the LaserWriter only until you turn it off. *Manual*—which is obviously based on an analogy to automatic and manual transmissions in cars—isn't exactly the right word either. *Preprint* downloading, or *batch* downloading, would be more accurate.)

Manual downloading is done with a program that comes on the disk with the fonts. Once the fonts are downloaded, printing is faster, because they don't have to be downloaded over and over again each time you print (automatic downloading takes about 5–15 seconds per font).

The main advantage of automatic downloading is that it's easier (manual downloading is an annoying chore, even though it only takes a few minutes). Another advantage is that the fonts get flushed out after each printing job, making room for new fonts on the next printing job.

very hot tip

As a rule, manual downloading isn't worth the trouble unless you're going to be using the same font(s) in three or more printouts (which might be the same document revised and reprinted three times). On the other hand, it often makes sense when you're printing from PageMaker, which flushes automatically downloaded fonts after each text block, rather than at the end of the printing job, and thus has to reload them for each subsequent text block.

🍎 *LaserStatus*

very good feature

LaserStatus is a very useful utility published by CE Software. It lets you check what's going on in a LaserWriter—which fonts are in memory, how much memory's left, whether or not the startup page is disabled and how many pages the printer has ever printed.

LaserStatus also lets you manually download fonts—and other files—to the printer. But the best thing about LaserStatus is that it lets you create and download *sets* of fonts to the LaserWriter. (You can even make a set that

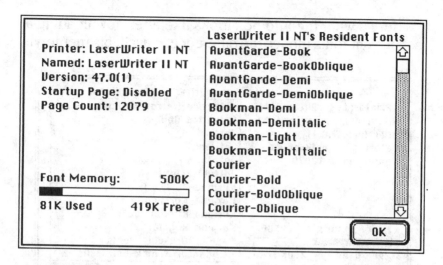

includes other sets.) This is an incredible convenience because you can download all the fonts that you need for a specific job.

You use LaserStatus to send them all to the printer in one fell swoop. I've even found that when Apple's and Adobe's downloaders can't handle a series of fonts I want in the LaserWriter (causing it to reset), LaserStatus can send them as a group with no problem.

very good feature

Here's what the info box looks like after downloading a set of eight fonts (notice the difference in available memory):

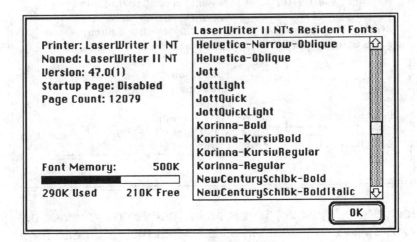

```
                            LaserWriter II NT's Resident Fonts
Printer: LaserWriter II NT   Helvetica-Narrow-Oblique        ⇧
Named: LaserWriter II NT     Helvetica-Oblique
Version: 47.0(1)             Jott
Startup Page: Disabled       JottLight
Page Count: 12079            JottQuick
                             JottQuickLight
                             Korinna-Bold
                             Korinna-KursivBold
                             Korinna-KursivRegular
Font Memory:        500K     Korinna-Regular
                             NewCenturySchlbk-Bold
290K Used     210K Free      NewCenturySchlbk-BoldItalic     ⇩

                                                   [  OK  ]
```

⚫ *where to store downloadable fonts* (AN/SZA)

esp. for beginners

Put the *printer files* for downloadable outline fonts either in the system folder or in the startup disk's window. (The matching screen fonts need to be installed in the System file or in an open *suitcase* file—see the font chapter for details.)

Why those restrictions? Because there can be so many files on a hard disk that the Mac could spend forever looking for the fonts, if it didn't limit its search to just those locations. (Lots of printer files can mess up your system folder, too—and besides the mess, lots of items in a folder makes it take longer to open when you doubleclick it on the desktop.)

very good feature

If printer files are stuck away in a folder anywhere else, the Mac won't be able to find them and they won't be downloaded to the printer—unless you use Suitcase, which lets you put them in any folder that contains an open suitcase, or Paul Snively's shareware program Set Paths, which lets you put them in any folder (you just show the Mac where they are). Both programs are described in Chapter 8.

By the way, don't change the names of a font's printer file; the automatic downloading process depends on its staying the same.

important warning

Unlike screen fonts that have the Font/DA Mover suitcase icon regardless of who created the fonts, icons for downloadable printer files vary with the publisher. (Sometimes the icon for a printer file will change when you copy it from the disk you get from the publisher, but don't pay any attention to that.)

Here's a small sample of printer font icons from Sharon's system folder:

♦ *how fonts affect laser printers' speed* (AN)

Laser printers process some kinds of fonts much faster than others. Outline fonts in ROM are the fastest. Downloadable outline fonts are slightly slower (in addition, ones that are downloaded automatically take 5–15 seconds longer than ones that are manually downloaded). Bit-mapped fonts are far and away the slowest, because the printer not only has to download them but also has to create a PostScript version of them.

Obviously, the more fonts (of any kind) you use, the longer it will take to print a page. So you'll get the very fastest speed out of a laser printer if you use just one font in ROM in just one style—and, because scaling also takes time, in just one size. But that's quite a sacrifice to make for a little speed.

If you use more fonts than a laser printer's RAM can accommodate, it won't print the page at all. This is particularly a problem on LaserWriter I's, with their skimpy 1.5 megs of RAM.

✖ *special characters on laser printers* (AN)

As a general rule, outline fonts give you a wider selection of special characters than bit-mapped fonts (for more details, see the font chapter). But many outline fonts borrow some of their special characters from the Symbol font. So if you want the full range of special characters, make sure Symbol's printer file is in the system folder on your startup disk.

✖ *type styles on laser printers* (AN)

very bad feature

On the ImageWriter, every font can be transformed into bold, italic, outline, shadow and any combination thereof—which comes to sixteen possible variations. On laser printers, however, no font I've seen can produce all sixteen variations. For example, Zapf Chancery (from Adobe) only gives you three: plain, outline and shadow (bold, italic and bold italic print out as plain and all the other variations print out as either outline or shadow).

Times and Helvetica do much better. Although outline shadow looks the same as shadow, eliminating four possibilities, the other twelve variations are there. (I've yet to see a outline font that will make the distinction between shadow and outline shadow—although with some type sizes in Word, characters are spaced farther apart in outline shadow than in shadow.) Adobe's Benguiat has the same twelve combinations, as does Casady & Greene's San Serif. Casady & Greene's Ritz provides eight of the possibilities—exactly half.

Bit-mapped fonts lose most of their style variations when they're printed on a LaserWriter. For example, when printed on a laser printer, Chicago retains just five of the sixteen styles it has on the ImageWriter. The only way to tell what variations a particular font will give you on a laser printer is to try them out.

All type styles on the ImageWriter are produced algorithmically—that is, by the application of a rule like *increase the width 10%* (to create boldface) *or slant right 11°* (to create italic). But on the LaserWriter, many fonts have their own separate *cuttings* for bold, italic and bold italic—that is, all the characters in those styles were individually designed, as if for a separate font.

If a font does have separate cuttings for certain styles, you'll have to put a separate printer file in the system folder for each one. But you'll get better-looking characters than with an algorithmically derived style. You can always tell whether the style you're using is algorithmic by looking to see if there's a separate printer file for it; if there's no file, the style is algorithmic.

Fonts with separate cuttings usually come with screen fonts to match but you can save room in your System file by not installing them. Just select the type style you want from the Style menu and PostScript will know to look for the font file before making the change algorithmically. But if you do install the special screen fonts, you'll get a cleaner representation of the characters on the screen.

Some fonts also have separate cuttings for variations with different names than bold, italic, outline or shadow. In these cases, you do have to install the screen font—unless the style is basically a variation on bold or italic. If it is, it will normally be "mapped" to the menu option. For example, demi type is bolder than regular, so selecting text set in Souvenir and then choosing Bold from the menu will give you Souvenir Demi (that is, if you don't have Souvenir Bold around).

Generally, font publishers try to do what makes sense; if a font comes with four variations, you can usually get them by choosing plain text, bold, italic and bold italic. (See the font chapter for more details.)

⚫ outline fonts in paint programs (AN)

esp. for beginners

Bit-mapped graphics programs like MacPaint can't output outline fonts. What you get instead is the screen font, just the way you see it on the screen.

To get around this, use a draw program like MacDraw or, even better, a draw/paint program like SuperPaint that lets you combine bit-mapped and object-oriented graphics.

⚫ bit-mapped fonts on PostScript printers (AN)

If you turn on Font Substitution in the Page Setup dialog box, a PostScript printer will substitute outline fonts for three basic bit-mapped fonts when it runs across them in a document. The substitutions are Times for New York, Helvetica for Geneva and Courier for Monaco (they deserve each other).

If you turn Font Substitution off, or use any bit-mapped fonts other than the four mentioned above, the printer creates special PostScript versions of the bit-mapped fonts it finds in a document. (Most people don't realize that PostScript can create bit-mapped fonts as well as outline fonts.)

These PostScript versions of bit-mapped fonts print more smoothly than the original fonts do on the ImageWriter and they also scale much better. But slanting doesn't work too well (which means that they may not look great in italic, for example). Two other disadvantages of the PostScript versions: they take much longer to print and they strip out most of the type style variations you get on the ImageWriter. (For more information on that, see the entries above called *type styles on laser printers* and *how fonts affect laser printers' speed.*)

⚫ more on Courier substitutions

In addition to substituting for Monaco when the Font Substitution box is checked, Courier also shows up whenever there's not enough room in the LaserWriter's memory to download the font you really want. So if Courier shows up someplace in your document instead of, say, Korinna, even though Korinna's been printed on the previous pages, it means that Korinna's been flushed out of the printer's memory to make room for something else.

❖ *using lots of fonts on LaserWriter I's* (AN)

Don't. (I'll resist the temptation to make this the shortest entry in the book.)

**important
warning**

After a LaserWriter I finishes imaging the page and doing other necessary tasks, it only has about 210K of RAM available for downloading fonts and other necessary information.

To give you an idea of just how limiting that is, consider that PageMaker takes about 50K for its header (the PostScript instructions it gives to the printer) and that the necessary QuickDraw information takes another 90K. This leaves only 70K for your downloadable fonts, which usually require between 20K and 35K each. (Other programs often have somewhat smaller headers and thus leave slightly more room for fonts to be downloaded.)

In addition to the space the fonts themselves take up, another 10K or so has to be downloaded along with the first font; it contains information that applies to all fonts.

PageMaker offers you a way around the problem. It flushes out the fonts after each text block, instead of at the end of the document, so the limitations that normally apply to fonts per document apply to fonts per text block. Since you can have as many text blocks as you want in a document, you can also have as many fonts as you want (within reason, that is; things can get pretty tedious with dozens of text blocks on a page).

But in most applications, you only have room to download three or four fonts; under some extreme circumstances, there may only be room for two. And remember that if bold, italic, bold italic or some other style comes in its own cutting (that is, if it's been separately designed and comes as a separate font file), it counts towards the total just like a completely different typeface.

(One exception to this is special cuttings labeled *oblique*. They're usually derived algorithmically—that is, by the application of a rule—and take up much less of the LaserWriter's memory. For example, ITC Glypha Oblique only takes up 3K if you already have Glypha Roman loaded, since all that needs to be added are the PostScript instructions on how to tilt the letters.)

If you use too many fonts, the Mac will show you one or more messages that tell you you're running short of memory. In a classic case of boneheaded design, these messages neither beep nor stay on the screen for very long.

So if you happen not to be completely catatonic and have therefore chosen to get up and do something rather than to stare blankly at the screen for the five or ten minutes it takes the LaserWriter to print a document with a lot of fonts, you'll miss the messages. When you come back into the room, the LaserWriter will be humming innocently away (*What do you mean, "Where's the printout?" What printout?*), with no indication on the screen of what happened.

(The above assumes your fonts are being automatically downloaded. If you're manually downloading fonts—sending them to the LaserWriter one by one with a downloading program prior to printing—and you overrun the LaserWriter's RAM, you'll flush out the earliest fonts. Or, if your downloading software isn't so hot, the LaserWriter may just restart itself and spit out a new startup page.)

If a document won't print, it's always worth trying to print it again; it often works the second time. If that doesn't work, try printing the document one page at a time. If that doesn't work, try breaking it into smaller documents.

very hot tip

If you're not sure that too many fonts is the reason the LaserWriter won't print your document, the easiest way to find out is to make a copy of it, change the entire copy to Times or Helvetica, and try printing that. If that works, your problem is almost certainly too many fonts.

To get around this limitation, some applications use *note format*, which gives half-inch margins all around (on the assumption that you're not going to want to print anything closer to the edge of the paper than that). This gives you room for more fonts, theoretically as many as eight or ten. But don't count on it.

The LaserStatus DA described above tells you how much RAM is left in the LaserWriter and what fonts—both downloadable and ROM-based—are already there; it also lets you reset the LaserWriter—that is, flush its memory—without turning off the power. Most font publishers offer similar software on their font disks.

very good feature

All in all, the limitation on how many fonts you can use is the LaserWriter I's most annoying shortcoming. The best way around this problem, of course, is to get a laser printer with at least 2MB of RAM, like the LaserWriter IINT or IINTX.

Laser printer supplies

⚫ *what kind of paper to use* (AN)

Laser printers put images down on paper in exactly the same way as photocopiers do; in fact, the guts of the LaserWriters (and of several other PostScript laser printers) are identical to those of many Canon copiers. So the kind of paper specifically designed for use in copiers—often labeled xerographic—is what you want for laser printers.

Copier paper comes in more than one grade. When you're preparing originals for presentation, you'll naturally want to use a nice-looking, heavy, opaque paper, or one of the special papers made specifically for high-quality laser-printer output (see the next entry). But for everyday use, and when you're preparing documents to be reproduced, use the cheapest kind you can find. Here's why:

very hot tip

When the humidity is high, pieces of paper tend to stick together. To help them separate more easily, paper manufacturers put powder between the sheets. This is called dusting, and the more expensive a paper is, the more dusting it tends to have. The problem with dusting is that particles of the powder tend to get bonded to the paper along with the image, producing a rough, uneven surface. So cheap paper, with little or no dusting, is best.

Cheap paper has another advantage: because of its low fiber content, it has a smoother surface than most expensive paper (except those specifically designed to be smooth). The smoother the surface, the more precise the image bonded to it will be.

bargain

If there's a discount paper supply house in your area that sells retail, you should be able to buy inexpensive copier paper for about $3 a ream (500 sheets). But the cheapest source for paper is generally a wholesale discount warehouse like Costco or Price Club. You have to be a member (small businesses, independent professionals, government workers, organization members, etc. qualify) and be willing to buy ten reams at a time, but if you are, you can get plain 20-lb. bond for about $2 a ream.

Except in an emergency, it makes absolutely no sense to go into a stationery store and pay $6–$7 a ream when you can get the same paper at half the price or less elsewhere.

✦ high-quality laser-printer paper

Paper specifically designed for laser printing (made by Hammermill, among others) can really make a noticeable difference in the printout, even to the unpracticed eye.

I'm not suggesting that your business correspondence will benefit from the added clarity, but if you're designing a newsletter or brochure that's going to be photocopied, it's wise to get the crispest original that you can. Use regular paper for all the drafts and the good stuff for the final output.

One supplier I can recommend for all sorts of laser stock—papers, labels and so on—is Imaging Products (see

Appendix B for contact information). They have a wide variety of products, including such special items as no-tear paper, and every time I check, it seems they've added something new to their lineup.

⁙ *labels and envelopes for the LaserWriter* (SZA/AN)

If you print on labels or envelopes, or anything else that contains glue, make sure they're made especially for laser printers or photocopiers. (Sharon has used regular envelopes in a LaserWriter with no ill effects, but we don't recommend it.) The heat in the printer can cause labels to peel off inside; it can also seal envelopes. (Hmm...if you put the letters inside the envelopes before you run them through for addressing, you won't have to lick them—no, that's probably not a good idea.)

important warning

Avery makes labels specifically designed for laser printers. Because a special adhesive is used, the labels don't peel off when subjected to the high heat inside the printer. We've been using them at Goldstein & Blair and haven't had any problems with jamming. They come in three sizes: 1" x 2-5/8" (product codes 5160 and 5260), 1" x 4" (product codes 5161 and 5261) and 1-1/2" x 4" (product codes 5162 and 5262) and are available at most office supply stores.

⁙ *printing on nonstandard stock*

If you're printing transparencies, you can use regular transparency film; it goes through the LaserWriter with no problems (but don't just use any piece of plastic—like, say, a report cover). For slightly more crisp output, try a transparency film made specifically for laser printers. Imaging Products sells laser transparency film in clear, red, yellow, green and blue.

On various occasions, I've laser-printed on nonstandard stock, like a manila folder. There was no problem feeding it through a LaserWriter II, but LaserWriter I's have much more trouble processing anything but plain (basically *thin)* paper. For example, I can't get disk labels on sheets to go through a LaserWriter I.

very hot tip

If you have trouble with thick stock going through a LaserWriter II, open the back and let the printed material come out there, instead of going through the second set of rollers to come out the top.

🍎 *getting the most from toner cartridges* *(AN/SZA)*

Before installing a new toner cartridge in a LaserWriter, you should rotate it gently from side to side (that is, lift the right side, then the left—it's *roll* you want, not *yaw*). If you don't do this, the images you get may not be dark enough. (You may also have to break in the cartridge by printing thirty pages or so.)

very hot tip

There are two things you can do to get more pages printed from each cartridge. First, use the print-density dial. It's on the outside of LaserWriter I's and on the inside of LaserWriter II's (it's green and to the right and front as you lift the lid). When the cartridge is new, set the dial at 9—which, in a masterpiece of counterintuitiveness, is as *low* as it will go.

When you're getting to the end of the cartridge and faint areas start appearing on your printouts, turn the dial up (in order words, towards 1). But wait—don't touch that dial! First, try rocking the cartridge, as described in the first paragraph above, and keep doing that whenever you have a problem. Only when this fails to produce the desired result, or only produces it for a few pages, should you turn the print density dial down...er, up...toward 1.

Using those two simple techniques, we both have been able to average about 5000 pages on both LaserWriter I and LaserWriter II cartridges, including refilled ones, with perfectly acceptable quality—except, of course, for solid blacks on LaserWriter I's, which you can't get even with a new cartridge.

🍎 *buying toner cartridges* *(AN)*

If you can't find an Apple-brand toner cartridge for your LaserWriter, a Hewlett-Packard LaserJet cartridge works just as well. The cost to the dealer for both brands is the same, so the price you pay should be, too.

If you have a LaserWriter I (the original or the Plus), any toner cartridge made for a laser printer with a Canon CX engine will work for you. If you have a LaserWriter II, you need a cartridge made for a printer with the Canon SX engine.

Be aware, though, that although Canon copiers use the same CX and SX marking engines, their cartridges won't work in laser printers.

⚫ *refilling toner cartridges* (Byron Brown)

Toner cartridges are far and away your greatest expense in operating a laser printer. Fortunately, you can have your cartridges refilled. If done by a reputable company, refilling won't hurt your printer and will provide printouts that are just as good as you get from new cartridges. (In fact, the image is often darker—one refilled LaserWriter I cartridge gave me blacks almost as solid as a LaserWriter II's.)

bargain

In general, cartridges shouldn't be refilled more than three times, and most companies mark them so they can discard them after the third refill. *(If the company recoats the drum, the cartridge isn't limited to three refills; in fact, with occasional drum-coating, refills are unlimited. Drum coating is much more difficult, and therefore less reliable, for LaserWriter II cartridges.—SZA)*

I'd guess my LaserWriter I refills give me about 90% of the life of new cartridges, and they only cost about $35–$50 (including replacing the green wand that keeps the rollers clean), instead of around $100.

There are many companies that refill cartridges, and some have 800 numbers. If they're in your local area, they'll usually pick up and deliver for free; if they're not, they'll usually split the shipping with you (you pay to send the cartridge, they pay to return it). If you have a problem with a refilled cartridge, any reputable refiller will replace it free of charge.

I've been told that the first LaserWriter II cartridges had a corrosive chemical in the toner that ate out the inside of the cartridge—so you couldn't refill them and had to buy new ones. Wasn't that thoughtful? Fortunately, this practice has been abandoned.

⚫ more on refilling cartridges

What Byron reports in the entry above about the built-in obsolescence of toner cartridges has been repeated to me by a number of cartridge-refill companies—and repeatedly denied by the cartridge makers. (I believe the refillers.)

That issue aside, there's another reason to go with refills: toner cartridges are not, by any stretch of the imagination, biodegradable. Picture the mountain of used cartridges we've already discarded and keep that picture in mind when your cartridge runs out of toner. Here's a chance to do something for the earth and save money at the same time. (And if you don't want to use refilled cartridges, sell your empties to a refill company—yes, many will buy them from you—and let them recycle them to someone else.)

⚫ throwing out toner cartridges *(AN)*

Here's yet another reason to refill toner cartridges: if you take a used one out of a laser printer and toss it immediately into a plastic waste basket (as I have), you may end up with a melted waste basket (as I have). Those suckers are hot when they come out of the machine. So unless you want your waste baskets to look like not-very-inspired modern art, let the toner cartridge cool down before throwing it away. (Or, better yet, refill it.)

⚫ the toner cartridge warning light

One of the lights on your LaserWriter II blinks when the toner in your cartridge is low. If your printout still looks OK, you can safely ignore the warning. I've stretched my printing for hundreds of pages beyond the blinking light, but I felt continually reproached by the blink, The solution?—I put the printer where I can't see its lights. *[Aren't neuroses fun?—AN]*

Advanced printing tips

⚫ *renting time on a PostScript device* *(AN)*

Businesses have sprung up all over (particularly in big cities and near universities) that let you come in with your Mac disk and print it out on one or more kinds of PostScript-compatible printers. Renting time can be surprisingly inexpensive: there's a place near me that charges just $5 an hour and 15¢ a page.

bargain

If you can't find a place in the phone book, check with a local Mac user group (in fact, do that first; unlike the Yellow Pages, they can tell you which businesses know what they're doing, charge the least and so on). If there's no user group in your area or they don't know of a rental place, check out the entry below on remote typesetting services; many of those services also provide LaserWriter output.

⚫ *getting your disks ready for a rented LaserWriter* *(DC)*

When you're planning to rent time on a LaserWriter, you might as well format your documents and set up your disks as completely as possible ahead of time, to cut down on the amount of time you have to pay for.

very hot tip

The first step is to make sure that the disk you bring with you has the software you need on it; the rental place will obviously have some software but they may not have what you used to create your document (or the same version of it). Call beforehand to make sure they have the outline fonts you want to use installed on their system; if not, be sure that the System file on the startup disk you bring has the appropriate screen fonts installed, and that the system folder contains the font files you need for the printer.

If you haven't been printing out on a LaserWriter, change the fonts in your document to outline fonts by selecting the text and choosing the screen fonts just the way you would any other font. (I'm assuming you proofed your document on the ImageWriter.) Next, open Chooser (on the ⚫ menu) and select the LaserWriter icon. Then open the Page Setup window (on the File menu), make any changes you want (or no changes) and click on OK.

Now go through your document. Remember: ImageWriter page setup has different margins from LaserWriter page setup, and there are other incompatibilities, so there may be changes you need to make.

When you've done that, you're ready for the shortest possible time rental on the LaserWriter.

There's one other hangup that gets more and more likely as time goes by—font ID conflicts. This complex issue is discussed in the font chapter.

⬢ *proofing on the LaserWriter before typesetting* (DC)

The Macintosh and the ImageWriter use QuickDraw routines to create their images, while the LaserWriter and many other laser printers and imagesetters use PostScript. Although a lot of brilliant work has been done to allow QuickDraw and PostScript to talk to each other, what you see on the Mac and on an ImageWriter is always going to vary somewhat from the output of a PostScript-driven device.

**important
warning**

This means there's no substitute for hard copies. If you're planning to do final output on a PostScript-driven imagesetter like the Linotronic, you definitely should proof your work on the LaserWriter. The differences between its output and the imagesetter's will be negligible. (The resolution will, of course be higher on the Linotronic—that's why you're using it in the first place—but the position of all the elements and the overall look of the page will be the same.)

There are two exceptions to that rule. First of all, the Linotronic can print all the way to the edges of the roll of paper it's using (which can be either 8.5" or 11" wide) while the LaserWriter can't print wider than 8". Secondly, the Linotronic won't smooth bit-mapped images. If you want the images smoothed, print them out on a LaserWriter and then paste them manually over the equivalent unsmoothed images in the Linotronic output.

⚫ *remote typesetting from Mac disks* (DC)

Let's say you've proofed your document on a LaserWriter until it's just the way you want it. Now you want to typeset it. But your budget's a little tight and you can't afford to buy a Linotronic this month (it probably wouldn't fit in the closet anyway). Don't despair. There are several services that will accept your Mac disks and print out from them on their own PostScript-driven imagesetters or laser printers.

The costs usually run from $5 to $15 a page (some places also have a one-time registration charge of about $50). Many of these services let you send data via modem—although if your document is at all long, it's going to take forever. Another advantage of mailing the disk (or, if you're in a hurry, sending it by Federal Express) is that you can send a printout along with it as a proof, so there won't be any questions about how you want the finished document to look.

Even if you send the document on the phone, you should send a message with it detailing exactly what you want. As mentioned in the previous entry, there's one other potential problem—font ID conflicts. See the advanced font tips section at the end of the font chapter for a discussion of this complex issue.

To find the names and addresses of services that offer typesetting from Mac disks, check out the various magazines on the Mac and on desktop publishing; they sometimes run updated lists of such services.

⚫ *halftoning on the LaserWriter* (AN)

The LaserWriter handles text so nicely, it's tempting to use it to produce everything that goes on the page, including pictures. But certain kinds of images have to be processed before you can print them. Here's why:

esp. for power users

All printed material is made up of either text or art (which is what every graphic element except text is called). There are two kinds of art—*line*, which contains no grays, and *continuous-tone*, which does (the name comes from the fact that the tones form a continuum, from black through gray to white).

Continuous-tone art presents a problem: since printing ink is black (or whatever) and paper is white (or whatever), how can the grays be represented?

Far and away the most common solution involves putting a screen over the photograph. (It's called a screen because the original ones were made of fine metal mesh, although many screens today are sheets of plastic with dots printed on them.) The screen converts light grays to tiny black dots on a white background, and dark grays to tiny white dots on a black background. From a normal reading distance, these dots—in many different sizes—look like various shades of gray.

Once a continuous-tone image has been screened, it's called a *halftone*. If you hold a magnifying glass to a half-toned picture (virtually any printed picture will do), you'll see the little halftone dots, but you won't find them on a continuous-tone photograph like a snapshot.

If you use the traditional screen approach to halftoning, you won't be able to integrate your graphics with your text and print them both out on the LaserWriter at the same time; you'll have to leave a space for the graphics and add them at a later stage. To integrate halftones with text, you need a device called a scanner that can capture continuous-tone images and halftone them electronically.

Scanners vary in sampling density (how many times per inch they evaluate the picture) and in how many levels of gray they'll pick up. They also vary in quality and price. ThunderScan is an inexpensive scanner that can produce images suitable for use in an informal newsletter—or maybe somewhat better than that, if you really know how to use it.

The next level of scanners have a resolution of 300 dpi and cost quite a bit more; their software makes it easy to capture an image as a PostScript file. Most scanners give you a choice of file types for saving an image—as TIFF, PICT or even paint files.

Once a scanner has captured the image, you can use various programs—usually software that comes with the scanner—to play with it. One unbundled program that does a great job with halftones is Silicon Beach's Digital Darkroom.

Everything else being equal, the quality of a halftone depends on how many lines per inch it breaks the picture into. The higher the number of lines, the better the photograph looks. The coarsest screen in general use is 65 lines per inch. Newspapers typically use an 85-line screen and magazines a 120-line screen. The finest screen in general use is 150 lines per inch.

Laser printers and imagesetters each have a default screen frequency that the manufacturer has picked to produce the best output on that particular device. On a 300-dpi printer like the LaserWriter, it's usually 60 lines per inch (lpi); on the Linotronic 100, 90 lpi; on the Linotronic 300, 120 lpi. You can vary this frequency somewhat (using simple PostScript programming), but if you go too far from the default, the results may not look very good.

The LaserWriter's resolution of 60 lpi is just below the usual minimum standard for halftones, and you can't expect an image printed at that resolution to look like the ones in magazines and books. But the quality is good enough for some purposes.

✦ *saving a PostScript file*

You can turn any Mac document into a PostScript text file that can then be printed on any PostScript device without any need for the application that originally created the document. To do that, open the document and choose *Print* from the File menu. Click the OK button and *immediately* (you have not much more than a second here) press ⌘ F .

esp. for power users

You'll get a dialog box that says *Creating PostScript file.* (If you don't, you didn't get to the key fast enough and you'll be printing the file instead. Try again and instead of clicking the OK button with the mouse use the ⟨Return⟩ key so you can get to ⟨⌘⟩⟨F⟩ more quickly.)

The file is saved to the disk as a text file that contains all the PostScript commands needed to recreate the document. It can be opened (and altered, if you know what you're doing) in any word processor.

Be aware that the phrase *printed on any PostScript device* in the first sentence doesn't mean that you can open the document and then print it. If you do, you'll just get the text listing of all the PostScript commands. A PostScript file, to be printed as such, has to be *downloaded* to a printer the same way fonts are.

Chapter 5

Miscellaneous hardware and accessories

Protecting yourself

✦ *screen filters and radiation shields (AN)*

There's some evidence that working at a computer monitor may have deleterious health effects. For example, a large-scale study in California found a *doubling* of miscarriage rates among women who worked more than 20 hours a week at computer screens. This may not be due to the equipment itself, however; stress is generally higher among computer users than other types of office workers (probably because most of them don't have Macs).

important warning

According to James Sheedy of the UC Berkeley optometry school, working regularly at a computer screen can accelerate presbyopia, the inability to focus at varying distances that usually hits people in their forties. (That's definitely been my personal experience, but since I started usirg computers heavily just as I was turning 40, I can't really tease apart the two causes.)

Other research has indicated that certain low-frequency radiation may have harmful health effects (see the next entry). In view of all this, it certainly can't hurt to cut down radiation coming from computers, so here's a bit of information on filters that screen out at least some of it:

There are two basic kinds of screen filters—glass and wire mesh. Wire mesh filters, like the ones made by NoRad, do a good job of screening out certain kinds of radiation, but I find them really hard to see through (it's like looking through finely woven cloth). For me, the strain of trying to focus through the mesh more than offsets any possible radiation-blocking benefit.

Many companies sell glass filters, including Kensington and Computer Covers Unlimited. Whichever type of screen you get, make sure it's grounded. Filters vary enormously in how easy or hard they are to ground. The best system has a three-pronged plug you stick into a wall socket (only the grounding prong is active, of course); the other end of the wire connects easily to the filter.

**important
warning**

Radiation comes in many frequency ranges, so it's easy for competing companies to claim superiority for their filters merely by restricting the scope of their comparisons (or by emphasizing different aspects of them).

This is a complex subject, and unless you really want to spend some time learning about it, you need to rely on someone else's expertise. The person I rely on is Mike Skaar of Ergonomic Computer Products in San Francisco. He sells excellent products at good prices and is extremely well informed. His customer service is great too.

**very good
feature**

By the way, many people buy screen filters to cut down on glare (that is, reflections). This is not a good approach. What you need to do instead is set up the place where you work so as to *eliminate* reflections (for details on how to do that, see the last section of Chapter 2).

❡ *ELF and VLF* (Byron Brown)

A study published in the *American Journal of Epidemiology* in 1979 indicated that children living near electric distribution lines have an increased incidence of cancer. A second study, published in 1986 by the New York State Department of Health, and a third study from Sweden, confirmed these results. The culprit seems to be sustained exposure to the *ELF (extremely low frequency)* electric and magnetic field created by the power line's 60Hz alternating current.

In 1982, a study in Canada discovered that the vertical scan rate of computer monitors also generates an ELF field of 60–75Hz. In addition, the monitor's horizontal scan rate generates radiation in the 10–30kHz range (i.e., 10,000–30,000Hz). This is called VLF (for *very low frequency);* it's easier to block with a screen filter than ELF, but there's a lot less of it and it seems to be less significant in creating the harmful magnetic field.

During the past five years, animal studies in California, Spain and Sweden have all confirmed the cancer-enhancing effects of sustained exposure to ELF. One theory is that cells become entrained to the particular pulse rate of the radiation, and that this unnatural rhythm then disrupts the normal activation of enzymes and cellular immune responses.

Macworld published an excellent, in-depth article on radiation from computers in its July, 1990 issue, which included its own tests of ELF emitted from ten Mac monitors. Apple's popular 13″ High-Resolution color monitor came out the worst. On all the monitors, the greatest amount of radiation was in the back and on the sides, which can particularly be a problem in crowded offices.

important warning

The strength of ELF radiation drops off rapidly as you move away from the monitor, but since there's no way yet to screen out ELF, no one should sit closer than four feet from the sides or back of a monitor, or 28″ (roughly arm's length) from the front of the screen.

Unfortunately, Apple didn't show any concern about this potential risk until January, 1990, and even then took a very conservative stance, claiming that there's still no evidence to indicate any risk. I'd like to see them include a notice with each computer, warning pregnant women against sustained exposure and recommending safe working distances for all users.

things to come

Protecting your Mac

🍎 *lightning only has to strike once* (C.J. Weigand)

A surge suppressor is a good way to protect your computer from sudden variations in electrical current, and every Mac (and major peripheral, like a disk drive or a printer) should be on one. But don't rely on it during a thunderstorm. Lightning can arc across open contacts and do extensive damage to your equipment.

important warning

So if it's thunderstorm season where you live, get in the habit of pulling the plug out of the wall whenever you shut down your system for any length of time. That's the only way to make sure it's safe. If you have a modem connected to your Mac, also unplug the incoming telephone line or disconnect the cable. Your computer can be zapped just as easily by lightning striking your telephone line.

⚜ *MacGard* (Larry Pina)

important warning

In the middle of a dry New England winter, just walking across the room can build up a terrific static charge, especially around synthetic fabrics, rubber-soled shoes and wall-to-wall carpeting. Under these conditions, touching anything connected to an electrical ground results in a painful shock. Sometimes it's so bad, it triggers an instant lockup.

very good feature

One solution is to use a $90 surge suppressor called MacGard. Besides superior surge protection (in lab tests I ran, it outperformed several units costing twice as much), it has an integral static-draining touch pad. When you tap it, you hear the same crackling noise that's normally associated with a painful shock but the discharge is much slower and completely painless. You can then touch your Mac safely.

⚜ *covering the Mac* (AN)

very good feature

To paraphrase an old saying, dust never sleeps, and the more of it that gets into your Mac, the worse off you are. Many people sell covers for the Mac, but the ones we like best are the Nycov brand, sold by Computer Covers Unlimited. They come in several colors, are attractive and well made, and are available for various models of the Mac, its peripherals, the keyboard and even the mouse. Best of all, they're made of high-quality, anti-static, rip-stop nylon, instead of vinyl with its nauseating, carcinogenic fumes.

Computer Covers Unlimited also makes The Keyboard Protector—a precisely molded piece of soft, flexible, relatively odorless, transparent plastic with little pockets for each key (there are models for many different keyboards). Unlike a dust cover, you leave The Keyboard Protector on while you work (always, in fact). It interferes with the feel of the keys less than I thought it would, but for my taste, it's still a bit too much like wearing a raincoat while taking a shower (to use the old analogy).

Still, it's a nice idea. Over the years, I've spilled many glasses of water near my keyboard (but somehow never directly on it). I now keep anything containing a liquid a good couple of feet away from my keyboard—a simple approach, but not foolproof (since my mouth is right over the keyboard). The Keyboard Protector *is* foolproof, and it protects against dust, staples and ashes as well as against spills.

¢ *AppleCare* (AN)

Apple's extended service contracts, which go under the name of AppleCare, provide the same coverage you get during the initial warranty period (free parts and labor for whatever goes wrong—unless, of course, you drop your Mac out a window, open its case or do something else Apple doesn't approve of).

AppleCare isn't cheap, and it's not as essential as it was back in the days of the power supply that blew more frequently than Old Faithful, so whether or not you get it basically depends on your temperament and your finances. If you're a cautious type and/or can't afford a big, unexpected repair bill, get it; if you're a gambler and/or can absorb that big bill in the unlikely event it comes along, save your money. (Since there's profit built into AppleCare, the financial odds are in your favor if you don't buy it. But that's usually less important than peace of mind.)

¢ *the best way to ship a Mac* (Paul Blood)

The best box to ship a Mac in is the one Apple shipped it to you in—except for one thing: it lets everyone know that a valuable computer is inside. The solution? Pull the box apart, then reassemble it inside out. All the same styrofoam packing materials will fit.

*very
hot
tip*

¢ *the Ergotron Muzzle* (AN)

What with viruses running rampant, leaving a Mac unattended in an office or other public place can be an invitation to disaster. Ergotron has the answer. Called The Muzzle, it's a piece of metal that covers the floppy drive slot, thus preventing anyone from putting software on your hard disk without your knowledge. There's even a model that prevents the Mac from being turned on.

⬤ *add-on fans* (AN/DC/Tom Swain)

All Macs since the SE have fans, so this entry only applies to Pluses and earlier models. (For a tip on how to quiet the loud fan in early SE's, see quieting the *original SE* in Chapter 2.)

Fanless Macs are cooled by convection—the basic principle of which is that hot air rises. The designers of the fanless Macs put hot components like the power supply near the vents on the top of the case, where they create an upward flow of air that cools things below.

According to Apple, fanless Macs can maintain an internal temperature no higher than 15° C (27° F) above the room temperature. While a 15° C difference is within Apple's guidelines and normally won't present a problem, the cooler a computer runs, the better (within reason).

Heat is a problem in a computer for two main reasons. First, cool chips last longer. For example, a chip that's fated to die after one year of operation at 170° F will last two at 80° F.

Second, the heat that's generated can warm and therefore expand floppy disks in the internal drive. If a file is written to the disk in this condition—say on a hot summer afternoon after your machine has been on for several hours—it can disappear the next morning when you turn your machine on. The disk drive will be searching for a track that moved a little during the night as the disk cooled. (If this happens to you, the file can most likely be recovered by letting the machine—and therefore the disk—warm up for a few hours and then trying to reread it.)

Here's a simple test of the temperature inside your Mac: Leave the machine on for at least an hour with a disk in the internal drive and then eject it. Immediately hold the top side of the disk's shutter mechanism (the sliding metal piece) to your face. The warmth (or lack thereof) will give you a benchmark against which to gauge the effectiveness of any subsequent cooling strategy.

So—a fan certainly isn't going to hurt the performance of any fanless Mac, and if yours has third-party additions (memory expansion upgrades and/or internal hard disks), a fan may well be a necessity. Unfortunately, fans have their own set of problems.

If they draw power from the Mac's power supply (as most of them do), then you're asking for more work out of a component which, in the early Mac Pluses, had a pretty poor track record.

Many people find the noise from a fan much more annoying over hundreds or thousands of hours in a quiet home or office than they thought they would when listening to it for a few minutes in a noisy computer store. So if you decide to get a fan, spend some time listening to it first and make sure you have the right to return it.

very
hot
tip

Some fans for the Mac are external; they mount on top of the case and boost the Mac's normal convective cooling. Because they're relatively powerful, they also draw dust, dirt and smoke particles into the Mac. You open the case after six months and it looks like the lint sock on a dryer vent. This isn't great for disk drives.

important
warning

So use external fans with caution if you're a smoker or work in a relatively dusty environment. (External fans also tend to be the noisiest.)

You should definitely avoid any external fan that draws air in and forces it downward into the Mac's case. Since the power supply is the major source of heat in the Mac, and it's near the top, these fans actually blow hot air down onto the delicate (and expensive) motherboard.

important
warning

Internal fans usually cost less than external ones. There are three basic kinds—rotary (blades twirling around), piezo-electric (two thin plastic flaps that vibrate back and forth) and squirrel-cage (a spinning cylinder with slots and fins on it).

Squirrel cages are junk; avoid them at any cost. Internal rotary fans are less noisy than external fans and piezoelectric fans are quieter still, making only a slight, dull hum. They're powerful enough to cool the circuit boards, but it's not clear how much they cool the disk drive.

Dale installed a 2MB memory upgrade in a Mac Plus. Since the clip-on daughter board mounted directly over the motherboard, he was skeptical that the little piezoelectric fan provided would be adequate. But after using the upgraded system for about five hours, the top of the unit was barely warm to the touch, dramatically cooler than a fanless Mac. This made him a piezoelectric fan fan. (Sorry.)

MacChimney, R.I.P. *(AN)*

**gossip/
trivia**

In my opinion, the ideal solution for cooling a fanless Mac was the MacChimney, invented by Tom Swain. It made the Mac look a little strange—sort of like the Tin Woodman in The Wizard of Oz—but that gave it a certain charm:

Basically, the MacChimney worked the same way as a fireplace chimney. Cool air entered the Mac through the vents at the bottom and got heated by the electronics and the power supply. As it entered the MacChimney, it acted as a buoyant mass and sucked about 60% more air through the bottom vents than if the MacChimney weren't there.

The MacChimney was primarily suited for people who tended to keep their Mac in one place, preferred to leave it on much of the time and were sensitive to sound (since MacChimney was, of course, totally silent). Unfortunately, it never sold very well, and Tom, who has moved on to fresh fields and pastures new, stopped making it.

I'm holding onto all three of my MacChimneys; I'm sure they're going to be worth a fortune someday, as early Macintosh memorabilia.

CD-ROMs

♠ *CD-ROM players* (AN)

CD-ROMs are a particular kind of compact disk. Depending on how they're formatted, they can hold about 550–600 *megabytes*, which is equivalent to more than seven hundred 800K disks and well over a quarter of a million typewritten pages.

There's just this one little problem—CD-ROMs are *slow*. Because of that (and perhaps for some other reasons as well), they haven't really taken off yet. Still, a lot of useful information now comes on CD-ROMs, and you'll find reviews of various specific CD-ROMs throughout the book (for example, some clip-art CD-ROMs are reviewed in the graphics chapter).

Several manufacturers make CD-ROM players; Apple's is called the AppleCD SC, because it connects over the SCSI port (why there's no space between *Apple* and *CD* I'm not sure, but that's how the name is spelled).

♠ *prolonging the life of CD-ROMs* (C.J. Weigand)

Although CDs are ballyhooed as being indestructible, don't believe it. The thin plastic coating can be easily scratched and that can cause data to drop out during the read cycle. Dirt can do the same thing, as can warping of the disk caused by excessive heat.

important warning

So keep your CDs out of direct sunlight, away from heat and in their protective cases when you're not using them. It's bad enough to ruin a $12 music CD, but it's a lot worse to ruin a CD-ROM that cost you $200.

🍎 *CD-ROMs under MultiFinder*

If you use a CD-ROM player and MultiFinder, you'll probably have to increase the Finder's memory allocation so it can handle all the CD's desktop windows. (There's more info on this in Chapter 6.)

🍎 *CD-ROMs on AppleShare networks*

very bad feature

If you have a CD-ROM player on an AppleShare network and want the Macs on the network to be able to access different CDs (a dictionary, say, and then maybe some clip art), too bad. The CD-ROM in the CD-ROM player gets installed as a volume when you start up, and you can't change volumes in AppleShare without closing down the whole network. If you want your workstations to access multiple CD-ROMs, you need multiple CD-ROM players on the network.

Scanners and other digitizers

🍎 *scanners* (AN)

Scanners are devices that convert images to digital form so they can be stored and manipulated by computers. Scanners vary in terms of how many *bits per pixel* they can store; those that store more than two bits per pixel can capture gray tones and are thus called *gray-scale scanners*. Some gray-scale scanners have as many as 256 *gray levels*. This can give you really high-quality pictures, including ones in color, but also costs a bundle.

Black-and-white (non-gray-scale) scanners can't produce pictures of book or magazine quality, but they're good enough for informal uses like newsletters and presentations. One of the least expensive black-and-white scanners is ThunderScan ($250 list). It attaches to an ImageWriter printer and can only scan loose sheets of paper.

There are a bunch of faster and more powerful 300-dpi scanners like Apple's (which is simply called the Apple Scanner); they tend to cost $1000 and up.

⚫ *camera-based digitizers* (DC)

Inexpensive black-and-white video cameras with high-quality lenses will provide much better images on camera-based digitizers like MacVision than the more expensive color cameras.

bargain

When using a camera-based digitizer, you can give the image dramatic depth by angling the object slightly. Be careful, though—just a little is enough.

⚫ *ThunderScan output on the LaserWriter* (DC)

Since the ThunderScan digitizer reads a picture on the ImageWriter, printouts on the LaserWriter often look no better than a MacPaint document at 72 dots per inch. But there's a way around this. Scan the image at 400%, then print it at 25%. That will give your image a resolution of 288 dpi.

But be prepared to wait a while. Scanning a whole page at 400% takes over an hour.

⚫ *avoiding stair-stepping on the ThunderScan* (DC)

One way to improve the quality of a ThunderScan image is to make sure you insert the original into the ImageWriter as straight as possible. If it contains horizontal lines, try to align them with the roller shaft. You can test the alignment quite easily—if the horizontal lines in the digitized image are slightly "stair-stepped," the alignment is off.

⚫ *vertical lines on the ThunderScan* (DC)

If the image you are digitizing with ThunderScan contains lots of vertical lines, put it in the ImageWriter sideways (but see the previous entry about aligning it precisely). You can then use MacPaint's Rotate command to properly orient the digitized image.

Miscellaneous hardware and accessories

✦ accelerators (Larry Pina)

As pointed out in the entry called *upgrading your Mac* in Chapter 2, one way to upgrade a Mac is to install an *accelerator card* in it. This gives you a more powerful processor chip and/or a faster clock rate (and sometimes extra memory as well).

The increased speed an accelerator card provides is especially important when you plan to use an external monitor. As the size of a screen increases, so does the time it takes to redraw it. Most monitors have extra memory on their video cards to take care of this problem, but even so, an accelerator board usually speeds things up.

Some accelerators have sockets for math coprocessor chips. These won't do much for you unless you work with complex formulas and large spreadsheets. If you're not absolutely sure that you need a math coprocessor, it generally means you don't.

Accelerators come in all shapes and sizes, and they're available for every model of the Mac from the 512K on up. Some of the older accelerators, like Levco's Monster Mac, use a special kind of *daughter board.* Others designed for the Macintosh SE and the Macintosh II are properly referred to as *cards* because they plug into expansion slots. (For more on this, and for other information that's relevant to accelerator cards, see the entry called *memory upgrade basics* in Chapter 3.)

✦ accelerators and interleave ratios

very hot tip

As discussed in Chapter 3, different models of the Mac need different *interleave ratios* in order to access their hard disks as quickly as possible. If you boost your Mac's performance with an accelerator, ask the manufacturer what interleave ratio you should use, to take advantage of your souped-up Mac's new speed.

✦ *the Z88* (AN)

About the size of an 8-1/2 x 11" sheet of paper, less than an inch thick, and weighing just 2-1/4 pounds with its four AA batteries installed, the Scottish-made Z88 is the ultimate laptop computer. (There are smaller ones, but they don't have a full-sized keyboard.) You can even get it with a nifty hardware-and-software package that makes it easy to load your files onto a Mac. And all this usually costs about $700—much less than most laptops.

bargain

So, what's wrong with the Z88? Well, a number of things. The basic software that comes built into it, called PipeDream, attempts to integrate a spreadsheet and a word processor. This makes very weird things happen when you hit the [Tab] key, and creates a number of other problems as well, none of which are very clearly explained in the documentation.

very bad feature

You can buy an add-on cartridge for the Z88 that contains a combination word processor and spelling checker called Spell-Master (I guess over in England they don't know about InterCapping and still use the old-fashioned hyphen). This will add about $100 to your cost, and Spell-Master, although better than PipeDream, is a fairly primitive program of the kind you'd expect to come bundled with the computer in the first place.

Whichever program you use on the Z88, you're going to have to remember a great number of arcane, PC-like commands—and that, after all, is what we turned to the Mac to escape.

very bad feature

Although the Z88's keyboard is full-sized and has a nice feel, the screen only holds eight lines of text. The screen could also be easier to read (although it's not terrible).

You can hook a printer up to the Z88. The tiny Diconix, described in Chapter 4, is perfect for this purpose, but the version that runs off a Mac won't run off a Z88. You're better off getting a generic Diconix and finding third-party printer drivers for both the Mac and the Z88.

**important
warning**

The main vendor of the Z88 in this country is a company called Cambridge North America. We've had a number of complaints about their support and service. You can also get Z88's from some computer stores; Microworld in Berkeley is an example.

If you want a *very* light and portable laptop, the Z88 is worth considering. But remember, what you'll be slipping into your briefcase or backpack is nothing like a Mac.

🍎 *MacRecorder* (AN)

Steve Michel thinks this dandy sound-capturing hardware-and-software package is the greatest thing since sliced bread. (Actually, he thinks it's even better than sliced bread, which he really doesn't like all that much.)

**very good
feature**

Made by Farallon Computing and sold for $250 list, MacRecorder lets you capture any sound (at 22,000 samples per second), mix it and add special effects. Once you have the sound the way you want it, you can use it as a replacement for normal Mac beeps (so your Mac will talk—or sing—to you), in many music and sound programs and in HyperCard stacks.

The hardware works very well and the software is generally slick and easy to use. But be aware that digitized sound takes up a *lot* of room in RAM or on a disk.

🍎 *use a mouse pad*

Invest a few dollars in a mouse pad to give the proper traction to the mouse roller—you won't regret it. The pad— usually about eight by ten inches and available in a range of colors and designs—also serves to stake out a reserved area of your desk for mouse movements.

🍎 *don't use a mouse pad* (AN)

I have three problems with mouse pads. One is that they should be unnecessary—the mouse should be designed so that any smooth desk surface will work fine. I use mine on a regular plastic laminate (Formica) desktop and usually have no problems with it. When I feel like I'm not getting enough friction, I simply use Dale's cheap mouse pad (see the next entry for more on this brilliant approach).

The second reason I don't like mouse pads is that they restrict how far you can move the mouse. I'm always running off the edges of them, which is annoying.

The third—and by far the most important—problem with mouse pads is the dreadful chemical stench almost all of them put out when new. I just don't understand how people can buy things that smell like Bhopal on a windy afternoon. And it's not as if the smell is just unpleasant—it's almost certainly carcinogenic too. That's not some hysterical comment: vinyl fumes are known to cause cancer, as do many other plastic and rubber fumes.

**important
warning**

If you do buy a mouse pad, at least leave it outside in the sun until it stops smelling. You're playing with your health if you don't.

◆ *Dale's cheap mouse pad* (DC)

My favorite mouse pad is a sheet of paper inside a good-quality spiral-bound notebook. It sells for a fraction of the cost of a commercial mouse pad and, unlike them, it doesn't attract dust and cat hairs. *(My mouse pad doesn't attract dust or cat hairs, and there's plenty of both in my house.—SZA)*

Best of all, when you want a new pad, all you have to do is turn the page. *(You probably pick up fibers from paper, which is bad for the mouse. And with mouse pads around $5, a pad of <u>good</u> paper that won't shred is not "a fraction of the cost."—SZA)*

If you already have a commercial mouse pad, you can prolong its life by covering its surface with a piece of heavy paper cut to size and attached with double-sided tape. *(Prolong its life? If you cover it, you're not using it—it <u>has</u> no life. The main reason for a mouse pad is the texture of the surface. This is like covering your sofa with vinyl to protect the upholstery. No, it's like putting bumpers on cars to protect the fenders, then bumper guards to protect the bumpers. I suppose bumper guard protectors are next.—SZA)*

⚫ stands for Mac II's, IIx's and fx's *(Fred Terry)*

Kensington makes an aluminum floor stand for the Mac II, IIx and fx that lets you stand it vertically next to your desk. It provides a stable support for the II and puts it about 2" above the floor, but it ignores the Mac II owner's manual warning to "keep your computer main unit flat, sitting on its rubber feet. Standing it on edge defeats the cooling design and is likely to make your computer over-heat." Apple technical support confirms this warning but Kensington (not surprisingly) claims that the stand provides enough clearance for convective cooling.

If you do use the stand, put the Mac II on it with the right side down. The power supply is on the left and if you put that side on the bottom, all of the heat from it will flow up over the motherboard and the chips. Unfortunately, putting the right side down places the floppy disk drive(s) near the floor and also deprives you of access to the programmer's switch (if you have it installed).

⚫ cables *(AN)*

For some reason I'm not clear on, many sources for Macintosh cables are flakes. A couple that aren't are Kensington and Monster Cable. The latter's MacCable line is extensive, and if they don't have what you want, they'll make it for you.

⚫ spaghetti control *(AN)*

Computer Cord Keeper (from Computer Covers Unlimited) is one of those simple ideas that makes you say, "Why didn't anyone ever think of that before?" It's a plastic tube about an inch in diameter with a slit down it (two come in a package). Tuck all the power cords from various pieces of equipment into the tube (or tubes) and you've cut down on some of the spaghetti behind your desk. (I *said* it was a simple idea.)

Chapter 6

Basic Mac software

⚫ basic terms *(SZA/AN)*

If any of the terms or concepts in this chapter are unfamiliar to you, you can either look them up in the glossary or go back and read the *Guide for beginners* section of Chapter 1. Meanwhile, here's a review of a few of the most basic terms:

esp. for beginners

A *file* is a collection of information on a disk, usually represented by an icon on the desktop. Although the information in a file is normally cohesive—that is, about one thing—it doesn't actually have to be; what makes it a file is simply that it's lumped together and called by one name.

There are two types of files—*programs*, which are instructions telling the computer what to do, and *documents*, which are collections of data you create and modify with programs—letters, drawings and mailing lists, for example. (On other computers than the Mac, documents are usually called *data files*).

There are several different kinds of programs: *applications*, which are devoted to relatively large, complicated tasks like word processing; *utilities*, which perform support tasks, like searching for a specific file on a disk or counting all the words in a document; *system software*, which controls the basic operations of the computer; *games*; etc. But there's a tendency among Mac users to call all programs *applications*, regardless of their type.

Tips on menus

⚫ indicators in menus

Back in the earlier days of the Mac (1984–85), menus were pretty simple—for example, they were never longer than the screen. Then the scrolling menu was born, and the hierarchical menu, so that now some menu commands are mere gateways to submenus (and sub-submenus).

esp. for beginners

There are four indicators you'll find in today's menus; they let you know what to expect when you choose a menu item.

The first is the ellipsis (...); when it follows a menu command, that means the program can't follow the command without further information and there's a dialog box on the way. (The *Open...*, *Save...* and *Print...* commands are examples.)

A down-pointing triangle at the bottom of a menu means there are more commands than can be displayed on the screen at one time. (You'll find this indicator almost exclusively in the menu, when you have lots of desk accessories, and in font menus.) When you get to the bottom of the menu and it starts scrolling, an up-pointing triangle appears at the top to remind you that additional items are up there out of sight:

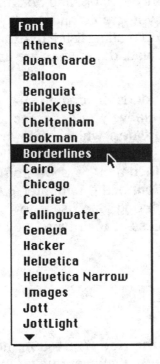 

When a menu item is followed by a right-facing triangle, it's not a command—it's the name of a submenu:

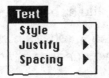 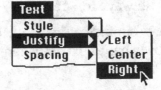

The fourth indicator is the checkmark you sometimes see in front of a menu command, like the one in front of *Left* in the illustration at the bottom of the previous page. This means the item is currently active or in effect. (See *toggles in menus* on page 287.)

esp. for beginners

escaping from menus (SZA/AN)

Once a menu's open, you don't have to slide the pointer back up to the top to get out without selecting anything; just slide the pointer off the menu anywhere onto the screen and let go of the mouse button. (This goes for submenus, too.)

Escaping *tear-off menus* is quite a bit harder. You can't just slide the pointer off the menu sideways, because that's what tears it off and lets you position it, permanently open, anywhere you want on the screen. You can always escape back out the top, of course—and, unless there's a downward-pointing triangle at the bottom of the menu, you can also go out there too. On HyperCard menus, there's a third way to avoid tearing the menu off—slide out the side while moving at an upward angle.

(If you manage to tear the menu off anyway, by mistake, it's no big deal—just click on its close box to put it away.)

keyboard equivalents and modifier keys

Sometimes a menu command is followed by a symbol (or symbols) and a letter. That's the *keyboard equivalent* of the command—it lets you execute the command without using the menu itself. Most menu commands use simply the ⌘ key along with the first letter of the command name, like this:

shortcut

File	
New...	⌘N
Open...	⌘O
Save	⌘S
Print...	⌘P
Quit	⌘Q

**esp. for
beginners**

Although the letters in keyboard equivalents are shown as uppercase, that's just because that's how they appear on the keyboard; you don't have to hold down the ⌈Shift⌉ key to use them. (We follow that convention in this book too. When we say ⌈⌘⌉⌈A⌉, we mean ⌈⌘⌉⌈a⌉; if we want you to hold down the ⌈Shift⌉ key, we say so: ⌈Shift⌉⌈⌘⌉⌈A⌉.)

Sometimes all the letters of the alphabet aren't enough—especially when you want to find a keyboard equivalent that has *something* to do with the name of the command. So other *modifier keys* are now used with ⌈⌘⌉ to extend the power of the keyboard. The most common is ⌈Shift⌉, which even acts as a modifier key on a typewriter (by converting lowercase letters to capitals). The other two modifier keys commonly used on the Mac are ⌈Option⌉ and ⌈Ctrl⌉.

Many of these extended keyboard equivalents aren't listed in menus, but when they are, each modifier key has its own symbol:

Here's what they look like in a menu:

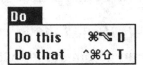

There are other symbols you'll sometimes find in menus—not for modifier keys, but for keys that, like the letters and numbers, *take* modifiers. Here's a guide to them:

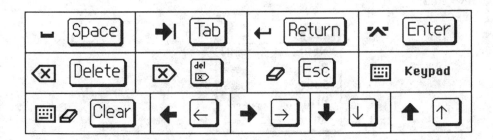

The ⊞ symbol is used to indicate the numeric keypad— that's the difference between ⌘1 and ⌘⊞1. Since there's no symbol for the Clear key, which is on the keypad, it's referred to as, in effect, *keypad esc*. The *forward delete* key (⌦) is only found on extended keyboards; it's in the cluster that includes the help and home keys.

Here's what some of these symbols look like in a menu. (The illustration also shows what a function key (F8) looks like in a menu—there's no special symbol for it.)

Sample Menu	
Plain Text	⌘⇧␣
Move up	⌘↑
Erase Next Word	⌘⌦
8x Magnification	F8

⌘ remembering keyboard equivalents

The basic, Mac-standard keyboard equivalents are:

File Menu		*Edit Menu*	
New	⌘N	Undo	⌘Z
Open	⌘O	Cut	⌘X
Save	⌘S	Copy	⌘C
Print	⌘P	Paste	⌘V
Quit	⌘Q	Clear	⌘B

esp. for beginners

Although these are supposed to be standard, I've seen most of them used for something else in one program or another. *[To some extent, this is justifiable, because the standards weren't chosen very thoughtfully. For example, how often do you need to open a new document? I customize all my programs so that ⌘N stands for Plain text, a command I use about a hundred times more often than New document.—AN]* The only standard keyboard equivalents that really seem to be sacred are ⌘Z, ⌘X, ⌘C and ⌘V.

Apple's original guidelines called for ⌘P to stand for *Plain text* rather than *Print*, and you'll still see that sometimes. Programs that use ⌘P for *Print* use various substitutes for *Plain text*. Word introduced Shift ⌘ Spacebar for plain text and some applications copy that; I like it, since the spacebar connotes for me nothing in the way of styles. *(Actually, in Word, this returns you to the default type style, not to plain text.—AN)* Works calls it *normal text* and takes ⌘N away from the *New* command, which I find highly annoying. *(And I find very sensible.—AN)*

The Edit menu commands are easy to remember—they're the first five keys on the bottom row of the keyboard, right above the ⌘ key itself. *Copy* is the only one that gets a letter that matches the command, but ⌘X for *Cut* makes sense if you think of x'ing out (if you wanted to cut a large portion of text from a hard copy, for example, you'd draw a big *X* through it).

Programs that have a keyboard equivalent for *Clear* usually use ⌘B. This used to be easy to remember, because it served the same function as the Backspace key—but the alliteration's been lost since the new keyboards have a Delete key instead.

The keyboard equivalents in the programs you use often eventually burn themselves into your neural pathways (unless they contradict each other). While you're waiting for that to happen, look for clues as to why particular letters were chosen for particular commands. For example, you can't use ⌘C for the *Close* command, because it's reserved for Copy. You might use ⌘K for the sound, or ⌘L because it's the second letter, or go to the second word and come up with ⌘W for *close Window* (this is the most popular).

If you can't figure out why the programmer used a certain letter (sometimes it's only because there weren't many left to choose from), make up your own mnemonic for it. Don't worry about how zany it might seem to someone else, as long as it helps you remember.

¢ toggles in menus

Some menu items are *toggles*—when they're off, choosing them turns them on, and when they're on, choosing them turns them off again. Often menu toggles get checkmarks when you choose them (and choosing them the next time removes the checkmark). Sometimes the command itself changes back and forth—between *Show Ruler* and *Hide Ruler*, for example.

esp. for beginners

¢ using hierarchical menus

The hierarchical menu is probably the single most elegant extension of the original Mac interface—a nice way to group commands and keep them readily available. The implementation is really elegant too. *(I hate hierarchical menus—they're cumbersome and slow. But that's what makes horse races.—AN)*

To use a hierarchical menu, just pause briefly on any item that has a right-pointing triangle. The submenu doesn't pop out immediately—if it did, you'd have submenus popping out all over as you dragged through a menu to reach something at the bottom.

Once the submenu appears, you don't have to drag over and down to the item you want—you can drag diagonally from where you are in the main menu to the spot you want in the submenu. *(This only works if you drag at a fairly shallow angle—that is, one with a significant horizontal component. If you drag at too vertical an angle, the Mac will think you want to move down the main menu and will close the submenu.—AN)*

shortcut

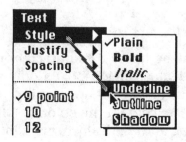

very good feature

Here's where some real design elegance is apparent. If you pause on a command till its submenu pops out and then drag the mouse very slowly to the next command, moving just a little to the right as you drag, the submenu stays popped for a few seconds—to give you time to get into it. Right, you figured that out already.

But here's the really elegant part: if you drag straight down or up, or slightly to the left as you move down, the submenu disappears right away—it knows there's no reason to hang around if you're not moving towards it.

Tips on icons, files and folders

❤ naming and renaming icons on the desktop

esp. for beginners

When you create a new icon on the desktop—either a new folder with the ⌘N command or a copy of a document with the ⌘D command—the new icon is automatically selected; to rename it, just begin typing.

If you rename an icon and change your mind while the icon is still selected, you can just use the *Undo* command (⌘Z) to revert to the original name.

❤ lowercasing file names *(AN)*

very hot tip

Since every inch of your screen counts, there's no sense in capitalizing an icon name except when necessary. Capital letters take up much more room than lowercase ones, and once you get used to the lowercase look (you can use the entry titles in this book for practice), filenames with gratuitous caps look clunky and old-fashioned.

❤ filename restrictions *(AN/SZA)*

A filename can be up to 31 characters in length—but keep in mind that most dialog boxes only show 22 characters. You can use just about any symbol you want in the name of a Mac file, except for the colon (:). If you try to put a colon in, the Mac automatically turns it into a hyphen.

This is because the Mac reserves the colon for *pathnames,* which show how to get to a file through all its folders. For example, the pathname for a file named *Dictionary,* nested inside a couple of folders on a hard disk called *HD20,* might look like this: *HD20:Applications:Word:Dictionary.*

For tips on how to control where filenames appear in list boxes and when viewed by name in windows on the desktop, see the entries that begin with the one called *keeping filenames at the top of lists* in the next section.

⚫ *the list views* (SZA/AN)

In addition to letting you view files by icon and by small icon, the Finder provides five kinds of *list views:* by name, by date, by size, by kind and by color. (Sometimes these are called *text views,* but we think *list views* is the more descriptive term.)   .

esp. for beginners

In all of these list views, the columns appear in the same order from left to right—making it hard to tell which view you've chosen. But you don't have to pull down the View menu to see what's checked—just look to see which column heading is underlined. (This won't work for viewing by color, of course, but it will usually be obvious when you're doing that.)

very hot tip

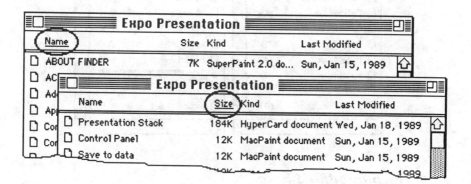

⚫ *the best way to view files* (AN)

**very
hot
tip**

View windows by name when they contain mostly folders (so the names stay in the same place on the list and can
be found easily) and by date when they contain mostly files
(so the ones you worked on most recently will be at the top
of the list). Viewing by icon is cute and Mac-like, but infinitely
less efficient than viewing by name or by date.

⚫ *long names*

**esp. for
beginners**

When files are in a list view, the filenames are only given
a certain amount of space. If a filename won't fit, it's short-
ened and a trailing ellipsis (...) indicates there's something
missing.

But if you click on the filename to highlight it, it expands
to its full length, even if that means overlapping the information in the next column. So if you have several files with
long names that all begin with the same words, you can
distinguish them by clicking on them one after the other.

🔲 System Folder 🔲		Kind		🔲 System Folder 🔲		Kind
Name	Size			Name	Size	
OptimAFM	17K			OptimAFM	17K	
OptimBol	65K			OptimBol	65K	
OptimBol.AFM	17K			OptimBol.AFM	17K	
OptimBol0bl	80K			OptimBol0bl	80K	
OptimBol0...	17K			OptimBol0...	17K	
OptimObl	78K			OptimObl	78K	
PageMaker...	14K			PageMaker...	14K	
PageMaker...	3K			PageMaker 3.0 Defaults		
PhonePad File	14K			PhonePad File	14K	
pmusdisk.dct	81K			pmusdisk.dct	81K	

⚫ *the unmodified date*

**important
warning**

Sometimes just opening a document to look at it is
enough to change the *modified* date that appears in list
views in windows on the desktop and in the Get Info box.

So be aware that the file may not have been modified at all on that date.

❖ *folder sizes and contents* (SZA/AN)

*very
hot
tip*

List views show you the size of files, but not of folders. Opening a folder's window (and viewing its contents by icon or by small icon) only tells you how many items are in the first level of the folder. To find out how many K are in the folder, or how many items are in folders *within* the folder, you need to use Get Info.

In the illustration below, we've selected a folder called *PageMaker* and opened it. The resulting window says there are five items in the folder. But when you select the PageMaker folder and Get Info on it, the Get Info window indicates eleven files. That's because one of the items in the PageMaker folder is a folder with additional files in it.

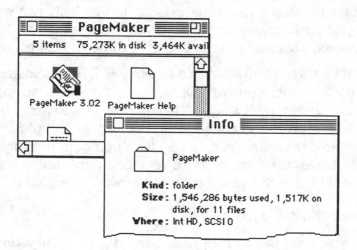

Notice that the Get Info window says *files,* not *items;* unlike desktop windows, Get Info doesn't count folders. So this PageMaker folder actually contains twelve items— four files that are loose and a folder (which the Get Info window doesn't count) with seven additional files in it.

✦ when an empty folder isn't

**important
warning**

Just because you have a folder on your desktop named *Empty folder*, that doesn't mean there's nothing in it. Whenever you create a new folder (with the aptly-named *New Folder* command), its default name is *Empty folder*. Putting something in it doesn't change the name.

(You think this isn't a tip? I used to get a lot of calls from beginners complaining about disappearing files. It took quite a while for me to realize just what was happening.)

Apple should change the default name of new folders to something less misleading, like *Untitled folder*.

✦ replace folder contents, not folders

**important
warning**

If you drag a folder from one disk to another and the destination disk already has a folder on it with the same name, the contents of the folder you're dragging completely replace the contents of the existing folder. This can be a big problem if the original folder (on the destination disk) contained files that the replacement folder doesn't.

To be safe, never replace a folder with a folder. Instead, work with folder *contents*. Open the folder you were going to drag, use ⌘ A for *Select All* and drag all the items into the folder on the destination disk. If any of the files you drag have the same names as files already in the folder, you'll be asked if you want to replace them—but any additional files in the destination folder won't be touched.

✦ disk-to-disk copies

**important
warning**

If you drag the icon of one disk on top of the icon of another disk of the same type (both 800K floppies, say), the contents of the dragged disk will replace the contents of dragged-upon disk. (Of course, you'll get a warning dialog box before this happens—this *is* the Mac.)

If you drag the icon of a smaller disk onto a larger disk—a floppy onto a hard disk, say—you won't have to worry about replacing the contents of the hard disk. The contents of the floppy will be placed on the hard disk in a folder that's given the floppy's name.

✎ dragging duplicates

Dragging a file from one disk to another actually drags a *copy* of the file—the original is left on the source disk. But when you drag a file from one *folder* to another on the same disk, the file moves from the first spot into the new folder.

If you want to move a *copy* of a file to a different place on the same disk, hold [Option] while you drag it; the original stays in place and a copy of it goes into the new spot (and with an identical name—not *Copy of*, as with the Duplicate command).

very
hot
tip

✎ locking files (SZA/DC)

To lock a file, select it on the desktop, choose *Get Info* from the File menu (or hit [⌘][I])and click in the *Locked* checkbox. To unlock it, just click in the checkbox again. Locked files can't be deleted or modified from within an application, although you can use *Save As* to make an unlocked, editable copy.

esp. for
beginners

On the desktop, you can tell if a file is locked without opening the Get Info dialog box. Put the pointer over a selected icon's name—if the pointer remains an arrow, the file's locked (it normally changes to an I-beam so you can edit the file's name).

✎ shades of gray

The way a disk's icon looks on the desktop tells you whether it's selected or not, whether it's window is open or closed, and whether it's in the disk drive or has been ejected:

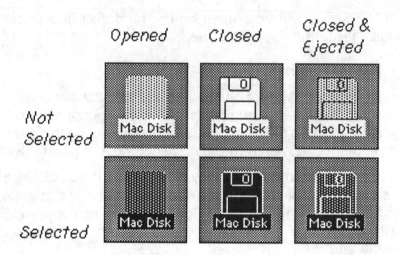

✦ *ejecting floppy disks*

esp. for beginners

The best way to eject a disk is to drag it to the Trash can. I've heard people gasp the first time they see someone do this—it does seem that this would erase the disk, but in this case, the Trash metaphor isn't strictly adhered to.

These commands below eject a disk but leave its dimmed icon (or *ghost*) on the desktop (for what a disk's ghost looks like, see the two icons on the right in the figure above).

⌘ E   ejects the selected disk(s). This is the keyboard equivalent for the Eject command in the File menu

⌘ Shift 1   ejects the disk in the internal drive

⌘ Shift 2   ejects the disk in the external drive

⌘ Shift 0   ejects the disk in a second external drive

Using the *Eject* button in an Open or Save As dialog box also ejects a disk and leaves its ghost on the desktop.

If you don't want the ghost, use Option ⌘ E (this is equivalent to dragging the icon to the Trash). This only works with the keyboard command; holding Option while choosing *Eject* from the File menu leaves the ghost.

● *disk ghosts*

Don't leave disk ghosts around on the desktop unless you're going to be reinserting the disk soon (the ghost will save you time, because you won't have to read the contents of the disk to create its windows all over again). Another reason to leave ghosts around is if you're comparing the contents of two or more floppies and only have one floppy drive.

If neither of those situations applies, drag the ghost to the Trash. Aside from the clutter, ghosts take up memory.

*very
hot
tip*

If the ejected disk had open windows, they'll be dimmed, too—but avoid the urge to be neat and close them before getting rid of the ghost. If you close a window, the Mac will demand that you insert the disk so the "change" can be recorded. If you just drag the ghost of the disk icon into the Trash, all its windows will disappear with it.

Sometimes you'll drag a disk to the Trash and its ghost will remain on the desktop, or will bounce right back up to where it was. This means there's a file on the disk that's being used. If you *know* that you have no documents open on that disk, the culprit is usually a suitcase file that you've opened with Suitcase or Font/DA Juggler.

Another tricky situation is when you're in MultiFinder and are trying to eject a disk that contains a document that was opened at some point after the disk was inserted, but which now is closed. Sloppily programmed applications sometimes don't "release" a document when you close it, but only when you quit the application. To eject the disk, quit the application that created the document on it, then drag the disk icon to the Trash again.

Tips on windows

● *the zoom box* *(AN/SZA)*

At the right end of the title bar on an active window, there's a small box with a smaller box inside it. That's the

*esp. for
beginners*

zoom box (the whole icon, both boxes). Click on it and the window expands to fill the screen (or almost—see the next paragraph); click on it again and it resumes its former size and shape.

Some programs don't actually expand the window to fill the entire screen. In the Finder, for example, a "full" size window stops about an inch short of the right edge of the screen, so you can still see disk icons and the Trash. (You can make it larger by manually sizing it to cover the full screen.)

More II lets you choose between two types of "full-size" windows; one is the size of the screen and the other leaves the right edge of the screen clear in case you're using MultiFinder. Word always leaves the right edge of the screen clear.

*very bad
feature*

These options shouldn't be left to individual applications, and the whole thing could be implemented better. On a large monitor, the whole-screen option is almost always ridiculous, whether it goes all the way to the edge or not; it looks as if someone has suddenly opened a bedsheet in front of your screen. The size and shape of the larger window should be user-adjustable, in the Control Panel.

✦ *moving inactive windows* (DC/SZA)

*very
hot
tip*

It can be annoying to always have to select a window before moving it. To move an inactive window (one that's not selected), just hold down ⌘ while dragging it. (This is a handy trick to know if you want to shift a background window to see something but don't want to lose the active window on the top of the pile.)

✦ *locating buried windows*

shortcut

If you have a lot of windows open on the desktop, sometimes the one you want gets buried. If you can't see a folder's window but can see its dimmed icon, just double-click on the icon to bring its window to the top of the pile.

✦ *keeping filenames at the top of lists*

very
hot
tip

Filenames are alphabetized both when viewed by name on the desktop and in list boxes inside dialog boxes (Open, Save, etc.). If you know the basics of the Mac's alphabetization rules, you can force the files you want (documents or folders) to the top of any list.

Alphabetic characters are sorted just the way you'd expect—and there's no difference between capital and lowercase letters. (So you can't have a file called *File* and one called *file*—one would replace the other.)

Numbers come before letters, so *9* is sorted before *A*. Punctuation marks and other symbols are sorted before, after or between the numbers and letters, according to their ASCII codes (there's a complete list of them in Chapter 7). Here are the first sixteen characters, in order; putting any one of these in front of a file name will jump it to the top of the list, even ahead of numbers:

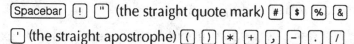

[Spacebar] [!] ["] (the straight quote mark) [#] [$] [%] [&]

['] (the straight apostrophe) [(] [)] [*] [+] [,] [-] [.] [/]

You can use these symbols to keep *groups* of files together. For example, you might put an exclamation mark in front of the names of all documents relating to one project, and an asterisk in front of the names of documents relating to another project. This lets you impose a hierarchical order on a list of files without having to move them into different folders, and order will be maintained no matter when the file names appear.

Option characters (the ones you type with [Option] or [Shift][Option]) may be sorted before, after or between alphabetic characters, and the order is different in desktop windows than it is in list boxes inside dialog boxes. The ones that are basically alphabetic appear within the alphabet; *å* sorts between *a* and *b*, for example. Ones that are not alphabetic (at least not in the *Roman* alphabet), like •, √, and Δ, sort to the *bottom* of desktop windows but to the *top* of list boxes—except for [Option]-space, which jumps to the top of both lists. To make it easy on yourself, just don't use option characters in filenames.

⚫ starting filenames with spaces

In the Save As dialog box, you can type a space at the beginning of a filename, but when you're renaming an icon on the desktop, you can't. There you have to first type a character, then a space, then delete the initial character.

You can, however, type an [Option]-space at the beginning of a filename on the desktop. Filenames beginning with [Option]-space will sort in front of filenames beginning with ordinary spaces in list boxes. So if you have two files named [Spacebar] *Chapter 1* and [Option][Spacebar] *Chapter 2* (well, those aren't actually their names, but you know what we mean), they'll appear in correct order on the desktop but *Chapter 2* will come first in list boxes.

⚫ sorting numbered filenames

esp. for beginners

The Mac isn't very smart about sorting numbers—for example, 10 comes after 1 and before 2. If you want numbers to show up in numerical order, use a space in front of the single digits, but none in front of the double digits:

Without space	With space
1	1
10	2
11	3
12	4
2	10
3	11
4	12

This works whether the numbers are the first (or only) characters in the filename or if they're embedded in the filename:

Without space	With space
Chapter 1	Chapter 1
Chapter 10	Chapter 2
Chapter 11	Chapter 3
Chapter 12	Chapter 4
Chapter 2	Chapter 10
Chapter 3	Chapter 11
Chapter 4	Chapter 12

If your list will include three-digit numbers, you'll need to put two spaces in front of the single-digit numbers, a single space in front of the two-digit numbers, and no space in front of the three-digit numbers.

⚫ *finding icons quickly*

If you have lots of icons in a folder in no particular order and you want to find one quickly, switch to viewing by name, find the file you want easily in the alphabetical list, click on it and then switch back to viewing by icon. The icon will be selected and easy to see. *[Yes, but why go back to viewing by icon?—AN]*

shortcut

⚫ *sorting by Color*

Once you've assigned colors to icons in any desktop window, you can use the *by Color* command in the View menu. Items are then shown in a list view, sorted according the order of the colors in the Color menu itself.

⚫ *moving icons into list-view windows* (DC)

Be careful when you move a file to a window that's displayed in any list view, especially if a number of the names on the list are folders rather than files. It's easy to accidentally select one of the folders, and then the file you're moving will end up hidden away inside the folder, rather than out in the larger window where you meant it to

important warning

be. You can have quite a time trying to find it, opening one folder after another.

very hot tip

The best way to avoid this problem is to drag the icons you want to copy to the part of the window just below the title bar (the rectangular space where the words *Name, Size, Kind* and *Last Modified* appear). Since no icons can appear there, there's no danger that the icons you're dragging will disappear into a folder.

● *automatic window closing with* Option *(AN/SZA)*

When you quit an application (and you're not using MultiFinder), the Finder recreates the desktop as you left it; if you left it in a mess with lots of windows open, that's what you'll get when you return. You'll also return more slowly, because the messier the desktop is, the longer the Finder takes to recreate it. Here are some ways to deal with that problem:

shortcut

In System 6.03 and earlier, you can open windows temporarily, so the Finder won't remember that you opened them. To do that, hold down Option when you doubleclick to open the windows. When you return to the desktop from an application, all those windows will be closed. (This works for both disk windows and folders.)

shortcut

From System 6.04 on, holding Option down immediately closes the window that the icon you're clicking is *in*. For example, in the illustration below, if you were to hold down Option while clicking on the folder icon called *New York publishers*, the window titled *dealing with psychopaths* would close.

▤▢▨▤▤▤▤ **dealing with psychopaths** ▤▤▤▤▤▨
Name	Size	Kind	Last
▢ Board of Ed	--	folder	⇧
▢ Post Office	--	folder	
▪ New York publishers	--	folder	
⇦			⇨ ▨

This cleans up things even faster and leaves the last window you were in open when you return to the desktop (so you can make up a backup copy of the document you modified, say, or have it there out on the desktop to re-open again sometime soon). This tip works under Multi-Finder too.

If you've left a messy desktop, you can have the Mac clean it up as you return from an application. Hold down [Option] while you choose *Quit* from the File menu—you'll be returned to a desktop with all its windows closed.

shortcut

Or you can just clean up your mess before you leave. To close all the desktop windows without clicking in each close box, hold down [Option] while you close any window—every other window on the desktop will close too. Another way to achieve the same result is to hold down [Option] and choose *Close* from the File menu; with [Option] down, the command becomes *Close All*. (The techniques described in this paragraph even work in MultiFinder.)

shortcut

☀ *cleaning up windows*

There's an invisible grid in every desktop window that you can use to align your icons neatly. Use the *Clean Up* command in the Special menu to do the straightening.

When nothing's selected in the window, the command reads *Clean Up Window* and shuffles all the icons around until they're in neat rows and columns. When something's selected in the window, the command is *Clean Up Selection* and only moves the selected icons.

If you hold [Option] down while opening the Special menu, the command reads simply *Clean Up* and gives you two advantages—it cleans up everything in the window even if something's selected, and it cleans up much faster than the standard *Clean Up Window*. The cleanup process proceeds differently too: with [Option] cleanup, everything disappears momentarily and then reappears in the right spots; without [Option], each icon moves individually.

You can also align icons manually. If you hold ⌘ while dragging an icon, it snaps to the nearest gridpoint when you release it.

⚫ *the desktop grid*

**very
hot
tip**

There's also a grid on the desktop itself, not just in its windows. If you hold ⌘ down while you drag a loose item, it will snap to the nearest gridpoint when you release it. And if all the windows are closed on the desktop and no icon is selected, the Clean Up command in the Special menu reads *Clean Up Desktop* and you can use it to align all the icons to the desktop grid.

⚫ *alphabetizing icons*

**very
hot
tip**

To alphabetize icons in a window, start by opening the folder whose contents you want to sort. Position the folder's window so that you can still see the folder icon itself. Assuming you're already in Icon view, select all the items in the window with the *Select All* command in the Edit menu (⌘ A) and drag the icons out of the window and into the folder icon. (Yes, you're dragging the folder contents from the folder back into the folder, as shown in the figure at the top of the next page. I call this the Möbius move.)

The items reappear in the window almost instantly, alphabetized and in neat rows.

This won't work if you've rearranged the icons manually after opening the window—you'll get neat rows, but in the order you specified when you moved the icons. If you've dragged your icons around since you opened the folder, close and re-open it before you try to alphabetize.

⚫ *Naimanizing* (AN)

On most icons, the name is wider than the picture, giving it the shape of a stovepipe hat (with the name as the brim). In addition, the names usually vary in length, so that

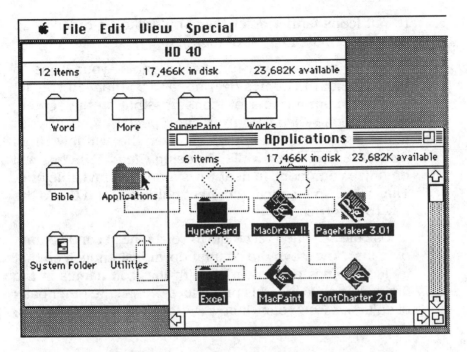

some icons have very wide brims, some have narrower ones and some have no brim at all.

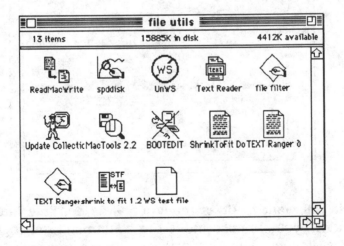

If you simply ignore this fact when you line up icons (as the *Clean Up* command does), the names will either interfere with each other (as shown above), or you'll be forced to put icons farther apart than you'd like (in order to ac-commodate the longest of them).

Here's a simple way to neatly organize your icons so that none of the names overlap, and so that you can get the maximum number of icons possible on the screen. First, choose *Clean Up* from the Special menu (if your icons are really scrambled all over the window, hold down the [Option] key while choosing *Clean Up*). This will organize your icons in neat rows along the invisible grid. They will also be aligned in neat columns, and that's the key to this trick.

Use the selection rectangle to select the second column of icons. Now move the column down just enough so that its icon names don't overlap with the icon names in the first column. Repeat this procedure with all the other pairs of columns. Now your window will look something like this:

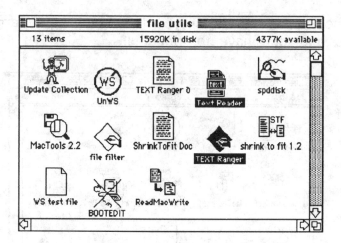

If you want to fit as many icons as possible into the window, you can also move the columns closer together and switch icons around to accommodate unusual shapes. This tightest possible packing looks something like the fig-ure shown at the top of the next page.

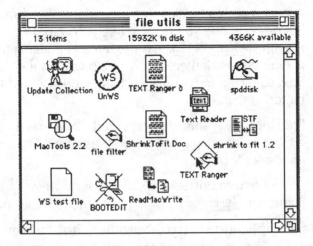

This technique of tucking the name of an icon under the names of its neighbors is known as *Naimanizing* (*NAY-mun-eye-zing*). The origins of this term are lost in the mists of history. Some scholars suggest that it's a play on the word *name*, but that wouldn't account for the spelling. Others trace it back to the famous 17th-century explorer, philosopher and bon vivant Balthasar Naiman. The debate goes on.

gossip/ trivia

Tips on dialog boxes

🍎 *using dialog boxes*

The simplest dialog boxes are *alerts*; they only contain a warning statement or a question, and an *OK* button so you can acknowledge that you've read it—or sometimes an alternative button for cancelling the procedure that produced the warning.

esp. for beginners

More complex dialog boxes contain more buttons of different types, one or more *text boxes* and sometimes even pop-up menus. Keyboard navigation through the elements of a dialog box varies from program to program, but the following are some basic elements that stay the same:

**esp. for
beginners**

- A button with a black frame around it is the *default* button—the one you're most likely to want to click. Pressing [Return] or [Enter] is the same as clicking the default button. If there's only one button in the dialog box, using [Return] or [Enter] usually works even if the button isn't framed.

- Pressing [⌘][.] almost always works as if you'd clicked a *Cancel* button. [Esc] also works, although less often, as the *Cancel* button.

- To move from one text box to the next, press [Tab]. Sometimes [Shift][Tab] moves you to the previous box.

Many applications also offer other shortcuts in their dialog boxes (Word started the trend). For example, in dialog boxes that have no text fields, hitting the first letter of the name of a button (either in combination with [⌘] or by itself), will often click the button for you.

⬥ *shortcuts in Open and Save As dialog boxes*

shortcut

The Open and Save As dialog boxes have lots of shortcuts (most are keyboard equivalents). First, here are ways to select things in a list box:

to move:	*use:*
up and down through the list	[↑] and [↓]
to the top of the list	[←] or [→] or [Delete]
the bottom of the list	[`] (The accent grave/ tilde key)

In the Open dialog box, hitting a key selects the first folder or file beginning with that character (or the next nearest character). You can do that for subsequent characters in the name of the file or folder, if you keep typing quickly (if you type slowly, the letters will be interpreted as single letters and you'll keep jumping around the list).

This method won't work in Save As dialog boxes, because typing enters the name of the file you're saving.

To move up to the parent folder (the one that contains the one you're in), hit ⌘↑ or click on the little icon that appears next to the name of the disk.

Instead of clicking on buttons with the mouse, you can use the keyboard shortcuts that other dialog boxes provide: ⌘. or Esc for *Cancel* and Return or Enter for the default button (the one with the thick line around it).

Finally, you can use Tab to change from one disk drive to the next.

✦ *selecting text box contents*

When a dialog box opens with a single text box in it, often the text in the box is highlighted (selected). If it isn't, and you want to replace it, you don't have to drag across the text to select it, or backspace all the way across it to get rid of it. Just hit Tab to select all the text in the box, then type in the replacement text.

shortcut

✦ *grammar alert* (AN)

When you choose the *Shut Down* command from the Finder's Special menu on any compact Mac (but not the Portable or any of the Mac II's), you get a message that reads: *You may now switch off your Macintosh safely.* What that means is: *You <u>can</u> now switch off your Mac safely.*

gossip/ trivia

The person who wrote this message obviously never recovered from grade-school teachers telling him to say *May I go to the bathroom?* instead of *Can I go to the bathroom?* (they assumed, probably correctly, that he had the *ability* to go to the bathroom pretty much whenever he wanted to).

Well, *may* is correct in that case (although it smacks of a sort of mundane fascism, as does so much of what was pounded into our heads in grammar school). But when you're asking for information about whether it's safe to shut off your Mac, and not permission to do so, *may* is incorrect. (It's also a perfect example of overcompensation—as epitomized by Anita Loos's classic line, *a girl like I.*)

The Mac is full of poorly written and often confusing messages. Apple ought to find a good writer and clean them up.

Clipboard tips

⚉ Clipboard basics

esp. for beginners

The Mac's Clipboard holds the material—text, graphics or both—that you cut or copied the last time you used ⌘X or ⌘C (or the *Cut* and *Copy* commands on the Edit menu). When you use the *Paste* command (⌘V), the contents of the Clipboard are what's pasted.

When you paste the Clipboard's contents, only a *copy* gets pasted. The Clipboard contents remain intact so you can paste them again and again; they only change when you cut or copy something new.

The contents of the Clipboard are usually held in memory, but if you cut or copy a lot of information, a temporary file is created on disk to store it. (The file is placed in the system folder, aptly named *Clipboard file.*)

⚉ special Clipboard contents

Some applications put special information on the Clipboard when you cut or copy. If you paste within that same application, the special information is also pasted; if you paste outside the application, the special information is lost.

For example, if you copy a paragraph in Word, the invisible paragraph marker, which contains formatting information, is also copied to the Clipboard. Pasted into another Word document (or the same one, in a different place), the paragraph retains its original formatting information. Pasted into an application that doesn't know how to interpret the special information, you'll only get the text of the original paragraph, and maybe some of its basic formatting, like tabs and indents.

❡ *preserving and restoring Clipboard contents*

To delete something without affecting the contents of the Clipboard, use the ⌑Delete⌑ key instead of ⌑⌘⌑⌑X⌑.

esp. for beginners

If you cut or copy something and then realize that you still need what was previously on the Clipboard, choose *Undo* (or hit ⌑⌘⌑⌑Z⌑). When it undoes the cut or copy, it also restores the Clipboard to its previous state.

❡ *flushing the Clipboard to free up memory*

There are times you might want to empty the Clipboard—to clear some extra memory, for example, or to make switching between applications in MultiFinder faster. You can't empty it completely, but you can reduce its contents to a bare minimum.

very hot tip

Select a single character in your document (or a very tiny piece of artwork if you're in a graphics program) and copy it to the Clipboard—*twice*. The first time you copy the character, it goes on the Clipboard, but the previous contents remain in memory in case you choose *Undo* (as per the previous entry). So to really free up memory, you need to copy the character a second time.

❡ *losing Clipboard contents in MultiFinder*

Sometimes the Clipboard comes up empty in an application under MultiFinder, even though you just cut or copied something into it in another application. If you go back to the first application, you'll find the Clipboard contents intact. (This shouldn't happen, but it does.)

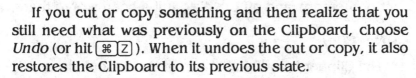

bug

I've found that just the act of pasting something into the Scrapbook, or using a *Show Clipboard* command (if available) in the first application, is sometimes enough to make the contents "stick" to the Clipboard so they're there when you move to the second application.

very hot tip

✦ *Save large Clipboard?*

Sometimes when you quit an application, you'll get a dialog box that asks *Save large Clipboard?* This means you have a lot of material on the Clipboard, and the application assumes that you won't have a use for it once you've quit. So you're given a chance to flush the Clipboard contents out of memory (and off the disk, if it's been stored there).

✦ *the Clipper*

The Clipper is a nifty utility program that enhances Clipboard operations by letting you crop or scale the contents of the Clipboard before you paste them into a document.

The Clipper's interface could be a little more friendly—after you open it (it's a desk accessory), you have to paste the Clipboard contents into it, and before you close it, you have to copy the Clipper contents back to the Clipboard. These should be automated procedures; you shouldn't have to go to the trouble of creating macros for them.

very good feature

But the Clipper can be invaluable. Once you've got the contents in the Clipper window, you can scale the image up or down (by percentage or by specific measurement) or crop it to fit a specific size. Since the Clipper window is moveable and transparent, you can see what the image will look like in your document; that makes it easy to get your image to the exact size and shape you need.

If you're using PageMaker, you should be using the Clipper. PageMaker doesn't let you scale graphics to specific dimensions—you can't, for example, make every one of your pictures 72% of its original size—but the Clipper does.

✦ *PostScript on the Clipboard*

very hot tip

If you want to copy something from a PostScript program like Illustrator or FreeHand and paste it into a program like Word that can't directly import PostScript material, hold down Option while you choose *Copy* from the Edit menu. This puts EPS (encapsulated PostScript) information on the

Clipboard—a combination of PostScript data for the printer and QuickDraw data for your screen.

The system folder and startup disks

❖ *system folder basics*

The system folder is special; to remind you of that, its icon incorporates a special mini-Mac icon:

System Folder

The two most important files in the system folder are the *System* and the *Finder,* which are described in entries of their own below. Here are some of the other files that go in the system folder:

- *drivers*—These programs allow the Mac to communicate with peripheral devices like printers; the ImageWriter and LaserWriter files are examples. Drivers are labeled *Chooser document* or just *document* when you view the system folder's contents by name.

- *inits*—These utility programs run automatically when you start the Mac. They're labeled *Startup document* when you view by name.

- *cdevs*—These utility programs appear in the Control Panel. Most are listed as *Control Panel documents,* but some just get the generic *document* label.

- *printer files*—These are downloadable fonts for laser printers.

- *prefs files*—Applications use these *preference* files to keep track of the settings that you want to use from one session to another—for example, whether you use Short or Full menus in Word, or where your tool palettes are

esp. for beginners

in SuperPaint. Each of the prefs files should have the application's name in it—*Word Settings, PageMaker Defaults*—and will be listed as a document of that application.

- *application support files*—Applications use these for special purposes; some examples are help files and spelling and hyphenation dictionaries. (Sometimes you can put these files elsewhere—usually in the same folder as the application itself—but lots of applications need them in the system folder.) As with pref files, support files are listed as documents of the application they work with.

- *temp files*—Applications create these files for temporary storage while you're working. If you crash, you can sometimes use the temp files to help you recover your data (see the entry called *temp file rescues* in the backup and recovery section of Chapter 9). Temp files are identified as documents of the application that uses them.

- *desk accessory information*—Most DAs store their information (like the pictures in the Scrapbook) in the system folder. Most of these files are listed as *System document* but some get the generic *document* label or are identified as documents of the DA that created them.

🍎 *organizing your system folder*

With all these different types of files, the system folder can turn into a jungle. Here are a few things you can do to keep clutter to a minimum:

- Some applications let you keep their support files in the same folder as the application itself, so take advantage of the opportunity when you can.

- Suitcase and Juggler let you put your desk accessories and screen fonts wherever you want.

- If you use a utility that directs the Mac to printer files when they're needed, you can put them in their own folder, either inside the system folder or elsewhere. FontShare, Set Paths, Suitcase and Juggler are some of the programs that let you do this.

- A utility called INITPicker lets you put most of your inits into their own folder within the system folder.

- A program called Tidy It Up! (available on The Macintosh Bible Software Disks, Third Edition) organizes all the files in your system folder into neat categories.

⚜ *paring your system folder*

If you have plenty of room on your hard disk, you may not much care if unused files are taking up space in your system folder. But you'll want to get rid of them if you're using floppies, or if you're running out of room on your hard disk. For example, if you're not using MultiFinder, you don't need *MultiFinder* or *DA Handler;* if you don't have a laser printer (or have one but don't use background printing), you don't need *Backgrounder* or *PrintMonitor.*

⚜ *invisible files in the system folder*

Use a utility like DiskTop, ResEdit or DiskTools to find and delete any invisible files in your system folder. They don't belong there and may be viruses (or their hell-spawned get). *(Yeah, that was me. Don't you love these literary touches?—AN)*

important warning

Versions of the system from 6.0 on won't run invisible inits, which gives you some minor protection against invisible viruses.

⚜ *trashing temp files*

Although well-mannered applications erase their temp files when you quit, if you crash, or turn off your machine without quitting the application, the temp file will remain in the system folder.

Word is notorious for leaving its temp files around—they're named *Word temp 1, Word temp 2* and so on. (My personal best is *Word temp 48.)* PageMaker creates files called *PM001* and so on; FileMaker creates a *FileMaker temp* folder and puts its stuff in there. It's generally safe to assume that any group of files that all have the same name except for a number that increments are temp files.

Check your system folder occasionally for errant temp files and throw them away (but don't do it when the application that created them is running).

❑ *System Folder vs. system folder* (AN)

*gossip/
trivia*

Although Apple capitalizes the phrase *System Folder,* I can't see the point of it. Aside from proper nouns, capitalization only makes sense when it helps avoid confusion (as it does with *System* and *system;* see the entry below). After all, this is English we're using, not German. Did we leave Saxony for Albion's fair shores only to remain under the thumb of German grammarians? *No!* I say. Excessive capitalization isn't just ugly—it's positively un-American (un-English too).

On a more practical note, the Mac doesn't care if you capitalize *system folder* or not; it will find the folder either way. So if you feel the same way I do about unnecessary capitalization (and any red-blooded American should), just rename your System Folder *system folder.*

❑ *the System file*

*esp. for
beginners*

The System file is the heart of the Mac's *operating system* (the basic software that controls a computer's operation); you can't run a Mac without it. Most of the information in the System file you can't change; it consists of programming instructions that work with, and supplement, the instructions in the Mac's ROM. You can, however, change three things that are stored in the System file—fonts, desk accessories and FKeys. (Fonts are covered in the next chapter, DAs and FKeys in Chapter 8.)

The size of the System file varies, depending on what version it is, what machine you're running it on and how many fonts, DAs and FKeys are stored in it. When you're running a floppy-based system, every K counts; not only should you clean out your system folder, but pare down your System *file* as well, by removing fonts and desk accessories you don't need. (For tips on how to do that, see the Font/DA Mover section of Chapter 8.)

You can also use the special small System that Apple supplies; it's in the Mini System Setup folder on one of the Utilities disks. But mini-Systems you set up will only run on one type of machine; if you use two different Macs, you'll need separate startup disks with separate Mini Systems on them.

🍎 *System vs. system*

There's an important difference between the words *system* and *System*. Capitalized, *System* always refers to the System file itself. Uncapitalized, system can refer to any of three things:

esp. for beginners

- a system *set*—the combination of System, Finder and related software you're using (the system set has a version number of its own, as do each of the programs in it)

- the customized environment you've created by adding and subtracting fonts and desk accessories to your System file, and inits and cdevs to your system folder

- the hardware setup you use— for example, a Mac IIcx with a 150-meg Magic hard disk drive and a DeskWriter printer

A system file (no cap) is any file in the system folder that helps run your computer—cdevs, printer drivers and the like (including *the* System file and the Finder).

🍎 *the Finder*

The *Finder* is the program that creates the desktop. It's not really as integral to the Mac as it seems—it's only an application and can be replaced. But since the desktop is usually the first and last thing you see when you work on a Mac, it's hard to think of a Mac as running without it. The term *Finder* is often used instead of *desktop*—as in *Quit the application and return to the Finder*. It doesn't usually work the other way, though—*Rearrange the icons on your Finder*.

esp. for beginners

♦ installing a new system

**very
hot
tip**

When Apple releases new system software, don't simply drag the new System and Finder (and other system files) to your startup disk. Instead, run the Installer program that comes with the new system. Here's why:

- When you use the Installer program, all the changes you've made to your System—desk accessories and fonts you've installed, for example—remain.

- The Installer optimizes the System for your hardware (a dialog box will ask you what Mac you're using). Later-model Macs have larger ROMs, and therefore more built-in information that applications can access. Earlier Macs don't have that information in their ROMs; they need it in the System file, so programs can find it there. Based on which model you're using, the Installer puts the necessary *patches* (little pieces of programming code) into your System file.

- The Installer won't put unnecessary files into your system folder. If you're installing a system for a Plus, for example, it won't copy the Color cdev to your folder.

Always start your Mac from the Installer disk (instead of your normal startup disk) when you're updating your system. There are two reasons for this. One is that the Installer program needs to access all the items in its own system folder, and it can only see the system folder the Mac is using at the present time.

The other reason is that the Installer needs to operate in a pristine environment. If you've started up from your normal startup disk, you may have all sorts of inits running. Switching to the Installer disk by simply doubleclicking on the Installer isn't good enough, because that leaves all your inits still in memory. So shut down and restart your Mac when you're going to run the Installer.

♦ re-installing a system

Since System 6.0, it's been possible to re-install the system. So if you've run buggy or beta software that's corrupted your system software, you can run the Installer again to fix it. (Earlier versions of the Installer program simply told you that you already had that version installed, and left everything unchanged; you had to do a manual update by dragging the new System and Finder into the system folder.)

⚫ *avoid first releases of system software* (AN)

important warning

The first releases of Mac system software are often pretty buggy. Unless you enjoy being a pioneer (and the arrows through the hat that go with it), you should generally avoid versions of the System and Finder that end in .0. Wait for .01 or .02 before switching over, or at least until the .0 version has been out for a couple of months and seems to be problem-free.

⚫ *system version numbers*

You have to use the compatible versions of the System and Finder; you shouldn't update one without updating the other. Here are the pairs that go together, starting with the last set developed for the unenhanced Mac 512:

System	Finder
3.2	5.3
4.0	5.4
4.1	5.5
4.2	6.0
6.0x	6.1

In October,1987, Apple realized we needed a way to refer to each *set* and started using the phrase *System Tools*. In its inimitable fashion, Apple called the 4.2/6.0 set *System Tools 5.0*.

Finally, in April, 1988, Apple got its numbering system ironed out, and presented System 6.0 and Finder 6.1 as *System Tools 6.0*. Now all you have to do is make sure that the main number of the System and the Finder match. Minor upgrades to either file will be compatible with the other file. For example, I'm running System 6.05 with Finder 6.1 right now.

(By the way, we call the System/Finder combinations *system sets*, or simply *systems*, instead of *System Tools*, because *tools* sounds to us like it refers to all the supplemental programs on the disk, not primarily to the System and Finder.)

esp. for
beginners

There are two ways to find out what versions of the System and Finder you're using. One is to choose *About the Finder...* from the menu on the desktop. The dialog box that appears gives the version numbers. (It used to only give the version number of the Finder, but all current systems supply information about both.)

The second way is to open the system folder, select the System and Finder files, and choose *Get Info* from the File menu. (Using the *About* command is much easier; this alternative is mentioned here only for the sake of completeness.)

Some desk accessories, like DiskTools II, also provide information about the system versions you're running.

when to use which system

If you're using an older Mac, you may be better off using an older system—usually because it takes less memory than newer systems. Here are the versions Apple recommends for each Mac:

Mac	*System*	*Finder*
512K, 512Ke	3.2	5.3
Plus, SE, II	6.02 or later	6.1 or later
SE/30, IIx, IIcx	6.03 or later	6.1 or later
IIci, Portable	6.04 or later	6.1 or later
IIfx	6.05 or later	6.1 or later

✦ startup disks

The disk that contains the System that's currently controlling the Mac is called the *startup disk*. The startup disk's
icon always appears in the upper right corner of the desktop. It's usually a hard disk or a floppy—but it can be a CD-
ROM drive or even a device on a network.

esp. for
beginners

✦ the startup scan

Usually it's obvious which is the startup disk. But what if
you've got a floppy (or two) in the machine and a hard disk
(or two) hooked up? Then you need to know the Mac's *scan
order* (where it looks first, then second, then third, for a
startup disk). Here it is:

1. the internal floppy drive

2. the second internal floppy drive (if there is one)

3. the external floppy drive (if there is one)

4. the Startup Device specified in the Control Panel (a
   feature that's only available for SE's and later models)

5. the external *serial* (non-SCSI) hard disk

6. the internal hard disk (or any other device with a SCSI
   ID number of 0)

7. other SCSI devices (starting with ID number 6 and
   working its way down to 1)

8. after a 15-second wait, back to the internal floppy drive

The first disk that the Mac finds that has a System on it
becomes the startup disk.

✦ avoid multiple systems

Never keep more than one system folder (or System file)
on any one startup disk, whether a hard disk or a floppy.
Multiple Systems make the Mac schizophrenic and you'll
have a lot of seemingly inexplicable crashes. (The record
at Montclair State College is held by Dr. Robert Stevens of

important
warning

the music department, who had *sixteen* Systems on his hard disk. We believe this may be a world record as well.)

Most people don't purposely put multiple Systems on disks, of course. What usually happens is, you insert a floppy that holds the new program you just bought and drag all the files on the floppy, including its system folder, over to your hard disk. Or you drag the icon of the floppy disk onto your hard disk icon, which puts all its contents into a new folder on your hard disk. Since the new system folder is buried in the new application folder, you never even notice it's there.

Periodically, and especially whenever you're experiencing more system crashes than usual, use a program like Apple's Find File to search your hard disk for the word *System*, and remove any extra System files you find.

✺ *switching startup disks*

Sometimes you want to switch startup disks without turning off your Mac, in order to access the fonts, DAs, Scrapbook pictures, etc., in the system folder of another disk. Generally, it's floppies you switch between; hard disks usually have room for all the fonts and desk accessories you need, and utilities like Suitcase and Juggler let you open additional fonts and DAs without changing your System.

There are two general rules to be aware of when switching startup disks:

- The system you're switching *to* must be the same or a later version than the one you're switching *from*.

- You can't switch *out of* MultiFinder, only *into* it.

To switch Systems (and remember—that means you're switching startup disks, because you *never* keep two Systems on the same disk), either open the system folder on the disk you want to switch to, hold down [Option] and [⌘] [,] and doubleclick on the Finder icon, or just hold down [Option] and doubleclick on any application on that disk. (Sometimes simply launching any application on the second disk switches systems, but not always; hold down [Option] to be sure.)

✎ *setting the startup application*

There's a Set Startup command in the desktop's Special menu that lets you set the Mac to start in the Finder or in MultiFinder, and with specific applications, documents and even desk accessories open.

Here's the basic Set Startup dialog box (it changes slightly depending on what you have running under MultiFinder and/or what you have selected on the desktop):

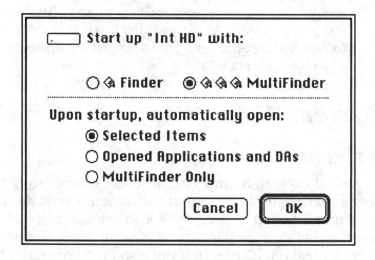

Here's how to use it:

- To choose between Finder and MultiFinder, click the appropriate button at the top of the dialog box. (The *MultiFinder* button will be dimmed if you don't have the MultiFinder file in your system folder.)

- If you want to start up at the desktop, click the *MultiFinder Only* button or the *Finder Only* button at the bottom of the dialog box—which one's available depends on which button you select at the top.

- To start up in an application, select its icon on the desktop, then choose *Set Startup*. Then just click on the button that will appear in the dialog box with the name of the application on it.

- To start up with two or more applications in MultiFinder, either select them on the desktop and click the *Selected Items* button that will appear in the Set Startup dialog box, or run the applications and click the button that's labeled *Opened Applications and DAs.* (This second method also lets you have DAs open automatically on startup; you must have them running as well.)

- To start up with particular documents opened, select them on the desktop and use the *Selected Items* button. Since opening a document automatically opens its application, you don't have to set the application as a startup. (When you use the *Opened Applications and DAs* button under MultiFinder, the documents you have open in the running applications are not set as startups.)

System 7

♦ System 7 vs. System 7.0 *(AN)*

Almost everybody says *system seven;* nobody says *system seven point oh.* But for some reason, everyone (but us) *writes* it *System 7.0.* And this is in spite of the fact that there will almost certainly be a System 7.01, a System 7.02, and so on, all of which will also incorporate the big changes that are coming in System 7.0. For both those reasons, we write it the way it's said—System 7.

♦ about System 7

things
to come

I expected to be writing tips for System 7 in one of the updates to the Second Edition of this book; then I expected to be rounding them up for this edition. But as I write this, System 7 is still months away, almost a year late (based on Apple's original announcements) and stripped of some of the features (like tear-off menus) that were originally planned.

Unlike many other Apple products, however, this version of the Mac's system software has been described in detail well before its release. So while we're not ready to do tips yet, we can explain some of the most important features you'll be seeing.

But first: do you *have* to switch to System 7? Absolutely not. In fact, unless you want to take advantage of some of the new features described below, you should wait until all the bugs are worked out of System 7. Apple will be supporting the 6.0x versions of the system software for at least another year, and probably for two.

● *what hardware you need*

System 7 will run on any computer from the Plus up that has at least two megs of RAM. But one of its features, virtual memory (described in an entry below), requires a PMMU chip. The PMMU is built into the 68030 chip and can be added to the original Mac II (which is built around the 68020 chip). You can even get virtual memory on a Plus, SE or Portable, by adding a 68020 accelerator card to it and then adding a PMMU chip to that.

● *Finder 7 and the new desktop*

With System 7, the Finder will finally live up to its name— it has a built-in Find function. Not only is the Find feature fast, it's also very sophisticated; for example, you can put key words in a file's comments box (in the Get Info window) and then search for files based on them. This doesn't just work on the desktop; applications will also be able to hook into these new capabilities to find documents much more quickly.

things to come

You'll be able to easily control the look of your Desktop; what now takes a program like Layout or a session with ResEdit is easily accomplished through dialog boxes, as shown at the top of the next page.

Finder 7 also introduces the *alias*: This is a copy of an icon that works just like the original—you can doubleclick on it to launch it, for example—but which takes up hardly any room on the disk (because it's just the icon that's copied, not the whole file). This means you can store a file in more than one place—for example, put WriteNow in a

folder with your other word processing applications, and also in a folder that holds a bunch of current WriteNow files you're working on.

very good feature

Another nifty new feature is *help balloons*. When you can't figure out what that odd-looking icon is for, or what a menu command does, you can ask for help and the balloon appears with appropriate information in it.

This is the kind of balloon we're talking about...

...not this kind

very good feature

The new Finder takes care of system folder clutter too; each *type* of system file—inits, cdevs, printer fonts, drivers, pref files, etc.—can be tucked into an appropriately named folder inside the system folder.

Another small but welcome enhancement in Finder 7 is being able to move through lists of files in windows on the desktop the same way you can in some list boxes—by typing the first letter of the filename you want. Finder 7 windows also scroll automatically when you move to the edge of them.

very good feature

Invisible improvements to the Finder make everything faster and let you have an unlimited number of files. (There's currently a limit on how many you can have.) But the main difference is that, under System 7, you're always in Multi-Finder; you can't run just in the Finder.

🍎 the 🍎 menu

Adding a desk accessory to the 🍎 menu will be as easy as dragging its file into the system folder. And, for easy launching, putting an application into the system folder puts *it* in the 🍎 menu too.

very good feature

🍎 *TrueType fonts*

Apple's new outline font technology—called TrueType—arrives with System 7. (For more about outline fonts, see Chapter 7.) TrueType fonts produce smooth characters in any size, on both the screen and printer (and that means *any* printer—dot-matrix, non-PostScript, whatever).

things to come

Apple plans to ship TrueType versions of the fonts it currently ships with the Mac, and possibly a few more. But they've made the TrueType specifications public so that third-party vendors can provide a wide variety of choices. (Apple's saying that hundreds of fonts in TrueType format will be available in the first few months of System 7's life. They ought to know.)

🍎 *new printing approaches*

System 7 includes something called New Print Architecture. This provides background printing for all printers and increases printing speed. It can also take the color Quick-Draw commands that Mac applications generate and translate them into color PostScript commands, or halftone color images for output on black-and-white printers.

There's also a new approach in the Print dialog box, with popup menus from which you can select the size of paper you're printing to.

🍎 sharing

things to come

Macintosh FileShare is a new capability that will let Macs talk to each other on a network without having to use a file server as an intermediary (and without using third-party software like TOPS or Public Folder).

There's also IAC *(interapplication communication)*, which includes PPC *(program-to-program communication)*. What all this alphabet soup means is that programs can exchange commands and data. PPC will even store data for a program that's not running, and then pass the message on when the program is launched.

The Clipboard lets you take information from one place and put it in another, but that's a one-way process and provides no link between the source document and the target document. System 7 has two new features called Publish and Subscribe that let you link documents through an intermediary file, so that when the original material is updated, the information you pasted into the second document is changed too. If, for instance, you've pasted a table of figures from a spreadsheet into a word processor document and then change the spreadsheet, the word processor document gets updated, too.

When you select part of a document and choose the *Publish* command (from the Edit menu), a dialog box appears so you can specify where to save the selection and what to call it. These saved files are called *publications* (guaranteed to confuse PageMaker users, at least initially) and appear as icons on the desktop.

When you're in another document (created by the same or a different application), the *Subscribe* command (also on the Edit menu) lets you incorporate any publication into what you're working on. It's easy to have multiple subscribers to a publication, even across a network. Individual subscribers can choose to be updated automatically when the publication's been changed, or ask that they be notified whenever a change has been made, so they can decide at that point whether or not to update the material in their documents.

Unlike most System 7 enhancements, which are automatically available to existing applications, Publish and Subscribe techniques will be available only to programs that are specifically designed to include them.

⍟ *expanded memory limits*

Currently, the Mac is limited to eight megabytes of RAM, but a new feature of System 7, called *32-bit addressing*, ups the limit to four *gigabytes* (almost 4100 megs). 32-bit addressing is available only on 68020 and 68030 machines— which means the SE/30 and the various Mac II's.

very good feature

Applications that have followed Apple's guidelines for developers will be able to make use of this extra memory right away; those that haven't will still run under System 7 but won't be "aware" that there's any memory available beyond eight megs. Which brings us to...

⍟ *virtual memory*

Virtual memory is a technique that uses disk space as if it were RAM (for more about it, see the end of Chapter 3). The main advantage of virtual memory is that disk space is always cheaper than RAM—even with RAM prices at an all-time low. You can currently get a one-meg SIMM for as little as $60, but some of the hard disks discussed in Chapter 3 provide disk space for $10/meg, or even less.

very good feature

As mentioned above, System 7 makes virtual memory available to any machine with a 68030 processor, to a Mac II with a PMMU chip added, or to a Plus or SE with a 68020 accelerator card to which a PMMU has been added.

MultiFinder tips

♦ MultiFinder basics

esp. for beginners

MultiFinder lets you run several programs at a time, one of them being the Finder (so you always have the desktop in the background, even if you can't see it on a small screen). The more memory you have, the more you can do in MultiFinder. You need at least two megs to really take advantage of its power; with a one-meg system, you can only run the Finder and one other program that doesn't require much memory.

To run under MultiFinder, you need to do two things: put the MultiFinder file in your system folder and set MultiFinder as the startup application (see the previous entry for details). Once you're in MultiFinder, a small icon appears at the far right end of the menu bar; it represents the application you're currently in. For example, when you're in the Finder, the icon is a mini-Mac:

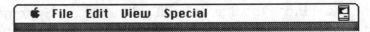

Under MultiFinder, each program you run gets its own *partition*—a portion of memory that belongs to only that program. Every program comes with a default partition assigned to it, but sometimes the program will tell you it isn't large enough. You can fix that by changing the size of the partition.

To do that, quit the application, select its icon on the desktop and *Get Info* on it. The Get Info box will list a *Suggested Memory Size* and an *Application Memory Size;* unless you've changed the latter, they'll be the same. All you have to do is make the Application Memory Size larger as shown in the figure at the top of the next page.

If your initial guess isn't big enough, repeat the process until you get it right. At some later point, when you're trying to squeeze more applications into existing memory, you may want to make the Application Memory Size smaller

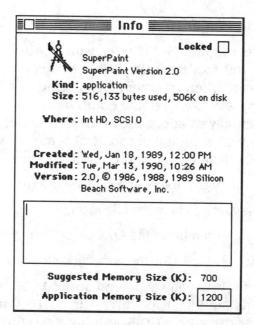

again. But never go lower than the Suggested Memory Size, since that's the minimum for safe operation.

**important
warning**

The *About the Finder* from the menu dialog box changes when you're running MultiFinder. It not only shows the memory allocated to the System and Finder but also to each program that's running, as well as how much of each partition is full (this illustration is slightly doctored—in the real dialog box, you can only see four bars at a time):

⚫ when the Finder runs out of room

If you're running MultiFinder with a 40-meg or larger hard disk, you may run into a *Not enough Finder memory* error message when you open lots of windows, have lots of items in any window, or some combination of the two. The Finder is actually an application that runs under MultiFinder and, like any other program, can be allocated more memory. To give your desktop more breathing room:

- Open the system folder and click on the Finder icon.
- Choose *Get Info* from the File menu.
- Change the number in the Application Memory Size box.
- Restart the Mac so the memory allocation takes effect.

The Finder is usually allocated about 165K as a default. 210K seems sufficient for drives up to 100 megs. If you use a larger drive or a CD-ROM player, you may need an even larger segment. (You don't have to restart the Mac when you change the memory allocation of any other application, but the Finder runs as soon as you start the Mac, so you do have to restart in this case.)

Another approach, which you can combine with this one or use on its own, is to partition your drive and mount only the partitions you're using at any one time. For more on that, see *partitioning* in Chapter 3.

⚫ memory fragmentation in MultiFinder (SZA/AN)

The first program you launch under MultiFinder gets the first chunk of available RAM, the second gets the next chunk, and so on. When you quit a program, the RAM it used doesn't get thrown back into the pool of available RAM—instead, it leaves a hole of empty memory between the program launched before it and the one launched after it. (Only if it was the *last* program you launched does the memory go back into the pool).

Notice that the dialog box at the end of the previous entry reports not how much memory is still available, but the *largest unused block*. If you were to quit Word, the largest unused block would still be 1508K; although you'd actually have over 3000K of memory free, you wouldn't be able to launch PageMaker (which needs a 1700K allocation) because you'd have only two *separate* chunks of 1500K memory available.

To get around these limitations, always begin by launching the program you use the most, and are therefore least likely to quit. Second, launch the program you use the next most, and are therefore the next least likely to quit. And so on.

why I don't use MultiFinder (AN)

Certain Mac jocks with serious cases of expertosis would have you believe that you've got to be some sort of Luddite, or have a serious learning disability, not to use MultiFinder. The fact is, lots of very experienced power users won't go near it.

For one thing, it's still buggy. You can depend on getting twice as many crashes in MultiFinder as you'll get, with exactly the same system and applications, using just the Finder. And that's not the worst of it. Here's why Charlie Rubin stopped using MultiFinder:

bug

He was working on two documents, a Works spreadsheet and a Word document. He finished his day's work, saved both files and went to bed. The next day, when he opened the Word file, he found that data and garbage characters (probably formatting codes) from the Works spreadsheet had been written over part of the Word file—that is, the words that had been in the Word file the night before were gone and the stuff from the Works file was there in their place.

bug

When Charlie called Microsoft, they denied that this is a problem (their typical response to this sort of thing), but when he called a large user group in his area, they confirmed that several other people had reported the same problem to them.

Now think of it: in the very act of saving to protect your work, that work is destroyed. That was enough for Charlie to kiss MultiFinder goodbye.

Another problem with MultiFinder is that you have to think about how much memory to give each program you're running, and adjust it if it's not right. A related problem is that you'll need more memory on your machine to use MultiFinder effectively than you will to use the same programs one at a time under the Finder. Finally, the memory fragmentation that results when you open and close applications (described in an entry above) is a real pain.

Sure, there are times in my work when it would be nice to be able to jump from one program to another without having to go back to the desktop. But as far as I'm concerned, there aren't enough of those times to make using MultiFinder worth the worry and trouble.

🍎 switching to MultiFinder

shortcut

If you're running in Finder-only mode, you don't have to set the startup and restart the Mac to go into MultiFinder; instead, simply open the system folder, hold down [Option] ⌘ and doubleclick on the MultiFinder icon.

🍎 moving around in MultiFinder

There are three basic ways to move from one opened application to another in MultiFinder. One is to click on the little icon at the right end of the menu bar; the icon will change as you cycle through all the programs you have open. Another is to select the application's name from the 🍎 menu (all the opened programs are listed there).

shortcut

The third way only works if you're on the desktop and can see the application's icon (it will be gray, because the application is running, just as the icon for an open disk, folder or file is dimmed). To move to that application, just doubleclick on its icon.

There are also utilities that let you launch and switch applications. They're covered in Chapter 8.

♦ *opening multiple applications*

Even if you don't set multiple applications to start up automatically, you can open several at the same time (as opposed to one after the other). Just click on the first application you want, shift-click on the others and then doubleclick on any one of them, or choose *Open...* from the File menu. (For this to work, the applications have to be in the same window, because you can't shift-click between windows.)

shortcut

♦ *temporarily disabling MultiFinder*

If MultiFinder is the startup and you want for some reason to disable it, hold down the ⌘ key as the Mac starts up. This forces the Finder to take over, but leaves MultiFinder still set for startup the next time.

♦ *shutting down with applications open* (AN)

If you choose *Shut Down* from the Finder's Special menu while in MultiFinder with other applications open, you'll get the standard *Save changes...?* dialog box for all open documents (a piece of idiot-proofing of which idiots like myself heartily approve).

♦ *the right edge*

Here's a MultiFinder housekeeping tip: move the right edges of your application windows in a little from the right edge of the screen. Otherwise, you'll find that when you're in the Finder, you won't be able to get to the disk icons or the Trash (you'll have to click on the offending windows, thus activating them and putting you back in their applications, just so you can move them out of the way).

very hot tip

♦ *no auto-empty for Trash*

When you're in MultiFinder, launching an application by doubleclicking on its icon empties the Trash. But using a launching utility like On Cue doesn't, and neither does moving to an already-opened application.

♦ getting DAs out of the way

shortcut

If you've used Suitcase or Font/DA Juggler to cram your ♦ menu full of desk accessories, it can be a real drag to scroll through all of them to get the applications listed at the bottom of the menu. To make all the DAs (except Suitcase or Juggler itself) temporarily disappear, hold down the [Option] key when you open the ♦ menu.

♦ making DAs application-specific

Some DAs add their own menus to the menu bar. If you only want that to happen in certain applications, you can assign the DAs to specific applications under MultiFinder. You do that by holding down the [Option] key while you choose the DA from the ♦ menu.

From then on, that DA will appear only when you're working in the application you were in at the time you opened it (although it's still in the ♦ menu no matter where you're working). Quitting or closing the DA as usual while you're in that application is all it takes to remove it from the menu bar.

There's another advantage to this: it lets the DA use the memory already set aside for the application, instead of having to carve out an additional chunk for itself from the portion set aside for all DAs to share.

At first glance, it would seem that you can't use this trick when you're using Suitcase or Font/DA Juggler, since both programs hide the DAs on the ♦ menu when you hold down [Option]. But there's a way around this. Just pop down the ♦ menu without pressing [Option], *then* press [Option] and choose the DA you want to assign.

(You can also actually install a DA into an application so it only appears in the ♦ menu when that application's running; see the Font/DA Mover section of the utilities chapter.)

♦ if your DAs have disappeared

very hot tip

If you just started using MultiFinder and find that there's little or nothing under your ♦ menu—or that you can't open anything that appears in the menu (all you get is a beep)—you need to put *DA Handler* file into your system folder. It's on the System Tools disk; just copy it over and restart your system.

Global software tips

The tips in this section should work in virtually all Macintosh programs, from the desktop to obscure DAs. If they don't, don't blame us; blame the people who wrote the program, because they're not following the standard Mac interface.

♦ shift-clicking *(Steve Michel/SZA/AN)*

Normally, when you click on something to select it, the thing you selected last is automatically deselected. But if you hold the Shift key down, the previously selected items stay selected.

esp. for
beginners

This technique, called *shift-clicking,* can be very useful. Let's say you want to copy a dozen files from one folder to another. Instead of having to select one, drag it, select another, drag it, and so on, you just select all dozen by shift-clicking on each one, and drag them all at once.

Shift-clicking usually acts as a *toggle,* so that not only do things that aren't selected get selected, but things that *are* selected get *de*selected when you shift-click on them.

There's another way to select multiple objects—by dragging a *selection rectangle* around them (described in the *Guide for beginners* section of Chapter 1). You can combine the two techniques. For example, if objects you *don't* want fall into the selection rectangle, just shift-click on them and they'll be deselected. Here's another way to combine them:

Let's say you have a single icon selected in a desktop window. If you hold down Shift while you drag a rectangle around four other icons, you'll have five icons selected when you're done. It also works the other way. If you have

esp. for beginners

ten icons selected in a desktop window and then hold down Shift while you drag a rectangle around four of them, they'll deselect and you'll end up with six icons selected.

All these techniques work the same way in object-oriented graphics programs like MacDraw or the Draw layer of SuperPaint as they do on the desktop. (They don't work in paint programs because there are no objects to shift-click on.)

Shift-clicking can also be used to select portions of continuous material like text. Let's say you want to select three paragraphs of a word processing document. You'd click in front of the first character in the first paragraph, then place the I-beam pointer after the last character of the third paragraph, hold the Shift key down and click again. This causes everything between the two clicks—all three paragraphs, in this case—to be selected. (Some word processors have easier ways to select a lot of text, but this basic technique should work in all of them.)

After you've selected a hunk of text, you can use shift-clicking to deselect some of it (in other words, make your selection smaller without having to do it all over again) or to extend the selection. As long as you hold the Shift key down, each subsequent click will select text from the original click to the latest shift-click. To start at a new beginning point, just click without the Shift key down.

So to make a text selection smaller, simply shift-click anywhere within it. Only the portion from the beginning of the selection to your latest shift-click will remain selected.

To extend a selection, position the I-beam at either the beginning or end of the selected text, hold down the Shift key, click and drag in the appropriate direction. (You can only do this at one end or the other, not both.)

(There's more about shift-clicking text in the *General word processing tips* section of Chapter 10.)

Shift-clicking works in spreadsheets too. If you click in one cell, then shift-click in another, a rectangle of cells will be selected, with those two cells in the corners (it will be a thin rectangle if both clicks are in one column or one row, but a rectangle nevertheless).

Some dialog boxes let you shift-click to make more than one selection at a time from a list box. Usually shift-clicking already selected items in the list deselects them, but some-times it selects everything from the initial selection to the new one (and shift-clicking *within* the selected area short-ens the selection to that spot in the click).

Some of these techniques may be a little hard to visual-ize as we describe them with words, but when you use them a bit, they'll quickly become obvious, and then au-tomatic.

✦ *the doubleclick drag*

To select text word-by-word, doubleclick on the first word, keep the mouse button down and drag. The selection will be extended one word at a time.

✦ *cancelling shortcut (AN)*

In most places on the Mac, ⌘ . will cancel what you're doing (printing, for example). It will also push the *Cancel* button in most dialog boxes. We've mentioned this short-cut elsewhere (because there are so many places where it works), but it's worth repeating (because there *are* so many places where it works).

✦ *the Esc key*

The Esc (for *escape)* key on ADB keyboards works, in most instances, as a substitute for ⌘ .—to cancel print-ing, for example. It usually also pushes the *Cancel* button in dialog boxes. (One exception I know of—in More II's Save As dialog box, the *Cancel* button highlights when you press Esc, but a missing character box is printed in the text field and the dialog box remains on the screen.)

✦ *deselecting with arrow keys*

In almost all applications, hitting ↑ or ← while text is selected places the insertion point at the beginning of the

shortcut

selection and deselects the text. Using ⬇ or ➡ does the same, but puts the insertion point at the end of the selection. This can save you some time. Let's say you've selected some text and made it boldface. Instead of having to go to your mouse again so you can click at the end of the selection to begin typing again, you can just hit ➡. This will deselect the text and position the insertion point directly after it.

This works even in dialog boxes, where you often have some default text selected when the box opens. It's especially convenient in the Save As dialog box that usually comes up with the current title of a document already highlighted. If you want to name the new document something similar to the original (like changing *Title* to *Title2*), you don't have to retype the original name. Just hit ➡, then add what you want to the end of the document name.

🍎 *global nudge commands*

*very
hot
tip*

SuperPaint's nudge commands, that move objects by one pixel, should be part of every object-oriented program. But since they're not, you can make your own, using Apple's Easy Access (whose other features are described in Chapter 8). With Easy Access in your system folder, you can turn it on any time and control the mouse with the numeric keypad.

To nudge an object on the screen:

• Select the object.

• Position the pointer on top of it.

• Press [Shift][⌘][Clear] to activate Mouse Keys.

• Press [0] on the keypad to lock down the mouse button.

• Use [2], [4], [6] and [8], on the keypad to move the object a pixel at a time down, left, right or up.

When you're done, press [Shift][⌘][Clear] again to turn off Mouse Keys.

♦ using templates to change defaults *(Michael Bradley/DC)*

All applications have default settings for things like font and type size, ruler, print quality, spreadsheet size and data format. Sometimes you can change the defaults, but often you can't. This means every new document will always start out formatted the standard way, whether you like it or not. If you don't like it, you should try using templates to format new documents the way you want them.

*very
hot
tip*

A *template* is a document with a special format that you use repeatedly—for example, one containing your letterhead, so you don't have to recreate the letterhead every time you want to write a letter. They're easy to make. All you have to do is open a new document and choose the formatting you want. When you're done, save the document with a name like *biz ltr, memo* or *standard Excel template.* There's no limit to how many different kinds of templates you can make.

To format a new document like one of your templates, don't use the *New...* command on the File menu. Instead, open the template and immediately save it with the name you want to give your new document (*Save As...* on the File menu). This automatically transfers the template's formatting to the new document.

Because of the way templates are used, they run a special risk of being overwritten. You can avoid this risk by locking them (in the Get Info box). This will prevent you from saving a modified template under the original name and will force you into the correct habit—always Saving As as soon as you open the template.

If you need to change the template itself, it's easy enough to unlock it. But don't forget to lock it again when you've finished making changes to it.

♦ beeps and other sounds *(AN/DC)*

The Mac's basic warning sound is a *beep* (it usually means *you can't do that here).* You can control how loud it is in

esp. for
beginners

the Control Panel. Setting the volume all the way to zero turns the beep off completely (the menu bar flashes instead). You can also block the sound port at the back of the Mac with a mini-jack that you can buy at any electronics store, or with Walkman-style earphones.

The current system software lets you change the beep to three other sounds. To do that, you open the Control Panel and select the Sound icon from the column on the left (you may have to scroll down to get to it). Then you can choose a monkey's screech, a clink-klank (which sounds just like its name) or the aptly named boing, which sounds a lot like Gerald McBoing Boing's favorite sound.

Arthur favors the boing, because it's the funniest and also the softest. That means he can set Speaker Volume to 7, so he can hear music and sound effects nice and loud but still not be startled by loud beeps while he's working. (The Simple Beep is the loudest of the four sounds; Clink-Klank is next, followed by Monkey.)

You can install many more choices for beep sounds with a piece of $10 shareware called SoundMaster, which is described in Chapter 8.

Miscellaneous desktop tips

♦ *easy launching of applications* (AN)

shortcut

In the previous section, we talked about using templates to change a program's defaults. But templates have another important use—making it easy to launch applications.

It's hard to leave applications out near the *root level* (the window of your hard disk) because they often demand folders of their own with dictionaries and all kinds of other stuff with them. My solution is to bury the application as deep as I like, in some folder filed logically away (a *Nisus* folder within a *word processors* folder within a *misc programs* folder, say), but to keep a template for each program I commonly use in a *common templates* folder.

I put a space in front of the name *common templates,* so that it will sort to the top of any list, and I put it right at the root level (that is, the only window it's in is the one for the hard disk I'm running off of). I usually leave the *common templates* folder open on the desktop as well, so its contents are just sitting there, waiting for me to doubleclick on them.

To launch the program, I just doubleclick on its template. If I don't actually want to create a new document, I simply close the template when it opens and proceed with my other work (opening a buried document, say, or import a text document into the program). It only takes a second or two longer (if that) to open an application and a template than it does to open an application with its Untitled window.

You're not restricted to one template per program, of course. My common templates folder contains three different Nisus letterheads, one nonletterhead Nisus template, a horizontal and a vertical Claris CAD template, an Excel template, three PageMaker templates (one-page, two-page and horizontal)—not to mention a bunch of documents that actually have a lot of contents, like my to-do list (in Nisus) and my address and phone number list (in Dynodex), but which qualify as templates because they're constantly being modified.

✍ Trash options

There are three things you can't throw away without some extra effort: applications, locked files and files in use. With applications, you get a dialog box asking if you *really* want to throw it away. With locked or in-use files, you get a dialog box telling you you're not allowed to throw out the file.

You can't get rid of files that are in use, but you can throw out locked files; just hold [Option] while you drag them to the Trash.

✍ emptying the trash

A file isn't deleted from the disk just because you've placed it in the Trash (on current systems, you can see that this is the case, because the trash can bulges whenever there are items in it).

You can use the *Empty Trash* command from the Special menu to empty it, but there are also five ways to flush the Trash automatically:

- launch an application by doubleclicking its icon on the desktop

- copy a file to or from the disk that the trashed file came from

- duplicate a file on the disk that the trashed file came from

- eject the disk that the file came from

- shut down the system

There is one thing that doesn't hang around in the Trash—an empty folder. When you drag it to the Trash, it disappears immediately.

¢ retrieving files from the Trash

shortcut

As long as the Trash hasn't been emptied, you can take things back out of it. Doubleclick to open the Trash window and drag out whatever you want to rescue. If you select any item(s) in the Trash window and choose *Put Away* from the File menu, the files will zip back into the folders that they originally came from. *(Put Away* also works for any files left loose on the desktop itself.)

¢ escaping from switch-disks nightmares

(Michael Bradley/SZA)

*very
hot
tip*

To escape from one of those interminable switch-disks nightmares (the kind that make you want to scream at your Mac, *You want that disk again? There's something sick about your obsession with that disk!*), press ⌘ . . Sometimes you have to press it more than once and sometimes it won't work at all—but it's worth trying.

❖ why Shut Down is important

Using the *Shut Down* command from the Special menu instead of just shutting off the power is important because it allows the Mac to write any information it's holding in memory to disk (you may think it's already there, but it's probably not).

**important
warning**

Global and desktop macros

❖ basic terms

A *macro* is a command that incorporates two or more other commands or actions. For more about them, how they work, and the various programs that make them, see the *Macro programs* section of Chapter 8.

**esp. for
beginners**

Most of the macros we present throughout this book are what I call *LCD macros* (for *lowest common denominator)*—watch-me recordings that you can make and play back with the simplest macro utilities, like Apple's MacroMaker. They should work in any macro program that lets you make recordings.

There are lots of macros you can create to speed up operations on the desktop. *Global* macros work no matter where you are, on the desktop or in any application.

❖ basic macros for Finder commands

Many commands on menus in the Finder don't have keyboard equivalents, but you can assign them ones with any macro utility. Just start recording a macro, choose the menu command, stop the recording and assign whatever keys you want to the macro.

**very
hot
tip**

Some commands have to be active in order for you to make the macro; others, like *Print*, don't have to be (you can select the greyed *Print* command when making the macro and it will work later, when you have something selected that can be printed). Some commands can't be recorded at all with MacroMaker—*Set Startup*, for example, puts you in a dialog box that doesn't let you access MacroMaker's *Stop Recording* command.

shortcut

It's important to plan ahead when assigning keystrokes to macros, to prevent conflicts and to make remembering the keystrokes easier. Here are some suggestions:

File and Edit menus:

Print	⌘ P
Put Away	⌘ Y
Clear	⌘ B

View menu:

by Small Icon	Shift ⌘ M
by Icon	Shift ⌘ I
by Name	Shift ⌘ N
by Date	Shift ⌘ D
by Size	Shift ⌘ S
by Kind	Shift ⌘ K
by Color	Shift ⌘ C

Special menu:

Clean Up	⌘ U
Restart	⌘ R
Shut Down	⌘ T

⌘ P is currently assigned to Get Privileges, but how often do you use that command? Even though the ⌘ P will still show in the menu next to the Privileges command, macro commands take precedence over menu commands, and ⌘ P will execute the Print command.

You're better off if you *don't* assign keyboard equivalents to the Empty Trash or Erase Disk commands. Neither is a command you want to give by accident and the extra effort of using the menu helps avoid mistakes. *(Personally, I'd say the same thing about Restart and Shut Down.—AN)*

important warning

The macro you make by recording the *Clean Up* command plays back as *Clean Up Window* or *Clean Up Selection*—whichever is in the menu when you use the macro. A better approach is to hold Option down when you choose the *Clean Up* command; that gives you the all-purpose command that cleans up the whole window even if something in it is selected (there's more on these commands in the windows section above).

very hot tip

switching applications in MultiFinder

Of all my simple-but-useful macros, these are the most useful; they switch me to specific applications running under MultiFinder. All you have to do is record yourself choosing whichever application you want to switch to from the menu. If you use Suitcase or Juggler, use Option to get to the application names without scrolling through all the DAs—the Option press will be included in the macro.

shortcut

(If you use this macro in MacroMaker and the application isn't open, you'll wind up with a desk accessory pulled out instead. Programs like Tempo can read the actual name on the menu, rather than just record its position, and they'll tell you they can't find what they're looking for.)

I use Ctrl for these application-switching macros, followed by a letter that indicates the application. If you're not using an ADB keyboard with the Ctrl key, you can use some special combination like Shift Option ⌘.

Remember to store the switching macros under Global macros so they're always available, no matter what program you're working in; and, remember to include the Finder as one of the switching macros, so you can get back to it when you want.

♦ taking out desk accessories

shortcut

It's a good idea to assign a macro key combination for each of the desk accessories you use often. I use [Caps Lock] as the modifier key for DA selections because it's awkward (you have to unlock it after you use it) and I don't want to use it for macros that I need constantly; at the same time, it doesn't interfere with any other global or application-specific key assignments. I also just use numbers for each DA because I know which ones I use the most—[Caps Lock][1] is the Phone Pad, [Caps Lock][2] is the Calendar and so on.

If you do more than just open a desk accessory each time you use it, consider recording your next step as part of the macro. For example, when I pull out the Phone Pad, the first thing I do is hit [⌘][F] because I want to find a name or other piece of information. MacroMaker won't let you do this specific macro because you can't stop the recording while a dialog box is on the screen, but Tempo lets me record both the selection from the ♦ menu and the [⌘][F] sequence.

Another two-step example—possible with MacroMaker—is the way I use the Clipper (reviewed in the Clipboard section earlier in this chapter). The first thing I do each time I take out the Clipper is to paste the current Clipboard contents into it, so my Clipper macro incorporates both the ♦ menu selection and [⌘][V].

♦ a macro that closes all windows

*very
hot
tip*

Holding down [Option] while clicking in a close box closes all the windows on the desktop. But you can't record a macro for this, since the window whose close box you click on won't always be in the same place when you play back the macro. Instead, record yourself choosing *Close* from the File menu while [Option] is down (which makes the command appear as *Close All* on the menu.)

I use [⌘][Option][W] for this macro because [⌘][W] is used as the *Close* command in so many applications and because you need the [Option] key on the desktop to close all the windows.

⬥ *a macro for opening disk icons*

Disk icons appear in specific places on the desktop. The startup disk is always in the upper right corner, the next disk is below it, and so on until there's no room left in that column; then the next disk appears to the left of the startup disk and on down in that column. Because of this predictable arrangement, you can create macros that open specific disks by recording doubleclicks on the spots where their icons appear.

When you record these macros, assign ⌘1 to the startup disk, ⌘2 to the next and so on. I use ⌘0 (that's the zero key) for opening the Trash, but Arthur suggests ⌘- (command-minus).

⬥ *closing everything but the disk window*

Many times, you'll want to clean up your desktop by closing everything except the main window—the one for the hard disk you're running off of (this macro is pretty unnecessary on a floppy system). To do that, just string together the macros in the previous two windows. (You can record previously-created macros as part of a new macro.)

shortcut

Assuming you've followed my recommendations in the last two entries, all you have to do to make the new macro is record ⌘ Option W, then ⌘1. You can also make macros that close everything and then open just the second disk, or just the third. Recommended keys: ⌘ Option 1, ⌘ Option 2 and so on for the different disks.

⬥ *date stamp*

If you have the Alarm Clock accessory in your ⬥ menu, you can create a macro that pastes the current date into any document you're working on. Record:

- Choose *Alarm Clock* from the ⬥ menu.
- Press ⌘C for Copy.
- Close the Alarm Clock.

- Press ⌘ V for Paste.
- Press ← 7 times.
- Press Delete 12 times.
- Press → 7 times.

Because the Alarm Clock puts both the time and date on the Clipboard, the ←/→ operations move the insertion point through the date to erase the time, and back through the date again so your insertion point is after the date again so you can continue typing.

Make sure you store this as a Global macro, so it's available no matter what application you're in.

🍎 *Control Panel settings*

shortcut

If you change certain Control Panel settings with any regularity, you can record macros to do it for you. The Control Panel macros I use are for changing the monitor display from black-and-white to color and vice versa, and three for adjusting the sound volume (off, minimum or medium).

If what you're changing is in the General settings in the Control Panel, there's not much of a problem—the Panel comes up each time with General information display. But if you record macros for other Control parts of the Control Panel (like Monitors, say), you'll have to click on the icon in the left-hand column first, If you add or remove items from the Control Panel, the position of the icons in the left-hand column will change, and you'll have to redo the macro.

Chapter 7

Fonts

Font basics

🍎 *what is a font?* (AN)

In regular typesetting, a *font* is a particular typeface in a particular size and a particular style (bold, italic, etc.) On the Mac, however, *font* has come to mean a typeface in every size and every style (what a regular typesetter calls *a type family*).

esp. for beginners

For example, Geneva comes supplied in six sizes and, on the ImageWriter, it can be transformed into sixteen different type styles (bold, italic and so on; see the entry below on font styles for details). A regular typesetter would call that 96 different fonts; to a Mac user, it's all one font—Geneva.

With the introduction of laser printers, which much more closely approximate regular typesetting, there's a move on to bring the two terminologies closer together. In the glossary of one of the LaserWriter manuals, for example, the definition for *font* is followed by one for *font family—a font in various sizes and styles.*

But I think Mac users have gotten too used to their own meaning of the word to be pushed back into line with the old terminology. When you change the size or style of some type, you don't think of it as changing the font. So, throughout this book, *font* is used in the classic Mac sense: a typeface in every size and style.

🍎 *some basic font terms* (SZA/AN)

- *Monospaced* fonts, like Monaco and Courier, give all characters an equal amount of horizontal space—an *i*, for example, gets as much room on a line as an *m*, even though the character itself may only be a third as wide. This is the way typewriters (and inferior computers) handle letters and numbers. *Proportional spacing* gives characters different amounts of horizontal space, depending on their actual widths.

esp. for beginners

- *Baseline, cap height, ascender, descender* and *x-height* are easier to show than describe:

- *Leading* (pronounced *LEDD-ing*) is also called *line spacing*—it's the distance from the baseline of one line of text to the baseline of the next. (In typesetting, it's actually the *extra* distance added to the spacing, but that meaning is dying out, and *leading* is coming to mean exactly the same thing as *line spacing.)*

**gossip/
trivia**

- Both leading and the size of a font are measured in *points* (both on the Mac and in regular typesetting). Points are 72nds of an inch. (Actually, to be more precise, a point is .0138″ and a 72nd of an inch rounds to .01389″. But since the difference between them is less than one ten-thousandth of an inch, the distinction is…well…pointless.)

- *Kerning* is adjusting the horizontal space between letters. Normally, each letter lives in its own little rectangle and letters on either side of it don't encroach on its space. But type is easier to read, and looks better, when certain letter combinations nestle into each other—like a lowercase vowel tucked under the overhang of a capital T, or the letters in the following illustration:

WAVE   WAVE
Normal spacing   *Kerned letters*

- *Serif* fonts have little hooks, lines or blobs added to the basic form of their characters; *sans serif* fonts have none (*sans* is French for *without).*

The   The
Serif   *Sans Serif*

▲ *bit-mapped, outline, screen and printer fonts* (AN)

Every Mac comes equipped with fonts designed for printing on non-PostScript laser printers like the LaserWriter SC, dot-matrix printers like the ImageWriter, ink-jet printers, and so on. They're called *bit-mapped fonts*, because they're made up of dots. Bit-mapped fonts are also what's used on the Mac's screen; one example is Chicago, the font used on menus and in dialog boxes.

*esp. for
beginners*

You install bit-mapped fonts with Font DA/Mover. They either go directly into your System file or into *suitcases* (described below), which are then activated by programs like Suitcase or Font/DA Juggler (described in Chapter 8). Wherever you put them, fonts are said to be *installed,* or *available,* when they show up on an application's font menus.

There are 72 dots per inch in the characters that make up a bit-mapped font—or, to put it a different way, bit-mapped fonts have a *resolution* of 72 dpi. (It's no coincidence that the standard Mac screen also has a resolution of 72 dpi.)

Although designed for the screen and the ImageWriter, bit-mapped fonts will also print out on laser printers, but not as attractively as *outline fonts,* those designed specifically for that purpose.

The characters in outline fonts aren't made up of dots— they're composed of instructions for forming an outline of each character, which is then filled in. The instructions are usually in a programming language called PostScript, which was specifically designed to handle text and graphics and their placement on a page. For this reason, outline fonts are also known as *PostScript* fonts, although some outline fonts don't use PostScript—they use QuickDraw or something else (for an example, see the next entry).

Technically, not all PostScript fonts are outline fonts. For example, when you send a bit-mapped font to a PostScript printer, a special, bit-mapped PostScript version of it is created. (How good it looks depends on the ratio of the size you're printing to the size you have installed. A ratio of four to one is ideal—a 48-point bit-mapped font installed to print at 12-point, for example.) But when people speak of a PostScript font, they're virtually always referring to an outline font, not to one of these recreations of bit-mapped fonts.

(Some font publishers provide *EPS outlines* of their fonts—graphics of individual characters that you can manipulate in programs like Freehand or Illustrator. Don't confuse these with *outline fonts*; they're entirely separate from the font itself.)

The Mac's screen can't display outline fonts directly, so each outline font comes in two parts. The actual PostScript instructions that get sent to the printer are called the *printer font.* Then there's a bit-mapped font that's used to represent the font on the screen, and which is therefore called a *screen font.*

Like any bit-mapped font, a screen font will print out on dot-matrix printers like the ImageWriter, but it won't look a whole lot like the actual printer font does when printed on a PostScript printer—both because of the lower resolution and because the person who designed the screen font knew it was only going to be used as an approximation for the screen, and therefore probably didn't spend a lot of time fine-tuning it for printing.

[Most writers and publications don't make the distinction between screen fonts, as Arthur defines them here, and other bit-mapped fonts; they just use screen font *as a synonym for* bit-mapped font. *I prefer our approach, but you should be aware of the common usage.—SZA]*

When you send a printer font to a PostScript laser printer or *imagesetter* (a digital typesetting machine that can also handle graphics), the printer reads the instructions and then draws the characters in as much detail—as high a resolution—as it's capable of. (For some comparative printer resolutions, see the second entry in Chapter 4.) Sending an outline font to a printer is called *downloading* it, and that gives us the final alias for this kind of font—*downloadable.*

For more information on which fonts are the right ones to use on various kinds of printers, see the entry title *which fonts for which printer* in Chapter 4.

🍎 *Apple's outline fonts*

With System 7 (described in Chapter 6), Apple will intro- duce—or has introduced, depending on when you're read- ing this—its own outline-font technology. Called TrueType, this new kind of outline font is supposed to provide both high-quality screen display and terrific-looking printing— on dot-matrix as well as laser printers. (Well, OK, what it's *really* supposed to do is to break Adobe's stranglehold by introducing high-quality, non-PostScript fonts.)

things to come

It's too soon to list the pros and cons of this new technol- ogy and what it means to you. Just be aware that there are going to be conflicts and make sure that the fonts you're using are the ones your software and printer can handle.

🍎 *font styles* (AN)

On non-PostScript printers like the ImageWriter, every font can be made bold, italic, outline, shadow and any combination thereof—which amounts to sixteen possible combinations in all: bold italic, bold outline, bold shadow, italic outline, italic shadow, outline shadow, bold italic out- line, bold italic shadow, bold outline shadow, italic outline shadow, bold italic outline shadow and, of course, plain (which is called *Roman* in regular typesetting).

esp. for beginners

Some of these combinations may seem foolish to you, but it's not just a case of meaningless overkill—quite often one variation will have just the look you want and no other variation will be quite right. And you'll find that in another font, that particular variation will look terrible and a differ- ent one will be just right. (For an easy way to see them all, see the entry on font templates below.)

On laser printers, you don't get all sixteen variations; for example, it's common for outline shadow to look just the same as shadow. How many variations you get depends on the font, the application and/or the printer, At least one outline font—Zapf Chancery—has only three style variations: plain, outline and shadow.

As was mentioned in Chapter 4, there's an important distinction to be aware of when thinking about outline fonts. Sometimes italics and boldface type styles are separately designed by a human being; these are called *cuttings* (from the days when type was designed by carving blocks of wood). Other times, the computer *algorithmically* derives the type style—that is, it applies a formula like *increase the width 20%* (to create boldface) or *slant right 15°* (to create italic). This doesn't look as good, but it's better than nothing. (Type which is slanted algorithmically is usually called *oblique* rather than *italic.)*

✦ bit-mapped font sizes *(AN/SZA)*

Bit-mapped fonts come supplied in various sizes and, on dot-matrix printers like the ImageWriter, they should be used only in the sizes you have installed, or in halves or quarters of those sizes. *Scaling*—shrinking or enlarging—a bit-mapped font can result in some pretty horrendous characters.

Picture a bit-mapped character as a series of filled-in squares on a piece of graph paper; each square represents one *pixel* (one of the dots that make up the image on the screen). To double the size of the character, you'd take a larger area of the graph paper and color in four squares for every one that was filled in the original. To double the size again, you'd take every square in the second grid and fill in four on the third grid (so every square from the original grid is now represented by *sixteen* squares on the third grid).

The illustration shows the letter *P* being enlarged on just such a grid. (The smallest letter is actually using an grid that's half the size of the one shown—including all those lines in the illustration made the shape of the letter hard to see.)

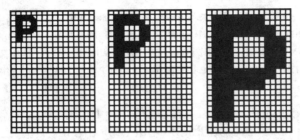

You can see that what was an acceptable curve in the small letter gets worse with each size increase, producing the dread *jaggies* (staircasing like that on the right side of the rightmost *P* above).

Scaling to a size that's not double, quadruple, half or a quarter the size of the original creates even more jaggies. It's not so bad if you're tripling the size, since each original square can translate into nine new filled squares, but let's say you're going from 12-point to 30-point (2.5 times bigger). You can't use half-squares (since each square on the grid represents a single pixel on the screen, and pixels are the smallest unit the screen can display). So each original filled square will sometimes get replaced by four squares (twice the original size) and sometimes by nine squares (three times the original size). This produces a mess:

11 point (not installed)

12 point (installed)

15 point (not installed)

18 point (installed)

20 point (not installed)

24 point (installed)

32 point (not)

esp. for beginners

The installed sizes of bit-mapped fonts (including screen fonts) are shown in outline type on the font size menu (which is sometimes part of the Font menu or another menu):

Size
9 Point
10 Point
12 Point
14 Point
18 Point
24 Point

On pop-up menus inside dialog boxes, no font sizes are outlined—but only the installed sizes are listed at all. (There's usually a text box where you can type in uninstalled sizes.) The illustration below shows Word's Character dialog box. The larger illustration on the right shows the sizes available for Geneva (yes, it really is available in all those sizes); the smaller inset on the left shows the sizes available for Benguiat.

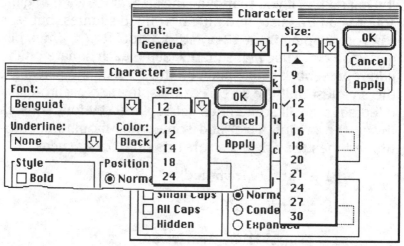

The standard type sizes that almost all applications give you on the font size menu are 9-, 10-, 12-, 14-, 18- and 24-point. Many applications (including all high-end word processors and page-layout programs) let you type in any other size you want—even, sometimes, fractional sizes like 11.5 points.

outline font sizes *(AN/SZA)*

Outline fonts scale beautifully, since they're composed of instructions, not bitmaps; you don't have to worry about limiting your choices to the sizes that are outlined in the menu. But what's displayed on the screen depends on the (bit-mapped) screen fonts, which *are* subject to the scaling problems described in the last entry. (See the entries on ATM and FontSizer in the font utilities section below for some ways to improve the screen display.)

🍎 *why font sizes aren't* (AN/SZA)

Font sizes don't measure the actual height of the charac- ters, but rather the distance from one baseline to the next. (See some basic font terms above, if you don't understand any of the terms in this entry.) Fonts that are nominally the same size often vary quite a bit in actual size. For example,

very hot tip

this is 18-point Zapf Chancery, but this is 18-point Benguiat.

The letters in Zapf Chancery are smaller in order to leave room for the font's exuberant ascenders and descenders (that's usually why fonts appear small for their size). If the letters were bigger, the ascenders and descenders would hit each other; as it is, they just barely clear each other (unless you add extra leading):

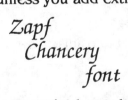

Zapf
Chancery
font

Benguiat has a high x-height, which means that its as-cenders and descenders are proportionally smaller (look at how squished-down the descender on the *g* is, for ex-ample). This makes the type itself bigger for a given (base-line-to-baseline) type size. So here are the basic rules:

- The higher the x-height, the shorter the ascenders and descenders, and the bigger a font looks at a given size.

- The longer the ascenders and descenders, the lower the x-height, and the smaller a font looks at a given size.

⚫ *tiny fonts* (AN/SZA)

Remember that the smaller the type size, the more the resolution of the printer matters. (At any given resolution, it's obviously easier to form a nice-looking 12-point character than a 6-point one, because you have more dots to work with.)

Well-designed 9-point fonts work fine on dot-matrix printers like the ImageWriter, and specially designed 8-point fonts can also be quite readable. On 300-dpi laser printers like the LaserWriters, 6-point and 7-point fonts are quite readable (depending on the font) and even some 5-point type is legible. For smaller sizes than that, you'll need an imagesetter, or a laser printer with better resolution than 300 dpi.

⚫ *font weights* (AN)

very
hot
tip

There are many levels of boldness (how thick each character is). Here are some common names for the various levels, from lightest to heaviest:

- ultra light
- extra light, or thin
- light
- Roman, book, regular, plain, normal or no adjective (just the name of the font)
- medium
- demi
- bold
- extra bold, heavy or black
- ultra bold

⚫ *special type styles* (AN)

Some fonts offer type styles far beyond the standard sixteen (only on the Mac could you call *bold italic outline shadow* "standard"). In addition to all the different levels of boldness just mentioned, there are *condensed* fonts (letters squeezed together and stretched vertically) and *expanded* fonts (letters spread apart and stretched horizontally). To get special type styles like condensed and expanded, you obviously have to install the screen fonts, since there are no menu items that correspond to them.

✦ renaming fonts

Screen fonts can be renamed in programs like Fontographer or Fontastic (or in ResEdit). You might want to do this if there's a particular font you want at the top of the menu for quicker access (or if you're using fonts from Page Studio Graphics, which uses *numbers* instead of names!).

very hot tip

If you don't alter the ID number of the screen font, but just its name, the right printer font will be found. If you rename a printer font, however, it won't be found, and you'll get a crummy, bit-mapped printout.

✦ printer font file names (AN/SZA)

There is some method to the seeming madness of printer font file names. The first five letters are the first five letters of the font name; the rest of the letters, usually in groups of three, describe the style or further specify the font. So, for example, the printer font file for Bitstream's Berkeley Old Style Black Italic is named *BerkeOldStyBlaIt*.

Here are some of the common style codes used:

bd	bold	*lig*	light
boo	book	*lit*	lite
bla	black	*med*	medium
bol	bold	*nor*	normal
con	condensed	*obl*	oblique
dem	demi	*reg*	regular
ext	extra, or extended	*rom*	Roman
hea	heavy	*sem*	semi
it	italic	*thi*	thin
ita	italic	*tit*	titling
kur	kursiv	*ult*	ultra

🍎 *font menu shorthand*

Some fonts appear in your menu with cryptic letters in front of them. (For the reason behind this, inadequate though it is, see the entry called *font families and menus* in the advanced font info section below.) The initials are the modifiers of the main font name. Here are the ones you're likely to see, and what they stand for:

B	bold	L	light
Bk	book	N	narrow
Blk	black	O	oblique
C	condensed	P	poster
D	demi	S	semi
E	extended	Sl	slanted
H	heavy	U	ultra
I	italic	X	extra
K	kursiv		

Sometimes you'll see them in combination—*XBO*, for example, would stand for *extra bold oblique.*

🍎 *picking fonts* (AN)

esp. for beginners

Which fonts to use is a matter of personal taste, of course, but there are a couple of general principles that will help you do it efficiently. The first rule is that it takes a while to learn which fonts you like, so spend some time playing with them before making your choices.

Second (and this may also be obvious), be aware that different kinds of jobs require different fonts. You might choose one group of fonts to use for your business letters, another for your personal letters, a third for your drawings, and so on.

🍎 *font sets* (AN/SZA)

If you're working on a floppy disk system, it makes sense to put together a set of fonts for each purpose, and to create separate System files with different font sets in them.

Then, when you set up a new disk, you just transfer the appropriate System onto it. (By the way, it's worth your while to reduce the number of fonts on each of your disks to the number you really need; messages telling you the disk is full can get really frustrating.)

If you're running off a hard disk, you may still want to put together various font sets and put them in different suitcase files that you can access with Suitcase or Juggler. You can keep certain suitcases open all the time, because you always need the fonts in them, and only open other suitcases as you need them.

♠ *a template for viewing fonts* (AN/SZA)

Some font publishers don't give you full printouts of their fonts, so in order to evaluate which fonts you want to use, it makes sense to make up a template like the one below. Once you've set it up—which might take twenty minutes—all you have to do is select the entire template and then change the font in order to get a printout of every character a given font can produce, as well as samples of the sixteen possible type styles in that font.

(We also provide this template on *The Macintosh Bible Software Disks,* in two of the formats most commonly read by various word processors—MacWrite 4.5 and Word 3. See Chapter 19 for details.)

It doesn't matter which font you choose to make the original template, since you're going to be changing it when you use the template anyway. I've picked the one this book is set in.

font: ITC Benguiat (BENG-*gat) from: Adobe*

9 point: 1234567890

abcdefghijklmnopqrstuvwxyz

ABCDEFGHIJKLMNOPQRSTUVWXYZ

10 point: 1234567890

abcdefghijklmnopqrstuvwxyz

ABCDEFGHIJKLMNOPQRSTUVWXYZ

12 point: 1234567890
abcdefghijklmnopqrstuvwxyz
ABCDEFGHIJKLMNOPQRSTUVWXYZ

14 point: 1234567890
abcdefghijklmnopqrstuvwxyz
ABCDEFGHIJKLMNOPQRSTUVWXYZ

18 point: 1234567890
abcdefghijklmnopqrstuvwxyz
ABCDEFGHIJKLMNOPQRSTUVW

24 point: 1234567890
abcdefghijklmnopqrstu
ABCDEFGHIJKLMNOPQR

unshifted symbols: ´ - = ( ) \ ; ´ , . /

shifted symbols: ~ ! @ # $ % ^ & * ( ) _ + { } | : " < > ?

option keys:

´ ¡ ™ £ ¢ ∞ § ¶ • ª º – ≠
œ ∑ ´ ® † ¥ ¨ ^ ø π " ' «
å ß ∂ ƒ © ˙ ∆ ˚ ¬ … æ
Ω ≈ ç √ ∫ ~ µ ≤ ≥ ÷

shift-option keys:

Ÿ / ¤ ‹ › fi fl ‡ ° · , — ±
Œ „ ‰ Â Ê Á Ë È Ø ∏ " ' »
Å Í Î Ï Ì Ó Ô Ò Ú Æ
Û Ù Ç ◊ ı ˆ ˜ ¯ ˘ ˙ ¿

accent characters:

á É é í ó ú

À à è ì ò ù

â ê î ô û

Ä ä ë ï Ö ö Ü ü

Ã ã Õ õ Ñ

This is bold. *This is italic.* Outline. Shadow. ***Bold italic.*** Bold outline. **Bold shadow.** *Italic outline. Italic shadow.* Outline shadow. *Bold italic outline.* ***Bold italic shadow.*** Bold outline shadow. *Italic outline shadow. Bold italic outline shadow.*

Here are some pointers on how to set this template up for yourself. You might as well begin by just typing in ours, or copying it from *The Macintosh Bible Software Disks*. Then you can customize it any way you want.

The shifted and unshifted symbols are shown in the order in which they appear on most keyboards, from left to right and top to bottom. Because the characters produced by the [Option] key (with and without the [Shift] key) don't appear on the keyboard, we've set it up so that each row represents a row of keys. This makes it easy to find the symbol on the keyboard.

Since the last edition, we've added accent characters to the template. For more about them, see the special characters section below.

Although all fifteen type styles are shown at the bottom of the template (plain text is omitted because most of the rest of the template is in it), it makes sense to give yourself a bit more of a look at the three most useful ones: **bold,** *italic* and ***bold italic.*** So we've put the title (font and publisher) in bold italic, the type sizes in italic, and the subheads below the type sizes (unshifted symbols, shifted symbols, etc.) in bold. We've also underlined those subheads and the type sizes, so you can see how underlining looks with the font.

Because the 8-1/2 x 11 page you'll use to print out the template is wider than this 7 x 9 page, the template we supply on disk completes the 18-point and 24-point alphabets that are cut off above. It also puts the Option and Shift Option keys side by side. If you're typing the template in yourself, be sure to make both of those changes. You may also want to make the special characters or the style variations bigger, so you can see them better; with most fonts, the whole template will still fit on a page.

Each time you select the template and change it to a different font, you may have to readjust line breaks and even lop a few letters off some of the larger alphabets. That's because, as explained above, fonts of the same nominal point size vary quite a bit in actual size, both in height and width.

When using the template for a bit-mapped font, it makes sense to only show the sizes that are installed, because scaled sizes of bit-mapped fonts generally look wretched. For outline fonts, you can use all the sizes in the template, and even add more if you want.

Like Benguiat in the sample template above, most outline fonts have special characters for every possible slot. Bit-mapped fonts almost never do. When a font doesn't have a given special character, it will produce *the missing character box:* ☐ (its appearance varies with the font, but it usually looks pretty much like that). But the missing character box will only print on a dot-matrix printer, not on a laser printer.

♦ *The Macintosh Font Book* (AN)

Font maniacs like myself always like nice new books on Macintosh fonts, and *The Macintosh Font Book* by Erfert

Fenton (Peachpit Press) is the best I've seen. It's full of useful information and is clearly and engagingly written.

There are lots of illustrations, a glossary and several helpful appendices. The book costs $24, but if you use Mac fonts frequently, want to develop a good grasp of typographic principles or just have a thing about fonts, I think you'll find it a good investment.

very good feature

🍎 *a free book on type* (AN)

Compugraphic, which publishes a wide range of Mac fonts (their samples didn't get to me in time to show them in this edition), distributes an excellent 60-page booklet called *The Art & Technology of Typography*. It's a terrific introduction to all the basic concepts, and it's thoroughly (and well) illustrated. Best of all, they'll send you it for free, just for the honor and privilege of having you on their mailing list. To request a copy, write the Compugraphic Type Division, 90 Industrial Way, Wilmington MA 01887.

very good feature

bargain

Special characters

🍎 *the standard special characters* (AN/SZA)

There are some pretty bizarre characters on the Mac's—or just about any computer's—keyboard. For example, there's the backslash (\ ), the vertical bar (|), the lesser than and greater than signs (< >) and so on. But when people talk about special characters on the Mac, they mean ones that aren't shown on the keyboard at all. To get one of these special characters, you hold down the Option key while pressing another key.

esp. for beginners

Let's say you want to type: *Hein, salopard! Parlez-vous français?* To get the special character ç in *français*, you hold down Option while hitting C. To get certain other special characters, you have to hold down the Shift key as well. For example, if you hit Shift Option C, you get an uppercase Ç instead of a lowercase one. (In this case, the two characters are related, but sometimes the [Option] and [Shift][Option] characters have nothing to do with each other.)

Some fonts have idiosyncratic special characters of their own, but there's a set of standard special characters that virtually all fonts share. No bit-mapped font contains all of them—Geneva and Chicago seem to have the most—but most outline fonts have the full set. Here they are:

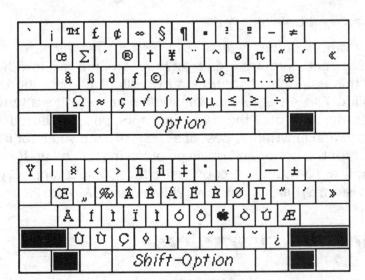

We've listed these standard special characters by category in the next entry. Some special characters do double duty; for example, the square root sign can serve as a check mark. When a character has more than one function, we list it under each category where it can be used.

♦ *special characters by category* (AN/SZA)

accent marks for foreign languages

Two foreign accent marks—the tilde (~) and the accent grave (`)—are regular characters on the Mac's keyboard, marked right on the keys. But it's not clear what you're supposed to use them for, since if you just press one of those keys, the character always appears on a space of its own, not above another character.

The accent marks in the table below—including a different tilde and a different accent grave—work the way they should. When you hit the key combination shown in the last column, nothing shows up on the screen. But when you type the next character, it appears with the appropriate accent mark above it. So, for example, typing Option E - does nothing, but then typing *e* produces *é*.

´	acute accent; accent aigu	{á é í ó ú É}	Option E
`	grave accent; accent grave	{à è ì ò ù}	Option `
^	circumflex; circonflexe	{â ê î ô û}	Option ^
¨	dieresis; umlaut	{ä ë ï ö ü Ä Ö Ü}	Option u
~	tilde	{ã ñ õ Ñ}	Option n

These accent marks won't appear over just any letter you type—it has to be one the Mac thinks makes sense. If you try to put an accent over a different letter, the accent appears by itself on one space and the letter on the next—like this: ´A. The third column in the table above shows the letters you can put each accent mark over. (If you want to produce an accent over a blank space, you can always do that simply by hitting the appropriate key, then the space bar.)

foreign letters, letter combinations & abbreviations

å	Option a	Å	Shift Option A
æ	Option ¨	Æ	Shift Option ¨
ç	Option c	Ç	Shift Option C
ø	Option o	Ø	Shift Option O
œ	Option q	Œ	Shift Option Q
a̲	Option 9	o̲	Shift Option ' o
ß	Option s		

foreign punctuation marks

¿   begins questions in Spanish   `Option` `?`

¡   begins exclamations in Spanish   `Option` `1`

«   European open quote mark   `Option` `\`

»   European close quote mark   `Shift` `Option` `\`

These last two symbols are called *guillemets (gee-may).*

monetary symbols

£   pound sign   `Option` `3`

¥   yen sign   `Option` `Y`

¢   cent sign   `Option` `4`

legal symbols

§   section mark   `Option` `6`

¶   paragraph mark   `Option` `7`

™   trademark   `Option` `2`

®   registered mark   `Option` `R`

©   copyright symbol   `Option` `G`

well-known mathematical & scientific symbols

−   minus sign   `Option` `-`

÷   division sign   `Option` `/`

√   square root   `Option` `V`

∞   infinity sign   `Option` `5`

π   pi   `Option` `P`

°   degrees   `Option` `Shift` `8`

not-so-well-known mathematical & scientific symbols

Since some of the symbols below can represent about a dozen different things, depending on the field of study, we simply give you their Greek names and/or what they most commonly stand for.

≠	not equal to	Option =
≈	more or less equal to	Option x
≤	less than or equal to	Option < ,
≥	greater than or equal to	Option > .
«	much less than	Option \
»	much greater than	Option ¦ \
±	plus or minus	Option + .
Å	Angstroms	Shift Option A
∂	delta; differential, variation	Option D
Δ	capital delta; increment	Option J
μ	lowercase mu; micro-	Option M
Ω	capital omega; ohms	Option Z
ƒ	function, f-stop	Option F
Σ	capital sigma; sum	Option W
∫	integral	Option B
Π	capital pi; product	Shift Option P
¬	logical not	Option L

typographic, graphic & miscellaneous symbols

"	double open quote	Option [
"	double close quote	Shift Option [

'   single open quote   Option]

'   single close quote   Shift Option]

–   en dash   Option –

—   em dash   Shift Option –

√   check mark   Option V

◊   diamond   Shift Option V

†   dagger   Option T

•   bullet, for lists   Option 8

…   ellipsis   Option ;

       Apple symbol   Shift Option K

·   dot accent   Option H

¤   currency   Shift Option 2

mnemonics for special characters (SZA/AN)

very hot tip

The easiest way to find special characters is to keep them in memory—yours, not the computer's. Many of the special characters are placed logically, and if you're lucky, the ones you need most often will have some reason for being on the keys they're on. If they don't, you can always look for a connection that means something to you.

The fact that the bullet and the degree mark are both on the 8 key is easy to remember, because they resemble the asterisk (Shift 8) that's printed on the key. The dagger (†) looks like a *T,* and you get it with Option T . The diamond (◊) and square root/checkmark (√) are on the V key, and the shapes of both incorporate *V's.*

The copyright symbol can't be on the C key, since ç and Ç are already there, but its shape is similar to the G and that's where you'll find it. The ellipsis (…) is on the same key as the colon (:); since the ellipsis has three dots and the colon two, that's easy to remember too. Other easy connections to make are π and Π on [P], ® on [R], μ (mu) on [M], ¢ on [4] along with the $ sign and ¥ (the yen sign) on [Y].

hyphens and en dashes in different fonts (Michael Bradley)

bug

Hyphens should always be shorter than en dashes (which you get with [Option][-]) but sometimes they're not. It varies with the font. For example, it's true in Benguiat but not in Chicago or in Geneva:

	hyphen	*en dash*
Benguiat	-	–
Chicago	–	-
Geneva 10	-	-
Geneva 12	–	-

The only way to tell for sure with any font is to type a hyphen and an en dash and compare them.

characters you can't type

very hot tip

There are four characters in most outline fonts that you can't type from the keyboard—there just aren't any key sequences that supply them. But since some utilities and applications (like Word) let you enter a character's ASCII code, here are the elusive characters, their names and their ASCII numbers:

¸	cedilla	252	˝	Hungarian umlaut	253
˛	Ogonek diacritic	254	ˇ	Carib diacritic	255

Zapf Dingbats has arrow characters for three of the codes (the fourth is blank):

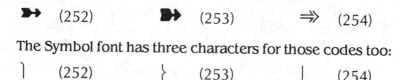

➼ (252) ➽ (253) ⇛ (254)

The Symbol font has three characters for those codes too:

⎫ (252) ⎬ (253) ⎭ (254)

Those characters may not seem very useful (or even recognizable) at first glance, but here's what they look like when you type one underneath the other:

**very
hot
tip**

If you don't have a program that lets you generate characters by their ASCII codes, find a friend who does and have him or her create a text file containing the three characters. Paste the contents of this file into a DA like the Scrapbook or the NotePad and then just paste the characters into documents and change them to the right font, whenever you want them. (Most DAs use bit-mapped fonts, so you won't see the special characters; they'll be shown as the missing character box, but the correct ASCII character will still be there.)

jury-rigged fractions

**very
hot
tip**

Some fonts give you fractions, but most don't. Here's how to jury-rig them:

- First, don't use subscripted numbers. The denominator (bottom number) of a fraction should sit on the baseline, not below it.

- Change the size of the numbers in the fractions to just over half of the point size of the main text. If the regular text is 12 points, make them 7 points; if the regular text is 10 points, make them 5.5 points (if the application you're using will let you, 6 points if it won't).

- Some applications automatically change the size of superscripted numbers, and generally make them too small. If this happens, select the number and change its size after it's been superscripted.

- Don't use the regular slash—use a special character (⁄) you get with Option Shift 1. Its got a shallower angle than the regular slash (/). Use it in the regular point size.

- If your application lets you kern numbers, move both numbers in towards the slash.

Fine-tuning fractions takes some time—you'll want to try different superscript offsets if your application lets you. But once you've worked things out for a given font, it's easy to do it again. (For an easier approach, see the entry below called *fraction fonts.)*

￼ *creating special typographic effects* (AN)

To distort a headline or other piece of display type for special effect, type it first in any draw program (but not a paint program; you need object-oriented graphics). Then paste it into a word processor or page-layout program, either through the Clipboard or the Scrapbook. (You can actually do the whole process in Word. To find out how, see the entry called *the graphics dump* in the Word tips section of Chapter 10.)

very
hot
tip

Once it's there, select it and reshape it to stretch the type horizontally, vertically or both. It will look terrible on the screen but when you print it out on the LaserWriter, the characters will have the same crisp, clean edges that outline fonts normally do. Here are some examples of the kinds of effects you can get:

(The fonts being distorted are Adobe's Cooper Black italic, Casady & Greene's Kells and their Gazelle.)

You can also use a draw program to drop out (reverse out) type—that is, to give you white type on a dark background. First create a solid shape filled with black (or gray, or any other pattern you want for the background). Then either drag some outline type on top of it or, with the filled-in shape selected—choose *Outline* from the Style menu and start typing.

You can combine both these techniques, creating white writing on a dark background and stretching it once it gets into your word processing program. These typographic special effects also work on the ImageWriter, but you don't get smoothing and the results don't look anywhere near as good.

(There are programs out that will give you much fancier effects than these, and much more control over them. They're described in the font utilities section below.)

Special fonts

☀ *pictorial characters* (AN)

very good feature

One of the best features of the Macintosh is the availability of pictorial characters—little images you can place in a document with nothing more than a keystroke or two. The best-known pictorial fonts are two bit-mapped ones from Apple—Cairo and Mobile (formerly know as Taliesin).

Casady & Greene offers some useful pictorial fonts for the ImageWriter, including one that contains architectural symbols and drawings (like a little toilet, or an overhead shot of a person walking), and a whimsical one called Images. Dubl-Click publishes several pictorial outline fonts, including laser versions of Cairo and Mobile. (See the bit-mapped font sampler section below for more details.)

The best way to arrange a pictorial font for reference is by categories, rather than by the keys that generate the characters. That way you can look for what you want instead of having to scan a whole list or table. Every publisher of a pictorial font ought to provide a printout of it by logical categories, but since they don't, the following entries give you some. They cover four of the most widely used pictorial fonts—Cairo, Carta and two outline fonts that come with most LaserWriters—Zapf Dingbats and Symbol.

One final note: if a pictorial character (or any other kind of nonstandard special character) uses one of the foreign accent mark keys, you'll have to hit the key twice (or hit it and then hit another) to generate the character (because normally that key waits for you to type a letter to put the accent mark over). So, for example, to get the character ① in Zapf Dingbats, you have to hit (Option)(U) (which normally generates an umlaut, ¨) twice; if you just hit it once, nothing will happen.

important warning

In general, whenever you have to hit one key (or keys) and then another, rather than all together, we separate the keys with a comma (e.g. (Option)(U), (Shift)(O)).

⁜ *key-caps fonts*

Needless to say, you need a special font to produce key-cap characters like (⌘), (Option) and (Shift) (not to mention (A), (B) and (C)). The second edition of *The Macintosh Bible* used a bit-mapped key-caps font from Dubl-Click called Manhattan (aside from the special characters, it's basically New York, hence the name).

This is Manhattan. It gives you Macintosh symbols like ⬛ ⬛ ⬛ (Tab) (Click) (Option) (Enter) (Drag) and (⌘). Manhattan is showing its age, however—it has no (Delete) key cap (only (Backspace)) and no key caps for many keys on the extended keyboard.

Casady & Greene's Hacker is another bit-mapped key-caps font. (H)(A)(C)(K)(E)(R) (l)(o)(o)(k)(s) (l)(i)(k)(e) (t)(h)(i)(s) (a)(n)(d) (i)(n)(c)(l)(u)(d)(e)(s) (c)(h)(a)(r)(a)(c)(t)(e)(r)(s) (l)(i)(k)(e) (Return) (CapsLock) (Save) (Copy) ⬛ ⬛ ⬛ ⬛ ⬛ ⬛ ⬛ ⬛ ⬛ (a)(n)(d) **File** (.)

Page Studio Graphics offers ten key-caps fonts; we are using two for the key caps in this book. The first one—

PIXymbolsCmdKeys—has the cap letters and most of the special keys. My only quibble with it is that there's no Control key with the word spelled out as it is on Mac keyboards—they provide only Ctrl.

The other font we're using—S2113PIXymbols (yes, that's its name—isn't that stupid?) has lowercase letters (a b c), symbols for the special keys like those used in menus (⇧ ⌥) and key caps for certain keys that have two characters on them ('₁ '₂ '₃), just like the keyboard.

*very good
feature*

Both fonts have a simple, thin line for the key shape, so the characters print nicely at the LaserWriter's 300 dpi. Variations on the key outline—light or heavy, shadowed, gray, double (sort of three-dimensional)—is what's different about the other PIXymbols fonts. There's even a roll-your-own key font in which you type the left half of the key, the character you want and then the right half of the key.

For more on Page Studio Graphics' other special fonts, see the next entry.

🍎 *PIXymbols fonts*

*very good
feature*

Page Studio Graphics offers a line of specialized picture fonts—*very* specialized. There's one, for example, for the travel and recreation industry that has icons for lodging and transportation and includes all the standard icons used by the Department of Transportation and the National Park Service. Others include international road signs, business images, telephone buttons and images, form construction, digital characters and clocks, apothecary measures, braille and astrology. (There are also a number of key-caps fonts, covered above.)

One of the PIXymbols fonts is full of Macintosh icons and symbols, like:

Here's a sample of the font for travel and recreation:

Did you notice that I didn't refer to either of these fonts by name? That's because neither one *has* a name. Page Studio Graphics, having decided that they have too many fonts to be able to assign meaningful names to them, has assigned each a number. When I spoke to them about it— noting that, with four of their fonts on my menu, I was having trouble remembering which was which,they said that most people have trouble remembering font names.

very bad feature

When I suggested that most people would have even more trouble remembering numbers, they said that after thousands of sales, no one had ever complained about the numbering system, but that I was certainly entitled to my opinion. (By the way, if you want either of the fonts shown above, they're called 2002 and 4108. No, wait, that's 2020 and 4018...I think.)

Page Studio's fonts are nicely designed, but the company's not great on details. First, there's the name/number problem. Then there's the problem of font conflicts. Because they haven't converted to NFNTs, some of their font ID numbers clash with some of the lower-numbered standard fonts. They've said they're converting to NFNTs eventually, but there's no target date and apparently no rush. (Again, no one's complained yet.) Conversion isn't a big deal (you can do it yourself, by running the fonts through Font/DA Mover) and certainly not time-consuming, so the delay isn't really understandable.

very bad feature

Another annoyance is the lack of standardization in Page Studio's reference cards. The two I have are set up entirely differently, which makes it hard for me to figure out what key combination is needed to generate a character.

This is a situation where I have to recommend a product in spite of the publisher's attitude (after all, how much support are you going to need for a font?). If you need these fonts, you can deal with the problems. But complain! And if you can find a suitable font from another company, get that instead.

Utility City

bargain

Utility City is a font that's included on the disk with all of Dubl-Click Software's World Class outline fonts. It's a *derived font*—that is, it borrows characters from Times, Helvetica, Symbol and Zapf Dingbats to create its own characters.

very good feature

Among its many talents, Utility City gives you true fractions (without the jury-rigging described on pp. 374–75). It also lets you combine buttons, boxes and checkmarks. Here are some of the checkmarks:

And here are some of the boxes:

important warning

Utility City's checkmarks have *negative width*—when you type one, the insertion point ends up to the *left* of the character, so the next character you type is printed on top of it. (Be aware that this makes it very difficult to edit what you have typed.) Typing a box over a checkmark looks like this:

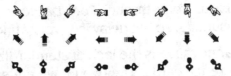

Utility City also gives you different angles on some of the Zapf Dingbats:

Symbols Galore and MathWhiz, also from Dubl-Click, take a similar approach to combining characters from other fonts to create new ones.

✦ Zapf Dingbats by categories *(AN/SZA)*

When Zapf Dingbats is the selected font, all you have to do to generate any of the pictorial characters shown is hit the key(s) indicated.

arrows (fat tails)

➳	Shift Option B	➴	Shift Option X
➶	Shift Option N	➸	Shift Option <
➹	Shift Option >	➷	Shift Option M
➻	Shift Option Z		

arrows (hollow)

➫	Shift Option D	➬	Shift Option F
➩	Shift Option G	➪	Shift Option H
⇨	Shift Option I	➭	Shift Option S
➯	Shift Option J	➱	Shift Option L

arrows (solid)

→	Shift Option ']	➔	Option ']
⟶	Shift Option 4	➙	Shift Option 5
➡	Shift Option 9	➛	Shift Option ~`
➚	Shift Option 1	➝	Shift Option 2
↔	Option /	↕	Shift Option V
➧	Shift Option Y	➨	Shift Option U
➥	Shift Option R	➦	Shift Option T

arrows (stylized)

�	`Option` `h`	➤	`Option` `k`
➡	`Shift` `Option` `6`	➤	`Shift` `Option` `7`
➢	`Shift` `Option` `W`	➢	`Shift` `Option` `'₀`
➤	`Shift` `Option` `E`	⊃	`Shift` `Option` `:;`

arrows (hard to get at)

There's no keyboard access for these characters, so they're shown with their ASCII codes in parentheses. See the entry above called *characters you can't type* for information on how to generate them.

| ➤➤ (252) | ➤➤ (253) | ⇒ (254) |

asterisks (florettes, snowflakes, starbursts)

❄	`d`	❄	`e`	❄	`f`
✳	`g`	❋	`h`	❋	`i`
✷	`j`	✳	`k`	❀	`` ` ``
❉	`[`	✴	`]`	❊	`\`
✢	`Shift` `B`	✤	`Shift` `C`	♣	`Shift` `D`
✥	`Shift` `E`	✱	`Shift` `Q`	✻	`Shift` `R`
✳	`Shift` `S`	✶	`Shift` `T`	✽	`Shift` `U`
✦	`Shift` `V`	✷	`Shift` `W`	✸	`Shift` `X`
✺	`Shift` `Y`	✹	`Shift` `Z`	❁	`Shift` `6`
❖	`Shift` `-`				

braces and brackets

❬ Option U , Shift U   ❭ Option E , A

(Option U , Shift A   ) Shift Option A

(Shift Option C   ) Option E , Shift E

[Option U , A   ] Option N , E

❰ Option ` , A   ❱ Option I , A

⟨ Option N , Shift N   ⟩ Option U , Shift O

[Option A   ] Option C

boxes and bars

■ n   ❑ o   ❐ p   ❒ q

❏ r | x   ❘ z   ❙ y

card suits

♠ Option e   ♣ Option r

♥ Option 2   ♦ Option g

check marks and x's

✔ 3   ✔ 4   ✕ 5

✖ 6   ✗ 7   ✘ 8

crosses

✚ 9   † =   ✛ ;   ♰ Shift ?

✜ Shift :   ✢ Shift <   ♱ Shift >   ☩ Shift 2

fat quotes

99 Shift ~

6 Shift '

66 Shift '

6 Shift {

geometric shapes (miscellaneous)

● i   ○ m   ◗ w   ▲ s

▼ t   ◆ u   ❖ v

hands

☜ -   ✌ ,   ☞ Shift 8   ☞ Shift *

miscellaneous

❧ Option s   ❦ Option 7

❧ Option 8   ⸿ Option Shift 8

numbers (sans serif, black on white)

① Option Shift ?   ⑥ Option x

② Option 1   ⑦ Option j

③ Option L   ⑧ Option \

④ Option V   ⑨ Option Shift \

⑤ Option F   ⑩ Option ;

numbers (sans serif, white on black)

❶ Option Spacebar   ❻ Option Q

❷ `Option` `` ` ``, `Shift` `A`   ❼ `Option` `–`

❸ `Option` `n`, `Shift` `A`   ❽ `Option` `Shift` `–`

❹ `Option` `n`, `Shift` `O`   ❾ `Option` `[`

❺ `Option` `Shift` `Q`   ❿ `Option` `Shift` `[`

numbers (serif, black on white)

① `Option` `u`, `Option` `u`   ⑥ `Option` `Shift` `+`

② `Option` `=`   ⑦ `Option` `,`

③ `Option` `Shift` `[`   ⑧ `Option` `.`

④ `Option` `Shift` `O`   ⑨ `Option` `y`

⑤ `Option` `5`   ⑩ `Option` `;`

numbers (serif, white on black)

❶ `Option` `d`   ❻ `Option` `9`

❷ `Option` `w`   ❼ `Option` `]`

❸ `Option` `Shift` `P`   ❽ `Option` `z`

❹ `Option` `p`   ❾ `Option` `]`

❺ `Option` `b`   ❿ `Option` `o`

objects (miscellaneous)

✂ `Shift` `1`   ☎ `Shift` `5`   ✀ `Shift` `3`

✆ `Shift` `7`   ✄ `Shift` `"`   ✈ `Shift` `(`

✂ `Shift` `4`   ✉ `Shift` `)`   ☮ `'`

pens and pencils

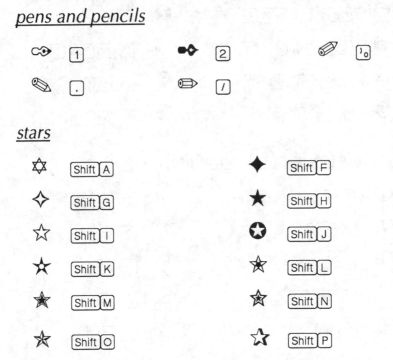

stars

✡	Shift A	✦	Shift F
◇	Shift G	★	Shift H
☆	Shift I	✪	Shift J
✬	Shift K	✴	Shift L
✯	Shift M	✩	Shift N
✶	Shift O	☆	Shift P

● *Zapf Dingbats by keyboard*

Here's how the dingbats are arranged on the keyboard. To get the characters on the top of each square, you hold down Shift; to get the characters on the right side of each square, you hold down Option (so the character in the upper right is Option Shift and the one in lower left is just plain—neither Shift nor Option held down).

And at the top of the next page are the key sequences for the characters that require more than one combination of keystrokes:

First, ↓ then→	Shift A	a	Shift E	Shift O	Shift U	Shift N
Option e		❯	)			
Option `	❷	(				
Option i		)				
Option u	(	[		)	❮	
Option n	❸	]		❹		{

Zapf Dingbats by logic

For those of you who think the arrangement of Zapf Dingbats' characters defies all logic, here they are in order of ASCII number:

See? There is some order, after all.

⚫ Cairo by categories *(AN)*

When Cairo is the selected font, all you have to do to generate any of the pictures shown is hit the key(s) indicated.

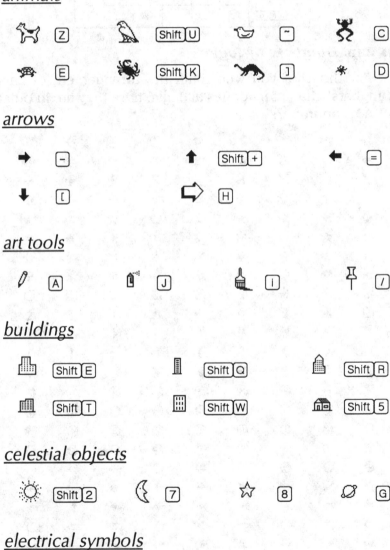

animals

🐕 Z   🦅 Shift U   🐦 ~   👾 C

🐢 E   🦀 Shift K   🐪]   ✳ D

arrows

➡ -   ⬆ Shift +   ⬅ =

⬇ [➡ H

art tools

✏ A   ✒ J   🖌 i   📌 /

buildings

🏢 Shift E   🏢 Shift Q   🏛 Shift R

🏢 Shift T   🏢 Shift W   🏠 Shift 5

celestial objects

☼ Shift 2   ☾ 7   ☆ 8   🪐 G

electrical symbols

⊣⊢ Q   ⊣⊢ R   ⋀⋀ S   ⁄ ¹₀

everyday objects—bigger than a breadbox

▯ `;`   📺 `Shift` `D`   🪑 `3`

🧳 `Shift` `-`   🔔 `Shift` `{`   ⚓ `T`

everyday objects—smaller than a breadbox

🔑 `F`   ✉ `Shift` `S`

🎲 `'`   💡 `Shift` `?`

🚚 `L`   🕯 `U`

⚾ `Option` `U` , `Shift` `A`

food and drink

🍳 `` ` ``   🍦 `Shift` `1`   🍰 `5`

☕ `\`   🍾 `4`   🍷 `6`

fruits

🍓 `Shift` `B`   🍇 `Shift` `C`

🍐 `Shift` `4`   🍍 `Shift` `:`

miscellaneous

〰 `Shift` `|`   ※ `9`   ✤ `Shift` `9`

𓂀 `Shift` `O`   ☥ `Shift` `V`   ✚ `x`

🗡 `Shift` `P`   🔫 `k`   🔫 `Shift` `}`

musical symbols

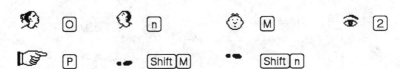

parts of the body

plants & parts of plants

things you wear

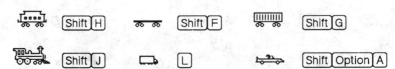

transportation

⬥ *Cairo by keyboard*

Here's Cairo by keyboard. You'll notice there are only two characters per key; that's because Cairo has no Option characters and only one Shift Option character. The upper character on each key is the one you get if you hold down Shift . The *A* key does have a third character, the convertible (⇨ , Shift Option A). Cairo also has one special accent character, shown in the inset.

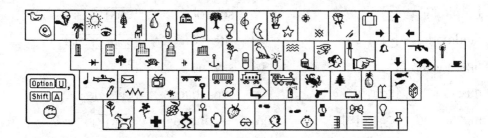

⬥ *Carta by categories* (AN/SZA)

Carta is a font of map-making symbols designed by Lynne Garell and published by Adobe. The list below groups the symbols into logical categories and tells you what they normally represent. (When a symbol can't be produced with keystrokes, we give you the ASCII number for it.)

arrows

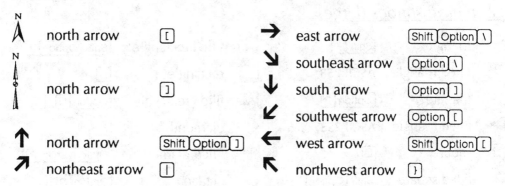

buildings, etc.

🏛	bank	`Shift` `Q`	✴	police	`Option` `W`
†	cemetery	`Shift` `Option` `B`	⊠	post office	`Option` `Z`
🛠	church	`b`	�III	prison	`Shift` `Option` `Q`
⚖	courthouse	`q`	∴	ruin	`+`
✚	hospital	`Shift` `Option` `X`	🛰	satellite dish	`Option` `,`
✛	hospital	`x`	🏳	school	`Shift` `V`
🏴	landmark	`=`	⊡	site	`Shift` `Option` `=`
☀	lighthouse	`-`	🏙	skyline	`C`
🕯	mission	`Shift` `B`	✡	synagogue	`Option` `v`
☪	mosque	`Option` `B`	ℭ	telephone	`Shift` `Z`
🏛	museum	`Option` `Q`	🎓	university	`v`
🏯	pagoda	`Shift` `Option` `V`	🌬	windmill	`Shift` `-`

cities and towns

◉	city	`t`	✪	national capital	`Shift` `R`
◎	town	`Shift` `T`	✪	state capital	`Option` `R`
○	village	`Shift` `Option` `T`	☆	county seat	`Shift` `E`

geometric shapes (large)

▽	triangle	`Shift` `P`	■	filled rectangle	`Shift` `Option` `3`
▼	filled triangle	ASCII 253	☐	rectangle	`L`
▷	triangle	`Option` `P`	■	filled rectangle	`Option` `N`, `A`
▶	filled triangle	ASCII 253	◇	diamond	`P`
☐	square	`L`	◆	filled diamond	`Option` `Shift` `P`
■	filled square	`Shift` `Option` `7`	○	octagon	`Option` `O`
☐	rectangle	`Option` `L`	●	filled octagon	`Option` `U`, `Y`

○ circle ☐O☐   ⬭ oval ☐Shift☐☐O☐
● filled circle ☐Shift☐☐Option☐☐4☐   ⬮ filled oval ☐Shift☐☐Option☐☐5☐

geometric shapes (small)

△ triangle ☐Shift☐☐3☐   ★ star ☐E☐
▲ filled triangle ☐Option☐☐3☐   ☆ inline star ☐Shift☐☐Option☐☐E☐
☐ square ☐Shift☐☐2☐   ✬ half-filled star ☐Option☐☐E☐ , ☐E☐
■ filled square ☐Option☐☐2☐   ☆ circle in star ☐Shift☐☐Option☐☐R☐
◇ diamond ☐Shift☐☐4☐   ✪ star in circle ☐R☐
◆ filled diamond ☐Option☐☐4☐   ○ circle ☐Shift☐☐1☐
+ thin plus ☐Shift☐☐Option☐☐˙·☐   • small filled circle ☐Shift☐☐Option☐☐W☐
× thin cross ☐Option☐☐˙·☐   ● filled circle ☐Option☐☐1☐
⬡ hexagon ☐Shift☐☐5☐   ● larger filled circle ☐Shift☐☐Option☐☐1☐
⬢ filled hexagon ☐Option☐☐5☐

highway signs

⛉ Interstate hwy ☐I☐
⬤ Interstate hwy ☐Shift☐☐Option☐☐2☐
⬭ US highway ☐U☐
⬭ US highway ☐Shift☐☐U☐
⬤ US highway ☐Shift☐☐Option☐☐`☐
⌂ California hwy ☐Shift☐☐Option☐☐O☐
⬣ California hwy ☐Option☐☐N☐ , ☐Shift☐☐O☐
⬠ county highway ☐Shift☐☐I☐
⬟ county highway ASCII 252
⬡ hwy in nat'l forest ☐Option☐☐U☐ , ☐Option☐☐U☐
⬢ hwy in nat'l forest ☐Option☐☐`☐ , ☐Shift☐☐A☐

♡	hwy on Ind. reserv.	`Shift` `Option` `U`
♥	hwy on Ind. reserv.	`Shift` `Option` `8`
♘	Trans-Canada hwy	`Shift` `Y`
⛊	Mexican hwy	`Y`
⛊	Mexican hwy	`Shift` `Option` `9`
♡	Mexican hwy	`Option` `Y`
♠	Mexican hwy	`Shift` `Option` `'`₀
⌂	hwy school sign	`Shift` `Option` `Y`
⬠	hwy school sign	`Shift` `Option` `K`
⊠	hwy RR crossing	`Shift` `Option` `I`
✕	hwy RR crossing	`Shift` `Option` `Z`

mining and industrial

⚗	chemicals	`Option` `X`	◿	mine shaft	`Shift` `?`
⛏	coal	`Option` `M`	⚒	mining	`.`
-⋄-	dry well	`Shift` `Option` `;`	⚏	nuclear reactor	`Shift` `Option` `N`
🏭	factory	`Shift` `Option` `.`	⛁	oil	`M`
☼	gas well	`Shift` `Option` `/`	⛏	oil well	`Shift` `M`
◈	gems	`Shift` `Option` `M`	✕	placer	`>`
▱	gold	`,`	☢	radiation	`Shift` `N`
⚒	gravel pit	`Option` `.`	⛙	refinery	`Shift` `Option` `,`
⬡	metals	`<`	⚛	uranium	`N`

miscellaneous symbols

✈	airport, large	`Option` `J`
✢	airport, small	`Shift` `J`
⤛	Amtrak	`K`

)(bridge   [Shift] [Option] [H]

    children crossing   [~]

    compass   [|\]

    dam   [Shift] [K]

    hammer & sickle   [W]

    handicapped   [Shift] [X]

    heliport   [Shift] [Option] [J]

    maple leaf   [Shift] [W]

    pedest. crossing   [`]

    port of entry   [Option] [K]

    registration mark   [Shift] [Option] [P]

    scale   [Shift] [[ ]

    traffic light   [Shift] [Option] [I]

    tunnel   [Option] [/]

    world   [C]

outdoor recreation

bicycle trail	[Option] [F]		game preserve	[S]
bird refuge	[Shift] [S]		golf	[Shift] [Option] [F]
boat	[Option] [H]		hiking	[Shift] [F]
boat launching	[⇧] [H]		horse trail	[Shift] [Option] [G]
campsite	[D]		hostel	[F]
campsite	[Shift] [D]		marina	[H]
fire	[Shift] [Option] [S]		pack station	[Shift] [Option] [D]
fish hatchery	[Option] [S]		picnic area	[Option] [D]

↟	ranger station	G	⬛	US Fire Svc facil.	Shift G
⚞	skiing	A	❄	winter sports	Shift A
♠	state park	Option G			

surveying and land use

⊙	benchmark	;	◐	gauging station	\
⊡	boundary	:	⬡	lookout	'
△	control	Option ;	⬠	lookout control	Shift "

warfare

⚓	aircraft carrier	Option 6
⚔	battlefield	Option –
⚓	battleship	Option 7
♜	castle	Option =
✺	explosion, flat	Shift Option 6
✦	explosion	Shift 6
★	explosion, filled	Shift 8
✸	explosion, filled	Shift 7
⊥	fort	Shift Option –
╎	ICBM	Shift)
╎	IRBM	Shift (
✈	military air base	J
⚉	soldier	Option '
⛏	tank	Option 9
⛴	tanker	Option 8

❡ *Carta by keyboard*

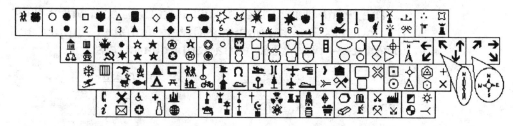

❡ *non-Roman alphabets* (AN)

Another exciting aspect of fonts on the Mac is the ability to generate foreign—that is, non-Roman—alphabets, especially since you can mix them in freely with regular text. (Roman alphabets—like the ones used for English, French and Spanish—have more or less the same characters as Latin does. Non-Roman alphabets—like the ones used for Greek, Russian, Hebrew, Japanese and Chinese—have different characters.)

very good feature

There's a wide variety of both laser and ImageWriter non-Roman fonts available—everything from common ones like Greek, Hebrew, katakana (Japanese phonetic characters) and Cyrillic (Russian, etc.) right down to totally obscure ones like Linear B (an early form of Greek writing dating from around 1500 BC).

This last was designed by Gary Palmer, who teaches anthropology at the University of Nevada in Las Vegas and also helps run the Center for Computer Applications in the Humanities Department there. Here's a short sample of it:

Pretty hot, huh?

One last note about non-Roman alphabets: remember that generating the characters may be only half the battle. For example, unless a Hebrew font comes with a word processor that lets you write from right to left, you'll have to type out the Hebrew text backwards (from left to right).

Symbol's Greek alphabet

The Symbol font that's built into the LaserWriter Plus, NT and NTX has a complete Greek alphabet—upper and lowercase—plus a few extra script characters:

name	uppercase		lowercase	
alpha	A	Shift A	α	a
beta	B	Shift B	β	b
gamma	Γ	Shift G	γ	g
delta	Δ	Shift D	δ	d
epsilon	E	Shift E	ε	e
zeta	Z	Shift Z	ζ	z
eta	H	Shift H	η	h
theta	Θ	Shift Q	θ	q
iota	I	Shift I	ι	i
kappa	K	Shift K	κ	k
lambda	Λ	Shift L	λ	l
mu	M	Shift M	μ	m
nu	N	Shift N	ν	n
xi	Ξ	Shift X	ξ	x
omicron	O	Shift O	o	o
pi	Π	Shift P	π	p
rho	P	Shift R	ρ	r
sigma	Σ	Shift S	σ	s
tau	T	Shift T	τ	t

upsilon	Y	Shift U	υ	u
phi	Φ	Shift F	φ	f
chi	X	Shift C	χ	c
psi	Ψ	Shift Y	ψ	y
omega	Ω	Shift W	ω	w

script characters

ϖ	omega (lowercase)	v
φ	phi (lowercase)	j
ς	sigma (lowercase)	Shift V
ϑ	theta (lowercase)	Shift J
ϒ	upsilon (uppercase)	Shift Option 8

⬥ Symbol's symbols

Besides the Greek alphabet shown in the last entry, the Symbol font contains arrows, card suit symbols, a wealth of mathematical and scientific symbols, and pieces of brackets and braces you can use to surround multiple lines of numbers in formulas. (When scientific symbols are also Greek letters, like Σ and π, we haven't repeated them below.)

arrows

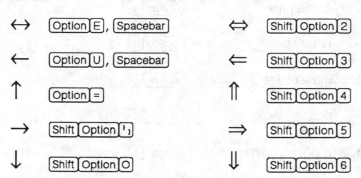

↔	Option E, Spacebar	⟷	Shift Option 2
←	Option U, Spacebar	⟸	Shift Option 3
↑	Option =	⟰	Shift Option 4
→	Shift Option 'ı	⟹	Shift Option 5
↓	Shift Option O	⟱	Shift Option 6

card suits

♣	Option S	♦	Option R
♥	Option G	♠	Option 2

mathematical & scientific symbols

∞	infinity	Option 8
ƒ	derivative	Option 7
∝	proportional	Option M
∂	partial differential	Option D
≤	less than or equal	Option 3
≥	greater than or equal	Option .
≠	not equal	Option P
≡	identical	Option B
≈	approx. equal	Option 9
⊗	circle multiply	Option F
⊕	circle plus	Option X
∅	empty set	Option J
∩	intersection	Option \
∪	union	Shift Option \
⊃	proper superset	Option ;

⊇	reflexive superset	Option Spacebar
⊄	not subset	Option ~ , Shift A
⊂	proper subset	Option N , Shift A
⊆	reflexive subset	Option N , Shift O
∈	element	Shift Option Q
∉	not element	Option Q
∠	angle	Option -
∇	gradient	Shift Option -
√	radical	Option /
¬	logical not	Option U , Y
∧	logical and	Shift Option ~
∨	logical or	Shift Option 1
Σ	summation	Option i , Shift A

(it's larger than the regular capital sigma)

brackets and braces (pieces)

⌠	integral, top	Shift Option Z
	integral, center	Shift Option X
⌡	integral, bottom	Shift Option B
⎛	left parens, top	Option i , Shift E
	left parens, middle	Shift Option Y

⎧	left parens, bottom	Shift Option U
⎫	right parens, top	Shift Option N
⎪	right parens, middle	Shift Option M
⎭	right parens, bottom	Shift Option ,
⎡	left brace, top	Shift Option F
⎰	left brace, middle	Shift Option G
⎪	left brace, extension	Shift Option J
⎣	left brace, bottom	Shift Option H
⎤	right brace, top	ASCII 252
⎱	right brace, middle	ASCII 253
⎦	right brace, bottom	ASCII 254
⌈	left bracket, top	Shift Option I
⎪	left bracket, middle	Shift Option S
⌊	left bracket, bottom	Shift Option D
⌉	right bracket, top	Shift Option .
⎪	right bracket, middle	Option H
⌋	right bracket, bottom	Option K

❖ Symbol by keyboard

At the top of the next page is a diagram showing where Symbol's characters fall on the keyboard:

– ‾	∧	! 1	∨ 5	≡ 2	⇔ ♠	≠ 3	⇐ ≤	∃ 4	⇑ ′	% 5	⇒ °	⊥ 6	⇓ ∫	& 7	◊ ƒ	* 8	Γ ↔	(9 | ⟨ ≈ |) 0	® …	_ –	∇ ∠	+ =	± ↑

Θ θ	∈ ∉	Ω ω	© •	Ε ε	™	Ρ ρ	Σ ◆	Τ τ	⌈ ∎	Ψ ψ	| ×	Υ ψ	⌊ ×	Ι ι	⌈ ↑	Ο ο	↓ ⌋	Π π	÷ ≠	{ ⌈	⊗ ⊘	} ⌉	Π ™	| ∴	∪ ∩

Α α	‖ ‖	Σ σ	⌊ ♣	Δ δ	⌈ ∂	Φ φ	⌈ ⊗	Γ γ	⌋ ♥	Η η	⌊ ⌊	ϑ ψ	⌊ Ø	Κ κ	♦ ♣	Λ λ	⟩ ℜ	: ;	∫ ⊃	" ′	→ —

Ζ ζ	⌈ ⌊	Ξ ξ	‖ ⊕	Χ χ	‖ ‖	ς ϖ	· ℘	Β β	⌉ ≡	Ν ν	⟩ –	Μ μ	| ∝	< ,	⌋ ˘	> .	] ≥	? /	× √

And here are the accent characters that are available:

First, ↓ then→	[Shift] [A]	[a]	[Shift] [E]	[e]	[i]	[Shift] [O]
[Option] [e]						
[Option] [`]	α		–			
[Option] [i]						
[Option] [u]						
[Option] [n]	⊂					⊆

⬥ *fraction fonts*

There are several fonts that will give you real fractions, but forget about getting them to match your favorite typeface. Your basic choices are serif and sans serif—Helvetica and Times.

It doesn't make sense to assign specific fractions to each key—there aren't enough keys to go around. What fraction fonts let you do is type a numerator, a dividing slash and a denominator. The numerators (top numbers) are raised well above the baseline. The denominators are on the baseline (as they should be) and both numbers are the right size for the font you're using.

Fraction fonts beat building your own (see *jury-rigged fractions* in the special characters section above) not only because of the time they save you but because of the way the numbers nestle against the dividing slash. You don't have to do any manual kerning (assuming the program you're using allows that)—the kerning's built in.

very good feature

Dubl-Click provides the Utility City font free on all its outline font disks. This is a *derived font*—it actually uses the Times and Helvetica fonts that are built into your laser printer, doing all the superscripting and kerning on the fly. You use the number keys on the keyboard to type the numerator, and [Shift] plus the number for the denominator. That gives you fractions in Helvetica (the first two examples below); for Times, just add [Option] to the commands (the second two examples below).

$\frac{1}{32}$ 5 $\frac{3}{4}$ $\frac{11}{16}$ 21 $\frac{3}{8}$

Another derived fractions font is MacTography's *Caps & Fractions.*

Page Studio Graphics, which specializes in specialized fonts, has two fraction fonts—one serif, one sans. Neither is a derived font, and they both include numeric and monetary symbols. As with most of its other PIXymbols fonts, these don't have names, just numbers—8020 and 8022.

small caps

The Small Caps option available in many word processors and page-layout programs uses two different sizes of uppercase letters, So That Your Text Looks Like This (assuming you capitalize the first letter of each word). It does this by combining two different sizes of caps—say, 12-point for the larger caps and 10-point for the smaller ones. (This means that to print in high-quality on a dot-matrix printer, you'll need the 20-point, as well as the 24-point, font installed— or whatever the other size is.)

The problem with this approach is that the line thicknesses of the two font sizes differ, and that makes them look like they don't go together (notice how the *L, &* and *S* in the illustration below look heavier than the other letters).

Large & Small

The way around this problem is to use a font specifically designed for small likes, like the

Times Small Caps Font
from The Font Company

Notice how much more even that looks than what the Small Caps command produces:

Times Formatted in Small Caps

A bit-mapped font sampler

Apple's bit-mapped fonts (AN)

One of the standard fonts used by the Mac, Geneva, is a bit-mapped version of the classic, standard typeface Helvetica. It's called Geneva because Helvetica was designed in Switzerland. Helvetica, gets *its* name from the official name for Switzerland, *Confoederatio Helvetica*, "the Swiss Confederation" (that's why the international license plate tag for Switzerland is CH).

gossip/ trivia

The Swiss use a Latin name to describe their country so as not to favor any of their four official languages—German, French, Italian and Romansch—over the others. *Helvetica* comes from the name of a Celtic people, the Helvetii, who inhabited Switzerland during the time of Julius Caesar. I don't know how they came by *their* name, but tell me—what other computer book gives you trivia of this caliber?

Unlike New York—a bit-mapped version of Times, the font Stanley Morrison designed for the *London Times* in 1922—Geneva is quite pretty and pleasant to read (which is fortunate, because it's used by the System to display things). But it doesn't hold a candle to Chicago.

You look at Chicago so often on menus and the titles of windows that it's easy to forget what an attractive font it is. Created by master type

very good feature

craftsman Charles Bigelow specifically for use on the Mac, it's probably the most beautiful and functional bit-mapped font ever designed. To get this kind of style out of 72 dots per inch is an incredible accomplishment.

(Chicago looks great on the screen and in ImageWriter printouts, but for some reason it doesn't look so good in this printout. The Laser-Writer makes it too skinny. It looks more like the screen font in boldface.)

Apple supplies Chicago only in 12-point, but Dubl-Click Software's World Class fonts gives you 9-point, 10-point and 24-point versions of it as well.

very good feature

Another Apple font I love is San Francisco (it used to come on System disks, but doesn't anymore). When the Mac first came out, a lot of grave warnings were issued about not using this "ransom note" font for business letters—as if most Mac users had IQs down in the room-temperature range.

Well, you shouldn't use San Francisco for your will, either—

unless you want it challenged on the grounds that you weren't of sound mind when you made it. But that doesn't mean you should never use San Francisco. Remember the first commandment: This is the Mac. It's Supposed to be fun.

❤ an inexpensive luxury *(AN)*

There are lots of beautiful collections of bit-mapped fonts on the market (two examples are shown in the following entries). I love bit-mapped fonts; they're one of the cheapest luxuries around.

❤ Fluent Fonts *(AN)*

Casady & Greene's 66 bit-mapped Fluent Fonts come on a two-disk set that costs $50. In addition to fonts of architectural, astronomical, astrological, biological, chemical, electronic, mathematical, meteorological and even a few yachting symbols (and Hacker, mentioned in the keycaps entry above), it includes some of the most useful and beautiful bit-mapped typefaces I've seen. My personal favorites are:

bargain

Nordic (Isn't this a beauty? I could look at it all day. It was all I could do to control myself and not set the whole book in it.)

very good feature

Oblique (this is another font you never get tired of looking at)

Chubby Shadow (for when you want to get really dramatic) and last, but certainly not least,

DREAM, A MOUSY LITTLE FONT THAT'S PERFECT FOR SPREAD-SHEETS.

World Class Fonts (AN)

Dubl-Click Software puts out a series of bit-mapped fonts that boggle the mind and dazzle the eye. They go by the name of World Class Fonts; there are many three-disk volumes, each of which only costs $80—about $1 a font!

World Class Fonts gives you Chicago in three other sizes than the 12-point Apple supplies, and Venice in two other sizes than the 14-point Apple supplies. You also get several foreign alphabets (Greek, Hebrew, Japanese, Russian) and a vast quantity of unique special characters that are hard to find elsewhere.

Other fonts give you chess pieces (a black set and a white set), postal labels, religious symbols (34 different crosses, among much else), architectural symbols and border designs. There's also Manhattan, described in the key-caps entry above.

Hollywood gives you what must be the ultimate in special characters–not merely 🏃, 📽 and ⟡ but also
very good feature

HOLLYWOOD**. ("You know the Hollywood sign that stands in the Hollywood hills? I don't think the Christ of the Andes ever blessed so many ills." A little something for you Dory Previn fans.)**

There are dozens of other useful and interesting fonts and, as if all that weren't enough, you get some great utilities with the disk. (See the entries on BigCaps, Font Charter and DefaultFont in the font utilities section below). The manual is terrific, the selection is astounding and the value is incredible.

very good feature

🍎 *public-domain bit-mapped fonts* (AN)

There are lots of public-domain bit-mapped fonts available, but my favorite is Santa Monica, designed by Paul Hoffman. As you can see, it's just about the widest font you'll ever find (this is just 10-point, believe it or not), which makes it a little hard to use, but I love the way it looks.

very good feature

(Santa Monica is included on the Macintosh Bible Software Disks, Third Edition, described in Chapter 19.)

bargain

An outline font sampler

⁙ *choking on fonts* (AN)

I love fonts and would have been delighted to show you ten zillion of them in this section. But even with a Laser-Writer IINTX with five megs of RAM and a 40-meg hard disk attached to it (and five megs of RAM in my ci), my system chokes on the sort of font madness to which I'm so devoted.

I'd call the tech people at Adobe and Bitstream and they'd say things like, *"How* many fonts did you say you have on that page?" Everyone seemed to agree that I was pushing the Mac beyond its present limits. (I could go to eight megs on the ci and twelve megs on the printer, but no one seemed to think that would solve the problems.)

So in order to actually get this book into your hands, I've had to compromise. I've had to give up on showing you ten zillion fonts. You'll have to be satisfied with five zillion.

But seriously, folks, the main thing I had to do was *refer* to weights and styles of fonts without showing them. So where I might want to write, "this font also comes in **bold,** *italic* and ***bold italic,***" I've often had to write instead, "this font also comes in bold, italic and bold italic." And I've also sometimes had to adjust page breaks to control the number of fonts on a page.

Sorry about that, but I'm dancing as fast as I can (and my equipment is clumping along with me).

⁙ *ITC* (AN)

very good feature

The *ITC* you see before the names of various fonts stands for the International Typeface Corporation of New York City, a powerful force for excellence and innovation in typography. They've been responsible for many beautiful new fonts and for tasteful redesigns of classic fonts like Garamond as well. Part of their agreement when they license a typeface is that their initials be shown as part of the name.

✦ *Apple's standard PostScript fonts* (AN)

The original LaserWriter came with four fonts built in:

Times—the standard, boring serif typeface. Look at how much smaller it is than Helvetica at the same point size (11-point).

Helvetica—the standard, boring sans serif typeface. Look at how much bigger it is than Times at the same size (11-point).

```
Courier—an excellent choice if you want to make
your laser printer look like a typewriter. To be
fair, Courier is also useful when you need a
monospaced font for some reason. Even we use it to
display programming listings and HyperCard
scripts, where precise spacing is often important
(and an even right margin isn't).
```

Finally, there's Σψμβολ—that is, Symbol, which supplements the other fonts by supplying symbols to them (although you can also get some great stuff by using it directly, as described in the previous section).

The LaserWriter Plus, IINT and IINTX contain a bunch of other fonts that Adobe also sells separately on disk (Bookman, Palatino, *Zapf Chancery,* Zapf Dingbats, Helvetica Narrow, etc.—the complete listing is in Chapter 4). In general, it's a useful and sensible selection—if not terribly exciting.

✦ *Adobe fonts* (AN)

Adobe is the company that developed PostScript, so it's not surprising that they were also the first to publish PostScript fonts. Their library now contains hundreds of typefaces, including the ones this book is set in (ITC Benguiat, with tables in Optima and headers in ITC Zapf Chancery).

The first Adobe font I'll describe is the beautiful Benguiat.
IT'S OFTEN USED FOR HEADLINES—THE
CAP A, B AND Q ARE REALLY BEAUTIFUL—

*very good
feature*

but for all its sensuous lushness, it's also an extremely readable font. Aren't you glad I used it for the book instead of something pedestrian like Times or New Century Schoolbook?

gossip/ trivia

Benguiat is named after the man who created it, Ed Benguiat (BENG-gat), who is certainly one of the greatest type designers who's ever lived. (I love names, so I took the trouble to find out that his is Spanish, originally from Córdoba. Actually, going all the way back, it's Moorish, *ben* meaning *son of* in Arabic.)

Anyway, Ed Benguiat, who was born in 1927, is responsible for more than five *hundred* typefaces, including classics like Bookman, Souvenir, Korinna, Tiffany and Charisma. In addition to being a designer and a vice-president at ITC, he's a pilot and a jazz drummer who's played with Stan Kenton and Woody Herman.

very bad feature

Adobe's version of Benguiat—of Benguiat Book, to be precise—is fine as far as it goes, but that isn't far enough. No italic or italic bold is provided, so everywhere you see those type styles in this book, they're algorithmic (calculated by the computer, rather than designed by a human being.) That's a pity, because *real* Benguiat italic—the kind used on phototypesetting machines—is *beautiful.* (See the Bitstream entry below for a description of a much fuller offering of Benguiat, which unfortunately got to us too late to use throughout the book.)

very good feature

If there's a prettier sans serif typeface than Optima, I've never seen it. It was designed by another titan of 20th-century typography, Hermann Zapf (1918–). Why anyone would ever use Helvetica when they could use Optima is something I'll never understand.

Optima is much smaller than Benguiat in a given size (11-point, in this case). IT'S A GREAT DISPLAY FACE TOO, AND LOOKS EVEN BETTER AT THE HIGHER RESOLUTION YOU GET FROM AN IMAGESETTER.

As its name implies, Zapf Chancery was also designed by Hermann Zapf. Adobe's version is of the medium italic and is really quite deficient. It's somewhat understandable that you can't make it italic, since it's <u>already</u> italic, although that's still annoying—look how I had to underline that word because I couldn't put it in italics. But why shouldn't you be able to make it bold? Ah, well.

Notice how much smaller Zapf Chancery is even than Optima (this is 11-point). Zapf Chancery also works nicely as a display font. For example, we use it for our logo: Goldstein & Blair. How do you like that ampersand?

Hermann Zapf also designed this font, which is built into the LaserWriter Plus, IINT and IINTX. It's probably the most popular font among people just discovering type—and also with those who've been immersed in type for fifty years. Classy, elegant, readable, luscious to look at—it's Palatino.

A fourth Adobe face designed by Zapf is Dingbats. There's a whole chart of the symbols in it, arranged by categories, in the special characters section above.

Another Adobe offering is Korinna, a beautiful redesign by Ed Benguiat of a turn-of-the-century typeface. It has the sensual grace that marks all his fonts—not to mention a really great capital U and lowercase italic *f*. It's also very readable and big for its size (this is 11-point). Here's how it looks in **bold**, *italic* and ***bold italic***.

very good feature

A third Adobe font of Benguiat's is Souvenir (in Light and Demibold). I once wrote a book for kids that was set in Souvenir and it worked great. It has an informal feel but, at the same time, it's elegant. Here's how it looks in **bold,** *italic and* ***bold italic.***

A fourth Adobe font of Benguiat's is Tiffany. (it's a display face, which is why I'm showing it to you at a larger size). You can make it bold but if you really want some weight, **use Tiffany Heavy, which comes on the same disk. (You can't make that bold, though.)**

very good feature

Cooper Black is one of my favorite display faces. Adobe's implementation of it is fine, except for the numbers, which vary in size. *I think Cooper looks best in italic. You can't make Cooper bold, because it's already black, which is bolder than bold.*

Brush Script is another nice display face, and on the same disk you get STENCIL, WHICH COMES IN CAPS ONLY, and the much-beloved (and much-used) Hobo.

Hobo is unusual in that it has no descenders (parts of letters that extend below the baseline). This cuts down on legibility but gives it a great lowercase g. Unfortunately, you can't make the Adobe version of Hobo italic or bold.

These three fonts make quite a nice package, but Adobe's got a lot more to tempt you with. **This is Futura extra bold, terrific for titling and headlines. *It looks good in oblique too.***

Belwe is a classy, ornate font you might use to complain to the lord of the manor about the predatory new crop levies—

SOMETHING YOU WOULDN'T WANT TO DO WITH ITC MACHINE, AN ALL-CAPS FONT WITH A MARKEDLY DIFFERENT FEEL. IT'S GREAT FOR HEADLINES, IF YOU KNOW WHEN TO USE IT (AND WHEN NOT TO).

LITHOS IS A REAL BEAUTY THAT SIMULATES GREEK WRITING. IT COMES IN A VARIETY OF WEIGHTS, FROM EXTRA LIGHT AND LIGHT **TO BOLD AND BLACK (IT'S SO DRAMATIC!).** I USED THIS FACE ON THE LABELS FOR THE MACINTOSH BIBLE SOFTWARE DISKS—I REALLY LOVE IT.

very good feature

As long as we're in Europe, let's look at Aachen (AH-khen) bold. It's named after the city in northwestern Germany that was the imperial capital of Charlemagne (or Big Charlie, as we used to call him around the palace school).

Skipping over the Alps, we come to an even prettier Adobe font—Italia. Aren't those diagonal serifs great? Look at that lowercase *i!* **Lucida Sans Roman** is another beautiful font. **Here it is in bold,** *italic* *and **bold italic.***

Goudy Heavyface is terrific for headlines, *especially in italic.* Antique Olive Nord is another good headline font, and it comes compact and bold condensed as well.

BUT THESE FONTS ARE ALL SO ORDINARY! HERE'S UMBRA, FOR WHEN YOU REALLY WANT TO MAKE AN IMPRESSION. SIMILAR IN FEELING ARE TWO OTHER ALL-CAPS FONTS— TRAJAN (WHICH IMITATES THE LETTERING ON ROMAN MONUMENTS) AND CHARLEMAGNE. (HE JUST KEEPS POPPING UP HERE, DOESN'T HE? I GUESS THE PEOPLE AT ADOBE HAVE A THING ABOUT THE HOLY ROMAN EMPIRE.)

Dom Casual is...well...casual; Helvetica 95 Black is not. (There's also a Helvetica 25 ExtraLight, and a bunch of other weights in between.) **Last but certainly not least is Arnold Böcklin (or Boecklin, for you conscientious umlaut refusers), a sinuous and sensuous Art Nouveau font.**

♦ *Bitstream fonts* (AN)

things to come

With almost a thousand PostScript fonts so far, Bitstream is one of the major suppliers (along with Adobe, The Font Company and the Image Club). And they're ready for System 7, since they'll be offering fonts in the TrueType format as well.

For a long time I've been complaining about Adobe not offering a Benguiat italic, thereby forcing me to use an algorithmic italic generated by my Mac. Well, here comes Bitstream's Benguiat to the rescue (it's what you're reading now). Compare it to the regular Benguiat that we've been using throughout the book (and in the last paragraph). As you can see, it's somewhat smaller for its point size, but otherwise looks pretty much the same.

And—Bitstream offers Benguiat in italic, in bold, and in bold italic—all separate cuttings. This is how the algorithmic italic looks in Adobe's Benguiat, so you can compare them. Bitstream also offers a medium weight of Benguiat, and a medium italic (again a separate cutting), and condensed (this is it), condensed italic, bold condensed, bold condensed italic, medium condensed and medium condensed italic.

very good
feature

I'd show them all to you, but then I wouldn't be able to print the page. Bitstream is one of the few font publishers I've come across that has enough different styles of a font to really push the limits of Mac hardware in a chapter like this. (In normal use, it won't make a difference, because you won't be using that many styles on a page. But you'll be able to pick the one you want from a meaningful range of choices.)

Ed Benguiat also put his name on a sans serif face—Benguiat Gothic. Bitstream offers it in its regular weight and style (book), in book italic, bold, bold italic, medium, medium italic **and heavy. This is how fonts should be supplied (and are, on phototypesetting machines)—you can choose the exact style that's right for the job.**

Another of Ed Benguiat's fonts supplied by Bitstream is Korinna. Since I've already got Adobe's Korinna, I asked Bitstream to just send the weights I don't have (they publish nine in all).

This is extra bold you've been reading **and this is Korinna heavy. (I'm showing them big because they're basically display faces in these weights.)** This beauty is Korinna bold outline.

Zapf Chancery is another font I have, but Adobe only supplies it in medium italic. This is Bitstream's Zapf Chancery light, and you can make it italic (although the effect is subtle). To get medium, you just make the light bold (or bold italic). **Bitstream also gives you a demibold, and to get a full bold, you just make it bold on the type style menu (or with** ⌘ Ⓑ **).**

Seagull calligraphic comes in light, which you can make medium with the Bold command, and in bold, which you can make **heavy with the Bold command. God, I love fonts!**

OK, let's cut loose a bit. This is Ronda Geometric, which also comes bold and light. (I know, I know, my snappy patter is beginning to falter. Well, you try doing this for page after page after page—let's see how long you last.)

Formal 421 looks a little like a cross between Casady & Greene's Dorovar and Gazelle (see below) but it has a look that's distinctly different from either. It really looks like it was written with a pen.

Here's Vineta. Impressed? No? OK, you

asked for it—THIS IS DECORATED 035 (A SUBTLE. LOW-KEY. ALL-CAPS FONT).

Bitstream publishes many weights of Cooper, from light to black. This is their Cooper black outline. Unfortunately, you can't make it italic; that's too bad, because I love Cooper in italic. Still, this is awfully nice just as it is.

Bitstream also publishes sixteen versions of Caslon. Given my terror of the ordinary, I requested Caslon Openface Engravers' Oldstyle, the most exotic of them. Isn't it gorgeous?

HERE'S A THIRD BITSTREAM OUTLINE FONT (I DON'T MEAN AN OUTLINE FONT AS OPPOSED TO A BIT-MAPPED FONT, AL-THOUGH IT'S THAT TOO; I MEAN THAT IT'S IN THE OUTLINE TYPE STYLE). IT'S CALLED ITC PIONEER AND IT'S CAPS-ONLY.

Finally, there's Poster Bodoni. I don't like Bodoni much in most weights, but I love this one.

**important
warning**

One important note about Bitstream fonts: Some of their printer font files have the same names as Adobe's, even though their names on the font menu are different. So if you're using both Bitstream's and Adobe's versions of a font (which may be unlikely, unless you're writing a chapter like this), make sure to put them in different folders. If you don't, the second one you drag into the folder will replace the first.

⌘ *Arthur's favorite Fluent Laser Fonts* (AN)

Richard Ware, the former type designer at Casady & Greene, came up with some really beautiful outline fonts (marketed as Fluent Laser Fonts).

**very good
feature**

ONE of THOSE is MONTEREY, AN AdAPTATiON of A cLAssic fAce cALLed PeiGNOT (pAiN-YOH). IsN'T iT exQuisiTe? I use iT iN my LeTTeRHEAd. THeRE's ALso A MONTEREY Medium (sLiGHTLy HEAVieR ANd wideR) ANd you cAN mAke eiTHeR THe ReGuLAR fONT OR THe **Medium bold** (buT THe Two **look THe sAme.** *HeRE's How iT Looks iN iTALic.*

One of my favorite Casady & Greene fonts is Dorovar. I often use it for notes or memos (it gives them a more personal touch). Isn't it gorgeous? Sometimes I find myself trying to think of what else I can put in a memo, just so I can keep on looking at this font.

Another favorite of mine is Gazelle. It's got a great lowercase d (which doesn't do a lot for readability, however). Gazelle really looks dra-

matic on the page. Here's how it looks in **bold**, *italic and* **bold italic**.

Casady & Greene also has an Old English (or "black letter") font called Gregorian. You may remember it from The Ten Commandments at the beginning of the book.

Another medieval font of theirs is Kells. It's what's called an uncial (UN-chul) font—that is, it resembles the lettering used in Irish and English manuscripts during the Middle Ages.

Another useful font is Ritz, a version of a classic (and classy) typeface called Broadway. If you find yourself suddenly transported back in time to the 30's (you never know when that might happen), this is the font to use.

Finally, there's Gatsby Light, which, as you can see, is an elegant face ideally suited for a fancy invitation or an ad for a store that sells expensive women's clothing. But it's sometimes nice to work against the grain of a font, so I think it might be fun to use this for, say, a boxing poster, or an ad for a demolition derby. Of course no one would *come*, but that's the price you have to pay for making art.

There are a lot of other beautiful Fluent Laser Fonts and they only cost $90 a disk (usually consisting of about four fonts, or four cuttings of a single font).

bargain

🍎 Sharon's favorite Fluent Laser Fonts

JottLight has a nice, informal feel without being too cute. It reminds me of the bit-mapped Los Angeles. Jott (hold the light) is a heavier version. Since neither translates well to italics, each has a special "quick" version: this is JottQuick and this is JottQuickLight. ("Quick" isn't an actual typographical term. The idea is just that if you write quickly, your letters are probably going to be a little more slanted.)

Collegiate, CollegiateBlack and CollegiateOutline are on the same disk. Collegiate is a combination of the other two and, for my money, is the nicest of the three. All three are *small caps fonts*—that is, the lowercase letters look like the capitals, except they're smaller.

THIS IS COLLEGIATE

COLLEGIATEBLACK AND

COLLEGIATEOUTLINE

Then there's what I (but not the publisher) call "the cowboy fonts disk":

ABILENE   DRYGULCH   Paladin

🍎 Arthur's favorite Font Company fonts (AN)

Although Adobe was for many years the largest supplier of PostScript fonts, that honor now goes to the Font Company of Phoenix, which offers over 1500 of them! Needless to say, there are a lot worth mentioning in there.

Before we get to the fancy stuff, let's look at a few of the Font Company's excellent text fonts. The LaserWriter Plus, IINT and IINTX come with Bookman Light and Bookman

Demi built-in (the demi is what you get when you choose bold). The Font Company provides a supplement for that—Bookman Medium (which is between light and demi—this is it here). **When you make it bold, it becomes a true bold, bolder than Bookman Demi.**

This is Barcelona—isn't it beautiful? Like Bookman, it's a very round font. This is Basilia, which is, as you can see, smaller for its size (all these text faces are 11-point) and is less rounded, more rectilinear. This is Caxton (I'll keep them all in the same paragraph to make them easier to compare). This is Novarese, which is elegant and thin. Slimbach is taller than most text fonts, and beautifully formed.

very good feature

Nicholas Cochin can be used for text, but it really works better as a display font, or at least as a text font in very large sizes—12- or 14-point, say (this is 16-point). It looks a little like the writing on ancient maps.

OK, ENOUGH TEXT FONTS. LET'S GET TO THE EXOTICS. THIS IS BALLOON, A SMALL CAPS FONT THAT RESEMBLES THE KIND OF WRITING YOU SEE IN CARTOONS (COMPARE IT WITH THE IMAGE CLUB'S CARTOON).

FRANKFURTER IS SOMETHING LIKE CARTOON AND SOMETHING LIKE THE IMAGE CLUB'S T.H. ALPHABET SOUP. IT GETS ITS NAME FROM THE FACT THAT THE SHAPES IT'S MADE UP OF RE-SEMBLE HOT DOGS.

LET'S KEEP GETTING FANCIER. THIS SMALL CAPS FONT IS CALLED PLAZA (AFTER THE HOTEL, I ASSUME). AS YOU CAN SEE, IT'S VERY THIN, TALL AND NARROW—EXCEPT FOR THE O'S.

LIBERTY IS AN ALL-CAPS FONT WHOSE LOOK REALLY FITS ITS NAME, I THINK (ALTHOUGH I'M NOT SURE WHY). ANYWAY, ISN'T IT A BEAUTY?

Paddington is one of those fonts you saw a lot of in the 60's, on Peter Max posters and the like, but which have more or less disappeared since then. Get this font (and the Image Club's Amelia) and when the 60's come back, you'll be ready.

Here's another font to add to your 60's revival package—Bottleneck. I don't know if it originated then, but you sure saw a lot of it on posters.

very good feature

This lush lollapolooza of a font is called Candice. It has caps to die for: A B C D E F G H I J K L M N O P Q R S T U V W X Y Z.

And we'll bring this entry to a close with Cabaret. I use this for letters to my senators, so they'll take me seriously. It's also good for a to-do list if you don't really want to get a lot done.

✎ *Sharon's favorite Font Company fonts*

bargain

The Font Company doesn't have a fancy name, but it does have some pretty fancy fonts, at prices ranging from $100 to $150. (Some of the fonts used as examples elsewhere in this chapter—like Times Small Caps and the six weights of Eras—are from the Font Company.) EPS outlines of every font are also available (they're included with some fonts, but are an extra-cost option with others). Here are some samples:

This is Golden Type, based on a font from the pen of the great 19th-century English designer, William Morris. [Isn't that hyphen in 19th-century great? It just makes you just want to hyphen-ate like cra-zy.—AN] Golden also comes in bold and in black. (Golden Black—it sounds like a contradiction in terms.)

𝕾𝖍𝖆𝖉𝖔𝖜𝖊𝖉 𝕺𝖈𝖙𝖔𝖕𝖚𝖘𝖘 (it also comes in unshadowed) is hard to read on the screen, but it's effective in a printout (depending, of course, on just what effect you're looking for).

This is Old English. It's similar to Casady & Greene's Gregorian, which we showed a few pages back; compare them to see which you prefer (or, for something better, see the Image Club's Daily Tribune).

This is one of my favorites—Van Dijk. I especially like the extra swirls on the s's (the cap S has them too).

Vivaldi is a very elegant script font. I love the flourishes on the lowercase g and f, and on the caps: A B C D E F G H I J K L M O P Q R S T U V W X Y Z.

This is Victorian, an Art Nouveau font similar to Adobe's Arnold Böcklin, but significantly different (as you'll see if you compare them).

● *Image Club fonts*

Image Club is one of the other big publishers of Mac fonts, with hundreds of Type 1 and Type 3 typefaces in their stable. They distribute them in an unusual way too—they send you a CD with *all* their fonts (and their extensive clip-art collection) on it. When you get the CD, all the fonts (and clip-art) are locked—except for some freebies. When you buy a font, Image Club sends you the code to unlock it, at which point you can download it from the CD and use it.

Some of their fonts are quite nice. The last paragraph was in Velijovic, and this one is in Citi Light, which is a little like Italia (shown in the Adobe entry above), but without the slanting serifs. **It also comes in what's called bold, but which to my eye is closer to extra bold or black.**

One really nice text face from Image Club is Caslon. *Nice* doesn't really do it justice, though—*clean, elegant, classy* are more like it.

Let's do all the text fonts together. This is Elan, which comes in six cuttings—book, book italic, bold, bold italic **and black and black italic. I'm a real sucker for a beautiful black font, and this is certainly one.**

Image Club gives you Gill Sans in a nice selection of weights, light, medium (that's what this is), bold **and ultra bold (my favorite, of course). There's an italic cutting for all the weights except this one (probably because it's too fat to lean over).**

If you're fortunate enough to own a copy of the Second Edition of this book, you can see this beautifully designed typeface at work on the cover (in bold, which is what this is).

I think Gorilla is a really beautiful font. In fact, when I was requesting review copies, I decided that if they'd only give me one font, this is the one I wanted. It looks a lot like Cooper—maybe that's why I like it so much.

Bauhaus is a font I've been waiting for for a long time. Image Club gives you a nice selection of weights in it too. This is light, and there's also a medium, **a bold (which is probably the weight most often used), a heavy and even** a heavy outline. (I'll give you more of the heavy, bold and medium in the next paragraph.)

very good feature

Bauhaus is named for the famous architecture school founded in 1919 in Weimar by Walter Gropius (*bauhaus* literally means *building house*), but I don't know if the typeface was actually designed there.

gossip/ trivia

Broadway is a classic font from the 30's (at least that's when it was the most popular). It looks particularly good in its *engraved* style—and I'm particularly glad that I can *show* you what *engraved* means without having to try to define it in words.

Amelia also harkens back to another era—in this case, the 60's. If you lived through those times, you're probably getting a contact high just from reading this.

BUSORAMA IS AN ALL-CAPS ART DECO FONT. YOU'VE BEEN SEEING IT AROUND YOUR WHOLE LIFE—ISN'T IT NEAT TO KNOW WHAT IT'S CALLED? IIMAGE CLUB PROVIDES IT IN LIGHT AND BOLD AS WELL AS MEDIUM (WHICH IS WHAT THIS IS).

Dingaling is a little like Busorama with lowercase letters. It's got a great *g*. (Did you know that one of the first letters font experts look at to distinguish a font is the lowercase *g*? As a result, font designers often go to town on that letter.) Dingaling comes in bold too (this is medium).

Harry looks a bit like Dingaling. This is medium, and there's also a thin (light) and a fat (black).

Here's Bamboo, your standard hand-written Chinese font. Compare it to Chinese Menu, a public-domain font shown at the end of this section, to see what you get for your money when you buy a commercial font (a great B, for one thing).

BANCO IS AN ALL-CAPS FONT AND, LIKE ALL OF THOSE FROM THE IMAGE CLUB THAT I'VE TRIED, IT WORKS THE RIGHT WAY. THAT IS, YOU GET A CAP WHETHER YOU HOLD THE SHIFT KEY DOWN OR NOT. (SOME FONTS PUNISH YOU WITH THE MISSING CHARACTER BOX IF YOU FORGET WHETHER THE SHIFT KEY SHOULD BE HELD DOWN OR NOT.

Guts is well-named. Tough and solid, it reminds me of Aachen Bold (see the Adobe section above), but it's more rounded and wider.

New Yorker is an elegant font, but it's nothing compared to New Yorker Engraved. Compare this beauty to Caslon Openface Engraved in the Bitstream entry above.

While we're doing elegant, let's do Firenze (which is, of course, the Italian name for the city we call Florence). Firenze

has extreme contrast between thick verti-
cals and thin horizontals, which is really
noticeable in capital letters like H, C and Q.

ALBERTUS IS AN ALL-CAPS FONT THAT ALSO
COMES BOLD AND BLACK. I'D LOVE TO SHOW THEM
TO YOU, BUT I COULDN'T PRINT THE PAGE WHEN I
TRIED TO.

very good feature

Daily Tribune is an Old English,
or black letter, font like Casady &
Greene's Gregorian and the Font
Company's Old English, but it's engraved, which makes it much nicer.

CARTOON IS MODELED AFTER THE KIND
OF LETTERING YOU FIND IN CARTOONS.
SINCE THAT LETTERING ONLY USES CAPS,
SO DOES THIS FONT.

THIS FONT IS CALLED TOO MUCH.
DON'T YOU LOVE THE SHAPE OF THE
LETTERS? IT ALSO COMES IN AN OUT-
LINE AND A SHADOW VERSION.

T.H. ALPHABET SOUP IS SIMILAR TO TOO
MUCH, BUT IT'S NOT AS FAT. IT'S A MORE
RESTRAINED APPROACH TO THE SAME LOOK
(IF YOU CAN CALL THIS RESTRAINED).

Finally, we have Rockabilly, which isn't restrained at all. It's perfect for the fine print on labels, when you don't want your customers to know that your mayonnaise contains machine oil. Isn't it the greatest?

🍎 *LetterPerfect fonts*

LetterPerfect is a new company whose initial offerings of PostScript fonts bode well for its success. Each font set comes not only with screen and printer fonts but also with a set of EPS outlines for each letter (for manipulation in programs like Illustrator). LetterPerfect's designer, Garrett Boge, is promising a new typeface every quarter. Prices range from $45 for single-font disks like Spumoni to $65 for a two-font set like Spring and SpringLight to $200 for a disk with six fonts (or six cuttings of a font).

bargain

Spring (the top example) and SpringLight (bottom) are two weights of a brush-style script. I like it better than Adobe's Brush Script, which seems blunt in comparison.

very good feature

Spring has sprung!

In Spring a young man's fancy ...

My favorite letters in Spring are the lowercase *f* (shown above) and the upper- and lowercase *Q's:*

Quiet!   *quiet?*

This is Florens, a chancery script with beautiful flourishes—and over 500 kerning pairs built in. Florens also has swash characters (ones with extra flourishes). Some of the lowercase swashes look good in double letters—gg, dd—and the swash caps look good anywhere: A, B, D, F, T, V, Z. There are even a few flourishes that aren't attached to anything: ✿ ⚘ ⌒

Florens also gives you old-style numbers. What are old-style numbers, you ask? Well, compare them to the regular numbers that follow them here: 1, 1; 2, 2; 3, 3; 4, 4; 5, 5; 6, 6; 7, 7; 8, 8; 9, 9; 0, 0.

very good
feature

AT THE OTHER EXTREME, HERE'S MANITO. PRETTY RUGGED-LOOKING, HUH? (MANITO IS AN AMERICAN INDIAN WORD FOR SPIRIT.) IT'S AN ALL-CAPS FONT, BUT THE SHIFTED CAPS ARE TALLER THAN THE UNSHIFTED ONES.

Spumoni is a playful font. It's based on the classic Bodoni, but looks as if it was hit by a small earthquake. The numbers (1 2 3 4 5 6 7 8 9 0) and punctuation (: " ? !) are not quite as shaken up as the letters, but they blend in perfectly.

World Class LaserType (AN)

Dubl-Click is one of the great publishers of bit-mapped fonts and their outline font collection, while small, has some real winners that they sell at just $80 a disk. They have a version of Hobo called Hoboken and a version of Stencil called Saigon that has lowercase letters as well as caps.

bargain

But my favorite World Class font is Metropolitan. Feast your eyes on these caps! ABCDEFGHIJKLMNOPQRSTUVWXYZ. Gorgeous, aren't they? Look how the L and M cross.

very good
feature

Mmm! The lowercase letters are beautiful too; for example, look at the ch combination—it almost makes a heart.

CALAIS IS AN ALL-CAPS FONT, WITH VARIANTS FOR SOME OF THE LETTERS (S AND *S*, FOR EXAMPLE). YOU MIGHT USE IT TO RESPOND TO AN IRS AUDIT NOTICE. THEY'LL PROBABLY THINK YOU'RE SO CRAZY THEY'LL DROP THE WHOLE THING.

IXTAPA IS ANOTHER ALL-CAPS FONT. IT'S AN IMITATION OF A FAMOUS FACE CALLED BABY TEETH. *ITALIC LOOKS OK*, BUT BOLD FILLS IN TOO MUCH.

 two hours after you use this font... (AN)

bargain

Chinese Menu is a public-domain outline font, designed by Andrew Faulkner, that looks like...hey, wait a minute! I get it! So *that's* why he calls it *Chinese Menu.* I always wondered about that. (Chinese Menu is included on The Macintosh Bible Software Disks, Third Edition, described in Chapter 19.)

 throw away that old clay tablet (AN)

Sure, we've shown you a lot of interesting and useful fonts. But what if your job calls for something in cuneiform (perhaps a memo to the main office back in Babylon)? You could just haul out your old clay tablet (it's over there behind those ewers) and knock one off, but you're wearing your good suit and you're afraid you'll get the cuffs dirty.

No problem. Just use Cuneifont, the public-domain outline font you're reading right now. It's missing some characters, like an em dash, curly apostrophe and curly quotes, and it doesn't quite work right (line lengths and justification are screwy, for example), but when you really need cuneiform, nothing else will do.

Font utilities

⬥ *Font/DA Mover, Suitcase and Font/DA Juggler* *(AN)*

These are the most important programs for handling fonts, but since they handle DAs as well, they're discussed in Chapter 8 rather than here.

⬥ *Key Caps* *(AN/SZA)*

esp. for beginners

It's often hard to remember which key combination to hit to produce the special character you need, or even whether the font you're using has that character. That's what Apple's Key Caps desk accessory is for.

When you choose Key Caps from the ⬥ menu, it displays a representation of the Mac's keyboard and puts a new menu title, Key Caps, at the right end of the menu bar. You select the font you're interested in from that menu and the Key Caps display switches over to it. (This is the display for an extended keyboard.)

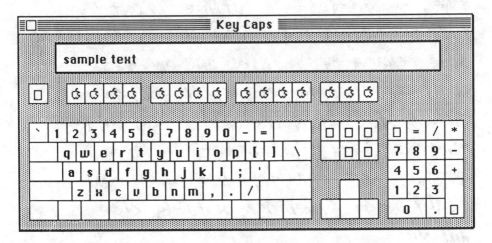

When you hold down the [Shift] key, Key Caps darkens the [Shift] keys on its display and shows you the the characters you get in the selected font when you hold down [Shift] and press another key.

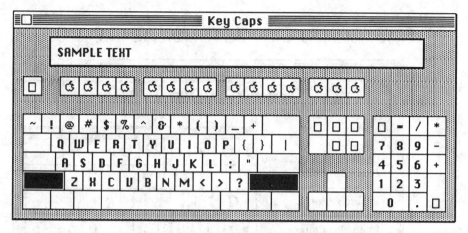

But you already know what the [Shift] characters are (except in fonts composed entirely of pictures and symbols). Where Key Caps really comes in handy is in showing you the characters generated by the [Option] and [Shift][Option] keys.

You can enter text in the sample text area by typing on the keyboard or by clicking on the key you want on the Key Caps display. You can cut or copy this text from Key Caps into any document. (It won't appear in the font you chose in Key Caps, but it's easy enough to change the font once you're back in your document.)

If you need a string of special characters, it's usually easier to type them in Key Caps, copy them to your document and then change the font than it is to remember where each symbol is on the keyboard and type them directly into your document.

very hot tip

If you use a lot of special characters and have trouble remembering which keys generate them, you can resize your text window to leave room at the bottom of the screen for Key Caps to be displayed at all times. But it's probably easier just to print out a chart of the font and pin it to your wall.

⌘ *BigCaps* (AN/SZA)

BigCaps is a replacement for Key Caps that comes with all of Dubl-Click Software's World Class fonts. It has several advantages: it displays characters in various sizes and styles, its window is resizable and it can display fonts even when you're not using them and they're not on the menu.

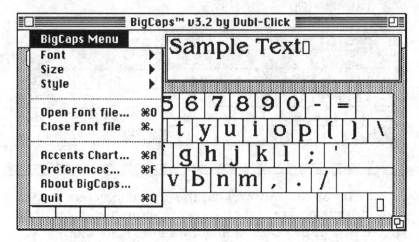

BigCaps also shows a chart of the special accent characters, something that's missing from the Key Caps display.

Prefix:	A	a	E	e	i	O	o	U	u
option+e		á	É	é	í		ó		ú
option+`	À	à	-	è	ì		ò		ù
option+i		â		ê	î		ô		û
option+u	Ä	ä		ë	ï	Ö	ö	Ü	ü
option+n	Ã	ã				Õ	õ		

If you have BigCaps, there's really no reason to use Key Caps.

 *Font Charter* (AN)

The Font Charter is another utility that comes with Dubl-Click Software's World Class fonts. It prints out a chart of all the characters in a font, arranged either by their location on the keyboard or by ASCII number, on both dot-matrix and laser printers.

This is quite handy for comparing fonts, (if for some reason you don't like our font template, described above). It's a good idea to make a printout of all the fonts you use, either with Font Charter or our template, and put them in a notebook. Then you can refer to them when deciding which font to use.

🍎 *DefaultFont* *(AN)*

This DA is third utility that comes on Dubl-Click's font disks. It lets you change the font an application defaults to when it first opens. So if you're tired of having to change from Geneva every time you select *New* from the File menu, you'll love this desk accessory. (The World Class Font disks are almost worth the money just for the utilities that come on them—never mind the terrific fonts.)

very good feature

🍎 *FontDisplay*

FontDisplay is a utility by Jeff Shulman that lets you display and print fonts. You can view each font as either a table (by ASCII number) or as a series of pictures of the keyboard, in whatever size and style you want. FontDisplay also shows you the ID number for each font. You can also set it up to print a full catalog of many fonts without having to do each one separately—for example, you could have it do a chart of all the fonts in a particular suitcase file.

🍎 *MenuFonts*

This is another terrific utility by the Dubl-Click people—but it's a separate product, not just a freebie on their font disks. It puts the font names on the menu in their own fonts, instead of in the usual Chicago font. Unlike the similar feature built into WriteNow and MacWrite II, MenuFonts is smart enough to keep certain fonts in Chicago (so Zapf Dingbats doesn't show up as ✹❖□✸ ✦✸■✳❂❖▼▲). And unlike Suitcase and Juggler, which also provide true-font menus, there's no delay when you access the font menu—with MenuFonts, it pops down just as quickly as any other menu.

MenuFonts also puts a bar along the edge of the menu that lets you access samples of the font in different sizes.

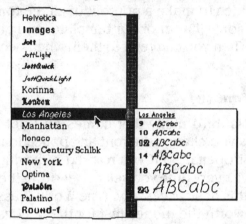

very good feature

But the niftiest thing about MenuFonts is that once the font menu is open and the pointer's in it, you can scroll by using the keyboard—press [Z] and Zapf Chancery jumps up to where you're holding the pointer.

⚫ *Set Paths* (Paul Hoffman/SZA)

very good feature

This terrific utility (described in Chapter 8) is very handy for dealing with outline fonts. When you use a lot of them, they really clutter up your system folder. With Set Paths, you can put the printer files in another folder—within the system folder or elsewhere—and just show the Mac where to find them.

⚫ *ATM* (SZA/AN)

Adobe Type Manager ($100) draws outline fonts on the screen based on the information in their printer files, rather than their bit-mapped screen fonts. This lets you display type at even the largest sizes without the dreaded *jaggies*. (You just need a single size of the screen font installed, so that the font name will appear on the Font menu.)

Here's what 72-point Benguiat looks like on the screen without ATM running:

Benguiat

And here's what it looks like *with* ATM running:

Benguiat

ATM also lets you print outline fonts on dot-matrix printers with the same quality (although of course not the same quality as on a 300-dpi laser printer, since both the ImageWriter and the Mac's screen only have a resolution of 72 dpi).

If you *absolutely* need accurate screen representations of large type (or great-quality dot-matrix printouts) ATM's the best thing since sliced bread. But it's *slow.* On anything less than a IIcx or an SE/30, it'll drive you nuts. In tests we ran, scrolling slowed significantly on a Mac Plus, but not on an SE/30. Likewise, on a Plus, converting a page of text took 30 seconds with ATM on and 5 seconds with it off, while on an SE/30 it took 3 seconds in either case.

But printing to an ImageWriter was slowed on either machine (understandably, since the ATM output is far superior). One page took a Plus 5:10 with ATM on, versus 2:35 with it off; on an SE/30, a page took 2:30 with ATM on, versus 1:40 with it off.

ATM also makes some smaller fonts virtually unreadable. For example, 12-point Benguiat bold italic looks like this:

12-point Benguiat Bold Italic

with ATM running. Without ATM running, it looks like this:

12-point Benguiat Bold Italic

Bold, italic and bold italics suffer the most under ATM. Sometimes it improves the look of small fonts. For example, here's Korinna 9-point plain (the ATM version is on the right):

Korinna 9 point   Korinna 9 point

bug

The most complaints we've heard about ATM have to do with bugs like unexpected font substitutions while you're in the middle of working on a document. But most of those problems seem to have been cleared up in version 1.02.

Another problem with ATM is that it forces you to keep printer files in your system folder for fonts that are built into your laser printer (or that you've downloaded permanently to a hard disk attached to an NTX).

FontSizer

FontSizer ($100) offers another approach to coordinating screen fonts and printer fonts. It will create a screen font in any size from 12- to 127- point *from* a printer font. You can also make a true bold, italic or bold italic version of a font (a *cutting,* in other words) to replace the algorithmically derived one the Mac creates when there's no cutting available. (Since FontSizer uses the PostScript interpreter in your laser printer to create the screen fonts, the printer has to be on, and selected in the Chooser, for it to work.)

The larger the size of the screen font you create, the better FontSizer works. And it works reasonably quickly too; in one little test I ran, it took six minutes to create two new screen fonts. But FontSizer doesn't do as well with smaller sizes. For example, at the top of the next page is what three sizes of Times looked like on the screen before I created screen fonts for them with FontSizer:

Times 16-point

Times 32-point

Times 48-point

And here's what they looked like after:

Times 16-point

Times 32-point

Times 48-point

As you can see, the improvement is wonderful at 48-point and considerable at 32-point, but the 16-point—although truer to the printed version in height and width—still isn't much of a screen font.

ATM creates screen fonts on the fly while you use your Mac, and therefore slows things down; but since its screen fonts don't exist until they're needed, they don't take any room on your disk. FontSizer creates regular screen fonts that are used like any others; they add to the clutter in your System file or suitcases, and you have to install every size you want. But if you need only a few large screen fonts for headlines, FontSizer is a faster, better and cheaper approach.

✦ *type-manipulation programs*

Graphics programs let you manipulate text to a certain extent, but the type itself isn't changed much—the characters are forced to bind to a specific path, say, but the letters themselves don't get squeezed or stretched (see the illustration on the left). Programs specifically designed to manipulate type do a whole lot more, as the illustration on the right makes obvious.

🍎 *TypeStyler*

TypeStyler ($200, from Broderbund) lets you get right to work (or play) by providing editable fonts and a library of basic shapes in which to put them. Here are two—the double slope and the pennant shape.

You can make the shapes larger or smaller, fatter or skinnier just by changing the size of the rectangle they're in. You can edit the basic shapes in the library, or create your own. The first illustration below shows the shape I started with. The one on the right shows it being edited (you drag on the handles to change the curves of the shape). The bottom illustration shows the result. (These are pictures of what they look like on the screen—printing them on a laser printer will eliminate the jaggies.)

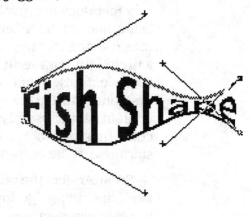

TypeStyler only works with Type 3 fonts (described in the next section). You have to convert them to TypeStyler's *Smoothfont* format, but a utility's included, so you can do that painlessly.

🍎 SmartArt 2.0

SmartArt ($150, from Emerald City Software) is a nifty font-manipulation utility that's worth your time and money despite its somewhat awkward user interface. It lets you distort outline fonts into any of a number of styles:

SmartArt is currently available in three different packages: I, II and III. Each contains the desk accessory that does the manipulating and some "effects" (basic shapes for the text, which you can edit to some extent). While the first and third packages

contain a lot of useful effects, Smart Art II is a disappointing collection of blocky, mostly 3-D shapes like boxes and starbursts. (The current version of each package is 2.0.)

SmartArt lets the processor in the laser printer do all the work, including figuring out out how things should look on the Mac's screen.

What I don't like about SmartArt is the way you have to set each of the elements of your effect separately—you click on *Font,* then choose the font; click on *Size,* then choose the size, etc.

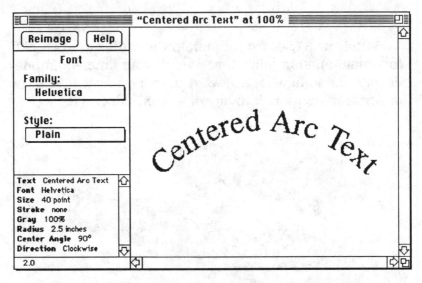

One large dialog box where you can set everything at once would be better. But at least when you choose *Font,*

you're actually choosing the type family and a separate menu lets you choose the family member:

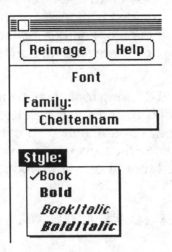

Version 2.0 lets you save the effects as EPS files. It also remembers where you left your folder of effects and automatically goes there when the DA opens.

The manual's a problem, though. There aren't enough picture samples and it must have been written by programmers—when was the last time you heard *yes/no* buttons referred to as *Boolean choices?*

If you're working with color, be aware that SmartArt effects pasted into PageMaker can only be assigned spot color, and even if you're using Adobe Separator on the file, you can't separate an effect.

Since Smart Art lets you display an EPS file on the screen, you can view any EPS file in the Smart Art window—just open it as if it were a SmartArt effect.

❤ *FONTastic Plus*

FONTastic Plus (from Altsys) was the first bit-mapped font editor (not counting ResEdit, for which that was a sideline). FONTastic is still fantastic. FONTastic lets you create a font bit by bit. You draw each character with a limited though sufficient set of tools and—voilà! A font!

very good feature

❖ *Fontographer*

When the Mac grew up to use laser printers, Altsys grew along with it and provided Fontographer to design PostScript fonts. The latest version of Fontographer can create Type 1 fonts (see below) complete with hinting to improve type at small sizes.

Fontographer's drawing tools may be a little disappointing to people used to the fuller palettes in Illustrator or Freehand, but they're sufficient. You can paste a bit map for a character and trace over it, but you can't import a whole bit-mapped font in one fell swoop.

Advanced font info

❖ *Type 1 and Type 3 PostScript fonts*

There are two standards for PostScript fonts—*Type 1* and *Type 3*. (There is no Type 2—it was a dead-end technology that Adobe dropped.) Adobe's own fonts are Type 1—they're *locked (encrypted)* so you can't alter them. They also contain special information called *hinting* that helps small sizes of type print well at the 300-dpi resolution of most laser printers.

Type 3 fonts aren't locked or hinted. Type 3 has been the standard for non-Adobe fonts, although many of these are now Type 1 as well. Fonts created with Fontographer are Type 3. On laser printers, at small type sizes (less than 9-point, say), Type 3 fonts may have uneven spacing and irregular base lines for curved letters.

Don't worry about Type 1 versus Type 3 if you're printing at a higher resolution than 300 dpi, or if you never print at small sizes. The only other time it will make a difference is if you're using a program that works with only one kind of font or the other—most font manipulation programs, for example, only work with Type 3 fonts, and Adobe Type Manager only works with Type 1.

✦ *font ID conflicts and NFNTs* (AN/SZA)

In the beginning, the Mac came with a selection of eleven bit-mapped fonts, and Apple allowed for a total of 256 different ID numbers, the first 128 of which it reserved for its own use. This has to be one of the most incredible underestimates in the history of computing.

It wasn't long before the available ID numbers were used up. Apple responded—belatedly—with new numbering system called *NFNT* (for *new font numbering table)* that has 16,000 font ID numbers (the old numbers were called, descriptively enough, FONTs).

Even with NFNTs, there are still *font ID conflicts* (two fonts with the same number). At present, they're the result of sloppiness on the part of font publishers or of Apple (which assigns the ranges). But soon they'll become inevitable, because it won't be long before we run out of NFNTs.

**things
to come**

Font conflicts are fixable, because font ID numbers are reassignable. When you install a font that has the same number as another font that's already installed, Font/DA Mover simply assigns the newcomer a different number. But this can become a real problem if you use another system, where that font's ID number *hasn't* been changed.

**important
warning**

The easy solution is to always bring your own System file and/or suitcase files when printing out at a service bureau or on a friend's Mac. For other solutions, see the next entry.

All old and even some current fonts have FONT numbers. There are two ways to convert them to NFNTs. One is to check with the font's publisher to see if they've come out with an NFNT version. This is the preferred method, because it makes sure the NFNT ID numbers are correct.

The other way is to do it yourself. Suitcase II, Font/DA Juggler Plus and FONTastic Plus all do NFNT conversions. But you have the perfect tool right at your fingertips: version 3.8 of Font/DA Mover (and later versions, we assume) automatically convert FONTs to NFNTs. Just create a new suitcase, open the suitcase with the old fonts in it and then move the fonts to the new suitcase.

Using Font/DA Mover to install every one of the fonts in the System, or in one gigantic suitcase file, will solve all internal ID conflicts. That won't work if your fonts are in separate suitcases, but Suitcase and Juggler both come with utilities that solve ID conflicts in multiple suitcases.

important warning

Versions of Font/DA Mover earlier than 3.8 don't handle NFNTs, so upgrade to the current version. NFNTs also won't work on:

- an original 128K Mac or a Mac 512 (you need a Mac 512e or later)

- much early software, including versions of PageMaker prior to 3.02

- systems earlier than 6.0

- WordPerfect 1.03 and earlier (maybe later versions as well)

✺ *font ID conflicts on foreign systems*

As mentioned in the previous entry, solving internal conflicts by font renumbering only adds to the probability of conflicts with other systems. The easy solution is to bring your hard disk and use that to run the other system. But there are other approaches.

One is to find out the ID numbers of your fonts and the fonts on the other system, and see if they match. (If they do, you're home free.) A utility called FontDisplay shows you the ID numbers of fonts, as does a handy little DA called Font Info (from Regional Typographers). Font Info also counts the fonts you have installed, points out any conflicts, and tells you how many there are. Both FONTastic and ResEdit show ID numbers and let you change them too. You can even display them in Word (believe it or not). Here's how:

very hot tip

Start a new document and choose *Save* from the file menu. Click the *Format* button and choose *Interchange*

(RTF) as the format you want the file saved in. Click the *OK* button in the Format dialog box, name the document and click the *Save* button. The document on your screen will look something like this (depending, of course, on the fonts you have installed):

≣ test ≣

```
{\rtf1\mac\deff2 {\fonttbl{\f0\fswiss Chicago;}{\f2\
froman New York;}{\f3\fswiss Geneva;}{\f4\fmodern
Monaco;}{\f5\fscript Venice;}{\f6\fdecor London;}{\f7\
fdecor Athens;}{\f11\fnil Cairo;}{\f12\fnil Los Angeles;}
{\f13\fnil Zapf Dingbats;}{\f14\fnil Bookman;}{\f16\fnil
Palatino;}{\f18\fnil Zapf Chancery;}{\f20\froman Times;
}{\f21\fswiss Helvetica;}{\f22\fmodern Courier;}{\f23\
ftech Symbol;}{\f27\fnil Benguiat;}{\f31\fnil Optima;}
{\f33\fnil Avant Garde;}{\f34\fnil New Century Schlbk;}
{\f50\fnil Fallingwater;}{\f79\fnil Images;}{\f104\fnil
```

The number appearing after the *f* between the backslashes in front of the font name (as in Geneva) is its ID # (in this case, *3*—the regular ID number for Geneva). Just ignore the lowercase words before the font names *(swiss, modern, script, etc.)*.

You can get font ID numbers many other ways. If the other system you're printing out on is at a service bureau, they may already have a list of ID numbers you can check against your own.

A final option is to print from a PostScript file instead of from the document you've created—PostScript files identify fonts by name. Some programs, like PageMaker, give you the option of saving a PostScript version of your document. (You can create a PostScript file from most Mac programs—see *saving a PostScript file* on page 259.) But the identify-by-name approach doesn't always work either, as the next entry makes clear.

esp. for
power users

✦ dimmed fonts on PageMaker's menus

Sometimes a font's name appears dimmed on Page-Maker's menu. This means you've created a document that contains a certain font and then reopened it (on your system or someone else's) when that font is no longer available. (It happens because PageMaker keeps track of fonts by name rather than by number.)

✦ two font menu puzzlers

very hot tip

Sometimes you know you have a font installed but it doesn't appear on the Font menu. Other times you choose a font from the menu but a different font is applied to the selected text. Both problems are caused by conflicting ID numbers. You have different fonts with the same ID number in separate suitcases, which confuses the Mac. It looks for its screen fonts in this order:

- in the current application (Chapter 8 describes how to install fonts directly into applications),

- in the System file,

- in any open suitcases (that is, one which is available to the System), starting with the most recently opened one

If you have fonts with conflicting ID numbers in various places, the first one the Mac runs across wins. If you can't resolve the conflict, install your important fonts in the System file, so they get priority.

(There's another possible reason for the first problem. If you open a suitcase with Suitcase or Juggler *after* you launch your program, the program can't update its Font menu. Both programs warn you of this problem, however.)

✦ installed sizes not noted on the menu

very hot tip

Suppose you know you have five sizes of a font installed, but only two of them show up on the Size menu (as outlined numbers). This occurs because you have the same font, with the same ID, in two different places, but not all the sizes are in both locations.

If the Mac finds Times-10 and Times-12 in the System file, it will ignore the Times 9 through 24 you have in an opened suitcase, because it always ignores fonts with duplicate ID's. You have to consolidate your fonts so all the sizes are in one place.

✦ *font size conflicts* (AN)

There's a bizarre bug in some screen fonts that I haven't been able to track down the reason for; knowledgeable tech support people don't seem to understand it very well, or give reasons for it that don't make sense. Still, it's worth telling you about it, so your heart won't stop the way mine did the first time you see it.

bug

Under certain circumstances, where there are *no* font ID conflicts (as verified by Font Info or some other utility), one screen font will be substituted for another in a certain small range (or ranges) of sizes. Increase or decrease the size significantly, or even leave it the same and go to a different view (200% or 50%, say), and the invader font disappears. The real font shows up on the font menu, and the text prints out correctly in that font. The invader font only appears when the real font is *displayed* at a certain size, but you get it no matter what program you're in and no matter what type style you change the text into.

The first time I saw the problem was in the Ten Commandments section of Chapter 1, when Adobe's **Arnold Böcklin** was substituted for Adobe's *Zapf Chancery.* Let me tell you, Arnold Böcklin was not meant to be a text face; I thought two fonts were printed over each other. (Amazing, when I just now went back to see what size the Zapf Chancery was, I couldn't reproduce the problem. I'd removed Arnold Böcklin from the suitcase and then reinstalled it, so maybe that helped somehow.)

One difficulty is that there's no way to tell what the invader font is unless you happen to recognize it. Some relatively heavy sans serif font is substituted on the screen for all the 18-point Adobe Benguiat bold italic section heads throughout this book. (I'm so used to it by now that I think if I actually saw them in Benguiat, I'd faint.) I thought it was **Vag Rounded**, but that's not installed at the moment, so I guess it's something else.

I'll work on finding out why this happens and will let you know about it in an update, but in the meantime, if it happens to you, you'll know not to panic. It's an annoying problem, and a mystifying one, but it doesn't seem to do any real damage.

❡ *FONDs and font families*

Both NFNTs and the original font numbering system just describe the basic font itself. To be able to choose *Bold*, *Italic* or both from a style menu and have the real cutting used—instead of just an algorithmically derived version of the basic font—you need FONDs *(font family descriptors)*.

A FOND acts as a sort of lookup table, so the Mac can find the styled versions of a font without having to keep them all in the menu. FONDs also provide a way to keep track of kerned pair and character width information.

A FOND can only handle a family of four related font cuttings. These are usually plain, bold, italic and bold italic. But what happens if they're not? Well, that depends. If there's no bold version of the font in the family, the next heavier version of the font is usually substituted. If there's no italic, you normally get the cursive or oblique version.

Here's an example. The three font names on the left were the ones on the menu. The second column is how they look without any style applied, and the third column shows how they look when I made them bold.

Font chosen	Plain style	Bold applied
LEras	Eras light	Eras book
Eras	Eras medium	**Eras demi**
BEras	**Eras bold**	**Eras ultra**

(Of course, not all font families have six weights. Often when you make a font bold or italic, nothing happens.)

¢ font families on menus (AN/SZA)

The Mac was designed to handle a limited number of type styles— bold, italic, underline, etc. (It didn't seem limited at the time, compared to what other computers let you do.) You'd just pick a font and apply a style to it.

But now Mac fonts, like regular typesetting fonts, come in a myriad of styles. You want bold? Well, which one— medium, semibold, demibold, bold, extra bold or ultra bold? So you have to pick the style, as well as the font itself, from the menu.

The second problem comes from the narrowness of list boxes. If they were wider, fonts could be named more logically, as in the illustration on the left below. But if you did that today, you'd get something like the illustration on the right whenever you open a list box.

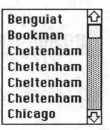

Which Cheltenham is which? That's why font publishers put a code letter in front of their fonts: *L Helvetica Light, CL Helvetica Condensed Light, N Helvetica Narrow,* etc. Even if you can't see the end of the font name, you can figure out what it is.

But this is a stupid approach, because all the styles of a particular font are scattered everywhere. If you have hundreds of fonts on your menu (as many people do), it's easy to completely forget that you've got, say, *T Vag Round Thin* under the T's. Even if you can keep all the far-flung styles in mind, you still have go all over hell-and-gone to get them.

very bad feature

The *sensible* approach is to shorten the font *name* (it's heresy, we know) and put the style codes *after* it. So you'd have *Helv L, Helv CL, Helv N,* etc. Pretty obvious, huh? Well, if common sense were common, we'd be living in a different world.

Adobe publishes an init called Type Reunion (originally called Family Reunion, a much cleverer name) that organizes fonts into families, and puts all the styles of the font family onto a submenu. It works OK, but slows down the menu quite a bit. It also prevents you from using QuicKeys to change fonts from the keyboard (unless you're choosing a solo font—one with no other members of its family on the menu; QuicKeys can handle those).

The illustration below shows you how the font menu works with Type Reunion installed. The selected font family is underlined in the main menu and the particular weight or style is checked in the submenu.

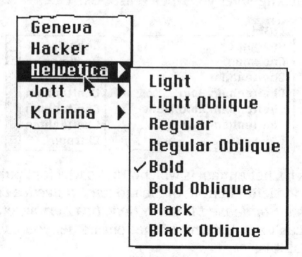

🍎 *a font by any other publisher*

important
warning

Many fonts are published by more than one company; Brush Script, for example, is available from both Adobe and Bitstream. Although most fonts with the same name look a lot alike (not surprisingly), they're never identical. If you use Bitstream's Brush Script in a document and then print it out on a system that has Adobe's Brush Script installed (using a program that identifies fonts by name, like PageMaker), you're in for an unpleasant surprise. Not only will the font itself look different, the spacing will be thrown off too.

₡ *kerned pairs*

Well-designed fonts contain *kerned pairs*—special spacing between certain pairs of letters (*Ta, To, Tr, We,* etc.). But kerned pairs work only if the program you're using supports them. Most word processors don't, but most page-layout programs do.

You don't have to worry about kerned pairs—you just type as usual and the printer substitutes the kerned pairs for the plain pair that you typed.

₡ *AFM files*

AFM (*Adobe Font Metrics*) files are supplied with many PostScript printer fonts. For the most part, you can just ignore them. If an application needs them (it's rare), the documentation will tell you so, and it will also tell you where to store them (usually in the system folder).

₡ *the ASCII chart*

As mentioned elsewhere, ASCII is a widely used system for referring to letters, numbers and common symbols by code numbers. (On the Mac, ASCII files are usually referred to as *text files.*)

esp. for power users

Some programs—Word, for example—let you enter characters by their ASCII numbers. See the entry called *the characters you can't type* in the special characters section above for some examples of where that might prove useful.

Here's a chart of the ASCII numbers that generate visible characters (0–31 generate tabs, returns, line feeds, etc.), and the key(s) you use to produce each character. (Note that 127 and 215–55 have no standard characters assigned to them, and so are omitted from the chart.)

32		Spacebar	60	<	Shift <
33	!	Shift 1	61	=	Shift =
34	"	Shift '	62	>	Shift >
35	#	Shift 3	63	?	Shift ?
36	$	Shift 4	64	@	Shift 2
37	%	Shift 5	65	A	Shift A
38	&	Shift 7	66	B	Shift B
39	'	'	67	C	Shift C
40	(	Shift 9	68	D	Shift D
41	)	Shift 0	69	E	Shift E
42	*	Shift 8	70	F	Shift F
43	+	Shift =	71	G	Shift G
44	,	,	72	H	Shift H
45	-	-	73	I	Shift I
46	.	.	74	J	Shift J
47	/	/	75	K	Shift K
48	0	0	76	L	Shift L
49	1	1	77	M	Shift M
50	2	2	78	N	Shift N
51	3	3	79	O	Shift O
52	4	4	80	P	Shift P
53	5	5	81	Q	Shift Q
54	6	6	82	R	Shift R
55	7	7	83	S	Shift S
56	8	8	84	T	Shift T
57	9	9	85	U	Shift U
58	:	Shift :	86	V	Shift V
59	;	Shift ;	87	W	Shift W

88	X	`Shift``X`		116	t	`T`
89	Y	`Shift``Y`		117	u	`U`
90	Z	`Shift``Z`		118	v	`V`
91	[	`Shift``[`		119	w	`W`
92	\	`Shift``\`		120	x	`X`
93	]	`Shift``]`		121	y	`Y`
94	^	`Shift``6`		122	z	`Z`
95	_	`Shift``-`		123	{	`Shift``[`
96	`	`Shift``` `		124	l	`Shift``\`
97	a	`A`		125	}	`Shift``]`
98	b	`B`		126	~	`Shift``~`
99	c	`C`		128	Ä	`Option``U`, `Shift``A`
100	d	`D`		129	Å	`Shift``Option``A`
101	e	`E`		130	Ç	`Shift``Option``C`
102	f	`F`		131	É	`Option``E`, `Shift``E`
103	g	`G`		132	Ñ	`Option``N`, `Shift``N`
104	h	`H`		133	Ö	`Option``U`, `Shift``O`
105	i	`I`		134	Ü	`Option``U`, `Shift``U`
106	j	`J`		135	á	`Option``E`, `A`
107	k	`K`		136	à	`Option``~`, `A`
108	l	`L`		137	â	`Option``I`, `A`
109	m	`M`		138	ä	`Option``U`, `A`
110	n	`N`		139	ã	`Option``N`, `A`
111	o	`O`		140	å	`Option``A`
112	p	`P`		141	ç	`Option``C`
113	q	`Q`		142	é	`Option``E`, `E`
114	r	`R`		143	è	`Option``~`, `E`
115	s	`S`		144	ê	`Option``I`, `E`

145	ë	Option U, E	172	¨	Option U, Spacebar
146	í	Option E, I	173	≠	Option =
147	ì	Option ~, I	174	Æ	Shift Option '
148	î	Option I, I	175	Ø	Shift Option O
149	ï	Option U, I	176	∞	Option 5
150	ñ	Option N, N	177	±	Shift Option =
151	ó	Option E, O	178	≤	Option ,
152	ò	Option ~, O	179	≥	Option .
153	ô	Option I, O	180	¥	Option Y
154	ö	Option U, O	181	µ	Option M
155	õ	Option N, O	182	∂	Option D
156	ú	Option E, U	183	Σ	Option W
157	ù	Option ~, U	184	Π	Shift Option P
158	û	Option I, U	185	π	Option PgUp
159	ü	Option U, U	186	∫	Option B
160	†	Option T	187	ª	Option 9
161	°	Shift Option 8	188	º	Option 'o
162	¢	Option 4	189	Ω	Option Z
163	£	Option 3	190	æ	Option '
164	§	Option 6	191	ø	Option O
165	•	Option 8	192	¿	Shift Option ?
166	¶	Option 7	193	¡	Option 1
167	ß	Option S	194	¬	Option L
168	®	Option R	195	√	Option V
169	©	Option G	196	ƒ	Option F
170	™	Option 2	197	≈	Option X
171	´	Option E, Spacebar	198	∆	Option D

199	«	Option \
200	»	Shift Option \
201	…	Option ;
202	(nonbreaking space)	Option Spacebar
203	À	Option ~ , Shift A
204	Ã	Option N , Shift A
205	Õ	Option N , Shift O
206	Œ	Shift Option Q
207	œ	Option Q
208	–	Option -
209	—	Shift Option -
210	"	Option [
211	"	Shift Option [
212	'	Option]
213	'	Shift Option]
214	÷	Option /
215	◊	Shift Option V
216	ÿ	Option U , Y
217	Ÿ	Shift Option ~
218	⁄	Shift Option 1
219	¤	Shift Option 2
220	‹	Shift Option 3
221	›	Shift Option 4
222	fi	Shift Option 5
223	fl	Shift Option 6
224	‡	Shift Option 7
225	·	Shift Option 9
226	‚	Shift Option 0
227	„	Shift Option W
228	‰	Shift Option E
229	Â	Option i , Shift A
230	Ê	Option E , Shift E
231	Á	Shift Option Y
232	Ë	Shift Option U
233	È	Shift Option I
234	Í	Shift Option S
235	Î	Shift Option D
236	Ï	Shift Option F
237	Ì	Shift Option G
238	Ó	Shift Option H
239	Ô	Shift Option J
240		Shift Option K
241	Ò	Shift Option L
242	Ú	Shift Option ;
243	Û	Shift Option Z
244	Ù	Shift Option X
245	ı	Shift Option B
246	ˆ	Shift Option N
247	˜	Shift Option M
248	¯	Shift Option ,
249	˘	Shift Option .
250	˙	Option H
251	°	Option K

Chapter 8

Utilities

Managing utilities

⚫ utility basics *(AN)*

Utilities are programs that perform relatively simple tasks—like searching for a specific file on a disk, setting an alarm, clipping a picture or counting the words in a document. (Some utilities perform relatively complex tasks, but in that case, they're support tasks for the creation of documents—managing fonts, for example.) Utilities come in various forms—as *stand-alone programs, desk accessories* (usually called *DAs*), *inits, cdevs* and *FKeys* (all defined in entries below).

esp. for beginners

When it makes more sense to do so, we cover some utilities in other chapters; for example, Acta, an outliner in the form of a DA, is covered in Chapter 10 (word processing), and the Clipper, which supercharges the Clipboard, is in Chapter 6 (basic Mac software). In this chapter, we cover Apple's basic utilities, other general-purpose utilities, and utilities that span categories, like programs used for clipping art from paint files and pasting them into word processing documents.

⚫ desk accessories *(DC/AN)/SZA*

You open *stand-alone programs* by clicking on their icons on the desktop, but you open *desk accessories* by choosing them from the ⚫ menu. (In System 7, this distinction breaks down—you can put an application into the ⚫ menu, and you can doubleclick on a DA's icon to run it.)

things to come

The advantage of DAs is that they can be used without leaving the application you're in, since no matter what you're doing on the Mac—with a few rare exceptions—the ⚫ menu will be in the upper left corner of the screen and will contain all the items it does on the desktop. For example, you can open up the Scrapbook in the middle of a word processing session and paste in a picture from it.

esp. for beginners

Some desk accessories are complex enough to be considered applications, but most are utilities. They let you take notes, dial the phone, open documents created by other programs than the one you're in, create new folders, check spelling, play games and move, rename and delete files.

Officially, you're limited to fifteen DAs installed in any one system file—in other words, at any one time—but you can get around that with programs like Suitcase and Font/DA Juggler, both discussed below.

Desk accessories are installed (and removed) with a utility called Font/DA Mover (there's a whole section on it later on in this chapter). You can put DAs in:

- the System file (once a DA is there, it always shows up in the menu).

- a *suitcase file*, named after the shape of Font/DA Mover file icons, which look like this:

Fonts   DAs

A suitcase can contain a single DA or many, and can include fonts as well. You create and alter suitcase files with Font/DA Mover. If a DA is in a suitcase file, it can be added to (and taken off) the menu with utilities like Suitcase or Juggler.

- an application—in which case, the DA only appears in the menu when that application is running. (For how to do this, see the Font/DA Mover tips below.)

desk accessory files

Some desk accessories—the Calculator, for example—are self-contained; others create, or let you create, files to hold information—just the way applications create documents.

Some DA files are automatic; for example, the Scrapbook automatically creates and maintains a Scrapbook file which holds all the information you put into the Scrapbook (it's opened automatically when you choose *Scrapbook* from the ⬝ menu). Like most automatic files, the Scrapbook file is stored in the system folder.

Other DAs let you open and save files the same way applications let you create documents. You can name these files anything you want, and store them anywhere on any disk.

⬝ DAs on floppy disk systems

If you don't have a hard disk, you've got two potential problems with desk accessories. One is that you won't have much room for them. Whether you put DAs in the System file or in suitcase files, some of the more powerful ones take up a lot of space—as do the documents you create with them.

The second problem is that the DA (or DA file) you want is often going to be on a different disk. For example, you'll have a different Scrapbook file on every startup disk, and the one you have at any given time will seldom be the one you need.

⬝ inits and cdevs

Inits (short for *init*ialization files; in System 7, they're called *startup files*) are loaded automatically into the System when you start up your Mac; as that happens, the inits' icons appear at the bottom of your screen. (Some inits let you suppress this display.)

esp. for
beginners

Inits do things as minor as replace straight quotes with curly ones as you type, or as major as letting you access a remote E-mail system. They take up memory—anywhere from 2K to 200K (I haven't seen one larger than that)—so if you don't have a lot of memory, you have to be careful how many you add.

Cdevs (Control Panel *devices*) are similar to inits but, as their name implies, they appear in the Control Panel, where you can adjust their settings. Many inits incorporate cdevs (so you can set preferences for how the init works), but an init doesn't have to have a cdev and a cdev doesn't have to have an init.

● *and then there are rdevs*

Rdevs are like cdevs, except they appear in the Chooser rather than in the Control Panel. (The *r* is just the last letter of *Chooser,* since *c* was already taken.) Printer drivers and network devices are rdevs.

● *FKeys*

FKeys are an almost-obsolete form of Mac software; they're invoked by pressing ⌘ Shift and a number. They never really took off as a concept and have been entirely overshadowed in the last year or two by inits and cdevs.

Confusion abounds because other commands can be assigned Shift ⌘ -number combinations with macro programs, and because people think the term refers to the function keys (F1 , F2 , etc.) at the top of the extended keyboards.

FKeys normally reside in the System file, and can be moved in and out with ResEdit. FKeys not in the System file can be accessed by Suitcase or Juggler, like DAs.

There were four FKeys in the very first version of the system software (for the 128K Mac). Now there are six:

- Shift ⌘ 1 ejects the floppy disk in the internal drive (or, if there are two internal drives, in the bottom or right one).

- Shift ⌘ 2 ejects the floppy disk in the external drive (or, if there are two internal drives, in the top or left one).

- Shift ⌘ 0 is for dual external floppy drives; it ejects the disk that Shift ⌘ 2 doesn't.

- Shift ⌘ 3 takes a picture of what's currently on the screen (called a *screen shot* or a *screen dump*) and saves it to disk as a MacPaint document. The first image is named *Screen0,* the next *Screen1,* and so on up to

Screen9. [Shift] [⌘] [3] works only in black-and-white, and on large screens it only captures what will fit (sideways) into a standard MacPaint window. More powerful capture programs are described in a section below.

- [Caps Lock] [Shift] [⌘] [4] prints out a picture of what's currently on the screen, but only on an ImageWriter or compatible printer.

- [Shift] [⌘] [4] prints a picture of the current contents of the active window, but only on an ImageWriter or compatible printer.

❡ taking more than ten screen shots

The [Shift] [⌘] [3] FKey only takes ten screen shots—*Screen0* through *Screen9*. Once you have *Screen9* on the disk, you'll get only a beep if you try it again. To make [Shift] [⌘] [3] work again, just rename one or more of the files or drag them into a folder.

very
hot
tip

❡ throwing inits away

Since inits are loaded into the System when you start up your Mac, you get the *file is locked or in use* alert if you try to throw them in the Trash. To throw one away, drag it out of the system folder (you're allowed to *move* a file that's in use) and restart the Mac. *Then* you can Trash it, because it won't have been loaded at startup.

❡ init clashes

The main problem you'll run into once you start adding inits to your system is that one will eventually clash with your system files, with other inits, or with some specific application. The only way to finger the culprit is to drag the suspect (the most recently-added init) out of the system folder and restart the Mac. If everything's fine, it was that init causing the problem.

To find out which old init the new one is clashing with, put the new one back in and take out all the old ones. Then add them back in, restarting the Mac each time you make a change, until the problem reappears.

If an init clashes, you don't have to give it up—sometimes simply renaming it helps. That's because inits are
loaded into memory in alphabetical order, and putting a
trouble-maker at the beginning or end of the line sometimes
solves the problem. (For more info on how to do this, see
the entry called *keeping filenames at the top of lists* in
Chapter 6.)

⚫ *init managers*

An *init manager* is an init that lets you turn inits on and
off (without having to drag them out of the system folder).
A good init manager also lets you rename inits to change
their loading order, and can be called up on startup before
the other inits load (so you can specify which inits should
be turned on or off this time around, without having to
restart again to make your choices take effect).

When inits have associated cdevs, some init managers
simply prevent the init from loading but leave the cdev's
icon in the Control Panel; other init managers remove the
cdev's icon from the Control Panel as well.

Aask, from CE Software, was the first init manager. It lets
you turn your inits on and off simply by clicking on their
icons, and you can do that at startup (simply by holding
down [Spacebar]) or in the Control Panel (init managers always have associated cdevs, which you use to control them).

INITPicker from Microseeds is the most versatile of the
init managers. As its package declares, it "helps you manage the tangled web of inits that are supposed to make
your system more productive, but frequently only serve to
screw things up."

Like Aask, INITPicker lets you check the inits you want
to run, either at startup or in the Control Panel; it will also
create sets of inits to run together and tell you how much
memory is being used by each of the active inits. There's
even a special utility, BombGuard, that detects init clashes
and prevents one of the clashers from loading.

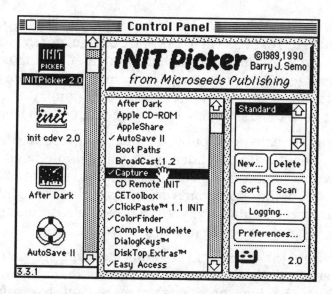

Init and Init Manager are public-domain init managers that work in the Control Panel (but not at startup). Unfortunately, Init Manager can't keep certain inits from loading even after you've turned them off.

bargain

[Init CDEV is another public-domain init manager. Although less sophisticated than INITPicker, it does have the advantage of being free—although its author, John Rotenstein, does ask you to send him a postcard in Australia (the address is in Appendix B) if you like it.—Chris Allen]

bargain

 *public-domain and shareware utilities*

Because utilities are usually small and relatively simple programs, many are available as public-domain software (i.e., free) or as shareware (try it and pay for it only if you like it and continue using it). You get shareware and public-domain software (also called *PD* or *freeware)* through *user groups* and on *bulletin boards.* (There's also a two-disk set of it called *The Macintosh Bible Software Disks;* see Chapter 19 for details.)

esp. for beginners

Once you get a shareware program, you'll find the author's name and address, and the amount of the fee—usually featured quite prominently. Be aware that most shareware authors won't actually send you the software, because the expense of a disk and postage, not to mention time and effort involved, is hardly covered by the usually nominal fee. But registered users sometimes receive documentation or upgrades not available to nonpaying users, so be sure to register any shareware you end up using.

One advantage of public-domain software and shareware, besides its low price, is that it gets updated quite often (most authors are very responsive to user feedback). And a lot of these programs do things too minor to interest a commercial publisher, yet are nonetheless quite useful (QuickFolder comes to mind).

important warning

The major drawback of public-domain software and shareware is that it's tested much less than commercial products. So these programs are more likely to crash your system or clash with other programs than are their commercial cousins.

The Control Panel

❤ *using the Control Panel* (AN/SZA)

esp. for beginners

When you first choose *Control Panel* from the ❤ menu, you may think it gives you more choices than you want. But in time you'll be glad to have them.

On the left side of the window is a scrolling list of icons (cdevs); you choose various ones to set various preferences. When you click on an icon, its controls appear in the window on the right. The basic Apple cdevs are *General, Keyboard, Mouse, Sound, Color* and *Monitors*. In the entries that follow, we describe what these controls do, and give you our recommended settings for them.

❤ *recommended General settings* (AN/SZA)

The General icon is always at the top of the list. All of the settings made using this icon are kept in a portion of memory called *parameter RAM* (also called *PRAM*)—except for the desktop pattern, which is stored on disk.

Because parameter RAM is powered by the Mac's battery, these General settings aren't lost when you turn the Mac off. And because these settings are held in memory, not on disk, they stay the same (until you change them), regardless of what startup disk you're running from.

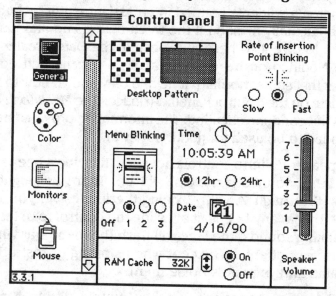

The first control is the setting for Desktop Pattern. On a black and white system, you should probably stick with the default pattern, a medium gray, because it's quite pleasant for daily use. If you run off floppies (and therefore have a variety of system files), you may find it convenient to use a different desktop pattern to identify the different systems. You can also get fancy; for details, see the last entry in this section.

Not surprisingly, Rate of Insertion Point Blinking controls how fast the insertion point blinks. This is a totally subjective matter, so set it wherever you like—but do try *Slow* some time and see if you don't find it less distracting, as Arthur does. Sharon doesn't like the slow speed—it takes too long to find the insertion point if she's glanced away from the screen and then looks back. Without the blinking to catch her eye, the insertion point is hard to find.

Menu Blinking controls how many times a menu command blinks after you choose it. If you don't think subtle feedback is important, try setting Menu Blinking to *Off;* most people find it disconcerting to select a command and not have it acknowledged.

gossip/ trivia

The Time and Date settings—well, we recommend you use reality as your guide. But here's an interesting sidelight. One of Sharon's students handed in an assignment late, but said he had actually finished it the week before and had just forgotten to give it to her. As expected, the Date Created and Date Modified on his disk file showed that he had done it earlier that same morning. If he had only known how to reset the date on the Control Panel.... (Notice: *The Macintosh Bible* does not condone cheating. The information provided here is intended to be used for good, not evil.)

Speaker Volume controls how loud the Mac's beeps (and any other sounds it makes) will be. There are eight settings, 0 through 7, with 7 being the loudest. If you don't want to hear any beeps at all, slide the control to 0; instead of making sounds, the Mac will flash the menu bar when it wants your attention (except when starting or restarting—the Mac always makes noise then).

When you change the Speaker Volume setting, the Mac gives you a sample of what the new beep sounds like, making it easy to find the volume level you want. We recommend starting with 1, then trying 2 or some higher number if you want it louder. After you've been using the Mac for a while and have a good feel for how it works, you may also want to try 0.

The RAM Cache settings are discussed in Chapter 3.

⌘ *Keyboard settings* (AN)

In the Keyboard section of the Control Panel, Delay until Repeat controls how long it takes before a key you're holding down begins to automatically repeat, and Key Repeat Rate controls how rapidly the key repeats after it begins repeating. I recommend you set Key Repeat Rate at either of the two fastest speeds and Delay until Repeat at either of the two middle choices.

■ *Mouse settings* (AN)

There are two settings in the Mouse section of the Control Panel. Doubleclick Speed tells the Mac how long it should wait after one click to see if you're going to doubleclick. With the longest interval set, the Mac will treat clicks that are fairly far apart as doubleclicks; with the shortest interval set, you'll have to doubleclick pretty fast or the Mac will think you're giving two separate clicks rather than doubleclicking.

I recommend either the short interval or the medium one; if you use the long interval, you'll always be accidentally doubleclicking on things and opening them when you only wanted to select them. (But if you have some impairment of your fine motor control, from age or illness, the long interval can be useful.)

The other setting is for Mouse Tracking. I like this set to the fastest (or next to the fastest) setting, because this really helps me get the pointer to where I want it quickly. It may take a little getting used to, but it's worth it in the long run.

■ *Sound settings* (SZA/AN)

The Sound section of the Control Panel lets you choose which of several sounds the Mac will use to get your attention. Current system software gives you a choice of the normal (simple) *beep*, *boing*, *clink-klank* (both of which sound exactly like their names) or *monkey* (a screech).

You can add to this selection of sounds; for example, in the illustration at the top of the next page, Sharon has added *ouch*, a dignified little beep that comes with the outliner called More. Many sounds are available—especially on electronic bulletin boards—that you can install in your System or in suitcase files with shareware utilities.

bargain

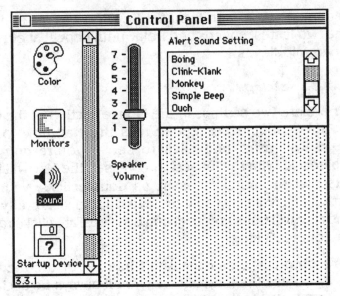

Sound Mover works like the Font/DA Mover, letting you install sounds in your System file from other files. Sound-Master is a cdev that lets you assign different sounds to different system events—so you can have one sound for startup, one for restart, one for when you've inserted a bad disk and so on. (You can also move sounds around with ResEdit; Chapter 17 describes how.)

The volume control appears again in the Sound section of the Control Panel. If you change it here, the change will carry over to the volume control in the General section, and vice versa.

⬛ using the Color Wheel

The Color section in the Control Panel lets you change the color in which highlighted text is shown. When you click in the *Change* button, the Color Wheel dialog box at the top of the following page opens.

The wheel has a dot in it that shows the currently se-lected color. You can click anywhere in the wheel to move the dot, or you can drag the dot around.

- To change the *hue* (the actual color) move around the circle.

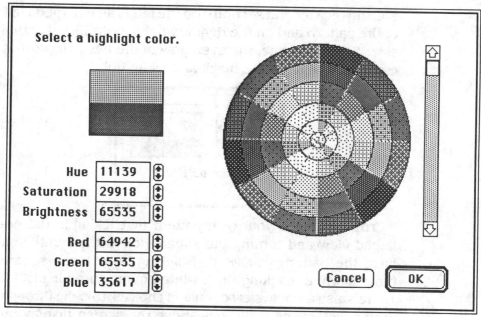

- To decrease the *saturation* (the intensity of the color), move in towards the center of the circle.

- To change the *brightness*, use the scroll bar to the right of the wheel. (When you move the scroll box all the way to the bottom, you get black no matter what the hue or saturation is.)

There's a square patch of sample color in the upper left; the lower half shows the current color and the upper half shows the new color. In the lower left are numeric representations of the current color. You can work directly with them if you like, by typing in new numbers or by using the arrows next to each number.

Adjusting the color in the Wheel and then clicking *OK* changes the highlight color. Keep the color relatively light—selected text doesn't invert to white against a highlight color, so dark colors make selections unreadable.

⚫ *changing the desktop pattern and color*

The Control Panel lets you change your desktop pattern and color. There are two pictures in the Desktop Pattern area (in the General section); on the left is an enlarged view of the pattern and on the right is what it looks like at actual size. As you can see, the even gray of the basic desktop is composed of alternate black and white dots.

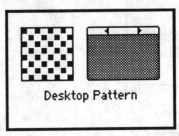

Desktop Pattern

You can make your own pattern by clicking in the enlarged view and turning the squares on and off until you have the pattern you want. (Clicking on a black square turns it white; clicking on a white square turns it black.) There's also a whole slew of built-in choices; to cycle through them, click in the white bar above the screen display on the right. When you find or create the pattern you want, click on the right display and the pattern will immediately be applied to the desktop.

If you're working in color, there will be a strip of eight colors underneath the desktop patterns. Click on any of them and then click on any dot in the display on the left; it will change to the color you're chosen (clicking on it again will return it to the previous color).

To change your choice of colors, doubleclick on any one of them to open the Color Wheel. Create the color you want, click *OK* and you'll be back in the Control Panel with the color changed. When you're happy with the pattern on the left, click in the display on the right to change the actual desktop to that colored pattern.

Monitors settings *(AN)*

The Monitors section of the Control Panel lets you specify how many colors or shades of gray will appear on your monitor (as described in Chapter 2). If you have more than one monitor, it also lets you decide which one gets the menu bar, and tells the Mac where you put them in relation to each other.

¶ who's responsible (AN/SZA)

For the names of the people who programmed the version of the Control Panel and Chooser you're using, click on the version number at the bottom of the window.

*gossip/
trivia*

Some basic Apple utilities
(and substitutes for them)

¶ the Chooser

The Chooser desk accessory is most often used to choose a printer (how to do this is described in Chapter 4). But the Chooser also lets you select *zones* and *file server volumes* when you're working on a network (that's covered in Chapter 15).

¶ adding Chooser drivers

Each time you open the Chooser, it scans the system folder for drivers (the kind of programs it recognizes). So you can add printer and network drivers at any time—you don't have to restart your system as you do with inits. (By the way, Chooser drivers are listed in list views as *Chooser documents*—logically enough.)

¶ the Calculator

What's to know about using the Calculator? Well, for one thing, you can copy the number it's displaying and paste it into the document you're working on. For another, you can paste things *into* the calculator—not just simple numbers, but chains of calculations, like 15*17*92*3, as well.

¶ Calculator Construction Set (AN)

If Apple's regular calculator DA is a bit too primitive for you, Calculator Construction Set is what you want. Published

**very good
feature**

by Dubl-Click Software, it lets you assemble the ultimate monster calculator of your dreams (you can stretch it to any size you want and keep loading in the keys). Then when you're done, you can install it as a desk accessory.

Rather than go into endless detail about all the functions Calculator Construction Set makes available, we'll just say that if you want it, they've almost certainly got it. And the user interface is good, so you won't have any trouble creating what you want. *(You don't have to create a monster calculator—you may only want a simple one, but with a "tape" so you can see what you've entered.—SZA)*

the Scrapbook

The Scrapbook is a standard Apple desk accessory, but it doesn't follow the standard Mac interface. For example, when you cut or copy something from the Scrapbook, you don't have to select it first—you just get whatever's showing. Adding something to the Scrapbook isn't very intuitive either—it *feels* like you're pasting it on top of the item that's showing, but when you give the *Paste* command, the Scrapbook creates a new page to receive what you're adding.

The Scrapbook window is not resizable, but even though you can see only part of a large graphic you've pasted in it, the entire graphic *is* stored. The things you store in the Scrapbook are kept in a file named *Scrapbook file* in the system folder. If you change the name of that file or move it out of the system folder, the Scrapbook will be empty the next time you open it.

Since the Scrapbook contents are in that file, you can transfer them from one disk to another. You can even have several Scrapbook files (with various names) on the same disk—just rename whichever one you want to use at the moment *Scrapbook file.*

Apple's Scrapbook DA was an elegant concept back in 1984, when it was introduced, but as far as features are concerned, it's been surpassed by the commercial DAs described in the next two entries.

✎ SmartScrap

SmartScrap (from Solutions) is a terrific Scrapbook sub-stitute, and it comes with the Clipper DA described in the last chapter (just $90 for both). With it you can select all or any part of a stored image for copying. It lets you name each page of the Scrapbook and then search through the con-tents by name. It also lets you build a pictorial table of contents—miniature pictures of the contents of each page (to go to the page you want, you just doubleclick on its little picture). Finally, SmartScrap lets you access multiple Scrap-book files, without having to constantly change their names.

very good feature

✎ ClickPaste

ClickPaste ($100) is a great idea—a hierarchical Scrap-book. To retrieve items from it, you just hold down the keys you've assigned to ClickPaste and click on the screen where you want the Scrapbook contents to be pasted. Holding down the mouse button makes a menu appear with a list of folders you've created; as you drag down the menu with the pointer, pausing on a folder name pops out a list of the items in the folder. When you select an item, it's automatically copied to the Clipboard and then pasted into your document.

very good feature

You can use ClickPaste as a glossary for any word pro-cessor that doesn't provide one, instantly retrieving phrases and even paragraphs that you use often. I use it in PageMaker for items I used to leave on the Pasteboard (which I found aggravating, because I'd have to scroll so far, or zoom in and out of different views, to get to them).

Unfortunately, ClickPaste needs a little more attention to detail. You can only delete items by throwing them into the Trash, and there's no New Folder option in its Save dialog box. ClickPaste annoyingly requires a folder named *Scrap* on the desktop at the root level (I hate being told where to put folders and what to name them). Still, ClickPaste is so useful that I can live with the small defects until an upgrade is available.

♦ *Multi-Scrap*

bargain

Multi-Scrap is an oldie but goodie among public-domain programs. It's not as powerful as SmartScrap or ClickPaste but, then again, it's free. It works like Apple's Scrapbook except that it lets you access multiple Scrapbook files without having to change their names.

♦ *Easy Access* (DC)

very good feature

Easy Access is a free system software from Apple that's designed for people with disabilities who have difficulty using the mouse or issuing multiple key commands (Shift Option F8 , say). There are two parts to Easy Access—Sticky Keys and Mouse Keys. To make them work, you simply put Easy Access in your system folder and follow the instructions below.

Sticky Keys lets you type key combinations one at a time instead of having to press the keys simultaneously. You turn Sticky Keys on by pressing the Shift key five times in a row. (Be sure not to move the mouse while you're doing this or you'll have to start over.) You turn it off by pressing the Shift key five times again or by pressing Ctrl or any two of the following keys simultaneously: ⌘ , Shift or Option (Apple recommends using Option ⌘ because they're close together).

Mouse Keys lets you use the numeric keypad to do all the things you usually do with the mouse (but be aware that it doesn't work with the original, separate numeric keypad—just the more recent, built-in ones). To turn on Mouse Keys, you press Shift ⌘ Clear simultaneously (or sequentially, if you're using Sticky Keys).

The number keys on the numeric keypad move the pointer up, down, left, right and diagonally—except for 5 , which is the same as clicking the mouse. The 0 (zero) key is the equivalent of holding the mouse button down, and . (the decimal point) is equivalent to releasing it.

Let's say you want to open a menu with Mouse Keys. You use 1 through 4 and 6 through 9 to move to the menu title, then hit ⎡0⎤ to make the menu drop down. The ⎡8⎤ and ⎡2⎤ keys move you up and down the menu. When the command you want is selected, you execute it by hitting ⎡.⎤ (the decimal point on the keypad, not the period on the regular keyboard). To leave the menu without selecting anything, you simply move the pointer outside of it, then hit ⎡.⎤.

You can get very precise control of pointer movement by tapping the keys. Each brief tap will move the pointer one pixel. The longer you hold a key down, the faster the insertion point moves. To slow it down, change the mouse speed on the Control Panel (the option labeled *Tablet* is the slowest).

Here's how to shift-click with Easy Access. First, turn on Sticky Keys, then press ⎡Shift⎤ twice to lock it down. Hit ⎡5⎤ to mark where you want your selection to begin, use the keypad to move the pointer to where you want the selection to end and hit ⎡5⎤ again. Everything between the two positions will be selected.

Managing fonts and DAs

♠ *suitcase files*

The Font/DA Mover, whose icon looks like a moving van, creates files whose icons look like little suitcases (isn't that cute?). The suitcases for fonts and DAs look different :

esp. for beginners

Fonts in here   DAs in here

You can mix fonts and DAs in the same file (in which case the icon will have the look of whatever went into it first). Here's how to do that:

Let's say you've used Font/DA Mover to put some fonts into a file. Click the *Desk Accessory* button and the fonts will disappear from the list box. If you now click the *Open* button, the file you just created won't appear, because it contains fonts and the DA button is selected. The trick is to hold down (Option) while you click the *Open* button; all files will appear in the list box, so you can reopen the font file and put desk accessories in it.

⚹ *Suitcase and Juggler*

very good feature

In the beginning, all fonts and desk accessories were stored in the System file, and you could only have fifteen DAs on the ⚹ menu. Then came Suitcase—it broke the fifteen-DA limit by letting you open fonts and DAs stored in suitcase files, not just in the System file. Font/DA Juggler came close on Suitcase's heels, and there's no better example of the leapfrog effect than these two programs—each release of each product surpasses the last.

Of the two, I like Suitcase better; Juggler has too many hierarchical dialog boxes for my taste, and doesn't seem as elegant. But both programs do basically the same thing and you definitely should use one or the other of them.

Suitcase and Juggler both let you open suitcase files automatically at startup, or at any time while you're working. They also handle system sounds and FKeys, and both include utilities that help resolve font ID conflicts (details in Chapter 7).

⚹ *Suitcase and rebuilding the desktop* (AN)

important warning

When you restart your Mac and rebuild the desktop by holding down (Option)(⌘) (as discussed in Chapter 3), Suitcase won't be active when the desktop appears. If you don't notice that, you can go into an application and wonder where all your fonts went. To reactivate Suitcase, you have to restart again.

⚹ (Option) *at launch* (DC)

When the Font/DA Mover opens, it normally displays fonts. If you want to install or remove a desk accessory, you have to click on that button and sit around while it dumps the fonts and loads the desk accessories. A faster way is to hold down the [Option] key when clicking on the Font/DA Mover icon (or right after). Keep it held down until the Font/DA Mover window appears, and it will come up with desk accessories rather than fonts displayed.

shortcut

❖ auto-open Systems

If you insert a floppy disk with a System file on it while the Font/DA Mover is open and one of its list boxes is empty, the System on the inserted disk is automatically opened and its contents appear in the list box.

❖ selecting multiple items

You don't need to hold down the [Shift] key to select multiple items in the Font/DA Mover—just drag across them. You can even select items that aren't contiguous, but for that you will need to hold down the [Shift] key.

very good feature

❖ putting fonts and DAs in applications or documents

You can install a font or desk accessory in any file—not just the System or a suitcase. Holding down [Option] while you click the Open button lists all files, no matter what their type (as long as they're visible), and you can open any one of them and install a font or desk accessory in it. Then the DA or font will only appear (in the ❖ or font menu) when that application or document is open.

very hot tip

❖ ejecting disks with [Option]

Holding [Option] while clicking the *Close* button closes the file in the list box and ejects the disk that it's on. Holding [Option] while clicking the *Quit* button takes you out of Font/DA Mover and ejects any floppy disk(s) that contains files that were open in Font DA/Mover.

shortcut

❖ getting font and DA info

When you click on a font name in the Font DA/Mover window, you get a sample of the font and how much room it takes on the disk. Select multiple fonts and you get the total size of all the fonts.

*very
hot
tip*

The size of desk accessories is also displayed when you click on them, but if you want more information, hold down (Option) while you click on the DA's name; you'll get a breakdown of how much of the DA is taken up by graphics *(picture data)*, how much by the program *(program data)* and how much by other information *(other data)*.

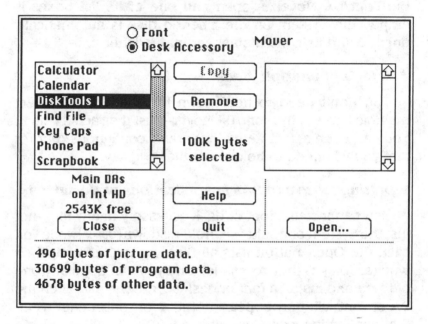

File handlers and
Finder substitutes

⬥ DiskTop *(Charles Rubin)*

*very good
feature*

DiskTop is a desk accessory that does so many things so well that it's hard to describe them all. For openers, it lets you find, open, delete, copy, move and rename files or folders (and eject disks) from inside any program. It also gives you information on files—either the kind provided in the Finder's Get Info window or the more technical information that's useful to programmers.

You can even switch applications from within an application, without having to go back to the Finder; DiskTop will close the current program and give you a chance to save your files before launching the new program. DiskTop performs all these operations at least twice as fast as the Finder—and sometimes much faster than that.

DiskTop is a delight to use. If you install a special init in your system folder, you can call up the DiskTop window by typing from the keyboard, rather than by selecting it from the menu, and you can even choose the keystroke combination you want to use to do that.

shortcut

Instead of simply showing you disk icons, DiskTop tells you the capacity of each disk and how much free space remains on it. Clicking on a disk icon displays its contents, just as with the Finder. You can navigate into and out of folders by doubleclicking on them, and you can also search for files by name, type, creator, date created, date last modified or size—and in the case of these last three categories, you can enter ranges (e.g., find me all the files that were modified in the last two weeks, or that are between 10 and 20K). You can search for files whose names begin with, contain or exactly match the letters you type.

very good feature

DiskTop can search multiple disks at the same time. When it finds a file, it lists it and keeps on going. When you select the name of a file it's found, DiskTop displays a graphic map of where that file is located. You can launch the application straight from that map by doubleclicking on its name (and when you do, DiskTop quits the application you're in, giving you a chance to save if necessary).

very good feature

Ah, but that's only the beginning of what you can do with DiskTop. You can also set a default folder, so the application you're running always looks for files in the same place. You can add up to 20 documents or applications to the DiskTop menu, so you can simply select them from the menu bar instead of having to root around for them. You can set preferences for how DiskTop sorts files, whether it shows file sizes in K or in bytes, and which level of information (technical or normal) you see when you get information about a file.

DiskTop comes with a really decent manual and two bonus utilities. One of these, LaserStatus, is described in the Printer chapter. The other is Widgets, which does various little things like turn off the LaserWriter's startup page and adjust the System heap (which is described in Chapter 3).

bug

[I've found that DiskTop's popup menus interfere with Word's menus—Word's keyboard commands work but its menus don't respond (although they do drop down). I've heard that Microsoft plays games with Apple's programming standards, so it's probably Word's menus that are at fault, but I use Word all the time, so I had to give up DiskTop.—SZA]

🍎 *PowerStation* (Paul Hoffman)

very good feature

This is the easiest Finder substitute to use and by far the most useful. Its most powerful feature is the ability to launch documents. Instead of putting all your choices on one screen, PowerStation gives you sixteen screens of buttons, so that you can group your buttons by type (such as graphics programs or utilities) or by project (all of the documents for one project on each screen).

PowerStation works particularly well with MultiFinder, and since it takes up much less memory than the Finder, it leaves more memory for your programs.

🍎 *Findswell* (Charles Rubin)

Findswell is a file-finding utility that appears as an extra button in the Open dialog box. Click the button and a window opens that lets you search for files; when you find one, its pathname (all the folders it's in) is shown. You can also navigate through files and folders the way you do in an Open window, and you can open any file you come across that was created by the application you're currently running (which saves you the trouble of quitting Findswell and going into the application's own Open window).

A number of other file-finding programs, including Apple's Find File, are available free or for less than $20 from user groups or bulletin boards. So why pay $60 for Findswell? Well, it has a few advantages that most of the competition don't.

Findswell will match a complete file name, the first part of a file name or any part of a file name; these choices let you specify a search more precisely, so you don't have to look at a whole slew of files with similar names. Another (somewhat minor) advantage is that you don't have to go up to the menu to access it. Because it's an init, it loads itself when you start up your Mac, and then its button is there whenever you choose *Open...* or *Save As....*

But Findswell's nicest, and most unusual, feature is its ability to remember the last files you opened (you tell it how many to remember) so you can return to them quickly—whether it's an hour or a week later. Findswell also lets you mark frequently used files so that they always appear in the Findswell window; if they're stuck deep inside two or three folders, this gets you to them much faster.

shortcut

DisKeeper (Chris Allen)

bargain

DisKeeper is a $10 shareware utility written by J. Geagan. It helps you manage disks that are cluttered up with multiple copies of applications and files, that have junk buried several folders deep, or that just have too many files. It will list all your files (you can't turn this feature off), as well as ones that are locked, invisible, identical to each other, have no data in them, and are "orphans" (their creator application can't be found, and thus they appear as the plain, generic-document icon). It will also find empty folders, invisible folders, and folders that only contain one item.

DisKeeper saves this information to a Word text file that can be read by most word processors and spreadsheets. It will also move identical files, empty files and the like to a folder called *DisKeeper Trash*. Quite a lot of value for $10, don't you think?

(DisKeeper is on The Macintosh Bible Software Disks, Third Edition, *which are described in Chapter 19.—AN)*

⚘ *Find File shortcuts*

shortcut

When you've found a file with Apple's Find File DA, you don't have to memorize its location and wade through folders to get to it. Instead, use the *Move to desktop* command in Find File's menu. This puts the file out on the desktop where you can see it.

You don't have to worry about remembering where the file came from, either: when you want to put it back, just select it and choose *Put Away* from the Finder's File menu. The icon zooms back to where it used to be—even if you've left it out on the desktop through a shutdown and restart.

⚘ *Icon-It!* (Steve Schwartz)

Even though pop-down menus are easy-to-use, I've often wanted a quicker way to choose commands (and one that's easier than memorizing sets of key combinations). Wouldn't it be nice to have your most frequently used commands available at the click of a button? Icon-It!helps you do just that by letting you design miniature icons to represent any command in any program (and FKeys and desk accessories as well).

Icon-It! provides templates of icons for the Finder and for about forty major word processors, databases, graphics programs and programming languages. Even though the templates may not have every option you want, they're a good place to start. You can replace any icon with one of your own design or copy one in from another template.

You modify icons (or build them from scratch) in Icon-It!'s editor. Another part of the editor lets you specify the number of icons in the menu, as well as their height, width, spacing and screen placement. Each icon can be assigned to a menu position, a menu name or a macro command.

Icon-It!is a well-designed product and many people will find it worth the $90 it costs.

❡ On Cue

On Cue lets you place a special menu just about any-where you want: at either—or both—ends of the menu bar, or anywhere you click on the screen while holding down certain keys (you choose the keys). The menu lists any applications you install in it; choosing an application from a menu launches it.

shortcut

You can also install documents in submenus on the main On Cue menu, and selecting such a document will also open the application that created it (if necessary). Under MultiFinder, the menu also lists all the applications cur-rently running, so you can get to any one directly.

On Cue sounds pretty nifty when you read about it, but after you've used it for a while, you'll be thinking, "how did I ever live without it?" On Cue is extremely configurable to your own needs and working habits. I recommend it very highly.

very good feature

❡ Layout *(Michael Bradley)*

Tired of the standard 9-point Geneva font used in the Finder? A public-domain program called Layout lets you change the font and/or type size. It also lets you change other defaults, like the size and shape of new windows, the spacing of icons and text, and how files are viewed in the default windows (by icon, by name or whatever).

bargain

Layout is good, bug-free software. It's available through the usual public-domain channels—bulletin boards, user groups, etc. We haven't given you the author's address in Appendix B because it's freeware, not shareware. It was written by Michael O'Connor. *[Layout is included on* The Macintosh Bible Software Disks, Third Edition, *which are described in Chapter 19.—AN]*

❡ Tidy It Up! *(Chris Allen)*

Tidy It Up! organizes cluttered system folders by group-ing files in logical categories. This not only pretties things up but also makes out-of-place files more obvious, so that you can eliminate them. Tidy It Up! comes to us from Belgium and was written by Guy Fiems. It's shareware and costs just $20, so if you use it, please send in your fee. *[It's included on* The Macintosh Bible Software Disks, Third Edition, *which are described in Chapter 19.—AN]*

🍎 *QuickFolder*

Some of the simplest utilities are also the most useful, as QuickFolder proves. It's a shareware init that puts a *New Folder* button in every Save dialog box. QuickFolder's registration fee is $5, which you send to Mark Igra, #2, 1588 Henry St, Berkeley CA 94709. (But get the program itself from a bulletin board or user group; $5 doesn't cover the cost of mailing out a disk.)

🍎 *Set Paths* (AN)

This incredibly useful $20 shareware utility (from Paul Snively) helps prevent clutter in your system folder (and interminable waits when you open it). With it you can specify up to five additional folders that programs will look in when they normally look in the system folder.

This lets you put away all those things that have to be in the system folder, like help files, printer fonts, AFM files, etc. (but be aware that some kinds of files—printer drivers, for example—have to be right out in the system folder).

Normally you put the additional folders in the system folder, but they can be anywhere on the disk. All you have to do to set them up is open the Set Paths DA and click on them.

I've been using Set Paths for years and couldn't work without it. Apple should make it part of the basic system software. (Note: Set Paths does not work with Multifinder.)

🍎 *Shortcut*

Here's another idea that's so useful Apple should include it in the system software. You know how tedious it is to move up three folders in an dialog box and then move back down four or five levels to get to the file you want? Well, with Shortcut, you can go *directly* to the folder you want by, either selecting it from a popup menu or by using keyboard commands.

You can also create new folders, go directly to a the disk you want without having to cycle through several with the *Drive* button or the Tab key, open a specific file without having to go to its folder, use the Find function to search the disk for something you've misplaced—and if that's not enough, you can automatically unstuff a stuffed file. (Raymond Lau, author of StuffIt, wrote this utility, too. Too bad he got out of high school and went off to college recently—it's slowing down his production of Mac utilities.)

Shortcut puts a little arrow to the left of the disk icon in every Open and Save dialog box. Pressing it pops down Shortcut's menu. You can use the menu and its submenus to navigate Shortcut's options, or take advantage of any of the many user-assignable keyboard equivalents.

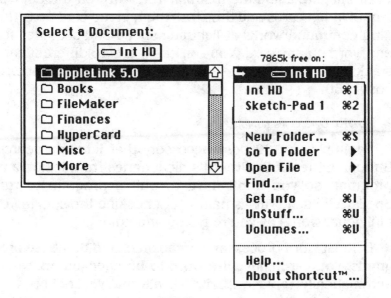

Text tools

⚫ miniWRITER (AN)

bargain

This is most people's favorite note-taking DA. Written by David Dunham of Maitreya Design, it's fast, slick, has a great (and accurate) word-count function, and only costs $12. I couldn't live without it.

⚫ JoliWrite (Paul Hoffman)

bargain

This little-known DA is a $20 shareware gem from France. Like the Note Pad, it lets you create and edit text-only documents while running other programs. It's much more powerful than miniWRITER and is compatible with more software, because it doesn't take up any space on the menu bar.

⚫ QuickDEX (Paul Hoffman)

very good feature

This is the ultimate note-taking DA—so intuitive I can't even imagine using the manual. You write on the equivalent of index cards and then toss them in the card box. The Find command works at lightning speed and searches for any word on any card. You can easily create different card stacks; QuickDEX keeps track of all of them at once. It costs $60.

⚫ Lookup (Charles Rubin)

Lookup is a $60 desk accessory that lets you search through either of Spellswell's dictionaries from inside any program, so you don't have to quit a program to run Spellswell itself. This is handy for checking the spelling of individual words as you're typing and editing.

In most word processor, spreadsheet and database programs, you can highlight a word to be checked and then automatically replace it with an alternative Lookup suggests (it often gives you several choices). In some programs, you can only look up words but you can't automatically replace them.

If you don't like the alternate word Lookup suggests, you can scroll through Spellswell's dictionary to find another. You can also add words to, or delete them from, the dictionary. When you add a word, you can specify variants such as plurals, adjectives and adverbs in one dialog box, so you don't have to add all these separately.

You have to choose Lookup from the DA menu and locate the Spellswell dictionary for it the first time, but after that you can check words during the same work session by typing Option ⌘ ~ from the keyboard.

It's nice to have access to a large dictionary from inside any application, but Lookup only checks individual words. For just $20 more, you could buy Thunder, a desk accessory that will check the spelling of whole documents from inside most applications, and which includes a glossary feature to boot.

GOfer

GOfer is a text-search utility—you tell it what text you're looking for and it searches through your entire hard disk (if necessary) to find every occurrence of it. You can set GOfer to look only in certain folders or only through certain types of documents, and you can tell it to find exact matches, ignore case, etc. This is an incredibly handy utility for those times when you know you wrote (or saw) something somewhere, but can't remember where.

Quote Init (AN/SZA)

As you type, this public-domain init substitutes true open and close quotation marks (" ") for the Mac's standard vertical quotation mark (") and a right-leaning apostrophe (') for the Mac's standard vertical one ('). It also supplies open and close single quotation marks (' ')—even when they're nested within double quotes.

Quote Init is smart about what to do when (for example, it can recognize the continuation of a long quotation through multiple paragraphs) and on the rare occasions when it makes a mistake (usually when you're inserting punctuation into existing text), corrections are relatively easy—you just backspace over the character and type it again.

Once active, Quote Init works in every application (including the Finder). You can choose to have it automatically install itself at startup or wait for your command, and you can toggle it on and off with ⌘ Option ' (or any another key combination you choose) as you work. The toggling is very rapid, so it's no trouble going back and forth.

That's good, because you'll find you have to turn the curly quotes off occasionally. Straight quotes are often used to indicate repeated information in databases and text in spreadsheets; FileMaker needs them in its formulas; and programming languages and terminal emulation programs use them too.

Toggling is useful for removing straight apostrophes from existing text. You just call up the find-and-replace dialog box (in whatever program you're in), hit ⌘ Option ' (or whatever key combination you've assigned to Quote Init), type ' in the Find field, Tab to the Replace field, hit ⌘ Option ' again, type a curly quote, and proceed to replace.

Quote Init also does other on-the-fly replacements. For example, it will insert an em dash whenever you type two hyphens in a row. This means you don't have to hold down Shift and Option when you want an em dash.

You can get Quote Init from all the usual places (bulletin boards, user groups, etc.). The program's author, Lincoln D. Stein, asks that you write him (at #2, 44 Boynton St., Jamaica Plain MA 02130) if you think of ways that Quote Init might be improved.

⚫ *SmartKeys* (Chris Allen)

SmartKeys is a cdev that prevents you from typing more than one space in a row, automatically converts two consecutive hyphens into an em dash, and automatically turns straight quote marks into curly ones. You can turn all these features on and off in the Control Panel, and you can specify applications in which you don't want SmartKeys to work.

The program was written by Maurice Volaski and is free-ware. *[It's included on* The Macintosh Bible Software Disks, Third Edition, *which are described in Chapter 19.—AN]*

Graphics tools

◆ *Artisto+* *(DC)*

If you deal with a large collection of clip art and often find yourself searching for just the right picture, you'll really appreciate the flexibility that Artisto+ provides. This desk accessory allows you to open any MacPaint or FullPaint document on any disk, copy all—or any portion—of it to the Clipboard (using a standard selection rectangle) and paste it directly to any application that accepts pictures.

Tom Taylor, the program's author, asks only that if you find Artisto+ useful, you send him a donation in any amount you like. His address is #137, 3707 Poinciana Dr, Santa Clara CA 95051. *[It's included on* The Macintosh Bible Software Disks, Third Edition, *which are described in Chapter 19.—AN]*

◆ *Clarity* (Chris Allen)

Clarity is a little program that takes bitmapped images (MacPaint-type pictures) that are on the clipboard and re-duces them for optimum resolution on a LaserWriter or an ImageWriter. It comes as an application and as a DA, and has complete documentation. This is a handy tool for desk-top publishers.

Clarity was written by Andrew Welch, and its shareware fee is a measly $5. *[It's included on* The Macintosh Bible Software Disks, Third Edition, *which are described in Chapter 19.—AN]*

⚫ *The Curator* (Eric Alderman)

The Curator is a tool for managing graphic files on disk. It lets you browse through folders and look at thumbnail versions of all the graphic images in them. You can also search by filename or by keyword (to do that, of course, you first have to attach keywords to the images).

The Curator automatically reads and displays graphic images in a variety of formats—paint (i.e., bit-mapped), PICT, EPS, TIFF and Glue—and can also convert between some of them (TIFF to paint, for example, or EPS to PICT).

The Curator comes both as a DA and an application. While some of its interface tends toward the cute side, it's nonetheless a useful and clever utility for those of us whose graphic libraries are starting to get—or have already gotten —out of hand.

Screen savers and
capture programs

⚫ *screen savers* (AN)

esp. for beginners

Most computer monitors (like most TVs) are cathode ray tubes. They're coated on the inside with phosphors that glow when a beam of electrons hits them, creating the image on the screen. Leaving static images on the screen for long periods of time can exhaust the phosphors in certain areas, causing them to shine less brightly, or not at all. That's where *screen savers* come in.

They keep track of how long it's been since you hit a key or the mouse button and automatically black out the screen after a certain amount of time has passed. Hitting any key or moving the mouse brings back the image that was there before the screen saver kicked in.

Most screen savers today don't merely black out the screen —they put a moving image on it. Some of these images can get quite complicated, and beautiful. The ones that move the most give your phosphor the best protection (but pure black is, of course, the best).

⚫ *Pyro and After Dark*

Pyro was the first really popular screen saver on the Mac. Its name comes from *pyrotechnics,* another name for fireworks, and that's what you get on the screen (on color monitors, they're in color). Another screen saver, After Dark, comes with a choice of display options (described more fully in the next entry). Pyro's newest release is a reply to After Dark—it has a choice of displays too.

Both programs let you specify how long they wait before they take over the screen. You can also turn them on immediately—the Sleep Now feature—by moving the pointer to a corner of the screen (useful when you've got something on the screen you don't want everybody to see).

⚫ *After Dark* (Karen Faria)

After Dark 1.1c is a fun screen saver cdev. It's compatible with MultiFinder (not all screen savers are) and gives you 26 patterns to choose from. You can create your own pattern by importing a graphic or by writing a message.

If you're the kind of person who doesn't like other people messing with your Mac, After Dark offers a feature called Anti-Snoop Sleep. Once you invoke it, your screen can't be reactivated until you key in a password. If someone tries to turn the screen saver off, by hitting a key or moving the mouse, the screen freezes for about ten seconds and then a password box appears. If the correct password isn't entered, the screen saver resumes until the next time someone tries to deactivate it.

very good feature

One bad feature of After Dark is that you can't turn off its Never Sleep corner (the place where you put the pointer to deactivate the screen saver). Since it's easy to accidentally leave the pointer in that corner, this defeats the whole purpose of having a screen saver.

very bad feature

[I understand the need for a Sleep Now corner, but not for a Never Sleep corner. After all, if the screen blacks out, you can just touch the mouse and bring it back again. Any decent screen saver should let you deactivate this "feature" permanently.—AN]

♦ BlackOut (Chris Allen)

bargain

Blackout is a screen blanker init that sends your Mac on an animated interstellar voyage. It's shareware (the fee is just $5) and was written by Andrew Welch.

♦ capturing screens

Sometimes you need a picture of what's on the screen to include in a document. The Mac's standard FKey for this function (Shift ⌘ 3, described on page 215) has a lot of limitations: it only works on black-and-white screens; you can't take a picture of *part* of the screen, or of an opened menu; and you have to open a MacPaint document to get at the picture of the screen. Fortunately, third-party screen capture programs overcome all these limitations, and then some.

♦ Capture

Capture ($80, from Mainstay) is a simple, straightforward utility. When you call it up (by whatever key combination you've assigned to it), the pointer changes to a crosshairs; you then drag a selection rectangle around whatever part of the screen you want to capture, and indicate whether you want it saved to disk as a PICT image or sent directly to the Clipboard. Capture works even when menus are down and dialog boxes are open.

♦ Exposure

Exposure ($100, from Preferred Publishers) is a super-duper screen-capture utility that's perfect for anyone who writes about the Mac. Even if you don't, you may find it useful.

When you invoke Exposure, an *image* of the screen (including menus and dialog boxes, if any are open) fills the screen—you think your program or the desktop is still there, but it's just a picture. Then Exposure's "control panel" appears, with a variety of tools that let you alter the screen image just about any way you want.

You can make everything disappear but a particular window, remove the desktop pattern, or bleach a color screen to black-and-white. There's even a menu cutter that draws a jagged edge at the end of a section of a menu to indicate that there's more to it than you're showing. When you're done editing the screen, the final picture can be sent to the Clipboard, the Scrapbook or a disk file.

very good feature

Make sure you get version 1.02 or later. The initial release of Exposure had a fatal bug that made your whole system freeze a few minutes after you started up, if you had MacroMaker installed. Speaking of which...

bug

Macro programs

✿ macros defined (AN)

A *macro* is a command that incorporates two or more other commands or actions. (The name comes from the idea that macro commands incorporate "micro" commands.) A macro can be as simple as a keyboard equivalent for a menu command—using ⌘ S for *Save*, for example—or so complex that it really amounts to a miniprogram.

esp. for beginners

Macro programs create macros by recording your keystrokes and/or mouse clicks, or by giving you a sort of pseudo programming language to write them in. Entries on some of the more popular macro programs follow.

✿ Tempo II

Tempo's been around for a long time. I've never understood why it didn't become a standard instantly, because it's an amazing piece of work—and it was even more amaz-ing (relative to what else was around) when it first came out. Maybe it was before its time.

Tempo is the most powerful macro utility you can get. It may not be the *best* one you can get, because if you don't need the power, MacroMaker—which is cheaper and easier to use (and is described below)—might be enough for you.

Tempo lets you do all sorts of amazing things, like:

very good feature

- record mouse moves *relative to* the window or screen—so if you record a click in a zoom box, it will still play back in the zoom box no matter where the window is when you use the macro

- chain macros together

- repeat a macro a specified number of times

- play back a macro at a specific time, at a specified speed or at the actual speed at which you recorded it

- branch to a submacro from a main one, based on what's in the Clipboard

- use keyboard combinations or a popup menu to recall macros—or play them back by their *names* instead of their assigned keys

- make dialog boxes pop up on the screen, to request information for pasting or branching

bug

Tempo isn't entirely compatible with Word, which can be a real problem for people like me, who refuse to give up either program. You can still record and play back macros in Word, but you have to control Tempo just with keyboard commands—you can't access its menu.

⚫ *QuicKeys* (AN)

I've been using QuicKeys to generate "dumb quotes" (see the entry in Chapter 10 for more details) and to create keyboard equivalents for menu commands. In this limited use, it's performed flawlessly; the keys I hit for my dumb quotes and keyboard equivalents respond as quickly as any unmodified key (or so it seems, anyway).

Unfortunately, I've found QuicKeys too complex and hard-to-use to do much more with it than that, but it's very popular among the computer experts I know, and they use it for a wide variety of purposes.

QuicKeys is a cdev, so you access it through the Control Panel. It costs $100 (from CE Software), and with it you get DialogKeys, which gives you keyboard equivalents for buttons and checkboxes in dialog boxes.

(I know people who swear by QuicKeys, but I can't stand it. You can only record a single action at a time, so if you want a macro that does two things in a row—saves and then prints, for example—you have to build two separate little macros and then link them together in a third macro. Even with an extended keyboard, you run out of key combinations very quickly.—SZA)

● MacroMaker

MacroMaker has a number of things going for it—not the least of which is that it's free (it's part of Apple's system software). MacroMaker is a straightforward, "watch-me" recorder. You can use it to play back mouse moves and keyboard input. There's nothing fancy about it—it won't let you link macros, for example. But you can use it until you learn the ropes, and then move on to something more powerful, if you feel the need to.

bargain

● turning MacroMaker off

To make MacroMaker's menu appear on the menu bar, just put the MacroMaker file in your system folder. To turn it off, choose *Open MacroMaker* and click on the on/off switch in the window that appears (the icon will remain on the menu bar, so you can turn it back on again if you want). To remove the icon from the menu bar, take the MacroMaker icon out of the system folder and restart the Mac.

esp. for beginners

❡ *moving macros in MacroMaker*

Don't worry if you've stored a MacroMaker macro in the wrong place (on the list of Finder macros instead of as a Global macro, for example); it's easy to move it. Here's how:

- Choose *Open MacroMaker* from MacroMaker's menu.

- Find the macro you want to move in the macro list, and select it.

- Click on the *Load* button. This moves the macro to the editing area at the left of the recorder.

- The menu box above the list of macros contains the name of the current location for the macro—the application to which it's assigned. Press on the box and a menu will pop up.

- Choose the application you want the macro to be moved to. (Only applications that already have macros appear in the list.) The *Global* choice means the macro will be available no matter what application you're in.

- Click the *Load* button to move the macro from the editing area into the list for the selected application.

This procedure *copies* the macro into a new list. If you want to remove the macro from its original location, you have to do that separately, by selecting it in that list and clicking the *Erase* button.

Miscellaneous utilities

❡ *AutoSave*

very good feature

AutoSave does something almost everybody needs done—at regular intervals (you choose what they are), it generates a ⌘S, thereby saving the document you're working on. (You can change the command if you need to, but virtually all programs use ⌘S.)

In earlier versions, you listed the applications where you *didn't* want AutoSave to work (the Finder, for example, or databases like FileMaker, that do their own saving), but in the latest version (AutoSave II), you list the applications where you *do* want it to work. This is a big improvement, because there didn't used to be any way to keep it from working while a DA was open.

Now what I want from AutoSave is for it to keep track of different applications under MultiFinder, and save every time I've racked up ten minutes (or whatever) in any one application. As it is, switching around under Multi-Finder may mean that some documents never happen to get saved.

[AutoSave could be more slickly written, but it's the only program I know of that does what it does, and that's something that's totally essential. When you get wrapped up in your work, you're going to forget to save—and that means you are going to lose work. Since I've been using AutoSave, crashes hold no terror for me. I just get curious about whether I was unlucky and will have to reconstruct nine minutes worth of work, or whether I was lucky and will only have to reconstruct two.—AN]

⬤ *Address Book* (Chris Allen)

bargain

Address Book (not to be confused with Address Book Plus, described in Chapter 11) is a handy little shareware database program specifically designed for storing names, addresses and telephone numbers. The program will also dial any phone number in its files at a click of the mouse, either directly onto your modem or by generating tones on the Mac's speaker.

It comes as an application and as a DA. The application works well under MultiFinder, handles multiple address lists, and lets you customize a number of features. The DA can only access a single list file in your system folder.

Address Book's main limitation is that it doesn't print, but you can export to a text file which can be printed with your favorite word processor.

Address Book was written by Jim Leitch. Send him the $20 shareware fee and he'll send you some additional, related utilities: Addr_list Merger, which merges two address book files; Text to Address Book Convertor, which imports text files from other applications; and SideKick Convertor, which (needless to say) converts SideKick files so Address Book can read them.

[Address Book is included on The Macintosh Bible Software Disks, Third Edition, *which are described in Chapter 19.—AN]*

🍎 *Calendar DA* (Chris Allen)

bargain

This is an elegant little shareware desk accessory for planning and scheduling. When you first open it, it displays the current month, with the current date selected. There's a text area at the bottom of the window for listing today's events (it will be empty, of course, since the program isn't psychic). Entering text into this area outlines the date, so you know there's something there. Clicking on other days, months, or years changes the calendar to show the appropriate day.

	Calendar 2.1							
Tuesday, July 3, 1990						10:58 AM		
Sun	Mon	Tue	Wed	Thu	Fri	Sat	Jan	Jul
	1	2	3	4	5	6	7	Feb	Aug
8	9	10	11	12	13	14	Mar	Sep
15	16	17	18	19	20	21	Apr	Oct
22	23	24	25	26	27	28	May	Nov
29	30	31					Jun	Dec
							89	91

About Calendar 2.1

Calendar DA doesn't print calendars, nor is it an alarm clock, but I've been using it continuously (in one version or another) for about five years now. The companion application, Calendar Tools, lets you convert text files to Calendar files, and Calendar files to text files (for printing).

Calendar was written by David Oster, who asks just $5 if you regularly use this DA, or just $8 if you use Calendar Tools as well. (*It's included on* The Macintosh Bible Software Disks, Third Edition, *which are described in Chapter 19.—AN*)

⚫ *To Do!* (Chris Allen)

To Do! is a neat little shareware desk accessory for making to-do lists. You can check off things you've done, lower or raise the priority of the things you have to do and attach notes to items. The things to do list and the notes can also be easily printed out so you can take them with you.

To Do!'s author, Andrew Welch, asks that you send him a meager $10 if you use the program. *(It's included on* The Macintosh Bible Software Disks, Third Edition, *which are described in Chapter 19.—AN)*

⚫ *SF Scroll Init*

This public-domain init, written by Mac programming wizard Andy Hertzfeld, gives you a little more control over list boxes. Instead of always seeing the start of the list each time a Save or Open dialog box opens, you'll see the part of the list you last worked with. (The *SF* in the title stands for *Set File*.)

⚫ *Scroll Limit*

One problem with faster Macs is that the lists in list boxes scroll by too fast. Well, there's a great freeware init called Scroll Limit that lets you control that. You control it through an associated cdev (see the illustration at the top of the next page).

(This is a great idea, but the rate you pick controls the scroll bars as well. I want the lists in list boxes to scroll by fairly slowly, but I want scroll bars to go as fast as possible. The way Scroll Limit is set up, you have to compromise between the two.—AN)

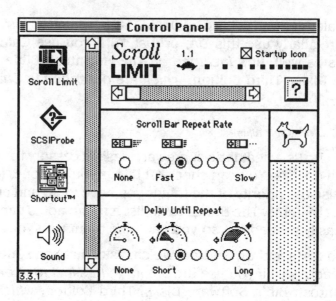

⚜ UnScrolly

bargain

UnScrolly is a nifty freeware utility that lets you choose between icons or text in the Control Panel. When you have lots of cdevs, this is a must. Here's how the Control Panel looks, before and after UnScrolly:

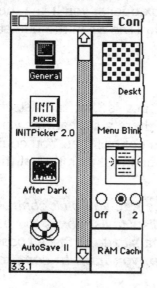

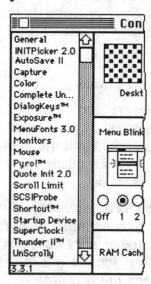

Stepping Out (Steve Schwartz)

If you've been drooling over large-screen displays but can't justify their cost, here's a $100 alternative. Stepping Out will make the standard Mac screen act like a big screen (or a window onto one). You can choose from a variety of preprogrammed screen sizes, or create and save custom-sized screens of your own.

When you move the pointer to the edge of the screen, the view automatically scrolls over. There are also options to view the screen at a magnification of two-to-sixteen times its original size, and at a 25%, 50% or 75% reduction. The menu bar and tool palettes stay in place no matter where you scroll, and the type on them stays normal Mac size.

Stepping Out can be set to run automatically whenever you turn on your Mac, or you can switch it on and off from the Control Panel or by holding down the [Option] key when launching an application. (Since some applications, like Font/DA Mover, use the [Option] key during launch for other purposes, you'll occasionally get a change in screen size as a side-effect.)

However you turn Stepping Out on, keep an eye on how much memory you have available. It takes a fair amount to emulate a big screen—from 100K for the simplest to over 600K for a three foot by two foot blueprint layout.

Although extremely handy, Stepping Out takes getting used to. For example, if you're in the Finder and use the Control Panel to turn off Stepping Out, your disk icons will occasionally be stranded somewhere off-screen. To get to them, you'll have to reactivate the program temporarily. Also, zooming icons open or closed occurs in slow motion when you're working on a very large screen or with MultiFinder.

The screen-locking function is quite useful when you want everything to hold still for awhile (and not scroll)— when you're editing a detailed drawing, say. Unfortunately, there are certain display modes where it doesn't work.

If your work demands a large display and you're willing to take the time to learn the ins and outs of Stepping Out, I think you'll find it one of your most useful programs.

bug

But be aware that in PageMaker, Stepping Out is more a hindrance than a help. PageMaker's tool palette disappears from the screen when you scroll, rulers either disappear or don't adjust as you scroll, and the *Fit in window* command is rendered useless (a major annoyance, since this is one of the most commonly used commands in PageMaker).

¢ StuffIt

very good feature

When you're sending files over phone lines, or squeezing them onto floppy disks, it's great to be able to make them as small as possible. To do that, you need a file-compression utility, and the one just about everyone uses is called StuffIt. It not only compresses individual files but also lets you archive combinations of files into a single compressed file; you can even compress a folder and its contents in one fell swoop.

bargain

StuffIt started out as shareware (written by a high-school student, Raymond Lau), but it's now a commercial product ($25). StuffIt is very fast and very efficient at compressing files. Keep your eye out for StuffIt Deluxe, a major upgrade that will be out by the time you read this.

¢ Set Clock *(Chris Allen)*

bargain

Set Clock is a useful utility that uses your modem to accurately synchronize your Mac's internal clock with an atomic clock in Virginia, thereby assuring millisecond accuracy. You just indicate your time zone, click the dial button, and within 30 seconds your Mac is on time. (Be aware that you'll be charged for a 30-second long-distance call to Virginia.)

Set Clock is by Jim Leitch and is freeware. *[It's included on* The Macintosh Bible Software Disks, Third Edition, *which are described in Chapter 19.—AN]*

❤ *SuperClock!* (Chris Allen)

SuperClock! is a cdev that puts a small clock on the right side of your menu bar. It has a number of customizable features including a timer with an alarm and the ability to sound on the hour. SuperClock was written by Steve Christenson and is freeware—but if you like the program and want to pay something for it, Steve asks that you send a donation to Stanford Children's Hospital, 520 Sand Hill Road, Palo Alto CA 94304.

bargain

[SuperClock is included on The Macintosh Bible Software Disks, Third Edition, *which are described in Chapter 19.—AN]*

❤ *Complete Delete* (Charles Rubin)

When you put a file in the Trash, or use a standard delete command from inside a program, you only remove the file's directory listing from the disk—the file is still on the disk, and it can be recovered with an undelete utility like the one in MacTools. Complete Delete is a public-domain program that completely erases a file from the disk, so that there's no way it can be recovered. (Don't confuse this program with Complete Undelete, which is described in Chapter 9.)

bargain

❤ *SUM II* (Chris Allen)

SUM stands for *Symantec Utilities for the Macintosh*. SUM II ($150) is a collection of utilities that I consider essential for every Mac owner who has a hard disk. The most important tool is Shield; it makes a backup copy of the vulnerable directory tracks on the disk, and keeps track of deleted files. Since I've started using SUM Shield, I've never lost a file because of a hard disk crash or an accidental deletion.

very good feature

If a disk does crash, Disk Clinic and Recover can help. I've used Recover on a number of occasions to recover clients' crashed hard disks. Even though they didn't have SUM Shield installed, I was able to recover most of their files.

The rest of the utilities in SUM II are also of good quality. They include Backup, Tuneup (a hard disk optimizer), Encrypt, Tools (a disk editor), Partition and QuickCopy (a floppy disk copier). There may be individual utilities from other publishers that do as good a job (or even a better one), but the ones that come with SUM are more than sufficient.

Screen Gems (Chris Allen)

This is a package of five color utilities for the Mac II family. Color Desk makes the desktop a piece of colored art, Dimmer is a screen blanker, TN-3 lets you configure the Finder's color menu to your own selected palette of colors, and Globe is just a color animation of the earth rotating.

For me, the most useful part of Screen Gems is Switch-a-Roo. This is a function key that changes your screen between any two color modes instantly. I find switching between black-and-white and eight-bit color useful, since some programs require one mode or the other, and since working in black-and-white speeds up your Mac.

Chapter 9

Trouble-shooting

✦ what this chapter is for *(AN)*

Some of the stuff in this chapter is covered elsewhere in the book (although a lot of it isn't). In any case, the purpose of this chapter is to bring together and summarize all the basic troubleshooting warnings and procedures, so you'll have one place to look when things go wrong. (For the same approach, but a much more comprehensive treatment, check out *The Macintosh Bible "What Do I Do Now?" Book* by Charles Rubin.)

Identifying and avoiding problems

✦ isolating the problem

esp. for beginners

The main skill in troubleshooting is figuring out what's wrong; once you know that, fixing it is usually pretty easy. To isolate the problem, you first have to think of all the things that *might* be wrong. Then you just check out each one in turn.

Start with the one that's most likely to be the problem, *or* with the one that's easiest to fix (cross your fingers—maybe the easy one will be the one that works.) It's all a question of logically eliminating possibilities—and not panicking.

The first thing to ask yourself is: *What have I changed lately?* If you just started experiencing the problem, the most recent change to your system (a system update, a new init) may be the culprit. Either that, or the new item is just the catalyst and something you've been using a long time is the actual culprit (it was designed poorly, but the flaw hasn't shown up until now).

Let's say you have a document that won't print. Here's a list (in no particular order) of the possible causes:

- something's wrong with the document
- something's wrong with the application you're printing from

- something's wrong with the printer
- something's wrong with the Mac system

Let's try the easiest thing first: Try printing a different document from the same application. If it prints, the document's probably the culprit. If it doesn't, check that the printer's plugged in, turned on, connected to the computer and chosen in the Chooser desk accessory. If you're using an ImageWriter, also make sure you've indicated the right connector port in the Chooser.

Now try printing something from another application. If that works, your printer's OK. The system's probably not the problem, since other things are printing. So try replacing the application (from the master disk or a backup floppy).

If *that* doesn't work, it still might be the application, since maybe there was something wrong with the original application. (Have you printed from it before? Had problems with it before? Either way, it's probably time to call the manufacturer's help line.)

Now, if you're not able to print anything from *any* application—you've got a system or printer problem. Check to see if the printer will print its test page. Are you sure the cables are OK? Have you tried resetting it (turning it off and back on again)?

If the printer seems fine, look back to your system. Do you have the correct printer drivers—up-to-date and compatible with the system version you're using? Are you running any new inits or DAs that might be causing the problem?

This is the point where it's great to have a friend with a similar setup. Will the document print from his machine? Yes? Aha...it's not the document then. And so on.

[This is just an example, of course, but hopefully it demonstrates how to approach a problem. The basics are: Don't panic—take a deep breath (or three). Then eliminate possibilities logically. Remember—computers aren't smart enough to be illogical.—AN]

❤ *before calling for help*

Before you call a manufacturer's technical support line because you're having a problem:

esp. for
beginners

* Narrow down the problem, as described above, until you're reasonably sure that it's either the application or a specific document that's giving you trouble.

* Have your registration number ready (if the publisher requires it) and know which version of the program you're using.

* Have a list of inits that are in your System. (You should also have tried to get things to work with no inits in your System at all. See Chapter 8 for details.)

* Know which version of the System and Finder you're running and be familiar with the rest of your software and hardware setup. How much RAM do you have? If you're running MultiFinder, how much memory have you allocated to the program? And so on.

❤ *an ounce of prevention*

Many problems—from minor ones like disk slowdowns to major ones like crashes and virus attacks—can be avoided or minimized by following basic preventive measures. Here are some general housekeeping guidelines:

esp. for
beginners

* Make sure you have only one System and Finder on a disk. Use Apple's Find File or some other disk-searching utility to check that there are no duplicate System or Finder files hiding on the disk. (For more details, see the entry called *avoid multiple systems* in Chapter 6.)

* Rebuild the desktop occasionally. (For more details, see the entry called *rebuilding the desktop* in Chapter 3.)

* Use an antivirus program to check out your whole hard disk, and then to monitor all incoming disks for viruses. (For more details, see the section on viruses later on in this chapter.)

* Defragment your hard disk to keep it running quickly. (For more details, see the entry called *defragmenting hard disks* in Chapter 3.)

**important
warning**

- Electronic bulletin boards are notorious breeding grounds for viruses. So practice *safe software*—know where your programs come from and where they've been. Make sure anyone with access to your computer also practices safe software. (For more details, see the section on viruses later on in this chapter.)

Backing up disks

● *about backups* (AN/SZA)

**important
warning**

There are only two kinds of computer users: those who've lost data and those who are about to. The latter obviously haven't had their computers very long.

Since it's *guaranteed* that you'll someday lose data, the thing to do is to reduce the *consequences* of it. And you can do that to such an extent that losing data is no big deal. For example, if you back up every ten minutes, you can never lose more than ten minutes' work.

● *same-disk backups*

If your hard disk crashes, it's a major catastrophe, because of all the data on it. But it's much more common for a single *file* on a disk to become corrupted (and unopenable, and unrecoverable), either because of a system crash or a virus. When that happens, a copy of the document right on the same disk is all you need to get going again.

**very good
feature**

Some programs let you automatically make a backup copy of the document you're working on—every time you save it, a copy is also saved. You should turn this feature on in any program that has it; in programs that don't, you should get in the habit of saving double copies of important documents by hand—either by using *Save As* from within the application or by duplicating files on the desktop at the end of a work session.

Other files you should remember to duplicate (because redoing them can take so much effort) are the little ones in your system folder, like the Scrapbook file, the file your macro utility uses to store your macros, files created by desk accessories, and user-created dictionaries for spelling checkers.

⬥ how many backups to make *(AN)*

An 800K floppy disk costs about a buck and holds at least 25 hours' work. So if you value your time at more than 4¢ an hour, the moral is simple: you should always have enough disks around to make multiple copies of your work.

very hot tip

I make three copies, each on a separate disk, of every piece of work I do. Tony Pietsch got me into that habit years ago, when he described the following scenario: *Let's say you only have two copies of something and your disk drive screws up. You insert the first disk and see garbage on the screen. Naturally you assume there's something wrong with that disk, but you're not worried, because you have a second disk with the same document on it. So you insert the second disk and the drive zaps that too. At that point you realize the problem is with the drive, not the disk, but it's too late—unless you have a third copy.*

⬥ backup of previous entry *(C.J. Weigand)*

I second what Arthur just said. Two backups let you recover from losses caused by program crashes, system crashes, undetected errors, viruses or disk failure. (The shelf-life of a diskette is two to three years at most and the potential for random media problems can increase dramatically as time goes by.)

If you really want to be safe, rotate in a third backup and keep it in a separate building, so you can recover your files even if you suffer a fire or a burglary. (For more on guarding against fire, see the entry titled *disks melt before paper burns* in the floppy disk section in Chapter 3.)

⬥ more backup tips *(Paul Hoffman)*

Here's another reason to back up your hard disk: someone may steal your Mac and hard disk. With a backup, you can rent another Mac and start working again.

As C. J. suggests, you should store at least one set of backups away from your computer and probably in a different building. If the building burns down, having a stack of backups next to the computer won't do you much good. Also, if someone steals the computer, the thief may steal all the disks near the computer as well.

If your Mac is on a network, you might consider backing it up by copying to unused space onto the hard disks of other computers. For example, if you're networked to a minicomputer with a large hard disk, filling up 20 megabytes may be perfectly acceptable to the system administrator. This is usually *much* slower than backing up to floppies, but it doesn't cost anything since no floppies are used.

*very
hot
tip*

Be sure to label your backup disks with the complete date of the backup, including the year. Since it's likely that you will own your Mac for more than a year, finding information on old backups is almost impossible otherwise.

✦ what not to back up

You don't have to back up everything on your hard disk. Why waste your time backing up a few megs' worth of fonts in the system folder when you have the master disks stored safely away? (You *do* have them stored safely away, right?) There's no need to back up applications, either, since you've got them on masters too. Concentrate your efforts on backing up files that don't exist anywhere else—the documents that you create yourself.

✦ backup programs and strategies

*esp. for
beginners*

Since backing up the contents of floppy disks is simply a matter of putting a copy of each file on at least two different disks, the rest of this section assumes that you're backing up from a hard disk. You can do that onto floppies, another hard disk, a removable cartridge or a tape.

Removable hard-disk cartridges are by far the most convenient and cost-effective. And a removable-cartridge drive can do double duty as your regular, everyday hard disk.

(See the entry on SyQuest cartridges in Chapter 3 for more about them.)

Backing up onto floppies is the least expensive method. But backing up a full 40-meg hard disk requires about *fifty* 800K floppies—just think about the *time* it will take. (Of course, you don't usually have to back up the whole hard disk at once.)

A good backup program should be reliable and fast (of course). It should also be able to split a large file across two disks (if you're backing up on floppies) and make global, incremental and archival backups.

A *global* backup makes a mirror image of the information on your disk. An *incremental* backup only backs up the files you've modified since you last time backed up (or from any date you specify). An *archival* backup saves the previous version(s) of your backups. Most backup programs insist on doing an initial global backup and then let you choose to back up just the files you want.

Some backup programs compress files when they back them up. This makes them work more quickly and efficiently, but it means that the same program has to translate the file on its return trip—you can't just insert the backup disk and drag icons back to the desktop.

shortcut

There are dozens of backup programs available, and many of them are good. Rather than trying to survey the field, here are a couple I'm familiar with.

⚫ *Redux*

Redux is a terrific backup utility from Microseeds. It does incremental backups and you can also specify that only certain *types* of documents (Excel spreadsheets, say) be backed up.

very good
feature

Redux writes to all kinds of media—floppies, hard drives or cartridges. Its manual is friendly and understandable, and the names of the files in its illustrations carry through the rabbit theme of the logo. Somebody at Microseeds was obviously an English major. *(For those of you who weren't,* Rabbit Redux *is the name of a book by John Updike.* (Redux, *by the way,* means brought back *or* returning. *A less pretentious author than Updike would have called the book* The Return of Rabbit *or* Rabbit Returns.*)—AN]*

🍎 *HD Backup*

Apple provides the HD Backup utility on its System Tools disks, so it's free. Unfortunately, you get what you pay for.

very bad
feature

First of all, HD Backup only works with floppies. Secondly, it duplicates files (slowly) even if they haven't been modified since the last backup. This means your backup disk collection will keep growing. If you're serious about backing up your work and have a hard disk larger than a 20 megs, forget HD Backup.

One final note: If you sometimes begin filenames with a period (to change where they sort to in lists), be aware that HD Backup ignores filenames that begin with a period.

bug

🍎 *back to square one* (AN)

I've used many different backup programs, some of which worked just fine, but in the fullness of my years, I've come back to the simplest method. When I quit whatever application I'm working in and return to the Finder, I simply drag the new documents I've worked on over to my removable-cartridge drive. That's it.

Once every few months, I do a full-disk backup (just documents, not programs) to catch any files I may have missed. For that I use the backup program that came with my SyQuest drive (all the manufacturers provide them). In my case, this is something called AIC MacBak AR (since I have an AIC drive). The name could use some work, but the program itself is easy to use and does just what I want.

Recovering data from disks

♦ recovering data from crashed floppies (SZA/DC)

Eventually it happens—you insert a floppy disk with important data in a drive and get one of these dreaded messages: *This is not a Macintosh disk: Do you want to initialize it?* or *This disk is damaged: Do you want to initialize it?* (The answer is no, unless you want to lose all the data on the disk.)

Here are some possible rescue procedures, none of which is guaranteed to work:

- Hold down ⌘ and (Option) while inserting the disk and keep them held down. A message will appear asking if you want to rebuild the desktop. Click on *Yes*. If the recovery succeeds, the desktop will appear after a minute or two (how long it takes depends on how many files are on the disk).

- Launch the application that created the documents you want to save. Once inside it, choose *Open...* from the File menu and, while the dialog box is on the screen, insert the problem disk . If the documents you're worried about appear in the list box, you're home free; just open them and immediately do a *Save As* onto another disk for each one.

  If the documents you're trying to rescue were created by more than one application, just repeat the process for each application (or use a program that can read lots of different kinds of files).

- Check that you haven't inserted a high-density disk formatted as 800K into a high-density drive. If you have, put it back into an 800K drive (and see the entry *high-density disks initialized as 800K* in Chapter 3 for more information).

- Try the disk in another drive. Sometimes a drive is bad, and sometimes a disk written on by one drive can't be read in another, because the heads are slightly out of alignment.

- Try rotating the disk's hub a quarter-turn or so and then reinserting it.

- Wait and try again later. If a disk is too cold or too warm, it might not be read correctly.

- Use a disk rescue utility. There are many available, and a not-very-powerful one, Disk First Aid, comes free on the System Tools disk that came with your Mac.

These tricks won't work with every disk that goes bad, but they're worth a try. If none of them works, remember the entire episode the next time you think you just don't have time to make backups of your documents.

recovering deleted files

When you empty the Trash, files don't actually get erased from the disk—their names just get erased from the directory. Since the information is still on the disk, you can get it back (until the computer reuses the space). The sooner you try, the more likely you are to be able to recover it—the longer you wait, the more likely it is that other information will be stored right over the old file. So as soon as you realize you need something you've deleted, stop using the disk and run a recovery utility.

There are utilities that let you go in and find pieces of your files, but the best approach is to plan ahead, by using a program like Complete Undelete (from 1st Aid Software) or Guardian (it's on the SUM disks from Symantec).

very good feature

Complete Undelete is an init that keeps track of everything you delete from your hard disk—well, not *everything*, but as much as it can in the space you assign to it. When you Trash something, Complete Undelete keeps a record of the information that used to be in the disk directory— that is, which tracks and sectors your file is stored in. Then, if you need the file back, Complete Undelete knows where to go get it—or as much of it as is still around.

Here's what an Complete Undelete record (accessed through the Control Panel) looks like:

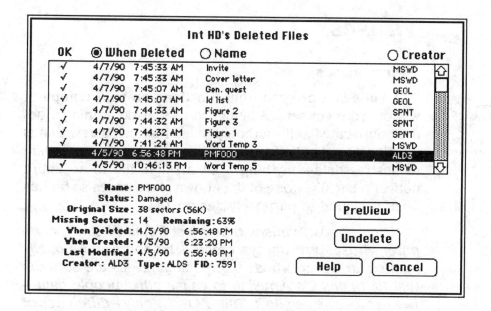

You'll notice that—unfortunately—records are kept for every temp file that an application makes and then erases. Programs that automatically make backup copies of documents also clog up Complete Undelete, since every time you save, the old backup is recorded as a deleted file. Because of these problems, make sure you leave Complete Undelete enough room to log your *real* deleted files.

❡ recovering unsaved files

If you crash with unsaved changes to your file, you may be able to piece some of it back together from the temp files many applications leave in the system folder.

Word, for example, leaves files named *Word temp 1* and so on. While you can't open a temp file directly, you can use a utility like DiskTop to change its type from WTMP to WDBN (the utility's manual will explain how to do it). This makes it openable by Word.

Viruses

⚫ virus basics

*esp. for
beginners*

A *virus* is a program that functions on your computer without your consent. A benign virus may do nothing more than duplicate itself—although even that can screw things up if it gets out of hand. Some viruses, however, are *meant* to destroy data—anything from a single file to an entire network. Luckily, none of the known Mac viruses so far has been designed to purposely destroy data.

[Unlike (most) viruses that infect human beings, computer viruses are always created by some emotionally stunted little nerd whose interpersonal skills are so weak that he thinks it's amusing to cause other people pain— just to prove he can do it. There's really only a difference of degree between creating computer viruses and creating biological ones, and no doubt little difference in personality between the puerile misfits who make computer viruses and the moral zeros who engage in biological warfare. (It is, of course, possible to create viruses for moral purposes. But even if you're on the side of the angels, this sort of sabotage does nothing to sway public opinion.)—AN]

You get a virus by using an infected program or disk— that is, one that already has the virus on it. Electronic bulletin boards are notorious for spreading viruses. When strange things start happening—unexplained crashes, files being corrupted or disappearing—that's reason to suspect that you're infected.

There are various utilities for detecting and eradicating viruses; just as in the world of medicine, it's a game of leapfrog—the viruses evolve to outwit the cures and the cures get more sophisticated to handle the new viruses.

⚫ common viruses

Here's a brief roundup of some common (or formerly common) Mac viruses:

- *Peace*: This didn't do anything except display a World Peace message on the first anniversary of the Mac II introduction and then erase itself. The first widely known Mac virus, it's simply an init in the system folder.

- *nVIR, hpat, nFLU*: The second widely known Macintosh virus, but the first real trouble-maker. It spreads through system files (System, Finder and DA Handler, but not inits and cdevs) and applications. It causes random system crashes; sometimes it beeps when you start up an infected application. nVIR has gone through several evolutions, but virus detectors are generally keeping up with it. hpat and nFLU are variations of nVIR.

- *Scores*: Apparently the first malicious Mac virus, this damages applications and modifies the System file, the NotePad file and the Scrapbook file. It creates two invisible files in the system folder—*scores* and *desktop*. One infection clue is that your Scrapbook and NotePad files, instead of being little Macs in icon view, turn into generic document icons (rectangular pages with down-turned corners). Scores was created by a disgruntled employee to infect his employer's products—which were never released to the general public.

- *ANTI*: One of the few viruses that doesn't create additional resources in existing files—which means that many anti-virus programs can't deal with it. It infects only applications and, so far, doesn't appear to do anything.

- *wDEF*: This virus alters the desktop file, which makes it easy to identify on networks: a work station will constantly access the file server to the point where everything slows down incredibly (say, ten minutes for a folder to open after you doubleclick on it) and finally freezes up. wDEF also causes startup crashes on IIci's and Portables.

🍎 *virus detection and eradication*

Antivirus programs work in three ways: as *detectors*, letting you know you're infected; as *eradicators*, getting rid of viruses; and/or as *preventers*, screening inserted disks for viruses before they can be passed on to other files.

It's really worth keeping abreast of public-domain and shareware antivirus programs. It's a lot easier to download the latest update from a bulletin board (or get it from a user group) than it is to contact the publisher of a commercial product to see if there's an update.

Since it's virtually impossible to maintain an up-to-date list of which program takes care of which viruses, I'll just list some of the better-known (and best-working) antivirus programs around. Those followed by an author's name are public-domain or shareware, Apple's is free, and the other three are commercial products.

AntiToxin (Mainstay)

Disinfectant (John Norstad)

Eradicate'Em (Dave Platt)

Ferret (Larry Nedry)

Virex (Microcom)

SAM (Symantec)

Vaccine (CE Software)

Virus Detective (Jeffrey Shulman)

VirusRx (Apple)

shortcut

Disinfectant is a terrific antivirus program generously placed in the public domain by its author, John Norstad (and/or his employer, Northwestern University—I'm not sure exactly who to thank, since some of the program was a collaborative effort).

very good feature

Disinfectant can find and remove all the known Mac viruses and even offers protection against mutant strains of the known viruses. It's simple to use and even has a mode that handles multiple floppy disks automatically—when one is cleaned and ejected, you just insert the next. This is a product that can't be praised highly enough.

important warning

 invisible files in the system folder

As we mentioned in Chapter 6 (it bears repeating), invisible files in the system folder are almost always due to a virus. (You can find and delete invisible files with utilities like DiskTop, ResEdit or DiskTools.)

We say *almost always* because it's not inconceivable that at some future date Apple may introduce invisible system files as part of the Mac system. So the rule is: make sure you know what every invisible file is there for.

⚫ *simple virus protection for applications*

You can protect an application from viruses simply by locking it in its Get Info box. Since viruses alter files and locked files can't be altered, this is the easiest way to protect your programs. (It is possible to build a virus that's designed to unlock files, but so far it's not common.)

very
hot
tip

⚫ *simple virus protection for master disks*

You can protect your floppy disk masters from picking up viruses simply by keeping them locked. Just slide the little plastic tab so you can see through the disk, and nothing can be written to it. Of course, you should keep your master disks locked anyway, since you shouldn't change any information on them—that's why they're masters. If your hard disk system is infected and you don't know it, the infection is easily passed to a master disk as soon as you insert it.

very
hot
tip

If your *data* disks get around—as you move back and forth between work and home, say—only unlocking them when you're writing to them yourself is an easy protection scheme. (Maybe keeping those little plastic sleeves on them when...no, I guess not.)

System errors, crashes & bombs

⚫ *errors, crashes and sad Macs* (SZA/AN)

An *error* is the general term for any kind of software problem that keeps the Mac from doing what you want it to do. Errors most often arise from some mistake in the programming of the application you're using. Sometimes the

esp. for
beginners

result is conflicting instructions being given to the Mac about what to do next, and sometimes it's an instruction that's impossible to carry out under the circumstances—for example, trying to open a file that doesn't exist or that's corrupted in some way that makes it impossible to read.

There are three basic classes of errors on the Mac: *general errors, system errors* (also know as *crashes)* and *sad Macs.* Simple *general errors* generate alert boxes telling you what went wrong—perhaps a file can't be opened because it's already in use, or a printer can't be found. Such situations are handled adroitly by the Mac; you simply click the *OK* button to let the Mac know you've seen the alert box, and you can continue to work.

When general errors are more serious, the alert boxes contain negative numbers that are codes for what the problem is. You'll find explanations of these codes in the *alert error codes* entry below, but don't expect them to tell you what you need to *do* in a given situation—they're rarely that practical.

gossip/ trivia

The messages in these more serious alert boxes often contain arcane messages; Sharon's two favorites complain about the *curlist object (Isn't that what Scottish curlers push around on the ice?—AN)* and the *line walker. (I know all about this one. I've been walking the line for years.—AN)*

Really serious errors cause a *system error* or *crash.* Unlike general errors, crashes normally mean you have to restart the Mac.

The term *crash* only applies to software problems. If it's a hardware problem, you usually say, *My power supply (or my floppy drive, or whatever) blew up*—even though there was no explosion and no smoke. (If there *were* an explosion and smoke, you'd probably have to say, *My Mac blew up last night—I mean, it <u>really</u> blew up.)*

Some crashes fill the screen with dots, strange patterns or garbage characters; sometimes the Mac makes a noise like a muted machine gun. (If you're really lucky, you get both together.) Some crashes are so dramatic that it's hard to believe that software, not hardware, is causing the problem.

Two kinds of less dramatic crashes have special names: *hangs* and *bombs*. In a *hang* (or *freeze*), the screen looks OK but the pointer is frozen in place (sometimes it disappears) and keyboard input is ignored. Sometimes, however, just the pointer freezes, and the Mac still responds to the keyboard. So don't hit the *reset* button on the programmer's switch without first trying to hit ⌘ S and save your work.

very hot tip

Bombs produce alert boxes that contain a cartoon of a bomb, a message that reads: *Sorry, a system error has occurred,* and an ID number that tells you what kind of error it was (they're listed in the *bomb ID numbers* entry below). Sometimes bombs also involve hangs, so you have no choice but to push the *reset* button.

> **Sorry, a system error has occurred.**
>
> ID = 02

Sometimes you think you've just got a serious general-error alert box (the ones with the code numbers), but when you click the *OK* button, you get a bomb, because the Mac is hopelessly confused by unexecutable commands.

When you're working in MultiFinder, you're less likely to see a bomb alert box; instead, you get an alert box that says: *The application Word (or whatever) has unexpectedly quit.* (The Mac brooks no nonsense; if it doesn't like how an application is behaving—blam, that application is *history.)*

The last sort of basic Mac error message is the *sad Mac* you sometimes get on startup. Instead of the normal smiling Mac icon, the screen goes black and a very unhappy Mac icon appears, indicating that the Mac (or the drive you're using) failed one or more of the system and memory tests that Macs automatically perform when you start them up.

Sad Macs also have code numbers indentifying what the problem is; they're discussed in an entry below. On Mac II's, sad Macs are accompanied by broken chords that indicate what the problem is (if you've been trained to distinguish the chords).

₡ *what to do when you crash* (SZA/Todd Corleto)

Usually you don't have much choice—you just have to restart. Bomb alert boxes usually give you a choice of *Reset* and *Resume* buttons, but more often than not, the mouse and keyboard also freeze up, so you can't get at either button.

very hot tip

Not that it would matter much if you could—in five years of intermittent bombs on the Mac, I've never seen a *Resume* button that worked. It always just restarts the Mac—just as if you'd clicked the *Restart* button. (That's probably just as well; you should always restart after a bomb, because things are very unstable.)

If the *Restart* button in the bomb alert doesn't respond, or if the pointer is frozen, try this:

- Press the *interrupt* button (not the *reset* button) on the programmer's switch

very hot tip

- If you're lucky, you'll get a dialog box on the screen with nothing in it except this symbol: >). If you have a debugger like MacsBug installed, type ES ⌐Return⌐ . Otherwise, type SMFA700A9F4 ⌐Return⌐ PCFA700 ⌐Return⌐ G ⌐Return⌐ . (You don't have to press ⌐Shift⌐ , but anything you type appears as capital letters on the screen.)

- If you're still lucky, the dialog box will disappear and you'll be back on the desktop. You might even be able to save some files, or at least whatever's on the Clipboard.

If pushing the *interrupt* button doesn't work, push the *reset* button (on the programmer's switch). This will always restart your Mac (unless you have a hardware problem).

The next few entries give you suggestions on how to avoid repeated system errors.

✖ crashes on startup

If you're crashing on startup (with a bomb, hang or whatever), it's usually because of a problem on your startup disk. Often, the problem is with one of the programs on the disk that runs automatically—inits in the system folder, the System or Finder, or an application you've set as the startup application.

The first thing to do with a crashing startup disk is also the easiest: try it again, while holding down [Option] [⌘]. This rebuilds the disk's desktop file. If that doesn't cure the problem, use another startup disk (usually a floppy, if you normally start from a hard disk) and try any or all of the following:

very
hot
tip

- Remove all inits from the system folder (at least temporarily)—or at least pull any you've added recently.

- You may have to increase your System heap to allow extra memory for lots of inits. (See the System heap entry in Chapter 3 for more information about this.)

- Check the disk for viruses.

- Re-install the System and Finder with the Installer program on the System Tools disk.

- Zap the PRAM (as described in Chapter 2).

✖ crashes during use

When you're having a lot of system crashes while running and you can't pin down the reason, first try the four suggestions in the last entry, then try these:

- Use Find File or a similar utility to see if there's more than one System on your disk (and get rid of any extras).

- If you think the crashes may have started after you installed a new desk accessory or started using a new init, get rid of it (or them) and restart. (If the problem is an init clash, you won't necessarily have to give up using the init; see Chapter 8 for suggestions.)

- Replace the application you're using with a fresh copy from the master disk.

- If you're running MultiFinder, check that the memory you've allocated to your programs, including the Finder, is sufficient. An easy check for this is to see if running *without* MultiFinder stops the crashing.

ƒ *alert error codes*

As mentioned in the entry above called *errors, crashes and sad Macs,* general error alert boxes contain negative numbers that describe the source of the problem (in ways that aren't likely to be intelligible to you). Here's what these number codes represent:

−33	File directory full
−34	All allocation blocks on volume are full
−35	Specified volume doesn't exist
−36	Input/Output error
−37	Bad file name or bad volume name
−39	File not open or end-of-file error
−41	Memory full
−42	Too many files open
−43	File not found
−44	Volume is locked (hardware)
−45	File is locked
−46	Volume is locked (software)
−47	File is busy; one or more files are open

–48	File with specified name and version number already exists
–49	File already open
–53	Volume ejected
–55	Volume already mounted
–56	No such device or disk
–57	Not a Macintosh disk
–59	Problem during renaming
–60	Bad master block on disk
–61	Tried writing to a read-only file
–64	Drive isn't connected
–65, –66	Font Manager errors
–91 to –99	AppleTalk errors
–100, –101	Scrap Manager errors
–108 to –117	Storage allocation errors
–120 to –123	HFS problems
–192 to –199	Resource Manager errors
–200 to –206	Sound Manager errors
–290 to –351	Startup Manager errors
–1024 to –1029	AppleTalk errors
–1096 to –1105	AppleTalk errors
–3101 to –3109	AppleTalk errors
–4096 to –4101	Print Manager errors
–5000 to –5302	Apple Filing Protocol errors
–8132 to –8160	LaserWriter Driver errors

⚫ *bomb ID numbers*

Here's a list of the common ID numbers that accompany bombs and, in the few instances where there is something you *can* do about the problem, what you should do:

esp. for power users

01 Bus error

The Mac is trying to get at memory that isn't there. It may be just reporting the wrong error code, because the application you're running has a bug in it or has been corrupted, but sometimes 01 can indicate a hardware problem. If you get the 01 code, try replacing the application(s) you've been using with fresh copies.

02 Address Error

The Mac can put something into memory one byte at a time, or in larger chunks (two bytes, a *word*, or four bytes, a *longword.*) It doesn't matter where a single byte of information is stored, but for machines with 68000 chips, the larger chunks have to be stored beginning in an address that has an even number. The *address error* occurs when the Mac puts a *word* or *longword* into memory starting at an odd-numbered address.

Again, as with so many bombs, the cause of this problem is usually a buggy or corrupted application.

03 Illegal Instruction

Sometimes a buggy or corrupted application (the culprit again!) gives the computer an instruction that just isn't in its vocabulary. That's when you get this bomb.

04 Zero Divide

The Mac (quite reasonably) refuses to deal with math problems where the divisor is zero.

05 Range Check Error

If the Mac is told to check if a number is within a certain range, and it's not, this error results. (This sounds pretty temperamental to me.)

06 Overflow

A specific amount of space is allowed for each number the Mac has to remember in its processing. (Remember, everything's a number to the Mac.) Larger numbers need more space. When a program tries to squeeze a number into a space that's too small, this error results.

07 Privilege Violation

Not that it makes any difference to you or me, but the Mac can run in either *Supervisor* or *User* mode. It's supposed to always be in Supervisor mode, but if it happens to be in User mode when it's supposed to follow a Supervisor-mode instruction, it bombs.

08 Trace Mode Error

If the Mac is put into Trace mode (this is programmer's jargon for something that's too complicated to bother explaining) and there's no debugger installed to do the tracing, you get this bomb.

09–10 Line 1010 and 1111 Trap

This bomb means the Mac was looking something up in a special instruction table but didn't find what it was looking for. A buggy or corrupted application causes this one too.

12 Unimplemented Core Routine

If the Mac hits a *breakpoint* in a program (a spot where the programmer expected to do some debugging and thus put a little stop sign there) and there's no debugger installed, you'll get this bomb. (You shouldn't have any software with breakpoints still in it.)

13 Uninstalled Error

This bomb means that the Mac doesn't have, or can't find, instructions on how to deal with a device (a keyboard, mouse or drive, say) that's asking for attention.

15 Segment Loaded Error

Some programs are only partially loaded into memory when you run them; other parts—*segments*—are loaded into memory only as you need them. When a segment can't be loaded, you get this bomb; it's usually caused by a bad application.

17–24 Packages 0-7 not present

Packages are routines in your System file that handle certain tasks, like disk initialization. Bombs 17 through

24 indicate that a needed package is missing, and that your System file is damaged and needs replacing.

25 Memory Full

bug

You've run out of memory, or the Mac *thinks* it's run out of RAM due to some mistake in the program you're running.

26 Bad Program Launch

This is my favorite, because it's the easiest to fix. *Bad Launch* means the Mac couldn't run the program you just opened. You need a fresh copy of the application because something's wrong with it.

27 File System Map trashed

Something's wrong with the information about what's stored on the disk. Try rebuilding the desktop.

28 Stack ran into Heap

The *stack* and the *heap* are two areas of memory, so this generally equates to running out of memory.

✦ sad Mac code numbers

As mentioned above, you get a sad Mac because the Mac failed one of the initial startup diagnostics. On the Plus and the SE's, the code number beneath the sad Mac icon identifies the problem. (The SE/30 and all the Mac II's use tones to report errors.) The codes are *hexadecimal* numbers (base 16), where the letters A–F stand for the numbers 10–15. The codes differ on the Plus and the SE.

On the Plus, the saddest Mac of them all is the one whose first two digits are 01; that indicates a problem with the ROM of the machine (probably time for a new board). The last four digits don't make any difference if you get an 01. Codes that begin with 02, 03, 04 and 05 are RAM failures.

Sometimes you think everything's going OK because the disk starts spinning (you've passed the ROM and RAM tests) and then you get a sad Mac. The codes for these failures start with 0F.

A code of 0F000D usually means that the *interrupt* button on the programmer's switch is being pressed. Check that it's not being accidentally pushed by some clutter on your desk. (The programmer's switches on early Macs were especially easy to press.) If nothing's leaning on it, remove it and try putting it in again—or leave it out and test the machine.

Codes of 0F0064 and 0F0065 are a cinch. They indicate, respectively, a bad (or missing) System or Finder file. Just start the computer with a different disk and reinstall the System and/or Finder on the problem disk.

The SE has two rows of eight digits beneath its sad Mac icon. The SE's failures are most often due to bad RAM chips and the numbers indicate which chips are no good.

Security and protection software

computer security

Computer security isn't about preventing the theft of computer equipment; it's about preventing the theft (or destruction) of *information*. There are a number of approaches you can use to safeguard your data.

*esp. for
beginners*

Which approach you need depends on just how private your private files are and whether you're protecting them from casual lookers or a sophisticated hacker who really wants to get at them. Maybe you don't care if files are *used*, but don't want them *copied*.

Keep in mind that, as a general rule, the more secure your files are the more inconvenient they'll be for *you* to use as well—so, for your own sake, avoid overkill.

*very
hot
tip*

protection schemes

Password protection means that you can't get at a particular file (folder, volume or hard disk) unless you know its password. Many programs have *levels* of password protection—restricting access, restricting privileges (look-but-don't-change, change-only-a-copy, etc.), or both.

File encryption is the best—and therefore the most dangerous—protection scheme. An encrypted file has been scrambled, so that the computer can't make any sense out of it—and it takes the right password to unscramble it.

Why is this dangerous? Because if you forget the password, you can forget the file. Even the people who make the encryption schemes, or the best hacker, won't be able to help you recover it. So if you use encryption, make sure your password is stored somewhere and that at least one other person knows where it is. (This is no joke. I know of someone who died recently and took his password with him—his employers needed, but never recovered, those encrypted files.)

● *low-level protection*

Mild security is often enough for many people—sometimes you just want to protect your files from being accidentally modified by fellow workers who are basically Mac-illiterate.

Most low-level protection comes from just figuring out what you know that everybody else around you doesn't. When we first set up a Mac lab at a school where I teach, we didn't want the students using the master work station. So we simply unplugged the mouse but left it where it belonged—no one could figure out why it wasn't responding. That worked for a semester.

Some utilities (like DiskTools, ResEdit and DiskTop) let you make files invisible. The invisibility is easily reversed and in any case is strictly a desktop feature—the file still shows up in the Open dialog box of the application that created it.

You can take this a step further if there are just a few special files you want to protect from unsophisticated users who have access to your machine. In addition to making the file invisible, use any of the same programs to change the Creator information (this tells you which application created the file). This will prevent it from appearing in an Open dialog box—unless you know that a particular application (Word is one example) lets you list *any* document by holding down [Shift] when you choose the *Open...* command.

If you have a hard disk with multiple partitions, it may not even be necessary to password-protect the partition with your private files in it. If no one knows it's partitioned, or how to mount the partition, your documents are safe.

⚅ *invisible applications* (C.J. Weigand)

very
hot
tip

One way to prevent programs stored on your hard disk from being pirated is to make them invisible (using Disk-Top's Technical level Get Info box, for example). But then how do *you* use them? Well, QuicKeys lets you launch a program with a keystroke combination, regardless of whether or not its icon is visible. (Both QuicKeys and DiskTop are described in Chapter 8.)

Using this trick gives you full access to all your programs, but no one else who sneaks a peek at your Mac will even know that they're there.

⚅ *security software tips* (Steve Schwartz)

Here are a few tips you may find helpful when working with security software:

- It's easy to be cavalier when assigning new passwords and to create so many you lose track of them. Remember— if you forget the password, you can kiss the file goodbye. *[Sharon said this already, but it's worth repeating.—AN]*

important
warning

- If you work with the files as a set, use a password for the whole set, and only use an additional password for the extremely sensitive documents inside it.

- Don't use obvious passwords. One company I worked for used everyone's first names as their passwords into the accounting system. (That's a hard one to crack, huh?)

- Unless there's a cryptographer in your office or you're required by contract to use the DES encryption standard, use the fast encryption method for most files.

- Remember to lock all files whenever you leave your Mac.

❖ *Empower*

Empower ($400) is a versatile and powerful protection program. It offers two types of protection—with and without data encryption. You can use it to assign passwords to individuals or groups and assign different privileges to different users, much as you do under AppleShare on a network.

❖ *StuffIt protection*

very
hot
tip

The StuffIt utility (described in Chapter 8) also provides optional protection for stuffed files—you can't unstuff them without the proper password.

❖ *unerased files*

important
warning

As has been mentioned several other places, when you throw a file in the Trash, it's not actually erased—only its name is erased from the disk directory. The information is still on the disk and can be recovered with the right software.

To keep that data from falling into the wrong hands, use a utility like Complete Delete (described in Chapter 8). Or, if the files were on a floppy, you can simply reinitialize the disk.

Created using Adobe Illustrator.
© *1987 by Adobe Systems Inc.*
All rights reserved.

Chapter 10

Word processing

Word processors

✎ about word processing

Word processors (also called *word processing programs)* are designed for entering, editing and formatting text. Some closely related activities (that aren't word processing proper) include jotting down your thoughts in an outlining program, looking in a thesaurus for the right word, keeping track of bibliographic references and running your finished product through a spelling checker.

esp. for beginners

✎ two basic word processing rules

- Don't press Return at the end of each line, only at the end of paragraphs.

esp. for beginners

- Don't use spaces to line things up (they won't line up straight). Use Tab for tables, the *Center* command (or whatever it's called in the program you're using) to center lines, and margin or indent settings to change the margins.

✎ some word processing features

Word processors get more powerful every year. Here are some features you should know about:

esp. for beginners

- *Headers and footers.* Virtually all word processors have them, but multiple-line headers and footers are rarer. If you need them, make sure the word processor you're considering can produce them.

- Built-in *spelling checkers* are almost the norm now. Make sure you can add your own words to a supplemental dictionary.

- *Word count.* This is a very useful feature. Sometimes you also get other, less useful statistics, like the number of lines or paragraphs.

- *Multiple columns.* Unfortunately, they usually all have to be the same width, which can be a real constraint.

esp. for
beginners

- *Variable leading.* The ability to vary line spacing independently of the size of the font, in one-point increments (or smaller).

- *Page layout.* This can involve anything from multiple columns to placing text blocks or graphics at specific spots on the page.

- *Glossaries.* This isn't what *glossary* usually means— a list of definitions like the one at the back of this book. In Word and some other programs, a *Glossary*— capital G—is a collection of often-used words, phrases, paragraphs or even graphics that you can recall with a keystroke and place in your document.

- *Outlining* capabilities are sometimes built into a word processor, as are other powerful features like *table of contents* and *index*-building.

- *Footnotes.* If you need them at all, make sure the word processor you choose can give them to you in the format you need (on each page, at the end of a document, with repeating numbers, or whatever). Whatever your basic requirements are, don't assume that they're the norm for footnoting.

very
hot
tip

Remember, just because you can get all these features doesn't mean you need them. For example, if most of your word processing is business correspondence, or even straightforward manuscripts, you won't need a word processor that lets you work in multiple columns.

The next two entries describe another couple of important word processing features.

♦ import/export *(AN)*

very
hot
tip

One very important (but often overlooked) consideration when choosing a word processor is what formats it will accept files in, and what formats it's capable of exporting files in. Some programs can take text from just about any other program, and give it back just as generously. Others make you jump through hoops to export and import, or only recognize a limited number of formats.

♦ *Styles*

A Style (capitalized to differentiate it from *type styles* like *italic* and *bold)* is a collection of paragraph and character formats that you can apply in one fell swoop to selected text. (A *style sheet* is a collection of Styles that you use in a particular document.)

What makes Styles so powerful is this: if you change the definition of a Style, every paragraph defined as that Style changes. For example, as I write this, I'm using a Style called *body*, whose definition includes the font, which for easy readability on the screen, is now 12-point Benguiat. For the book, the definition will be changed to 11-point Benguiat. When that happens, it won't be necessary to select all the text and tediously change it to 11-point (being careful to avoid section heads, etc.); we'll just change the Style to 11-point and all the entries will automatically change to that.

very good feature

Another advantage of Styles is that they can be based on each other. For example, the entry titles here (the lines that begin with an ♦) are in a Style called *entry*. It's based on *body*, but with no indent and with bold italic added. If I change the definition of *body* to Helvetica instead of Benguiat, the entry titles will also change to Helvetica—but remain bold italic and unindented.

Another great feature, which isn't available in every program that provides Styles, is the *next style* or *next paragraph* option. This lets you define whether the next paragraph you type remains the same Style as the current one or switches to another Style. For example, the Style called *body* doesn't change when I move to the next paragraph, but the Style called *entry* does have a *next paragraph* definition. So when I type an entry title and press ⌐Return⌐, I'm automatically shifted into the *body* Style.

♦ *how to choose a word processor* (SZA/AN)

- Word processors are the programs most people use most often, so choosing one isn't a decision to be made lightly.

- A good place to start your research is the reviews of word processors in recent issues of Macintosh magazines. Read the ads too.

- Talk to people at a user group and see what they love or hate about their word processors. But keep in mind that most people love the one they're using and that no opinion is objective.

- See if a local dealer will give you a demonstration of one or more major programs. Know ahead of time what kind of word processing power you need and focus on whether each program is capable of performing those functions.

**very
hot
tip**

- Remember that more important than features is that elusive thing called *feel*. If features were all Arthur were interested in, he'd use Word. But he can't stand its feel.

- Call the publisher of any program you're interested in to see if they have a demo version of it (or ask a dealer).

- Buy or borrow a book about the program. Reading through a book about a word processor will give you more of an idea what the program can do than any magazine review.

- Check out the brief reviews of some major programs that follow. They're organized into three groups, according to price. And because word processors are so important, we've given two separate reviews of many of the major programs.

the high-end word processors

At the top of the (price) list for Mac word processors are Word, Nisus, WordPerfect and FullWrite Professional. They each cost $400 and are loaded with features.

Word 4

Although Microsoft Word has its detractors, a lot of people obviously like it, since it's far-and-away the best-selling word processing program on the Mac. I'm a Word fan myself. It's true that some of Word's most powerful features—like table creation, page layout and typesetting commands—are hard to get the hang of. Its built-in outliner is the worst in any word processor. And Word is pretty slow until you get to an SE30 or beyond; even on the original Mac II, there's a noticeable delay just waiting for a menu to drop down.

But Word's faults are minor compared to its advantages. Even if they're difficult to grasp at first, the power features *are* there. The fact that no other Mac word processor has true Styles keeps me from even considering moving to another program. Thanks to the wealth of keyboard commands, I don't have to reach for the mouse when the words are flowing from my fingertips.

very good feature

All of Word's menus are totally configurable—you can put commands where you want them and assign them the keyboard equivalents you want. You can even add Ruler or dialog box options to the menus. This is a great feature, although it must drive Microsoft's support people nuts.

very good feature

Word gives you a choice of three views: the *galley* (standard view), *print preview* (a page view that shows miniature pages) and *Page* view, which is WYSIWYG *(wiz-ee-wig;* it stands for *what you see is what you get)*—everything formatted, with headers and footers showing, and yet still editable.

There are lots of nice little touches. The I-beam pointer slants when placed over italicized text—no more guessing whether you're clicking in front of or behind a slanted letter. *[But selection highlighting doesn't always work right in italics.—AN]* There's a word-count function, which also counts characters, lines and paragraphs and which works for headers and footers as well as the main document. The Ruler has a drop-down menu that lists Styles. You can hide graphics temporarily, to make scrolling through a document faster.

All in all, Word 4 has a lot of power. If you don't need it, don't succumb to the snob appeal of buying an expensive product. But if you do need it, Word provides it.

🍎 *why I don't like Word* (AN)

Because many of the people I work with send me files in Word, I end up spending a fair amount of time working in it. Since Sharon is one of those people (and since I didn't want to be constantly converting files), I used Word to edit this book.

Word has a lot of wonderful features, and my life would be a lot simpler if I used it for all my word processing. But after being immersed in it for several months, I dislike it more than ever.

That's because Word isn't very carefully thought through and has, at least for me, a very unMaclike feel. Many of its clunky, ham-handed ways of doing things remind me of programs I used to use on my CP/M machine, back when software standards were really low. Here are some examples:

- When a document is saved, it often shifts position on the screen. This is disconcerting when you first encounter it, and it remains annoying even after you come to expect it.

- Equally annoying is the fact that when you reopen a Word document, it always puts you at the beginning, instead of where you left off working.

very bad feature

- If you accidentally delete the space at the end of a paragraph that includes the formatting codes, the font, size and style of the paragraph will often change. This means you can't drag down by lines to select a whole paragraph, because that selects the space at the end of the paragraph as well.

- Similarly, if you hit Return to go to a new line, then change your mind, you can't simply hit Delete to remove the line break (the way you can on every other Mac word processor) if the formatting of the paragraphs is different.

- Word's spelling checker is one of the dumbest and hardest to use of any I know. Its suggestions for correct spellings are particularly lame-brained, as is the fact that it puts any word it queries on the *top* line of the window (so you often have to exit the spelling checker and use the scroll arrows to see the context the word is in).

very bad feature

- Word's search and replace function is equally primitive and thoughtless. You can only *Change All* before you start a search; once you've begun, that button disappears. Since the only safe way to do global changes is to do a couple by hand to make sure they're working the way you want them to, this is really a bad approach. *[There is a way to get the* Change All *button back. Click in the main window twice (once to make it active, and again to deselect the selected word), then click in the Change window again.—SZA].*

very bad feature

Even the buttons in the *Change* dialog box are needlessly confusing. You have a choice between *Change* and *Change Selection*. (Now there's a clear distinction.) The first one means *change this occurrence and find the next occurrence* and the second one means *just change this occurrence.* Why don't they read *Change and Find* and *Change only?*

One other thing I hate about Word's search and replace function is the way it demands you to tell it if you want to *Continue search from beginning of document?* What's so special about the beginning of a document? How often do you only want to search from where you are to the end of a document, rather than search the *whole* document? (Whenever I click that stupid button, I think "Yes, *of course* I want to continue the search from the beginning of the document." It's a continuing annoyance.)

Amazingly, even when you tell Word to *Change All,* it asks you if you want to continue changing from the beginning of the document. What sophisticated software—it doesn't even understand the meaning of the word *all.*

- Word's command hierarchy pays little or no attention to the actual needs of users. Basic commands (like ⌘ B for bold and ⌘ I for italic) are assigned instead to ⌘ Shift keys while commands you use much less often (if at all) are given simple ⌘ equivalents. (Fortunately, Word does let you reassign any keyboard commands you want.)

This wouldn't be so bad if other programs, like PageMaker, didn't follow Word's lead, but they do—as if Word were the standard and every other Mac program some sort of aberration.

very bad feature

- I've dealt with Microsoft for many years, as have many of my friends, and I've also known people who've worked there. Based on all this, it's my impression that Microsoft is a company more interested in its bottom line than in serving its customers. As a result, I don't feel safe depending on them for support and product upgrades.

- Microsoft's lack of concern for its users also shows up in its manuals, which I find more trouble to use than they're worth. Unfortunately, you need them, since Word—like other Microsoft programs—is counterintuitive, and filled with powerful but obscure capabilities.

✦ *Nisus 3* (AN)

Unlike most computer writers, I'm not fascinated with every new program that comes along. In fact, I'm very conservative about the software and hardware I use; I don't want to spend the time it takes to learn about something unless I'm going to end up using it frequently—and enjoy that use. (Along the same lines, I drove a 1965 Plymouth Valiant until 1989, and spent eighteen months deciding what to replace it with.)

But every once in a great while I run across a product whose intelligence of design shines like shafts of sunlight breaking through the clouds. Paragon Concepts' Nisus *(NY-sis)* is one of those programs (at least 90% of the time it is).

I'm not alone in liking Nisus, by the way. In London, *MacUser UK* voted it the best word processor, and *MacUser* here in the US gave it an honorable mention.

A few of Nisus's very intelligent features are listed in Chapter 1, in the *Why don't they all...?* section; there are dozens more. In fact, Nisus has more features I'd like to see made standard parts of the Mac interface than any other program I've ever used. Paragon Concepts' telephone support is great and even the manual is pretty good—although, as with virtually every one I see, the index needs some work.

very good feature

Probably my favorite feature in Nisus is multiple undos, which we unaccountably forgot to put on the *Why don't they all...?* list (it definitely belongs there). I often find myself accidentally making two mistakes in a row (usually rapidly), at which point, in most programs, the text I *really* want to recover is lost (all I can recover is my first typo or mistake). But with Nisus, you can *always* recover the text you really want, because it gives you *32,767 levels of Undo.* (This is overkill, I admit; even I seldom make more than 10,000 mistakes in a row.)

very good feature

Nisus has the most powerful search and replace feature of any Mac word processor, and once you get to know it, you can use it to get many of the same effects that Styles provide. Version 3 also has something called *named rulers* that are closer to Word's Styles, although still not all the way there.

Nisus 3 lets you put as many as three character keys after the modifier keys (⌘, Shift, Option, etc.), and thus create keyboard commands like, say, Shift Option ⌘ S C R. This gives you up to 125,000 possible key combinations (Nisus's programmers seem to revel in overkill).

Another nice feature of Nisus 3 is *noncontiguous selection,* something I've wanted for a long time. It lets you select separate, disconnected pieces of text, as many as you want, and then do the same thing to them all at once (change them all to bold, say, or change the font, or cut and paste them as a unit).

very good feature

Page-placed graphics is another feature of Nisus 3. They give you a way to place independent text blocks or graphics anywhere you want on the page, as in a page layout program. But what you're placing are actually windows that contain other documents.

You can have side-by-side columns, for example, but each column is a separate file, in a separate window, within the larger window of your document. It's a little like linking fields in a relational database (explained in Chapter 11) or the new System 7 *Publish* and *Subscribe* commands (explained in Chapter 6).

For all its virtues, however, Nisus has some problems:

- You can only import directly from Word 3, Word 4 and MacWrite 5 (or earlier). Files in all other formats (Works, MacWrite II, WriteNow) have to be converted into text before Nisus can read them, which is an incredibly annoying extra step and also strips out fonts, type sizes, type styles, etc.

- To export into PageMaker, you have to save your Nisus files in Word 3 format. This is a bother—but since you used to have to save your file as text and lose all your formatting, it's an improvement. (Nisus documents can be imported directly into PageMaker, but to do that you have to throw out PageMaker's filter and substitute Nisus's—something I'd be loathe to do, since I import into PageMaker from all sorts of applications.)

bug

- The spelling checker is very dumb about em dashes; it queries you on every one, treating the em dash and the words on either side of it as a single word. For someone who uses as many em dashes as I do, this makes the spelling checker virtually useless.

very bad feature

Paragon Concepts knew about this bug and yet didn't bother to fix it for Version 3, preferring instead to concentrate their energies on developing an elaborate, arcane, built-in programming language! (After all, which would you rather have in a word processor— a usable spelling checker or the ability to program?) This is a classic case of tertiary expertosis, where the sufferer's tiny area of expertise becomes all that's real, and normal people, walking around in the world, seem as insubstantial as ghosts.

- In line with this nerdy approach, some of Nisus's screen messages read as if they were written by machines. My favorite is the one that asks you to *Name file as*. I mean, do English-speaking human beings talk like this? —

gossip/ trivia

> Jan: *Hey, Karen, congratulations on your new baby. What did you name her as?*
>
> Karen: *Thanks, Jan, we're really in heaven. We named her as Susan.*

Stuff like this makes me feel that Paragon Concepts only understands its users' needs up to a certain point, or only in a certain way, which makes me reluctant to switch over completely to Nisus. That's too bad, because I've been using it for most of my work and I like it a lot. Hopefully, Paragon Concepts will eventually get on the ball and iron out the remaining problems. In the meantime, Nisus is still definitely worth checking out.

By the way, I know you've been assuming that Nisus is named after the Trojan soldier who was killed avenging a friend's death in book IX of the *Aeneid*. Well, you're wrong— it's just your extensive classical education leading you astray again. No, *nisus* is an ordinary English word (well, not *ordinary*, perhaps, but it's in most dictionaries) that means *an effort* or *an endeavor*.

gossip/ trivia

♠ *Nisus*

Nisus has something called Easy-GREP, a search-definition language that originated in the Unix world. With it, you can search and replace by font, size and style—through a list of opened *and closed* documents. You can specify exactly what you want to find and exactly where you want to find it—dollar signs at the beginning of a line, say, or any digit between two uppercase characters. Easy-GREP is not all that easy to learn, but it's worth the effort.

Nisus' other super-powerful feature is its macro editor, but you might be happy just using the 80 macros that come with the program. It also has a built-in graphics capability and basic page layout features, but it's missing footnotes and true Styles.

Since Nisus keeps your whole document in RAM, it's very fast, but this approach also limits the size of documents you can work with. The speed of its spelling checker is also amazing.

When I consider Nisus for daily use, or for recommendation to others, I only see what's missing—like Styles and mail merge. I think that every good word processor that wants to be great has to have real Styles, like Word's.

⬥ *WordPerfect*

very bad feature

WordPerfect is far from perfect (in fact, I've heard it referred to as WordImperfect). It's hard to learn, has a decidedly unMaclike user interface and is painfully slow in multicolumn mode. Its main attraction is the compatibility of its files with those created by WordPerfect on the PC, which transfer with formatting intact. Is this reason enough to buy it? Maybe if you have an office that combines PC's and Macs...but maybe not even then.

⬥ *FullWrite Professional*

very bad feature

FullWrite Professional is crippled by its inability to handle large documents (in one little test I ran, it couldn't handle 60 pages of text on a two-meg machine) and by its incredible slowness (it took *five seconds* to respond to a drag on the size box of the document window, and it didn't even give the usual gray outline of the window's new size as I dragged—and that was working on a cx with 1200K of memory in MultiFinder).

It's a shame, because FullWrite has some great features. Besides handling standard footnotes, it compiles bibliographic references for you. It also has electronic Post-it notes. Its outliner is well-integrated with the rest of the program and drawing capabilities are built in. I'd like to say that FullWrite might be for you if you have plenty of memory and a fast computer, but I wouldn't recommend it even then.

🍎 *more on FullWrite* (AN)

A letter in *Macworld* accused *The Macintosh Bible* of doing a "hatchet job" on FullWrite—or, at best, of being "ill-informed." But Paul Hoffman, who wrote the review the letter was complaining about, sticks by the following facts:

bug

- FullWrite originally shipped with serious LaserWriter printing bugs that had been reported to Ashton-Tate during the beta test.

- the program is very slow ("leisurely," as a review in *Macworld* described it).

very bad
feature

- the documentation is poorly organized and wrong in many parts.

🍎 *the mid-range word processors*

WriteNow, MacWrite, MindWrite and Microsoft Write cost between $200 to $300 and offer a surprising range of features for the money.

🍎 *WriteNow*

WriteNow ($200) is just about perfect—so close, in fact, that I can't think of anything remotely bad to say about it. It's fast and has the best kind of user interface, one that's *transparent* (you don't even notice it).

very good
feature

WriteNow is the only current Mac word processor that will run even on a 128K machine and that requires only a single 800K drive. But don't let those minimalist requirements fool you—WriteNow is no slouch on features or performance. While it doesn't have Styles, you can copy character and paragraph formats from one place to another.

🍎 *WriteNow 2.2a* (Susan McCallister)

I've loved WriteNow for years because it's fast, reliable, easy to learn, easy to use and takes up so little room on a disk. It has good control over display and page formatting, keystroke commands that are easy to remember, and all the features you'd normally use for day-to-day writing, including the ability to have several documents open at once, as many as four columns (all of the same width), mail merge and footnotes.

WriteNow acts smart; for example, when you use [Delete] to delete a word, it deletes the extra space (something MacWrite II will only do when you use the *Cut* command). Its spelling checker is fast to load, easy to use, makes good suggestions for words it catches and stays open (if you want it to) as a window behind your document(s).

My only serious problem with WriteNow has been with its inability to convert Word documents (since other people *persist* in using the thing) and that's been fixed in version 2.2a. Besides that, 2.2a has added a lot of other goodies without compromising WriteNow's speed and grace.

very good feature

Let me start with a feature that I think should be on the *Why don't they all...?* list in Chapter 1. When you get a *This document was set up for a different printer* dialog box, WriteNow puts a *Page Setup* button right there in the box (saving you the trouble of cancelling printing, going to Page Setup and then giving the *Print* command again).

There's a 135,000-word spelling dictionary and a 1,400,000-entry thesaurus, and you can add to any dictionary by selecting a text file and having the spelling checker "learn" it. It's easy to count words, characters and paragraphs, and as with everything WriteNow does, it's *fast*. Search and replace goes forward, backward and wraps around the document, and can search and replace [Tab] and [Return] characters (especially useful for reformatting database files).

You can control the font size directly from the keyboard. (Most of WriteNow's features now have keyboard commands.) There's also a new font/style/size format accelerator, which functions sort of like Styles (though you can't invoke it as you are creating a document, so it's not really the same thing).

WriteNow also has useful dotted lines that extend down the page when you adjust margins or tabs. Doubleclicking at the top (or bottom) of a page will get you a header (or footer).

very good feature

Most of what I like about WriteNow is what isn't there—problems and barriers. It becomes such a transparent tool, it reminds me of a favorite jacket, the one that has just the right number of pockets in all the right places, and never feels too warm or not warm enough.

MacWrite II

MacWrite ($250) is an oldie but a goodie—but not goodie enough compared to its competition in this price range. It lacks anything even mimicking Styles; although you can apply combinations of character styles to text, there's no way to copy existing paragraph formatting to other paragraphs. It has a slow and limited spelling checker, and its new-ruler-for-every-paragraph-change approach is tiresome.

MacWrite handles multiple columns very intuitively and its mail merge is great—the easiest to use of any word processor except perhaps for Works' (but that's integrated with its database). But you can only merge with text files. Even Claris' own FileMaker files can't be used unless you export them first as text.

MacWrite II too (AN)

The staff at Goldstein & Blair (publishers of this book) have been using MacWrite II for over a year and are quite happy with it. It's true that WriteNow has more power, but what's great about MacWrite is how intuitive and easy to learn it is. Here's one example out of many: when you choose the *Insert Header* (or *Insert Footer)* command, a text box opens on the page in the exact position where the header (or footer) will appear. This is so simple, so obvious, so right, and yet no other word processor I know does it that way.

Not everything about MacWrite makes sense. The font menu shows font names in the fonts themselves, which makes it just a bit hard to identify ones like Cairo and Zapf

Dingbats. WriteNow has this same "feature," but at least gives you a way to turn it off.

Another thing MacWrite is missing is the ability to customize keyboard commands. Without this feature, you're stuck with whatever choices MacWrite's programmers made, which include ⌘T for the *Plain text* command. (You can, of course, go in with QuicKeys or some other macro program and change things around, but this should really be built into the program, the way it is in Word, Nisus and many other word processors.)

We haven't put a section of MacWrite tips in this edition. That's partly because not all that many people are still using MacWrite (its sales haven't been great), and partly because some of the MacWrite tips from the last edition were moved into the general word processing tips. But it's also because MacWrite II has so few hidden or poorly explained features that it doesn't have the same need for tips as other programs.

very hot tip

(Here's one tip we would have put in if we'd had a section: Doubleclicking on a word in MacWrite highlights the word, but not the spaces on either side. So if you hit Delete to delete a word, you have to hit it again to delete the remaining extra space. The solution? Use ⌘X instead. It deletes the space to the left of the highlighted word as well.)

I have a lot of affection for MacWrite, since it's the word processor I used for my first four years on the Mac. I hope Claris brings out a new, more competitive version. If they don't, I hope that, at the very least, MacWrite's competitors will appropriate some of its extraordinary intuitiveness. It really sets the standard for ease of use.

MindWrite *(Charles Rubin/SZA)*

MindWrite ($200) is a nice word processor that has the best integrated outliner in this price range; it makes organizing and re-organizing documents a breeze. MindWrite's window-handling is great, with automatic tiling, and the program has a lot of unusual extras. For example, there's an accumulating clipboard that stores everything you cut until you specifically delete it; this is very handy when you want to rearrange a lot of text.

MindWrite will keep track of the date you enter text and then let you select portions of a document that were changed since a certain date or between two dates. (This is great if you collaborate with other people on your writing.) You can also get an instant word count at any time.

The search commands are particularly impressive. For example, you can search for sections of documents that have changed since a particular date, and you can have MindWrite automatically copy all the occurrences it finds of a string and place them in a new document window. (This is handy for gathering all pieces of text marked with a special character—for indexing, for example.) You can search through text in headers and footers, or you can limit searches to open sections of outlines.

very good feature

MindWrite's *Preferences* command lets you set the font, size, heading markers and other default options you want to have with each new document you create. There's also a table of contents generator that creates a new document window listing the section headings in an outline.

very bad feature

Unfortunately, MindWrite is missing a lot of features—superscripting, subscripting, small caps, footnotes, a way to set different headers/footers for odd and even pages, the ability to copy existing paragraph formats, mail merge, multiple columns and other basic page layout features.

🍎 *Write*

Microsoft Write ($300) is sort of a limited edition of Word. It's no match for comparably priced word processors like WriteNow, but what may make it worth considering is the fact that you can upgrade from it to Word for only the difference in price between the programs. If you start out with another mid-range word processor and then need to move up, you'll have to shell out the entire cost of a high-end word processor. *(Still, there are a couple of major ifs in this scenario—if you need to move up, and if it's Word you want to move up to.—AN]*

🍎 low-end word processors *(AN)*

These programs are for people on limited budgets (or who do word processing very seldom). We've Microsoft Works here, even though it costs $300, because Works not only offers word processing but also includes a database, a spreadsheet, a communications program and draw capabilities. We figure that brings Works' word processing module down into the $100 range, but if you have no use whatever for Works' other modules, you should compare it against the programs in the mid-range category above, not against the other low-end programs below.

🍎 Works' word processing module

Works' word processor is perfectly adequate. Version 2.0 has integrated drawing tools, basic page layout functions (through the Text tool of the drawing layer), a built-in macro editor, mail merge (from the database module and all sorts of tables (from the spreadsheet module). It's still missing a lot of basics, though: separate headers/footers for even and odd pages (and it uses a really lame way of constructing a basic header or footer), footnoting and character formatting like small caps.

🍎 WordMaker *(Karen Faria)*

Although WordMaker costs just $125, it can do mail merge, search and replace, and can import formatted text from databases or spreadsheets. It also lets you change margins and tabs (left, right, center or decimal) throughout a document, adjust leading and kerning, set the ruler to measure in inches, centimeters, picas, points, etc., and change text to all caps, lowercase or mixed case.

WordMaker has a 100,000-word spelling checker and lets you insert automatic page numbering, time and date. Once you paste a graphic into WordMaker, it's treated independently of text (as opposed to being embedded in it). You can move it around, resize it and even wrap text around it.

Although WordMaker has a lot of good features, I really didn't like using it. As you key in the text, the line of text you're working on flickers every three-to-eight keystrokes. I found this very irritating.

very bad feature

🍎 *Letter Writer Plus* (Karen Faria)

Letter Writer Plus ($90) is a desk accessory, which is handy. If you don't work in MultiFinder, it lets you dash off a letter without quitting the application you're in.

Letter Writer Plus can do mail merge and search and replace. It's designed to import directly from Address Book Plus, and can import formatted text from databases or spreadsheets. But it has very little formatting flexibility. You choose one set of margins for the first page, one set for the rest and that's it for margins; you get one set of (left) tabs for the entire document and that's it for tabs.

very bad feature

If you use more than one letterhead, Letter Writer Plus has a *save as stationery* feature. It also has an *insert paragraph* feature that enables you to insert a previously saved paragraph into a letter. And it's set up to address and print envelopes quickly and easily.

I found Letter Writer Plus too limited, but then I run MultiFinder and thus don't have a need for a word processing DA. People who work in the Finder may find it useful.

General word processing tips

🍎 *insertion point vs. I-beam pointer* (AN)

A common confusion among beginning Mac users (and even some who've been using the machine for a while) is between the *insertion point*—the thin, blinking, vertical line that indicates where the next character of text will appear (or disappear)—and the *I-beam pointer*, which looks like this: ⌶ .

esp. for beginners

Basically, the I-beam pointer *places* the insertion point. You move the I-beam to where you want the insertion point to be and click the mouse button once. To move the insertion point, you simply move the I-beam to another place and click again.

Unlike more primitive machines, the Mac has no *cursor*. This term from the world of the PC—and, before that, CP/M —is sometimes incorrectly applied to either the pointer or the insertion point.

(The people who *program* the Mac do use the term *cursor,* and there's a danger that this techie jargon will filter down to ordinary people like you and me. We should resist that, because the terms *pointer* and *insertion point* are both more precise and more elegant.)

✺ em dashes, en dashes and hyphens (AN)

very
hot
tip

Em dash is the technical name for what people normally just call a dash—there's one right there. (It gets its name from the fact that it's more or less the same width as a capital *M.)*

An *en dash* is half the length of an em dash and is used to indicate ranges of numbers (1926–66) or as a minus sign. (It gets its name from the fact that it's more or less the same width as a lowercase *n.)*

Hyphens are shorter than either. Here's a comparison of the three:

em dash	—
en dash	–
hyphen	-

On the Mac, you get an em dash by holding down [Shift] and [Option] while hitting [-], and you get an en dash by holding down [Option] and hitting [-].

✺ spacing after italics (DC)

On dot-matrix printers like the ImageWriter (and on the Mac's screen), italics bend so far over that they crowd, or even run into, the plain-text characters that follow them.

This is particularly a problem when the last italic character and/or the first plain character is a capital letter or a lower-case b, d, f, h, k or l. (On laser printers, things are easier. Outline fonts are designed so that the italic characters don't crowd the following plain text—except when they're computer-generated, as they are with Benguiat, for example.)

Putting two spaces after the italics gives you too much room. The solution is to use the option space, which usually produces a space that's larger than a regular one but smaller than two (you get it, of course, by holding down [Option] while hitting [Spacebar]). See the next entry for more details.

very
hot
tip

the option space (AN)

This character, generated by holding down the [Option] key while using [Spacebar], has two unique features. The first is that it's always a *hard space*—which means that if it falls at the end of a line, it won't break; instead, it will drag the word before it down to the next line, along with the word after it. This is useful when you want to keep phrases like WW II and J. B. S. Haldane all on the same line, but can make for a very uneven right margin (or, if your text is justified, for lines with very loose spacing).

The second feature is that, in some fonts, the option space is wider than a regular space (but narrower than two). This is also useful for keeping italic characters from leaning into the plain text that follows them in dot-matrix printouts (see the previous entry for details).

The easiest way to see if a font makes the option space wider is to type a character (let's say you use X), hit the [Spacebar] five times, type another X, hit [Return], type X, hold down the [Option] key, hit [Spacebar] five times, and type a final X. If the option space is wider than regular spaces, the second X on the second line will be to the right of the second X on the first line; if the option space is the same width as the regular spaces, the X's will line up.

The wider option space occurs only in proportionally spaced fonts (which is what most Mac fonts are); in monospaced fonts like Monaco, hard spaces are always the same width as regular spaces.

This combining of two features into the option space is far from ideal. When you want a hard space, you normally don't want a wide space, and when you want a wide space, you normally don't want a hard space. Hopefully savvy font designers will soon start providing hard spaces and wide spaces as separate characters (Option Spacebar and ⌘ Spacebar , say).

🍎 *left and right quotation marks*

If your word processing program doesn't automatically give you left- and right-leaning (" ") quotation marks (also called *curly quotation marks),* and if you're not using Quote Init (described in Chapter 8) or some equivalent utility to produce them, you can use your word processor's find-and-replace function to substitute curly quotes for all your straight quotes (").

To do that, you have to assume that every *open,* or *leading,* quotation mark will be preceded by a space—which is almost always the case. *(Close,* or *trailing,* quotation marks aren't necessarily followed by a space, since the next character may be a punctuation mark or, in programs like Word, a paragraph marker.)

very hot tip

Given that assumption, you can change to curly quotes in two passes. First, replace every instance of " that's preceded by a space with an open quotation mark, which you get by hitting Option [. Then replace every remaining instance of the straight quotation mark with a close quote, which you get by hitting Option Shift [.

🍎 *curly quotes in Benguiat* (AN)

In Benguiat, the font used for regular text in this book, left- and right-leaning quotes don't look very different: " " (they actually are slightly different—one's narrower at the top and the other's narrower at the bottom—but it's very subtle). So when we're talking about curly quotes, I'll sometimes put them in Times, where they look more different: " " .

Interestingly, Benguiat's quote marks are curly in the *screen* font, so you don't know that they're going to look so similar to each other until you print them out. Benguiat is the only font I've seen where this situation has come up, but there are probably others.

bug

❡ *dumb quotes* (C.J. Weigand)

Using smart-quote utilities like Quote Init can be annoying, because backspacing over or selecting a quote or apostrophe and then retyping it can leave it facing the wrong direction. I prefer the "dumb quote" approach.

very hot tip

Using QuicKeys from CE Software, I reassign the curly apostrophe (') to the straight apostrophe key ([']) and the curly quotes (" ") to the left and right curly bracket keys ([{] and [}] , i.e., [Shift][[ ] and [Shift][ ]]). That way I'm always sure of typing the correct symbol. If I ever need to type a straight apostrophe or curly brackets, all I have to do is temporarily turn QuicKeys off, by hitting [Option][⌘][.].

[Although I once was a fervent Quote Init fan, CJ's approach made more sense to me. I used QuicKeys to do him one better—I assigned the curly quotes to the (unshifted) [[ ] *and* [ ]] *keys, to make them even easier to get to than the straight quote mark is normally.*

While I was at it, I made [Shift][,] *and* [Shift][.] *print out as* [,] *and* [.]*, instead of as* [<] *and* [>]*. I moved* [<] *and* [>] *to the* [\ ] *key, and moved* [[ ] *and* [ ]] *to where the curly brackets* [{] *and* [}] *normally are (* [Shift][[ ] *and* [Shift][ ]] *). I even thought of getting rid of the letter Z, since I hardly ever use it. But then I thought, zees may be fooleesh. So I relented, and decided to let Z stay.—AN]*

[I don't agree with either of these guys (that's nothing new). I don't want to have to relearn what touch-typing I know by having to reach for a different key for opening and closing quotes and the apostrophe. The problem with getting a wrong-facing quote or apostrophe when editing is easy to deal with if you understand how Quote Init decides which one to use.

If I surround a word in quotes as I type, like "this", the first one I type is an open quote because it's preceded by a space, and the second is a close quote because it's preceded by a character. If I go back to surround an already-typed word with quotation marks, the marks may be facing the wrong way, because it cues off of the last thing I typed (before I clicked by the word I wanted to put in quotation marks).

So I just select or backspace over the space in front of the word and then type [Spacebar] [·] *and the quote faces the right direction. At the end of the word, I retype the final letter and then the quote mark again. The tiny extra editing effort is nothing compared to relearning three typing positions—and not having them all fit on the old home row of keys (asdfghjkjl;") for easiest access.—SZA]*

(I don't agree with Sharon on this (that's nothing new). Moving off the home row is a lot *easier than having to hold down the* [Shift] *key, so curly quotes are much easier to access where I put them than they are in their normal position. I found relearning the three key positions virtually effortless, even though I'd been touch-typing on the old key positions for almost thirty years. And once I'd converted, I was done with it, which isn't the case with "tiny extra editing efforts" that continue for eternity. But, hey, gentle reader, why not just try these various approaches for yourself and see what's easier for* you.—*AN)*

🍎 *low-rent Glossary substitutes* (DC/AN)

Many word processors don't have *Glossaries* (often-used words, phrases, paragraphs or even graphics that you can recall with a keystroke and paste into your document). But there's an easy and obvious way around that:

Just use two or three unique characters as abbreviations for the longer text. For example, you might type *tmb* every time you want the phrase *The Macintosh Bible* to appear. Then, when you've finished entering your text, just before you check the spelling in the document, you do a global search for *tmb* and replace it with *The Macintosh Bible* everywhere it appears in the document.

Some people find this technique of using abbreviations more convenient than permanently setting up Glossaries. *(But remember to check the* Whole Word *option when doing this kind of global change. I forgot to when changing all the* RW's *after entries in Chapter 15 to the full name,* Rich Wolfson, *and wound up with dozens of* LaseRich Wolfsonriter's, *several* otheRich Wolfsonise's *and one* straightfoRich Wolfsonard.—SZA)

gossip/ trivia

🍎 *bargain-basement leading* (AN)

Leading refers to the space between lines of text. Some word processors don't let you vary it other than by selecting a certain size type and choosing single-spacing, double-spacing and the like, but even in these programs you can exert some limited control over leading by using the following (admittedly klutzy) technique:

To change the leading between two lines of text, select a blank space in the second line and change it to a different size. (You're limited to six sizes: 9-, 10-, 12-, 14-, 18- and 24-point.) That line will then adjust itself accordingly. When you're satisfied with the results, repeat the procedure for each successive line of text.

🍎 *cheap, ersatz Styles* (AN)

If your word processor doesn't have Styles, the following techniques will save you some time and trouble:

Let's say you're writing a document in 12-point Bookman plain with subheads in 18-point Avant Garde bold italic. Switching between the two can cost you a lot of keystrokes and/or trips to the menu bar. But there's an easier way to do it (it may sound a little confusing when you read about it, but just try it).

Let's say you just finished typing a paragraph (in 12-point Bookman) and now you want to type a new subhead. Just go to another subhead somewhere nearby and select any character (or doubleclick on any word) in it. Then copy that character (or word), paste it where you want the new subhead to be, select it and start to type. What you type will be in the font, size and style of the other subhead (18-point Avant Garde bold italic, or whatever).

When you're inserting text into some already-existing text (instead of adding it on to the end of a new file you're creating), you often don't have to do any copying. Let's say you've finished typing the subhead and want to go back to your text font. If the text immediately after the subhead is in the text font, just select the first character in it and begin typing. The character you selected will be deleted, so be sure to retype it at the end of what you're inserting.

(The reason for selecting the first character is that the space in front of the text may be in a different font, style and/or size than the text itself. Often it will be the same and all you'll have to do is click in the space, but it's different enough of the time that you're better off always selecting the first letter as a matter of habit.)

shortcut

This also works if the text immediately before the place where you want to make your insertion is in the font you want. In that case, you begin by retyping the character you selected, then go on to type your insertion. *[You can also record the selection of various paragraph and character formatting commands in a macro program and play them all back with a single keystroke combination.—SZA]*

🍎 *custom letterhead* (AN)

esp. for beginners

There are no particular tricks for creating a letterhead—although creating a nice one requires a great deal of skill and taste. But here's a trick on how to deal with one once it's been created:

Assuming you have access to the Mac and a laser printer on a regular basis, don't waste your time printing out blank sheets of letterhead that you'll then have to feed one by one into the printer when you want to use them. Instead, create a dummy document with your letterhead at the top and a few words in the font you use for the text of letters below it. Here's a sample, using Fluent Fonts' Monterey and Monterey Medium:

Jack Twiller
512 Pet-de-Loup Boulevard
Halitosis ND 58353
701/ 555-1941

Date, 1991

Dear

Save this document as *letterhead* or some similar name. Then every time you want to write a letter, open it and immediately *Save As...* under whatever name is appropriate for the letter you're going write. Many word processors give you *stationery* for this purpose, which is even easier, because you can't forget to save it.

Then doubleclick on *Date* and change it, place the insertion point after *Dear* and begin writing. (Some programs let you insert an active date marker in your document, which saves you this step.) When you print out the letter, the letterhead will print out at the top.

You can (and probably should) have more than one letterhead for use with different sorts of letters (business, personal, etc.). In programs that have Glossaries, it's sometimes simpler to store your letterheads as Glossary items and just pop them into a document when you need them—but only if you're happy with the standard margins, font, etc.

If you have a specialized signature, you can either make it the last item in your dummy letterhead document or drop it in from the Scrapbook or SmartScrap. Here's one I use:

Of course there's no need for you to feel limited to something as stodgy as this.

(The gorilla was drawn by master Mac artist Mei-Ying Dell'Aquilla and is available on the ClickArt Personal Graphics disk from T/Maker.)

🍎 *estimating the number of words in a document* (AN)

shortcut

Most word processors have a word count feature by now, and if yours doesn't, you can use a DA like miniWRITER, or a spelling checker, to get that information. But you can also can get a quick-and-dirty word-count estimate simply by dividing the number of characters by six.

(Some people divide by five to count words, but it's hard to figure how they arrive at that number. Anyone with a word processor or other program that counts both words and characters can easily see that the ratio is always close to six. I just checked this chapter and got 5.76 characters per word. Since I don't use a lot of fancy, sesquipedalian words—except for that one—most normal writing should average about the same or slightly higher.)

Another way to roughly estimate the number of words in a document without having to wait for a word count is to multiply the number of K by 170. (There are 1024 characters in a K—except when someone's trying to sell you a disk drive—and 1024 divided by 6 equals 170.67...for you, 170.)

shortcut

Here's a table with some convenient (but approximate) conversions:

1K = 170 words		30K = 5000 words
3K = 500 words		50K = 8500 words
6K = 1000 words		60K = 10,000 words
10K = 1700 words		75K = 12,500 words
15K = 2500 words		100K = 17,000 words

To make your estimate more accurate, you should subtract some figure for *overhead* (described on page 137). As you add formatting instructions, the amount of overhead increases. Graphics in particular will inflate the figures for both the number of K and the number of characters in a document, thus throwing your calculations off (since there's no way to estimate exactly how much to subtract for overhead).

⚫ *different length rulers*

Does the Ruler in your word processor sometimes display six inches across the window and sometimes six and a half? That's because the length of the Ruler in the window changes according the printer driver software you've selected in the Chooser desk accessory. You get the six-inch Ruler if you've chosen the ImageWriter driver and the six-and-a-half-inch Ruler if you've chosen the LaserWriter driver.

*very
hot
tip*

⚫ *double-sided printouts* (DC)

You'll seldom find instructions in a word processor manual for printing on both sides of the paper so that the correct pages will print back-to-back. Here's how you do it:

*very
hot
tip*

First print half as many copies of the document as you need. Then arrange them so that the copies of page 2 are on the top, followed by the copies of page 1, followed by page 4, then page 3, page 6, page 5, and so on, continuing to count up by even numbers and subtracting 1 in between. If there are an odd number of pages in your document, set aside the copies of the last page and substitute blank pages for them in the pile.

Place the pile of arranged pages in the paper tray face up, with the top edge of the pages pointing towards the end of the tray that goes into the LaserWriter. Insert the tray and print the other half of the copies.

The same technique works on the ImageWriter II with a sheet feeder. The only difference is how you place the pile of arranged pages (printed on one side)—in the case of the sheet feeder, put them upside down, with the printed side facing you.

⚫ *importing word processing files to the Mac* (DC)

esp. for beginners

If you need to import a word processing document to a Mac from another type of computer (and you don't have a *filter* for translating the file), you have to first save the file on the foreign computer as a text, or *ASCII*, file.

If you neglect this step, the document will be a mess when it gets to the Mac, because word processing programs embed formatting codes in the text that will appear as gibberish on the Mac's screen.

⚫ *text markers* (DC)

esp. for beginners

Few word processors have a specific function that lets you mark places in a document so you can return to them later. But it's easy enough to do that in any program, simply by inserting unique characters (like *##1, ##2* and so on, or any other combination of characters that wouldn't appear in normal text). Then you just use the Find command to move to these points in your document quickly.

⚫ *distorted graphics* (DC)

You may notice some distortion when you paste bit-mapped graphics, especially ones that contain circles, into word processing programs. This is because word processors typically squeeze the image of the page to make it narrower, in order to make text look better when printed out on dot-matrix printers like the ImageWriter.

One way to correct this distortion is to choose *Tall Adjusted* in the Page Setup window. Your text will now print out wider on the ImageWriter than usual, but graphics will look just the way they do when you print them directly from a paint program.

🍎 *a reverse-letters macro*

The macro below will reverse two letters that you just typed in any program that lets you select something by holding Shift while you pass over the character by using an arrow key. (For more about macros and how they work, see the section on them in Chapter 8.)

- Shift ← selects the second letter of the two
- ⌘ X cuts the selected letter
- ← moves the pointer in front of the first letter
- ⌘ V pastes the second letter in front of the first
- → moves the pointer past the second letter, so you can start typing again

Use this macro when you type *teh* instead of *the,* or any time you accidentally reverse two letters.

Word tips

These tips work in Word 4, and many will work in Word 3 as well.

🍎 *the "selection bar"* (AN)

Beginning Word users must often be confused by the term Microsoft uses to refer to the narrow, invisible column to the left of your text (it's used for selecting text—you know you're in it because the pointer changes from an I-beam to an arrow). Although *bar* virtually always implies a

esp. for beginners

horizontal line—so much so that another Microsoft program, Excel, uses it to distinguish a *bar chart* (horizontal lines) from a *column chart* (vertical lines)—Microsoft calls this vertical column the *selection bar.*

❡ toggling window sizes

There are four ways you can toggle between the size and shape window you've created and one that fills the whole screen:

- click on the zoom box (at the right end of the title bar)
- doubleclick on the title bar itself
- doubleclick on the size box in the lower right corner
- press [Option] [⌘] [ ]]

❡ window splitting

shortcut

You don't have to drag the split bar to split a window— [Option] [⌘] [S] has the same effect. The command works as a toggle, so you can use it to unsplit the window as well.

❡ cycling through windows

When you have multiple windows on the screen, use [Option] [⌘] [W] to cycle through them (this sends the topmost window to the bottom of the pile).

❡ Go Back between windows

**very
hot
tip**

The *Go Back* command in the Utilities menu moves the insertion point back to its previous position. That's not the tip. The tip is: *Go Back* works not only within a document, but also back and forth between open document windows.

❡ hot spot shortcuts

shortcut

Word provides shortcuts with *hot spots* in its document window.

doubleclick on	to
any tab mark on the Ruler	open the Tabs dialog box

the page number in the lower left corner of the window	open the Go To Page dialog box
the Style box at the bottom of the window	open the Define Styles dialog box
a margin marker or the numbered area of the Ruler	open the Paragraph dialog box
the split bar in the vertical scroll bar	split and unsplit the window without dragging the bar
the title bar or the size box	toggle the window between full-screen size and the user-defined size

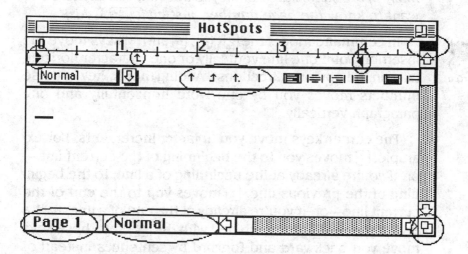

■ *keyboard scrolling*

You can scroll a window from the keyboard, just as if you were using the vertical scroll arrows. To scroll up, use Option ⌘ [or * on the keypad; to scroll down, use Option ⌘ / or + on the keypad. (As with regular scrolling, the insertion point stays where it was.)

shortcut

If you have an extended keyboard, you can use the PgUp and PgDn keys to scroll, but that also moves the insertion point.

🍎 *using the numeric keypad*

The numeric keypad has two modes—one in which it issues commands that move the insertion point, select text and the like (let's call this *command mode)* and one in which it enters numbers into the text. This second mode is called *Num.* (for *numeric) Lock.* The ⌈Clear⌉ key toggles you between them.

When you're in Num. Lock, it says so in the status box in the lower left corner of the window. (Unfortunately, it doesn't trigger the NumLock light that's available on extended keyboards.) *(The number of the page you're viewing is normally in the same little box. If you see* Num. Lock *there and want to know the page number, just hit* ⌈Clear⌉.*—AN)*

shortcut

In command mode, the ⌈2⌉, ⌈4⌉, ⌈6⌉ and ⌈8⌉ keys move the insertion point one line vertically or one character horizontally (in the obvious directions). Adding the ⌈⌘⌉ key to these numbers moves you by one word horizontally and one paragraph vertically.

The corner keys move you in larger increments. For example, ⌈7⌉ moves you to the beginning of the current line— or, if you're already at the beginning of a line, to the beginning of the previous line. ⌈1⌉ moves you to the end of the current line—or, if you're already at the end of a line, to the end of the next line. Combined with the ⌈⌘⌉ key, these keys move you backward and forward by sentences instead of by lines.

The other corner keys, ⌈9⌉ and ⌈3⌉, move you backward and forward a screenful at a time. Combined with the ⌈⌘⌉ key, ⌈9⌉ moves you to the beginning of the document and ⌈3⌉ to the end.

The ⌈5⌉ key doesn't do anything by itself, but ⌈⌘⌉⌈5⌉ jumps the insertion point to the top left corner of the current screen.

Here it all is in diagram form:

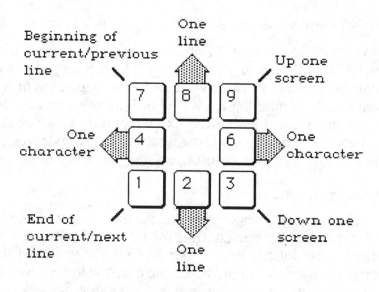

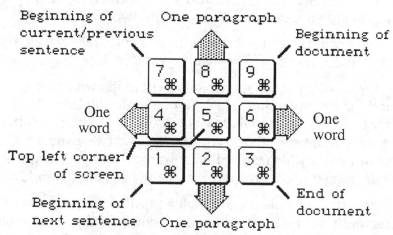

The ⓪ (zero) on the keypad works the same as choosing the *Go Back* command on the Utilities menu. Say you're typing and see a mistake. You can go to the mistake and correct it, then press the keypad ⓪ to jump right back to where you were. (Word remembers your last four positions, so you can use the keypad ⓪ for even more complicated series of jumps around your document.)

very good feature

✎ ⌘ *arrow keys*

shortcut

You can extend the basic arrow-key movements with the ⌘ key. Combining ⌘ with ← or → moves you to the beginning of the previous word or to the beginning of the next word. Combining it with ↑ or ↓ moves you to the beginning of the previous or next paragraph. (When you're in the middle of a word or paragraph, ⌘ ← moves you to the beginning of that word or paragraph.)

✎ *using the Ruler*

There are two triangular markers at the left end of Word's Ruler. The bottom one controls the left margin and top one controls the indentation of the first line. If you drag the bottom marker (the margin), the top one (the indent) moves with it, but the top marker moves separately—that's how you change the distance between the two.

(You can move the bottom marker separately as well, by holding down the Shift key while you drag it.)

If you want to set a margin or indent to the left of the zero mark on the Ruler, just slide the marker to the left; after an initial hesitation, the window scrolls so you can get to the negative numbers. (To scroll to the left of the zero mark without moving anything on the Ruler, just hold the Shift key down while using the left scroll arrow at the bottom of the window.)

The default unit on the Ruler is inches, but you can change it with the *Preferences...* command on the Edit menu. To change the default tab stops, use the *Document* command and type the new distance you want in the Default Tab Stops box.

✎ *moving several tabs at once*

*very
hot
tip*

When you have a series of tabs on the Ruler, moving one doesn't affect the others—unless you hold down Shift, in which case all the tabs to the right of the one you're dragging move together. This is very useful when you have tabbed columns set up and want to shift them all.

✦ *customizing menus with the mouse*

You can add many commands to (or subtract them from) Word's menus without using the *Commands* command. To add them, first press [Option] [⌘] [+]. This gives you the *plus pointer,* which looks something like this (only bigger): + . (Calling it [Option] [⌘] [+] helps you remember the command, but you don't actually have to hold down the [Shift] key; in other words, [Option] [⌘] [=] works just as well.)

shortcut

Once you have the plus point, click on the item you want added to the menu. You can click on:

- items on the Ruler, including the various kinds of justification, line spacing and paragraph spacing, as well as Styles on the menu that pops down from the Ruler

- any of the commands on the Outline Ruler

- items from most dialog boxes—for example, paragraph and character formats

- Glossary entries

- Styles

Pressing [Option] [⌘] [−] gives you the *minus pointer,* which looks something like this (only bigger): − . Select something from a menu with the minus pointer and it's deleted—no matter how it got there to begin with.

You can add several items to (or delete them from) your menus without having to call up the plus or minus pointer each time. Just hold down the [Shift] key when you click on an item or select it from the menu. It will be added or deleted, and the pointer will remain a plus or a minus.

✦ *keyboard control of menus*

Word allows total control of menus from the keyboard. This involves four steps—activating the menu bar (getting it ready for keyboard control), choosing a menu to display (the equivalent of clicking on its title with the mouse), choosing a command from it (the equivalent of dragging down to that command with the mouse) and executing the command (the equivalent of releasing the mouse button).

To activate the menu bar, you press ⊡ on the keypad or ⌘ Tab. To choose a menu, you either type the first letter of its name or the number that corresponds to its position on the menu bar. (The menu is zero.) Or you can move to the menu title with the ⟵ and ⟶ keys. (After one menu is down, only the arrow keys will take you to another.)

To choose a command, hit the first letter of its name. If more than one command begins with the same letter, repeated pressings of the letter key will select each of the commands in turn. Or you can move up or down in the menu with the ⬆ and ⬇ keys.

To execute the command, you press Return or Enter. (As with almost everything in Word, you can cancel the procedure at any time by pressing ⌘ ⊡ or Esc.)

Keyboard sequences are handy for often-used commands that don't have command keys assigned to them. If you're a decent typist, they take far less time than reaching for the mouse. Here are some of my favorites (you don't type the commas, of course; they're just there to indicate that you press the keys one after the other, not at the same time):

Print Preview   ⊡, F, P, Return

Save As   ⊡, F, S, S, Return

Sort   ⊡, U, S, S, Return

Here's my very favorite (it saves a document as text only):

⊡ F S S Return [document name] ⌘ F T Return Return

This sequence opens the Save As dialog box, in which you type the document name, then clicks the *File Format* button (you need the ⌘ key because there's a text field in the dialog box), then clicks the *Text Only* button (you don't need the ⌘ key because there's no text field in that dialog box), then closes the File Format dialog box and clicks on the *Save* button. *(Isn't Sharon amazing?—AN)*

⏏ *keyboard commands in dialog boxes*

Word gives you several ways to choose buttons in dialog boxes without having to take your hands off the keyboard. Here are the basic techniques:

shortcut

- If there isn't a text field in the dialog box, pressing the key that corresponds to the first letter of the name of a button chooses the button (Ⓒ for Cancel, Ⓞ for OK, etc.).

- If there's a text field in the dialog box, you have to hold down ⌘ while pressing the first letter of the button. (This also works when there aren't text fields.)

- In addition to ⌘Ⓒ, ⌘. and Esc also select the Cancel button.

Word also has keyboard commands that let you cycle through the *items* (buttons, text fields, lists and popup menus) in a dialog box. When you move to an item, a flashing underline appears beneath it.

- To move from one item to the next, use the period on the keypad or ⌘Tab.

- To move to the previous item (that is, to move backwards through the items), use Shift. or Shift ⌘ Tab.

- When buttons are clustered in groups, you can jump from one group to the next by using the arrow keys.

- To activate a button or open a popup menu once you've moved to it, use ⌘Spacebar or hit the zero on the keypad.

There are also keyboard commands for choosing from lists or popup menus.

- To choose from a list, use the ⬆ and ⬇ keys. In some dialog boxes, typing a letter selects the first word in the list that begins with that letter (the Commands dialog box is one that works like that).

- To choose from an opened popup menu, use the ↑ and ↓ keys or type the first letter of the item's name. Press Return when the item you want is highlighted.

- To close a popup menu without selecting anything from it (or to close it and return to the original selection), press Esc or Delete.

⚫ *basic selection commands*

shortcut

To select:

a word	doubleclick anywhere in it
a sentence	⌘–click anywhere in it
a line	click in the selection bar
a paragraph	doubleclick in the selection bar
the entire document	⌘–click in the selection bar or press ⌘ Option M

(And, of course—as with virtually all Mac programs—you can also select any amount of text either by dragging across it or by clicking at one point and then shift-clicking at another.)

⚫ *using* Shift *to select*

shortcut

If you use any pointer-movement technique with the Shift key held down, you select the area the pointer moves across. So, for example, Shift ⌘ ← selects the last word you typed.

To extend the selection, just hold the keys down. So, for example, holding Shift ⌘ ← down will continue the selection backward, word by word, until you release the keys.

Note that shift-clicking to extend a selection works in the original unit of the selection. So, for example, if you ⌘–click to select a sentence, shift-clicking someplace else extends the selection to include the whole sentence you've shift-clicked on, regardless of where in that sentence you shift-clicked.

⚫ *using* Option *to select*

Holding down the Option key as you drag lets you select any rectangular area of the screen, regardless of where there's text.

If you want to delete an [Option] key selection, you have to cut it: you can't use [Delete]. (The Mac just beeps at you if you try.)

Note that if any part of a graphic is selected this way, the entire graphic is affected by the deletion or formatting.

🍎 *special deletes*

As you no doubt know, the [Delete] key erases the character to the left of the insertion point. And you can also use it to delete whatever amount of text you've selected. But Word has other delete commands as well:

[Option] [⌘] [F]   erases the character to the right of the insertion point. If you have an extended keyboard, the [⌦] key does the same thing.

[Option] [⌘] [Delete]   deletes the previous word—or, if you're in the middle of a word, everything from the insertion point to the beginning of the word.

[Option] [⌘] [G]   deletes the next word—or, if you're in the middle of a word, everything from the insertion point to the end of the word.

🍎 *an optional way to cut or copy*

You can do the equivalent of a cut (or copy) and paste without using the Clipboard—or the cut, copy, or paste commands. (This can be useful if you have something in the Clipboard and don't want to lose it.) To move text (and/ or graphics) without the Clipboard:

very
hot
tip

• Select the material you want to move and press [Option] [⌘] [X]. The words *Move to* appear in the status box in the lower left corner of the window.

• Click in the spot you want the text moved to, or select the material you want it to replace. (A clicked spot shows as a dotted vertical line; a selection is underlined in gray.)

• Press Return or Enter.

To copy text (and/or graphics) without the Clipboard, follow the same procedure but use Option ⌘ C instead of Option ⌘ X (the words in the status box will read *Copy to* instead of *Move to).*

To remember which key you have to add to the normal cut and copy commands (⌘ C and ⌘ X), think of these commands as *optional cut* and *optional copy.*

♦ the "top of paste" jump

shortcut

After you paste something into your document, the insertion point is left at the bottom of the pasted-in material. To move it back to the top of the pasted material, just hit the keypad zero or Option ⌘ Z. (Since all pastes are done at the insertion point, the top of the paste is always the previous position of the pointer.)

♦ keyboard character formatting

shortcut

There are ⌘ Shift keyboard commands for all of Word's character formats, even if they're not noted on the menu or in the character dialog box:

Bold	⌘ – Shift – B	S̲h̲a̲d̲o̲w̲	⌘ – Shift – W
Italic	⌘ – Shift – I	SMALL CAPS	⌘ – Shift – H
U̲n̲d̲e̲r̲l̲i̲n̲e̲	⌘ – Shift – U	ALL CAPS	⌘ – Shift – K
Word U̲n̲d̲e̲r̲l̲i̲n̲e̲	⌘ – Shift –]	H̲i̲d̲d̲e̲n̲	⌘ – Shift – X
D̲o̲u̲b̲l̲e̲ U̲n̲d̲e̲r̲l̲i̲n̲e̲	⌘ – Shift – [	Smaller Font	⌘ – Shift – <
D̲o̲t̲t̲e̲d̲ U̲n̲d̲e̲r̲l̲i̲n̲e̲	⌘ – Shift – \	Larger Font	⌘ – Shift – >
~~Strikethru~~	⌘ – Shift – /	Super script	⌘ – Shift – +
O̲u̲t̲l̲i̲n̲e̲	⌘ – Shift – D	Sub script	⌘ – Shift – –

♦ copying character formats

shortcut

You can copy existing combinations of character formats (font, size and styles) and apply them either to existing text or to the insertion point, so that they affect whatever you type next.

To copy character formats to existing text:

- Select some text formatted the way you want and press
  Option ⌘ V . The words *Format to* appear in the status
  box (in the lower left corner of the window).

- Select the text you want the formats applied to. (This
  second selection is underlined rather than highlighted.)

- Press Return or Enter .

**To copy character formats to the insertion point (so that
what you type next will have the new formats):**

- While nothing is selected, press Option ⌘ V . The
  words *Format from* appear in the status box.

- Click in any text that's formatted the way you want. The
  click leaves a dotted vertical line.

- Press Return or Enter . The dotted "insertion point"
  disappears, the regular insertion point begins blinking
  again and you can continue typing with the new
  character formatting.

You can cancel either procedure at any time with ⌘ . or
Esc (the words *Format from* in the status box will disappear).

⌘ plain text

To specify plain text, hit Shift ⌘ Z . Option ⌘ Spacebar
doesn't remove character formatting—it returns the selected
text to the formatting that's defined in the Style of the
paragraph it's in. That's why the equivalent command in
the Format menu is called the *Plain For Style (whatever that
means—AN)*.

⌘ soft and hard hyphens

Word gives you a choice of three different kinds of hyphens. *Regular hyphens* are what you get when you hit the
hyphen key (-); they're always displayed, and the words
they connect split when the hyphen falls at the end of a line.

*esp. for
beginners*

A *soft hyphen* (also called a *discretionary hyphen*) is only
displayed when it falls at the end of a line (and the words it
connects are split). To enter a soft hyphen, type ⌘ - .

A *hard hyphen* (also called a *nonbreaking hyphen)* is always displayed, but it won't let the words it connects be split across two lines. To enter hard hyphens, type ⌘ ~.

🍎 *kerning*

**very
hot
tip**

Using Word's Condensed spacing (in the Character dialog box) removes some of the space between letters, but it doesn't do true *kerning,* which lets letters overlap into each other's vertical space on the page. But Word can kern letters with its special (if arcane) typesetting language.

To kern letters, use the *Displace* command to move the second letter of a pair backwards. Start the typesetting formula by typing Option ⌘ /. (That's the backslash character, not the regular slash that's on the same key as the question mark.) This shows up simply as a backslash, but with Show Paragraphs turned on, you can see it's the typesetting character—a backslash preceded by a period.

Use *d* for displace, *ba* for backwards and then the number of points by which you want the next letter shifted. The basic formula looks like this:

.\d.\ba10()

The 10 near the end of the formula is the number of points you want the letter moved and, yes, that's a set of empty parentheses at the end. (I told you it was arcane.)

By nesting this formula between pairs of letters, you can turn

WAVE into WAVE

With Show Paragraphs turned on, the command for the kerned word *WAVE* looks like this:

W.\d.\ba10()A.\d.ba10()V.d.ba4()E

Put the basic kerning formula .\d.\ba10() into the Glossary so you can retrieve it anytime you need it; all you'll have to do is change the number of points you want the letters to move.

♦ keyboard paragraph formatting

Here are the keyboard equivalents for the formats listed in the Paragraph dialog box:

Unlike character formats, they don't act as toggles. Sometimes (as with *Indent First Line* and *Double Space*), nothing at all happens when you apply the format a second time; sometimes (as with *Hanging Indent* and *Nest*), the text is further affected by the command, with margins being moved again, beyond where they had already been moved to.

shortcut

Plain ("Normal")	⌘ – Shift – P		Indent First Line	⌘ – Shift – F
Side-by-side	⌘ – Shift – G		Nest	⌘ – Shift – N
Left Justify	⌘ – Shift – L		UnNest	⌘ – Shift – M
Right Justify	⌘ – Shift – R		Hanging Indent	⌘ – Shift – T
Centered	⌘ – Shift – C		Double Space	⌘ – Shift – Y
Full Justify	⌘ – Shift – J		Open Space	⌘ – Shift – O

♦ copying paragraph formatting

To copy paragraph formatting, follow the procedures described in the entry above called *copying character formats*, with one difference: to select the text that's formatted the way you want, doubleclick in the selection bar to select the entire paragraph.

shortcut

♦ line spacing and paragraph spacing

There are two sets of spacing icons on the Ruler, with related commands in the Paragraph Format dialog box—line spacing (the space between the lines within a paragraph) and paragraph spacing (the space before and/or after a paragraph). These options are entirely independent of one another.

esp. for
beginners

♠ leading control

very good feature

Word gives you a lot of power to control *leading*—the spacing between lines of text (it's pronounced LEHD-*ing*, not LEED-*ing*; in the old days of metal type, it consisted of actual pieces of lead).

To change the leading, go to the Paragraph dialog box (the keyboard shortcut is ⌘M) and type the number of points of leading you want into the Line Spacing box. (You don't need to type *pt* or anything after the number; Word knows you mean points if you don't specify inches or anything else, and in fact automatically puts *pt* after the number the next time you open the dialog box.)

So, for example, if you want to print out text 11/13 (11-point type on 13-point lines, which is what you're reading now), you first select the text, then go to the Character dialog box and type *11* in the *Size* box, then go to the Paragraph dialog box and type *13* in the *Spacing* box.

♠ an improved Shift Return

very hot tip

When you use the Shift Return option to start a new line without starting a new paragraph (this keeps all the paragraph formatting but ignores the first-line indent, which is very useful on occasion), the last line of a fully justified paragraph is stretched from margin to margin.

To avoid this, use Option Return instead to start the new line. Actually, it makes sense to simply use Option Return all the time, but the Word manual—for no justifiable reason— says Shift Return is the way to do it.

♠ eliminating shifting text

If you're inserting new text in the middle of an existing paragraph, it can be really distracting to have the rest of the paragraph shifting to the right and down. To avoid this, put a paragraph marker to the right of the insertion point, by pressing Option ⌘ Return. This pushes the rest of the paragraph down and leaves the insertion point where it was.

When you're finished inserting text, use Option ⌘ F or ⌦ to remove the temporary paragraph marker; this joins the two paragraphs again.

● *supercharging Change To:*

The *Change To:* text box in the Change dialog box (on the Search menu) has a limit of 255 characters, and it doesn't let you specify font or type styles in the replacement text. You can get around both those limitations by inserting the contents of the Clipboard into the *Change To:* box.

very hot tip

To do that, you use *^C*—that is, the caret (Shift 6) followed by the letter *c* (cap or lowercase, it doesn't matter). This lets you replace something short with something very long, or something plain with something fancy.

For example, let's say you want to change every occurrence of *Apple* to **Apple**. Make the first occurrence of *Apple* bold, select it and copy it to the Clipboard. Choose the *Change* command. In the *Find What:* box, type *Apple* and in the *Change To:* box, type *^c*. Then click on the *Change All* button and every occurrence of *Apple* in your document will be changed to boldface.

● *searching for special characters* (SZA/Paul Hoffman)

You can search for invisible and other special characters like paragraphs and tabs by using the following *caret* (^) *combinations* in the text field of the Find or Change dialog box. (You get the caret with Shift 6 .)

very hot tip

^n   newline

^p   paragraph

^t   tab

^s   hard (nonbreaking) space (i.e., Option Spacebar)

^ -   soft hyphen (i.e., Option -)

^d   section or page break

^w   white space (any combination of spaces, tabs, paragraph marks and page breaks)

^\   formula character

^1   graphic

^5   footnote reference mark (You can only search for
this, not add it to your document with the *Change*
command.)

^*x*   where *x* is the ASCII code for a character—i.e., don't
type *x*, type the ASCII code (for details, see the *ASCII
chart* entry in Chapter 7)

^^   caret

^?   question mark

Here's an example of how you can use these special
characters. Let's say you want to change the indent at the
beginning of each paragraph in a document to a tab. First,
you select the entire document and adjust the indent marker
on the Ruler so there's no indent. Then you just search for
every ^*p* and replace it with ^*p*^*t* (you can type them just
like that; you don't need anything between them).

♦ the Again command

very
hot
tip

The *Again* command (⌘ A) repeats the last command,
your last edit, or the last thing you typed. For example, if
you've just applied a Style to a paragraph, you can click in
another paragraph and use *Again* to apply the Style there too.

If you want to use *Again* to apply a group of character or
paragraph formats (bold, outline and italic, say, or justified,
indented and double-spaced), use the Character and Paragraph dialog box rather than the keyboard or the Format
menu. That way the *Again* command will apply all the formats
in the dialog box, instead of just the last one you applied.

♦ finding again

shortcut

To find another occurrence of the word, phrase or format you last searched for, you don't have to open the Find
or Change dialog boxes again—just press Option ⌘ A , or use
the = key on the numeric keypad.

Combining this with the general *Again* command (⌘ A)
lets you search for something, apply a format to it and then
search for the next occurrence, all from the keyboard and
without using dialog boxes.

⚫ *unusual Glossary entries*

The Glossary can store anything that you can select in
the document. Here are some entries that may not have
occurred to you, but which can be quite useful:

*very
hot
tip*

* Graphics (for example, a logo or a letterhead).

* Section breaks. All the section definitions (number of
  columns, page number position, etc.) are stored in the
  section-break symbol (a double line that runs across the
  page). Keeping them in the Glossary lets you apply
  section-formatting options quickly.

* Character format combinations. To do this, select a
  single character with a variety of formats—14 point
  Times bold italic, for example—and store it in the
  Glossary. When you retrieve it, hit Shift ← to select it
  and then type whatever you want—the new typing will
  have the retrieved format.

* Paragraph formats. First press ⌘ Y (or choose *Show* ¶
  from the Edit menu). Then select a paragraph marker
  (¶) and open the Glossary window. (Why retrieve
  paragraph formats from the Glossary instead of using a
  style sheet? Because the style sheet includes character
  formatting, and sometimes you won't want that.)

* Tables. Create tables with the number and size of rows
  and columns you need, and store them in the Glossary
  for quick retrieval.

You can put a Glossary entry into the Work menu (using the *Commands* command. You can also retrieve
graphics, character and paragraph formats, section breaks
and tables with keyboard commands (again, using the
Commands command).

⚫ standard and nonstandard Glossaries

When you create a Glossary entry, it's only good for the current session—unless it's specifically saved into the Standard (default) Glossary that Word starts with in each session. You'll be prompted to do that when you quit Word, but you don't have to wait till then—just choose *Save* from the File menu while the Glossary window is open.

To save a specialized Glossary as something other than the Standard Glossary, use *Save As* when the Glossary window is open. To retrieve a nonstandard Glossary, use *Open* when the Glossary window is open.

To create a new Glossary with nothing in it (except the default entries of New, Date and Time) just open the Glossary window and choose *New* from the File menu.

⚫ sorting

Word is smart enough to know the difference between punctuation marks and other symbols (which it sorts first), numbers (which it sorts second) and letters (which it sorts last). Capital letters are put before their lowercase equivalents (e.g., *Mac* before *mac)* *(that doesn't seem very smart to me—AN)* and accented foreign characters are put with their unaccented equivalents (e.g., *e* with *é, u* with *ü,* etc.) Word is even smart enough to sort alphanumeric combinations correctly, so you get *9a* and *9b* before *10a* and *10b.*

To sort in descending order (highest numbers first or *z* to *a),* press Shift as you select the *Sort* command from the Utilities menu. (You'll notice that the command becomes *Sort Descending* when Shift is down.)

⚫ creating and changing default Styles

There are default Styles that Word always uses, like the Normal Style and those used for automatic page numbers and index entries. You can change their definitions and add new defaults of your own.

Why should you want to add your own defaults? Because nondefault style sheets are stored with the document in which they were created (or into which they were imported; for details, see the entry below called *importing or merging style sheets)*. So if you create a Style for one document and forget to define it as a default, you'll have to import it into each document you want to use it in.

To make a Style a default, just select it in the Define Styles dialog box and click the Set Default button.

Changing default Styles is easy. Just hold down the (Shift) key, choose *Define Styles...* from the Format menu and select the Style you want to change. The names of the default Styles have a bullet (·) in front of them. (If you don't hold down (Shift), they won't appear).

Prime candidates for changes are:

• The Normal Style (the default for a new document)

• Page Number (used for the automatic page number)

• Line Number (used with the number lines paragraph format)

Page Number and Line Number are based on the Normal Style, so if you change Normal to Times 10-point, the page numbers and line numbers will also be in that font.

✦ *no retroactive default Styles*

When you change the definition of a default Style, paragraphs defined as that Style automatically reflect the changes—but only in the current document and future ones. A pre-existing document using that Style will not show the changes—unless you either open the document, Select All and paste it into a new, empty window, or import the new style sheet into it (see the next entry for how to do that).

important warning

✦ *importing or merging style sheets*

If a document has no style sheet, you can import one from another document. If it does have a style sheet, you can merge it with one from another document.

To import or merge, open the Define Styles dialog box and choose *Open* from the File menu. Select the document whose style sheet you want and click the *Open* button.

Note that when both documents have Styles with the same name, the imported one replaces the current one.

🍎 *combining Styles in a document*

To merge two Styles in a document (turn all your *Unit Title* paragraphs into *Chapter Title* paragraphs, say):

• Open the Define Styles dialog box.

• Select the Style you want to get rid of. (You can't just cut it, or all the paragraphs you've formatted in that Style will revert to Normal Style.)

• In the text box that displays the Style's name, type a comma and then the name of the Style you want to change to. (In this example, you'd select the Style *Unit Title* and change its name to *Unit Title,Chapter Title*).

• Click the *Define* button. You'll get a dialog box asking if it's okay to merge the Styles. Click the *OK* button.

• Now select the new (combined) Style and change its name, deleting the old name. (For example, change *Unit Title,Chapter Title* to simply *Chapter Title*.)

When you're finished, all the paragraphs that used to be formatted for the *Unit Title* Style will be *Chapter Title* Style, and the *Unit Title* Style itself will be gone from the Style sheet.

🍎 *Next Style override*

very hot tip

When you define a Style to have a Next Style, pressing Return to start a new paragraph switches to that next Style. When you want to stay in the current Style, you can override the Next Style option by pressing ⌘ Return instead.

🍎 *doubleclicks in Print Preview*

shortcut

Doubleclicking the page number icon puts the page number in its default position in the upper right corner of the page. Doubleclicking the printer icon opens the Print dialog box. (Doubleclicking on the page margin or single/double page icon does nothing but confuse you; the clicks are interpreted as two single clicks and therefore simply put you into, and right back out of, the modes they stand for.)

✎ *paging and scrolling in Print Preview*

There are keyboard equivalents you can use instead of the scroll bar in Print Preview. Any of the following will move you backward or forward one page:

shortcut

- the ⬆ and ⬇ keys
- the ⑧ and ② keys on the keypad
- Option ⌘ / and Option ⌘ [
- Option ⌘ O and Option ⌘ ,

In addition, you can jump to the first page with ⌘ 9 (keypad) and to the last page with ⌘ 3 (keypad).

✎ *deleting the automatic page number*

To get rid of an automatic page number while in Print Preview, just drag it off the page. It won't look like anything has happened, but if you click the margins icon to update the display, you'll see that the page number is gone.

✎ *adding a page break in Print Preview*

To add a page break while in Print Preview, click on the margins icon, then drag a page break up out of the bottom margin of the page.

✎ *run-in headers and footers*

The body of a document is automatically adjusted to make room for headers and footers, but you can circumvent this feature. If you have a header or footer that's higher than it is wide, you can run it down the left or right margin of the page, overlapping the area that "belongs" to the body of the text by defining the header or footer as a *run-in*.

shortcut

To do that, use a negative number for the top paper margin (for a header) or the bottom paper margin (for the footer) in the Document dialog box. Or, in Print Preview, adjust the header or footer position while holding down the [Shift] key.

❤ *removing paragraph borders*

shortcut

Removing paragraph borders by working in the Borders dialog box is time-consuming. You have to click on each bordered side of a paragraph to take the lines off. If you're working on multiple paragraphs with differing border styles, it's even worse, because it's hard to tell which lines you're turning on and which you're turning off.

It's easier to use the *No Paragraph Border* command to remove all the borders from selected paragraphs. Here's how to put the command in the Format menu:

- Choose *Commands...* from the Edit menu.

- Choose *Paragraph Border:* in the command list. The *Paragraph Border:* command appears to the right, above a menu box displaying *L Thick Paragra...* (one of the four basic border commands you can add to the menu).

- Click in the menu box, or on the arrow next to the box, and choose *No Paragraph Border* from the menu that appears.

- Click on the Add button.

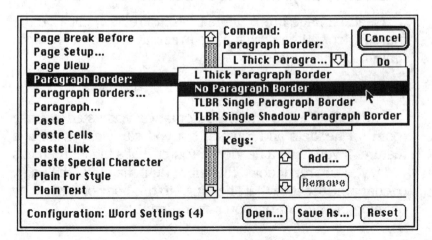

❦ *framing a whole page*

You can frame an entire page with a simple box (thin, thick, or shadow), just by combining two of Word's special capabilities.

very
hot
tip

First, create a header or footer that consists of no text but has paragraph formatting for the border you want. Set the left and right margins as needed and press Return as many times as necessary to set the length of the box. (Word 4 lets you define borders to apply to a block of paragraphs, but in Word 3, you have to press Shift Return so you won't get a series of boxes, one for each paragraph.)

Then set the Top margin to a negative number—so, if you want the body text to start a half-inch from the top of the page, type -.5. (Negative numbers let the header/footer run into the body of the page.)

❦ *sizing and cropping graphics*

Dragging the handles on the frame that surrounds a selected graphic resizes the frame, but not the picture. Making the frame smaller than the graphic crops the image, leaving the upper left part of it showing. Making the frame larger centers the picture in the frame.

very
hot
tip

To change the size of the picture instead of cropping it, hold the Shift key as you drag on the frame. To return a graphic to its original size, doubleclick on it.

❦ *the graphics dump*

To turn any part of a Word document into a graphic, select it and hit Option ⌘ D. This puts a snapshot of it on the Clipboard. Although this feature is meant to allow you to transfer complicated formulas (constructed with Word's typesetting commands) into other programs, it also can be handy within Word, because it lets you distort text by turning it into a graphic and then stretching or shrinking it. (For more details, see the entry called *creating special typographic effects* in Chapter 7.)

very
hot
tip

◉ scanning a long document

shortcut

When you switch to Outline mode, the first line of each paragraph in your document is displayed. This makes it very easy to skim through a long document when you're looking for something.

◉ disabling Fast Save

Word's Fast Save option is fast because it doesn't save your edited file all over again; it simply takes the changes you've made and adds them to the file on the disk. You get speed, but the trade-off is file size—the more often you edit and Fast Save a document, the larger it gets.

The *Fast Save* button (in the Save As dialog box) is always checked as a default—which means you always get a fast save when you simply use the *Save* command (because unless you *Save As*, the Save As dialog box doesn't open and you can't uncheck the button).

You can disable the automatic fast save by putting the *Fast Save Enabled* command in your Edit menu (so you can turn it on or off whenever you want). This command is a toggle—choosing it alternately turns it on and off. When it's off (no checkmark in front of it), the Fast Save button in the Save As dialog box is *disabled*—dimmed so it can't be selected at all. Then when you use the *Save* command, you get a regular save.

To add the command to your menu:

*   Choose *Commands...* from the Edit menu.

*   Choose *Fast Save Enabled* in the command list.

*   Click the *Add* button below the word *Menu:* (not the one farther down).

Once you've disabled the button, you can remove the command from the menu—the button stays dimmed even with the command gone. But it's smarter to simply leave the command in the menu, in case you ever want to turn *Fast Save* on again.

⚫ *Screen Test*

Word has its own built-in screen saver, called Screen Test, but like so many of Word's capabilities, it's pretty well hidden. Here's how to add it to your menu or assign it a keyboard combination:

- Choose *Commands...* from the Edit menu.

- Scroll to the command *Screen Test* and select it.

- Click the *Add* button if you want to put in your Utilities menu.

  OR

- Assign it a keyboard command and click the *Add...*button next to that box.

You can, of course, do both—put it in the menu *and* assign it a keyboard equivalent.

Screen Test puts on a terrific display (especially if you have a color monitor). Once it's on, hit any key or click the mouse button to bring up a dialog box that lets you change various options for the display. Have fun with this one!

(If you want to see what Screen Test looks like before installing it, click on the Do *button instead of the* Add *button in step three above.—AN)*

⚫ *Word credits*

Just for fun, choose *About Microsoft Word...* from the ⚫ menu and ⌘-click on the Word icon in the dialog that appears.

gossip/ trivia

⚫ *dynamic dates and times*

Date and time entries inserted by the Glossary into a document are static—that is, they don't change once you insert them. To make them reflect the time of printing rather than the time of insertion into the document, use the Header or Footer window to make Glossary entries:

very hot tip

- Open the Header or Footer window.

- Click on the date or time icon.

- Select the date or time entry in the window.

- Open the Glossary window, give the entry a name (but not time or date, since those are taken already) and click on the *Define* button.

● *date style macros*

Word's Glossary offers three styles of dates: abbreviated *(7/30/91)*, short *(Sun, Jul 30, 1991)* and long *(Sunday, July 30, 1991)*. You can't change them, since they're default entries, but you can create a macro (using any Macro utility) to alter or combine elements from different styles to get what you need.

Say you need this style: *Sunday, 7/30/91*. The following macro, which plays back in less than a second, provides it.

press ⌘ Delete	prepares the status box for a glossary entry name
type *date - now - long* and press Return	inserts the long-style date into the document
press Delete 13 times	erases everything but the day of the week
press ⌘ Delete	prepares the status box for a glossary entry name
type *date - now - short* and press Return	inserts the short-style date into the document

Another convenient date-style macro is any of the available styles with the year removed (by backspacing over it).

(Note that you can't record a macro of selecting an entry from the Glossary window, because as you add and delete entries, the position of other entries in the list changes; when you play the macro back, it will choose the wrong entry. To retrieve Glossary items in a macro, you have to use the ⌘ Delete option.)

❡ *the footnote window*

To review or edit text in the footnote window, press [Shift] while you drag the split bar, or press [Shift][Option][⌘][S]. To close the footnote window, drag the split bar to the top or bottom of the window, or press [Option][⌘][S].

You don't have to close the footnote window after typing text into it. You can just click in the main part of the window to continue working on your document, or use the *Go Back* command (it will place the insertion point immediately after the footnote reference mark in the main document).

❡ *removing returns from imported documents* (DC)

Sometimes when you transfer a document created on another computer into Word, you'll find carriage returns at the end of each line. (Use [⌘][Y] to see where all the carriage returns are; they show up as ¶'s.) Since Word uses carriage returns only to mark the ends of paragraphs, you'll need to remove all the ones that fall elsewhere. Here's how to do that:

🔥
**very
hot
tip**

Select the entire document. Now choose *Change* from the Utilities menu, and change each occurrence of *^p^p* (Word uses *^p* to represent carriage returns) to some unique characters that don't appear anywhere in the document, such as *##*. Click the *Change All* button.

Next, choose *Change* again and change each occurrence of *^p* to a single space (just use the space bar). Click the *Change All* button. Now choose *Change* for a third time and change each occurrence of *##* (or whatever you're using) to *^p*. Again, click on the *Change All* button.

All the carriage returns in your document should now be at the ends of paragraphs. ([⌘][Y] will reveal if any unwanted ones remain.)

❡ *removing blank lines from merge printouts* (DC)

Since the dawn of mail merge, users have put up with the problem of blank lines in their mailing labels and merge letters. You set up fields for Title, Name, Company, Address,

*esp. for
power users*

City, State, and ZIP, and the first thing you discover is that half your records have no company name associated with them. In many word processors, this leaves you with no option but to print the labels with a blank line where the company name would go. Officially, Word is no different, but there is a way around the problem.

Word's manual states that each ELSE statement must be enclosed with *guillemets* (which look like this: « » and are pronounced *gee-may*). But if you leave off the last » , Word will not advance to the next line, and blank lines will be eliminated when the document is printed.

The official Microsoft approach shown below will leave you with blank lines if the title, name, or company field is empty:

```
«IF  title»«title»
«ELSE»
«IF  name»«name»
«ELSE»
«IF  company»«company»
«ELSE»
«ENDIF»«address»
«city», «state»  «zip»
```

But the following Print Merge document will not leave blank lines, regardless of whether or not the title, name, or company field is empty:

```
«IF  title»«title»
«ELSE
«IF  name»«name»
«ELSE
«IF  company»«company»
«ELSE
«ENDIF»«address»
«city», «state»  «zip»
```

WriteNow tips

⬥ *suppressing menu fonts*

very hot tip

In WriteNow's font menu, the font names appear in their own typefaces. This makes the menu a little slower to pop down than other menus. *(It also makes it impossible to read pictorial fonts, and difficult to read ornate display fonts. It also makes the menu ugly, cluttered and jumbled. Mac-Write uses the same approach but, unlike WriteNow, doesn't give you a way to turn it off.—AN)*

To suppress this "feature," hold down (Option) when you open the Font menu. *(There should be some way to turn it off as a default, so you don't have to do this each time.—AN)*

✺ closing all documents

To close all open documents in one fell swoop, hold down (Option), open the File menu and choose the *Close* command (which will now read *Close All)*. This trick also works on the desktop but not in every program—just those that, like WriteNow, have wisely chosen to implement it.

shortcut

✺ moving with the arrow keys

The arrow keys ((↑)(↓)(←)(→)) move the insertion point left and right by a single character and up and down by a single line. You can use the (Option) and (⌘) keys with the arrow keys to move in different increments:

shortcut

(Option)(←)	left one word
(Option)(→)	right one word
(⌘)(↑)	to the top of the current screen, then to the top of the next screen
(⌘)(↓)	to the bottom of the current screen, then to the bottom of the next screen
(⌘)(←)	to the beginning of the line
(⌘)(→)	to the end of the line

Adding (Shift) to any of these keyboard commands selects the text from the initial position of the insertion point to where it ends up.

✺ keyboard text changes

There are three ways to change the font size of selected text from the keyboard:

shortcut

⌘0   increase by a single point

⌘9   decrease by a single point

⌘8   change to specific point size

When you use ⌘8, immediately type the point size that you want. When you use ⌘0 or ⌘9, you can hold the keys down to continually increase or decrease the size.

You can also superscript and subscript selected text with keyboard commands (the mnemonics are *higher* and *lower):*

⌘H   superscript (by one point)

⌘L   subscript (by one point)

If you hold ⌘H or ⌘L down, the superscripting or subscripting increases continually, in increments of one point. To remove superscripting or subscripting, use ⌘T. This puts the text back at the baseline no matter how far you've offset it with ⌘H or ⌘L.

♠ *keyboard ruler changes*

shortcut

You can change paragraph alignment and spacing from the keyboard, without having to click on the Ruler. Here's how:

⌘ Shift L   align left

⌘ Shift R   align right

⌘ Shift C   align centered

⌘ Shift J   justify margins

⌘ Shift I   increase line spacing

⌘ Shift D   decrease line spacing

⌘ Shift X   toggle between fixed/flexible line spacing

♠ *creating new default formatting*

To change the formatting for new documents, create a document with the settings you want. Name it *Stationery* and put it in either your system folder or in the same folder as WriteNow. From that point on, each time you use the *New* command, the Untitled document that opens will have the stationery's settings.

If you want a new document to use WriteNow's regular defaults instead those of the Stationery file you've set up (but don't want to change them permanently), hold down (Option) while you choose *New*.

⚫ *tabs and returns in dialog boxes*

When you want to indicate a (Tab) or (Return) character in a Find or Replace dialog box, you can do it in one of two ways —use (Option)(Tab) or ^t for (Tab), (Option)(Return) or ^r for (Return).

⚫ *relative margin changes*

If you select all the paragraphs in a document and move the left margin marker in half an inch (say), all the paragraphs will start at the half-inch mark. To make a *relative* change to paragraph margins—like moving all of them in a half-inch *from their current positions*—hold (⌘) while you move the margin marker.

very
hot
tip

⚫ *custom leader characters*

WriteNow lets you use any character as a *leader* (that is, to fill the blank space between tab stops). To specify a leader, just press (Tab) and the character at the same time. So if you wanted a dotted line as a leader, you'd press (Tab) and the (.) key at the same time.

The space between tabs—and whatever leader character is in it—can be selected and formatted. So if you have chapter titles and pages in 18-point bold:

Chapter One..................1

you can select the dots and make them look more reasonable:

Chapter One....................1

⬧ WriteNow and Word merge documents

**very good
feature**

WriteNow's merge documents are identical to Word's—in fact, a merge document created in Word can be opened directly in WriteNow and used without editing. (Kudos to T-Maker for admitting that other software actually exists.)

⬧ bulk editing of the dictionary (DC)

shortcut

To add a lot of words to the dictionary, select them all and click on the *Learn* button. To delete a lot of words from the dictionary, select them all and click on the *Forget* button.

⬧ creating unique paragraphs

While WriteNow doesn't provide Styles, it does let you copy existing paragraph formats and apply them to other paragraphs. It also lets you change all paragraphs in a selection that have identical formatting to some other format—ignoring paragraphs in the selection that don't share that formatting.

One way to uniquely identify paragraphs for later global changing is to add invisible formatting to them. Let's say your document has primary and secondary heads. Add a tab to the end of the Ruler—even beyond the right margin—to identify the primary heads; add two tabs to identify secondary heads. Adding tabs that you know you won't use doesn't affect the look of paragraphs at all, but it gives them distinct formatting.

Works word processor tips

⬧ nontoggling Undo (AN)

**very bad
feature**

In Works, ⌘Z doesn't toggle between *Undo* and *Redo*, the way it does in virtually every other Mac program. This may not sound like much of a problem, but it's amazing how much work you can lose as a result of it. For example, if you accidentally hit ⌘Z, all the text you typed since the last time you clicked the mouse is irretrievably lost!

Incredibly, this ridiculous mistake was not corrected in Works 2.0, thereby slipping over the line from gross negligence to willful misconduct (and, in the process, winning the much-coveted Naiman Prize for Brain-Dead Software Design).

♦ the four tabs

It's not immediately apparent, but Works provides four different types of tabs: left, right, decimal, and centered. Here's what they look like on the Ruler:

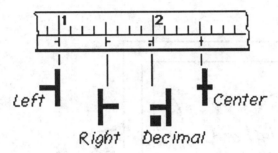

To get a left-aligned tab, click once; to get a right-aligned tab, doubleclick; to get a decimal tab, triple-click; and to get a center tab, quadruple-click (there's a word you don't see too often).

very hot tip

Clicking on an existing tab changes it to the next type, and it goes around in a circle (from the center tab back to the left tab again). So if you're moving a tab on the Ruler, make sure you hold the mouse button down as you drag—if you release it too soon, the tab will change to a different type.

♦ automatic entry of search text

If any text is selected when you use the *Find* or *Replace* command (both on the Search menu), it's automatically entered into the *Find What:* text box.

very good feature

♦ margins vs. indents

As the Works manual tries to make clear, margins are set in the Page Setup dialog box while Indentations—left, right and first line—are set on the Ruler. It may help you avoid confusion if you think of the Ruler as controlling left and right *text* margins while Page Setup controls *paper* margins.

The zero mark on the Ruler is set wherever the left paper margin is. So with a one-inch page margin and a zero setting on the Ruler, the text begins one inch in from the left edge of the paper. If you set the margin on the Ruler at one inch, the text will begin two inches in from the edge of paper. Paragraphs on a page can have various right and left margins, but the paper margins remain constant.

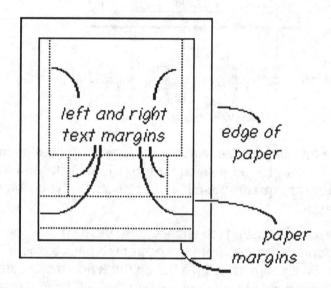

If you put the right margin marker on the Ruler beyond the right paper margin, it turns into a hollow triangle. Since Works won't print anything beyond the paper margin you've set in Page Setup, you'll lose some text (or graphics) at the ends of your lines.

(I hate this old-fashioned, pre-Mac way of treating margins, which is a leftover from the primordial ooze of CP/M. After all, the only thing that counts is how far the text is from the edge of the paper; to indent a paragraph, you just increase that one, single measure. There are no such things as text margins and paper margins—there are just margins.

*This is a good example of the opposite of transparency—
instead of being invisible, the mechanics of the software
show through and distract you from your work.—AN)*

⬢ page zero

When you use the *Title Page* command, the header and/
or footer isn't printed on the first page of the document,
but the next page is marked Page 2 (assuming, of course,
that you have a command that reads *Page &p* in the header
or footer). To make the second page read Page 1, choose
the *Set Page* command (on the Format menu) and set the
starting page number to zero.

⬢ page breaks

You can use [Shift][Enter] instead of the *Insert Page Break*
command to put a page break in a document. Both commands insert a forced page break (that is, one that moves
you to a new page regardless of how much text is on the
current one).

Forced page breaks can be removed by backspacing
over them, but there's another way to do it: [Shift][Enter] acts
as a toggle—that is, it also removes a page break if the
insertion point is immediately beneath it.

⬢ drawing room

If you turn Draw on, but the crosshairs pointer doesn't
appear when you place it where you want to start drawing,
you're probably trying to draw past the end of the document. Just add some empty lines with the [Return] key and
the Draw function should work.

⬢ pasting text and graphics

If you have both text and graphics stored in the Clipboard, pasting will insert both into the document—unless
you have Draw on, in which case only the graphic object
will be inserted.

If you're pasting a graphic at the end of the document, remember that you first have to make space for it, by pressing [Return] as many times as necessary.

♦ multiple (repeating) labels

To print address labels that all have the same name and address (either because you're sending a shipment of many boxes or because you repeatedly ship to the same address), set up the merge document the way you would for regular multicolumn labels, but don't check the *Multiple Labels* option. Go to the database window and select the record that contains the information you want. Then move back to the word processor and use the *Print Merge* command.

Outliners

♦ what's an outliner?

esp. for beginners

Outliners are, in effect, word processors that specialize in making it easy for you reorganize your material. You enter text on indented *levels* or in *headlines*, and then you drag it around. If you're thinking that you can do that in your word processor, by using tabs for indenting and then cutting and pasting to reorganize—you're wrong. Picture yourself cutting and pasting icons on the desktop every time you want to move something, and you'll get an idea of the difference in convenience.

very good feature

The various levels or headlines don't have to be single words or phrases—they can be multiple paragraphs of text or even graphics. And best of all, you can *collapse* or *expand* the outline—looking at, for example, only all of the first level headlines, or everything up to the third level, or all the levels that are subordinate to the third first-level headline. Being able to get an overview of your document's structure, and to zero in on any section of it, is invaluable.

The usefulness of outliners isn't limited to organizing large text documents. You can, for example, use them to create calendars, or to-do lists on which you can reprioritize items simply by dragging them to a different spot.

● *More II*

ThinkTank begat More which begat More II, a smooth, beautiful, powerful piece of software. When More II came out, *presentation software* was the latest buzzword and Symantec tried to position the product in that market. Bad move. They have since come to their senses and returned to the outliner-organizer category in their advertising.

More lets you create multiple-line headlines and attach a window to any or all headlines for further text or graphic information. It automatically labels headlines and subheads by any of a number of schemes—including ones you make up yourself.

very good
feature

You can define formatting for any group of headlines (including font, size, style, color and leader characters) and you can store and retrieve the combination (like style sheets in a word processor). More lets you view your information in more than just the straightforward text view. You can choose bullet charts or tree charts, and there are lots of additional choices within those categories. Here's a basic outline view:

very good
feature

```
    + Main Title
      + First Level Headline
        - This is a second level headline
        - So is this
      - Another First Level Headline
      - Still Another First Level Headline
```

And here's a tree chart of the same information:

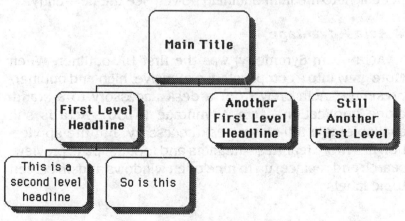

Here's the first screen of the bullet chart for the same outline:

> # *Main Title*
>
> ■ First Level Headline
> ■ Another First Level Headline
> ■ Still Another First Level

The next bullet chart would have the First Level Headline in the place of the Main Title with the second level headlines bulleted underneath (by default it would be formatted the same, but you can define different styles of charts for different levels).

More hasn't forgotten its presentation pretensions—you can easily design slides and/or handouts from the information in your outline. More also provides a slide show option, with special effects from one screen to the next.

If you need heavy-duty outlining, you should consider shelling out the $400 More II costs, whether or not you need presentation graphics. If you don't do presentations and only need light-to-medium outlining power, see the next entry.

❡ *Acta Advantage*

Acta (from Symmetry) was the first DA outliner. When More grew into a complicated, expensive, high-end outliner/ presenter, Acta grew from a desk accessory to a stand-alone application—Acta Advantage ($130). Acta is still available as a full-blown desk accessory, but the application has more features—headers and footers, page preview, search and replace, up to nine open windows and on-screen topic labels.

Acta Advantage is perfect for anyone who needs an outliner (and that's almost everyone) but doesn't need the high-end power of More II. The Acta Advantage package includes the DA, which is useful for accessing your application's files from the menu.

Tips on More

about "document window"

The tips in this section reluctantly stick to LivingVideo-Text's confusing and unMaclike term *document window*. A More *document window* is not the window that has your outline in it, the one with the close box and the title bar (as it would be on any other Mac application)—it's the expandable scrolling area that stores text for a headline.

very bad
feature

the zero-level headline

A currently-selected headline is always considered the zero level; headlines immediately beneath it are level 1 and so on.

underlined document names

Opened documents are listed in the Window menu. If the title is underlined, that means you haven't saved the latest changes. *(This is a great feature. All programs should do this.—AN)*

very good
feature

character formatting from the keyboard

Since there are no keyboard equivalents listed in the Style submenu, it's not obvious that you can apply character formatting to selected text from the keyboard. But you can. The keyboard commands are:

shortcut

Shift ⌘ B	bold
Shift ⌘ I	italic
Shift ⌘ U	underline

Shift ⌘ D	shadow
Shift ⌘ O	outline
Shift ⌘ P	plain

The *Plain* command, whether chosen from the menu or accessed with Shift ⌘ P, doesn't strip selected text of all styles—it removes just the formatting that doesn't belong in the *rule* (in other words, the Style) for that headline. So if all your second-level heads are defined as 14-point bold, and you've underlined one of them, applying *Plain* to that one leaves it bold but removes the underline.

You can make selected text larger with Shift ⌘ , or smaller with Shift ⌘ . . You can cycle through all the fonts in your System, applying them to headlines or document windows, with Shift ⌘ [and Shift ⌘] .

⚫ tabs and returns in headlines

To use tabs or returns within a headline, press Option Tab or Option Return .

⚫ splitting and joining headlines

very hot tip

To split an existing headline into two headlines, click where you want to split and press ⌘ Return . To join two headlines into one, click at the beginning of the lower one and press ⌘ Delete . Then insert a space to separate the words at the joined spot. (If you click anywhere other than at the beginning of the headline, ⌘ Delete acts as a regular backspace.)

Here's a macro that lets you join headlines no matter what part of the lower headline you're in (it adds the needed space between the joined headlines automatically):

- ⌘ A   selects the entire headline
- ←   deselects the headline, putting the insertion point at its beginning
- ⌘ Delete   joins the headlines
- Spacebar   inserts a space

To play the macro back, just click anywhere in the lower headline before you call the macro. Suggested playback command: [Option] [⌘] [Delete].

⬤ *moving around*

To jump right to the Home headline, press [Shift] [⌘] [↑]; to jump directly to the last headline, press [Shift] [⌘] [↓]. To jump up a windowful at a time, press [Shift] [↑]; to jump down a windowful at a time, press [Shift] [↓]. If you have an extended keyboard, you can use the [Home], [End], [PgUp] and [PgDn] keys.

shortcut

⬤ *selecting text*

To select text in headlines or in document windows without using the mouse, hold down the [Shift] key and use the arrow keys to move the insertion point (it will select the text it passes over).

⬤ *the triple-click trick*

Triple-clicking selects a paragraph in a headline or in a document window. (If your headline is a single line or paragraph, as most are, triple-clicking selects the entire headline.)

shortcut

⬤ *in and out of document windows*

[Option] [Enter] moves the pointer out of a document window and back into its headline without closing the window. The same command also moves you the other way—from a headline into its open document window.

shortcut

⬤ *clicking buttons from the keyboard*

In a dialog box, the first letter of a button's name will click it. For example, if your choices are *Yes, No* and *Cancel,* you can simply press [Y], [N] or [C]. ([⌘] [.] and [Esc] also work for *Cancel.)*

shortcut

⬤ *automatic Search For entries*

If any text is selected when you use the *Search* command, it's automatically entered into the *Search For:* text box.

very good feature

✦ importing and exporting

To save a More II outline as a Word document, to open a More 1.0 document in More II or to do any of a number of other import/export operations, you use the pop-up menus in the Open and Save dialog boxes. If the menus aren't popping up, then you forgot to move the *import/export drivers* into your system folder. They're in the *Driver* folder on the More II utilities disk.

✦ counting words

You can use More's search function to count the words in an outline (or any part of it). First, select the part you want counted. (Selecting a headline will count all its subheads and document windows; to count the whole document, select the Home headline.) Then type the following in the *Search For:* text box (in the Search dialog box):

[a-z]*

Click on the *Whole Word* and *Match Pattern* check boxes and the *Find All* button.

✦ bypassing the Sort dialog box

shortcut

To bypass the Sort dialog box when you want to use the current settings anyway, hold down Option while choosing *Sort* from the Outline menu.

✦ restoring a graphic to its original size

shortcut

When you've resized a graphic by its handles, restore it to its original size by doubleclicking on it.

✦ formatting shortcut

shortcut

The formatting rules you apply to headlines—and therefore to their subheads—can be cut or copied as a group, without even opening the Rules dialog box. You can then paste the group of rules onto another headline. The commands are Option ⌘ X, Option ⌘ C and Option ⌘ V.

⚫ *indented pastes*

When you paste a headline into an outline, it appears directly beneath the current headline, on the same level. To make it subordinate to the current headline, use this macro:

shortcut

- ⌘ V pastes the headline beneath the current one

- Tab indents the lower headline

⚫ *the open-next-document-window macro*

Here's a macro I think of as the "leapfrog" macro. It's for when you're in a document window and you want to move to the document window attached to the next headline (which isn't currently open).

shortcut

- Enter closes the first document window

- ↓ selects the next headline

- Enter opens the next document window

The playback command I use is ⌘ Enter. If you prefer to work with full-size document windows, record the macro with Shift Enter and use Shift ⌘ Enter as the command.

⚫ *removing subheads*

Here's a macro that removes all the subheads from under a headline.

shortcut

- ⌘ A selects the whole headline

- ⌘ X cuts the contents of the headline

- ⌘ B clears the headline itself, with all its subheads
  (the previous headline is then selected)

- Return inserts a new headline

- ⌘ V pastes the original headline text back into
  the outline

Note that this works only on the headline and not on any document window attached to it.

gossip/ trivia

At LivingVideoText (the program's publisher), this macro used to be called *the infanticide command.*

Spelling checkers

¢ finding the right spelling checker (Scott Beamer)

**esp. for
beginners**

Everyone who does word processing on a Mac should use a spelling checker. It doesn't make much difference whether you consider yourself a good speller, because most errors are typos. Spelling checkers not only help you to find these, they let you correct them quickly and efficiently.

**important
warning**

But remember: No spelling checker can find errors in which you inadvertently substitute a valid word for the one you intended *(form* for *from,* say, or *tow* for *two).* So you should proofread a document one last time after running it through a spelling checker.

Virtually all Macintosh word processors now come with built-in spelling checkers, and they're generally pretty good. But some people may still want a stand-alone spelling checker to use with other applications, and to get features not included in a particular built-in checker.

Some spelling checkers offer *batch checking,* which processes an entire document, or a selected portion of it, at once. Some also offer *interactive checking,* which means the program interrupts you every time you type something it doesn't understand. Interactive checking makes me lose my concentration, but you may prefer it.

A big dictionary is one of the most important features of a good spelling checker, because it cuts down on the number of *false alarms*—correctly spelled words it doesn't recognize. The fewer of these, the faster you'll finish checking a file. Another advantage of a large dictionary is that it's more likely to offer a correct spelling as an option, which is the fastest way to make a correction.

I like a dictionary of at least 80,000–100,000 words. Much smaller than that and there may be more false alarms than actual spelling errors, which is a real annoyance. Most stand-alone checkers offer statistics, including word count— a feature which, as a journalist, I'm very fond of.

Many programs of both types offer extras. A *Glossary* function is one of the more useful of those. This allows you to make a list of abbreviations and the full text they represent. Type the abbreviation and the full text appears (e.g., you might type *td* when you want today's date). The text to be substituted can be quite long, so whole paragraphs of boilerplate can be put in the Glossary. Some Glossaries even accept carriage returns, which makes it possible for you to insert your whole address (or somebody else's) by typing a simple abbreviation.

very good feature

Other extras offered by some programs include the ability to recognize the entire ASCII character set, not just the standard alphabet. This lets you put words with foreign accents and even mathematical formulas into the dictionary.

Another useful extra feature is flagging double words (like *and and)*, which are both very common and among the most difficult mistakes to spot when proofreading. Some spelling checkers also look for correct capitalization and simple punctuation errors like unmatched parentheses or quotation marks. Automatic hyphenation and hyphenation checking are offered by many programs.

very good feature

Being able to view the actual dictionary and make changes in it is very useful (especially since virtually all dictionaries contain some errors).

very good feature

A final consideration when choosing a spelling checker is how many different applications it can work with without having to change the formatting. Some DA spelling checkers have some problems with formatting, because they use the Clipboard as part of their correction routine. This sometimes causes problems with applications that don't follow Apple's guidelines (some Microsoft products, for example).

Thunder II

Thunder II ($80) is a terrific spelling checker that works both in batch and interactive mode. It now works under MultiFinder (you go to the Control Panel and designate the applications you want Thunder to be active in, and the

bargain

Thunder menu title—a checkmark—appears in the menu bar when you run them).

There are two other improvements from earlier versions: you can now add items to Thunder's dictionaries and its word-count feature (which Arthur justifiably panned in the last edition) is now solid and consistent.

very good feature

I find Thunder indispensable for two reasons: its Glossary feature and its on-the-fly spell checking. The glossary lets you define misspellings that will be automatically fixed as you type them. So *hte* turns into *the* without your doing anything. You can turn *mf* into *MultiFinder*, *mb* into *Macintosh Bible*, and create a complete shorthand dictionary.

In interactive mode, Thunder watches as I type; I don't have to wait and check the entire document later. *(Isn't it amazing how much people's tastes differ? I'd rather be tortured by some CIA-trained goon than have a spelling checker flash or beep at me while I'm typing.—AN)*

Well, Arthur, you don't ever *have* to have interactive checking turned on (although you need it for the glossary feature). You can set the beep to any sound at any volume (independent of the System sound setting), or you can just have it flash silently, so I don't see the problem.

♦ Spelling Coach Professional

Spelling Coach Professional is the son of Spelling Coach and the grandson of MacLightning, one of the earliest Mac spelling checkers (that's where Thunder got its name—the reply to lightning). It has a large basic dictionary (licensed from Merriam-Webster) and also provides specialized legal and medical dictionaries that you can add terms to. Definitions are supplied for many of the words in main dictionary, and there's a built-in thesaurus.

The program works both interactively and as a batch checker. It's annoyingly slow in batch mode and once you've asked for suggestions, you can no longer type in your own choice. The interactive checker isn't as powerful as Thunder's;

it doesn't have a powerful Glossary feature and it doesn't check for capitalization mistakes or for for doubled words (like those—did you notice them?).

At $200, Spelling Coach Professional, is twice the price of Thunder, so you have to decide what's more important to you—Coach's thesaurus, dictionary with definitions and specialized medical and legal dictionaries or the lower price and better interactive checking of Thunder.

⚫ *Spellswell* (Scott Beamer)

One of the most popular spelling checkers, Spellswell works with a large number of applications (the current version, 2,2, costs $75). Options include medical and legal dictionaries (expensive at $100 each) and LookUp, a DA that allows you to look up the spelling of a word from anywhere you have access to the ⚫ menu. It will also paste a word selected from the dictionary into almost any program.

Spellswell checks homonyms, double words, capitalization and some punctuation (as well as spelling, of course), but it's only an average guesser. Its dictionary is 105,000 words.

⚫ *Spellswell* (AN)

Is it Spells Well or Spell Swell? Only its publisher knows for sure. Either way, their spelling checker is one of the better ones on the market.

I used Spellswell for a while but fell afoul of its inability to ignore special characters like dashes—which, as you can see, I use all the time—and foreign accents (I was writing a book on Central America and got tired of adding words like *Jos* to the dictionary because Spellswell couldn't deal with the *é* in *José*). But aside from that, this is an efficient, well-written program.

⚫ *Spellswell* (SZA)

One thing drives me nuts about Spellswell is the placement of the *Skip* and *Replace* buttons. If you select the

very bad feature

correct spelling of a word from the suggestions in the list, your first move will be to the button immediately below the list box—and that's the Skip button. So after you've typed in the correct spelling, you tend to tell Spellswell not to use it. (If you're working mostly from the keyboard, this isn't a big problem, since you can use keyboard commands.)

Spellswell's main problem, though, is the fact that it's not a DA; if you're not in MultiFinder, you have to quit the application to run it. Basically, Spellswell is an OK product, but when you can get something like Thunder (reviewed above) for just $5 more, why not do that?

♦ *Word Finder* (AN)

Word Finder isn't a spelling checker—it's a thesaurus in the form of a desk accessory. It's one of those products that makes you wonder how you lived without it.

very good feature

Word Finder's thesaurus contains 220,000 synonyms for 15,000 words. That sounds like a lot, but I'd like it to be even more extensive. Still, it's so useful to have a thesaurus as a DA that I hardly ever consult my paper one anymore.

bargain

Word Finder's operation is slick and obvious; it finds words fast and usually gives you a lot of them. If you need the manual to use this program, you don't know much about the Mac. At $60, this is a must-own product. *(I second that.—SZA)*

♦ *Dictionary Helper* (Larry Pina/AN)

bargain

Dictionary Helper is a file of 1313 words (how's that for a lucky number?) that normally aren't found in the dictionaries of spelling checkers. Instead of having to add these words to the dictionary one by one whenever you happen to use them in something you write—which can be an incredible nuisance—just open Dictionary Helper, run your spelling checker on it and add all the words at one sitting.

That's a tedious task but it's a lot better than doing it piecemeal. Some spelling checkers will let you import all the words in bulk, so you don't have to click *OK* or *Add* for each one.

Dictionary Helper adds less than 9K to your spelling checker's dictionary(ies) but it greatly reduces the number of "false alarms"—flagged words that are actually correct. Here's what it contains:

- contractions (with both straight and curly apostrophes)

- everyday abbreviations like Thurs, Apr, St, etc.

- the 26 letters of the alphabet as stand-alone words

- the names of the 50 states, their standard two-letter abbreviations, their capitals and other major US cities

- the names of foreign countries and large foreign cities

- common US first names and nicknames

- common US last names

- common brand names

- the names of some famous people (inevitably a very subjective—and incomplete—list)

In all the above categories, names are omitted when they're also words. So, for example, the first names list omits Art, Bill, Bob, Dawn, Frank, Pat, Ray, etc.; the cities and states lists omit Little Rock, New, South, etc.; and the days of the week abbreviations omit Sat and Sun.

We may have missed a few, or decided to err on the side of caution, but it doesn't matter—if words on this list are already in your spelling checker's dictionary, all that will happen is you won't be queried about them, or if you're importing the whole file in bulk, your dictionary(ies) will contain a few extra words.

Names are also omitted when they're in some other list. So, for example, Jan isn't in the list of first names because it's in the list of month abbreviations, and Lincoln, Jefferson and Madison aren't in the list of famous people's names because they're in the list of state capitals.

bargain

If you want to type out the file yourself, here it is (we don't envy you). For those of you who can't handle the boredom, we've included Dictionary Helper on the Third Edition of the Macintosh Bible Software Disks (described in Chapter 19). Feel free to add and/or delete words from the file to make it fit your particular needs.

aren't can't couldn't didn't doesn't don't hasn't haven't he'd he'll he's I'd I'll I'm I've isn't it'd it'll it's she'd she'll she's shouldn't should've that'd that'll that's there's they'd they're they've they'll wasn't we'd we'll we're weren't we've who've won't wouldn't would've you'd you'll you're you've

aren't can't couldn't didn't doesn't don't hasn't haven't he'd he'll he's I'd I'll I'm I've isn't it'd it'll it's she'd she'll she's shouldn't should've that'd that'll that's there's they'd they're they've they'll wasn't we'd we'll we're weren't we've who've won't wouldn't would've you'd you'll you're you've

Mon Mo Tues Tue Tu Thurs Thur Thu Th Fri Fr Sa Su Jan Feb Mar Apr Jun Jul Aug Sep Oct Nov Dec Ave Av bldg Blvd Cir Ct dept Dr hwy Ln Rd Sq St Ste Wy NW NE SW SE amp avg cc cm ext ft gal lb ml mm mph mpg pkg pp qt tel yd yr TV VCR UHF VHF Mr Mrs Ms Jr Sr II III IV MD DDS BA AB BS MA PhD meg megs MB cps dpi Hz MHz CP/M MS DOS PC el le la los las de des di von van der San Santa a b c d e f g h i j k l m n o p q r s t u v w x y z

AL AK AZ AR CA CO CT DE DC FL GA ID IL IA KS KY LA MA MD MI MN MS MO MT NE NV NH NJ NM NY NC ND OH OK PA PR RI SC SD TN TX UT VT VA VI WA WV WI WY

Montgomery Alabama Juneau Alaska Phoenix Arizona Arkansas Sacramento California Denver Colorado Hartford Connecticut Dover Delaware Tallahassee Florida Atlanta Georgia Honolulu Hawaii Boise Idaho Springfield Illinois Indianapolis Indiana Moines Iowa Topeka Kansas Frankfort Kentucky Louisiana Augusta Maine Annapolis Maryland Boston Massachusetts Lansing Michigan Minnesota Jackson Mississippi Jefferson Missouri Helena Montana Lincoln Nebraska Carson Nevada Concord Hampshire Trenton Jersey Fe Mexico Albany York Raleigh Carolina Bismarck Dakota Columbus Ohio Oklahoma Salem Oregon Harrisburg Pennsylvania Rhode Columbia Carolina Pierre Nashville Tennessee Austin Texas Utah Montpelier Vermont Richmond Virginia Olympia Washington Charleston Madison Wisconsin Cheyenne Wyoming Columbia Juan Puerto Rico

Angeles Chicago Francisco Philadelphia Detroit Dallas Houston Nassau Pittsburgh Baltimore Minneapolis Newark Anaheim Cleveland Diego Miami Seattle Tampa Bernardino Cincinnati Milwaukee Portland Orleans Antonio Lauderdale Tucson Memphis Jacksonville Paso Tulsa Toledo Oakland Albuquerque Omaha Charlotte Louisville Wichita Birmingham Norfolk Corpus Christi Fresno Rochester Petersburg Akron Jose Ana Shreveport Lexington Yonkers Dayton Arlington Vegas Lubbock Huntington Knoxville Riverside Spokane Chattanooga Wayne Syracuse Stockton Tacoma Worcester Greensboro Berkeley Cambridge Jolla

Afghanistan Albania Algeria Andorra Angola Argentina Australia Austria Bahamas Bahrain Bangladesh Barbados Belgium Belize Benin Bhutan Bolivia Botswana Brazil Bulgaria Burma Burundi Cambodia Cameroon Canada African Chad Chile Colombia Congo Costa

Rica Cuba Cyprus Czechoslovakia Denmark Dominican Ecuador Egypt Salvador Ethiopia Fiji Finland France Gabon Gambia Germany Ghana Greece Grenada Guatemala Guinea Guyana Haiti Honduras Hungary Iceland India Indonesia Iran Iraq Ireland Israel Italy Jamaica Japan Jordan Kenya Korea Kuwait Laos Lebanon Lesotho Liberia Libya Liechtenstein Luxembourg Madagascar Malawi Malaysia Maldives Mali Malta Mauritania Mauritius Monaco Mongolia Morocco Mozambique Nauru Nepal Netherlands Zealand Nicaragua Niger Nigeria Norway Pakistan Panama Paraguay Peru Philippines Poland Portugal Qatar Romania Rwanda Marino Saudi Arabia Senegal Sierra Leone Singapore Solomon Somalia Africa Spain Sri Lanka Sudan Swaziland Sweden Switzerland Syria Taiwan Tanzania Thailand Togo Tonga Trinidad Tobago Tunisia Uganda USSR SSR Volta Uruguay Vatican Venezuela Vietnam Samoa Yemen Yugoslavia Zaire Zambia Zimbabwe

Addis Ababa Ahmedabad Alexandria Algiers Amman Amsterdam Ankara Antwerp Athens Auckland Baghdad Baku Bandung Bangalore Bangkok Barcelona Barranquilla Beijing Beirut Belfast Belgrade Belo Horizonte Berlin Bern Bogotá Bogota Bombay Brisbane Brussels Bucharest Budapest Buenos Aires Cairo Calcutta Calgary Cali Canton Caracas Casablanca Chittagong Chongqing Cologne Copenhagen Cordoba Cuenca Dacca Damascus Delhi Dhaka Dnepropetrovsk Donetsk Dresden Dublin Düsseldorf Dusseldorf Edinburgh Edmonton Essen Frankfurt Fukuoka Geneva Genoa Glasgow Gorky Guadalajara Guayaquil Hague Haifa Hamburg Harbin Havana Helsinki Ho Chi Minh Hyderabad Ibadan Istanbul Jakarta Jerusalem Johannesburg Kanpur Karachi Kharkov Kiev Kinshasa Kobe Kuala Lumpur Kuilbyshev Lagos Lahore Paz Lausanne Leipzig Leningrad Liege Lima Lisbon Liverpool Lódz Lodz London Lyons Madras Madrid Managua Manchester Manila Marseilles Mecca Medellin Melbourne Milan Minsk Monterrey Montevideo Montreal Moscow Munich Nagoya Nanjing Nantes Naples Novosibirsk Odessa Osaka Oslo Ottawa Oxford Palermo Paris Peking Porto Alegre Prague Pusan Pyongyang Quebec Quezon Quito Rangoon Recife Rio Janeiro Riyadh Rome Rosario Rotterdam Saigon José Santiago Santo Domingo São Sao Paulo Sapporo Seoul Seville Shanghai Sheffield Shenyang Singapore Sofia Stockholm Stuttgart Surabaja Sverdlovsk Sydney Taipei Tashkent Tbilisi Teheran Tel Aviv Tianjin Tokyo Toronto Tripoli Tunis Turin Valparaiso Valencia Vancouver Venice Vienna Volgograd Warsaw Wellington Winnipeg Yokohama Zurich

Aaron Adam Alan Albert Alexander Alfred Alice Alicia Allen Allison Amanda Amber Amy Andrea Andrew Andy Angela Angie Ann Anna Anne Annie Anthony Arnie Arnold Arthur Artie Ashley Audrey Barbara Barry Beckie Becky Ben Benjamin Benjy Bennie Bernard Bernie Beth Betty Beverly Billy Bobby Bobbie Bonnie Bradley Brandi Brandon Brenda Brent Brian Bruce Caitlin Candace Candice Carl Carol Carole Carolyn Carrie Catherine Cathy Chad Charlie Charles Chelsea Cheryl Chris Christina Christine Christopher Christie Christy Corey Cory Courtney Craig Cynthia Dale Dan Dana Daniel Danielle Danny Darlene Darryl Dave David Deborah Denise Dennis Derek Derrick Diana Dick Don Donald Donna Doris Dorothy Douglas Dustin Earl Ed Eddie Edith Edward Edwin Elaine Eleanor Elizabeth Emily Eric Erica Erin Ernest Esther Ethel Eugene Eva Eve Evelyn Florence Frances Francis Franklin Fred Frederick Gail Gary George Gerald Gerry Glenn Gloria Gordon Greg Gregory Harold Harry Harvey Helen Henry Herbert Howard Jackie Jacob Jacqueline James Jamie Jane Janet Janice Jared Jason Jean Jeff Jeffrey Jennifer Jenny Jeremy Jerome Jerry Jesse Jessica Jessie Jill Jim Jo Joan Joanne Joe John Johnny Jon Jonathan Joseph Joshua Josie Joyce Judith Judy Julia Julie Juliet Juliette Justin Karen Karl Kate Katherine Kathleen Kathy Katie Keith Kelly Ken Kenneth Kevin Kim Kimberly Kristen Kristin Kyle Lacey Lakisha Larry Latoya Laura Lauren Lawrence Lenny Leonard Lewis Linda Lindsay Lisa Liz Lizzy Lois Lorraine Lou Louie Louis Louise Lori Lynn Lynne Maggie Malcolm Mandy Marcia Marc Marcus Margaret Maria Marianne Marie Marilyn

Marion Marjorie Mark Marsha Martha Martin Marty Marvin Mary Matt Matthew Maureen Megan Melissa Michael Michelle Mick Mickie Micky Mike Mildred Mollie Molly Monica Nancy Natalie Nathan Ned Nicholas Nick Nicole Norma Norman Pamela Patricia Patrick Paul Pete Peggy Peter Phil Philip Phillip Phyllis Rachel Ralph Randy Raymond Rebecca Renee Renée Rhonda Richard Richie Rick Ricky Rita Robert Roger Ron Ronald Ronnie Ronny Ross Russ Russell Ruth Ryan Sally Samantha Samuel Sandra Sarah Scott Sean Shane Shannon Sharon Sherry Shirley Stacey Stacy Stanley Stefanie Stephan Stephanie Stephen Steve Steven Stewart Stu Stuart Sue Susan Susie Suzanne Suzy Tammy Tara Ted Teddy Teri Theodore Theresa Thomas Tiffany Tim Timothy Tina Todd Tom Tommy Tony Tracy Travis Tricia Tyler Vic Victoria Virginia Walter Warren Wendy William Yvette Zachary

Smith Johnson Williams Jones Miller Davis Martin Anderson Wilson Harris Harrison Taylor Moore Thompson Clark Roberts Robertson Walker Robins Robinson Peters Peterson Allen Morris Morrison Wright Nelson Rodriguez Richards Richardson Lee Adams Mitchell Phillips Campbell Gonzalez Carter Garcia Evans Turner Collins Parker Edwards

Macintosh Mac Sony Motorola IBM DEC NEC GE Toshiba Panasonic Toyota Honda Acura Nissan Mazda Chevrolet Buick Pontiac Cadillac Oldsmobile Chrysler Plymouth Jeep Porsche Volkswagen Audi BMW Saab Volvo

Sigmund Freud Einstein Marx Engels Darwin Plato Socrates Isaac Newton Pascal Kant Ludwig Beethoven Johann Sebastian Bach Wolfgang Amadeus Mozart Brahms Mendelssohn Corelli Vivaldi Ellington Armstrong Parker Gillespie Coltrane Goodman Basie Pablo Picasso Orson Welles Humphrey Bogart Marlon Brando Hepburn Ali Shakespeare Milton Dickens Orwell Eliot Auden Yeats Whitman Kafka Dante Goethe Nietzsche Hugo Shelley Keats Byron Dylan Hemingway Fitzgerald Faulkner Reagan Nixon Kennedy Eisenhower Truman Roosevelt Hoover Coolidge Taft Monroe Adams Paine Gorbachev Stalin Lenin Mao Winston Churchill Adolph Hitler Napoleon Bonaparte Jesus Christ Moses Jehovah Mohammed Allah Buddha Confucius Luther Brahma Vishnu Shiva Krishna Rama

From the WetPaint clip-art collection.
Copyright © 1988–89 by Dubl-Click Software Inc. All rights reserved.

Chapter 11

Databases

Database basics

♠ database terms

Strictly speaking, a *database* is a collection of data and the program that creates and handles it is a *database manager*, but in common usage and in this chapter, *database* refers to the application and *database file* or *document* refers to the information itself.

esp. for beginners

The three main database terms you need to know are all analogous to an index-card system:

A *file* is an entire collection of information—it's the box you keep the index cards in.

A *record* is a grouping of related information, like a person's name, address and phone number—it's the index card.

A *field* is a single item of information in a record, like a name or an address—it's a line on the index card. The *field name* is the label you use to refer to the field—*First Name, Last Name,* etc. The *field data* is the information you put in the field—John, Smith, 123 Elm St, etc.

Other basic terms aren't so easily related to a pencil-and-paper system, since they take advantage of the computer's capabilities:

- A *calculated* or *computed* field is one that contains a formula that draws data from other fields in the same record. For example, you can have a calculated field called *Subtotal* that totals the numbers in a list of price fields and another calculated field called *Grandtotal* that takes the *Subtotal* and adds sales tax (another calculated field) to it.

- A *report* is printed information compiled from records in the database. This can be a simple list of information, like mailing labels, or it can include computations. These *report calculations* differ from calculated fields because they gather data from more than one record.

esp. for beginners

For example, while a calculated field might total all the items on a single invoice, a report might total your sales for the month.

- The meaning of *sorting* is pretty obvious—it lets you arrange things backwards or forwards alphabetically, numerically or chronologically. Most databases let you do *multi-level sorts,* so you might have your customer file sorted by zip code, and within each zip code, sorted by the customer's last name.

- *Selecting* is finding a group of records that match certain criteria. For example, you might look for all invoices that have outstanding balances more than 60 days old. Or you might select all customers in Colorado with total sales of $500 or more.

- A *multi-user* database is one that can be used on a network by more than one person at a time (although only one person can *change* a particular record at any given time).

✦ flat-file vs. relational databases

There are two main types of databases: *flat-file* and *relational.* The first, which are also known as *file managers*, create files that are independent of one another (some examples on the Mac are FileMaker, Panorama, File and Works), while relational databases (4th Dimension, Omnis, Double Helix) create files that can exchange information with each other.

With a relational database, you might set up three interrelated files: *Invoices, Customers* and *Inventory.* When you use the Invoice file to make up an order and enter the customer's last name, the rest of the relevant information (such as address and phone number) is filled in automatically, taken from the Customers file. At the same time, the Customers file is updated to note the additional purchases and the number of each item purchased is subtracted from the Inventory file.

If you don't need the power of a relational database, *don't* get one, because they're more expensive and much more difficult to set up. A real relational database is actually a specialized programming environment. It takes hours (and hours and hours) of designing and programming to get what you need. (And that's not counting the hours—that add up to *days*—that it will take to learn how to use the program.)

very
hot
tip

Don't let a program like Double Helix fool you—just because it takes a Mac-ish iconic approach to programming, it's still programming and anything beyond simple setups takes specialized skills. If you like buying programs that do more than you actually need at the time—giving yourself room to grow—then buy a fancier flat-file database.

important
warning

Database programs

FileMaker

There's no doubt that FileMaker is *the* flat-file database of choice for Mac users, and it has been for several years. Because of its lookup function, which lets data be automatically entered in a field based on the contents of a field in another file, it straddles the flat-file/relational line just well enough to keep its price down and be easy to learn, yet still be versatile enough to serve thousands of personal and business uses.

Here's an example of the lookup function: I use FileMaker to keep track of all the products I write about in this book. I have a separate file that lists all the vendors of those products. When I create an entry for Microsoft File in my *Products* file, I put *Microsoft* in as the vendor. FileMaker looks up *Microsoft* in my *Vendors* file and fills in the company's address and phone number. I don't have to enter that information five times for the five Microsoft products I put in the *Products* file— I only had to enter it once in the *Vendors* file. And I don't have to look to the *Vendors* file to get the information I need—it's right there in the *Products* file.

Why isn't this relational? Mostly because the information can only be pulled into, not sent out of, the active file. For example, if I rate Microsoft File software as only OK on a scale of Poor to Great, there's no way I can enter that rating in the *Products* file and have it sent to the *Vendors* file.

very good feature

FileMaker provides terrific touches like pop-up scrolling lists for fast data entry. You can also create dozens of different views for each file and make simple *scripts* that, accessed from a special menu, automate such operations as switching to a different view, sorting or searching for specific records, and printing.

FileMaker also has some glaring design problems. For example, in the Define Fields dialog box, fields are listed in order of creation and you can't change that order. When you have a lot of fields, this can make the one you're looking for hard to find. This is annoying in a $300 product.

things to come

Still, unless you need a relational database, FileMaker is the one to get—at least as I write this, it is. By the time you read this, you'll have to take a close look at FileMaker's upgrade, FileMaker Pro, and compare it to the new low-end database manager from Acius (the developers of 4th Dimension), which should also be out by then. (I thought they should call it *2nd Dimension*, but they called it *File Force* instead.)

♦ 4th Dimension

esp. for power users

Ah, 4th Dimension! Promise and potential stunted by lack of speed, miserable documentation and all-round disease of use. But that was the first version, and now there's 2.0, with more than reasonable speed and entirely new manuals. They're still pretty daunting, but then they have to cover a program that has all the power of the original version as well as over 300 new features.

4th Dimension 2.0 is easy-to-use on its basic level. Of course, if all you ever need is the basic level, you don't need 4th Dimension. Anything beyond basic is not for the faint-of-heart but if you know some programming (or you're willing to learn), 4th Dimension can be made to do some amazing things. For example, you can use it to create something that looks like a Macintosh stand-alone application, complete with buttons, checkboxes, scrolling lists and popup menus.

very good feature

If you're planning to develop specialized databases, 4th Dimension is a rich environment to work in. But if you need only one specialized database for your business, it will probably be more cost-effective to hire an outside 4th Dimension consultant to design and program it for you than to invest the hours you'll need to learn how to do it yourself.

very hot tip

♦ *Panorama* *(John Kadyk/Byron Brown)*

(It seems a little unfair to give Panorama so much more ink than other databases we talk about in this chapter, but I accidentally assigned the review to two people and got back two good reviews. They come at the program from slightly different angles, so here they both are.—AN)

JK: Panorama is a single-user, flat-file database with lookup capabilities for linking different files. It offers extensive and unusual processing and presentation features, including several of its own user-friendly innovations that ease data entry, reporting and form design.

One example is *clairvoyance.* This feature reads data as it is being typed in and finishes the entry for you when what you're typing matches data in existing records. (If clairvoyance guesses wrong, you can just continue typing over the guess.) You can also set fields for automatic first-letter capitalization or a variety of other "smart" default values.

very good feature

Panorama keeps your entire database file in RAM, which makes it very fast but limits the size of your files to the space you have in memory, not on disk. It's even worse under MultiFinder, where files are limited to the application memory size you've set for Panorama.

None of the changes you make to a Panorama file are saved to disk until you tell the program to do that. This lets

important warning

you change files and manipulate data, get the reporting results you want, then "revert to saved" with your original data unchanged. On the other hand, it means you can lose all the work you've done since the last save if your computer crashes (with programs like FileMaker, that automatically save everytime you move from one record to the next, all you can lose is your work on the current record).

Panorama's graphics mode provides advanced "draw" features like magnification, pixel-accurate drawing and cluster resizing (so that you can adjust one field's size and other fields will resize and reposition similarly). The FlashArt feature lets you link graphics to data, allowing different records to show different graphics. Panorama's graphic cookbook contains a wide selection of icons to include in designing forms. You can even set up buttons right on a data entry form that will execute your own macros.

Panorama's interface has many thoughtful touches. For example, when you select a draw tool from the tool palette in graphics mode, a pop-up title tells you what the tool does.

very bad feature

One annoyance is the overuse of submenus. To select certain commonly-used features, you have to select an item in one menu, drag across to the menu that pops up, select another item, drag across to a second pop-up menu and *then* select the feature you wanted. If your arm's vertical and horizontal tracking aren't accurate enough, you may never get to see, let alone select, the item you're after.

Given Panorama's strengths in other areas, I was surprised to find that the Print Preview mode won't tell you what page you're looking at, allow you to select a page number for display or scroll backwards through pages.

very good feature

Panorama has made a lot of data processing power accessible in one application. The manual is thorough, well-written and well laid-out. ProVue proved very accessible for tech support (although the techies varied in their expertise). It's a strong rival to FileMaker among flat-file databases. For small files on a single Mac, I'd probably choose Panorama for its superior reporting, graphics and data manipulation.

BB: Panorama's basic file structure is called a *data sheet;* it looks a lot like a spreadsheet, with each record forming a row and each field a column (thus the marketing slogan, "the database that thinks it's a spreadsheet"). This lets you see all your records at once, limited only by the size of your screen. As in Excel, the width of the fields can be altered simply by clicking on the field name and dragging the double-headed arrow left or right.

I'm presently using Panorama to invoice my customers (with three linked files), for my own financial records and those of my business, to keep track of book inventory for a small local publisher, and for a department store mailing list and mail merge for a local craft business. I love how easy it is to set up a new database and enter data, especially repetitive items like addresses or financial records.

Many of Panorama's tools are shown as icons on a palette. The top icon toggles you back and forth between a design window and the actual data window. In the design window, you can assign each field any of sixteen possible characteristics: data type (text, numeric, date, picture), number of digits, alignment, etc.

Clairvoyance (described in the previous entry) is especially useful for mailing lists when you have a few cities repeated over and over again or in financial records when you invoice or pay the same vendors over and over. Not only does it speed entry but it also reduces the chance of different spellings of the same name due to retyping. All of these features greatly help inputting. I can avoid having to use the shift key to capitalize words, select from preset values from the keyboard, tab through fields that seldom change, have the program fill in repeated names, and so on.

very good feature

There are excellent and easy methods for creating, editing and accessing macros. Though the form layout could certainly be simpler, it is effective and, with a little patience, you can create some very impressive results. You can create simple mail merges within the program but

very hot tip

I've found combining Panorama with Word works even better—exporting fields for a merge is a breeze.

I've yet to make use of many of the features in this program including storing graphics and sound, working with charts, doing extensive calculations with various summary levels, making cross tabulations, using color, etc. But I like Panorama because it gives me what I find most useful in a basic database program: transparency in construction with great flexibility and power in operation.

very good feature

I like to be able to control the many variables of accessing my information and be able to experiment with different approaches and methods and not feel that I'm wasting time. Panorama gives me all of this with its speed, its reliability, its shortcuts and its ability to undo. Provue's customer support is free, and I've found it to be prompt and helpful.

Although Panorama lists for $400, it's generally available for significantly less than that.

I'd strongly recommend this program for anyone looking for a fast, flexible database to store words, numbers, graphics and even sounds. It's simple enough for you to grasp immediately what the basic principles are and yet powerful enough to let you build quite sophisticated databases for working with information through the use of linked files, macros, multiple forms, extensive graphic capabilities within forms and fast, efficient data storage.

❤ Microsoft File

I like all of Microsoft's Macintosh programs, except this one. It was innovative (if slow) when it first came out, but it's hardly changed over the years.

very bad feature

Some of File's crippling limitations include: only being able to open one file at a time; only two views of your data in any one file; no search and replace; no special Mac-like features like buttons or pop-up fields; and no way to link files, even for basic lookup functions.

File lists for only $200, but you still probably won't get your money's worth from it.

✦ *Works' database module*

The database module in Microsoft Works is usable, but it's nothing great. Here are its major limitations:

- You're limited to only two views of your data—a spreadsheet-like list view and the form you design.

- Fields can't be any longer than the width of the window—no multi-line entries for, say, comments.

- The draw function you get in the word processor and spreadsheet modules isn't available in database module.

- The Report function has one of the ugliest, most counter-intuitive interfaces on the Mac.

Still, if you only need basic data records and mailing labels, the database is functional, and many of its design limitations can be overcome by merging the information into the word processor module where you can arrange things more attractively and use the draw function to add visual interest.

✦ *Address Book Plus and Dynodex* (Chris Allen)

The purpose of both of these programs is the same—to allow you to manage your address book/phone list on your Mac, and to print it out so you can take it anywhere. If you want to print to an ImageWriter, choosing between them is simple—only Address Book Plus can handle pin-feed paper. Your decision is also simple if you want double-sided pages in your address book (which cuts down on its weight)—only Dynodex can do this. Otherwise, choosing between these programs is difficult.

Dynodex is superbly easy to use, but you're limited to its printing formats. On the custom-perforated paper that comes with the program, you can print three sheets of 3.33" x 6.75", six-ring paper plus a 1.5" x 3.33" mini address book. You can also print a full 8.5" x 11" page, or two half-page sheets. All three options only allow you four lines per record.

Both programs have desk accessory modules that can dial any phone number on your list, but only Dynodex lets you edit your address and phone list from the DA.

Address Book Plus is much more difficult to use, but also more flexible. You can print on all kinds of paper, pin-feed or sheet-feed. You get some of the former with the program, which comes preset with formats for a variety of popular address-book binders.

Address Book Plus gives you many more options when printing—for example, you can choose which fields in a record you print—and you can configure it to your own page sizes. The software will also print envelopes, labels and pin-feed Rolodex cards.

The custom paper that Dynodex uses is slick, but refills are expensive (25¢ a sheet—although you can get six pages out of one sheet). You don't have to use custom paper for Address Book Plus, although the publisher does sell it. Address Book Plus sells for $130 with a leather binder and some sample paper, and for $100 without the binder. Dynodex sells for $100 with some sample paper and a six-ring plastic binder.

Retriever *(AN)*

This desk accessory database lets you access data while in another application, and is thus an ideal place to keep a phone list or the like. Actually, the more I think about it, the menu is the right place for lots of database files.

Retriever gives you all the normal database functions, like searching, sorting, selecting, hiding columns and printing. The publisher's commitment to this product seems genuine; they sent a free "maintenance" update (called version 1.01, it fixed a few minor bugs) to all registered users just a few months after the product was released.

Retriever only costs $90, but for $130 you can get DAtabase (see the next entry) which gives you about ten times more functionality.

♠ *DAtabase*

As its name implies, DAtabase is a database in the form of a desk accessory. It comes with both an application for designing and altering databases and a DA for entering and retrieving information. You can put pop-up menus in a field, use checkboxes for yes/no situations and install external commands like a time or date stamp or a phone-dialer.

DAtabase is almost terrific. Polished and expanded, it could rival FileMaker as a stand-alone database. The potential is there, but the program's not great yet.

There are minor design annoyances, like having to format each field separately for font, size and style. More importantly, DAtabase allows only fifty fields in a record—and the field count includes any labels you type on the screen. DAtabase's printing options are severely limited, although you can export information to a "real" database for printing.

♠ *FoxBASE 2.0* *(John Kadyk)*

This dBASE clone works on Macs and PCs, and comes in single- and multi-user versions. The Mac version is fast, handles relational tasks well and combines the power of dBASE with the Mac's user-friendly interface.

esp. for power users

You can select commands via pull-down menus or type them in à la PC. If you open the command window and then select commands from the menu, the command sequence that's generated appears at the same time in the window, where it can be edited, printed or saved as a program. This is an excellent way for aspiring dBASE/FoxBASE programmers to learn commands and syntax.

You can access up to ten files at once in separate windows. FoxBASE's "browse" mode lets you resize and reposition fields in relation to one another. The versatile FoxReport function uses a graphic interface to create reports or labels and lets you execute logical functions that relate data from different files.

Fox is a powerful, versatile tool for anyone who wants to run dBASE applications on the Mac, handle and interrelate large files or produce reports requiring complex manipulations of data. It's not an entry-level Mac program, though. For those who want user-friendliness and don't need a programmable relational database, FileMaker is a much easier program to learn and use.

General database tips

⚫ plan ahead

There are two things you should think about when you're designing a database—what information you need stored and how it will be organized or extracted. The first question is pretty straightforward but the second may require some thought.

As an obvious example, if you have a vast mailing list and want to print labels sorted by zip code, you'll need the zip to be in a separate field, not part of a larger address field. Or, if you send form letters to clients, you'll want a separate field for a title, so the Mr.'s will get *Mr.*, the Ms.'s will get *Ms.* and the Dr.'s will get *Dr.* in front of their names.

The opposite holds true as well—you don't need a separate field for data that's never going to be picked apart. The list of companies in Appendix B, for example, is from a FileMaker file where the address—street, city, state and zip—are all in one field.

⚫ special zip code formatting

important warning

Unless the database you're using lets you specify a special type of field for zip codes, make sure you make your zip code fields text and not numeric. A numeric field will strip off the leading zero from a zip like 07461 and will perform a subtraction on a zip like 07461-8976.

♠ duplicate database files before working on them
(Steve Michel)

It's good practice to keep at least two copies of any database file, and three of any active one. But if you're too lazy to do that, at least do yourself the favor of duplicating a database file before launching the application to work on it. Most databases keep their files on disk, and constantly update them while you work. So the file you had on disk when you began to work is not the file you'll return to when you're done.

very hot tip

This constant, automatic saving to disk is a good feature, since it means that you don't have to worry about losing any appreciable amount of work if the system crashes. But if you make some changes you later want to discard, you're stuck—unless you made a copy of the file before you started (or unless you're using a database like Panorama, which only saves when you tell it to).

♠ annotating databases (Steve Michel)

One of the drawbacks of most Mac databases is that they don't give you a good way to document what you're doing as you do it. For simple files, this isn't much of a problem. But for more complex ones, it's easy enough to forget what a particular report, sort or calculation is supposed to do. I have one file I use at least three times a week, but recently when I went to make some changes to it, I lost a couple of hours' work because I hadn't made extensive notes while I was designing it.

Keeping notes is particularly important if you're designing an application for someone else to use, even if it's just a mailing list. They'll help you to explain it to the person using it, and to yourself when you go to modify it weeks or months later.

It's most convenient to make the notes in a desk accessory. I use Mockwrite or miniWRITER, which are nice text editors. Another good choice is Acta, the outlining desk accessory.

✦ multilevel sorts

Some databases only let you sort on a single field at a time. If you need a multilevel sort (for example, records arranged by zip code, by city within zip code and by last name within cities), just do three sorts in reverse order of importance. In other words, in the example above, you'd sort *first* by last name, next by city and *last* by zip code. (This may not work with all databases, but it will with most.)

FileMaker tips

✦ a larger-type Help file

The Help file that Claris provides for FileMaker is itself a FileMaker file. So once you know how to use FileMaker, you can easily change the size of the Help file's window, or the size of the text in any of its fields.

✦ bypassing the Delete alert

When you use *Delete* to remove a record from your file, FileMaker asks you if you're sure you want to delete it. This is a normal Mac touch—giving you a chance to change your mind before an irreversible operation is performed. But if you're *sure* you want to delete the record, Option ⌘ E will avoid the dialog box.

✦ loose fingers sink databases (John Kadyk)

When choosing *Delete* from the menu, be careful not to select *Delete Multiple* by accident. This an easy way to delete your whole file (as we've done).

✎ selecting from a list of values

When a field is formatted to display a list of values for you, you don't have to scroll through the list to find the one you want. There are two alternatives. One is to use the ⬆ and ⬇ keys to move through the list. The other is to start typing the word you want; if it's in the list, it will be highlighted. As soon as that happens, you can stop typing and hit ⟨Return⟩—you don't have to finish typing the whole name.

shortcut

A list of values is only a *suggestion* list—you can always type something else in the field instead, or edit an entry that was made from the list. If you want the field to return to a blank state, just select the information in it and hit ⟨Delete⟩.

✎ default field entries

The *List* option lets you pop up a list of suggested entries for any field. But let's say you have a field that's going to be the same in most records (say, your local area code). In that case, use the *Auto-enter Data* option in the Entry Options dialog box. This puts the suggested item in the field automatically (you can change it in any record where it doesn't apply).

shortcut

✎ to relookup a single record

When you've changed information in a file that's used as a lookup (say, you've updated names and addresses that are looked up by your invoicing file), the *Relookup* command in the Edit menu updates all the records in your file. This wastes time when you only need to update the record you're looking at.

To force an update for only the current record, move to the field that does the lookup. Make a minor change to it—say, add a space and then delete it. When you move out of the lookup field, the "new" information in it will force a lookup and the rest of the record will be updated.

shortcut

⬥ getting today's date

FileMaker gives you three ways to insert today's date: you can use ⌘ - (or the *Paste Date* command in the edit menu) to insert the current date into a field, you can type *today* in a formula, or you can type a double slash (//) in a layout. (You'll always see the double slash on the screen, but in Preview mode and in printouts, the current date is substituted).

important warning

But be aware that while both the *today* and // give you dates that change along with the calendar, the date you enter with *Paste Date* is static—so it remains the same as the date you first inserted it, no matter when you subsequently open the file.

⬥ resizing in one direction

To change the size of an object in Layout in only one direction (just vertically or just horizontally), hold down Option while you drag on the object's handle.

⬥ fast field label styling

shortcut

When you use the Text tool in Layout to type field labels or enter other text, you'll get the currently selected font, size and type style. Don't tediously reset these options; it's faster to just copy and paste an existing label that has the settings that you want and then edit it.

⬥ overriding grids and magnets

To move something in Layout without the movement being affected by the Grid or the magnetized T-squares, you don't have to turn them off—just hold down ⌘ while dragging.

⬥ searching and sorting repeating fields

FileMaker's special repeating field option (which gives you multiple entries in a single field) is great, but it's sometimes also confusing. For example, if you *sort* by a repeating field, only its first entry is sorted on. But if you *search* for something in a repeated field, all its lines are searched.

❡ cancelling repeating fields

If you change your mind and don't want a field to be a repeating field, you don't have to delete it and start all over again. Just go to Layout, select the repeating field, choose *Repeat* from the Format menu, and type the number *1* in the dialog box that appears.

shortcut

❡ changed field names in formulas

If you change the name of one of your fields and it's used in a calculation in some other field, you don't have to go back and change the name in the formula—it's changed automatically.

❡ adding record numbers

If you use the *Auto-enter serial number* option when you're defining a field, each new record gets a number one higher than the previous record. Unfortunately, when you import records from another source, numbers aren't assigned in such a serial field—it stays blank.

If you've imported a few hundred (or more) records, you certainly don't want to manually enter numbers for all them. Here's the shortcut:

Use a spreadsheet to create a column of numbers as long as you need for your records. (Use 500 rows for 500 records.) Put a 1 (or whatever your starting number is) in the first cell and in the second cell use a formula that adds 1 to the number in the cell above. Copy this formula down through as many rows as you need—you'll wind up with column of numbers in increments of one.

shortcut

Save the spreadsheet as text and then go back to FileMaker. Use the *Input From* command to insert the list of numbers directly into the serial field (make sure you specify *update existing records* instead of *add new records*). If you care which numbers go into which records, sort or otherwise arrange the records in FileMaker before you do the import.

Then go to the *Auto-enter serial number* option and set the serial number to one greater than the highest serial number you imported, so that new records will be numbered correctly.

● *alphabetizing by last name*

FileMaker lets you alphabetize by last name even when you've got both first and last names in a single field. There are a few different approaches, depending on the complexity of your problem—just how many separate words might be in the name field, for example.

In every case, though, you'll be defining a new field—*LastName*—that you'll eventually sort on. *LastName* doesn't have to be a part of any layout, so it won't clutter up your screen or printout; as long as it exists, you'll be able to sort by it.

If all your *Name* fields contain just first and last names, the *LastName* field can contain a simple formula that takes the length of the entry in the *Name* field, subtracts from it the position of the space, and uses the *right* function to give you all the letters that follow the space:

LastName=

right(Name,length(Name)-position(Name," ",1))

esp. for power users

You need a more complicated approach when you have to deal with the possibility of a three different names (maybe a middle name or initial) in the *Name* field. The *if* formula below takes care of that by using nested position functions to start the search for a possible second space after the position of the first space found:

if(position(Name," ",position(Name," ",1)+2) >1
    ,right(Name, Length (Name)-position (Name," ",position
    (Name," ",1)+2)),right (Name,Length (Name)-position
    (Name," ",1)))

With this formula, *Jones* would be extracted from *John Paul Jones* and *Fields* from *W. C. Fields*.

● *formatting phone numbers*

Unfortunately, FileMaker can't define a field to contain a phone number format—(201) 555-1234 or 201/555-1234.

But you can "read" the phone number from the field in which it's entered, format it the way you want it, and put the result in another field.

First, define a numeric *PhoneEnter* field. Then, no matter how the phone number is typed in—with or without dashes, slashes or parentheses, the field is going to store only the digits (2015551234, for example), because all the non-numeric characters will be stripped out.

Next, you make another field, *ShowPhone*, to display the phone number. Make it a calculated field and use this formula to get the numbers from the PhoneEnter field and format them:

ShowPhone=

"(" & left(PhoneEnter,3) & ")" & middle(PhoneEnter,4,3)
    &"-" & right(PhoneEnter,4)

This puts parenthesis around the area code and a hyphen after the exchange. If you want the area code separated from the rest of the number by a slash, use the formula instead:

left(PhoneEnter,3)&"/"&middle(PhoneEnter,4,3) &"-" &

    right(PhoneEnter,4)

If you want to set up the formula to allow for the possibility that some phone numbers will be entered without area codes, use an *if* statement to check the number of digits in the PhoneEnter field:

ShowPhone=

if(length(PhoneEnter)>9,"(" & left(PhoneEnter,3) & ")" &
    middle(PhoneEnter,4,3) & "-" &
    right(PhoneEnter,4),left(PhoneEnter,3) & "-" &
    right(PhoneEnter,4)

❡ *splitting and combining repeating field entries*

This is my favorite FileMaker tip. In fact, it's probably my favorite application-specific tip in this whole book. Claris' technical support helped me with a problem I was having in a file, and this technique is the result.

Here's the problem: you've designed a database with a repeating field (say, for phone numbers—work, fax and home). Now you want those three items of information in three separate fields. (Or you have the opposite problem: you have separate fields that you want combined as entries into a single repeating field.) Here's how you handle the first problem:

First, export the information from the repeating field into a text file. Use the *Output to* command in the File menu, and click the *Text only* and *Unformatted* buttons. Save only the information from the Phones field into this export file.

Next, open the file in Word. You'll see each group of phone numbers on its own line, with boxes between the phone numbers:

```
555-6985□555-8721□555-3287
555-2378□555-1245□555-3641
555-1286□555-3491□555-6398
555-3678□555-9743□555-9312
```

The box is the character that FileMaker uses to separate items of information in repeating fields. Since the Tab character is used to separate information in *separate* fields, you have to replace each box with a Tab. But don't do it manually—let Word do the work.

The box character has an ASCII code of 29. Since Word can search and replace based on ASCII codes, this is a cinch. Use the *Replace* command and in the *Find what* box, type *^29*. (You get the caret, ^, with [Shift] [6]). In the *Change to* box, type *^t* for [Tab]. Click the Change All button to make the changes.

Next save the file. (Since it was a text-only file when you opened it, Word defaults to text-only when you save it, which is just what you need.)

Now, back to FileMaker. Use the *Input from* command in the File menu and select the text file you altered in Word. When the Input dialog box appears, select the three new phone fields that you want the information stored in. Click the *Text file* and *Update current records* buttons, then click Input. (This illustration shows how the dialog box would look if these phone fields were the only ones in the file.)

```
┌─────────────────────────────────────────────────────────────┐
│  Field List                          Input Order             │
│  ┌──────────────────┐  ┌──────────┐  ┌──────────────────┐    │
│  │ Phones        🔼 │  │ Move All │  │ WorkPhone     🔼 │    │
│  │ WorkPhone        │  └──────────┘  │ Fax              │    │
│  │ Fax              │  ┌──────────┐  │ HomePhone        │    │
│  │ HomePhone        │  │  Move    │  │                  │    │
│  │                  │  └──────────┘  │                  │    │
│  │                  │  ┌──────────┐  │                  │    │
│  │                  │  │  Input   │  │                  │    │
│  │                  │  └──────────┘  │                  │    │
│  │               🔽 │  ┌──────────┐  │               🔽 │    │
│  └──────────────────┘  │  Exit    │  └──────────────────┘    │
│                        └──────────┘                          │
│  "Breakup" is a:                     Use it to:              │
│  ◉ Text file (tabs)                  ○ Add new records       │
│  ○ BASIC file (commas)               ◉ Update current records│
│  ○ SYLK file                                                 │
└─────────────────────────────────────────────────────────────┘
```

All the information that used to be in the Phones field is now split among the three new fields.

If you want to take information from separate fields and combine them into repeating fields, you do basically the same thing, but change all the Tabs that will be in the text file into the special code 29 box character. Just reverse the information in the Replace dialog box—put ^t in the *Find what* box and *^29* in the *Change to*.

Works database tips

These tips apply to Works 2. Also see pp. 687–88 and 889–95.

⬥ date and time

You can enter the date into any field by pressing ⌘ D and the time by pressing ⌘ T.

shortcut

⬥ ditto fields

To enter the same information into a field as is in the equivalent field in the previous record, just press ⌘ " . Think of it as *ditto* (″) to make it easier to remember (the ″ is on the same key, but you don't need to use the Shift key for this command).

shortcut

Remember that if you're using Quote Init, or if you've reassigned the quote keys using QuicKeys or some similar program, you'll have to turn the curly quotes off for this command to work.

☀ computed fields

If the results of the calculation in a computed field don't seem to be turning out the way you expect, you may be forgetting something called *priority of operations*. See the entry called that in the spreadsheet chapter.

(By the way, these are normally called *calculated* fields, but Works calls them *computed* fields.)

☀ back and forth

shortcut

To switch back and forth between the Form view and the List view, you can do any of the following things:

- choose the *Show List / Show Form* command (on the Format menu)
- press ⌘ L
- doubleclick in any empty area of the Form window
- doubleclick in the space in front of a record in the List view to go directly to that record in the Form view
- doubleclick in an empty cell in the List view to go to the currently selected record

☀ pasting from the List view

very good feature

There's a slightly unexpected result when you copy from the database's List view and paste into the word processor or spreadsheet, but it's done on purpose and is very useful. The field names will appear at the top of the pasted columns, even though you can't select them when copying.

☀ doubleclicking on fields

esp. for beginners

In the Form view, fields have two distinct parts: the field name and the field data.

Doubleclicking in the field name area lets you rename the field; it's the same as using the *Change Field Name* command on the Edit menu. Doubleclicking in the field data area opens the Field Attributes dialog box; it's the same as using the *Set Field Attributes* command on the Format menu.

In other words:

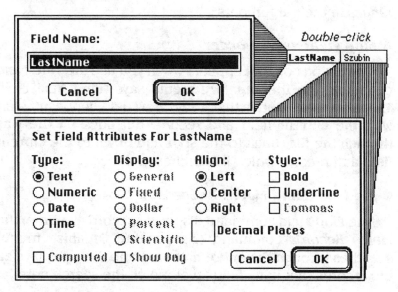

❡ deleting fields

If you use *Cut, Clear* or Delete when a field is selected, the field data, not the field itself, is affected. The only way to get rid of a field is by using the *Delete Field* command (on the Edit menu).

❡ multilevel sorts

Works' spreadsheet lets you sort by up to three columns at a time but its database allows only a single-level sort. To get a multilevel sort, see the entry with that title in the section above on general database tips.

❡ A is for arrange

⌘ S is for Save, so it can't be for Sort. Works uses ⌘ A instead (to remember the command, think of *arranging*).

✺ using spreadsheet functions

**very
hot
tip**

Many of the spreadsheet functions can be used in the database's computed fields. For example, you can use the *Average* function to construct a formula that averages the contents of other fields in the record. The only spreadsheet functions that can't be used are the ones that require cell *ranges* in their arguments.

✺ Find Field search order

**important
warning**

The dialog box that appears when you use the *Find Field* command (on the Organize menu) says "Find Next Field That Contains:" Notice that it says *next* field. It doesn't start with the current field and record, but goes all the way through the file, back to the start and down to the current field and record, which it searches last.

✺ Find Field and Match Records

The *Find Field* command displays a record at a time; the *Match Records* command (also on the Organize menu) searches through the entire database and then displays all the records that have fields that match the search criteria.

Neither command is case-sensitive—that is, they pay no attention to upper- and lowercase (search for *Mac* and you'll find *mac* and *MAC* as well). Nor do they care about whole words (search for *Mac* and you'll find *Mac, Macintosh, machine, Machiavellian* and *stomach*).

✺ Record Selection command

Neither *Find Field* nor *Match Records* is field-specific—that is, they'll both find records that contain *John* no matter what field *John* is in. So you'll get first names of *John*, last names of *Johnson*, addresses of *St. John Street*, etc.

But the *Records Selection...*command (also on the Organize menu) lets you specify which field Works should look in. In addition, it lets you decide whether the search criteria (*John*) should be a whole word, part of a word, at the beginning of a word or whatever.

❡ stuck in subfiles

When you're viewing and/or working with a subfile created by the *Record Selection* command, it's hard to tell the difference between that subfile and the main "parent" file. To find out which you're in, look in the Organize menu. If *Record Selection* is checked, you're working with a subfile; if *Show All Records* is checked, you're not.

❡ reports and selections

If you're working with a subfile created by the *Record Selection* command and you start a new report, the report initially includes only that subfile. To include all the records in the report, use the *Show All Records* command (on the Organize menu) while the Report window is active. (The main database window will continue to display only the selected records.)

very
hot
tip

If you use the *Record Selection* command while the Report window is active, the selection rules you create affect only the report. The main database window is independent of rules you create for a report.

❡ totaling on the first character

The original version of Works (1.0) had a command in its TotalsPage menu named *Total-1st Char Field*. The minor improvement in Works 2.0 changed it to *Take a sub-Total on 1st Char*. Nice try, Microsoft (*A* for effort, no change in the overall grade).

This command creates subtotals in a report when the first character of a field changes instead of when the entire field contents change. This means you could do a subtotal for a column that contains stock part numbers and have the subtotals for all the parts with numbers in the 100's, then those with numbers in the 200's, etc. (Normally (without the *1st char* option) you'd get a separate subtotal every time the field contents changed—so you'd have a subtotals for 101, 102, 103 and so on.)

❡ *AND and OR hierarchy*

esp. for power users

When you use multiple selection rules in the Record Selection dialog box and you're mixing ANDs and ORs as connectors between the rules, you have to be careful how you arrange the rules.

For example, if you're looking for customers who owe you more than $200 and also either live out-of-state or have owed the money for more than 60 days, you can't use the following rules:

Amount is greater than 200

AND   Invoice Date is less than 10/01/88

OR   State is not equal to NY

because Works will interpret them to mean:

[Amount is greater than $200 AND Date is less than 10/01/88]

OR

[State that is not NY]

In other words, you'll wind up with all the records that don't have NY addresses regardless of what the customer might owe.

The AND connector for a rule always takes priority over the OR connector in a list of rules. Unfortunately, you can't just use parentheses to circumvent this, as you can in a spreadsheet or database formula. Instead, you'll have to redo the rules as follows:

Amount is greater than 200

AND   Date is less than 10/01/88

OR   Amount is greater than 200

AND   State is not equal to NY

These rules will be interpreted as:

[Amount is greater than 200 AND Date is less than 10/01/88]

OR

[Amount is greater than 200 AND State is not equal to NY]

Chapter 12

Spreadsheets

General spreadsheet tips

❡ what's a spreadsheet?

A spreadsheet is a grid of *cells* arranged in rows and columns. You put numbers in the cells and have the spreadsheet perform mathematical operations on them.

esp. for beginners

Picture a column that represents your monthly budget, with a cell each for rent or mortgage, utilities, food and so on. Then picture twelve of those columns, one for each month of the year, next to each other. A spreadsheet can calculate the total for each *column*—your budget for the month—and/or the total for each *row*—how much you spent (or will spend) in a single category for the year. It can also calculate the average amount you spent in any category or month.

Even in this simplest of spreadsheet scenarios, you could use the *what if* capability of a spreadsheet. Change a number or two *(if I move, my rent goes up, but utilities are included in the new rent, so that figure goes down)* and see what happens to your budget.

The great strength of spreadsheets is that if you change a number in one spot, everything that needs to be recalculated as a result of that change is done automatically. That's what gives the spreadsheet its great power and popularity.

very good feature

Want to figure out how large a mortgage you can afford at a various rates of interest? Or see how much you're *really* paying over the life of that car loan? Would you like an electronic checkbook so you can sort things into categories for expenditure subtotals? Spreadsheets can do all this.

Most spreadsheets also contain charting capabilities to turn your numbers into pictures, but if you're not in a business environment, you'll need minimal charting capabilities at most. *[I find charting very useful for all kinds of purposes, not just business ones.—AN]*

❡ Excel

Excel is fast and handles all sorts of charts. Its macro editor not only can speed up repetitive tasks but also turns

very good feature

Excel into a programming environment where you can design spreadsheets for other, less sophisticated users—even adding dialog boxes to help them out.

Version 2.2a (the latest as of this writing) includes a bewildering number of keyboard commands—but that's OK, you only have to use the ones you need. The disappointment is in how Microsoft chose to implement its keyboard control of menus (for people who don't want to reach for the mouse in the middle of something else).

Basically, instead of making Excel on the Mac look like Word on the Mac (and other Mac programs), they chose to make it look like Excel on the PC—so when you activate the menu bar (from the keyboard; you don't need to do that if you're using the mouse), a letter in each menu title is underlined (*File, Edit, Formula*) to indicate which key you use to pop it down. This is both aesthetically and philosophically unpleasing.

Excel is still far and away the most popular of Mac spreadsheets, partly because it has a lot of power, and partly just because it's *been* the most popular of Mac spreadsheets for a long time and lots of people are used to it.

new features of Excel 2.2

**important
warning**

Microsoft jumped directly from Excel 1.5 to Excel 2.2—not passing Go but collecting well over $200. Excel 2.2 ($400) has everything 1.5 had and then some; just the updated manual pages in the reference section fill the original binder to overflowing. *[But make sure you get 2.2a; it fixes some sixteen bugs that were in 2.2.—AN]*

Here are some of 2.2's features:

**very good
feature**

- You can change the font, size and style of individual cells.

- You can change the height of rows.

- You can control *everything*—menus, dialog boxes, cell outlines, number formatting (and on and on)—from the keyboard.

- There's a status bar at the bottom of the screen that keeps you posted as to what's going on; it says *ready* when it's waiting for you to do something and it functions as an automatic help screen too. It describes more fully what, say, the menu command you're pausing on will do. (You can turn this status bar off, and you'll probably want to if you're working on a small screen.)

- A separate window is available for each cell into which you can type notes (an explanation of how a convoluted formula works, for example). The notes don't print when you print the spreadsheet (unless you want them to).

- 2.2 has nearly 200 more macro functions than 1.5.

- The Excel Startup document is a new feature; if you put it in the system folder, it opens automatically when you launch Excel. (There's a tip on it in the Excel tips section below.)

- The Info window displays information about the currently selected cell. It lets you see the cell's name, its contents (in both formula and value views) and its notes all at the same time.

Wingz

Wingz (from Informix) is another major contender in the Mac spreadsheet marketplace. It survived nearly two years of prerelease hype that included spaceships, giveaways and Leonard Nimoy hawking it on videotapes.

Wingz has two things that are better than what you'll find in Excel: a scripting language that lets you develop customized applications, and powerful charting capabilities—3D charts, for example. This power, of course, comes at a price—the scripting requires more programming ability of you than Excel's macros, and the charts, though easy to set up, draw pretty slowly on the screen. (Although Wingz is a speed demon on spreadsheet calculations.)

Because Wingz' charts are one of its most powerful features, Informix has been pushing the program as a tool for presentations—they probably encounter fewer head-to-head comparisons with Excel that way.

Wingz costs $400, and *may* be worth it if you need super-duper charts. (But for another reason why it may not be, see Arthur's quick take on Wingz on page 38.) Excel is easier to use for basic functions, and it's spawned so many consultants, support products and user groups that you'll always have someplace to turn for help. Full Impact, MacCalc and even Works are also worth considering, so read on.

⬤ *Full Impact* (AN)

Full Impact 2.0 (from Ashton-Tate) doesn't make the same mistake that Wingz did (see page 38)—that is, it recognizes the existence of Excel and lets you import your existing Excel spreadsheets without making you jump through hoops to do it. I did just that and played with Full Impact for a bit. It's similar enough to Excel (and to the standard Mac interface) to make it virtually effortless to learn; there's a lot of new power as well, but it all seems very intuitive and easy to figure out.

very good feature

Full Impact has some commands that I've been dying for in Excel ever since I started using it—⌘B boldfaces the contents of a cell and ⌘I italicizes them. Instead of Excel's primitive, clunky cell borders, it has a full-bore drawing function with lines, rectangles, rounded rectangles, ovals, etc.

very good feature

Like Wingz, Full Impact has 3D graphs. It has customizable icon bars on which you can put commonly used functions, so you can get to them with just one click. It lets you integrate data, charts, text, drawings and graphics all in one document.

The manual looks good, and even seems to have a decent index! Unfortunately, as is the case with many manuals, it smells—I mean, literally. I don't know if it's the vinyl cover or the ink they used, but I can't bend over it for more than a few seconds without getting a slight headache. If it weren't for that, I would have already used Full Impact a lot more.

I'm putting the manual out in the sun a lot, and when the smell is gone, I'll spend some more time with the program and give you an updated report. But from my first glance, it looks like it might be a winner.

🍎 *Works' spreadsheet module*

The spreadsheet module in Microsoft Works is all most people need for their personal work; it's even enough for most business tasks. It has over a million cells (you'll use a lot since you can't link separate spreadsheets) and all the basic mathematical, statistical and financial functions. It lets you format cells various ways, has cell notes, and even provides basic charting.

The most frustrating lack is its inability to handle text. You can enter text, but you can't manipulate it at all—there are no text functions. In fact, the spreadsheet considers a cell with text in it a blank cell—so you can't even write a formula that says *if the contents of cell C34 is "yes" then....*

🍎 *MacCalc*

This gem of a program fills the bill for lots of personal spreadsheet users. It has no charting capabilities and is small (999 rows by 124 columns) compared to Excel, Wingz and Full Impact, but it's incredibly fast. It lets you assign differ-ent fonts and styles to cells and even has cell notes. All this for just $140. If you need a basic spreadsheet program but have no use for Works' other modules, MacCalc is the answer.

bargain

🍎 *101 Macros for Excel* (Steve Schwartz)

If you don't have the time or patience to learn how to create macros for yourself, you can buy canned macros (sort of like clip art for a spreadsheet). Individual Software's 101 Macros for Excel range from the simple and obvious (removing all borders, or removing the outline from a selection) to the interesting (charting a biorhythm or creating a recalculation timer) to the supremely useful (creating a new database or defining hot spots). All in all, they can vastly simplify your day–to–day work with Excel.

very good feature

Each of these macros can be executed in two or three different ways. First of all, they can be accessed the way any Excel macro can, with the *Run...* command on Excel's Macro menu. Secondly, almost half of them can also be called up with a preassigned [Option][⌘] combination.

Finally, you can run the Macro Launcher (itself one of the 101 macros) by pressing [Option][⌘]. This produces the dialog box below. Each macro has a short name (one to three characters long); you simply type it into the dialog box to run the macro. (The one in the illustration, *tg*, toggles grid lines on and off.)

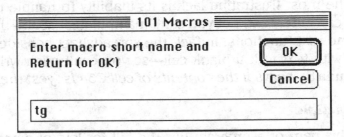

101 Macros for Excel gives you a quick reference guide that lists each macro's [Option][⌘] key and its short name. If the manual's not handy, there's even a macro that will recreate this list for you as an Excel worksheet.

The excellent manual keeps things simple by describing each macro in the same, organized manner. Since each macro description is completely self–contained, after reading the first four chapters of the manual (37 pages), you can skip immediately to the macros that interest you. A few of my personal favorites swap two columns (or two rows), toggle between two hot spots, save all worksheets and change zeros to blanks.

Admittedly, several of the macros—most of those for formatting, alignment and borders, for example—could easily be created using Excel's macro recorder. Others, however, would require fairly sophisticated macro programming skills. So even if you're a macro hot-shot, this package will save you an enormous amount of work—both in programming effort and in efficiency gained from using the macros. After all, why reinvent the wheel simply because you can?

If you're a macro novice, a careful examination of these macros may be all you need to push you into the ranks of those who "build their own." What better place to start than with 101 carefully debugged and commented examples? But whether or not you ever write a macro of your own, this excellent package adds enough functionality to Excel to justify its purchase by virtually any user.

⬤ *Excellence and Cobb Group books* (AN)

Getting the most out of Excel takes a lot of advice and one way to get it is by subscribing to *Excellence,* a journal of Excel tips and tricks published by the Cobb Group. It costs $50 a year so you'll only want to do that if you make fairly extensive use of Excel; if you do, Excellence should be a real help. The Cobb Group also publishes as number of books on Excel.

General spreadsheet tips

⬤ *printing large worksheets* (DC/AN)

When you're printing a very large spreadsheet, use forced page breaks to divide it into sections of related data, rather than just letting the program insert page breaks arbitrarily. This makes the printout easier to read, since logically related information is grouped together on the same page, without irrelevant information to distract you.

This approach also lets you print out selected portions of the spreadsheet simply by specifying the pages you want in the Print dialog box. In Excel, you do that with the *Set Print Area* command. (To remove a print area you've set up, choose *Define Names* from the Formula menu and delete *Print_Area.)* In Works, you simply select an area before you print, and only it is printed.

✤ displayed vs. stored numbers

In a spreadsheet, the format you set for numbers only affects how they appear, not their actual stored values. If the number in a cell is 1.457 and you've formatted the cell for two decimal places, you'll see 1.45 or 1.46—some spreadsheets truncate numbers and some round them. In either case, the spreadsheet remembers that the number you entered in the cell is actually 1.457 and uses that number in any calculation.

important
warning

This can lead to some confusion. For example, you might have the numbers 1.23, 9.18 and 8.32 in three cells, which add up to 18.73. If you've formatted all four cells for no decimal places, what you'll see is 1 + 9 + 8 = 19. Remember this when you see calculations that don't seem to be coming out right.

✤ turn off curly quotes

important
warning

If you use a utility like Quote Init or SmartKeys to automatically substitute curly quotes for straight quotes, turn it off when you're working in a spreadsheet. Spreadsheets accept only straight quotes in formulas.

✤ save time with Manual Calculation

shortcut

Since the automatic calculation mode in most spreadsheets recalculates the entire spreadsheet each time you change an entry (or create a new one), it can waste a lot of time. The shortcut? Switch to manual calculation, make all your changes, then either manually calculate the spreadsheet or turn automatic calculation back on.

This isn't always necessary in Excel, since it only recalculates the necessary parts of the spreadsheet—but if you're working in cells that are part of a large calculation (involving many other cells or linked worksheets), using manual calculation still speeds things up,

✤ relative vs. absolute cell references

When you refer to a cell in a formula, the spreadsheet thinks of it *relatively*—that is, as the cell that's three columns to the left and two rows above this cell (or wherever it is). This is so the formula will still work if you copy it to a new cell (a sum, for example, will add up the cells above it, rather than the cells above the cell where the formula was copied from).

esp. for
beginners

Sometimes, though, you don't want cell references to change when you move a formula—you want them to be identified by their actual, *absolute* locations *(A1, 4F* or whatever). To do that, put dollar signs before both the column and the row—for example, *4F.* You can also make just the column, or just the row, absolute—for example, *A$2* or *$B14.*

You can type the dollar signs in yourself, but most programs also have a command that does it. In Works, it's the *Absolute Cell Ref* command in the Edit menu; in Excel, it's the *Reference* command in the Formula menu.

♠ *priority of operations*

When you create a formula for a spreadsheet cell, you have to be careful how you arrange the mathematical operations. Some operations have a higher priority than others, and are performed first no matter where they are in the formula. If there are multiple operations of equal priority, they're performed left to right.

5+3+2 is a simple example. Because all the operations are additions and are thus of equal priority, the calculation is done from left to right, and the result is 10. Addition and subtraction are also of equal priority, so 5–3+2 is also calculated left to right, with the result being 4 (if it were calculated right to left, the result would be zero).

Multiplication and division are of equal priority to each other but are of higher priority than addition or subtraction. So 5+3*2 gives you a result of 11, not 16, because the multiplication is performed before the addition.

You can circumvent the natural priorities by using parentheses: operations within parentheses take priority over everything else. So if you change the last example to (5+3)*2, the result is 16.

As with other equal-priority operations, if you have multiple parenthetical operations, they're performed left to right. If you have nested parentheses, the innermost parenthetical operations are done first.

It works like this:

innermost parentheses	5 + (10 + (6–1) *4) / 2
multiplication (in parens)	5 + (10 + 5 * 4) / 2
parentheses	5 + (10 + 20) / 2
division	5 + 30 / 2
	5 + 15
	20

🍎 *freezing numbers*

very hot tip

Let's say you've created a spreadsheet to take care of your checkbook. Instead of typing in every check number, you've created a formula that adds 1 to the value in the cell above and then copied it down a column. That works fine until you have a break in the series (for a deposit, maybe) or until you do some sorting (to pull out certain expenses, say).

The solution isn't to type in the check numbers one at a time; a computer is supposed to save you time. The solution is to freeze the numbers after the formula has created them.

To do that, select and cut the cells that contain the check numbers, click in the cell where you want them to begin (which can be the same place you just cut them from) and then choose the Paste option that lets you paste only the *values* in the Clipboard instead of the *formulas*. In Excel, use the *Paste Special* command in the Edit menu. In Works, it's the *Paste with Options* command.

Excel tips

These tips work with version 2.2, and many work with version 1.5 as well. (Most will probably work with the next version too.) Marty Sobin and Bob Umlas contributed many of the entries in this section. If you want to hire an expert Excel consultant, you'll find their contact information in Appendix B.

● *learning Excel* (AN)

Sharon says Excel's manuals have improved, but I still find them so frustrating that I seldom use them. The program's help screens are pretty good, however, so you can turn to them instead of to the manual. You still may have to look things up in the manual, but the less time you spend with it, the happier you'll be.

● *short and full menus* (Marty Sobin)

Both Excel and Word allow their menus to be modified, creating a common confusion for beginners—missing menu commands. Excel's *Short menus* command (in the Option menu) removes commands that are less often used from menus, while the *Full menus* command restores them all.

esp. for beginners

● *selecting the whole spreadsheet* (DC/AN)

To select the whole spreadsheet, click in the box in the extreme upper left corner—that is, above the number *1* and to the left of the letter *A*.

shortcut

● *selecting a cell range with Go To* (Marty Sobin)

The standard way of selecting a group of cells is to drag through them, or to click at one corner and Shift-click at the other. But here's another, more elegant way: use the *Go To* command and type a *range* of cells (*B3:D10*, say) in the dialog box. When you click *OK*, all the cells in the range will be selected.

shortcut

● *the Go Back command* (Bob Umlas/SZA)

The *Go To* command will take you back to the cell you came from (assuming you used it to go to a single cell and not to select a range of them, as in the previous entry). Just choose *Go To* again, and the dialog box will suggest the cell you were last in as a destination. Just press `Return` or `Enter` and you'll be moved right back to where you started. You don't have to wait for a dialog box to appear; just type `⌘` `G`, `Return`.

⚫ *selecting noncontiguous cells*

very hot tip

Excel lets you select noncontiguous cells or groups of cells (that is, ones that don't touch each other). Just hold down `⌘` while you click in or drag through cells in different parts of the spreadsheet. Each `⌘`-click adds the current cell choice to the selection but, unlike `Shift`, it ignores the cells in between.

The *Select Special* command also lets you select noncontiguous cells, but only in categories like *all the cells with formulas* or *all the blank cells*.

⚫ *localized scrolling*

Excel's default is to scroll you through just the part of the spreadsheet you're using, instead of through the whole thing. So if your last entry is in row 100, putting the vertical scroll box in the middle of the scroll bar will put you in row 50, not row 8192 (it works the same way for columns).

To supersede localized scrolling and get the scroll box and scroll bar to represent the entire (possible) spreadsheet—all 4.2 million cells of it—hold `Shift` while you drag the box or click in the bar.

⚫ *cycling through opened worksheets* (Marty Sobin)

You don't have to select a window's name from the Windows menu to activate it. `⌘` `M` takes you to the next window in the stack of worksheets you have open, and `Shift` `⌘` `M` takes you to the previous one.

⚫ *the Close All command*

In Excel 1.5, there was a *Close All* command on the File menu. To get that command in Excel 2.2, hold [Shift] down before opening the menu.

⚫ *the uses of cell protection* (DC/AN/SZA)

If you're designing a worksheet that will require the re-peated input of varying data, you'll want to protect the cells that contain text or formulas so they don't get accidentally changed during the data-entry process. Here's how to do that:

very hot tip

With the document unprotected, select the cells where the data is to be entered. Use the *Cell Protection* command (on the Format menu) to unlock them. Then choose *Protect Document* from the Options menu. This will lock all the cells that have not been selected.

It will also let you (or the person you design the worksheet for) jump directly to cells that need input by using [Tab] or [Return]. Once the document is protected, only the unpro-tected cells can be used—and the normal methods of mov-ing from one cell to another in the spreadsheet (like [Tab] and [Return]) will move you from one unprotected cell to another.

⚫ *shortcuts for row and column insertion*

You don't have to use the *Insert* command to insert a row or column into your worksheet—you can do it with the mouse. [Option]-click inserts an empty row above the row number you click on, or an empty column to the left of the column letter you click on. If you [Option]-click in a cell, a row is inserted above that cell.

shortcut

⚫ *swapping rows or columns* (Bob Umlas/SZA)

Here's a nifty way to swap rows or columns without hav-ing to cut and paste (this example assumes you're swapping columns, but the same concept applies to rows):

To swap equal sections of columns A and B (five rows, say), type a *2* in the cell below the column A section and a *1* in the cell below the column B section. Select those rows in both columns—including the cells that you just put the *1* and *2* into—and choose *Sort* from the Data menu. In the Sort dialog box, click the *Columns* button and type the name of the cell that you typed the *1* in. (In this example, it would be B6, and since you should use absolute referencing, you'd type *$B$6*—except that you'll find that's the suggested cell anyway and you won't have to type it in at all.)

Excel sorts the two columns, putting the one with the 1 in it (column B) before the one with the 2 in it (column A). (Note that relative cell references in formulas aren't retained when you do this kind of swapping.)

✿ *opening hidden columns*

When you've hidden a column in the worksheet, you can drag it open again with the mouse. When you position the pointer over the dividing line between column headings *(A, B,* etc.), it changes to a thick vertical line with arrows pointing right and left. (You don't have to be very precise—you'll get this pointer as long as you're within about an eighth of an inch of the dividing line.)

When there's a hidden column, dragging on the divider line itself or in the sensitive area immediately to its left adjusts the column you can see. Dragging from the area immediately to the *right* of the dividing line, though, opens up the hidden column.

Start here for this

Start here for this

✦ outlining cells *(AN/SZA)*

Although it's right there in the Border dialog box (on the Format menu), many Excel users don't realize that they can outline a cell they've selected simply by clicking on *Outline*. This is a lot easier than clicking on *Left, Top, Right* and *Bottom* all the time.

If you're working with a group of selected cells, *Outline* borders the group as a whole. There's even a keyboard command for outlining a cell or group: ⌘ Option ‚o.

✦ seeing the borders *(AN)*

Sometimes it's hard to see what borders you've drawn in an Excel spreadsheet. An easy and fast way to make them more visible is simply to select the area you're interested in; the borders show up much more prominently when they're white against a black background.

shortcut

✦ the Copy Picture command *(DC)*

There's a hidden command on Excel's Edit menu called *Copy Picture;* to make it visible, hold down the Shift key when you pop down the menu. This will copy the selected portion of the worksheet (along with the relevant row and column headings), in PICT format, to the Clipboard. You can then paste the selection into a draw program (to manipulate the parts of it individually) or into an application like PageMaker (which lets you stretch or shrink it).

very hot tip

✦ copying down contents vs. values *(Bob Umlas/SZA)*

⌘ ‚' copies the contents of the cell above into the current cell. Shift ⌘ ‚' copies just the *value* of the cell above. So if the cell above contains *=$C$4/3* with a result of *27*, ⌘ ‚' copies *=$C$4/3* to the current cell, while Shift ⌘ ‚' copies only *27*.

✦ paste shortcut

If you've just cut or copied a cell (or range of cells) or copied data from a chart, pressing Enter will paste the

Clipboard contents into the cell(s) you've clicked in. *But,* unlike an ordinary Paste operation, this [Enter]-Paste cancels the marquee around the original cells and also empties the Clipboard—so you can't do multiple pastes.

❁ *the Fill alignment* (Marty Sobin)

esp. for beginners

There's a special option in the Alignment dialog box called *Fill*—it takes the contents of a cell and repeats across the cell's width, no matter how wide you make the column the cell is in.

When you put a dash or an asterisk or some other special character in a cell, the *Fill* command makes special breaks between rows to separate sections of the spreadsheet—or just something as simple as an underline beneath a column of numbers that will stretch the width of the column.

❁ *Fill Up and Fill Left*

very hot tip

The *Fill Down* and *Fill Right* commands duplicate the contents of the first cell in all the selected cells. When you want to fill up, or to the left, hold [Shift] before you open the Edit menu and the commands will read *Fill Up* and *Fill Left*.

You can also fill in a selected area in any direction— even in more than one direction at once. Just select the cells you want the duplicated information in, type the information in the entry bar and press [Option][Enter]. What you typed will appear in all the selected cells.

If there's already data in any of those cells, you won't get any warning that you're about to replace it—but you can undo the maneuver with [⌘][Z], if you realize your mistake in time.

❁ *using* [⌘][B] *for Clear* (Marty Sobin)

When you choose *Clear* from the Edit menu, you have four ways to clear the selected cells: *All, Formats, Formulas* or *Notes*. When you use the [⌘][B] keyboard equivalent, though, the options dialog box doesn't appear and you don't get a choice—the contents of the cell disappear but the formatting and cell notes remain.

♠ *importing worksheets from large-screen Macs* (DC/AN)

If you import an Excel document created on a Mac with an external monitor to a Mac with a 9" screen, the spreadsheet's window will probably be larger than the screen, and you won't be able to resize it, because the size box will be off the screen. The solution is simple: just doubleclick on the title bar and the window will automatically resize to fit the Mac's screen.

very
hot
tip

♠ *previews of printouts* (AN)

One of Excel's nicer features is the ability to preview on the screen what printouts will look like on paper (by checking the *Preview* box in the Print dialog box). The text in the Preview window is too small to read (unless you're using giant type) but you can zoom in on any part of it by clicking with the magnifying-glass pointer. You can move around while zoomed in by using the scroll bars. Click again and you're back at the overall view of the page.

♠ *doubleclicking on radio buttons* (Marty Sobin)

Doubleclicking on a radio button does the same thing as selecting it and then clicking an *OK* button. And just as you can click a button from the keyboard by typing the first letter of its name, you can also doubleclick it with the key.

shortcut

For example, this is the small dialog box that you get when you start a new worksheet:

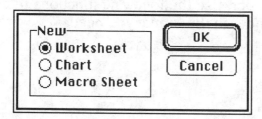

Instead of reaching for the mouse, clicking the *Macro Sheet* button and then clicking *OK*, you can just hit Ⓜ Ⓜ. This means you can start a new Macro Sheet with the following series of keystrokes:

You don't have to wait for the dialog box to open; in fact, if you type at a reasonable speed, you'll never even see the dialog box—you'll go straight to the new Macro Sheet.

◉ *the Repeat command* (Bob Umlas/SZA)

shortcut

⌘Y repeats the last thing you did. This is especially useful for repeating a dialog box action without having to open the dialog box again. If you've just protected a cell by making it locked and hidden, for example, you can click on another cell and press ⌘Y to lock and hide it too.

◉ *autonaming cells*

When you use the *Define Name* command, Excel suggests as the name the text in the cell to the left of the cell being named—which is where you'd normally type a label. So after you've typed a label, simply tab right to the next cell, press ⌘L and then Return (which confirms the suggested text).

You can use this same technique to autoname a whole column of cells. Just type their labels in the column to the left, select the next column of cells to the right and press ⌘L and then Return.

◉ *time and date functions* (DC/Fokko Du Cloux)

Use the *NOW( )* function to retrieve the current date and time from the system clock and enter it into a formula as a serial number. Use the following functions to convert the serial number to the format you need:

DAY
WEEKDAY
HOUR
MINUTE
MONTH
YEAR

For example, the formula *=FORMULA("=HOUR(NOW())")* gives you the current hour.

You choose how the date or time appears. For example, if you specify *m/d/yyyy* (with the *Number...* command on the Format menu), you'll get it in this form: *5/12/1989.* If you specify *dddd,* you'll get just the day of the week. *Mmmm* will give you the month written out in full and *hh:mm am/pm* the time in this form: *22:01 pm.*

⚫ *formula bar activation* (Bob Umlas/SZA)

Little things mean a lot. One of Excel's little things is ⌘U, which activates the formula bar and places the insertion point at the end of the data there. No more reaching for the mouse (unless, of course, you'd rather).

shortcut

⚫ *cancelling changes in the formula bar* (Marty Sobin)

There are three ways to cancel any change in the formula bar:

- Click the *Cancel* icon (the *X* in the box to the left of the formula bar)

- Press ⌘ .

- Press Esc

⚫ *escaping from cells with invalid formulas* (DC)

Excel won't let you close a cell until the formula in it meets the program's formatting rules. You'll keep getting a message that says your formula is wrong and you'll be put right back in that cell. This can be maddening when you're working on a complex formula and can't seem to get it right.

very
hot
tip

To escape, just remove the = (equal sign) at the beginning of the formula. Excel will now treat the entry as text and thus won't analyze it for correctness, allowing you to move on to another cell. After a little while away from the troublesome formula, you may be able to go back to it and spot your mistake.

⚫ *calculating part of a formula* (Marty Sobin)

You can calculate part of a formula in the formula bar by selecting the part you're interested in and hitting ⌘=. The selected part of the formula is immediately converted to a value:

= SUM(B1:B12) / 12

= SUM(B1:B12) / 12

=172 / 12

If you want the value to stay, hit ⟨Return⟩, or edit it further first. If you wanted only a sneak preview of that part of the formula, cancel the calculation before you do anything else, and it will return to its original state.

⌘ the Calculate Document command *(Bob Umlas/SZA)*

When you use the *Calculate Now* command, all open worksheets are recalculated. To save time when you have several worksheets open, hold ⟨Shift⟩ before you open the Options menu; this changes the *Calculate Now* command to *Calculate Document*, which recalculates only the current worksheet.

⌘ counting things *(Marty Sobin/Todd Corleto)*

The COUNT function merely counts the number of cells in a given range that contain numbers. To see how many times a specific item appears in a given range, use this formula:

=SUM(IF(C8:F14="YES",1,0)), followed by ⌘ ⟨Return⟩

This tells you how many times the number or text—in this example, *YES*—appears. (Numbers don't go in quotes, and must be in a continuous range.)

⌘ looking at both values and formulas *(Marty Sobin/SZA)*

There are two ways you can view both the formulas in your worksheet and the values that result—at the same time!

One way is to open the Info window and place it next to your worksheet. It will display any information you want about the current cell in the active worksheet, so set it (in the Info menu that appears when the window opens) to show both the formula and the value for a cell. Then move Around in your worksheet and click on any cell for which you want that information.

Another way is to use the *New Window* command from the Windows menu. This opens a second window for the current worksheet. You can format one to display formulas and one to display values and set them side by side on the screen.

⚫ *checking the spelling of functions* (Marty Sobin)

If you type the name of a function in the formula bar rather than using the *Paste Function* command, you run the risk of misspelling the function's name (is it *maximum* or just *max?*). But you'll know right away if the name is right or not if you always use lowercase letters when you type, because function names are converted to all caps when you enter a formula (so if the lowercase name you typed doesn't co-vert to all caps, you'll know you typed it wrong).

very hot tip

⚫ *paging through notes* (Bob Umlas/SZA)

Here's an easy way to review all the notes in your worksheet:

- Select all the cells in the worksheet that have notes (as described in the next entry).

- Choose *Show Info* from the Windows menu to open the Info window.

- Choose *Arrange All* from the Windows menu to tile the opened windows, so you can see both your worksheet and the Info window.

- Activate the worksheet window again by clicking in it, then use Enter to jump from one selected note cell to another.

As you go from cell to cell, the notes you made will be displayed in the Info window.

⚫ *four Notes notes* (Bob Umlas/SZA)

Here are four quick notes about cell notes:

- You don't have to use the *Note* command to open the Note window for the current cell—just press Shift ⌘ N.

- You can quickly select *all* the cells in the worksheet that have notes by pressing [Shift] [⌘] [O].

- When the Notes window is open, you can scroll your worksheet in the background—if the insertion point is in the *Cell* text box but not if it's in the *Note* text box!

- If you press [Return] while the Notes dialog box is open, that closes the box. If you want to move down a line in the Note text box, use [Option] [Return].

▲ the Excel Startup document (Bob Umlas/SZA)

You can create a worksheet that automatically opens when Excel is started—just name it *Excel Startup* and put it in the system folder. The best use of this startup document is to put all the macros that you use most often in it—since the worksheet will be open, they'll all be available to you.

There are two things you can do to make the Startup document more convenient for macro storage. First, hide it, by choosing *Hide* from the Windows menu—this keeps screen clutter to a minimum. (Excel will find the macros whether the document is hidden or not.)

Second, keep the Startup document from closing when you issue the *Close All* command. To do that, make it active, choose *Protect Document* from the Options menu and click the *Windows* button. This takes away the the Startup document's close box and keeps the *Close All* command from affecting it.

▲ zooming in and out (SZA/DC)

very hot tip

To get an overall picture of a large spreadsheet, use the *Standard Font* command in the Options menu to change the font size to 2 or 4 points. You won't be able to work in this view, but you can get a good feel for where everything is.

An even better approach is to build a macro to do that. Here's what to use for the zoom-out macro:

=STANDARD.FONT("Geneva",2)

For the zoom-in macro, simply substitute the font and size you normally work in. Put these macros in the Excel Startup document (described above) so they'll always be available.

✎ *speeding up macros* (Marty Sobin/Lee Hinde)

shortcut

The *Echo(False)* feature greatly speeds up the execution of macros (it particularly makes a difference in long ones). One of Lee's macros that takes two minutes without *Echo(False)* takes just fifteen seconds with it. (Just put *Echo(False)* at the beginning of the macro.)

Echo(False) works by turning off screen redrawing. (Being able to ignore that saves Excel a lot of time.) By the way, you don't need to reset Echo at the end of the macro so that screen redrawing will be turned on again; Excel does that automatically.

But if your macro involves several worksheets, there's a delay that *Echo(False)* doesn't prevent: each worksheet is activated when it's called and even though the contents of the worksheet aren't drawn on the screen, the window itself coming to the top of the pile slows things down. So before you run a macro involving a worksheet other than the active one, use *HIDE( )* to hide it—and use *ACTIVATE( )* when you're finished.

✎ *references in linked worksheets* (Marty Sobin)

If you move the contents of a cell that's referenced in a link, the reference won't be followed—that is, if Worksheet A references cell A12 in Worksheet B and you move the contents of A12 someplace else, Worksheet A is still going to look at cell A12—and not find anything there (or find something it didn't expect).

If however, you reference a cell by its *name* (the *Define Name* command lets you name it), you can move its contents around and the linked spreadsheet will find it—because a cell's name moves along with its contents.

✦ circular reference problems (Bob Umlas/SZA)

When you get a *circular reference* alert, it's easy to look through all the cells that are involved. Select the problem cell(s) (they'll be identified in the alert box), choose the *Select Special* command and click either the *Precedents* or *Dependents* button (click *All levels* too). *Precedents* selects all the cells on which the current cell depends; *Dependents* selects all the cells that depend on the current cell.

Works spreadsheet tips

These tips apply to Works 2. Tips for Works' other modules appear in the appropriate chapters—like word processing and data-bases. Tips for general Works use (and using its modules together) are in Chapter 18.

✦ clicking on the scroll box

very hot tip

A click in the gray area of the scroll bar shifts the contents of the window up or down by one screenful (and moves the scroll box accordingly). But Works spreadsheets can get so large, and the scroll box can get so close to the top or bottom of the scroll bar, that there's no gray area left for you to click in.

When that happens, just click in the scroll box itself. If it's closer to the top of the scroll bar, it will move up; if it's closer to the bottom, it will move down (and the contents of the window will move accordingly). This trick also works in the word processor module, but it's not often a document gets so long that you need to use it.

✦ two cell-click shortcuts

shortcut

You can doubleclick on a cell to open the Set Cell At-tributes dialog box instead of choosing that command from the menu. But if you want to set attributes for a group of selected cells all at once, you'll have to use the menu command, because doubleclicking on one of the cells de-selects the rest of the group.

Instead of using the *Open Cell Note* command in the Edit menu, sometimes it's faster to open the note window for a cell by holding ⌘ while doubleclicking on the cell.

❤ *the Paste Function command*

The main advantage to using the *Paste Function* command (on the Edit menu) instead of just typing in the name yourself is to make sure it's entered correctly. As an added convenience, the equal sign that signifies a formula is also typed for you, and the insertion point is placed inside the parentheses that follow the function name.

❤ *sorting*

Sorting in the spreadsheet doesn't work like sorting in the database. In the database, you can select a column to sort on in the List view and all the information in the rows (records) stays together. In order for the information to stay together in the spreadsheet, however, you have to specifically select which rows and columns are to be sorted.

esp. for beginners

Selected area		Sort result	
A	ape	A	ape
E	elephant	B	elephant
C	cat	C	cat
D	dog	D	dog
B	bird	E	bird
A	ape	A	ape
E	elephant	B	bird
C	cat	C	cat
D	dog	D	dog
B	bird	E	elephant

❤ *inserting rows and columns*

The *Insert* command in the Edit menu inserts a new row in the spreadsheet if you've clicked on the row's number along the left edge of the spreadsheet; it inserts a column if you've clicked on a column's letter at the top of the spreadsheet.

New rows are inserted *above* the currently selected one; new columns are inserted to the *left* of the selected one.

If you have a cell or range of cells selected in the spreadsheet when you choose *Insert*, a row is inserted above the first cell of the selection.

🍎 *blank cells*

As far as Works is concerned, any cell that doesn't contain a number is blank—even if it contains text. So, if you use something like the IsBlank function, it will return a *1*—for *true* ("yes, it's blank")—even if there's text in the cell.

🍎 *Go To Cell vs. Find Cell*

Both the *Go To Cell* and *Find Cell* commands (on the Select menu) search for a cell with contents that match what you type in their respective dialog boxes. But only *Go To Cell* lets you type the name of the cell (A1, say, or V12) you want to go to.

The second, more subtle difference between the two commands, is that *Find Cell* selects the found cell; *Go To Cell*, despite what seems like a direct order, merely makes sure that the named cell is visible in the window. It's not selected and if the cell is already displayed on the screen, you won't see anything happen at all.

🍎 *moving cell contents*

shortcut

You can move the contents of a selected cell by holding ⌘ Option and clicking in the cell you want the information moved to—the data jumps right to the new spot. This works with a selected group of cells too.

🍎 *the border commands*

esp. for beginners

If you have only a single cell selected in the spreadsheet, using the *Outline* command in the Borders submenu is the same as choosing *Left, Right, Top* and *Bottom* one after the other.

But if you have a group of cells selected, these commands work a little differently. *Outline* puts a border around the outside edges of the group as a whole; *Left, Right, Top* and *Bottom* work on *each* cell in the selection.

❡ *the print area*

If you have more than a single cell selected in the spreadsheet when you choose the *Print* command, Works assumes you want only the selected area printed, not the entire spreadsheet.

esp. for beginners

❡ *a Home macro*

Many spreadsheets have a *Home* command that puts you back at cell A1, in the upper left corner of the spreadsheet. Works doesn't have this capability built in, but you can create a macro to do it for you:

shortcut

- Press ⌘ F

- Type *A1*

- Press Return

Works has its own macro editor, but it's pretty lame—especially in the limitation on which keys you can store macros. But it will perform this macro, and the ones listed below.

❡ *activating the Entry bar with a macro*

When you click on a cell or move to it with some keyboard command, its contents are displayed at the top of the screen in the Entry bar. Although they're not highlighted, they are selected—if you type anything, it will replace what's showing in the bar. If you want to add to or edit the contents of the bar, you have to reach for the mouse—*unless* you make an *activate the Entry bar* macro.

shortcut

To do that, record a click in the far right end of the Entry bar. That's it! When you play back the macro, it will activate the Entry bar and put the insertion point at the end of the data that's there. (The click has to be all the way to the right, to make sure it doesn't get inserted into the middle of a formula instead of at its end.)

❖ cell border macro

shortcut

The Outline option for cell borders is probably the one that's used most often—and so it's a likely candidate for a macro. Just record the selection of *Outline* from the *Border* submenu (in the Format menu) and play it back whenever you want a cell outlined.

❖ copying charts

The charts that Works creates from spreadsheet information can be copied just by choosing Copy from the Edit menu when the Chart window is active. You don't have to select the chart first (which is good, since there's no *way* to select it).

❖ exporting charts

**very
hot
tip**

The charts that Works creates are object-oriented. That means if you paste them into a graphics application that handles objects (like MacDraw or SuperPaint's Draw layer), you can edit and move each element separately—change the fill patterns, pull out a slice of the pie, move titles around, etc.

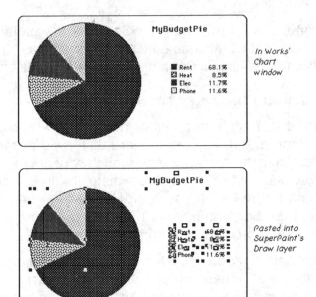

*In Works'
Chart
window*

*Pasted into
SuperPaint's
Draw layer*

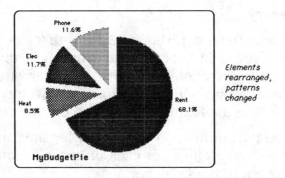

Elements rearranged, patterns changed

The rest of these tips for Works' spreadsheet module also apply to its database module.

● moving around

There are lots of ways to move around in the spreadsheet or in the List view of the database:

keys	*move you*
Tab or →	right
Shift Tab or ←	left
Return or ↓	down
Shift Return or ↑	up

If you select a portion of the grid, your movements will be restricted to it. For example, if you're at the bottom of the selected area and hit Return (or ↓, you'll be wrapped around to the top of the selected area and find yourself in the top cell of the leftmost selected column.

● entering data

When you enter information into a database field or a spreadsheet cell, it first appears in the text box at the top of the screen (which is called the *Entry bar*). It gets entered into the field or cell only when you leave it and move to another one (by hitting Return, Tab or whatever).

esp. for beginners

✺ text entry

If you want to enter text that begins with a + , – or = , you can't just type it in a cell, since Works will think it's a formula. So type a quotation mark—a regular, straight one ("), not a curly one—first. The quote mark won't appear in the cell, just in the text field at the top of the screen.

To enter the information without leaving the current field or cell, you can hit Enter or click on the checkmark icon just to the left of the Entry bar.

✺ using percents

Both the spreadsheet and the database understand percent signs. So there's no difference between typing 50% and .5—Works treats them both the same.

✺ too-narrow columns

esp. for beginners

Sometimes a column in the spreadsheet or a field in the database is too narrow to display its contents. If a database field contains text, Works simply displays as much as will fit in the space provided. In the spreadsheet, the text will overflow into the next cell if it's empty. But if the cell or field contains a number, you'll get a string of pound signs (#####), and you'll have to widen the column or field to get the number.

✺ dates and serial numbers

If you enter a date in a spreadsheet cell that's formatted for dates, it will always have the year appended to it. If you want dates without years, you have to leave the cell formatted as General. But you can't enter a date notation (like Nov 15, 6/20, or even 12-5) in a General cell without its being converted to a "serial" number: one that Works uses to calculate the number of days between dates. So if you type *Nov 14*, you get *31364* displayed in the cell.

To get a date that you type displayed as text instead of a serial number (if you want to have a date without the year, for example), first type quote marks ("), then the date. Initial quote marks force the cell contents to be treated as text, but the quotes themselves aren't displayed in the cell.

Chapter 13

Graphics

Graphics programs

🍎 *kinds of graphics programs* (AN/SZA)

Graphics programs for the Mac fall into four basic categories:

esp. for beginners

- *Paint* programs (like MacPaint) create bit-mapped images—that is, ones that are made up of dots. The dot is their basic unit, so if you want to move a bit-mapped image, you have to encircle all the dots that make it up and select them as a group. Bit-mapped images—which, on the Mac, are always at a resolution of 72 dots per inch—are saved and transferred in *paint* format (see the next entry).

- *Draw* programs (like MacDraw) treat each item you draw as a discrete object. All you have to do to select one is click on it. (On the down side, you can't fine-tune an object, removing a dot here and adding one there.) High-end draw programs go by the name of CAD *(computer-aided design).* and are sometimes specific to a particular profession (for an example, see the ArchiCAD entry below). Object-oriented graphics are transferred between programs in *PICT* format.

- Paint/draw programs (like SuperPaint) create both bit-mapped and object-oriented images, placing them on different levels (which work like transparent overlays, so you can see everything that's on each level).

- PostScript-based illustration programs (like FreeHand and Illustrator) create PostScript files that scale perfectly to all sizes. They're usually transferred in EPS format.

In general, bit-mapped images are better suited for artistic tasks and object-oriented graphics for business applications like drafting and diagramming. PostScript images are hard-edged like object-oriented graphics but are capable of much greater sophistication and subtlety (they still don't have that bit-mapped look, though).

This isn't an either/or proposition, of course. If you do a fair amount of graphics work on the Mac, you'll want to have at least a paint/draw program (or separate paint and draw programs) and probably also a PostScript-based one.

One last note: any of these types of programs may or may not handle color. If they do, they're often used just for that, but some programs—Illustrator and FreeHand, for example— are commonly used for both color and monochrome work.

❤ *kinds of graphics formats* (SZA/AN)

esp. for
beginners

Each kind of Mac graphics program saves its files in its own, *native* format, which may or may not coincide with one of the basic file formats used to transfer images from one program to another (or even between Macs and other kinds of computers). Some programs give you a choice of several different formats to save files in, and some also recognize many different formats.

- *Paint* files (MacPaint's native format) are 72-dpi, black-and-white-only, bit-mapped images; in addition, they're limited to an 8″ by 10″ page. The *file type* for paint files is PNTG (some utilities let you view and manipulate file types).

- Like paint files, TIFF files *(tagged image file format)* are bit-mapped, but they can be any size and have any resolution (number of dots per inch). TIFF is generally used for images created by scanners. (Although it was intended to provide a high-resolution bit-mapped standard, everybody wanted to improve it—and did, in different ways—so the TIFF standard isn't exactly standard anymore. Some TIFF images are black-and-white only, most support gray scale information and a few do color—it all depends on the software that creates the image.)

- PICT files (from *picture*) are used to transfer the object-oriented graphics created by draw programs. PICT files use QuickDraw, the programming routines that are also used to display things on the Mac's screen. (The original PICT only allowed for eight colors, but the current standard, PICT2, allows for full 32-bit color, which is the most the Mac can produce. You don't need to worry about which kind of PICT you're dealing with—almost everything uses PICT2 now.)

- EPS files *(encapsulated PostScript)* are combinations of the PostScript code that tells the printer how to print the image and a PICT image that tells the screen how to display it. (You can just use the PostScript code—place it in PageMaker, for example—but you won't be able to see it on the screen, because the screen doesn't know how to display PostScript instructions. You'll get just a gray box instead.)

MacPaint

MacPaint 1.0, which came bundled (included free) with the original 128K Mac, set the standards for Mac graphics. But version 2.0, ($125 from Claris) doesn't meet the standards that have been set since then.

MacPaint has some very elegant features like tear-off menus and a Magic Eraser that erases through only the artwork you've added since you last took a "snapshot" of the document, but it falls far short of what other paint programs are doing these days—for example, it can't rotate a selection in increments smaller than 90°.

If you're still working with MacPaint 1.0, it's worth the $25 upgrade fee to get version 2.0. But if you're shopping for a black-and-white paint program, shop a little further.

SuperPaint

SuperPaint ($200) has both a paint layer and a draw layer, so you get the benefit of both kinds of graphics. You can see both layers on the screen and in printouts (although you can hide either layer when you want to), but you work in only one layer at a time.

very good feature

SuperPaint 2.0 has significant printing problems when your draw layer is complex. (I usually copy the whole thing into PageMaker and print it from there.) It also has problems with Clipboard transfers of objects created with hairline widths. Its color capabilities are so limited they should be ignored.

bug

But in spite of those bugs, SuperPaint is a real workhorse and the best bet for all-around graphics work. It has all the

very good feature

basic paint and draw features, and then some; extendable tool palettes (you can add tools that are written by someone else), Bezier curves and autotrace are a few of its advanced features.

🍎 *MacDraw*

The first object-oriented graphics program, MacDraw went the way of MacPaint—from Apple to Claris, and from original to version II with elegant new features but not enough to rave about.

MacDraw is dependable and it allows for a lot of precision in the drawing and placement of geometric objects. MacDraw II has beefed-up text handling capabilities that make it suitable for basic (one- or two-page) layout jobs.

(I generally like MacDraw II. It has a fair amount of power, works well, is relatively easy to learn, and I don't run up against its limitations very often. It may not be anything to rave about, but I don't know anyone who uses a different draw program. But I agree that SuperPaint is probably a better bargain, since you get two programs for the price of one.—AN)

🍎 *FreeHand and Illustrator*

esp. for power users

Aldus FreeHand and Adobe Illustrator (both $500) are the two premier PostScript illustration programs. Both give you files of your artwork that will print at the highest resolution available on a PostScript printer or imagesetter.

If you're deciding which one to buy—good luck. Every Mac graphic designer I talked to says you need both. If you can buy only one, or if you want to start with just one, most people recommend Illustrator, unless you do a lot of text manipulation.

Illustrator has no text manipulation capabilities to speak of, but FreeHand lets you do things like bind text to a curved path. Everyone also seems to prefer FreeHand's method of dealing with colors, and with fills. And, unlike Illustrator, FreeHand accepts TIFF files.

What the designers like about Illustrator is its uncluttered design and fewer tools to do the same jobs. In FreeHand, for example, there's one tool for making curves with two corner points, another for making curves with a single corner point and a third for making a curve with no corner points. Illustrator has a single tool capable of making curves with any kind of control points. Illustrator is also better for fine detail work and technical drawing.

What most designers don't like about Illustrator—aside from its lack of good text manipulation—is that the working and preview modes are separate. (FreeHand lets you work in the Preview mode, so you can adjust things in the view that's most representative of the final product.) Both programs have autotracing, but only Illustrator can import drawings made by StreamLine (see the next entry); if you manipulate a lot of clip art, that's an important capability.

The designers I know tend to create graphics in Illustrator and then import them to FreeHand to do the fills. FreeHand is also preferred for complicated pieces of artwork, because you can put items in different layers and then hide every layer but the one you're working on.

StreamLine

StreamLine is a $400 program that does only one thing, but it does that one thing extremely well—it traces bitmapped graphics and converts them into PostScript. You then import the results into Illustrator for further manipulation and fine-tuning (they usually need it, but StreamLine is still an incredible time-saver).

very good feature

StreamLine 1.2 is much more accurate at tracing images than 1.1 was, so make sure you get that version. StreamLine is quite expensive for what amounts to a utility, but if you deal much with bit-mapped graphics, it's a must.

MacCalligraphy *(Fred Terry)*

MacCalligraphy's manual describes the program as a word processor (based on the idea that Japanese calligraphy is both writing and painting). I'm not persuaded that it would make a great word processor but it's an intriguing paint program, with tools specifically designed to emulate brushes on paper. A particularly appealing feature is the ability to leave a tail as you end a stroke.

very good feature

The program comes in a wooden box with several sheets of rice paper and its documentation is filled with Japanese art. The manual is quite delightful at times, despite some awkward sentences obviously translated from Japanese. The Desktop of the program's startup disk looks like a Japanese tea room with a treasure alcove.

MacCalligraphy is easy to learn, although it takes a while to get used to the way the painting surface picks up ink. The program's tutorials have you practice the strokes of the Japanese character for eternity and walk you through drawing bamboo stalks. When you tire of this, there's a "tea break" option that shows you a garden scene as you relax. There are even two short essays that you can read while taking your tea break.

bug

One of the few complaints I have about the program is that you have to enter a reduced view of your painting to move around in it. I also think the program needs a grabber hand, an essential tool in most graphics programs.

The Qualitas Trading Company is the American distributor of MacCalligraphy. They provide free support for the program but you have to pay for the phone call.

⁂ *Claris CAD* (AN)

esp. for power users

Since I feel barely competent in a regular draw program, the letters *CAD* (for *computer-aided design*) have always intimidated me. But when I tried out Claris CAD, I found to my delight (and relief) that it's just like a more powerful MacDraw. There are still plenty of things about it I don't understand, but it's easy to learn and use and I've yet to come up with something I wanted to do that it couldn't do.

CAD software should be reviewed by someone who really knows the programs and can fully use their power, rather than by a duffer like me, and maybe in a future edition we'll be able to do that. But in the meantime, you should know that even a relative beginner can make use of at least some of Claris CAD's very powerful features, and can do that without having to spend hours learning how.

♠ *finally, a program that includes the kitchen sink* (AN)

I'm not sure what you're supposed to expect from a $4000 piece of software, and I know it's not fair to rave and drool over something I get to review for free and you have to mortgage your house to buy. Having said that, stand back while I rave and drool.

esp. for power users

Whenever G&B's office has moved, I've spent many hours drafting the new premises in MacDraw, planning where the furniture would go, etc. This kind of map, drawn as if from directly above, is called a *plan* (as opposed to an *elevation*, which shows how something will look from the side; a *section*, which shows how it will look if sliced through vertically; or a *perspective view*, which shows how it will look in three dimensions, from a given point of view).

ArchiCAD (from Graphisoft) also begins with a plan, but instead of just drawing a line, you specify what the wall will actually be (or is)—say, reinforced cement block a foot thick on the outside, then six inches of insulation, a frame of 2x4's and sheetrock on the inside. Then, whenever you draw a line, that's what you get—that exact wall, in exactly the correct thickness, with each layer of it coded with the standard architectural patterns for the material used.

very good feature

To put windows in the wall, you choose what you want from a library of dozens of basic types, then customize the dimensions. Let's say you decide on a doublehung 30° bay window 6'7" high by 7'9⅝" wide, with a frame 2½" wide and 4" thick, with two rows of four panes in the center section, and two rows of two panes in the side sections. You just click anywhere on the wall with the mouse, and it inserts exactly that.

very good feature

There are also extensive libraries of doors (with and without sidelights, with and without transoms, as well as bifold, sliding glass and garage), toilets, washstands, showers, tubs, kitchen sinks, cabinets, stoves, refrigerators, tables, chairs, etc. etc. You just choose what you want and click to place it.

very good feature

But you ain't seen nothing yet. Once you've got things laid out in plan, ArchiCAD will show you how everything looks in elevation, in section or in perspective, with contours and shading, from any point inside or outside the building, with the light coming from wherever you want!! (That's the only time you'll see two exclamation marks in this book.)

Hmmm, that butcher-block table doesn't look quite right under that bull's-eye window, viewed from the couch over in this corner. Shall I change the window, use another kind of table or move the couch? By the time you're done playing around with all the possibilities in ArchiCAD, you'll have such an intimate knowledge of how the space is going to look that actual construction is likely to be anticlimactic.

I can't imagine spending $4000 for any piece of software, but if I could, this is the one I could imagine spending it on. ArchiCAD is designed for architects, of course, not individuals, and for them the price will be recouped quickly with the time they save having the program generate perspective drawings for their clients instead of drawing them themselves (or—even worse—constructing models; I did that once and couldn't *believe* how long it took).

very bad feature

Like several other terrific programs, ArchiCAD has a problem with its manuals. You get six (five more than I wanted), none of which has an index! What's more, something on the manuals—the ink, probably, but maybe a coating on the paper—smells so bad that I've had them airing out for several months and still can't bear to have them in the same room with me. Needless to say, this limits the use I can make of the program.

❡ *graphics utilities* (AN)

For reviews of three useful utilities that handle graphics, see pp. 497–98 in the utilities chapter.

General paint program tips

Most of these tips should work in any paint program, including desk accessories and SuperPaint's paint layer (because they're all ultimately based on the original MacPaint).

✎ *quick Undo* (AN)

The two standard ways to undo the last thing you did are to choose *Undo* from the Edit menu or to use the keyboard shortcut ⌘Z. Most paint programs offer a third alternative that only requires hitting one key. On ADB keyboards, hit [Esc]; on the older Mac keyboards, hit [`] (both keys are in the upper left corner of the keyboard).

shortcut

✎ *doubleclicking on tools* (AN/SZA)

Doubleclicking on icons in a tool palette usually produces some handy shortcuts, (To do this in MacPaint 2.0, you first have to tear off the Tools menu.)

shortcut

doubleclick on:	*to:*
🖌	change its shape
✒	enter the magnified view
✋	toggle between regular and reduced
▱	erase the whole window
⬚	select the whole window
⌔	lasso the whole window
a pattern box	change that pattern

✎ [Shift] *key effects* (AN/SZA)

The [Shift] key usually acts as a *constraint* in painting programs, keeping a tool moving in a horizontal or vertical direction (depending on which way you move initially) or keeping shapes that you're drawing of equal length and width. For example:

Shift +	lets you:
🖌	paint straight horizontal or vertical lines
✏	make straight horizontal or vertical lines
✋	shift the window contents horizontally or vertically
⬛	erase in straight horizontal or vertical
▭	create squares
◯	create circles

⬥ alternative erasers *(AN)*

very hot tip

Here are three alternatives to the standard Eraser:

- Use any selection tool (⬚ or ✑, for example) and then hit Delete to delete the selection.

- Use 🖌—in any convenient size and shape—with white paint (or whatever the background pattern is).

- For really detailed, bit-by-bit erasing (literally), go to a magnified view and use ✏—it changes black dots to white (and vice versa).

⬥ quick magnified views *(AN)*

shortcut

A quick and precise way to zoom into a magnified view is to ⌘-click with ✏. The magnified view will be centered around the point you clicked on.

⬥ shrinking ⬚

Holding ⌘ while selecting something with the selection rectangle (⬚) shrinks ⬚ down around the image as small as possible.

⬥ scaling bit-mapped images *(C.J. Weigand)*

very hot tip

When you shrink a bit-mapped image, adjoining pixels tend to clump together until you have unsightly blotches where once there was finely drawn detail. To reduce a bit map without significant loss of detail, copy it at full size into an object-oriented drawing program, shrink it there and then print it out.

When printing from an object-oriented program, the LaserWriter scales the image starting from a full-size representation in memory, not from the reduced on-screen image. If you're using an ImageWriter, you can shrink the image to 50% of its original size and get a beautiful printout at Best quality.

🍎 *quick lassoing* (AN)

You don't have to draw a complete loop around an image with ⌇ to select it. The loop you make is automatically closed with a straight line between where you start and end the Lasso drag.

shortcut

🍎 *stretching a selection*

If you press ⌘ while dragging on the edge of a selected area, the selection is resized—larger or smaller, depending on which way you drag. This always introduces some distortion in the image, but you can get interesting effects.

If you want the selection resized proportionately (in the same amount vertically and horizontally), hold Shift ⌘ while you drag.

🍎 *resizing while pasting*

If you draw a rectangle with ⸢⸣ and then choose *Paste* from the Edit menu, the pasted material is automatically sized to fit the selected area.

🍎 *the* Option *copy* (SZA/AN)

You can duplicate objects in a paint program by copying and pasting them, but there's an easier way. First, make the selection, then press Option while dragging it. Instead of moving the original, you'll peel away an exact copy. When you have it where you want it, just release the mouse button. Here's what happens with a lassoed rabbit (assuming you can manage to lasso one) when you Option-drag:

very hot tip

To make repeating copies, hold down ⌘ too—you'll leave images behind as you drag the selection. The more slowly you drag, the more copies there'll be:

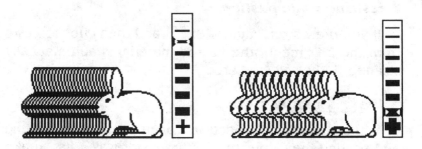

Holding down [Shift] as well (which means [Shift][Option]⌘ in total) keeps the dragged copies in a straight line.

To make the spacing even between the copies, adjust the line width and drag slowly. The width of the line defines the minimum spacing between the copies:

❡ the three-finger stretch

*very
hot
tip*

This tip was named by the original MacPaint's author, Bill Atkinson. It's actually the repeating-copies-in-a-straight-line technique explained in the [Option] *copy* entry above, but it's a different application of it—you can use it to "repair" parts of your picture.

Say you drew a musical staff of five lines and, after adding a few notes, realized you needed more room. All you have to do is first select part of the picture and drag it away from its original position—holding [Shift] so the piece moves in a straight line:

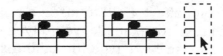

Then lasso the edges of one of the pieces and [Shift][Option][⌘]-drag the lassoed area. The repeating copies left behind fill in the empty area:

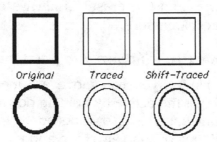

⚫ *shadowed traced edges*

The basic *Trace Edges* command traces around any black dots in the selection—and changes the original black dots to white. If you hold [Shift] while choosing *Trace Edges*, a shadow is applied to the tracing—extra dots to the right and bottom of the traced edges.

very
hot
tip

Original   Traced   Shift-Traced

⚫ *freezing text formatting*

When you type bit-mapped text, you can change the size, style, font, justification or spacing of *all* of it—as long as it's still active (with the insertion point still blinking). If you want to freeze the formatting of what you've already

very
hot
tip

typed, you can just click the mouse and start another block of text—but then the two text blocks probably won't line up.

The solution is to press ⁅Enter⁆, which freezes the formatting at that point. You'll be able to keep typing, but the text before the ⁅Enter⁆ will be frozen and new formatting commands won't affect it. So to insert a bold word in the midst of plain text, for example, you'd type the plain text, press ⁅Enter⁆; choose *Bold*, type the bold text, press ⁅Enter⁆ again, choose *Plain Text,* and continue typing.

SuperPaint tips

⁅ switching layers

shortcut

You usually toggle between the Paint and Draw layers by clicking on the icons at the top of the tool palette, but there's also a keyboard equivalent: ⁅⌘⁆⁅/⁆.

⁅ palettes and small screens

very
hot
tip

If you're working on a standard, 9" Mac screen, you'll find that reversing the positions of SuperPaint's floating tool and pattern palettes is much more convenient. With a horizontal or square tool palette, you can see eight paint tools at a time, and the eraser is always available for a quick doubleclick erasure.

⁅ moving inactive windows and palettes

As in the Finder, you can move a SuperPaint window without making it the active by holding down ⁅⌘⁆ while you drag it by its title bar. This also works on the tool and pattern palettes, so if they overlap anyplace and you want to move the bottom one without having it come to the top, hold ⁅⌘⁆ while you drag the floating window to its new position.

⁅ the Close All command

If you hold down ⁅Option⁆ while opening the File menu, the *Close* command changes to *Close All.* As in the Finder, you can also [Option]-click in the close box of any open document window and all the windows will close. (If any of the documents have been edited, you'll be asked if you want to save the changes.)

⚫ *zooming shortcuts*

There are two shortcuts for jumping from regular view to maximum magnification (8x). Doubleclicking on ⬚ in the palette centers the magnified view around whatever was in the center of the last view. [⌘]-clicking with ⬚ anywhere in the document centers the magnified view around the spot you click on.

shortcut

⚫ *keyboard zooms*

Unlike the *Zoom In* and *Zoom Out* commands in the View menu, which make the view one step larger or smaller than the current view, these three keyboard commands take you directly to the greatest or smallest magnification, or back to the regular view.

shortcut

[Shift] [⌘] [W]	reduced, "page" view
[Shift] [⌘] [E]	8x magnification mode *(forever known in our hearts as FatBits, no matter what any given program chooses to call it)*
[Shift] [⌘] [R]	regular view

When you use a keyboard command to zoom out or in, the new view is centered around the current position of the pointer.

⚫ *nudge arrows*

The *Left, Right, Up* and *Down* commands in the *Nudge* submenu (in the Edit menu) have easy keyboard equivalents: [←], [→], [↑] and [↓].

shortcut

⚫ *line patterns*

To change the current line pattern without having to click on it in the *Selection Indicator* (which shows whether you're selecting Line or Fill patterns), ⌘-click on any pattern in the palette. That pattern becomes the current Line pattern but the indicator remains pointing to the Fill pattern.

⬤ *Paint/Draw from Center or Corner*

shortcut

A shortcut for choosing the commands *Paint (Draw) from Center* and *Paint (Draw) from Corner* is to doubleclick on the rectangle, rounded rectangle and circle tools in the palette. When *Paint (Draw) from Center* is active, small crosses appear in the centers of the shape tools in the palette.

⬤ ✋ *tricks*

Pressing [Spacebar] gives you ✋ so you can move the document around. But if you're working with ⌶ for text, [Spacebar] of course just types spaces, so use ⌘ [Spacebar] instead.

If you hold down [Shift] when you're using ✋, the document will move only horizontally or vertically (whichever way you move first).

⬤ *smaller eraser*

Holding [Option] while you use ⟋ changes it from a sixteen-pixel square to an eight-pixel square.

⬤ *power-erasing the Paint layer*

Doubleclicking on ⟋ erases everything in the Paint layer that's showing in the window. Holding down [Option] and [⌘] while doubleclicking on ⟋ erases the entire paint layer regardless of what portion is showing in the window.

⬤ ⬚ *tricks*

As in most paint programs, if you press [⌘] while using ⬚, it shrinks down (as soon as you let go of the mouse button) to the smallest size that will enclose all the black pixels of the selected area.

If you hold down [Option] while using ⬚, the selection is lassoed as soon as you let go of the mouse button—and the current tool switches to ℘.

❡ ℘ *tricks*

Pressing ⌈Option⌋ while you use ℘ keeps it from shrinking when you let go of the mouse button. It stays where you traced it, enclosing any white space you selected.

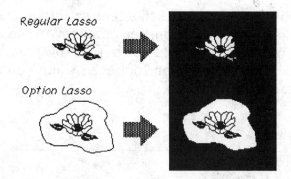

❡ *the x-ray* ℘

Holding ⌈⌘⌋ while you lasso activates "x-ray" mode. No white parts are selected, even if they're totally surrounded by black.

very hot tip

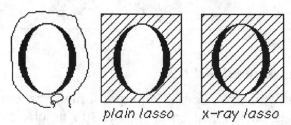

plain lasso   *x-ray lasso*

❡ *selecting all*

When used on the Paint layer, the *Select All* command (in the Edit menu) normally selects the layer in a rectangle as large as the page. If you hold ⌈⌘⌋ while you choose *Select All*, the rectangle shrinks to the smallest size possible that encloses all the black dots in the document. If you hold ⌈Option⌋ while you choose *Select All*, everything in the Paint layer is lassoed and the current tool switches to ℘.

⚫ *selections in selections*

*very
hot
tip*

Once you've made a selection in the Paint layer, the pointer changes to an arrow when you move it within the selection. (To be precise, within a *lassoed* selection it only changes to an arrow when you're over a black dot.)

If you want to make a different selection that begins inside the current selection, you don't have to deselect the current one first. Just hold down Tab. The pointer will remain the current selection tool even when you're within the already-selected area.

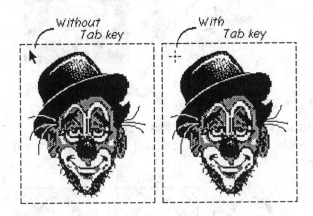

⚫ *paint modes and text*

When you use normal (Opaque) paint, the background is whited out as you type, for the full height of the text. When you use Transparent paint, however, you can type text without disturbing the background.

Typing in Opaque Paint mode

Typing in Transparent Paint mode

The Paint on Black mode isn't supported for text in QuickDraw, so SuperPaint can't do it either. If you use the

Text tool when Paint on Black is selected, you'll get the Transparent mode instead.

⚫ *temporary transparency*

No matter which paint mode you've chosen in the Paint menu (*Opaque, Transparent, Paint on Black* or *Invert*), if you hold ⌘ when using a paint tool, the paint type is temporarily changed to *Transparent*. This works not only for tools like 🖌 and ✍, but also for the shape tools:

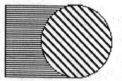 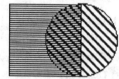

Opaque shapes   Transparent shapes

⚫ *limited pours*

When you use ✍, it normally fills an enclosed area, even if parts of that enclosed area are not visible in the window. If you hold Option when you pour, the paint pours only into the area that's visible in the window.

⚫ 📷 *shapes*

Did you think 📷 was forever restrained to its basic round pattern? So did I, until I very belatedly discovered that if you hold down Option while using it, the spray pattern changes to the currently selected 🖌 shape. (The spray pattern of the pointer doesn't change until you actually press the mouse button.)

⚫ *30° and 60° lines*

It's second nature to those of us who had MacPaint in the early days to use Shift to constrain movements of paint tools to horizontal and vertical, and to use it to get 90° (horizontal and vertical) and 45° lines with the Line tool. All this works in SuperPaint, but you can also get perfect 30° and 60° lines by holding down Option when using the Line tool.

very hot tip

⚫ *text boxes in the Draw layer*

When you click somewhere in the Draw layer with ⌶, the initial width of the text box extends from the point of the click to the right edge of the window. Although you can always resize the text box in the normal way (by dragging on a handle), it's easier to start with something close to what you want. So instead of clicking with ⌶, use it to drag the text box to the width you want.

⚫ *picking up patterns*

very hot tip

Here's a trick that works with both the Pattern Edit and Brush Shape dialog boxes. When the dialog box is open, move the pointer outside the box, press the mouse button and drag the pointer around. Anything beneath the pointer is "picked up" and sent to the edit area of the dialog box. This lets you take any pattern from the screen and make it either a defined pattern in the palette or a brush shape. (This also works in MacPaint.)

You don't have to keep the click inside the document window for the pickup: it works anywhere on the screen.

⚫ ⌘-*click invert*

very hot tip

In both the Brush Shapes and Pattern Edit dialog boxes, a ⌘-click in the edit area reverses the black-and-white pixels of the pattern.

⚫ *arcs*

The Arc tool makes either a wedge (like a slice of pie, if there's a paint pattern selected) or an arc (if the *None* pattern is selected) but either way, a quarter of an oval is created.

If you want more or less of an arc, you can do it in the Draw layer. Draw an arc, choose *Reshape Arc* from the Draw menu and drag one of the arc's handles to continue the curve or shorten it.

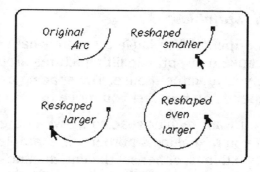

⚫ adding "corners"

When you use the *Reshape Polygon* command on a polygon in the Draw layer, you can not only drag the original "corners" to reshape it but you can also add new corners. Just hold ⌘ down as you move a handle and a new handle will be dragged out of it.

very hot tip

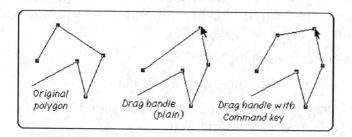

⚫ skipping dialog boxes

You can bypass some dialog boxes whose settings you don't want to change by holding down (Option) while you choose the command from the menu. For example, if you want to scale a selection to the same proportions as the last time you used the *Scale Selection,* just hold down (Option) while choosing *Scale Selection.* The dialog box won't open and the current settings will be used. This also works for the *Other* command (for point sizes, in the Text menu) and the *Rotate Selection* command in the Transform menu.

shortcut

🍎 spacing "sprinkles"

Many of SuperPaint's plug-in tools are what I call "sprinklers," because they sprinkle little pictures around at random when you drag the mouse. The spacing between the images depends on how fast you move the mouse.

When you want regular spacing between the sprinkled pictures (if you're making a border, for example), you can do one of two things: either set the line thickness to something other than the default single-pixel width (the line thickness then controls the amount of space between "sprinkles" when you drag the mouse slowly), or turn on a grid of about a quarter-inch (that's about the best spacing for these little pictures) and then [Shift]-drag the mouse to set the images at the grid points.

🍎 white outlines around graphics

very
hot
tip

When you want to place a solid black graphic against a black or patterned background and need a white outline around it to make it visible:

- Select the graphic with 〽️.

- Choose *Trace Edges* from the Paint menu.

- Drag the selection against the background (don't click anywhere to deselect it yet).

- Choose *Invert* from the Paint menu.

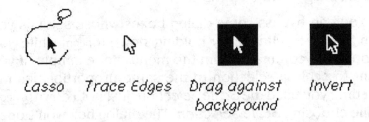

Lasso   Trace Edges   Drag against   Invert
background

To put a white outline around a more complex graphic, you need a few extra steps. (This tip only works for graphics with a solid outline, where there are no breaks in the perimeter of the figure for the Lasso to slip into.)

- Select the item with with ✏.

- Pull out a copy of the graphic by holding [Option] as you drag.

- Choose *Trace Edges* from the Paint menu.

- Drag the copied item against the background.

- Choose *Invert* from the Paint menu.

- Lasso the original graphic and drag it on top of the inverted figure.

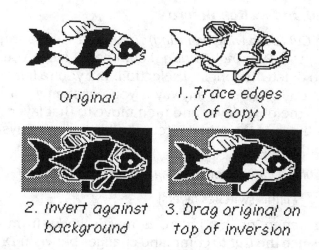

Original

1. Trace edges (of copy)

2. Invert against background

3. Drag original on top of inversion

🍎 paint and draw macros

Simple macro utilities like MacroMaker have limited abilities when it comes to painting or drawing tools. You can record a macro that plays back the use of a shape tool (rectangle, circle, etc.), but since a drag of the mouse is recorded simply as the start and the end points of the drag, and not the path the mouse took between those points, you can't record squiggly lines drawn with ✎ or 🖌.

important warning

Recorded   Playback

Also remember that if you only record the drag of a tool, and not the tool selection itself, the macro will play back your moves with whatever tool is currently selected in the tool palette.

You can use this simple playback ability to instantly paint or draw lines or shapes to specific sizes. Record them while using the Rulers so you get the size you need, then play them back at any time; the same size is drawn without your having to turn on the Rulers and measure.

✦ *a cut-and-switch macro*

shortcut

The *Cut to Drawing (Painting)* command saves a step over the *Copy to Drawing (Painting)* command, since you don't have to delete the original selection. But you're left with an extra step to perform anyway if you constantly cut something to the other layer and then move to that layer. To do the cutting and then the switching all in a single keystroke, record this macro:

- *Cut to Drawing* (or *Painting)* from the Edit menu

- ⌘ / [this switches layers]

The beauty of this macro is that it works from either layer, since the *Cut to* command changes between *Drawing* and *Painting* depending on what layer you're on.

✦ *line and fill macros*

shortcut

No matter what line and fill patterns you use, you usually wind up returning to two basic combinations: black line and white fill, and black line and no fill. You can record macros that instantly return you to either of these combinations. Record this sequence:

- Click on the Line pattern indicator.

- Click on *Black.*

- Click on the Fill pattern indicator.

- Click on *White.*

Store the macro under ⌜Option⌝ ⌜⌘⌝ ⌜W⌝ and replay it anytime you need the black/white combination. Then record the same sequence but click on *None* as the Fill pattern; store that under ⌜Option⌝ ⌜⌘⌝ ⌜N⌝. (Remember: the macros will work correctly only if the Patterns window is still in the same spot on the screen as when you recorded them.)

❤ *Multigon macros*

Here's a keyboard shortcut for selecting various Multigons:

shortcut

- Choose *Multigon Sides* from the Options menu.

- Click on the triangle.

- Click on the *OK* button.

Store this macro under ⌜⌘⌝ ⌜3⌝, the equivalent one for a rectangle under ⌜⌘⌝ ⌜4⌝, the one for a pentagon under ⌜⌘⌝ ⌜5⌝, and so on.

❤ *changing the order of plug-in tools*

The *plug-in* paint tools appear in the palette in alphabetical order, with the exception of the Airbrush, which always gets the first spot. So all you have to do to change the order is go out to the Finder and rename the files in the folder called *SP Pouch*. (See *keeping filenames at the top of lists* in Chapter 6 to find out how alphabetizing of special characters is handled.) To check the new order, just choose *by Name* from the View command while you're still in the folder.

General draw program tips

❡ drawing polygons (Lena McGuire/Carol Aiton/SZA)

very hot tip

This entry (and the next) will work in any draw program—including a PostScript-based one like FreeHand and Illustrator—so long as it lets you repeatedly replicate an object, specifying an angle between the copies. But be aware that some draw programs, like SuperPaint, have easier ways to create polygons (although none that we know of can draw stars, other than by using the technique in the next entry).

The step-by-step instructions here are for SuperPaint's Draw layer, but you can use the same approach in the drawing program of your choice (just the names of the commands will be different).

- Decide on how many sides you want, and then divide 360 (the number of degrees in a circle) by that number. In this example, we'll use a ten-sided polygon (called a *decagon*), which gives us 36°.

- Draw a vertical line with the Line tool.

- While the line's selected, choose *Replicate* from the Edit menu. Specify four copies of the line, rotated at 36° around the *center* of the object. (That's five lines all together, with ten endpoints.) This is what you'll get:

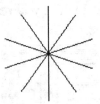

In some programs, you may find it easier to make this initial shape by using shorter rays that fan out from the center (radiuses, in other words) instead of longer lines that spin around a center point. The number of degrees between each spoke remain the same, so in this example, you'd need to specify nine additional rays at 36°. You'll have to take that approach, no matter program you're in, to create polygons with odd numbers of sides (five, say, or nine).

- Select all the lines, group them and then lock them so they won't be moved or changed while you draw the other lines.

- Now use the Polygon tool to click lines around the endpoints of the locked lines. When you're finished, unlock the background object and delete it. Here's what the process will look like:

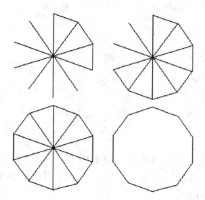

⚞ *drawing stars* (Lena McQuire/Carol Aiton/SZA)

By using techniques similar to those in the previous entry, you can also draw stars. Start the same way as for the polygon, replicating lines around in a circle. You need twice as many rays as you want points in the star—so, for a five-pointed star you'll need the ten rays. Then:

very hot tip

- Draw a circle that's the size you want for the *valleys* of your star. (The ends of the lines are for the points.)

- Center the circle over the lines. (You can draw the circle outward from the center point of the lines if you're in *Draw from Center* mode.) So far it looks like this:

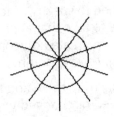

- Select the Polygon tool and click at the end of one line, then at the point where the second line intersects the circle, then at the end of the third line, then at the point where the fourth line intersects through the circle; and so on. When you're finished, delete the background lines and the circle. It looks like this:

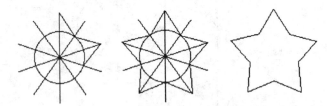

Changing the size of the inner circle makes a big difference in the overall look of the star. Here are some seven-pointed examples:

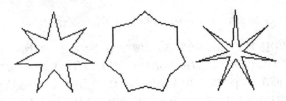

MacDraw tips

Shift menu commands

shortcut

There are keyboard equivalents for many of MacDraw's menu commands—they're just not listed in the menu. Here they are:

Open As Library	Shift ⌘ O
Save As	Shift ⌘ S
Unsmooth	Shift ⌘ E
Move to Front	Shift ⌘ F
Move to Back	Shift ⌘ J
Alignment	Shift ⌘ K
Ungroup	Shift ⌘ G
Unlock	Shift ⌘ H

There are also some Shift ⌘ combinations for commands that aren't in menus:

very
hot
tip

Shift ⌘ A selects all the objects in the *document* (as opposed to all the documents in the *layer*, which is what Select All does).

Shift ⌘ V rescales an image to the current ruler settings as you paste it

Shift ⌘ W cycles through the opened windows.

Shift ⌘ M toggles between 100% view and the last zoom level that you set.

Shift ⌘ 1 through Shift ⌘ 9 switch views.

❡ *moving horizontally or vertically* (C.J. Weigand)

As in most Mac graphics programs, you can force an object (or group of objects) to move exactly horizontally or vertically (and nothing in between) by holding down Shift as you drag. But in MacDraw, be sure to press the mouse button down before you press Shift or you'll simply deselect whatever object you click on.

important
warning

❡ *dragging to select objects*

In some object-oriented programs, you have to *completely* enclose an object in the rectangle you drag with the selection arrow in order for that object to be included in the selection. Other programs include an object in the selection as long as *any part* of it is within the dragged rectangle.

very
hot
tip

MacDraw works both ways. As a default, you have to completely surround an object for it to be selected by dragging. But if you hold [⌘] while you're dragging, the selection will include any object that was even partly covered by the drag.

selecting through layers

shortcut

When you click on an object and its handles don't appear (to indicate that it's been selected), it's probably in another layer. If you don't want to switch layers to get it, just [Option]-click on it.

selecting objects of a kind

I haven't ever needed to do this, but it's nice to know that it's there: you can select all the objects (in a layer or the entire document) of a specific kind—all the rectangles, for example, or all the ovals. Simply click on a shape tool in the palette before you choose *Select All* from the Edit menu.

dragging object outlines

When you move more than one object at a time, all you'll see is an outline of the last object selected inside a gray rectangle that shows the overall dimensions of the entire selection. (In the illustrations below, the cross-hatched circle is last object selected and the empty circle is the outline.)

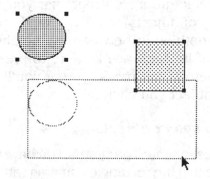

If you want to see outlines of the individual objects in the selection, hold [⌘] while you drag:

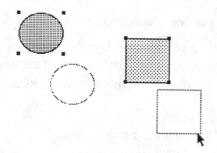

♦ retaining the tool you're using

When you draw a shape, or type text, the pointer normally reverts to the selection arrow as soon as you're done. If you want to retain the tool so you can use it again immediately, doubleclick on the tool in the palette to select it (instead of the usual single click).

esp. for beginners

♦ two ways to copy text *(C.J. Weigand)*

If you select a block of text with ▶ , copy it to the Clipboard and then paste it into a page layout or word processing program, it will become a PICT image that can be stretched or reshaped but not edited. (For more on this, see *creating special typographic effects* on pp. 375–76.) If you select the same text with the text tool (Ị), it will transfer as editable text.

very hot tip

♦ placing pastes

When you paste an object, it appears centered in a window. If you want it centered on a particular point instead, click on that spot before you use the *Paste* command.

♦ angled lines

When you hold ⌜Shift⌝ in almost any Mac graphics program, the line you're drawing is constrained to the horizontal or the vertical, or sometimes the 45° angle between. This is also true in MacDraw, but you can change that inbetween constrained angle to anything you want by typing in the desired angle in the *Mouse Constraint* text box in the Preferences dialog box.

very hot tip

☀ quick Pen pattern selection

shortcut

You don't have to click on the Pen Pattern box and then on the pattern you want for lines and outlines—instead, just hold (Option) while you click on the pattern you want for the pen.

☀ changing the ruler's zero point

shortcut

To change the position of the zero point on the ruler (it's usually at the extreme top and left of the ruler) just click anywhere on the ruler with ▶ . If you have the grid turned on, the zero point will jump to one of the grid lines.

If you don't want this to happen accidentally by a slip of the mouse, click the *Zero point locked* button in the Rulers dialog box.

☀ Bezier-like curves (C.J. Weigand)

*very
hot
tip*

You can draw and edit curves quickly and accurately in MacDraw without having to struggle with the limitations of the arc tool. The trick is to create the equivalent of a Bezier curve. Here's how you do it:

Draw an open polygon with four or more sides. While the polygon is still selected, choose *Smooth* from the Edit menu. Then choose *Reshape Polygon.* You'll end up with a Bezier-like curve having two end points and two control points. Dragging these points lets you reshape the curve to fit any path.

For more complex curves, draw the approximate shapes using the freehand tool. When you're done, choose *Smooth* and *Reshape Polygon* from the Edit menu. This will change your irregularly-shaped curves into nicely smoothed ones. You can then edit them like any other polygons.

Illustrator tips

❧ reduction and magnification

The magnifying glass can also be used as a reducer. Just hold down Option and the plus sign will change to a minus sign:

shortcut

When you don't see either a plus sign a minus sign, that means you can't zoom any further in the current direction.

When you click in the document with the zoom tool, the zooming is centered around the spot you clicked. If you want to zoom based on the center of the window, doubleclick on the zoom tool in the palette. A plain doubleclick magnifies the view; an Option doubleclick reduces the view.

❧ temporary tool changes

Three tools are used more often than others in Illustrator—the arrow pointer, the grabber hand for moving the page around on the screen, and the magnifying glass. You can temporarily change to any one of these tools without going to the tool palette, by pressing the following keys:

shortcut

❧ hand-y shortcuts

Doubleclicking on the hand in the palette will take you to the Fit in Window view. If you hold Option down, it will take you to Actual Size.

shortcut

❧ the Freehand-Pen tool switch

To temporarily switch from the Freehand tool to the Pen tool or vice versa, press Ctrl. When you release the key, you get the original tool back again.

shortcut

⚘ draw from center

To draw ellipses, rectangles and rounded rectangles from the center out instead of from the corner, hold down Option before you begin the drag.

⚘ the Shift constraint

As with most programs, holding Shift constrains the line you're drawing to the horizontal or vertical—or to the 45° angle in between. But the 45° angle changes according to the constraint angle you define in the Preferences dialog box—so if your lines aren't at the angle you expect, check the preferences settings.

⚘ ungrouping basic shapes

**very
hot
tip**

When you use a basic shape tool (ellipse, rectangle, round rectangle), it actually draws a series of lines and curves to make the shape. So you can take any shape you draw and ungroup it into its components. For example, this is the quickest way to get a half-circle:

- Draw a circle (hold Shift to keep it round).

- While the circle's still selected, choose *Ungroup* from the Element menu.

- Shift-click to select two of the circle's points that are across from each other.

- Choose *Split Elements* from the *Special* submenu in the Element menu.

- Select and delete the half of the circle you don't want.

- Select the two pieces of the circle that are left and choose *Group* from the Element menu.

⚘ the Option copy

The Option-copy trick that works in most paint programs also works in Illustrator—press Option as you drag a selected object and a copy will be dragged out of the original.

⚫ *using the arrow keys*

The arrow keys (⬆ ⬇ ⬅ ➡) move a selection a pixel at a time in the indicated direction—unless you specify a different unit of measure in the Preferences dialog box.

⚫ *missing page breaks*

If the dotted lines that indicate page breaks aren't showing in your document, that means you haven't yet selected a printer in the Chooser DA.

⚫ *partial tracings*

When you click on a bit-mapped shape with the Autotrace tool, it traces the entire item. If you only want to trace a section of a shape, don't click the tool. Instead, drag it on the shape—the tracing will start at the spot you started your drag and end at the spot you stopped dragging. In the illustration below, for example, dragging the line shown would cause only the wing to be traced.

very hot tip

FreeHand tips

⚫ *as goes Illustrator, so goes FreeHand* (AN)

If you notice some similarities between entries in this section and entries in the Illustrator section above, it's because FreeHand came out after Illustrator and copied many of its shortcuts and keyboard commands as well as its features. We would have just referred you to the other entries, but there are some subtle differences that would have only made that approach confusing.

🍎 *moving the info bar*

The thin info bar at the top of the screen (immediately below the menu bar) can be hidden by using the *Info Bar* command in the *Windows* submenu, and also can be dragged anywhere you want on the screen. If you only want to see the mouse coordinates, you can leave just the left end of the bar in sight, letting the rest of it hang off right side of the screen.

🍎 *temporary tool changes*

shortcut

Three tools are used more often than others in Free-Hand—the arrow pointer, the grabber hand for moving the page around on the screen, and the magnifying glass. You can temporarily change to any one of these tools without going to the tool palette, by pressing the following keys:

(Wouldn't you think that Aldus would try for a little standardization across its programs? PageMaker uses Option to get 🖐, and it doesn't appear when you press the key—only after you press the mouse button.)

🍎 *keyboard tool selections*

shortcut

You can switch to any of the basic shape tools simply by pressing a number key on the keyboard. (This is the same as actually clicking on the tool, unlike the temporary tool selection described in the previous entry.) The keyboard commands work even if the toolbox is closed.

```
    ▼ |   A
1 - □ | ◯ - 2
3 - ◯ | ╲ - 4
5 - ∿ | ⊓ - 6
7 - ◤ | ⌇ - 8
9 - ⌐ | ⌠ - 0
```

❡ deselecting from the keyboard

To deselect everything in the document, press [Tab]. (This is useful when you've selected a small element on top of a larger one and can't click anywhere to deselect it without selecting the larger one.) To deselect points on a path without deselecting the path itself, press [`].

very hot tip

❡ reduction and magnification

The *Scale* subcommands in the View menu reduce or enlarge the view, zooming in or out on the center of the window. If you want your zoom to be centered on another spot, use the magnifying glass instead, clicking on the spot you want to be the center of the new view.

shortcut

To use the magnifying glass to reduce a view, hold down [Option]: the plus sign in the tool changes to a minus sign to show you which way the zoom will work.

❡ draw from center

You can draw ellipses, rectangles and rounded rectangles from the center out instead of from the corner by holding [Option] before you begin the drag.

❡ ungrouping basic shapes

When you draw an oval, rectangle or rounded rectangle, you've actually drawn a series of lines and curves that are

very hot tip

automatically grouped. See the entry of this same name in the Illustrator section above for how you can use this information to, for example, draw a perfect half-circle.

♠ deleting elements or parts

When you press ⌊Delete⌋, what's deleted depends on what's selected. If an entire element is selected, it disappears. If just a corner of it's selected, the corner disappears and the path closes, joining the corners on either side of the deleted one.

♠ transformation dialog boxes

shortcut

Each of the transformation tools (scale, skew, rotate and so on) has a dialog box available. Instead of using the tool to drag an element on the screen, you can type the transformation values you need right in the dialog box—and get exactly what you need right away. To open the dialog box for any of the transformations, ⌊Option⌋-click on the element you want to transform.

♠ optimal resizing

To resize a graphic to its optimum size for the resolution of the printer you're using, hold ⌊Option⌋ while you drag on the element's handle to resize it. But first make sure you've selected the correct printer in the Document Setup dialog box. If you're, say, proofing things on a LaserWriter but will end up on an imagesetter, choose the imagesetter, so the graphics will be sized correctly for the final output.

♠ text kerning

very good feature

You can kern text in the Text dialog box by tenths and hundredths of an em:

⌘ Delete	subtract .01 em
Shift ⌘ Delete	add .01 em
⌘ Shift ←	subtract .1 em
⌘ Shift →	add .1 em

✎ scaling text on a path

The effect of scaling text on a path depends on whether or not you've grouped the text and the path. (Text on a path is always "stuck" to the path, so that selecting the path also selects the text—but that's not the same as the text and path being grouped with the *Group* command.) If the text and the path aren't grouped, scaling changes only the size of the *path* and doesn't affect the font size. If the text and the path are grouped, scaling also changes the font size.

very
hot
tip

✎ text block manipulations

Dragging the corner handle of a text block changes the size of the block and rewraps the text in it, but dragging any of its other handles, or dragging a corner handle with [Option] held down, changes the text inside. In each case, the change to the text mirrors the change to the text box so the box remains filled—top to bottom, side to side—even in its new size. Here's a summary of what happens:

- Dragging on a top or bottom handle changes the line spacing.

- Dragging on a side handle changes the letter spacing.

- Dragging on a side handle while holding down [Option] changes the word spacing.

- Dragging a corner handle while holding down [Option] resizes the type to fit in the new block size.

- Holding [Shift] while you resize the text with [Option] resizes it proportionately.

Clip art

✎ beautiful vs. useful? (AN)

There seems to be an idea afoot that business graphics need to be simple cartoons. Detailed, painterly drawings are seen as somehow frivolous and therefore not business-like. I don't understand this. With the exception of things like charts and graphs, business graphics *are* illustrations. They're there to make something clearer and/or more appealing, and the prettier they are, the better.

It is true, of course, that some kinds of illustrations are more likely to be useful than others. But given a choice between a beautiful drawing of a pair of pliers and an ugly drawing of a pair of pliers, a hardware store would be wise to use the former.

Even art that doesn't apply directly to your business can be seen as a challenge. A flyer with a gorgeous picture of a bird on it, say, might well sell more desks than one with nothing on it but minimalist cartoons of desks. I'm not saying you never need simple, practical drawings, but beautiful, seemingly irrelevant drawings have their place in business communications too.

✎ clip art formats

There are several graphics formats for the Mac (for the differences between them, see the first couple of entries in this chapter). Of the main four, all but PICT are commonly used for clip art.

✎ WetPaint (AN/SZA)

very good feature

This is far-and-away our favorite collection of bit-mapped clip art. It has ten packages—nine with three 800K disks and one with two 800K disks, for a total of over 22 megabytes of art.

We'd show you some samples but we like them so much we've used them between chapters and other places throughout the book; they're much more dramatic there than here. (To find them, just look in the index under *WetPaint, illustrations from.*)

bargain

WetPaint's three-disk sets cost $80 each (which amounts to about 3¢ per K for some of the best clip art around); it's two-disk Egyptian set costs $50. There are five packages of modern illustrations—Classic Clip Art, Publishing, Animal Kingdom, Island Life and All the People—and four pack-

ages of art from the turn-of-the-century—Special Occasions,
Printer's Helper, Industrial Revolution and Old Earth Almanac

Each WetPaint package comes with two desk accessories: ArtRoundup, which lets you open paint files from within
another application and edit them with all the usual paint
tools, and PatternMover, which lets you edit MacPaint patterns and transfer them between files. WetPaint's manuals
are well-written, clear and complete, and they contain
printouts of all the images on the disks.

**very good
feature**

🍎 *ClickArt* (AN/SZA)

T/Maker published the first package of Macintosh clip
art way back when; now it has five volumes of bit-mapped
images and two of EPS images. The bit-mapped packages
are Personal Graphics (the original ClickArt volume), Business Images, Holidays, Christian Images and Publications.
They all cost $50 except for Christian Images, which costs
$60 (God demands higher royalties, presumably).

bargain

Business Images contains a zillion or more arrows,
monetary and computer images, pieces of graphs, charts
and frames, and flags, state outlines and minor office items
like paper clips and pencils. Holidays contains everything
from turkeys and pumpkins to flag bunting, Easter bunnies
and mentors. Arthur's favorite illustration is one you could
use for a party anytime during the winter (or for a formal
party any time of year):

**very good
feature**

Please Join Us

Christian Images contains one file of 93 crosses, another of 36 stylized signs (Prayer Group, In Memoriam, Announcing, etc.) and that just scratches the surface. Any church or religious group should be able to find what it needs for newsletters and flyers in this collection. Here's one of Arthur's favorites (it shows the world's most famous seder):

The most recent ClickArt volume of bitmap images is Publications. All the images come both as paint files and in a HyperCard stack. If you use HyperCard, this is convenient, because HyperCard's Find feature can help you look for pictures, but it means you're only getting about 380K of art on an 800K disk. Also included is T/Maker's new ClipOut desk accessory that lets you access any paint file from within whatever application you're in.

Despite the short count on total art, Sharon thinks *Publications* is T/Maker's best bit-mapped offering so far. Here are a few examples:

T/Maker's two sets of EPS clip art, called Business Art and Illustrations, each contain four disks and cost $130.

The images on Illustrations vary from the useful to the striking, like the bear shown below. Among the most useful things on these disks are individual drawings of the fifty states (we've shown Louisiana and Alaska, which look particularly good with the drop shadow).

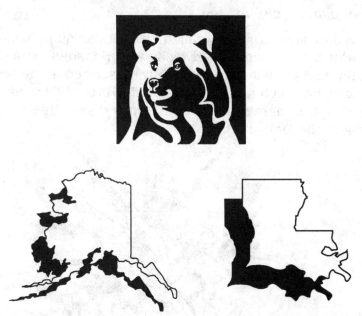

The Business Art set contains beautifully-rendered images of office items like staplers, scissors and tape dispensers, as well as borders and dingbats for memos and pictures of people and office equipment.

♦ McPic

Two oldies but goodies are volumes 1 & 2 of McPic. Both volumes are filled with high-quality, general-purpose images, and come with the best idea-filled manual you'll find. Here are some examples:

♦ Japanese clip art (AN)

A Japanese company called Enzan-Hoshigumi has a series of bit-mapped clip-art disks with Japanese subjects. (They also publish MacCalligraphy, described at the beginning of the chapter; both are distributed in the US by Qualitas Trading Co.) Here's an example from a disk of theirs called Year of the Dragon '88:

● *Images with Impact!*

If Dubl-Click software defines the word quality for bit-mapped clip art (and it does), then 3G Graphics defines it for EPS images. Each of its three collections comes packed with useful images and a clearly written, idea-filled manual.

very good feature

The Graphics and Symbols collection (two 800K disks for $100) comes with a variety of images—a mime in various positions, for example, or a mail-carrier pigeon (shown below) in different poses, so you can use them to establish a theme in your publication. There are also collages on various subjects (food, travel, and a very busy neighborhood); they're made up of grouped images that you can ungroup and use individually.

The second collection is called Business (four 800K disks for $130). It contains people, occupation logos, computers, office equipment and hands doing a variety of things—clicking a mouse, holding tickets, typing and shaking hands. Here are two examples:

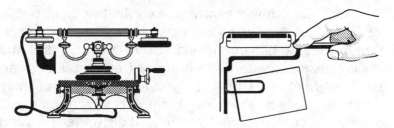

3G's final collection (so far) is Accents and Borders (four 800K disks, plus a bonus fifth disk of color art, for $130).

They provide a wide variety of borders and accents like the ones shown below, many of which come in matched sets so you can design an integrated line of stationery, publications or whatever.

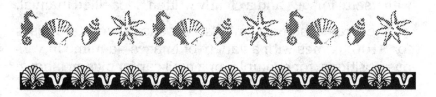

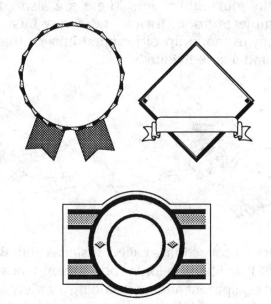

🍎 *Image Club Digit-Art* (AN)

very good feature

Image Club, many of whose excellent outline fonts we describe and display in Chapter 7, also offers a wide selection of exciting EPS graphics on CD-ROM. There are fifteen collections of various sizes (ranging from about two megs to about five) at $100 each (you send them your money and they send you the code that unlocks them on the CD, so you can copy them onto your hard disk). Here are some of my favorites:

Image Club also distributes photographic clip art in TIFF format; for more on that, see the last entry in this chapter.

Multi-Ad Services (AN/SZA)

If you've ever wondered how what you're doing will play in Peoria, there's an easy way to guarantee that it will do OK. Peoria-based Multi-Ad Services offers two collections of EPS clip art, and if they don't know how it will play in Peoria, who will?

The first collection has a name that simply shouts refinement and good taste: Kwikee In-House Pal Potpourri. Here are some samples from it:

Multi-Ad Services' second collection has a more restrained name: ProArt. It has pictures in six different areas—Business, Holidays, Sports, Food, People, and Borders and Headings— each priced at $1.40. Here are some samples:

photographs in TIFF format (AN)

Image Club sells a CD of black-and-white photographs in TIFF format; they're scanned from the Focus library of stock photos. You're allowed to use the black-and-white images for free, as long as you include a credit line; if you want the color image, however, you have to negotiate a fee with Focus.

very bad feature

There are two problems with this approach. The first is that the gigantic "credit line," which is dropped out in black at the bottom of the image and contains huge white letters, is so intrusive, so dominant, that I can't imagine a case where you'd want the picture enough to put up with it. Whatever mood or graphic effect you were going for would be spoiled by it.

The other problem is that, beautiful as these images are in full color in the catalog, they don't look all that great scanned, in black-and-white, printed on a laser printer— even though each TIFF file takes up more than a meg. They would no doubt look a lot better on an imagesetter—but you'd still have to deal with the credit line from hell.

very bad feature

Comstock, a stock-photo service in New York, also distributes black-and-white TIFF scans of color images on a CD. They don't have the big, ugly credit line, but then, they don't need one, because you're only allowed to use their black-and-white images for in-house publications (notices on bulletin boards, say, or internal newsletters) or for comps (detailed mockups you show to clients). For any other use, you have to buy rights to the picture.

Being able to use the TIFF images in comps isn't that much of an advantage; you could do almost as well with a good photocopy of the image from the catalog. So what this really amounts to is Comstock selling you their catalog on CD. Still, for in-house use, it *may* be worth having, so long as it doesn't cost too much. (I'd tell you what they're charging, but it doesn't say in any of the materials they sent me.)

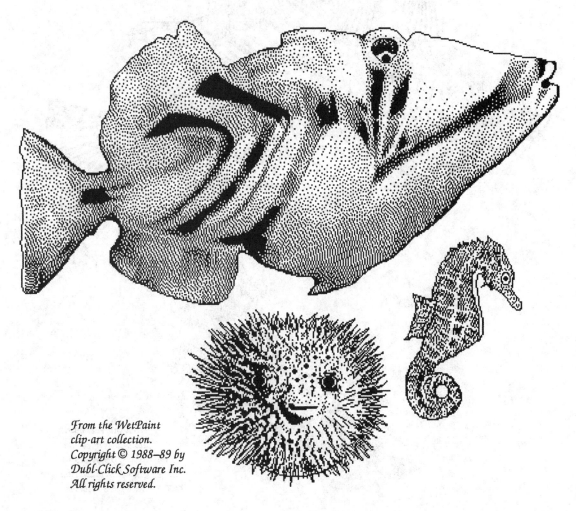

Chapter 14

Page layout

Page layout programs

⬥ *page layout choices*

Professionals who need super-fine control over text and placement of graphics should use QuarkXpress (which is called *Quark* by virtually everybody, even though that's the name of the company and not the program). It's also the only Mac page layout program that's specifically designed to interface with the ultra-high-end Scitex scanner, which makes it a must for many professionals.

Like Quark, PageMaker (from Aldus) costs $800; it probably has 90% of Quark's functionality (and that's probably the 90% you need). But there's more to a program than features; PageMaker's interface is simple and consistent, and it lets you do an amazing variety of things with very few tools. I've found it such a pleasure to work with that I recommend it to anyone who doesn't need Quark's special features. (For *much* more on these two programs, see the next entry.)

very good feature

Ready,Set,Go! ($500) has some fine-tuning controls lacking in PageMaker, and it lets you rearrange pages by dragging them around in a thumbnail view. *(But it's missing many more important features and doesn't begin to compare to Page-Maker or Quark in power.—AN)*

(The new high-end version of Ready,Set,Go!, which is called DesignStudio, has lots of features. It costs the same $800 that Quark and PageMaker do, but it doesn't have their track record. It also implements style sheets in an idiosyncratic (and possibly problematic) way.—Byron Brown)

Publish It! ($400 from TimeWorks), which used to be called Scoop, offers combined layout, word processing, painting and drawing. Despite its wealth of features, it's a small program, so you can run it on a 512e; it's also fast, so if you're working on a Plus with just a meg of memory, you might want to consider it. But its interface is...well...a little clumsy.

Springboard Publisher costs $200, although you can probably get it discounted for around $100. It's a good bet if you do fliers, brochures or simple, short newsletters. It's really aimed at ImageWriter output (although it doesn't say that anywhere explicitly).

things to come

There's also a page layout program with a lot of promise that's waiting in the wings as I write this: Personal Press ($300) from Silicon Beach.

very hot tip

Remember—you don't need a layout program to do basic layouts, or even some fairly fancy ones. Most high-end word processors can do lots of tricks on a page, and graphics programs can do good layouts as well, if they don't run to too many pages.

♦ *PageMaker vs. QuarkXpress* (Byron Brown)

[PageMaker and Quark are among the most powerful, full-featured programs on the Mac. I've always been interested in the real differences between them, as have many people I've talked to. So I asked Byron Brown, who's had a lot *of experience with both programs, to compare and contrast them. His original manuscript was 28 pages long! Even after editing it down, it's far and away the longest entry in the book. But these are important (and expensive) programs, and this is an insightful comparison, so I feel the length is well used.—AN]*

important warning

I should begin by mentioning that, although I was able to spend a lot of time with the release version of PageMaker 4.0, I had to review a beta version of QuarkXpress 3.0, with minimal documentation. But I have spent several years working with earlier versions of both programs on a wide variety of projects. (I haven't done much work with color, however, so I won't cover that in this review.

PageMaker and Quark represent two different approaches to page design, but they've been growing closer together. Version 3.0 of Quark joins PageMaker in using a *pasteboard*—a storage and work area outside the page, the contents of which don't print out.

In PageMaker, the pages of a document are stacked on top of each other like a book or pad—you can see either one page or a *spread* (two facing pages) at a time. The pasteboard is the same for all pages and is big enough to store entire pages. If you want to move a graphic or a piece of text from one page to another, you can drag it to the pasteboard, go to the new page and drag it back in from the pasteboard (you can also cut, copy and paste in the normal way).

very good feature

Quark's pages aren't stacked like PageMaker's—they're laid out in a vertical column, either one or two across. This allows you to literally scroll through the document rather than turning pages; it also means you can see more than a single spread in reduced views. To move items between pages, you can simply drag them as the window auto-scrolls. (The pasteboard is a smaller area to the left and right of each page or spread, and is unique to it.)

In PageMaker, you place objects on the page the way you do in actual, physical pasteup—stacking, overlapping, and moving discrete objects, completely independent of each other. If you draw a box around a text block or a graphic, it remains a separate object; to move them together, you have to select both. There are no boundaries constraining the movement of objects—only column guides to contain text, or guides you can snap objects to.

You size and position all objects—text blocks, graphics, lines or boxes—with the mouse. You can't position them numerically, by typing numbers in a dialog box. This is a surprising limitation, since another Aldus product, FreeHand, gives you both visual and numerical control—as does Quark, which takes a different approach.

very bad feature

To create text or graphics in Quark, you begin by drawing a box that defines an area of the page that will contain the text or an imported image. After creating this area with the mouse, you can redefine it numerically in a dialog box. This allows precise placement that's not dependent on the limitations of eye, mouse and screen. If you know the dimensions you want, typing numbers is a lot quicker than measuring with rulers.

very good feature

Boxes can have customizable borders called *frames,* which are linked with, and aligned to, the box's contents. Boxes can have a background fill of any color or shade. (PageMaker provides eight line thicknesses, but its lines and boxes are much less customizable than Quark's.)

**very good
feature**

Quark lets you *constrain* any box or line to a larger box that surrounds it; that means you can't move it out of the larger box, but moving the larger box moves all the items inside it with it. This can be useful for putting captions within graphic boxes, for example. In addition to constraining, you can group, align, space and/or lock objects. PageMaker has none of these features.

PageMaker's drawing tools are similar to those in graphics programs, but Quark has no actual drawing tools, other than two for straight lines. Instead, you use graphic boxes. For example, to create a rounded rectangle, you draw a graphics box, define a border for it, and simply leave it empty. Unfortunately, if you don't put a graphic in it, the shape has a double line around it with a big *X* in the middle. These *X's* inside what are simply empty shapes can get distracting, even though they don't print out.

Another difference in overall approach is how the two programs handle master pages. In PageMaker, whatever's on the master page (or pages, if you specify right and left) is like the bottom layer of any individual page, and yet it's not accessible from that page. On any document page, you can mask master page items, and you can choose to not have any of them show, but to actually remove or change them, you have to go back to the master page(s). On the other hand, whatever changes you make to a master page are immediately reflected on all the document pages. This is an important feature for long documents like reports, books and manuals.

The major drawback to PageMaker's master page approach is that you're limited to at most two master pages per document (right and left). This is especially limiting in book production. A chapter with *several sections* might need a different head for each section, which means you either have to use a separate document for each section (which requires that each starts on a new page) or manually add the heads on each page.

Quark has always taken a different approach to master pages (formerly called *default pages)*. Each document page is simply a copy of the default page, and any default item on it can be changed or removed at any time. In previous versions of the program, changes to the default page did not affect pages previously created (as in PageMaker). But in Quark 3.0, document pages are updated when you change the master page, can be assigned a master page before or after they're created, and can be changed from one master page to another after the fact. Even better, you can have over 100 master pages in any document.

very good feature

PageMaker also doesn't allow you to start automatic page numbering after the start of a document. This is bothersome in a book, for example, when you might want page number 1 to come after several pages of front matter. Aldus suggests getting around this by making the front matter a separate document. PageMaker 4.0 does, however, have a *Book* feature for linking documents to generate tables of contents and indexes—something Quark can't do. But Quark lets you have different page numbering in different parts of a document.

PageMaker has long suffered from a lack of basic word processing capabilities like spell-checking and search and replace. Version 4.0 will now do both, but requires that you first transfer the text from the normal page layout window to a separate Story Editor window (leaving a grey box in the layout window).

In the Story Editor window, all text is one font and one size (which you specify) with no page breaks, paragraph formatting, tabs or other modifications visible. The window scrolls easily and text editing is simple and direct. Both spell-checking and find/change work well. *(I found the spelling checker pretty primitive.—AN)*

*very bad
feature*

PageMaker *still* lets you have just one document open at a time (it must be the only remaining Mac program with that limitation), but the Story Editor can have many stories from a document open at once, and can open any story from any other PageMaker 4.0 document. This still isn't as good as several open documents, because you can't see or copy graphics or layout, but it's useful for copying text. It lets you preview stories before selecting them, or combine chunks of text from various places quickly.

Quark keeps all of its word-processing, finding and spell-checking in the document window, and is remarkably efficient about scrolling through the document pages for finding and spell-checking. But it can't search or spell-check selected text only (PageMaker can).

As you'd expect, both programs have sophisticated (and similar) paragraph and text formatting—except for PageMaker's tab dialog box. It does now let you set tabs numerically, and aligns the tab ruler with the left edge of the text block (unless that would put part of the ruler off the screen). Unfortunately, the ruler is a fixed length, which means you often have to scroll it when changing page view, which defeats the purpose of having it lined up over the paragraph in the first place. Quark's tab ruler is fixed at the top of the column and changes size with the page view.

Quark 3.0 has something I've always longed for—automatic drop caps! Simple and smooth, this feature is a real gem. Not all of Quark's text handling methods are so efficient, however. When you apply a style to text, all localized formatting is removed (e.g., single words in bold or italic). This can mean a lot of time spent redoing it if you have imported text from a word processor.

*very bad
feature*

Quark now has three floating palettes for streamlined document production. The *Measurement* palette has lots of very useful information about whatever's selected—all editable, so you don't have to open dialog boxes. *Library* palettes can be filled with objects for drag-copying into and out of documents at any time. And a *Document Layout* palette contains small page icons—each just big enough

*very good
feature*

for a page number and a letter that identifies its master page. In this palette, you can create new pages, rearrange existing ones and reassign master pages to them.

When you put a TIFF or EPS graphic in either PageMaker or Quark, it doesn't actually insert the whole graphic (if it did, the files would be gigantic). Instead, it notes where the TIFF or EPS graphic is on disk, and uses *that* when printing out. So if you go to a service bureau to print out on an imagesetter, you need to bring these linked TIFF or EPS files with you. To make that easier for you, both PageMaker and Quark provide a list of all the graphics linked to any of their files..

very good feature

Another thing that's handy to have when you're outputting at a service bureau is a list of the fonts used in a document. PageMaker still can't provide this, but Quark can. You can even do global searches for a given font and change it to another.

Both programs now offer *kerning* (closing up the space between letters to make them look better together). When the space is changed uniformly over a range of text (usually a line or more), it's called *track kerning* or simply *tracking*. Tracking lets you save a line by moving a word or two back up to the line above, or gain a line by spreading the letters in a paragraph ever so slightly to push the text down to an extra line. It's great for dealing with orphans and widows.

very good feature

Quark allows greater precision by allowing smaller adjustments to the interletter spacing than does PageMaker. PageMaker 4.0 is the first version to offer track kerning, so people will still be happy to have it, but it's too bad its capabilities are limited. Both programs make it easy to apply tracking from the keyboard, but only Quark lets you know how much you've already tracked (which is helpful in making adjustments later).

Quark 3.0 has a couple of clear advantages over Page-Maker 4.0. One is its ability to rotate text and graphics in .001° increments (with the mouse, or numerically). In PageMaker, you can only do that by 90° increments, which

very good feature

gives Quark a slight advantage in precision of 90,000 to 1! *(Being able to rotate text is the one thing I miss most in PageMaker.—AN)* Quark also lets you magnify any portion of the screen in 10% increments (up to 400%), which is useful when, say, 400% is too big and 200% is too small.

So, given all this, which program should you use? Well, first let's compare them as design tools. Design requires the ability to experiment with different layouts, to make changes and to be spontaneous while working—in a word, flexibility. Here PageMaker has tended to dominate.

very good feature

It remains an easier program to learn. The tools are simpler and more intuitive. It tends to feel cleaner and more fluid without all the boxes. Though it lacks a polygon or freehand tool, its graphic tools definitely provide more flexibility for simple drawing tasks like charts or simple shapes. For example, I was able to easily create the handicapped-accessible logo (a stylized icon of a person in a wheelchair)—something that would be next to impossible in Quark.

Quark has not been considered a designer's tool in previous versions, in part because it lacked drawing tools. This problem remains. And having to create a box before applying a new element to a page tends to stifle spontaneity. But you can now move objects as easily as in PageMaker, you can have many documents open at once and you can do a lot of things PageMaker can't (like rotate text).

The other major area of page layout work is production. It requires efficiency, precise control of output, and short-cuts for repetitive activities. PageMaker has improved its resources considerably, but Quark remains dominant here. When I work with an already created design, I generally choose Quark, because it's so easy to spec my work. An example would be a book with a lot of photographs that each require an outlined box of a certain size in the layout. It would be a painstaking job to measure each of a hundred boxes with the rulers on the screen in PageMaker. If your work is more of this type, you'll save time by using Quark.

I also find that it's easy to automate activities in Quark by stringing its many keyboard commands together in a sequence with a program like QuicKeys. Quark also offers the option of using the third party add-ons called Xtensions—these essentially allow major users to customize the program for specific purposes, and allow developers to collaborate with Quark to offer specialized features. This is part of the reason why Quark has been a big seller to newspapers and magazines across the country.

very good
feature

A final subject to mention is technical support. Quark, which has been clearly oriented to high-end users like newspapers and corporations, charges $250 a year for support—much more than Aldus's most expensive plan—and doesn't even offer an 800 number. What's worse, their support isn't very good. Sometimes I've been helped, but generally their tech staff has been unfriendly and not particularly knowledgeable. Often, I haven't even been called back when my question couldn't be answered on the phone. Other people have reported similar experiences with Quark. This is one of the most disappointing aspects of what is otherwise a fine program.

very bad
feature

Aldus has an 800 line for people who pay for the support and I've found the staff friendly and responsive, with pretty consistent return calls for questions that couldn't be answered immediately.

very good
feature

Basic design tips

⚫ *Rule # 1—break the rules* (AN)

Many professional designers would love to have you think that there's a right way and a wrong way to design something. That idea is not merely incorrect—it's absurd. Designs can't be right or wrong; they can only be better or worse. It's a subjective matter—although that certainly doesn't mean everybody's opinion is equally worth listening to.

very
hot
tip

The tips in the next entry (and in the books described at the end of this entry) are all good, sensible, basic guidelines to good design. But good design is, by definition, not boring (unless you think boredom is good). And yet it's easy to follow all those design rules and come up with something that makes phenobarbital seem like a stimulant.

If I had to come up with a design rule, it would be: *Never use Times or Helvetica for anything.* I think it's at least as universal as any of the others you're about to read. But let me give you a more general rule—*Fais ce que voudras* (as my old buddy Frankie Rabelais used to say): *Do what you want.*

✦ rule #2—follow the rules *(Rich Wolfson)*

If you don't have much of a design eye—and you *realize* that you don't—follow the rules. Times and Helvetica are eminently readable *[Nonsense. Helvetica is virtually unreadable as body text.—AN]* and have stood the test of time—they didn't become standards by accident. *[They became standards because most designers—and their clients—are afraid of their own shadows.—AN]* Using Times for body text and Helvetica for headlines is a safe, good-looking way to go *[Well, it's <u>safe</u>.—AN]*; their very unobtrusiveness lets the message get through.

[A layout that's too elaborate is like a stained glass window—beautiful, but hard to see through. Clear glass is boring to look at in itself, and you can see through it to other things. (And consider: clear glass took centuries longer to perfect than colored glass.)—SZA]

✦ basic design tips *(C.J. Weigand)*

Here are a few general design guidelines I've found useful.

- Mixing more than three typefaces or styles on a page is something a professional designer will do only very rarely.

- Use color to set your publications apart from others. Don't be gaudy. Spot color tastefully applied might be all you need to catch a reader's eye. In a market where color predominates, the absence of color can also be used to good effect.

- Leave plenty of white space to balance your compositions. A cluttered page is likely to be overlooked as being too "busy" to spend time with.

very hot tip

- Organize your message around a dominant visual element. A single large headline or graphic can help to focus your readers' attention; several will probably confuse them.

very hot tip

- Use subheads to break up your text and sustain interest. You can also separate large blocks of text by using well-placed pull quotes. Set them in a different font or type style from the main text.

- Additional emphasis can be given to text and graphics by accenting them with boxes or frames. Drop caps can further heighten interest, but should be used sparingly.

- Design facing pages together. Two pages that look great separately can clash terribly when placed next to each other.

very hot tip

- Above all, be consistent. Consistency lends credibility to your message.

🍎 *Looking Good in Print* (Steve Schwartz)

Thanks to desktop publishing software, millions of people now have the tools to create gaudy, unbalanced publications full of klutzy layouts and mismatched fonts. Just as easy-to-use financial software won't instantly make you a CPA, accessible desktop publishing tools won't magically give you taste.

A book called *Looking Good in Print*, by Roger C. Parker ($24, from Ventana Press), can help. It does a good job of covering design essentials, offers help in selecting typefaces and provides hints for effective use of the tools of the trade. Its heavy use of graphics makes it a quick read.

Although this book starts you thinking along the right lines, don't get the impression that knowledge of a few rules (coupled, of course, with a lot of creativity and imagination) will make you a good designer. If you're serious about learning design, treat *Looking Good in Print* as a jumping-off point to other reading and training. As that, it's quite good.

🍎 *The Makeover Book*

The Makeover Book ($18, from Ventana Press) is subtitled *101 Design Solutions for Desktop Publishing*. I didn't count the examples, but there are plenty of them. The book is divided into sections—brochures and fliers, advertisements, business correspondence, etc.—each of which contains general guidelines and lots of before-and-after layouts.

Many of us are willing to admit we can't draw a straight line, yet few seem willing to admit we can't lay out a good page. Get this book even if you *can* lay out a good page— it will teach you to lay out a better one.

PageMaker tips

🍎 *selecting near guides* (SZA/AN)

very
hot
tip

You may sometimes have trouble selecting something when a guide is right next to it (or, even worse, right on it). To get the object and not the guide, hold down ⌘ while clicking on it.

🍎 *selecting layered objects*

very
hot
tip

When you have elements lying on top of one another, use a ⌘-click to get beneath the one on the top (it selects the next one down). To get the *next* item down, ⌘-click again. And so on. (Once a buried item is selected, you bring it the top of the pile permanently with the *Bring to Front* command.)

🍎 *crowded text blocks* (AN)

When several text blocks are all in the same area, you may have trouble selecting the one you want. One trick is to grab them at the sides. You can facilitate that by making one flush left, another flush right, a third centered, and stretching their widths so that they extend onto different areas of the pasteboard. Of course this approach is only practical for blocks where the text is all on one line.

♠ *Send to Back and deselecting* (AN)

When you send an object to the back, PageMaker should deselect it. But, annoyingly, you have to click somewhere else to do that. (After all, why would you ever want to send something to the back and keep it selected? Even if you can think of a few bizarre examples, what would you *normally* want to do?)

♠ *some useful keyboard shortcuts* (AN)

Here are a few of the more useful commands that aren't covered in other entries. Commands listed on PageMaker's menus or common to many other Mac programs aren't listed.

shortcut

triple-click (with I-beam pointer)	select paragraph of text
⌥ Option ⌘ P (with I-beam pointer)	insert automatic page number
Shift (while dragging on graphic handle)	resize proportionately
Shift -click (on graphic handle)	return graphic to proportional shape after distorting

♠ *keyboard tool shortcuts*

You can select any of PageMaker's tools from an extended keyboard by using Shift and the function keys:

shortcut

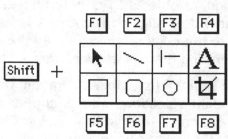

These commands work even when the tool palette is closed. Unfortunately, you can't do them comfortably with one hand—which means you have to take your other hand off the mouse. The solution? Create one-handed macros for the tools you use the most, like the arrow and text tool. I use F5 (unshifted) for the arrow and F6 for the text tool.

With 4.0 you can toggle between any tool and the pointer tool by pressing [⌘][Spacebar]. Avoid holding down the two keys or else you will get a strobe effect between the two pointers with no way to tell where you will end up. Also, if you are going from the text tool to the pointer, make sure you don't hit the [Spacebar] ahead of [⌘] or you will add a space where you may not want it, or worse, lose selected text.

✎ *seeing what you're moving*

When you drag something in PageMaker, what moves is an *outline* of the item; when you stop dragging, the item itself appears in the new position. But when you're trying to align something exactly (to the baseline of a line of text, say) or when it's a graphic you're moving (whose outline will be rectangular no matter what the actual shape of the graphic is), the outline isn't good enough.

very
hot
tip

To drag the item itself instead of its outline, pause for about two seconds between pressing the mouse button and starting to drag. When the pointer changes from an arrow to a cross with arrows at the end of each arm, the Mac is ready to show you the actual item when you drag.

✎ *centering objects on each other* (AN)

very
hot
tip

PageMaker desperately needs, but doesn't have, a command for aligning objects to one another (the way most draw programs do). Aligning the edges is easy—you just pull a guide to the edge of one and drag the other objects to it. But centering them is trickier. Here's how to do it:

When you select a text block, a graphic or a drawing in PageMaker, eight selection handles appear on it—one in each corner and one in the middle—aha!—of each side. Just pull a guide to that middle handle, and then align the middle handles of the other objects to that same guide. (This trick won't work with lines, since they only have two selection rectangles, one at either end.)

❡ *masking* (AN)

Every PageMaker expert I know uses *masking*, but many beginning users don't know about it. It couldn't be simpler—when there's something on the page that you don't want, it's often easier to cover it up than to try to remove it. To do that, you draw a rectangle or an oval and place it over what you want to erase. Then go to the Element menu (in 4.0) and select *Paper* under *Fill* and *None* under *Line*. In PageMaker 3 you will select *Paper* from the *Shades* menu and *None* from the *Line* menu. The rectangle or oval will disappear, and so will what's behind it.

esp. for beginners

❡ *measuring an object's size* (AN)

You can't point to an object (graphic, text box, whatever) in PageMaker and get its size (a major defect in the program). But when you move an object, "whiskers" that correspond to its edges show up on the rulers. Another way to measure an object's size is to drag guidelines to each of its four edges and see where they point to on the rulers. Both these methods involve subtracting one ruler amount from another—which can be a pain.

The best way to measure an object is to drag the zero-zero point (from the intersection of the left and top rulers) to the left top edge of your object and then put the pointer at the right bottom edge and see where the whiskers are on the rulers.

very hot tip

❡ *page-turning shortcuts*

The number of page icons that appear at the bottom of your window depends on the size of the window (and therefore on the size of your screen). When there are more pages than there's room for icons, scroll arrows appear at either end of the page icons:

| ◁ | 1 | 2 | 3 | 4 | 5 | 6 | 7 | 8 | 9 | 10 | 11 | 12 | 13 | 14 | 15 | 16 | 17 | ▷ |

⟨Shift⟩-clicking on either scroll arrow moves the icons by groups of six. For example, a ⟨Shift⟩-click on the right arrow of the icon group shown above would scroll it so that pages 7 through 23 were displayed.

⌘-clicking on the left scroll arrow displays the icon for the first page of the document; ⌘-clicking on the right scroll arrow displays the icon for the last page.

⌘ Tab moves you to the next page or spread and Shift ⌘ Tab to the previous page or spread. These commands work even when you have the horizontal scroll bars turned off (which makes the little page icons at the bottom of the screen disappear).

♠ the go-back-to-last-page command

To move back to the last page or spread you were working on, hit ⌘ G, which opens the Go To Page dialog box, and then immediately press Return, which presses the OK button. (If you do it immediately, the Mac won't even bother displaying the dialog box.)

This works because the Go To Page dialog box always suggests as a default the last page you were on before the current one. So if you were working on page 6 and then went to page 20, the dialog box would come up with a 6 in its text field. (This tip does not work in version 4.0.)

♠ flipping to Fit in Window

When you return to a page, it's displayed in the same view and position as you left it. If you want to see it in *Fit in Window* view no matter how you left it, hold Shift while you click on the page icon.

♠ clicking between page views

No matter what view you're in, an Option ⌘-click in the window will return you to *Actual size*. If you're already in *Actual* size, Option ⌘-click puts you in *Fit in Window* view. This means you can easily toggle back and forth between *Actual* and *Fit in Window* view.

⌈Shift⌉ ⌈Option⌉ ⌈⌘⌉-click puts you into *200%* and/or toggles you between *Actual* size and *200%* view.

❡ *400% view* (AN/SZA)

The 400% page view is listed on the menu in PageMaker 4.0, but there's also a way to get it in PageMaker 3: hold down ⌈Shift⌉ as you choose *200% size* from the View menu. (The changed command won't show up in the menu when you hold down ⌈Shift⌉, as it should, but it will still work.)

To give yourself a keyboard equivalent for this command, make a macro (with Apple's MacroMaker or any other macro utility) and assign ⌈⌘⌉⌈4⌉ to it—or whatever you want, but ⌈⌘⌉⌈4⌉ is easy to remember.

❡ *viewing the whole pasteboard* (C.J. Weigand/SZA/AN)

There's a special command that's still not listed on the menu in PageMaker 4.0. If you hold ⌈Shift⌉ as you choose *Fit in Window*, you'll get a view that includes the entire pasteboard. This makes it easy to drag graphics and text in off the pasteboard and onto your page. (Here again, the changed command won't show up in the menu when you hold down ⌈Shift⌉, but it still works.)

very
hot
tip

If you create a macro for this command, you might want to assign it ⌈Option⌉ ⌈⌘⌉ ⌈W⌉ (because its parent command, *Fit in Window*, is ⌈⌘⌉ ⌈W⌉).

❡ *the grabber hand*

You don't have to use the scroll bars to view different parts of the page you're on—there's a grabber hand you can use to slide the layout around in the window. To make it appear, you hold down ⌈Option⌉ and press (and hold) the mouse button. (This is one of PageMaker's few design flaws. The *right* way for this to work is to have the hand appear as soon as ⌈Option⌉ is pressed, not after the button is pressed.)

very
hot
tip

🍎 *slide shows*

To see a "slide show" of your document, hold ⌈Shift⌉ while you choose *Go To Page*. PageMaker will display each page (or spread if you're viewing facing pages) on the screen for about four seconds. To stop the show, just click anywhere with the mouse. To speed it up a bit, turn off the Rulers first—time won't be wasted redrawing them every time a new page is displayed.

🍎 *customized thumbnails*

You can print out pages in miniature with the *Scaling* option in the Print dialog box, but that only gives you one miniature page per sheet of paper. Or you can choose the *Thumbnails* option, and get as many miniature pages per sheet of paper as you specify. But to miniaturize just the specific pages you want, to just the size you want, and to be able to insert them into other PageMaker documents, use this technique:

For each page you want to miniaturize, use the *Print* command and specify that page. Then hold down ⌈Option⌉ while you click the *OK* button (in 4.0 click on the PostScript button). This brings up the PostScript Print Options dialog box below (the box is a little different in 4.0):

```
┌──────────────────────────────────────────────────────┐
│                                         ╔══════════╗   │
│  PostScript print options               ║    OK    ║   │
│ ─────────────────────────────────       ╚══════════╝   │
│                                         ┌──────────┐   │
│  ☒ Download bit-map fonts               │  Cancel  │   │
│  ☒ Download PostScript fonts            └──────────┘   │
│  ☐ Use default paper tray                              │
│  ☐ View last error message                             │
│  ☐ Make Aldus Prep permanent                           │
│ ─────────────────────────────────────                 │
│  ☒ Print PostScript to disk:  ○ Normal  ◉ EPS          │
│  ☐ Include Aldus Prep         ┌────────────────────┐   │
│                               │  Set file name...  │   │
│                               └────────────────────┘   │
└──────────────────────────────────────────────────────┘
```

Save the pages as EPS files. Then you can use the *Place* command to put the EPS files of your pages back into any PageMaker document and make them any size you want.

♦ sticky page number settings

Virtually all Mac software resets the page range in the Print dialog box to *All* after each Print command, and also resets the number of copies to *1*. But PageMaker has an annoying habit of remembering the page numbers you specified in the *From* and *To* boxes the last time you printed. So if you're used to following ⌘P with an immediate Return, you'll have to break the habit when you're using PageMaker. (To add insult to injury, PageMaker's downloading of fonts on a per-page basis drags out the print operation, so printing the wrong set of pages is even more time-consuming.)

[Although I'm very much in favor of all Mac programs following the standard Mac interface, I think sticky page numbers should be the norm. It's much easier just to click on All when that's the page range you want, than to have to repeatedly type in page numbers—as you would, say, if you were futzing with a couple of pages trying to get them right. PageMaker's approach takes some getting used to, but I prefer it.—AN]

♦ how PageMaker handles fonts (AN)

After PageMaker prints a block of text (in other words, by the end of each page at the latest), it's supposed to flush the fonts it used out of the laser printer's memory. This *should* mean that you can have as many fonts in a block as most applications let you have in a whole document. In practice, however, PageMaker doesn't seem to be able to handle more fonts than other programs, and it doesn't seem to flush them out at the end of each text block either.

When I was printing out the outline font sampler in Chapter 7, the printout was interrupted each time by messages saying that the printer had no more room for

bug

fonts. But all I had to do was start printing again at the page after the last one to come out of the printer, and everything would be fine. (It usually took me three print commands to get the whole chapter.) The implication is that there were residual fonts (or residual something) in the printer after a text block was finished, but that weren't there when I gave the print command again. This isn't how it's supposed to work.

shortcut

Another problem with PageMaker's approach to fonts is that it slows down printing, since the fonts have to be downloaded to the printer anew at the start of each block. One way around that is to manually download all the fonts you commonly use before you start the job. That's worth the trouble if you're printing a fair number of pages and/or documents in which the same fonts (or many of the same fonts) will be used.

⚫ *style name markers*

When a name in the Style palette is followed by an asterisk, it means the style was imported from a word processing document. When the name is followed by a plus sign, it means the selected paragraph was defined as that style and then "overrides" were applied (additional formatting beyond the style definition—like tabs, say). A style can, of course, have both an asterisk and a plus sign after its name.

⚫ *the Edit Style dialog box*

shortcut

To go directly to the Edit Style dialog box for a style, ⌘-click on its name in the Style palette.

⚫ *preserving special formats when applying styles*

*very
hot
tip*

When you apply a style to a paragraph, its font and size are automatically applied to the entire paragraph—even if you have some characters in it that are formatted differently (like Return and ⌘ in this paragraph). To preserve the special font and size formatting, Shift-click instead of double-clicking.

● *copying tabs and indents* *(Jerry Szubin/SZA)*

To copy tabs and indents from the first paragraph in a selection to all the other paragraphs, choose *Indents/tabs* from the Text menu. The tabs and indents in the first paragraph will be displayed in the dialog box. Now just click the *OK* button (don't do anything else). These settings will be applied to all the selected paragraphs.

very
hot
tip

To copy tabs and indents from one paragraph to paragraphs that *don't* follow it, copy part of the original paragraph and paste it at the top of the paragraphs you want to change. Select all the paragraphs, use the *Indents/tabs* trick and then delete the pasted paragraph (or piece of a paragraph).

● *page number reminder* *(C.J. Weigand)*

If you're having trouble getting automatic page numbering to work, make sure the [Caps Lock] key is up. If it's down, nothing will happen when you type [Option][⌘][P].

● *special spaces*

PageMaker lets you use four special kinds of nonbreaking spaces—spaces that "glue" words together so they won't be split at the end of a line.

The *em* space is as wide as the point size you're using. The *en* space is half the point size. The *thin* space is one-quarter the point size. The *fixed* space is the size of a normal space in the font and size you're using. Here's how to get them:

em space	[Shift][⌘][M]	en space	[Shift][⌘][N]
thin space	[Shift][⌘][T]	fixed space	[Option][Spacebar]

● *kerning* *(AN)*

To *kern* a pair of characters (i.e., bring them closer together), use [⌘][Delete]. They'll move by 25ths of an em. Or use [Option][Delete] and they'll move by 100ths of an em. To move the characters farther apart (also by 25ths of an em), hit [Shift][⌘][Delete], and [Option][Shift][Delete] for 100ths of an em.

Since an em is the same number of points wide as the font you're using is high, the larger increments will be one point with 25-point type, a half-point with 12-point type, a quarter-point with 6-point type and so on.

✦ changing point sizes

To change the point size of text from the keyboard, use [Shift] [⌘] [,] to make it smaller and [Shift] [⌘] [.] to make it larger. (The commands make sense when you realize the other characters on those keys are the *less than* (<) and *greater than* (>) symbols.)

shortcut

As in many Mac applications, this changes the size of the text to the next available size shown on the menu. (Note: Unlike most other programs, PageMaker 4.0 displays 11-point as a standard size on its font menu.) To change the point size by increments of one point instead, use [Shift] [Option] [⌘] [,] and [Shift] [Option] [⌘] [.].

My friend Adrian Coblentz points out that using the public domain utility Period-Comma (which lets you type periods and commas even when the [Caps Lock] key is down) keeps the one-point-size-at-a-time option from working.

✦ temporary text flow modes

You toggle between *automatic* and *manual* text flow by checking and unchecking *Autoflow* in the Options menu. To temporarily override the menu setting, hold [⌘] when you're ready to flow the text. The pointer icon changes to show the new flow mode.

✦ semi-automatic flow

When Autoflow is on, a click starts the text flowing onto as many pages as necessary. A click without Autoflow (*manual* flow) flows the text to the bottom of the page or column. PageMaker also provides *semi-automatic* flow—the text flows to the bottom of the page or column, as in manual flow, but the pointer remains loaded with text, instead of turning into the selection arrow.

To use semi-automatic flowing, hold [Shift] when the pointer is loaded with text—the pointer changes to the semi-automatic text flow icon, no matter which mode you were in.

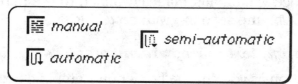

Text Flow Icons

✖ cancelling Autoflow

You can stop an Autoflow operation at any time by just clicking the mouse button. This doesn't undo the operation, however—whatever's already flowed into the document stays there.

✖ placing from the Scrapbook

The Place command lets you choose the Scrapbook as the document to be placed, so you can use the graphics on each of its pages without having to move back and forth between PageMaker and the Scrapbook, copying and pasting each page individually. You place the Scrapbook just like any other file: choose *Place...* from the File menu, open the system folder, and doubleclick on *Scrapbook File*.

shortcut

You'll get a special Scrapbook pointer, with a number in it that shows how many pages are in the Scrapbook. Clicking anywhere in the document pastes down a page of the Scrapbook (the top page is pasted first) and the number in the pointer changes to show how many pages are left.

✖ deleting a linked text block

If you have a "story" (i.e., text) running through multiple text blocks and you want to remove the middle text block without losing any of the story, *don't* select the middle text block and delete it—all its contents will be lost, and while the first text block will then be linked to the third, all the material in between will be missing.

important warning

Instead, close the middle text block by dragging its bottom border all the way up to the top border, so that the two of them together make a single line on the screen. Click anywhere on the screen and the line will disappear. Your first block will be automatically linked to the third (which will now be the second), with no text lost.

⚫ *delaying text rewrap around graphics*

shortcut

As soon as you change border on a graphic, text is automatically rewrapped around the new shape. If you're making several adjustments, waiting for constant rewraps can be annoying. To delay the text rewrap until you're finished futzing with the borders of the graphic, hold the [Spacebar] while you drag them.

⚫ *spreading a list without tabbing* (Byron Brown)

very good feature

There's a new alignment command in PageMaker 4.0 called *Force justify;* it lets you spread text out to fill a line. If there's just one word on the line, it puts spaces between letters; if there's more than one word, it puts spaces between the words.

This feature has a valuable side effect. In certain lists, you may want items flush left to one side of the column (or to one margin) and other items flush right to the other side, so that they'll look like this:

Hamlet	Richard Chamberlain
Ophelia	Sissy Spacek
Claudius	Sting

You can set this up with a right tab at the right margin and tabs between the items (which is how you'd do it in Page-Maker 3.) But *Force justify* provides a quick alternative, without any tabbing.

There's only thing you need to remember: If there are two or more words on either end of the split, put a fixed space ([Option][Spacebar]) between them. That way they won't be spread, and all the space will be put in the middle of the line.

● *spreading text to a specific width*

As mentioned in the previous entry, PageMaker 4's *Force justify* command spreads text out evenly over the width of a line. Here's the trick for doing that in PageMaker 3:

First, justify the line you want to spread. Then type a space between every letter and two spaces between every word. Then type a space after the last word in the line and hold down any letter key; let it repeat until the length of the "word" you're typing is too long to fit at the end of the line and its moved down to the next line. (Before that happens, the characters on the line will squeeze together to try to make more room for the word.) The operation looks something like this:

> **Void where prohibited**

> **Void where prohibited**

> **Void where prohibited aaaaaaa**

> **Void where prohibited aaaaaaaaaaaaa**

> **Void where prohibited**
> **aaaaaaaaaaaaaa**

Once the nonsense word is wrapped down to the next line, the words you formatted with the extra spaces are spread across to fill the width of the line. Just move the window shade (the bottom border of the text block) up to hide the nonsense word, and the text will be evenly spread across the line.

● *shrinking PageMaker files*

PageMaker files get larger as you work on them, because PageMaker simply appends all your changes to the existing file when you save it, instead of resaving the edited file on top of the original. To shrink a PageMaker file down to a more reasonable size (sometimes you can cut its size in half, or more), choose *Save As...* instead of *Save*. Use the same filename, so the old file will be replaced by the new, smaller one.

✦ *speeding up loading* (Steve Michel)

shortcut

One possible reason PageMaker takes so long to load is that it's searching for its spelling and hyphenation dictionaries. (It takes a long time no matter what, but this can make it take longer.) It looks first in the system folder, then in the folder named *PageMaker* and finally in any folders within the PageMaker folder. Putting both dictionaries in the system folder will speed up loading significantly.

✦ *getting out of buried dialog boxes* (Byron Brown)

shortcut

PageMaker 4.0 has many dialog boxes within dialog boxes which can get pretty tedious getting out of. Fortunately there is a shortcut for getting out: if you simply want to close all the boxes as if you were clicking *OK* in each, hold down the [Option] key as you click the first *OK* and they will all be closed at once. You can also type [Option][Return] from the keyboard.

✦ *mail merge*

very hot tip

Carol Aiton, a friend who practically lives in PageMaker, brought this terrific technique to my attention. You can do a kind of mail merge in PageMaker that's really useful when you want to personalize mailers or other single-page documents (assuming you're not doing *too* many of them).

The names and addresses need to be in a word processor or database file that PageMaker can access with its Place command. Each "mailing label" should have the same number of lines, although you can adjust that later in your document if you have to.

Next, create a master page that has everything on it you want except for the personalized info (leave a space for that). Now for the tricky stuff:

- Redefine the page margins in the Page Setup dialog box so that they surround the area for the personalized information. In the illustrations below, the gray lines are the original and redefined page margins.

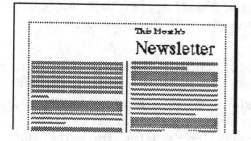

- Use the *Place* command to load the information from the file you created.

- Turn on *Autoflow* in the Options menu.

- Click on the first page. PageMaker will flow the text from the file, creating pages as necessary to hold the information.

- Change the page margins back to their original settings, so they contain the entire original page again. (This illustration shows the reset page margins after the text pour, with the personalized information inserted.)

🍎 *a threesome with a problem*

bug

Try to run PageMaker 3.02 on a IIci with Apple's portrait monitor (using the ci's built-in video card) and you're in for a lot of problems. Text looks fine on the screen but prints out with weird spacing—gaps and overprintings.

The apparent problem is the combination of the video card and the Aldus Prep file for printing (I'm not sure who's at fault here). According to Aldus, the two together somehow think they're dealing with an 80-dpi monitor instead of a 72-dpi monitor.

PageMaker 4.0 probably contains a fix for the problem, but we don't know anyone who has an Apple portrait monitor, so we haven't been able to check it out. The workaround for version 3.02 is to use Apple's printer drivers instead of Aldus's. (Of course, if you do that, you lose the extra printing area and features the Aldus driver provides.)

adapted from a Japanese woodcut by Steve Price

Chapter 15

Communi-cating between computers

Telecommunicating

✦ *telecommunicating on the Mac* (AN/DC)

Telecommunications (transferring information between computers over telephone lines) has a reputation for being one of the least friendly areas of personal computing. That's because, all too often, it *is* one of the least friendly areas of personal computing. But *communications* (as it's also called) can be tremendously exciting, useful and fun. If you get the right software, it can even be easy to learn.

esp. for beginners

You can telecommunicate directly with a friend's computer (it usually makes little difference whether it's a Mac or PC, or even something else), or with a *bulletin board system* or *information service* (both described in their own section below). When you do the latter, sending a file to the distant computer is called *uploading,* and retrieving a file from the distant computer is called *downloading.*

Telecommunicating on the Mac tends to be a little easier than on other computers. Many standards have emerged, and most Mac programs walk you through whatever nonstandardized decisions remain.

✦ *telecommunication basics* (SZA/AN)

To telecommunicate, you need a *modem (MOE-dum).* This small piece of hardware lets you hook up your computer to a phone line and transmit data over it. The name is short for *modulator-demodulator;* on the sending end, it modulates (changes) your computer's digital information into sounds, which then travel over telephone wires; on the receiving end, it changes the sounds back into digital data again (demodulates them).

esp. for beginners

Hooking up a modem is a cinch—there's a power cord to plug it in, a cable to connect it to the computer (unless it's an internal modem, of course) and a jack that connects it (by means of a regular telephone wire) to the phone jack in the wall. Since you probably have a single phone line for both the modem and a phone, there's a second jack on the modem to hook the phone into.

important warning

There's a de facto standard for modems, which is that they should be Hayes-compatible. Non-Hayes-compatible modems are virtually worthless (as Arthur discovered when he tried to sell one). Few people we know have actual Hayes modems, however; most get less expensive brands that use the same *protocols* (a set of standard procedures that control how information is transmitted between computers).

You also need *communications software* to set variables like the rate at which the modem transmits data, and to tell the modem how to dial out and receive calls. Communications programs can be general-purpose or they can be adapted for a specific job, like the software that's designed to connect you with the America Online information service and that's provided by them as part of their package.

The bad news is that most telecommunications terms are carryovers from the less friendly days of early computers. Even the barebones communications module in Microsoft Works has a dialog box that looks like this:

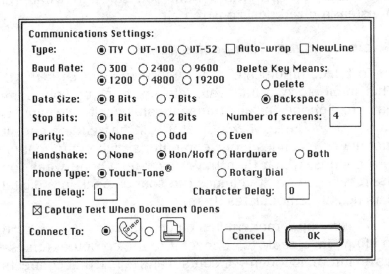

The good news is that, with the exception of the baud rate (described in the next paragraph), you can usually just leave the default settings suggested by your program and everything will be fine.

The *baud rate* is the speed at which the modem sends and receives information. When you're connecting directly to another computer over the phone, you have to make sure both modems are set to the same baud rate, but when you call an information service, it will notice what baud rate you're using and match it (if it can). Most modems are capable of handling their own top speed as well as anything below that; for example, a 2400-baud modem can work at 2400, 1200 and 300 baud.

Even when both computers are using the same baud rate, one or the other of them might receive information faster than it can handle it (it might need to pause to write information to the disk, for example). This situation is controlled by establishing a *handshake* with the other computer.

A common handshaking protocol is called XON/XOFF, in which an *off* signal is sent to the other computer to temporarily stop the flow of information and an *on* signal is sent to resume it (the *X* stands for *transmit*). When you can't establish a handshake with the other computer, you can establish a standard delay after each character and line, specifying how long a pause there should be before the next one is transmitted.

Data size and *stop bits* have to do with the chunks of information you send. Most programs expect every character (every *byte*, in other words) to be eight bits long, but some use only seven bits. A stop bit marks the end of one byte and the beginning of another.

Parity is a way of checking that the other computer received exactly what you sent. Since there are better ways to check this, most telecommunications transmissions use no parity at all.

You can telecommunicate in *real time*—which means that what you type appears on the other person's screen as you type it, and vice versa. (Most communications programs let you store everything you see on the screen to disk, so you can review it later.) You can also communicate in real time with a bulletin board or information service, where there's no human on the other end but everything you send and receive still appears on the screen.

But most of telecommunications involves *file transfers*—something goes directly from your disk to the other computer, or from the other computer to your disk, and you don't see anything on the screen except a report as to the status of the transfer (how much time is left until it's finished, and/or how many bytes have been transmitted).

Some communications programs include a basic programming or scripting language that lets you automate your telecommunications sessions. The next entry describes one of them.

⁙ *MicroPhone* (AN)

I used to hate telecommunicating for the same reason I'd hate trying to communicate in Urdu—I simply didn't know the language. That's why I like MicroPhone. It translates a lot of telecommunications jargon into English and makes it possible for me to do what I need to without a lot of effort. (Now if I could only find a good Urdu grammar.)

MicroPhone III is coming soon, and may even be out by the time you read this. But even Microphone II has a lot of power (it should, for $300). It works in the background under MultiFinder and supports transmission protocols that greatly increase file transfer speeds.

very good feature

As Dale Coleman put it, MicroPhone walks the thin line between maximum power and maximum user friendliness. Both strengths are obvious in its script feature, which records your every move in a short program you can then install on the menu as a command, as a button at the bottom of the screen, or both.

For example, you can devise a very complex script that calls several bulletin boards and information services in the middle of the night (when rates and usage are low) and uploads and downloads files based on any number of contingencies. To initiate this flurry of activity, all you have to do, once the script is written, is click on a button or choose a command from a menu.

FreeTerm (Chris Allen)

FreeTerm is a simple, free communications program for connecting with BBS's and information services. Many user groups have been recommending FreeTerm for beginning users since the mid-80's. Written by Bill Bond, it dials your information service and lets you interact with it and send and receive Mac files. No macros, no fancy emulations, no graphics—just a good, basic program.

bargain

StuffIt (AN)

StuffIt is a virtually indispensable utility developed by Raymond Lau while he was still in high school. It compresses files, making them an average of 25–30% smaller, so it take less time to transmit them. It also combines them into one document, so you can send several all at once. Then it reverses the process and unstuffs them at the other end.

very good
feature

This file compression can be really significant if you're paying long-distance charges or information service access fees (even if you're not, the shorter transmission times are a boon to Type-A personalities). File compression is also useful for saving disk space when you're maintaining archives.

If you ever telecommunicate, you need to have StuffIt. For $15, it's an incredible bargain. A commercial version, called StuffIt Pro, is coming out soon, but the old shareware version may be all you'll need.

bargain

E-mail (Charles Rubin)

Anybody who has a computer and needs to send stuff to anybody else with a computer should be on an E-mail system (the name is short for *electronic mail*). Once you realize you can send your stuff to someone else in a few minutes instead of a few days, you'll be hooked. Some of the more popular systems are CompuServe, America Online and MCI Mail.

esp. for
beginners

[Because I dread having another thing to do each day, I used to avoid E-mail systems. I was afraid that if I had E-mail accounts, I'd have all kinds of people sending me notes and being offended when I didn't have the time to respond. (I can't even get around to answering regular snail mail—whatever of it gets to me.) But to transfer the chapters of this book among Sharon, Byron and me, I opened accounts on AppleLink (which is only for Apple dealers, developers, universities, user groups, etc.) and America Online (which is open to all Mac users). Both are described in the section on information services below.

The main advantage, since Sharon lives three time zones away and I tend to work odd hours, is that the other people don't have to be around (and awake) when I upload or download something of theirs, and I don't have to be around (and awake) when they upload or download something of mine.

I still worry about getting mail I don't have time to respond to, so I didn't use my own name on America Online (AppleLink doesn't give you that choice). And I don't use either of them for anything but E-mail. But for that, they're both really convenient, and have saved me a fortune in Federal Express bills.—AN]

 *MCI Mail* (Charles Rubin)

very good feature

MCI Mail lets you send E-mail to other MCI Mail, CompuServe or Telex users (as well as several other systems); it also will convert your computer messages to paper and have them delivered overnight or by regular USPS snail mail (the advantage in that case being that the letter starts off in the destination city rather than where you live, which gives it more of a fighting chance). Even better, you can have your messages printed out on any Group 3 fax machine in the world (for 50¢ for the first half page and 30¢ for each additional page).

You address mail in most cases simply by typing a user's name (mine is *CRubin).* You can create and store address lists and then select groups of people to receive your messages en masse. You can create messages by typing them in online. There's also a text editor for altering messages before you send them, but it's pretty crude—you're better off deleting your draft and starting over again.

Aside from a yearly fee of $25 (which includes about $10 of free message credits), the only charges you pay are for sending messages or accessing special services (described in the next paragraph); receiving mail and simply checking for it is free (as is the phone call, since you connect with MCI mail over an 800 number). Sending messages costs 45¢ for up to 500 characters, 75¢ for 501-2500 characters and $1 for each 2501–7500 characters.

You can also use MCI Mail to access the Dow Jones News/Retrieval database. This costs from $12 to $72 an hour extra, depending on the database you read and the time of day you read it. But MCI Mail is primarily designed to make sending E-mail very easy (which it does).

✎ *Desktop Express* (Charles Rubin)

Desktop Express is a communications program that lets you transmit graphics, programs or formatted application files to the MCI mailboxes of other Desktop Express users, without having to wait for the recipient to be available to set up error-checking protocols.

shortcut

The Desktop Express screen has icons representing separate mailboxes for new mail, opened mail, unsent mail and sent mail. Another icon gives you access to an address book where you can store phone numbers for sending mail to CompuServe and other electronic mail boxes as well as to MCI. A file cabinet icon lets you find mail, delete it or move it to another folder or disk. From this one screen, you can create memos, specify other files to send, address mail, open and read mail, and perform a number of file-management functions.

Once you've stored your own MCI account information and local telephone number, you can click a button and Desktop Express will log on to MCI Mail, check for messages, send any messages you want and then log off, and you can go do whatever you want while it does it. Before you actually tell Desktop Express to dial, you can choose which messages in your outgoing mailbox you want to send and which you want to receive. (If you'd rather be involved, you can also call MCI Mail or Dow Jones interactively, and use their normal interfaces.)

If you're just sending a short memo, a built-in text editor lets you create it with Desktop Express. But Desktop Express also lets you send any Macintosh file—a formatted document, a program, whatever. It automatically recognizes MacPaint graphics and it comes with ImageSaver, a stripped-down version of Glue that lets you print graphic images from any program to a file that can then be transmitted.

There are some annoying things about Desktop Express. One is its inability to automatically redial telephone numbers. If your local MCI access number is frequently busy (as mine is), you have to keep telling Desktop Express to redial, and that of course eliminates the advantage of automated operation. And unlike Lotus Express, its MS DOS counterpart, Desktop Express won't run in the background and beep you whenever you have an incoming message.

Desktop Express is no speed demon. It occupies 544K, and all that code makes it somewhat glacial. For example, when you click the button to dial MCI, you sit and wait several seconds before your modem actually dials. When the program logs off MCI Mail, it takes about ten seconds after it says it's disconnecting to actually do it. It also takes a long time to open windows showing individual pieces of mail.

Connection costs are another possible drawback. Since Desktop Express makes it possible for you to send formatted files and programs, which tend to be quite large, your MCI bill could get pretty hefty.

While $150 may seem like a lot to pay for access to a service you can reach for free with the communications program you already have, Desktop Express's ability to transfer formatted files, graphics and programs may make the program well worth the money.

General telecommunications tips

⚫ *garbage*

Intermittent garbage (bizarre characters that have no apparent meaning) on the screen when you're communicating with another computer usually means you've got a noisy phone connection.

esp. for beginners

If you're just typing back and forth, don't worry about garbage as long as you can read through it. But if you're transferring files, garbage will probably ruin the transmission, so hang up and try again for a cleaner connection. Dropping the baud rate (from 2400 to 1200 or even down to 300) sometimes helps too.

If you're getting nothing but garbage on the screen, it may be because you and the computer you're connected to are trying to communicate at different baud rates. Most programs let you change the baud rate right in the middle of a session, so try that and see if it eliminates the garbage.

⚫ *disabling Call Waiting* (DC)

Many phone companies offer a service called Call Waiting that interrupts calls with signals when someone else is calling, and lets you switch between the two calls. Unfortunately, these signals disrupt data transmissions, thus forcing modem users to choose between giving up the convenience of Call Waiting or gambling on an interrupted connection.

very hot tip

But if your phone company uses electronic switching, you can temporarily disable Call Waiting for the duration of any outgoing call. You just precede the number you're dialing with *70 (on a tone line) or 1170 (on a pulse line). When the call is over, Call Waiting automatically comes back.

To see whether you can do this on your phone, just try putting the appropriate code in front of a number you're dialing. If the service isn't available, you should get a recorded message that the call can't be completed as dialed.

If you're using an autodial modem, instruct it to pause briefly between the Call Waiting disabling code and the number you're dialing. Two or three seconds is sufficient. The following command will cause a Hayes-compatible modem to give the code *70, then pause two seconds, then dial the number 555–1212:

ATDT*70,555–1212

(Needless to say, you should substitute whatever number you're dialing for 555–1212.)

✦ *protection against lightning* (AN)

important warning

As C.J. Weigand points out on pp. 265–66, lightning can hit a telephone pole, come down the wire, pass through your modem and fry your computer (and the modem too, of course). If you live in an area where there are a lot of thunderstorms, it's a good idea to disconnect the incoming phone line from your modem when you turn the system off. (Since lightning hits power poles too, it's also a good idea to pull the plug of your computer's power cord out of the wall socket.)

Bulletin boards and information services

✦ *bulletin boards* (DC/SZA/AN)

bargain

An electronic *bulletin board* (abbreviated *BBS*, for *bulletin board system)* is a lot like an electronic user group—you'll find plenty of people there who are willing and able to answer your questions. Most bulletin boards also have the latest versions of public-domain and shareware software available for downloading. And although they provide all this, most BBS's are free.

The person who runs a bulletin board is called a *sysop (SISS-ahp, for system operator)*. On small bulletin boards, the sysop does everything—takes care of the hardware, decides what's available for downloading, controls who's allowed to leave and retrieve messages, and so on. On bigger boards (and on information systems like America Online), sysops control sections that are dedicated to specific kinds of information.

A complete list of every active Mac BBS in the country would take up many pages of this book and would probably be out of date by the time you read it. One that Sharon can personally recommend is the one run by the New Jersey Mac User Group. Although it has a private section for members, there's also an extensive bulletin board open to the public, complete with 600 megs of online information and *gateways* to other bulletin boards (that is, you can call this board and access others thru it—post and pick up messages, for example—without having to make another call.

The number is 201/388-1676. If you drop in, let the sysop, Mike Bielen, know that *The Macintosh Bible* sent you. (Just use his name, or answer *yes* when you're asked if you want to leave a message for the sysop.

Here are a few other BBS's Mike recommends:

MacInfo BBS, Newark CA, 415/795-8862
maximum baud rate: 9600; sysop: Norm Goodger
no access fee

The Tiger's Den, Phoenix AZ, 602/996-0078
maximum baud rate: 2400; sysop: John Gillett
no access fee

Laserboard New York, Queens NY, 718/639-8826
maximum baud rate: 9600 HST *(high speed transfer,* a
    protocol used by some 9600-baud modems—like US
    Robotics, but not others); sysop: Adam Wildavsky
access fee: $18 a year

MACropedia, Lake Forest IL, 708/295-6926
maximum baud rate: 9600; sysop: Dave Alpert
access fee: $24 a year

⌘ request for feedback online *(SZA)*

If you want to make comments on my entries in this book—good or bad—you can get in touch with me through NJMUG bulletin board (described in the previous entry; just address your message to *Sharon Aker)* or through AppleLink (described in an entry below; my address is D6145). I won't be able to reply to your messages (with at least a third of a million Mac Bibles out there, I probably wouldn't be able to do anything else if I did) but I do promise to read them.

[You can also mail comments on this edition, or on what you'd like to see in the updates or the next edition, to Goldstein & Blair, Box 7635, Berkeley CA 94707. Here again, we don't have time to respond individually, but we do read your letters and consider them carefully.—AN]

⌘ information services *(DC/AN)*

esp. for beginners

Commercial electronic information services like CompuServe and America Online are great sources of info and software, but they have two drawbacks: they charge you for each minute you're connected to them, and they present you with a bewildering series of menus that can be frustrating for first-time users (and for many experienced users as well). Still, you can do an amazing number of things on them, including send messages by electronic mail, shop and make plane reservations.

Most large information services have Mac special interest groups (America Online is all Mac so far), which amount to bulletin boards with an area for messages and another area that contains public-domain and shareware software you can download. *[They also have conferences, which are really nifty. Several people sign into a conference "area" at the same time, and everyone in the conference can see what everyone else is typing. Comments are automatically preceded by the name or the "handle" (assumed name) of the person who typed it.—SZA)*

The major benefit of using a commercial information service rather than a bulletin board system is that you'll virtually never get a busy signal. If you need some information or software right away, you'll appreciate not having to dial repeatedly just to log on. There are many commercial information services available, but America Online and CompuServe (both described below) are particularly good sources for Mac info and software.

🍎 *CompuServe* *(DC)*

CompuServe is an extremely popular service, though its rates are higher than some others. To register, you need to purchase a CompuServe Starter Kit (available at most computer and software dealers for about $40). The kit includes a list of available phone numbers, a log-in code, and instructions for signing up. You'll also need a major credit card for billing.

🍎 *Navigator* *(Paul Hoffman)*

If you use CompuServe, and don't want to have to think while the meter is ticking, Navigator is the way to go. It gives you a quick-and-easy method for getting the messages in all the conferences you want to browse; you can then look at them offline at your leisure.

shortcut

You can answer the messages you want and create new ones, run Navigator again and have it send all of your responses to the right places in a single step. This sounds like it will save you money but it won't—since using Navigator is so easy, you'll find yourself signing up for many more conferences.

🍎 *AppleLink*

Apple's own online electronic mail and information service, AppleLink, isn't available to the general public. But I mention it here because user groups are one of the privileged classes that are eligible for an account (the others are developers, universities and dealers). If your group has a BBS, the sysop may already know about this, but a user group doesn't have to have a BBS to be on AppleLink.

very good feature

AppleLink is full of useful technical information and the latest product announcements and price lists (for third-party stuff as well as Apple products). One very useful category for user groups is the Third-Party Updates section. When Pyro had a few minor upgrades that were free to registered users, its publisher, Fifth Generation Systems, posted an update utility on AppleLink that updated the program (when run on any system that had Pyro already installed). Your user group rep can download those kinds of things and distribute them to the members who need them.

(By the way, if you use the educational network Bitnet but not AppleLink, you can leave messages for people on AppleLink from Bitnet by following their AppleLink address with @APPLELINK.APPLE.COM. So if you wanted to reach me, for example, you'd type D6145@APPLELINK.APPLE.COM.)

⁂ *America Online* (AN)

bargain

America Online used to be AppleLink Personal Edition—the version for people who weren't eligible for a regular AppleLink account. It's evolved into a large, Mac-only information service, and a very inexpensive one at that—the rates are currently $10/hour prime time, $5/hour other times, with a $6/month charge that includes one hour of nonprime time (and the rates are even cheaper than that if you join through a user group). If you only want to use one information service, this is the one I'd recommend. But it has a lot of drawbacks.

very bad feature

For one thing, the software doesn't recognize tabs, em dashes, curly apostrophes or curly quotes; if you type any of these, you get beeped at and nothing happens. For another thing, AO asks you a lot of dumb questions. For example, to sign on, you doubleclick the America Online program icon. After several seconds, you see a dialog box that asks you if you want to sign on *(no, I was just doubleclicking the icon for kicks)*.

Let's say you do, by some miracle, want to sign on. Instead of typing your password right there, you have to sit and stare at some dumb graphics while waiting for AO to connect with the network. When it finally asks you for your password, you have to wait again while it checks it. (AppleLink does this the right way. When you doubleclick on its program icon, a dialog box comes up within a second or two and asks for your password; you type it and are then free to do something else until you're logged on.)

Quitting AO is equally difficult. After giving the command, you have to reconfirm *twice* that that's what you want to do. (Well, you can understand why. Disconnecting from America Online is a major life decision that should be agonized over endlessly; if you do it by mistake, you'll have to go through the stupid sign-on procedure again.)

very bad feature

America Online compensates for the thoughtlessness of its software by saying things like *welcome* and *goodbye* in a dumb, synthesized voice. It also appears to transmit data slower than AppleLink. Sending the same file, at the same baud rate, in the same way (MacBinary Xmodem), will take twelve minutes on AppleLink vs. sixteen on AO. (Both programs estimate how long a transmission takes and I'm basing this comparison on that, not on actual timings. So it may be that AO just estimates more poorly. But that's not great either.)

For all its defects, America Online offers a lot of value for the money, and has become very popular with Mac users.

🍎 BIX *(Paul Hoffman)*

BIX is an information service run by *BYTE* magazine, one of the oldest technical microcomputer journals. Most of the people who participate in BIX's Macintosh discussion (and they include people who work at Apple and other major Mac companies) are not only technologically knowledgeable but also quite friendly and generous with their time. (But Dale wants to point out that the discussions on BIX can get quite technical; they're definitely not for beginners.)

⚫ *Prodigy*

Prodigy is an information service sponsored by Sears; there's a special version of the software for Mac owners. It's relatively young but, despite its name, it's no *wunderkind.*

very bad feature

Prodigy is *slooooow,* and it doesn't use the Mac interface. It doesn't run under MultiFinder and the ⚫ menu isn't available. If that's not enough to turn you off, the bottom of your screen is reserved for ads. *Ads!* For things like mouthwash! Prodigy is cheap—a flat fee of $10 per month. You get what you pay for.

I have a friend who works for Prodigy; she'll remain nameless, so she won't lose her job. (Hi, Kathy.) She handles calls from the (many) people who cancel their service after the three-month trial period. More than 90% of them are Mac users, and their major complaint is that the program isn't Maclike enough.

⚫ *saving time and money online*

very hot tip

There are three things you can do to make your communications sessions with information services more efficient, which saves you money both on your phone bill and on the hourly charges:

* Although many services have higher hourly fees for higher baud rates, you should still use the highest baud rate your modem can handle. Few services charge twice as much for a 2400-baud connection as for 1200-baud one, even though transmissions take only half the time.

* If your communications software lets you create scripts, or otherwise automate online procedures like posting and retrieving messages, use that capability. Scripts run faster than you can work in real time.

* Prepare your messages and files offline. Why pay for online time when all you're doing is writing?

Networks

❖ *what a network is* (Rich Wolfson/AN)

A computer network is two or more devices connected to share information. So, technically, a single Mac hooked to a LaserWriter is a network (although it's seldom called one). Among Mac users, *network* usually refers to a *local area network*, or *LAN*—one that's confined to a relatively small area, like an office. Macintosh LAN's are usually connected by LocalTalk or PhoneNET hardware, or imitations thereof.

esp. for beginners

Some complex *wide area networks* (abbreviated *WAN* in writing, but seldom in speech) contain thousands of devices from varied manufacturers communicating with each other directly over dedicated cables or phone lines and indirectly via modems or even microwaves.

❖ *networking basics* (Rich Wolfson)

Every device on a network (whether a computer, a printer or whatever) is called a *node*. Every node has an *address*—an ID number or name. On the Mac, a node's address is whatever name you've specified in the Chooser.

esp. for beginners

In addition, each node automatically gets an ID number when you turn it on; the number varies from one time to the next, but it's always unique on the network. Because of this, you don't have to halt the network to hook up additional nodes, and that makes Mac networks a cinch to set up.

This is thanks to the fact that the Mac has had networking software, called AppleTalk, built-in since the beginning— yes, even back in the days when 128K was a lot of RAM and virtually nobody had a hard drive. (PC's and most other computers need special, additional software to network.)

very good feature

Information flows through a network according to certain *protocols* that tell each device what to do with the information. Most Mac networks use the AppleTalk protocol, because that's the one that's built into the machine. Other protocols—sometimes used by Mac and mostly used by other machines—include DECNet, TCP-IP and Token-Ring.

Networks are often subdivided into smaller areas called *zones,* which show up in the Chooser. Separate networks can be connected by *bridges, routers* or *gateways* (in order of increasing intelligence). Such devices don't need to understand the protocols—just whether or not to pass the information on. When networks are connected with one of these devices, they're treated as zones.

⬥ *networking hardware* (Rich Wolfson/AN)

When the original LaserWriter was introduced, Apple also introduced the cabling and connectors (called *AppleTalk* at the time, but now called *LocalTalk)* needed to link up one or more Macs; this was the first Mac network. Not only was this hardware expensive, but it limited you to 1000 feet maximum, you had to use it in a daisy-chain configuration (see the next entry for details) and the connectors had a tendency to pull out.

Then a small company named Farallon introduced PhoneNET, which has several major advantages over LocalTalk:

very good feature

- It uses regular phone wire, which costs about a third as much as LocalTalk cabling. You save even more if you use the two unused (yellow and black) wires in existing phone lines that probably already run where you want your network lines to go.

very good feature

- Its connectors are like the standard modular plugs on phone cords. When was the last time a modular phone cord pulled out of your phone?

very good feature

- PhoneNET allows networks to run up to 3000 feet.

- It lets you use a variety of network configurations (described in the next entry).

LocalTalk has one minor advantage over PhoneNET. Apple's connectors are automatically terminated, while PhoneNET requires that you put terminators in any unused socket. (But this isn't a black art like SCSI termination—you can always see the resistors in the sockets and manufacturers always provide plenty of them when you purchase connectors.)

If you have a network of any size, PhoneNET hardware can save you a lot of money, and imitations of it can save you even more. At the college where Rich teaches, they use an inexpensive and reliable PhoneNET clone, Trimar's CompuNet.

bargain

(If you already have LocalTalk cabling, don't throw good money after bad—switch over to PhoneNET-type hardware for any additional needs. Farallon makes an adaptor for connecting LocalTalk to PhoneNET systems, so you won't lose whatever you have invested.)

❡ *network configurations* (Rich Wolfson/AN)

There are three basic network configurations (patterns of connecting devices):

esp. for beginners

Daisy-chain or *series* networks connect devices one after the other, in a chain. The problem with this configuration is that if one node is disconnected, so is everything beyond it.

A *backbone* configuration is an improvement over the daisy-chain, because each node has its own little branch off the main cable (like rooms off a hall). If one node is disconnected, it doesn't affect the others.

A *star* configuration (also available with PhoneNET) has a central node to which all other nodes are connected.

PhoneNET-type connectors allow all three configurations; as noted in the previous entry, LocalTalk restricts you to the daisy-chain.

You can combine various configurations—for example, you might daisy-chain several nodes on one branch of a star. The only limitation is that you can't link the first and last node together into a complete circle. That's called a *ring network* and is allowable on PC's and many larger computers.

On ring networks, electronic message *packets* circle ceaselessly; as a packet passes a node, the node grabs any information meant for it and loads any information it wants to send someplace else. (If the packet is full, the node waits for the next one.) Ring networks have the same disadvantage as daisy-chains, only more so—one node going down can disrupt the entire network.

⬢ *file servers and AppleShare* (Rich Wolfson/SZA)

esp. for beginners

A *file server* is a computer on a network that everyone can access and get applications and documents from. Some file servers are *dedicated* machines—that's all they do, and you can't use them as a workstation. (They might also take care of print spooling and E-mail for the network.) Some networks don't require dedicated file servers—see the entry below on TOPS.

AppleShare is Apple's file-server software; with it running, the file server appears to everyone on the network as another icon on the Desktop, with its own window, folders and files.

AppleShare has some security features; each file and/or folder can have an "owner" and only someone with appropriate access privileges can get at it. A network administrator can set up work groups with various levels of access privileges.

PC's can be connected to AppleShare with a card from Apple. To the PC's, the server looks like another disk drive, and they can access the documents on it (after all, what could they do with the applications?).

very good feature

At the college where I teach, we have four separate AppleShare file servers with six volumes (hard drives and their partitions) in four zones. We've never had any problems with the system crashing or failing in three years. Even during power surges, the networks go down only momentarily and then recycle and reconfigure on their own.

Although Apple recommends using an SE/30 or a Mac II as a server (because of their speed), we use Mac Pluses with four megs of memory, Radius accelerators and large RAM caches.

⬢ *AppleTalk Phase 2* (Rich Wolfson)

The original AppleTalk, referred to now as Phase 1, had only limited support for other vendors' protocols. The current version, Phase 2, supports Token-Ring (IBM's protocols), PC's on EtherTalk networks (Apple's implementation of AppleTalk on Ethernet wiring) and EtherTalk support for AUX (Apple's answer to Unix). Phase 2 also works with Apple's Internet router. (See the entry below.)

⚫ *TOPS* (Eric Alderman/SZA)

TOPS (the name stands for *transcendental operating system)* uses the AppleTalk networking capability built into every Mac and lets all the machines on a network access each other without any file server being necessary. (This is especially great for a small network—say two or three machines that need to share files.)

very good feature

When you *publish* a volume (a disk drive, directory or folder) onto the network—that is, when you make it available for others to use—you become a *server.* When you *mount* a server's published volume—that is, when you indicate that you want to use it—you become a *client.* Any computer attached to the network can act as a server, a client or both at the same time. The same software is loaded on each machine, regardless of whether it's intended to be a server or a client.

When you mount a published volume (which could be on a machine right next to you or up on the 12th floor), your computer treats it as if it were simply another disk drive attached to your system. When you open the window for this icon, you'll see the mounted volume's files. From the Open and Save As dialog boxes within an application, you simply click on the *Drive* button to access the new volume.

File transfer is as simple as copying a file from one icon to another. The fact that one of the volumes you're using is not actually attached to your system is almost completely transparent to you—your computer acts exactly as if you were using another disk drive.

You need a TOPS package ($150) for each Mac on the network.

bargain

⁜ *SneakerNet* (Rich Wolfson)

SneakerNet may be the most widely-used network. It's implemented by putting information onto a floppy disk (or even paper!) and walking it over to the person (or machine) you want it delivered to. Protocols include Reebok, Nike and Keds. Bridges include UPS, Federal Express and even the post office. SneakerNet sometimes loses data and is often slower than you'd wish, but it's one of the cheapest networks available.

⁜ *repeaters* (Rich Wolfson)

A repeater can extend an AppleTalk/PhoneNET network to as much as 6000 feet, by boosting the signals along the cabling. Install several, and you can go a long way. TOPS and Farallon repeaters are similar in function; both are reliable, but the TOPS unit is less than half the price.

Farallon's StarController and NuvoTech's TurboStar are multiport *repeaters*—they not only amplify the signal as it passes through but allow multiple branches on a star network (twelve for StarController, sixteen for TurboStar).

very good feature

Since each branch on an AppleTalk star network has its own 3000-feet limit (if you're using PhoneNET-type cabling) and can only contain 32 devices, using a star repeater can really expand your system. It has two other advantages: by breaking a large network into smaller pieces, everything happens faster and more reliably; and if any part of the network has a major problem, only that part shuts down, making troubleshooting much easier.

⁜ *EtherTalk/Ethernet* (John Kadyk/Rich Wolfson)

bargain

EtherTalk is one of the fastest networking systems available. LocalTalk can transmit data at 230 kilobits (about 5000 average-sized words) a second, while EtherTalk can go as high as 10 *megabits* (over 200,000 words) a second—more than 43 times as fast! (But be aware that most hardware can't go that fast.)

Each Mac in an EtherTalk network needs EtherTalk software and an interface card ($400–$650—the card and cabling are called Ethernet, the software and communications protocols EtherTalk). The cabling normally resembles the coaxial cables that connect VCR's to TV's, but some companies run EtherTalk on twisted-pair wiring—like phone wire. (Many networks that run off a VAX minicomputer already have Ethernet, and it's easy to connect Macs to them (individually or as a zone).

Several companies—including Apple, Asanté, Cayman, Dove, Excelan and 3Com—manufacture Ethernet cards. John used the Asanté cards at Goldstein & Blair. The speed difference over LocalTalk was incredible. With EtherTalk up, the server's hard disk and computer are what limit your speed—using a file server over EtherTalk is almost as fast as using a local computer.

Asanté's installation manual is brief and simple, and for questions the manual doesn't answer, the company is easily accessible by phone. Their techies seemed knowledgeable, although some have heavy accents that make them difficult to understand.

FlashTalk and DaynaTalk (Rich Wolfson/John Kadyk/SZA)

bargain

FlashTalk and DaynaTalk are network accelerators that are advertised as faster than AppleTalk and cheaper than Ethernet. At about $200 per node, they're certainly cheaper, but we've had mixed experiences with their speed-up performance.

Both products are priced similarly and offer basically the same advantages and limitations. John worked with DaynaTalk on a network of four Macs, two LaserWriters and a server, and Rich tried both at one of his Mac labs (eighteen Macs, two LaserWriters, an AppleShare file server and a FastPath connection to Ethernet). Rich didn't find either one acceptable—there was absolutely no speed improvement for his particular network. John found a great speed improvement for his setup, but later switched to Ethernet for even greater speed and data security.

As mentioned above, Macs communicate at 230 Kbps (kilobits per second) on a normal AppleTalk network. These accelerators make possible rates of up to 850 Kbps, and allow different devices to communicate at different rates within the same network (not all devices can handle 850 Kbps). For example, you might have a IIcx file server equipped with DaynaTalk communicating at 850 Kbps, a Mac II also communicating at 850 Kbps, a Mac Plus communicating at its maximum 740 Kbps and a Mac Plus without DaynaTalk communicating at 230 Kbps.

The problem with all this speeding up and communicating at different rates is that it increases the likelihood that two data transmissions will collide and be garbled in transit. DaynaTalk's SpeedGuard collision avoidance system guards against such collisions, but the best they can say for it is that it will allow "fewer data collisions and fewer delays" than unprotected DaynaTalk. (If your network includes a LaserWriter Plus, NT or NTX, you'll need to buy a special collision filter. You'll also need one for any AppleTalk Mac II's and SE/30's on the network.)

On the up side, Macs using DaynaTalk or FlashTalk can share the same network as those using AppleTalk without using any bridging software. On the other hand, if your network includes a Hayes InterBridge or Kinetics FastPath, FlashTalk performance slows down—unless the bridge or gateway is isolated from the network by a TOPS repeater (which will run you about another $200).

In sum, buying these accelerators is a risky proposition. They work well in certain situations but aren't always the magic wand the ads say they are. (Read the small print on the product boxes that warns about the possibility of lower speed improvements than promised; interestingly enough, those labels appeared only after reviews like this were printed.)

routers *(Rich Wolfson/John Kadyk)*

Liaison (from Farallon) is a software-only router that links AppleTalk networks, including those with different cabling systems (like LocalTalk and Ethernet), thus allowing them to share resources like file servers and printers. Liaison also lets you link networks (or single computers) at a distance, using just a modem. And it lets you organize a single network into zones, making the use of printers and other resources more efficient and allowing a LocalTalk network to expand beyond 32 nodes.

At G&B, we used Liaison on our file server to link the EtherTalk zone of our network to the LocalTalk zone. It was easy to install and, for the most part, worked seamlessly in the background to make the network function as a contiguous whole.

The Liaison manual is concise and informative, Farallon's tech support is knowledgeable and accessible, and their product works. It has provided us with a trouble-free means of sharing printers between the two zones in our office. Here's some info on some other routers:

very good feature

FastPath (previously from Kinetics, now from Shiva) was the first router of its kind, connecting networks through an intermediary Ethernet backbone. The current version, FastPath 4, can use a variety of cabling and handles Phase 2 AppleTalk (as well as many other protocols, including TCP-IP).

Rich has found FastPath to be very reliable and easy to use—it's invisible to network users. There's a trade-in for FastPath 4 for registered users of earlier versions. If you're planning to go to Phase 2 of AppleTalk, the upgrade is a must.

Shiva also makes the NetBridge, a router for LocalTalk-to-LocalTalk networks, and EtherGate, an EtherTalk-to-LocalTalk router which, unlike FastPath, doesn't handle non-AppleTalk protocols.

If your networks aren't connected with dedicated cabling, a Hayes InterBridge may be your answer. But since it uses a phone line to connect the two networks, InterBridge isn't as speedy as FastPath. (FastPath, NetBridge, EtherGate and InterBridge all include hardware as well as software.)

Apple's software-only Internet router supports up to eight ports simultaneously, is accessed through a desk accessory and can run in the background. It supports both AppleTalk-only networks and extended networks that use EtherTalk and TokenTalk.

♦ E-mail on networks *(Rich Wolfson)*

Some computer applications have the potential to change the way we work, and I think network E-mail is one of them. Up until now, E-mail systems have gained only limited use because they've lacked critical mass. But two recent products, CE Software's QuickMail and Microsoft Mail, make network E-mail so easy to use that I believe we're fast approaching the beginning of a chain reaction.

While you can use a file server as the dedicated mail server (to store messages and let people know that mail's waiting), both programs also let you use a nondedicated machine on the network for this purpose. Both programs provide gateways to other mail systems, including AppleLink, MCI Mail, All-In-One, VMS Mail and UNIX Mail. And they're both so Mac-like and easy to use that few users will need help getting started. Here's the basic scenario, from the user's point of view, for QuickMail:

When you start your Mac, the QuickMail init automatically notifies the mail server that you're online. If there's mail waiting for you, you'll be notified by a dialog box that lists how many messages are waiting. You go into QuickMail by choosing it from the ♦ menu or by using its special menu (which can be installed on the menu bar). After retrieving your messages and replying as you wish, exit QuickMail and go back to work.

very hot tip

If someone sends you a message at this point, your Mac will chime to let you know some mail has been delivered. If you were away from your computer when it chimed, you'll come back to find that the ♦ menu title has been replaced by a blinking QuickMail icon. *(This blinking icon may fool your screen-saver into thinking you're still using your Mac, even after you've left for the day. If this becomes a problem, you can turn the blinking icon off and tell QuickMail to notify you that you have mail in some other way.—John Kadyk)*

Both QuickMail and Microsoft Mail are constantly evolving, with many innovative features being added. They already allow for text messages as well as file transfers, real-time conference and even voice mail (the digital sound is input through a Farallon MacRecorder).

very good feature

We've used QuickMail here at Montclair State since its introduction with no problems. Installation was a breeze and administration takes very little time (it's even fun). *[QuickMail is the first piece of software that ever made me think that working in an office instead of at home might have its fun aspects. QuickMail is beautiful.—SZA]*

🍎 *Broadcast* (Rich Wolfson)

Because most of our students use Macs in open-access labs around campus and it would cost a fortune to buy a Microsoft Mail or Quick Mail address for each, we use Broadcast to introduce them to the concept of electronic mail.

Broadcast is a Chooser device. When you select it, it lists all the current users on the network who have Broadcast installed (and activated, since you can shut it off when you don't want anyone to bother you). You select a user, type a message, and click the *Send* button. The message pops up in a dialog box on the receiver's screen. Broadcast allows the receiver to make an immediate, direct reply.

The students love it and I think it's pretty neat too. It's shareware and costs $25 per zone or $100 for all the zones on your network. You can get it from Joachim Lindenberg, Sommerstrasse 4, 7500 Karlsruhe 1, West Germany (AppleLink GER.XSE0010).

bargain

🍎 *Public Folder* (Rich Wolfson)

Public Folder is one of my favorite utilities. Distributed *free* by Claris and available on most bulletin boards and information services, it allows anything that's placed in a root-level folder named *Public* to be seen and copied by any other Mac on the network (provided it has the Public Folder init running).

bargain

You access Public Folder through the Control Panel. You can copy the whole folder, or choose among its contents.

I sometimes even use Public Folder to transfer files even on my AppleShare network—the transfer is much faster than using an intermediary file server. But my favorite use for Public Folder is to accomplish something that used to be impossible:

Previously there was no way to connect two Macs with internal hard drives together to transfer the contents of one hard drive to another. You needed a spare hard drive or had to connect both machines to a file server for an intermediary transfer. With Public Folder, you just hook an ImageWriter cable into the printer port of both Macs and run Public Folder on both machines. With AppleTalk turned on in the Chooser, the machines can communicate with each other.

🍎 *network management utilities* (Rich Wolfson)

This is a software category that's beginning to grow—management and troubleshooting utilities for the network administrator. I've used various programs—CheckNet and TrafficWatch from Farallon, and LanRanger, Look and Echo from Kinetics; they've all been handy at times.

One of the niftiest things about these utilities is that some will actually draw a network map for you. On a large network, this is almost worth the price just by itself.

🍎 *Inter•Poll* (Rich Wolfson)

very good feature

Apple's Inter•Poll ($130) is a utility that lets you see who's on the network, what System, Finder and printer drivers they're using, as well as the name and ID number of each device, what type of computer it is and its zone name. It's great for troubleshooting and maintenance—you can find out, for example, who's resetting the LaserWriter because s/he has an old printer driver, or who needs a System update.

Inter•Poll's interface is functional, if not elegant. The program is simple to learn and use, and it works across network bridges. If you're a network administrator, it's a must-have.

☀ *Timbuktu* (Rich Wolfson)

Timbuktu ($150 per copy, $2000 for a 30-pack) should get an award for the cleverest product slogan: *The next best thing to being there.* When you use Timbuktu, your screen reflects what's happening on another machine in the network. You can either observe the other machine or actually control it.

very good
feature

This is invaluable when someone on another floor, or in the next building, needs help. Network administrators with out-of-the-way file servers will also love Timbuktu. In fact, if you have Timbuktu, your file server doesn't even need a screen, keyboard or mouse.

Timbuktu is slow but sure. Version 2.0 lets you do file transfers and remote operations—which means you can call in from home and work on your office computer (but even with a 9600-baud modem, response time will be agonizingly slow).

☀ *FontShare* (Rich Wolfson)

FontShare ($295, from Olduvai) lets you access downloadable printer fonts (but not their screen fonts) from anywhere on a network, which means each workstation doesn't need a System folder full of printer font files. FontShare is smart when it comes to finding fonts: first it looks in your System folder, then in folders inside your System folder. Then it asks where it should look next—and remembers to look there the next time. So if you tell it to look in a folder on a file server, for example, it finds the downloadable fonts there from then on.

☀ *Suitcase II on a network* (Rich Wolfson)

Suitcase II (described in more detail in the utilities chapter) can be used on a network to share downloadable and screen fonts that are stored on a file server. It has to be installed on each machine in the network for this to work.

(Be aware that once Suitcase has accessed files from a file server, you can't log off the server by dragging its icon into the Trash, because you'll be trying to cut the connection to the opened, active font files on the server.)

♠ *"hiding" Suitcase* (Rich Wolfson)

very hot tip

If you've set up Suitcase for network use but don't want anyone reconfiguring it, you can remove its name from the ♠ menu; it will still function, but users won't be able to select it. (Thanks to Steve Brecher, Suitcase's author, for this tip. I corralled him on the floor of a trade show and explained my problem, and he provided this solution.)

First, set up Suitcase the way you want it to work. Then, in ResEdit:

* Open the Suitcase file.
* Doubleclick on DRVR in the list of resources.
* Select the single item in the DRVR window that opens.
* Choose *Clear* from the Edit menu.

♠ *LaserOneCopy* (Rich Wolfson)

very hot tip

When we installed open-access labs at the school where I teach, one immediate problem was students printing multiple copies of a document—in other words, using the LaserWriter like a copy machine. Since we don't charge for laser output, we modified a LaserWriter driver to allow only one copy of a document to be printed at a time, and called it LaserOneCopy. It's been an effective way to limit LaserWriter abuse.

There are no problems using LaserOneCopy, since it's only a slightly modified Apple driver. It won't work with programs that have built-in printer drivers, but it doesn't interfere with them either.

bargain

We pass out LaserOneCopy for no charge (hey, it's Apple's software, after all). AppleLink is best way to contact me—the address is U0754. (If you want to use snail mail, my address is in Appendix B.) When new driver versions come out, we modify them and make them available.

All we ask is that you not remove the credits on the bottom of the dialog box. (Thanks to programmer Marsh Gosnell, who recently went off to Iowa to join CE Software.)

```
┌──────────────────────────────────────────────────────────────────┐
│ ┌────────────────────────────────────────────────────────────┐    │
│ │ LaserWriter  "Montclair State"              5.2  ┌──────────┐│   │
│ │                                                  │   OK     ││   │
│ │  ONLY ONE COPY     Pages: ◉ All  ○ From: │  │ To: │  │└──────────┘│   │
│ │                                                  ┌──────────┐│   │
│ │  Cover Page:   ◉ No ○ First Page  ○ Last Page    │ Cancel   ││   │
│ │                                                  └──────────┘│   │
│ │  Paper Source: ◉ Paper Cassette  ○ Manual Feed   ┌──────────┐│   │
│ │                                                  │  Help    ││   │
│ │ •-•-•-•-•-•-•-•-•-•-•-•-•-•-•-•-•-•-•-•-•-•-•-•-•-•└──────────┘│   │
│ │   LaserOneCopy (allows only one copy at a time) is brought to you by: │
│ │        Rich Wolfson, Sharon Aker, Marsh Gosnell and          │   │
│ │      the MacLab at Montclair State College, Montclair, NJ.   │   │
│ └────────────────────────────────────────────────────────────┘    │
└──────────────────────────────────────────────────────────────────┘
```

serial servers *(Rich Wolfson)*

Most modems, plotters and scanners connect to the Mac's serial port. They're not SCSI devices and can't normally be included on a network. If you need to network any such devices, you can do so with a *serial server.* Two that I've found reliable are the Solona R-server and Shiva's NetSerial.

NetModems *(Rich Wolfson)*

NetModems can be used by anyone on a network, providing dial-out and dial-in capabilities for everyone. When you dial in from a remote site, it looks like you're connected directly to the network—you can get at all the zones and access file servers and printers. But you need at least a 9600-baud modem to do any actual work; 2400 baud is too slow for anything except picking up mail or transferring small files.

Shiva has 9600-baud NetModem. Or you can use a regular 9600-baud modem with a serial server so it can be accessed throughout the network.

PC to Mac and back

⬤ trading with the enemy (AN)

If you use a personal computer at work, there's a frighteningly high probability that it isn't a Mac. Yes, the ugly reality is that most personal computers are IBM PCs or clones thereof—known generically as PCs or as DOS (pronounced *dahss)* machines, because the most common operating system they use is MS DOS or PC DOS (although *dross* machines might be a more appropriate name).

WARNING! HYSTERICAL RANT AHEAD.

*gossip/
trivia*

There's an ignorant trend afoot to call all personal computers—presumably even Macs!—PCs, as if there were something wrong with the simple and straightforward word *computers.* The people who use PC in that way tend to be the same ones who talk about *software programs*—as if you needed the word software to distinguish a program running on your computer from, say, a television program or a drug rehabilitation program. (And come to think of it, if we're warring on drugs, why are we spending all this money rehabilitating them?)

Maybe they feel that the *P* in *PC* helps make it clear that you're referring to a personal computer and that without that qualification, you might ask someone what kind of computer they use at home and get an answer like, "Do you mean my *personal* computer or the Cray in the basement?"

This is all by way of saying that—in this book—*PC* refers to an IBM PC or clone, *not* to a Mac.

END OF HYSTERICAL RANT. RESUME NORMAL READING.

Where was I? Oh, yes—the PC you have in your office. Although there's no way around the wrenching feeling in your gut you have to endure every morning when you travel back into the pre-Mac Stone Age of computing, you can at least transfer data back and forth between the office machine and your Mac at home. The tips below tell you how.

⌘ *easy reading with SuperDrive* (Rich Wolfson)

very good feature

Apple made a great move toward cross-machine compatibility with its SuperDrive which—with the help of the Apple File Exchange software that comes with your Mac—can read all DOS-formatted 3.5" disks. Of course, just because it can read the *disk* doesn't mean it can read the files *on* it—they have to either be text files or specially formatted by a PC program to be readable by the Mac.

⌘ *Apple's external 5.25" drive* (Rich Wolfson)

Apple has an external floppy disk drive that reads 5.25" PC disks formatted for 360K. it plugs into a card in your SE slot or one of the NuBus slots on Mac II's. The disks don't mount on your desktop—you need Apple File Exchange to transfer data in and out.

⌘ *direct connection* (DC)

shortcut

Even if you don't have a SuperDrive, transferring files back and forth between a Mac and a PC can be relatively simple—particularly if you can arrange to wire the two machines together directly. A cable is the only hardware you'll need. Simply connect it to the modem port on the back of the Mac and to the serial connector on the PC.

Next, you'll need a communications program for each machine. For the DOS machine, either PC-Talk or ProComm is a good choice. They operate at up to 19,200 baud and both support the error-checking file-transfer protocol called Xmodem. Both are shareware and can be obtained from most computer bulletin boards, commercial information services like CompuServe, or PC users groups.

On the Mac, run software that will transfer at 19,200 baud and that will allow you to disable MacBinary (a special kind of Xmodem file-transfer protocol) when you're doing the transfer. Most communications programs for the Mac meet both requirements—although the otherwise excellent TermWorks doesn't allow you to disable MacBinary. With both machines set to 19,200 baud, the data moves quite fast.

⌘ over the phone (DC)

Lugging machines around can be tedious, so you may prefer to transfer files over the phone. The main differences from the method described in the previous entry are that you need to add a modem at each end and that data transfer will be slower. (The faster the modem, the better—it should be at least 1200 baud.)

Let's assume you have a DOS machine at the office and a Mac at home (the opposite is a bit hard to imagine). Before you leave the office, turn on the PC (if it isn't already on), start your communications program and set it to answer an incoming call.

ProComm is particularly well suited for phone transfers, since it has a special option called Host Mode that gives you full access to the files on any disk when you connect remotely, while at the same time providing for extensive password protection, so that only you and the people you authorize can access the computer.

When you get home, you just start your Mac communications program and tell it to dial the number of the PC. When you've connected with the PC, it will ask you for your password, then provide you with a menu of files available for transferring (downloading) to your Mac. When you've transferred all the files you want, just tell the Mac communications program to hang up. That's all there is to it.

When you've finished working with the files, you can call the remote machine and send them back. And, by following the same procedures, you can set the Mac up so you can call it from the PC during the day.

⌘ TOPS (Eric Alderman/SZA)

TOPS, described in the networks section above, is especially good for an office with both Macs and PC's. To use it, each PC needs a LocalTalk interface card ($390, including software).

One of the nice features of TOPS is that PC users continue to use the PC interface—they don't need to learn a lot about Macintosh terms like *icon* and *folder*. You have just another drive letter (for a published Mac volume) to use for saving and retrieving files or for performing any normal DOS command. Folders on the Mac volume appear to your PC as subdirectories, so you can navigate around the Mac disk using the normal DOS subdirectory commands before copying the file.

very good feature

For example, Microsoft Excel reads and translates Lotus 1-2-3 worksheets automatically. Normally, you'd first transfer the worksheet onto your Mac disk and load the file. With TOPS, you can leave the file in place on the PC's hard disk. While in Excel, you'd click on the *Drive* button to access the 1-2-3 files on the remote PC disk and then retrieve one—straight into Excel, right across the network.

Another common use for TOPS is to transfer word processing documents between the Mac and the PC. A program called MacLinkPlus (from Dataviz) can translate documents from WordStar, MultiMate and DCA format to MacWrite format, and vice versa. It can also perform many spreadsheet translations—for example from the DIF format common on PC spreadsheets to the SYLK format used by Mac spreadsheets like Multiplan and Excel.

♠ what gets lost in the translation *(DC)*

If you use both a PC and Mac on a regular basis, you know that they're quite different animals. As a result, there are some limits to what the Mac can do with files transferred from DOS machines.

Two programs that impose very few limitations are WordPerfect and Microsoft Word, because they both have versions that run on PCs as well as Macs. This lets you work extensively on documents on both machines and send them back and forth with little or no loss of formatting.

If you're using another DOS word processing program, you may only be able to enter and edit text; you'll have to remember to save the document as a text file and all your formatting will be lost in the transfers between the machines. (One way around this limitation is to find a word processing program on the PC that offers a conversion utility to Word or WordPerfect format.)

Spreadsheet users are in better shape, thanks to some standards in the industry and to the flexibility of Excel, the most popular spreadsheet on the Mac. The standard spreadsheet in the PC world is Lotus 1-2-3 and you can read 1-2-3 files directly into Excel. After you've worked on the files in Excel you can save them in 1-2-3 format and transfer them back. (The main limitation is that macros written in one product won't work with the other.)

Database files also transfer fairly easily if the PC program uses the Mac standard format of [Tab] between fields and [Return] between records. dBASE is a popular PC database and several Mac databases can read PC dBASE files with no conversion.

All this transferring and modifying files can get to be a lot of work. If you're fortunate enough to have Macs at work as well as PCs, you should investigate one of the more direct—although expensive—solutions like TOPS.

⬤ *making your Mac work like a PC* (Rich Wolfson)

Not, of course, that you would want to do that, but other, less enlightened users might. (Do you think that lead will appease Arthur, so he'll leave this entry in?) *[No way, Rich. But that bribe did the trick.—AN]*

Mac 286 is a NuBus card from Orange Micro that allows your Mac II to run IBM applications in a separate window on the screen. We've used it at the college where I work and found it to be reliable—it works well enough to impress most PC users. The Mac 286 is basically a clone-on-a-card and, at $1600, costs as much as (or more than) a clone—that is, a whole separate computer. (So why not just buy a clone? Well, this approach saves desk space, cuts down on clutter, lets you use a single hard disk and just generally avoids the bother of dealing with two machines.)

Soft PC from Insignia Solutions, at $400, is a much less expensive alternative. It's a software-based PC emulator that requires a Mac II or SE/30 with at least two megs of RAM and three megs of disk space it can devote to the emulator. In using it extensively at the college, we've found that it can run most popular MS-DOS programs, and you can even copy text from its window and paste it into a Mac word processor.

bargain

🍎 *a good book on all this* (AN)

Bon vivant, raconteur and Macintosh Bible contributor Steve Michel has written a good book on this whole topic. It's called *IBM PC and Macintosh Networking.*

Macs and Apple II's

🍎 *making your Mac work like an Apple II* (Rich Wolfson)

Apple II emulation doesn't get as much attention as PC emulation, but it's often critical in school situations. Many schools have big investments in Apple II software, and even when they're ready to invest in new hardware, building a new software library (and losing their favorite Apple II-only programs) keeps them from switching to Macs.

II in a Mac runs Apple II software in a Mac window. It's proven very useful at our school on many occasions. Be aware, however, that it won't run any copy-protected software—which includes most games and a lot of educational programs.

🍎 *transferring AppleWorks files to the Mac* (Eric Angress)

There's nothing like buying a Mac to make you realize how slow and cumbersome your old Apple IIc or IIe was. But you've had the IIc around for a long time, and have accumulated a lot of documents on it. It sure would be nice to be able to transfer them quickly and easily to the Mac. Fortunately, there's an easy way to do that—if your Apple II files are in AppleWorks.

You'll need Microsoft Works for the Mac, and you'll have to transfer your II files from 5¼″ disks to 3½″ disks. This first step is most easily done on an Apple IIGS, which has both types of drives attached. (If you don't have access to a GS, some desktop publishing places have this setup.)

You'll also need Apple File Exchange, which comes with any Mac system, version 5.0 or later, and the Works-Works Transporter, which is on the Works program disk. Here are the basic steps:

- Copy the Works-Works Transporter file into the Apple File Exchange folder.

- Start Apple File Exchange on the Mac.

- Insert the 3½″ disk containing your AppleWorks files into the Mac's drive.

- Launch Works-Works Transporter.

- In the list box, select the files to be converted.

- Click the *Transfer* button. The Works-Works Transporter will convert the files to (Macintosh) Works format.

- Choose *Quit* from the File menu to quit Apple File Exchange.

The files won't be exactly the same on the Mac as they were on the II, but all the information and most of the formatting will be there. You'll probably want to reformat most of what you're working on anyway, because the Mac has so many more options than were even dreamed of on the Apple II. (Well, maybe they were dreamed of, which is why we now have Macs.)

If you prefer Excel or Word to Works, it is an easy matter to transfer files between these programs. When using the SYLK format to convert Works files to Excel, you'll probably get messages that say something like, *Can't read record 98,* with an option to click *OK* or cancel. I've always just clicked on *OK,* and everything has worked out fine.

Tips on Works' communications module

✦ dialing

You can store numbers in the Dial dialog box (from the Communications menu) or you can just type the number you want to dial right in the window. Type *atdt* in front of the number; when you hit [Return], it will dial through the modem.

✦ sending text

Despite its name, the *Send Text* command (on the Communications menu) can't send ordinary Mac text files— it only handles Works word processing documents, sending just the text of them (ignoring formatting and graphics). To send a text file, you have to use the *Send File* command (on the same menu) and click on the *Xmodem Text* button.

Another way to send text is to paste it from the Clipboard into the communications window. It gets treated just as if you typed it in—that is, it appears on the screen one character at a time (although more quickly than you could actually type it).

✦ changing the baud rate

You can change the baud rate even if you're right in the middle of a communications session, by choosing the *Settings...* command (on the Communications menu).

✦ control characters

Information services often require that you use control characters (key combinations involving the control key) as commands. With most Mac software, you can substitute the [⌘] key for the control key, but in Works, using the [⌘] key triggers a menu command. The [Option] key will work, however—even if you're using a Mac-specific service that tells you to use [⌘][S], using [Option][S] will get you the results you want.

very
hot
tip

🍎 *no curly quotes*

**important
warning**

If you use a utility like SmartKeys or Quote Init that changes your plain quotes to the curly ones, you won't be able to type any quotes or apostrophes at all in the Works communications window—you'll just get a beep if you try. So turn off your curly quotes program while you're telecommunicating with Works.

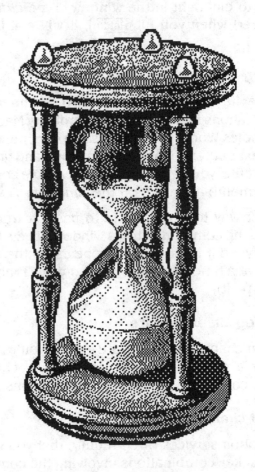

Chapter 16

Education and entertainment

Fun, games and learning

♦ games and hard disks

esp. for
beginners

Games (and educational programs, which are usually disguised as games) are often incompatible with a hard disk system. There are two reasons for this. The first is that, while few business products are copy-protected, many games are.

The kind of copy-protection used for games doesn't usually mean that you can't drag the program to your hard disk or run it from there. But as soon as you start the program, it will ask you to insert the master disk (the one you bought). Once you've done that, proving you're a legitimate user, the disk will spit out and you can get on with the game.

The second problem with running games from a hard disk is that they tend to do some pretty fancy things on a programming level to squeeze top performance out of the Mac. Thus they may use every K of memory, or need specific software to be in just the right spot, or both. Inits in your system may be using specific areas of memory that the game program wants, even if there's plenty of total memory.

If you run into memory problems, don't even bother trying to run the game from the hard disk. Boot from the floppy and run the game from there.

♦ games and hardware upgrades

Because of the neat tricks game programmers tend to do, games don't always conform to Apple's official programming guidelines. But following those guidelines is the only way to ensure upward-compatibility—so that what you wrote for a Plus also runs on an SE/30 and a II.

important
warning

You'll find that many games run only on compact Macs (ones with 9″ screens)—sometimes including the SE/30, sometimes not. Some run only in color, and many don't run under MultiFinder. So if you upgrade your system, you may have to leave some of your favorite playthings behind. We've tried to note with each product mentioned in this chapter which systems it's compatible with.

♦ educational, shmeducational

**very
hot
tip**

Why do we insist that computer games for young children be educational? Do we feel guilty just letting them play with an expensive machine? It's rare that young children don't learn *something* from anything they do, so don't rationalize that they're learning hand-eye coordination (even though they are). Just tell yourself they're having fun. That's what counts in a game, and when they aren't fun, kids don't play them and therefore don't learn from them.

Educational software for kids

♦ general considerations

**very
hot
tip**

It's usually easy to tell whether an educational program for older children is teaching what it's supposed to. But programs for very young children are harder to evaluate. Here are some things to consider:

- Can the children do everything by themselves? Of course you should do some of it with them, and three- or four-year-olds might need help in getting started, but after that, they should be able to handle things on their own. (This not only gives them a feeling of control, but saves your sanity too.)

- How are wrong answers handled? I remember once when my son kept getting wrong answers in an alphabet game when I *knew* he knew the answers. When I asked if he needed help, he said: "No, I like the sound it makes when you give the wrong answer."

  What does the program do after two or three wrong answers in a row? It should provide a hint, or the answer itself, and should let the user try the same problem again, after the answer's been shown or the hint's been given.

- Some programs try to teach too many things at once. You want ones that know how to focus on particular tasks and concepts, and how to dole them out in easily learnable chunks.

- Don't worry about the absence of color—young kids don't care about that, nor does it matter educationally (except, of course, in games that teach color recognition).

When my sons were younger, we had four computers: a black-and-white Timex-Sinclair, a color Timex-Sinclair, a color Commodore 64 and a black-and-white Mac. (Because of the Commodore, *RUN* was the first word both of them learned how to spell.) For a year they showed no preference until it was obvious they liked the Mac the best. It had the least software (I kept programming little games for them) but they were won over by how easy it was to use.

✎ *KidsTime*

KidsTime (from Great Wave) was one of the first Mac programs for young kids, and it's stood the test of time. The package consists of five separate activities, the first three of which teach prereading skills; ABKey builds character recognition, Match-it teaches recognition of same and similar objects, and Dot-to-Dot (shown below, in progress and completed) teaches number recognition and sequencing.

very good feature

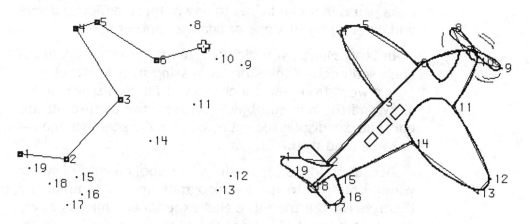

Although recommended for ages three to eight, the two other activities, StoryWriter and KidsNotes, still keep my ten-year-old involved. The former lets you type a story, interspersing pictures from a special font. The program then reads the story back to you, saying the word for the picture. KidsNotes is a terrific music program—no surprise, I suppose, since the same company publishes a music program called ConcertWare.

One weakness of KidsTime is that it uses Macintalk, Apple's speech-generating utility. The voice sounds robotic, especially compared to the digitized sound used in so many other educational packages. KidsTime works on all Macs.

✎ Dinosaur Discovery Kit

Dinosaur Discovery Kit is a talking program from First Byte. Its three activities—a coloring book, a matching game and a story maker—teach reading skills to children three to eight. Each activity uses—what else?—dinosaurs in the graphics.

In the Coloring Book, a word or phrase that describes an item in the picture—like *baby's head* (the baby dinosaur, that is) appears at the top of the screen. You can click on a button to hear the word read as many times as necessary. When you click on the correct item in the picture, it's filled in with the pattern you've chosen.

The Match game is a basic Concentration-like, find-the-pairs game that can be set to any of three difficulty levels and can be played alone or against another user.

In Story Maker, you pick one of three main story lines. Each sentence of the story is missing a word. When you pick a word from several choices, it fills the blank in the story and the related object goes into the picture. At the end, you can display the entire story on the screen to read— or to be read by the program.

Because all the instructions are spoken, it's easy for young children to get the program up and running by themselves. But the more Mac experience children have, the more minor frustrations they'll run into. For example, mine were constantly doubleclicking on items (as I would have) when only a single click was needed by the program.

Despite a few such flaws, Dinosaur Discovery Kit is a good package, but mostly appealing to the younger half of the recommended age group. It works on 512K Macs, Pluses and SE's (except the SE/30), but you can't print to laser printers.

✎ The ManHole

The ManHole is a fascinating Alice-in-Wonderland and Through-the-Looking-Glass visual adventure game for children—or at least those whose Macs have a meg of memory and a hard disk, because this game comes on five 800K disks and needs HyperCard to run. (The program works on all Macs that meet those hardware requirements.)

The ManHole takes advantage of HyperCard's user interface. Clicking almost anywhere on a screen makes something happen or takes you to the place you clicked. If you see a castle in the background and click on its tower, you're on it. Click on a picture on a wall and you're inside it. I've watched children not quite four contentedly play with this game for long spells, yet my eight- and ten-year-olds still like it.

The ManHole is also limited by HyperCard. First of all, there's the program's ungainly size. Then there's the really limited animation (swaying underwater plants just sort of flip back and forth—it's Hanna-Barbera, not Disney). It doesn't seem to bother kids, but I keep thinking how great a program this could be if the designer hadn't been hampered by HyperCard.

✎ The Playroom

The Playroom is like The Manhole, in that clicks on the screen make things happens or take users to the place where they clicked, but it uses real (not HyperCard) animation and clear, digitized voices and sounds.

The main screen in Playroom is just that—a picture of a playroom. Click on the bird and it sings. Click on the nightstand's drawer and it opens—and a balloon floats out. Click on the balloon and...well, I don't want to give away the plot.

Click on the computer and you're zoomed into it. Click on a letter on the keyboard on the screen (or press that key on your Mac's real-world keyboard) and the letter appears on the monitor and is identified.

Clicking on the mouse hole takes you inside, where you can choose from three simple board games you play with the mouse (the Mac's mouse, that is), either alone or with a partner.

Clicking on an odd-looking stuffed animal in the Playroom takes you to one of my kids' favorite activities: a game where you choose the head, body and legs for the figure on screen, mixing or matching elements.

very good feature

Playroom is terrific for three- to eight-year-olds. It works on any Mac from the Plus on up, including Mac II's. It requires two floppy drives or a hard disk, and if you run it from a hard disk, you have to insert the master disk when it's asked for.

♦ *Reader Rabbit*

Reader Rabbit is another program for early readers that uses three-letter words exclusively. The program has four activities, half of which I like. The illustration below shows one of the good ones. A letter appears to the left of the rabbit, and you have to choose words that have that same letter in the same position. Words that don't match get dumped into the garbage. When you've filled the shelves with correct words, the rabbit does a dance—with good sound and animation.

The other activity I like is the Word Train, where you have to fill the cars of the train with words that rhyme with the one in the engine. When the cars are filled, the train drives off the screen.

There's also a labeler game that's very confusing, and a nice Concentration-type game with a serious flaw—no matter how many times you turn over the wrong cards, you're never shown the correct answer.

Reader Rabbit has another flaw that's really annoying— at certain points in each activity, a little box comes up that says *Click mouse to continue.* It's a subtle little box—not a big dialog box in the middle of the screen—and a child who doesn't notice it will just sit there waiting for something to happen. More to the point, since no child who needs Reader Rabbit could possibly *read* the message in the box, this is not exactly a brilliantly thought-through feature.

very bad feature

gossip/ trivia

[This reminds me of a sign I once saw in an old New York elevator that read: To actuate elevator mechanism, press button corresponding to floor desired. *Now try to imagine someone who could read and understand that message but didn't know how to press a button in an elevator.—AN]*

Reader Rabbit is a good program, if you're willing to help children use it. It works on the 512K Mac, the Plus and the SE; you have to insert the master disk if you run it from a hard disk.

♠ *The Munchers*

This product contains two great educational games called Number Munchers (for eight and older) and Word Munchers (for six and older). Both games use the same scenario: you move a PacMan-like cartoon character (called *the muncher)* anywhere in a 6 x 5 grid of words or numbers and make him eat the correct words or numbers (by clicking the mouse).

For words, *correct* means matching a vowel sound. For numbers, it means finding a number that's equal to the target number, or a multiple of it, or a factor of it. In both games, you can set difficulty levels and children can get the correct answer when they make a mistake.

As the muncher moves around the grid, various bad guys chase it (of course). Some change the numbers they pass over, and some eat the muncher. If you munch all the right words/numbers, you get another board of them; after three boards, your reward is a cartoon. The cartoon is of the Road Runner ilk, with the bad guy's plans to catch the Muncher backfiring on him.

Both Muncher games work on all Macs from the Plus on, and special color versions are included for the Mac II family. Muncher, which originated on the Apple II, is intended for the classroom as well as for the home. Teachers can set difficulty levels and lock them in with a password, so they can't be changed by mistake.

♦ *CrystalPaint*

CrystalPaint is a nifty little doodling program from Great Wave Software. It's sort of an overgrown MacPaint/Super-Paint Brush Mirrors mode—you draw and the line is mirrored at whatever (and however many) angles you've chosen. You can choose one of three line thicknesses and one of three backgrounds (black, white or gray). You can invert your image at any time and flip the colors back again. Special copy and pastes are provided (so the paste is also mirrored at all the right angles).

I've found that my kids are just as happy with this kind of program as with a full-fledged paint program—perhaps even happier, because with fewer tools around they can just concentrate on the process. (It's sort of like finger-painting, instead of working with pots of tempera colors.) They've only been using CrystalPaint for a brief time, but I know the staying power of this kind of simple program—I wrote a similar one for them years ago (when they were too young for MacPaint) and they still use it.

♦ *Where in Europe Is Carmen Sandiego?* (Jessica Albert)

I don't know. I can find almost all her accomplices but never Carmen. Well, it's still a great game to play. It's not for people who want a lot of shooting and stuff like that, but if you like to think, this is for you. Whenever you come into a new country, it teaches you all about it, so you learn about Europe. I loved it, and hopefully you will too.

**very good
feature**

Educational software for adults

♦ *teenagers too* (AN)

Despite this country's ridiculous infantilizing of teenagers, they are adults in everything but name and legal status. And don't say that they don't have the life experience of people in their twenties. Of course they don't. Neither do people in their twenties have the life experience of people in their thirties, nor people in their thirties the life experience of people in their forties. Continue with this absurd line of reasoning and soon Ronald Reagan and Bob Hope are the only adults among us—you see why I call it "absurd."

By the way, do you know where the idea that people become adults at 21 comes from? From the old idea that people shouldn't be allowed to participate in community decision-making until they'd been adults *for seven years—* which, in those days of poor nutrition and relatively late puberty, was figured at 14 + 7.

This is all by way of saying that, in this section, software aimed at teenagers is lumped together with software aimed at other adults.

🍎 *The '88 Vote*

If you're a teacher with enough funding for a videodisc player, you may be interested in a new product from ABC News—a videodisc of the 1988 presidential campaign, from the first mudsling to the last. The disc contains everything from candidates announcements to their withdrawals (quick: who made two withdrawal statements?), election night coverage, the debates, the TV commercials—seemingly everything, in stills, sound and videos.

But we wouldn't be covering it here unless it had a Macintosh hook—the HyperCard stack you use to navigate your way through the information. It's based on the one Peter Jennings used to get through the election coverage (his Mac monitor was built into his desktop and he was clicking his mouse just off-screen). You can use the stack not only to look things up but also to create your own sequence of clips for a class or lecture. *[Quick: who won the election—Tweedledum or Tweedledee?—AN]*

The disc/stack package is excellent—although why they couldn't align their icons neatly on the opening screen is beyond me. (ABC News also has similar packages on Martin Luther King and AIDS.)

☀ *Hidden Agenda* (AN)

This is one of the most intelligent, interesting and beautifully designed computer games I've ever played. A corrupt dictatorship has just been overthrown in the mythical Central American country of Chimerica. Your job as the new president is to appoint a cabinet and guide your country through the many difficulties that await it, balancing the demands (and threats) of various groups struggling for power. At the end of three years, you receive a written report several pages long that summarizes your achievements and failures.

very good feature

I asked Davida Coady, who knows a lot about Central America and nothing about computer games, to play Hidden Agenda. She was very impressed with how challenging and involving it is as a game, and also with the thoughtfulness and knowledge that went into its simulation of reality. A lot of computer games claim to teach you something about the real world; this one really does.

Hidden Agenda (from Springboard) costs $60 and works on all Macs from the Plus on up.

☀ *Culture 1.0* (AN)

This is a terrific series of HyperCard stacks that cover world history from ancient times to the present. When it discusses an artist or architect, Culture usually gives you a representative piece of art, and when it discusses a composer, it often gives you a snatch of melody.

very good feature

I generally find HyperCard references tedious, because HyperCard is *soooo s...l...o...w,* but the addition of music really makes it worthwhile. The text is generally quite intelligent, the information is well organized, and the stacks are easy to use. For about $200 (I can't find the current pricing), it gives you over four megabytes of useful and interesting information. This product is definitely worth checking out.

◉ *The Electronic Whole Earth Catalog* (AN)

Stewart Brand's *Whole Earth Catalogs* are not only a fantastically successful series of books (over 50 *million* copies sold worldwide, I hear) but they spawned a whole new *kind* of book—the obsessively detailed, no-frills, ultrahelpful catalog of tools (in the widest possible sense of *tool*). Like many books, *The Macintosh Bible* was inspired by *The Whole Earth Catalog,* and we certainly see ourselves as a part of its tradition (although there are some obvious differences in approach).

Now there's a CD-ROM version—The Electronic Whole Earth Catalog (from Brøderbund). The HyperCard interface is pretty slick and easy to learn, and—like its hard-copy equivalent, it's *crammed* full of information. Its more than 9000 cards review 2500 items, with the help of 4000 pictures, 2000 text excerpts and 500 sounds.

I'd rather sit on a couch with a book on my lap to access this information, instead of staring into my Mac screen (something I do too much of already), but if you like getting your information in HyperCard, this is one of the most useful collection of stacks you can own. No home should be without *The Whole Earth Catalog,* in one form or another (or in both).

◉ *The Blind Watchmaker* (AN)

very good feature

The Blind Watchmaker, by the brilliant British evolutionary biologist Richard Dawkins, is one of the most interesting and important books I've ever read. Subtitled *Why the evidence of evolution reveals a universe without design,* it's the clearest and, at the same time, the most profound explanation of the theory of evolution (and its implications) that you'll ever find. So if you have the slightest interest in this topic, you should definitely buy this book ($8 in paper).

bargain

To help demonstrate his points, Dawkins has written a companion Mac program, which is also called *The Blind Watchmaker* ($18 from the book's publisher, W.W. Norton; there's a coupon in the back of the book). The software lets you "breed" *biomorphs* (animal- or plantlike shapes). This process is natural selection made concrete—almost tangible—and shows, as no mere explanation can, how extraordinarily complex an organism can be produced by selective breeding—one step at a time.

very good feature

Dawkins runs *Blind Watchmaker* breeding competitions, with $1000 prizes. The aim of the first (won by Thomas Reed of Oxnard CA) was to breed a biomorph that most closely resembled the Holy Grail! The aim of the second—which ended May 30, 1990—was to breed the most human-like biomorph (depicting "an entire human form or a part, e.g., a face, torso, limb"). Who knows what the third contest will be, but you'll find information on entering it in the back of the book *(The Blind Watchmaker,* that is, not *The Macintosh Bible).*

I could go on for another twenty pages describing what you can do with this fascinating piece of software (and another forty describing Dawkins' theories and arguments). But why not get it directly from the horse's mouth? (Speaking of which, he has some interesting things to say about the evolution of horses.) Both the book and the software are *highly* recommended.

Voyager (Jim Beime)

very good feature

Voyager ("The Interactive Desktop Planetarium") brings the night sky into your Mac with power, grace and speed. It's a valuable tool for the novice as well as the most experienced amateur astronomer. Its window full of stars can be resized for the largest of screens. A control panel shows the current location, time, chart position and size of the current field of view.

You have three operating modes to choose from: Star Atlas, a star chart of all the heavens; Local View—what the sky will look like at any time from any observation post on earth or from any other object orbiting our sun; and Celestial Sphere, which gives a view of the stars as projected onto a sphere which can be oriented to any position.

Most amateur astronomers use star charts to plan their evening's activities before going observing. What advantage does Voyager have over a good atlas? First, you can get anywhere quickly. Grab the scroll box and move it—the Right Ascension or Declination positions are displayed as you move. When you're where you want to go, just release the mouse button.

If you're looking for a specific constellation, use the *Center on Constellation* command from the Field menu; every constellation will appear alphabetically in a list box. Choose *Find and Center* and the screen is quickly redrawn, with the chosen constellation in the center. (You'll notice that the Big Dipper doesn't appear in the list. That's because it's not a constellation; it's an *asterism*, an arrangement of stars within a constellation—which, in this case, is Ursa Major.)

Voyager's graphic database has over 14,000 objects in it, from stars and asterisms to irregular galaxies and dark nebulae. You can choose what kind of objects, or magnitudes, you want to see. By selecting *10th magnitude* and *galaxies*, for example, you can come across some interesting objects that you may have previously overlooked.

A major strength of Voyager is the way it tracks the planets. You can go into the past, present or future, to any point in or above our Solar System, and see events with this program that would take months or years of observing and charting. A trail of dots will show the path of the planet through the sky. The time between dots can be varied from one minute to two years! Click on the *Track* box and sit back and watch the planets move through the fixed stars.

You can even see the path that a newly discovered comet will take through the local sky in the months to come. The program provides earth-to-sun and sun-to-comet distances at the click of a mouse.

Voyager is a great educational tool. The manual is very complete with good illustrations, tips for the user and sample situations walked through step by step.

⍟ *ArtWorx Bridge*

I wouldn't want this to get back to my parents, but I majored in bridge at college, with a minor in pinochle—no matter what the records actually say. (I don't think Rutgers offers those degrees anymore.) I haven't been able to play in years for lack of three other players but, hey, I've got my Mac.

very good feature

ArtWorx Bridge is really quite good. It bids predictably and pretty much by the book (Stayman and Blackwood, that is)—try replaying a hand and you'll get the same bids. It also plays well (it's a little humiliating being finessed by a computer program). Cards are displayed so you can click on them, but the screen isn't particularly attractive. The only serious flaw is that you can't take back a move—and it's easy to click on the card *next* to the one you really wanted to play.

very bad feature

Where ArtWorx Bridge really falls down, though, is when you want to throw a hand in. When you know you've won the hand and don't want to bother playing it out, you can use the *Claim Hand* command; when you know you can't make it and want to throw it in, you use the *Concede* command. In each case, though, the program seems to assume that the side that's going to win is going to make every possible right move and the losers are going to make every mistake short of reneging.

So when you throw in a hand because you know you're down by one, you'll get a dialog box informing you you've been set four tricks. When you claim a hand because you're sure of it—with maybe one overtrick if a finesse works—you'll find you've been conceded a small slam. I even got one dialog box that informed me that I took the bid—three hearts—with five overtricks (only four are available after a three bid). But these bugs don't matter if you're not playing for points—or if you're willing to play every hand down to the last trick.

Music programs

⚹ Deluxe Music Construction Kit *(AN)*

Years ago, when I was writing a computer book for kids, I played around with a program called Songwriter on an Apple II. Designed for musical dodos like myself, it couldn't have been easier to use. I wrote several "songs" with it (which I still listen to) and have seldom been happier.

very good feature

Ever since then, I've looked for an equivalently easy-to-use music program on the Mac, but I hadn't been able to find one—until I discovered Deluxe Music Construction Kit. Written by Geoff Brown for Electronic Arts, it costs $130 and seems to have quite a bit of sophistication and power. I wouldn't know about that. All I know is, unlike several other Mac music programs I've tried, it's musical-idiot-friendly and a whole lot of fun. Even the manual seems to be pretty good.

⚹ Music Mouse

Music Mouse doesn't write or store music, and it doesn't use musical notation (though it does use terms like *chords* and *ligatures)*. It just *produces* music, by turning the Mac into a mouse-controlled musical instrument. You use menus and keys to set things like the tonal range, but the mouse does the playing. As you move the mouse vertically, it changes the tone being played; moving it horizontally changes the background chord. Your moves are displayed on the screen.

This is a unique approach, but I don't care for the sounds you can produce with it. I asked a musician friend to play with it, and he said he'd grow very tired very quickly of the limited tonal variations within each setup.

[Music Mouse is the least Mac-standard Mac program I can remember using—it doesn't even have a Quit command! I got so frustrated with its total contempt for the interface that I didn't even have the patience to play around with it.—AN]

⌘ *ConcertWare Plus*

Great Wave Software does some great stuff, and ConcertWare is the proof. In its first incarnation, it got me to wire a speaker so I could plug it directly into the Mac, and it's only gotten better since that original release.

ConcertWare is actually three applications: the Writer, the Player and the Instrument Maker. In the Writer, you compose your music by placing notes on the staff with the mouse or by playing them from the keyboard. You can add all sorts of embellishments to the score—including lyrics. There's limited, though adequate, playing ability from within the Writer, so you can check your work in progress, but for the real playback, you'll want to switch to the Player.

The Instrument Maker lets you alter existing instruments or create entirely new ones by defining various waveforms and envelopes. You even get to design the icon the Player uses for your instrument.

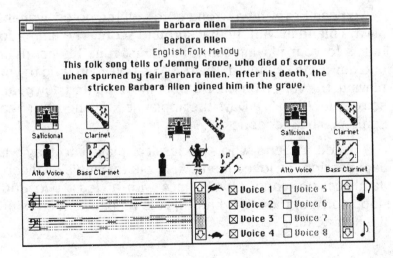

ConcertWare comes with such a large library of songs and instruments that you could skip the Writer end of things for months and still enjoy the software. The Player lets you set the speed and volume for the piece, as well as assign an instrument to each of the voices in the score. The illustration above shows the Player window, with its instrument

very good feature

icons (only a few of the dozens available) and the nonstand-ard but intuitive musical notation that which changes as the song plays. (In the Writer, you work with standard musical notation.)

♠ Jam Session

very good feature

Ah! A music program that can please both musicians and nonmusicians alike. It consists of five "scenes"—down-home country, classical piano concert, heavy metal band, rock group and jazz club—and a selection of appropriate background music to go with each.

You play along with the band by pressing keys on the keyboard. Each row of keys represents a different kind of playing or a different instrument. In the concert scene, for example, one row of keys plays single notes, another plays short riffs. In the country scene, one row plays the fiddle, another the banjo—and, OK, one row plays the rooster and chickens.

You can't ever hit a wrong note—all the notes available always blend in with the background score. The animation reacts to your playing too: the pianist runs his hands up and down the keyboard, the fiddle is bowed in time to your playing, the valves on the trumpet move up and down, and so on. And there's always the applause key when you need some positive feedback.

I asked a friend who's a classical pianist to play with Jam Session; he loved it and went out to get his own copy. Jam Session works on all Macs with at least two 800K floppy drives, though a hard disk is recommended (since it's a three-disk set).

Action and adventure games

♠ Arkanoid

Arkanoid takes a classic computer game—which goes by several names, including *brickbats*—and turns it into something entirely different. In the classic game, you smash bricks by bouncing a ball at them with a paddle.

Arkanoid gives you a large variety of screens, and also sends capsules falling down at you as you smash the bricks. The capsules provide various powers if you catch them with your paddle: laser beams, a larger paddle, a slower hit on the ball, extra points, etc.

Like so many arcade games, Arkanoid is utterly addicting. It works on the Mac 512, 512e, SE, SE/30 and II. It doesn't work under MultiFinder or if you have certain inits running, and it doesn't work on my cx either.

⬧ *Billiards*

Colour Billiards (by the spelling, it must be British—or maybe Canadian) shares a disk with its black-and-white predecessor, MacBilliards. I'll review the color version here (which has a few more options), but even as I write, my kids are playing the black-and-white version, arguing over whose turn it is—a sure sign of a great computer game. The older one has talked about how realistic the sounds are. (He's right, but how would he know? Is he hanging around the pool hall when I think he's out riding his bike?)

How do you shoot pool with a mouse? When you drag on the cue ball, a pool cue appears. The longer you drag, the harder the shot, and pressing ⌘ doubles the force of the shot.

Colour Billiards is terrific, and offers a variety of games—billiards, eight-ball, nine-ball, etc. You can have the balls leave a path as they move, which makes for an interesting effect and may even help you analyze your shots. You can even do an instant replay of any good shot you'd like to show off.

very good feature

Colour Billiards isn't MultiFinder-compatible, but it works on any Mac (just use the proper version).

⬧ *Tetris*

Tetris is one of those games that has become an instant classic. As with most classics, the rules are simple. Objects made up of four connected squares in various configurations slowly fall, one at a time, from the top of the game screen to the bottom. As a shape falls, you can rotate it and move it to the right or left.

The object of the game is to arrange the shapes so that when they land, there'll be a solid row of little squares from one side of the window to the other. When you accomplish that, all the squares in the row disappear, everything above it slides down, and you get some points.

For all its simplicity, Tetris is pretty addictive. It comes in two versions—a monochrome DA and a color version with some impressive background graphics. Both feature Russian theme music in the introduction, and you can choose to keep it on while you're playing. Tetris works on any Mac with at least 512K of RAM.

Airborne

**very good
feature**

An oldie but a goodie, Airborne was the first of Silicon Beach's games to incorporate RealSound—terrific digitized sounds that have been compressed to fit on a floppy disk. As with their other games, the action was designed to run from the mouse and keyboard, so you don't miss a joystick at all.

In Airborne, you're on the ground, under attack by both ground and air forces, with only a boulder for protection. (And when you hear that jet rushing in, before you can even see it on the screen...) As with so many computer games, there's no winning this one—the more enemies you destroy, the more come after you. You just try to survive a little longer each time, racking up points while you can.

Airborne works on all compact Macs from the 128K on up, but not on Mac II's.

Dark Castle and Return to Dark Castle

**very good
feature**

Dark Castle has been around for a long time, but it's still one of the best Mac action games there is. Black-and-white and mouse-driven, it was designed for the Mac from the ground up—and it shows.

In Dark Castle, you move the Prince from room to room through...well, through the Dark Castle and its dungeons. His enemies are legion and his only weapons are rocks. The only problem with the game (besides the raucous birds, which got me to attach earphones to the kids' machine) is that you can't save your position. Even if you stop before all your lives are used up, you have to start from the beginning the next time you play.

Return to Dark Castle is more of the same. Both versions are great; it's too bad that Silicon Beach has stopped developing new games.

Dark Castle works on the Mac 512 (you need version 1.0 on two 400K disks), the 512e (you can use version 1.0 on a single 800K disk), the Plus, SE, SE/30 and all Mac II's. Return to Dark Castle works on everything except the original 128K Mac, the Mac 512 and the Portable.

Apache Strike

Apache Strike isn't Cowboys-and-Indians—the Apache is a helicopter, and you're flying it. You're flying it *low*, between tall buildings; you duck under bridges, or pull up in time to avoid them, dodging bombs all the time. You only see what's directly in front of you—no peripheral vision, so you need quick reflexes.

The ever-changing maze of buildings (in various cities) shifts as you turn the helicopter, but they're just simple line drawings. Apache Strike is more difficult than it looks— but then, flying a helicopter is more difficult than it looks, too. It works on the Mac 512 (you need version 1.0 on two 400K disks) and the 512e (you can use version 1.0 on a single 800K disk). Version 1.1 works on all other Macs except the SE/30.

Mac•Man

As you might guess from its name, Mac•Man is a Mac version of the classic PacMan. Mac•Man looks like a Macintosh, and instead of being chased by ghosts and gobbling power pills, he's chased by PC's and eats apples.

The keyboard implementation of the game is terrific, but it's just not the same without a joystick. A one-inch mini-joystick is included—it sticks (lightly) to the 5 key on the numeric keypad and each of its four legs presses a key when you tip it. Aside from the fact that the stick slips off when you push it down toward the 2 key, this mini-joystick must have been an afterthought—my version of Mac•Man uses the 5 key, not the 2 key, for *down.* Years ago, Mac•Man came with a real joystick from Nuvo Labs, the developer of the program. I'm glad I still have it.

Mac•Man works on all compact Macs from the Mac 512 on.

✎ *Star Wars* (Jessica Albert)

Star Wars is stupid. In one day, I beat level 1 and in three days, I beat levels 2 and 3 (the last level), even though I only played for fifteen minutes a day—and I'm not that good at video games. Five- to seven-year olds might enjoy Star Wars for a day or two, but only an idiot would like the game if they were older than that.

[Despite Jessica's agonizing attempt to be fair, I think she may have done Star Wars a disservice here. As a sophisticated twelve-year-old—well, anyway, as a twelve-year-old—when she wrote this, she was forgetting how much she'd matured—well, grown—in the previous few years. I think Star Wars would be challenging and fun for kids up to the age of ten or eleven.—AN]

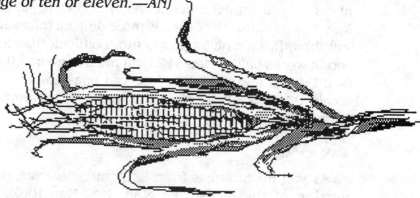

Chapter 17

Programming

Mac programming basics

♦ basic programming terms *(AN)*

esp. for
beginners

The first thing to understand is the difference between a *programmer* and a *user*. Programmers use *programming languages* to write programs; when bugs turn up in the programs, they fix them, and when new features are needed, they add them. Users simply use the programs—the programming language is invisible to them (or should be).

It's like the difference between an automobile mechanic and a driver. Just as you don't need to know how a carburetor works to be an expert driver (although you may), you don't need to know anything about programming to be an expert Macintosh *user*.

The actual statements or instructions in a program are called *code*. It's normally broken into *lines*. A relatively small piece of code, which does a specific task, is called a *routine*. Put a bunch of routines together and you have a *program*.

♦ compilers vs. interpreters *(AN)*

esp. for
beginners

There are two ways to implement a programming language—with a *compiler* or with an *interpreter*. Interpreters execute each line of a program individually each time the program is run, while compilers translate the whole program at once, before it's run. From that point on, you can run the compiled program whenever you want, without having to use the compiler to translate it again.

Compiling is more time-consuming when you're editing a program for mistakes, because you have to recompile the whole program each time you want to check out the effect of a change you've made (and large programs can take an hour or more to compile). But compilers are less time-consuming when you want to use the finished program over and over again.

Interpreters are better for learning, because there's no compilation time, but they run more slowly each time through.

⬤ *the Toolbox* (DC)

esp. for
beginners

One thing that makes the Mac's programming environment stand head and shoulders above that of other computers is a built-in feature called the Toolbox. It's part of the ROMs and works like this:

Let's say you want to draw a circle on the screen. With old-fashioned computers, you have to write a great deal of code specifying every aspect of making a circle. On the Mac, you simply have your program call the Toolbox and use the code already written there to draw the circle. Many wonderful things are included in the Toolbox, including all the information the Mac needs to create windows and pop-down menus.

⬤ *resources* (SZA/Michael Bradley)

very good
feature

Another thing that makes Mac programming so different from working on lesser machines is its use of *resources*. Simply put, resources are items that can be used over and over again in different parts of a program. The various pointer shapes are a kind of resource, as are icons, dialog boxes and patterns.

A Mac program might say something like *get dialog box #7, put icon #14 in it and the text from string #347.* Thus the way a program looks can be controlled just by changing its resources, leaving the main program unaltered. This makes it relatively simple to do a foreign-language implementation of a product, for example, because all you have to do is translate the resources (the text in dialog boxes and on menus).

Resources on the Mac are identified by four-letter names (although some are three letters followed by a space). Some are all caps, and some are all lowercase (there's no functional difference between them). The most common ones are:

ALRT   alert boxes—the boxes themselves, not the contents

CURS   pointer shapes (the name is short for *cursors)*

DITL   *dialog item list*—text in alert and dialog boxes

DLOG	dialog boxes—the boxes themselves, not the contents
FKEY	Fkeys
FOND	font family information
FONT	font characteristics
ICN#	icon list
ICON	icons
MENU	menu information
snd	sound
STR#	text of screen messages

ResEdit

♦ *using ResEdit*

ResEdit (pronounced *REZ-ed-it*, short for *resource editor*) is a utility program from Apple that lets you change the *resources* (see the previous entry) that Mac programs—including the System and Finder—use. ResEdit is available free through bulletin boards and is included on Microsoft's QuickBASIC disks.

Because it's meant for programmers, ResEdit lacks much of the friendliness of most Mac software and has a reputation for being a heavy-duty, hackers-only program. But anybody can use ResEdit, with just a bit of instruction.

The first thing to remember about ResEdit is that you can alter your System, Finder and applications with it. This means you can make a very serious mistake and ruin one of those important files. So make sure that you have a copy or two handy, in case you destroy the one you're changing.

important warning

ResEdit presents a series of windows with lists in them. Doubleclicking on an item in the list gets you another window with a list in it. For example, here's how you get to the Trash icon:

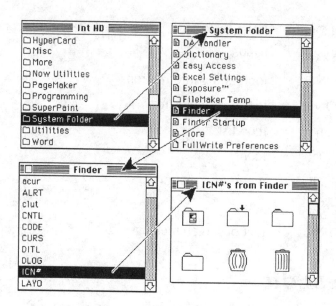

You can select items by typing as many letters of their names as are required to identify them—the same way you do in Open dialog boxes.

The last thing to remember about ResEdit is that it has no Save command. Only when you close a file (first closing all the windows within it) does ResEdit ask if you want to save changes. So if you're doing a lot of work on a resource and want to do an interim save, you'll have to close the file and then reopen it to continue working.

✎ ResEdit under MultiFinder

bug

Under MultiFinder, ResEdit's windows occasionally misbehave, turning transparent so you can see whatever's behind them, and you can't use it to alter the Finder or certain System resources. To change them, you have to choose *Set Startup* from the Special menu, set the Finder as the Startup, and restart the Mac.

✎ viewing PICT resources

very
hot
tip

When you view a PICT resource in ResEdit, you can't resize the display window, which means you can't see all of a large picture (it's even worse than working with a large picture in the Scrapbook). To view the entire thing, copy it and paste it into a desk accessory that can handle graphics at full size.

✿ *changing where DA's appear on the menu* (Paul Hoffman)

very hot tip

Desk accessories are listed alphabetically in the ✿ menu, but you can use ResEdit to change their names so they'll appear where you want them to. To do that, open the System file (or whatever file contains the DA) in ResEdit and then doubleclick on the DRVR resource. This opens a window with the names of the DA's in the file. Select the one you want to rename, then use the *Get Info* command from the File menu and change the name in the dialog box that opens. (To put a DA at the top of the list, add a space before its name.)

Close the windows and save your changes when ResEdit asks you. You won't have to reboot—the DAs will move to their new positions on the ✿ menu immediately.

✿ *altering a menu*

It's easy to change the names of, and the ⌘-key equivalents for, menu commands—*if* the application stores that information as a standard MENU resource (Word doesn't, but the Finder does—as do most programs). The example below shows how to add a ⌘-key keyboard equivalent for the *Show Clipboard* command in the Finder's Edit menu.

Enter ResEdit and open the Finder. Scroll through its list of resources until you see MENU, and doubleclick on it. The window that opens lists the menus that can be displayed in the Finder. (There will be more listed here than are actually displayed, because there are different versions of menus depending on which system you're using. Just because a resource is available doesn't mean it's always used.)

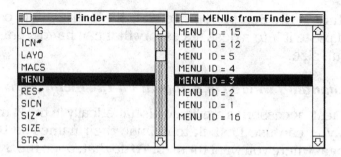

Doubleclick on MENU ID = 3 and the Edit menu's window will open. (You'll have to experiment to see which ID numbers correspond with which other menus.) Scroll down through the list of menu items to the *Show Clipboard* command listed. In the box labeled *key equiv*, type a K (cap or lowercase, it doesn't matter—it still shows as a cap in the menu).

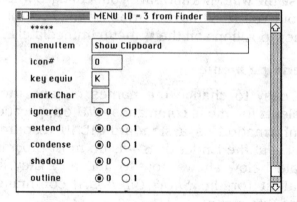

That's it. Click your way out of ResEdit, closing all the windows and saving the changes before you quit. When you get back to the Desktop, the Edit menu will be revised.

⚫ *changing an icon*

The Trash can is an icon resource in the Finder. To change how it looks, enter ResEdit, open the Finder file and doubleclick on the ICN# resource. This opens a window with icons in it, including the empty and full trash cans.

Doubleclick on the icon itself. A window will open containing two enlarged views of the Trash. Let's begin by considering the main icon, on the left. You can use the pointer to change white dots to black, and vice versa (by clicking on, or dragging over, them). Here's how you might draw a Trash can Oscar the Grouch would be proud of:

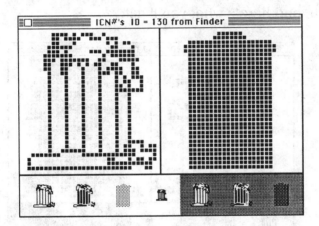

Across the bottom, you'll see three versions of the icon: the normal one, what it looks like when it's selected, and what it looks like when it's been opened. They change as you change the main icon.

The large icon on the right is the *mask;* it defines how an icon looks against a background (in most cases, the Desktop's gray pattern). It also has three smaller versions across the bottom.

The main icon and the mask are overlaid. Whenever there are black dots in both layers, the icon stays black against a background. Wherever there are white dots in both layers, the icon is transparent against the background. (That's why you can see the gray desktop around the Trash icon.) Where the icon is white and the mask is black, the icon stays white against the background (like the white areas of the can). The fourth combination is the tricky one: when the icon is black and the mask is white, the icon stays black against the background until it's selected—then those dots remain black instead of inverting to white (as would normally happen when the icon's selected).

The typical mask is an outline of the icon completely filled with black. This silhouette-type mask keeps the icon looking correct against any background and inverts all its details when it's selected. Luckily, there's a quick way to make the silhouette: select *Data—>Mask* from the ICN# menu, and here's what you'll get:

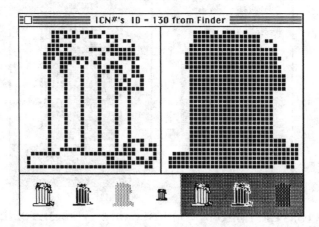

Once you've created the mask, close all the nested windows and save your changes on the way out.

￼ *moving a sound*

Sounds are resources too. When you open the Control Panel and use the Sound device to set the System sound, you get a list of available sounds: Beep, Monkey, Clink-Klank and Boing. ResEdit lets you add other sounds to this list—even move them from other programs.

I like the dignified little beep—it's more like a *blip*, really—in More. So I extracted it and installed it in my System file. To do that, you enter ResEdit and open More (or whatever program has a sound you like). Doubleclick on the resource called *snd*. In More, there's only one sound there—it's named *Ouch* and is referred to by a number as well. Select it and choose *Copy* from the Edit menu.

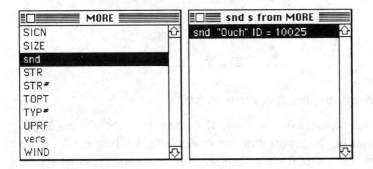

Now open the System in ResEdit. Select the snd resource (you don't have to open it) and choose *Paste*. If you open it after the paste (and I bet you will), it will look like this:

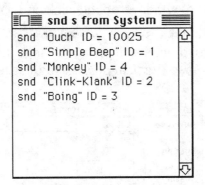

(Of course, you can open it first, and then paste, if you prefer to see what's happening while it's happening.) Then quit ResEdit, saving your changes as you leave, and the Control Panel will look like the illustration at the top of the next page:

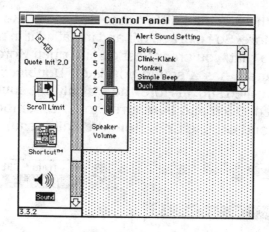

🍎 *changing the icon grids*

The default grid on the Desktop for icons is 64 x 64 pixels. But you can use ResEdit to put icons closer together, and/or to stagger them so their names don't run into each other. To do that:

- Enter ResEdit and open the Finder.

- Scroll to the *LAYO* resource and doubleclick on it.

- In the LAYO window, doubleclick on *LAYO=128*.

- Scroll through this window until you find the series of text boxes for icon spacing and change the numbers as shown below. *(Vertical phase* is the stagger amount.)

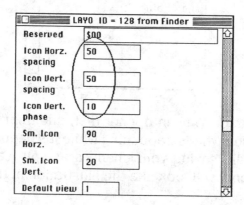

- Close all the windows you've opened and quit ResEdit, clicking *Yes* when you're asked if you want to save your changes.

To make the change immediately apparent, use the *Clean Up* command. Here are before and after views:

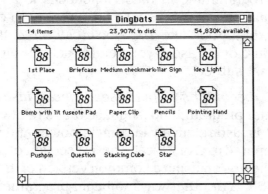

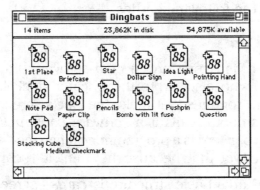

You can change the grid for *small* icons in the same way. Assign 70 for Small Icon Vertical Spacing and 17 for Small Icon Horizontal Spacing (the two boxes you see at the bottom of the ResEdit illustration above).

[Please note: The results produced by this method will never conserve space—or please the eye—the way icons hand-Naimanized by a skilled practitioner can. No mere machine can hope to master a craft that has been refined for centuries and into which living human beings have poured their hearts and souls, their hopes and dreams.—AN]

important
warning

Mac programming languages

◆ *C and BASIC (AN)*

*esp. for
power users*

Most Mac applications are written C or Pascal (most often C). Programming in these languages is an advanced activity that it makes no sense for us to try to cover, ever cursorily, in a book like *The Macintosh Bible*. If you're interested in C or in Pascal, you need to get a book (or books) just on that subject.

BASIC *(beginner's all-purpose symbolic instruction set)* is a popular programming language that's relatively easy to learn but is also relatively lacking in power and sophistication, compared to C or Pascal. The last section of this chapter gives some tips on using a common version of it, Microsoft's QuickBASIC. For other ways to begin programming on the Mac, see the following entries.

◆ *HyperCard*

Apple calls HyperCard *system software.* Its author, Bill Atkinson (who also wrote the original MacPaint, and the QuickDraw routines that make the Mac's screen display so fast and smooth) calls it a *software construction set.* Put simply, HyperCard is a programming language—but Apple is afraid to tell you that, because they think it'll scare you away.

HyperCard's basic structure is *cards*—screens of information—organized into *stacks.* You can flip through a stack in order, or jump directly to the card or stack you need—as long as the person who created the stack remembered to *link* related pieces of information. Cards can have pictures, text and buttons on them.

This makes HyperCard sound like a database, and in fact, when it first came out, there were a lot of complaints from database publishers who were afraid it was going to destroy their business. Actually, HyperCard is pretty poor as a database—it's incredibly slow both for entering information and for sifting through it to find something specific.

What HyperCard is great at is making Mac programming accessible to ordinary people. On all but its highest level (there are five) it's very simple to use. But HyperCard has severe limitations as a programming environment, so all stacks that are at all sophisticated use something called XCMDs (pronounced *x commands,* the name is short for *external commands).*

An XCMD is a compiled routine, written in another programming language than HyperCard, that does something that HyperCard can't do. Once you embed the XCMD in a HyperCard stack, HyperCard can run it. XCMDs are used to create things like menus, dialog boxes and multiple windows.

It's no surprise (at least to me) that commercial HyperCard stacks haven't really made it. For one thing, you can't compile a HyperCard stack into a stand-alone program. One of the early HyperCard stacks requires that *twenty* different files be available—which is messy. But the main problem is HyperCard's slowness—it takes at least a second to tab from one field to another once you're in a stack.

That's not to say that there aren't good stacks around. But the really wonderful ones use a lot of XCMDs, and usually restrict themselves to information retrieval. I love programming in HyperCard, but I never lose the feeling that its elegance is more appreciated by the programmer than by the end user of the stack.

⌘ *SuperCard*

SuperCard (written by Bill Appleton for Silicon Beach) is HyperCard and then some. You can do color, menus, multiple windows, graphics that aren't just bitmaps, cards that are any size, and simple animation. The programming environment is easier and friendlier than HyperCard's. You can import HyperCard stacks and enhance them. And you can turn your work into a stand-alone application. Quite a lot of power for $200.

I love SuperCard, but I'm also disappointed by it. It has no *Undo* command. The documentation is good as far as it goes, but it doesn't go far enough. The main problem, though, is that SuperCard is slow. For example, on a Mac Plus, many special buttons don't highlight as soon you press them—there's a noticeable, disconcerting delay.

SuperCard 1.5 is still a product to keep an eye on. With HyperCard 2.0 out soon, SuperCard may not remain as important a product as it was. It depends on how quickly Silicon Beach gets a matching SuperCard 2.0 out the door.

🍎 *SuperCard 1.5 and HyperCard 2.0* (Steve Michel)

very good feature

Probably the first thing you'll notice in SuperCard 1.5 is the vastly improved Runtime Editor. It's been rewritten from the ground up and is much faster and more reliable than the previous version. But SuperCard still isn't a fast program; large cards—especially those with color bitmaps and a lot of buttons and fields—still take a long time to load. To offset this, SuperTalk lets you open a window invisibly while a user is reading one card, then display it, thus hiding some of SuperCard's sluggishness from the user.

very good feature

SuperCard 1.5 also includes a powerful interactive debugger (called ScriptTracer) that lets you to examine and modify global and local variables, as well as send messages to SuperCard while script execution is paused. The only problem with ScriptTracer is that it takes up a lot of room on the screen, possibly hiding the effects of what the script is doing on the card underneath the dialog box.

Hierarchical and pop-up menus are now very easy to implement, and SuperTalk lets you create or remove menu items at runtime (before version 1.5, you could only create items in SuperEdit). But you still have to create the menus themselves in SuperEdit. Version 1.5 also lets you create "list" fields, which allow the selection of a line or group of lines simply by clicking on them.

Certainly SuperCard will continue to offer a number of things that HyperCard will not. This includes more powerful dialogs (without resorting to externals), object and draw graphics, integrated color and SuperEdit (which offers editing capabilites not available in other programs). But Hyper-Card 2.0 will also offer things not supported by SuperCard.

This will create something of a quandary for developers. Previously, the decision about which environment to support was pretty straightforward. Do you need to show color pictures, open multiple windows or create your own menus? Use SuperCard. But HyperCard 2.0 will let you do some of those things. And you used to be able to start a project in HyperCard 1.2.5, then convert it to SuperCard if you needed to do so. But it will be a while after HyperCard 2.0 comes out before SuperCard can translate stacks created by it.

things to come

⚫ *ProGraph* (Bill Hensler)

ProGraph 1.2 bills itself as an *object-oriented graphical dataflow language*. Computer techies have seen this hype from many sources over the years, none of which have been able to live up to their own press releases. But ProGraph is a different story.

esp. for power users

Every other graphical language I've ever tried was abstracted from a specific language, and only the problems that the designer could foresee could be programmed. ProGraph is the first that let me test out general-purpose algorithms right from a text-based language book. Anything you can do in BASIC, you can do in ProGraph.

But why would I use it instead of, say, Pascal? ProGraph's graphical nature doesn't in itself make it superior to a text-based language (VIP proved that). It's really no easier to use than Pascal and the initial learning curve is about the same. But combining graphics with object-oriented programming lets ProGraph reach areas untouched by most languages. Its designers went even farther and based the language on dataflow. As a result, ProGraph should be able to handle any problem C or Pascal can, and a few that would be too complex to even consider in a text-based language.

ProGraph's debugging environment goes beyond the normal debugging you find in other languages. It has standard *step, stop,* and *go* with breakpoints, and ways to look

very good feature

at variables to confirm that your code is working—all in a true graphical presentation. But it also uses a truly interactive programming environment. If it comes across a method that hasn't been programmed, it asks if you would like to create it, presenting you with the shell of the method, ready to have the code drawn in.

If an error is found, the program is stopped and the editor is switched on. You can interrogate anything in the system while trying to determine the cause of the error. Once you've corrected the error, the really cool part kicks in—ProGraph doesn't stop running the program when the code changes are made, it just performs a "rollback" to a part of the program at a point when the changes would have had no effect, then continues on from there. The entire edit-compile-run-debug cycle is gone. It's more like a run-debug combination.

very good feature

ProGraph's ease of use encourages experimentation in your code and lets you take a layering approach to your programming, starting with the simplest ideas and slowly, interactively, sculpting those ideas into solutions.

ProGraph isn't perfect. Its environment is tied a little too much to color, and it's only an interpreter at this point (no compiler). Its manuals are excellent, but they refuse to lie flat without the aid of a six-pack of Coke (there should be a law against this). But, in general, ProGraph is great.

Tips for HyperCard users

This section is for people who use HyperCard at anything but the highest, "scripting" level. (For that, see the next section.) All these tips work in HyperCard 1.2 and may or may not work in other versions.

✶ button, button, who's got the button?

esp. for beginners

If you can't tell where all the buttons are on a card and you think maybe you're missing something, press ⌐Option⌐ ⌐⌘⌐. All the buttons will be framed in gray rectangles for as long as you hold down the keys.

♦ *showing the menu bar*

If you're in a stack that has no menu bar and you want it, press ⌘ Spacebar. That toggles the menu bar on and off.

♦ *no visual effects on color displays*

The *visual effect* command works only on black-and-white displays. They'll be ignored if the stack is running on a color or gray-scale monitor. *(But HyperCard 2.0 does allow visual effects on color monitors, and SuperCard always has.—Eric Alderman)*

♦ *a quick Open command*

You can use the message box as an alternative to the File menu when you want to open a stack. (You get the message box by choosing it from the Go menu or pressing ⌘ M.) Type *go stackname* and press Return. If you've used the stack before, HyperCard will know where it is and open it without your having to go through a series of folders to find it in the standard Open dialog box.

♦ *selecting the Browser, Button and Field tools*

You don't have to use the Tools menu to select the main tool you're working with. ⌘ Tab chooses the Browser, ⌘ Tab Tab chooses the Button tool and ⌘ Tab Tab Tab chooses the Field tool.

shortcut

♦ *copying locked text*

If there's text in a field that you can't copy—the pointer remains the Browser hand instead of changing to the I-beam—that means the field is locked. You can unlock it to get at the text without having to know anything about stack-building. Just follow these simple steps:

- Choose the Field tool from the Tools menu. (If the menu bar isn't showing, or if the Tools menu isn't displayed, see the entries called *showing the menu bar* and *changing the user level.)*

- Doubleclick on the field you want to unlock. In the dialog box that opens, uncheck the Locked Field button. Click the OK button to put the dialog box away.

- Select the Browser tool again from the Tools menu.

Now you can select the text in the field to copy it.

important warning

Most fields are locked to prevent you from accidentally deleting or otherwise editing the text in them. So, to be safe, open the field after you've retrieved the text and lock it again.

◢ *improving HyperCard's dialer tones* (Michael Bradley)

HyperCard's Address Directory stack (and stacks like it) can output touch-tone dialing sounds through the Mac's speaker. This means you can hold your phone's handset up to the speaker and have HyperCard dial for you. (On a Mac Plus, hold the handset at the lower left side of the computer; on the SE, at the lower front; and on Mac II's, at the lower right front.)

For some phones, however, the Mac's speaker isn't good enough. There are two ways around this problem. One is to use an external speaker. Get the kind that's sold for Walkman-type personal stereos; it will plug right into the Mac's sound port. But a more effective and convenient solution is to buy HyperDialer—a $35 gizmo that connects the Mac to your phone.

◢ *changing the user level*

HyperCard allows five user levels for any stack. Each level provides new privileges for the user and includes everything allowed in the lower levels. (So, for example, the Painting level also lets you type in text fields.) The levels are:

1. *Browsing*—the read-only level.

2. *Typing*—allows you to type in text fields. When you're in level 1 or 2, you'll see only the File, Edit and Go menus in the menu bar.

3. *Painting*—lets you use the Paint tools. The Tools menu is added to the menu bar.

4. *Authoring*—allows use of the Button and Field tools. For this and level 5, the Objects menu is added to the menu bar.

5. *Scripting*—lets you edit scripts.

If you have a stack that you'd like to alter but can't get at, say, the Paint tools, here's the quickest way to change the user level:

- Press ⌘ M. This opens the *message box*, a small window with a line for you to type on.

---

set userlevel to 3

- Type *set userlevel to 3* (or whatever level you want) and press Return.
- Press ⌘ M again to put the message box away.

If a stack creator *really* didn't want the stack altered, the message might be ignored. But you'll find that you can reset the user level on most stacks. (Do yourself a favor— save a copy of the original stack before you start messing around with it.)

important warning

⚫ *keyboard card deletion*

The *Delete Card* command has a keyboard equivalent even though there are none showing in the menu. In fact, it has *two* keyboard equivalents: ⌘ Delete and ⌘ Clear.

shortcut

⚫ *copying text along with a field*

Using the Field tool to select a field, then copying and pasting it, pastes down the field itself (with all its attributes) but not the text that's in it. To copy the text along with the field, use the *Copy* command as usual, but hold Shift while you paste. (This works for *card* fields, but not *background* fields.)

⚫ *where've you been lately?*

The *Recent* command (on the Go menu) shows you a card with miniatures of the last 42 cards you've used; click on one and you go directly to it, no matter what stack it's

very hot tip

in. But the miniatures don't trace a history of where you've been in the order you were there, since once a card's picture is in the Recent card, it isn't repositioned when you go back to it.

To retrace your steps, use the *Back* command (in the Go menu). It moves you back through the cards you've used, in reverse order, starting with the current one. (You can go back through 100 cards.) The Go menu shows ⌘ ~ as the keyboard equivalent for *Back*, but you can also use ⌘ Esc.

❡ *quitting an application* (Michael Bradley)

When you open an application from within HyperCard, quitting the application takes you back to the card you were at. To quit to the Finder, press Option when you choose *Quit* and hold it down until the Finder's menu bar is displayed. (You have to choose *Quit* from the menu; pressing Option ⌘ Q won't work.)

❡ *importing Paint documents*

The *Import Paint* command imports paint (bit-mapped) documents into HyperCard, pasting them onto the current card. But since a card is so much smaller than a standard paint document, only part of it gets pasted on the card (and you can't scroll to see the rest). So, before you import a paint picture, use a paint program to make sure that the area you want is in the upper left corner of the document (that's the part that gets pasted on the card).

❡ *moving shapes while drawing them*

When you're using the shape tools for ovals, rectangles, rounded rectangles or polygons, you can drag the shape around on the screen before you've finished drawing it. To reposition the shape, press ⌘ *without* releasing the mouse button. Release the ⌘ key to continue drawing the shape after you've repositioned it, or release both the key and the mouse button if the shape is finished. (This feature was introduced in version 1.2.2.)

✻ *turning a rectangle selection into a lassoed one*

If you select a graphic with the selection rectangle and want to get rid of extraneous white space within the selection, press ⓢ while the selection is still active—the rectangle tightens into a lasso around the graphic.

very
hot
tip

This is a Power Key option, so it only works if *Power Key* in the Options menu is checked. (The Options menu only appears when you have a paint tool selected.)

✻ *Paste place*

When you cut or copy any element of a card—a button or field, or a graphic—and then use the *Paste* command, the pasted element is not placed in the center of the screen, as happens with most Mac graphic applications. Instead, it appears exactly in the position it was in when you cut or copied it.

very
hot
tip

So if there's a button or graphic you want to appear on several cards, copy it from one card, flip to the new card and paste. You won't have to drag anything around. This is especially useful to know if you're going to do some flip-card animation, since you can be sure that the main graphic will always be in the same spot on each card.

✻ *pasting a miniature*

To get a miniature view, like the ones in the Recent card, of any card, choose *Copy Card* or *Cut Card* and then paste the miniature down with ⬚Shift ⬚⌘ ⬚V.

✻ *HyperDA* (AN)

This useful desk accessory (from Symmetry) is a stripped-down version of HyperCard that lets you access stacks without having to either exit the application you're in or buy enough memory to run HyperCard and other applications under MultiFinder. It's designed for people who aren't techie but who still want to be able to refer to stacks. (Another advantage of HyperDA—unlike HyperCard, it can copy text even when a field is locked.)

very good
feature

❖ *The HyperMedia Group* (AN)

If you'd rather have someone else create stacks (Hyper-Card demos, etc.) for you, I recommend The HyperMedia Group. In the spirit of full disclosure, I should say that one of its principals, Eric Alderman (author of many juicy tips in this chapter), is a friend of mine, but I've seen the work they've done for clients like Apple, Claris and Novell and have been impressed by it. (If Apple likes their stuff, chances are you will too.) Contact info is in Appendix B.

❖ *The Automation Group*

The Automation Group, also listed in Appendix B, does great stack development too. They focus on CD-ROM appli-cations.

Tips for HyperCard programmers

These tips work in HyperCard 1.2.2 and may or may not work in other versions.

❖ *101 Scripts and Buttons for HyperCard*

very good feature

I didn't count the items in this package, but it also in-cludes fields, graphics, utilities, icons, cursors, XCMDs and XFCNs, as well as scripts and buttons. It's a terrific pack-age—a well-put-together stack of useful and *imaginative* utilities and routines. It's easy to navigate your way around the various categories, and you can ask for more informa-tion or a demonstration of any feature.

Most of the utilities and routines included are aimed at extending the HyperCard interface, by giving you things like animated buttons and special pointers. There are also time-saving utilities for the stack creator, like one that cre-ates a neatly aligned array of buttons.

❖ *CLR HyperArrays*

The folks at Clear Lake Research wrote such great exter-nal routines for Macintosh BASIC that Microsoft licensed them (the routines, that is, not the people) and included them in the language. CLR has now turned some of its talent towards HyperCard, and HyperArrays is the first result.

HyperArrays 2.0 includes 15 XCMDs and 33 XFCNs. Although it gives you true arrayed variables, that's only the beginning. Most of the routines handle *matrix* mathematical operations (they work on rows, columns or the whole matrix, and include straightforward adding and subtracting as well as finding minimum and maximum elements in any area). There are fancier mathematical functions too, like log, sine, cosine, square root and exponentiation. You can also do things like merge arrays.

very good feature

HyperArrays 2.0 also includes some routines that can be used outside the array structure, like sorting, generating random numbers (faster than HyperTalk can) and emptying a field of blank lines.

⚫ some scripting basics

HyperTalk works with *lines* of information. If the text of your command is too long to fit in the script window, press `Option` `Return` to move down to the next line. This inserts the line-continuation marker (¬) at the end of the first line and tells HyperTalk that it's not at the end of the command line.

esp. for beginners

When you want to insert comments into a script to remind yourself (or tell another user) what the routine is supposed to do, type a double hyphen (--) at the beginning of the comment. You can put it at the beginning of a line, or after a command in the middle of a line—HyperTalk ignores everything on the line after it.

⚫ shortcuts to scripts

The basic way to get to the script for a button or field is to doubleclick on the button or field (while the Button or Field tool is selected), then click the *Script* button in the dialog box that appears. A faster way is to hold `Shift` while you doubleclick on the button or field—the first dialog box is bypassed and you go directly to the Script editor.

shortcut

The basic way to get to the script for a card, background or stack is to choose the *Card Info*, *Bkgnd Info* or *Stack Info* command from the Objects menu and then click in the *Script* button in the dialog box that opens. A faster way is to hold Shift while selecting the *Info* command. And even faster way than that is to use one of these keyboard commands:

Option ⌘ C	script for the card
Option ⌘ B	script for the background
Option ⌘ S	script for the stack

⬥ new synonyms

Version 1.2 introduced some new synonyms and abbreviations for HyperTalk words. The left column shows the new synonym, the right column the word it stands for (and, in parentheses, any previous, still-usable abbreviations):

new synonym	for
bg	background (bkgnd)
bgs	backgrounds (bkgnds)
btns	buttons
cd	card
cds	cards
fld	field
flds	fields
grey	gray
pict	picture
sec	second
secs	seconds
tick	ticks

● *the Closest and Farthest commands*

Using the *Closer* (🌐+) and *Farther* (🌐-) commands moves a button or field one layer at a time—that is, only past a single other element. If you want to move the selected button or field all the way to the top or bottom of the pile, hold Shift while you choose *Closer* or *Farther* from the menu, or use Shift 🌐+ or Shift 🌐- .

shortcut

● *identifying buttons and fields*

There are three ways to identify a button or field: by its *number*, by its *ID* and by its *name*.

Fields and buttons are assigned numbers automatically. But the number merely notes where the object is in the objects layer on the card and changes when you move the object with the *Closer* or *Farther* command. Buttons number 1 and 2, for example, have their numbers switched if you move the first button closer. So, if you identify a button or field in a script according to its number, you'll regret it.

Instead, you can refer to an object by its ID; although this is also an automatically assigned number, it's safe to use in scripts, because it never changes. But since it's hard to remember what button ID 7 does versus button ID 9, name all your buttons and fields and use those names in your scripts.

● *changing pointers*

You don't have to stick to just four basic pointers, nor do you have to refer to them by number ID. There are eight pointer options available (although *none* isn't a pointer at all—it's the option to hide the pointer):

```
set cursor to "hand"
set cursor to "iBeam"
set cursor to "watch"
set cursor to "cross"
set cursor to "plus"
set cursor to "arrow"
set cursor to "none"
set cursor to "busy"
```

The last option, *busy,* changes the pointer to a beachball. Each time you call it, the beachball appears in a new position, which makes the ball look like it's spinning on the screen.

[Note that since you're programming *the Mac, you use the computerese term* cursor *rather than the Mac-friendly term* pointer.—AN]

♠ *visual effects within a card*

**very
hot
tip**

The *visual effects* command, normally used when moving from one card to another, can also be used within a card, to slowly reveal buttons and/or fields.

Start with the buttons or fields hidden, lock the screen and then show the button or fields (they won't actually be displayed because the screen is locked). Finally, unlock the screen with a visual effect in the *unlock* command. The script will look something like this:

```
hide card button 1
lock screen
show card button 1
unlock screen with dissolve very slow
```

Using this to slowly reveal a single button on an already-displayed card is a good attention-getter. And you can, of course, make buttons or fields disappear, by hiding them while the screen is locked and then unlocking the screen with a visual effect.

♠ *the 64-element limit*

HyperCard has a limit of 64 elements when it's doing calculations. A function is itself an element, as are all its arguments. So if you use *max (the List),* then *the List* can only contain 63 items.

♠ *attaching fonts & DAs* (Michael Bradley)

You can attach fonts and desk accessories to HyperCard stacks with the Font/DA Mover in just the same way that you can attach them to applications. Just hold down the

[Option] key when you click the *Open* button in the Font/DA Mover's window, then select the stack you want to add them to.

[Be aware that Apple doesn't recommend doing this and has stated that it may not work with future releases of the system software. The safest solution is to distribute a suitcase file of fonts and DAs with your stack.—Eric Alderman]

important warning

🍎 *simulating dimmed buttons* (Eric Alderman/SZA)

One Macintosh interface feature that isn't provided in HyperCard is the ability to disable—or dim—buttons. Here's how to achieve the same basic effect:

very hot tip

Make a gray image of the button in question. If you have a screen-capture utility, you can take a picture of the real button and paste it on an unused card to work with. Or, if you have a compact Mac, you can dump the entire screen to the disk and then get the button part of it by opening the document in a paint program. If you're working in Hyper-Card, you'll have to pour gray paint into each letter and the button frame separately. But in SuperPaint, you can use the Paint on Black mode with the Fill command to turn the button gray.

[**Button**]   [Button]

Once you have the gray version of the button, put it on the card underneath the real button. When you want the button to be disabled, hide it and the button picture will show; when you want to activate the button, just show it again.

🍎 *simulating list boxes* (Eric Alderman)

The key to simulating a list box in HyperCard is setting the lockText of a field to *true,* so the field will read the mouse click. Once clicked, the script of the field will set the lockText of the field to *false* and will use the mouse location to decide which line to select.

very hot tip

By checking for the mouseClick in the mouseUp handler, you can sense a doubleclick on the field. (A more dependable way to sense a doubleclick would be to keep track of the elapsed ticks since the original click and then vary that number based on the desired delay for the second click. But checking for the mouseClick usually works just fine, and it's a lot easier.)

In the field script, type the following:

```
on mouseUp
    -- allow the handler to edit the text
    set the lockText of me to false
    -- place insertion point at the same position
    click at the clickLoc
    -- use "the selectedLine" to find line number
    get the selectedLine
    -- select the entire line (all except RETURN)
    select it
    -- get a chunk expression of the selection
    get the selectedChunk
    -- add 1 to the end character (to include RETURN)
    add 1 to word 4 of it
    -- select the line with RETURN
    select it
    -- enable clicking again
    set the lockText of me to true
end mouseUp
```

Be sure you size the field so that it's the correct height for the size of text you plan to use. You can determine the height of a field by checking the *height* property of the field.

After you've selected a line, you can use the command *get the selection* or the functions *the selectedLine, the selectedChunk* or *the selectedText*. (SuperCard 1.5 adds a fanatastic feature for creating list boxes of this type. A new field style allows you to include snappy, professional list boxes in your application.)

very good feature

✎ *selected text and autohilite buttons* (Eric Alderman)

Clicking on a button which is set to autohilite causes the program to deselect any text which happens to be selected. This means that the script of the button can't do a *get the selection* to determine what text has been selected, and that means you have to use buttons that don't autohilite (which is really too bad—I prefer buttons that autohilite).

One alternative is to place the contents of the selection into a global variable as soon as it's selected (in the script of the field). Then it wouldn't matter if the text is deselected when a button is pressed, since the button's script could simply access the value of the global variable.

There's another possible solution: Instead of using the *Auto hilite* check box in the Button Info dialog box, you can simulate the autohiliting in the script after the selection has been grabbed. Here's a handler you can place in a button (with autohilite set to *off*) that puts the selection into a variable (which I call—quite cleverly—*aVariable):*

```
on mouseUp
   put the selection into aVariable
   set the hilite of me to true
   wait 5 ticks
   set the hilite of me to false
   -- continue with other steps for button
end mouseUp
```

[Note that the hilite function deselects the text the same way the autohilite function does. If you want the selection to remain selected—the way a standard Mac program would handle it—you have to include a routine in the script that reselects the selection.—SZA]

**important
warning**

✎ *hiding field scroll bars* (Eric Alderman)

Field scroll bars in HyperCard don't act like normal Mac scroll bars—they're always displayed, no matter how much text is in the field. This is disconcerting to most Mac users, who expect the scroll bars to disappear (become blank) when all the available information is already displayed.

**very
hot
tip**

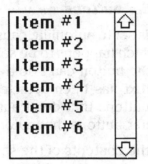 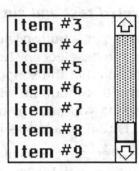

The way I've gotten around this is to create narrow, opaque fields (with lockText set to *true)* that cover the scroll bars when they should be blank; I call them *cover fields.* Once they're created, all that's left to do is to show or hide them as needed. Here's a script that does that:

```
on cover fieldtoCover
   get the rect of field fieldtoCover
   put item 4 of it - item 2 of it - 2 into fieldHeight
   put fieldHeight / the textHeight of field ¬
   fieldtoCover into numLines
   put "Cover" && fieldtoCover into coverField
   if the number of lines in field fieldtoCover ¬
   > numLines then
      hide field coverField
   else
      show field coverField
   end if
   set the scroll of field fieldtoCover to 0
end cardCover
```

Cover fields work best in list-box type fields like the ones shown above for a couple of reasons: since the text is usually inserted into the field in a controlled manner by a script, you can call the cover fields as needed; and since each line usually ends with a [Return] (rather than being word-wrapped), it's simple to determine the number of lines.

With wrapped text, there's no way to calculate the number of "lines," since a line by definition is a string of text ending in a [Return]. So it's very hard to sense when the number of lines has changed as you're typing. *On idle* doesn't work either, because it's too disruptive.

I developed a klugy but workable solution. I found that if you set the scroll of a wrapping field to some very large number, then did a *click at* to click the up arrow, the field would scroll to its bottom. Once at the bottom of the field, you can tell whether the cover field is needed by checking to see if the scroll is now greater than 0 (that is, if any text is scrolled off the top).

Hey—it works, OK? Here's the script for wrapped fields:

```
on cover fieldtoCover
   get the rect of field fieldtoCover
   set the scroll of field fieldtoCover to 10000
   click at item 3 of it - 5,item 2 of it + 5
   put "Cover" && fieldtoCover into coverField
   get the scroll of field fieldtoCover
   if it > 0 then
      hide field coverField
   else
      show field coverField
   end if
end cover
```

Both of these handlers assume that the name of the cover field (the one that's used to cover the scroll bar) is named *Cover,* followed by a space, followed by the name of the field it will affect. To use the routine, you place one of these handlers into the card, background or stack script of your stack. Then a command like *cover "card field 1"* will perform the cover routine on any given field.

⚫ *hiding dialog boxes* (Eric Alderman)

When you want to hide a dialog box you've popped up over a screen (one you've created yourself, not the Ask or Answer dialog box), it's best to set lockScreen to *true.* (If you don't, you get a much messier effect as each element of the dialog box disappears.) If there are a lot of elements to the dialog box, it might take a few seconds to be hidden, so change the pointer to the wristwatch or the beachball, with *watch* or *busy.*

⬥ *zooming fields* (Eric Alderman)

**very
hot
tip**

You can simulate the action of a zooming window with a HyperCard field. For example, you might want to have a small field on a card that can expand to a larger size and then contract back to its original size. Here's a script that will do that:

```
on mouseUp
  -- the variable oldRect tracks the field's ¬
  original size
  global oldRect
  -- check to see whether it's time to zoom
  if the rect of the target is not "3,23,509,339" then
    -- remember original size
    put the rect of the target into oldRect
    -- to produce visual effect without going anywhere
    visual effect zoom open
    go to this card
    set the rect of the target to 3,23,509,339 -- zoom
  else -- unzoom the field
    -- produce visual effect without going anywhere
    visual effect zoom close
    go to this card
    set the rect of the target to oldRect -- unzoom
  end if
end mouseUp
```

By placing this script into any locked field, you can zoom it to full size by simply clicking on it and then return it to normal size by clicking again. Of course, you could modify this to only work when, for example, the field is [Option]-clicked.

If you want to be able to zoom a field which isn't locked, use the same script but hold down [⌘] when you click on the field.

The rectangle used in the script is about full-size in the HyperCard window, but you can easily modify it to make the field expand to any size and position you wanted.

You'll have to watch out for other cards or fields that appear in front of the zoomed field. To deal with that, either use the *Bring Closer* menu command to bring the zoomed field closer to the front, or hide some of the buttons and fields each time you zoom the field.

[Remember that visual effects don't work on color or gray-scale monitors unless they're set to black-and-white.—SZA]

important warning

✎ *changing the pointer while over a button* (Eric Alderman)

very hot tip

You may want the pointer to change its shape when it is moved over a button on the screen, as a way of letting the user know when to press the mouse button. For example, you might want to turn it into a picture of a mouse or of a finger pointing.

You can do this by placing a *mouseWithin* handler in the card, background or stack script of your stack which changes the pointer as long as it's within the rectangle of a button. Here's the handler:

```
on mouseWithin
   if "button" is not in the target then exit ¬
   mouseWithin
   set cursor to "watch"  -- or whatever you want
   repeat while the mouseLoc is within ¬
   the rect of the target
     if the mouseClick then
       click at the loc of the target
       exit mouseWithin
     end if
   end repeat
end mouseWithin
```

QuickBASIC tips

♦ activating the Command window

⌘ . stops programs that you're running—you'll find it in the default File menu for any program that you write. But in the QuickBASIC environment itself, ⌘ . activates the Command window.

♦ LaserPrinter listings

esp. for power users

QuickBASIC prints its program listings in Geneva—even if you're using a LaserWriter. To force QuickBASIC to use Helvetica instead, execute this command from the Command window before choosing *Print* from the File menu:

```
POKEW &h984,21
```

If you want to change the size of the print in the listing, use

```
POKE &h987,n
```

where *n* is the point size you want.

Poking these values also affects the font in the List window on the screen. Poking a new size affects menus, dialog boxes and other text in the program. The changes are limited to QuickBASIC when you're working in MultiFinder and they only stay in effect until you quit the program—or poke new values.

If you want to return to 12-point Geneva in the List window after you've printed your listing, use

```
POKEW &h984,1:POKE &h987,12
```

in the Command window.

♦ dropping CALL

esp. for power users

The CALL statement isn't necessary for ROM routines (except for one, noted below). And when you drop CALL, you also get to drop a set of parentheses. So instead of typing CALL PENSIZE (3,3), you can use PENSIZE 3,3.

When you drop the CALL from more involved ROM routines, you still drop a set of parentheses—so you get FRAMERECT VARPTR (pat%(1)) instead of CALL FRAMERECT (VARPTR (pat%(1))).

The only time you can't drop CALL is for CALL LINE—without the CALL, QuickBASIC thinks you're using the standard LINE statement, which needs a different set of arguments than does the ROM routine LINE.

♦ macro keyboard shortcuts

QuickBASIC doesn't have the keyboard shortcuts that earlier versions of BASIC had—the obscure combinations of [Option] plus a character to type in a command word. But you can make your own shortcuts with a macro program—and while you're at it, you can make them less obscure.

shortcut

Just record as a macro the typing of any keyword you use often. In fact, you can record more than just the keyword—store phrases like WINDOW 1,,( )-( ) and just fill in the blanks with the numbers you need after you play the macro back.

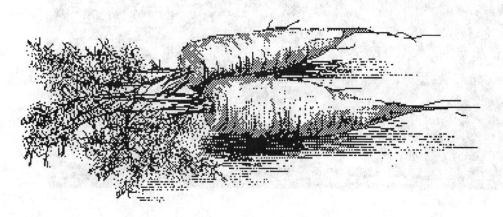

Chapter 18

Miscellaneous applications

Financial and accounting programs

⚫ *Quicken*

Quicken ($70) is a terrific checkbook program for home or a small business. It lets me print checks on a LaserWriter or ImageWriter (check forms are available from the publisher), or I can use my own checkbook and enter the amounts into the program as transactions. Best of all, Quicken doesn't force me to understand or use double-entry bookkeeping. I can mark checks as "outgo" for different categories (child care, business, utilities, etc.) but I don't have to keep track of where my income comes in from (I don't care).

**very good
feature**

Quicken makes checkwriting and bookkeeping easy in a number of ways. One of the best is the Recurring Transaction List, where you can store information about checks you write frequently; all you have to do is doubleclick on that transaction in the list and all the information is entered on the check. Recurring Transactions don't have to have an amount filled in ahead of time, so you can use it for bills like the telephone and electric, as well as for your rent or mortgage, where the amount is always the same.

Unfortunately, the Quicken interface needs quite a bit of work. You have no choice about the font—on the screen or in printouts. The Recurring Transaction List only displays a limited number of characters—so I can't tell the difference between *Manufacturer's Hanover MasterCard* and *Manufacturer's Hanover Visa* because all I see in the list is *Manufacturer's Han* (although the full name gets entered on the check).

This list and the Category List (which shows your budget categories, so you can note what each check is going for) are regular windows, not floating windows (palettes). That means you have to click on the Transaction window to activate it, *then* doubleclick on the transaction you want (the extra click wouldn't be necessary if the windows were palettes). And these windows always open to a default position, instead of where you left them (it's annoying to have to arrange your screen every time you open the program).

But even if the interface needs polishing, Quicken has all the features I need. This is the first friendly Mac checkbook I've found (and at a user-friendly price).

⬤ *Managing Your Money* (Steve Schwartz)

very good feature

Although it only came to the Mac in 1988, Managing Your Money has been around on other machines since 1984. It's a mature, well-conceived program that can handle all your home financial activities. *[Andrew Tobias, author of the program and of books like* The Only Investment Guide You'll Ever Need *is one of the clearest and most entertaining writers around. He made sure the program was nonthreatening, easy-to-use and fun.—AN]*

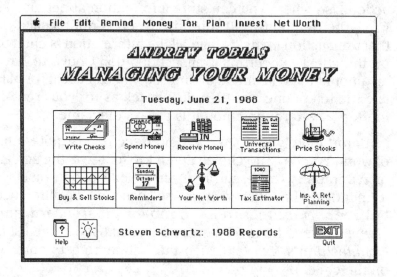

The opening screen/main menu (above) looks like HyperCard. To move to any part of the program, you can click an icon, select a command from a menu or—in many cases—doubleclick an item on one of the many data entry screens. I initially found this duplication confusing, but the thing to remember is that whatever makes sense usually works. You can get there from here—usually by two or three different routes.

After setting up asset-and-liability accounts and customizing the budget categories, you can begin to enter transactions. Each transaction has two components. In the case of money you spent, for example, the components are where it came from (checking, savings or cash, say) and what it was spent on (groceries, gasoline or whatever).

As you record the bills you've paid and the money received, and update the current value of your investments and possessions, the information is automatically entered into a net-worth statement. A report of your overall financial status (with accompanying graphs) is only a keystroke away. Simply marking items as tax-related kicks them into an impressive tax-estimator component, which duplicates major IRS forms and provides on-screen worksheets for the hard parts.

What distinguishes Managing Your Money from its competition is that it's all-inclusive. In addition to the normal check-writing and budgeting functions, it lets you handle IRAs and other investments; do tax, insurance, retirement and college-tuition planning; and perform financial calculations for things like mortgage refinancing, loans and annuities, and bond yields.

very good feature

There's also a feature that lets you set reminders for appointments and projects, and specify a frequency for each (one time only, weekly, etc.). I just wish the program would automatically let me know that something is pending, instead of expecting me to remember to check my reminders.

The only serious problem I have with Managing Your Money is the price. Is any home financial package worth $220? I suppose it depends on how much money you're managing. If the price doesn't bother you and you've made a commitment to keep better track of your money, Managing Your Money will do a fine job of it.

✦ *In-House Accountant* (Steve Schwartz)

In-House Accountant ($200) is a double-entry accounting system that offers invoicing, budgeting, bank reconciliation, check and statement printing and more useful reports than you can shake a stick at. (Double-entry accounting requires that each credit transaction be balanced by an equal debit and vice versa. For example, if you make a sale and deposit the money, you'd debit your bank account and credit one or more income accounts—product sales, say—by the same amount.)

Some of the more useful features include:

- no need to "post" transactions

- provision for recurring transactions

- on-screen preview of reports and "batch" printing

- invoicing, statements and aging reports

- bar and pie charts that compare this year's, last year's and budgeted amounts for any account or group of accounts

- a financial calculator with formulas for present and future value, loan payments, interest and principle, and three kinds of depreciation

Learning to use the program is facilitated by context-sensitive help, a guided tour of the program with sample data, a question-and-answer section in the manual and an introduction to accounting for novices. If you're new to double-entry accounting, you should supplement this material with other reading.

Since it uses standard menus and a normal Macintosh interface, you'll spend most of your time learning how double-entry accounting works and setting up a chart of accounts. The issue isn't whether you're a Macintosh novice or expert but whether you're an accounting novice.

Because In-House Accountant is designed for accountants and nonaccountants alike, the program's greatest weakness is its lack of flexibility. Reports—although plentiful—can't be customized, invoice and check printing only work on specific forms and data can't be imported from other accounting programs. Still, it is easy to use and should suffice for many small businesses.

SuperMOM (AN)

National Tele-Press's SuperMOM (for *mail order manager)* is an order-entry program that's easy-to-learn, even for novice users. It manages everything from accounts receivable and payable to inventory and sales tax.

We used an earlier version of the program (called simply MOM) at Goldstein & Blair for over a year and National Tele-Press's support was a delight. There was always a technically knowledgeable person available to return calls, answer user questions and patiently walk people through problems.

MOM let you edit or reverse any transaction you make, and you never had to key information in twice—the relevant fields are interconnected and the information is automatically entered in all of them. The problem with MOM was its rigidity. Making changes in how it did things required customization by a programmer.

National TelePress no longer provides custom modification. Instead, they've built in a certain amount of customizability to SuperMOM. Beyond that, they claim to incorporate into updated versions of the program 75% of the changes customers request.

If you don't want to take the time and trouble to customize a database like FileMaker for your own use, and you want all the connections between files thought through and set up for you ahead of time, MOM is definitely worth considering.

business accounting packages (AN)

I'm told there's a saying in business accounting circles that no one is ever happy with their accounting package. Although I didn't appreciate hearing this from the people who had just customized and installed ours, as a response to the blizzard of problems that ensued, it's certainly been my experience.

In the hope of finding a decent system for ourselves, we've done an enormous amount of research in this area. We finally gave up on finding a package that will process our mail orders quickly *and* give us the accounting we need.

Instead, we're setting up a customized database to process orders; data from that will be exported to a separate accounting package. This seems to be the best solution for businesses like ours; we'll let you know how it works out.

**very
hot
tip**

If you need to find something now, all I can say is, do plenty of research, and don't be surprised to find that your accounting package dictating how you run your business.

ShopKeeper-4 *(Larry Pina)*

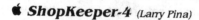

ShopKeeper-4 is an amazing "cash register" program designed by Apple retailer Mike Nudd specifically for small, independent, retail businesses. The program comes in single- and multiuser versions and can track over 8000 charge customers and 8000 inventory items.

Combined with an APG cash drawer, a hard disk and a bar code reader, it can turn your Mac into a high-tech electronic cash register, just like the ones used in supermarkets and department stores—but at a fraction of the cost. And, in true Macintosh fashion, it's much easier to get started with and to maintain.

When merchandise is received, you enter it on ShopKeeper's supplier invoice screen, which looks just like a supplier invoice. Then you print stock number/price stickers on 3.5" mailing labels and sticker the inventory. When merchandise is sold, all you have to do is copy the stock numbers off the stickers. If a sticker is missing, you can also look up prices and stock numbers right on the screen.

**very good
feature**

ShopKeeper's data searches are incredibly fast. Given the correct stock number, ShopKeeper fills in a complete item description, enters the current price, calculates tax and discounts, adjusts the inventory, rings up the sale, opens the cash drawer, calculates change and prints the invoice—on plain paper or Deluxe-brand computer forms.

The program works with any ImageWriter-compatible printer (and even some that aren't ImageWriter-compatible). At the end of the day, ShopKeeper prints detailed sales reports and also totals the register. All this from a program that only costs $300.

If it sounds too good to be true, order the $5 demo disk and see for yourself. You get the full working program with all features enabled (except that it's limited to 50 invoices) and a nicely printed ten-page minimanual.

● *MacInTax*

I'm a strange enough person to always have taken a sort of perverted pleasure in designing a spreadsheet to handle my income taxes. But then I met MacInTax. It's absolutely beautiful, and I've recommended it to everyone. My sister called towards the end of last tax season to say she and her husband had put aside a weekend, as usual, to get the taxes done, but they were finished in under three hours.

very good feature

What you see on the screen are replicas of the paper tax forms you get from the IRS, and you fill in the blanks just as you would on paper. But since there's a program behind the forms, all the calculations are done for you automatically, and all the forms you've used are included in those calculations.

So if you fill out form 2441 (Child Care Credit), for example, it already contains the figure, taken from the 1040A, on which the total allowable credit is based. Then the final figure from form 2441 is automatically entered back on the 1040.

Get Info on any line on a form and MacInTax shows you the official IRS instructions (too bad they didn't get permission to use text from one of the more popular—and understandable—tax guide books). When you think you've finished, MacInTax will show you any spot you've forgotten to fill in. When you *are* finished, you just print out the forms, which are acceptable to the IRS (special fonts are included with the package).

**very good
feature**

MacInTax is so easy to use that I never looked at its documentation until I wrote this review. And I never used its telephone support until I was audited. The documentation's fine and the telephone support was phenomenal. I called to get help rescuing a file created with the 1987 version of MacInTax—which the tech support guy didn't even have around anymore. He spent nearly two hours on the phone with me as we worked through the problem (and he didn't know I was a journalist).

[As a reviewer, my dealings with MacInTax's publisher, Softview, have been so unpleasant that I refuse to have anything further to do with them. That may not make any difference to you when using the program, but I thought you should know it.—AN]

Miscellaneous software

¢ *WillMaker* (AN)

Nolo Press, publisher of scores of extremely useful self-help law books and crusader against the ruling shysterocracy, has a terrific program that helps you write your will. (Dying without a will is really a mistake. The legal and judicial buzzards will feed off your financial corpse, greatly reducing what your friends and family get. After all, do you really want your Mac sold to pay the predatory fee of some troll at the courthouse?)

**very good
feature**

WillMaker comes with an entire book that gives you background on the various choices making a will confronts you with, but you can just let yourself be walked through the program and only consult the book when you want (or not at all). When you're done, WillMaker prints out a will (on virtually any dot-matrix or laser printer) that's a legal document in any state except Louisiana (whose laws are based on the Napoleonic Code rather than English common law) and the District of Columbia.

WillMaker costs $60, which is a small fraction of what a lawyer will charge to draw one up, or of what the probate court will extract as tribute if you're foolish enough to die intestate (without a will). Making a will is an easy thing to put off, but WillMaker makes it easy and almost fun, so don't put it off too long.

bargain

¢ For the Record (AN)

Another useful product from Nolo is *For the Record* ($50). It helps you organize all your personal, financial and legal records so you can find them when you need them. The program lets you protect your records with a password, and print them out, in whole or in part. The 270-page manual gives you legal background and practical tips on record-keeping and personal planning.

very good feature

Like making a will, organizing your personal records isn't the sort of thing you plan a weekend around. But, also like making a will, it's something you shouldn't put off too long—and that you'll feel great about getting out of the way.

¢ MacProject (Karen Faria)

MacProject II 2.0 is a powerful project-management tool. You start a project by graphically mapping it out on the Schedule Chart, using boxes to represent tasks and drawing lines between the boxes to show dependency relationships. As you draw the map, you enter project and task information such as scheduling, resources and budgets.

MacProject II then coordinates the data and displays it in seven additional charts. It coordinates schedules, lets you know when you've over-allocated resources (a very helpful feature) and keeps track of costs and income for both individual tasks and and an entire project. The Resource Timeline and Task Timeline charts are "bare-bones" Gantt charts (for more on that, and on how to improve them, see the next entry). I like the Resource Timeline because it lets you see at a glance what tasks a particular resource is being used for.

very good feature

The Task Cost Entry Table shows you fixed costs and income for each task and provides a way to review expenses for each task at a glance. The Cash Flow Table displays planned, actual and cumulative costs and income for the entire project by date ranges. The Resource Table shows all resources, their cost information, availability and where to find their schedules. The Resource Histogram is a bar chart that shows how your resources are being used on a given date. The Project Table presents all information about a project in a table form and is particularly useful if you're planning several projects at once and want to input the information quickly.

MacProject makes it easy to manage complex projects. Let's say you're working on a project and you realize that one of its tasks is fairly complicated and should actually be a project of its own. It's easy to split it off, and MacProject will automatically adjust all its calculations.

MacProject is a good computer planning tool that can save you a lot of human planning hours. (But it does cost $500.)

♦ *Great Gantt!* *(Karen Faria)*

Great Gantt! 1.2 ($200, from Varcon) is exactly what it says it is—an easy-to-use application that produces great Gantt charts. And *what,* you ask, is a Gantt chart? Well, it uses bars to chart tasks on a timeline. (At the top of the next page is a sample, made at Arthur's instigation, that illustrates the creation of the world in seven days.)

Great Gantt! lets you see at a glance the planned and actual start and end dates of each task in a project, which tasks are ahead of or behind schedule, and how near each task is to completion.

Great Gantt! also lets you customize your Gantt charts, making them as plain or fancy as you like. You can also create style sheets by saving customized formats. Great Gantt! imports files from MacProject—which is good, because MacProject only offers two Gantt chart formats, and they're both bare-bones.

Creation of the World

Name	Description	Days 1	2	3	4	5	6	7	8	Planned Start	Planned End
create heavens and earth	formless, dark									01	01
create light										01	01
name light and darkness	day and night									01	01
create firmament	heavens									02	02
gather waters together										03	03
dry lands appear										03	03
name waters and land	seas and earth									03	03
create plant-life										03	03
create great light	sun									04	04
create lesser light	moon									04	04
create lights in heavens	stars									04	04
create animals										05	05
create humans										06	06
rest										07	07

There are a couple of drawbacks to Great Gantt!. For one thing, while you can change the font and style of column headings, you can't change the point size. For another, the way Great Gantt! moves text blocks is clumsy. If you create a text block and want to move it immediately, you have to click on the pointer tool, click outside the text block and then move the text block. It seems like a small thing, but it takes some getting used to.

Great Gantt! comes with a good manual that's written by humans for humans, and good technical support. All in all, it's a good application that does what it says it does.

very good feature

♦ *SmartForms vs. Fast Forms* (Karen Faria)

Both SmartForms ($400, from Claris) and Fast Forms ($180, from Power Up) are designed to make it easy for you to create forms, and both include supporting applications for filling out and/or printing the forms you create. They both have data fields capable of making automatic calculations, and can import data from spreadsheets or databases. But SmartForms has better graphic tools and other important features that Fast Forms lacks.

very good feature

In SmartForms, you can create multipage forms and work in up to seven documents at a time. In Fast Forms, you can only create single-page forms and have only one document open at a time. While both programs have vertical and horizontal rulers, with hairlines that show the exact location of an object as you draw or resize it, only SmartForms' Spec Box gives you the object's dimensions and location numerically.

In SmartForms, you can rotate objects, pin them down and group them. I really missed these features when working with Fast Forms. And SmartForms has simplified leading and kerning capabilities, and the ability to center text vertically.

Although both programs work perfectly well, SmartForms is obviously more powerful. It's up to you (and your budget) to decide whether or not the greater power is worth an additional $220.

MacInUse

MacInUse is a terrific init that's invaluable if you do time-billing and need to know how much time you've spent working on a projects for each client. It keeps track of how long you spend in each application, and/or on any document, putting the information in a text file that's readable by any word processor, database or spreadsheet program. This also makes it a great tool for network administrators, who can see how files are being utilized, and by whom.

very good feature

Version 3.0 has a lot of small but important improvements over previous versions (which were pretty nifty already). You can tell MacInUse when to start the clock ticking—so, for instance, if you go into an application for five minutes just to read a document, that doesn't have to go into the data sheet. You can make MacInUse ignore any time spent in the Finder, and define an "idle time" that won't be included on the time clock—so if you walk away from the computer, MacInUse knows you're not there if nothing's happened for the last five minutes (or whatever interval you choose).

Another useful option prompts you for specific information or a general comment each time a new application or document is opened for time-tracking—the information you enter in the dialog box is stored along with the rest of MacInUse's data. (You can design your own dialog boxes for the prompts, including even radio buttons and checkboxes for input.)

(My dealings as a reviewer with this program's publisher, Softview, have been so unpleasant that I refuse to have anything further to do with them. That may not make any difference to you when using MacInUse, but I thought you should know it.—AN)

General Works tips

Microsoft Works is an integrated program that includes a word processor, a spreadsheet, a database and a communications module. Each of these modules is briefly reviewed in the chapter that covers that topic, and the tips for those modules are also in those chapters. What we cover here are tips that are common to all (or most) of its modules, or that relate to how the modules interact with one another.

⚫ doubleclicking for New

When Works' large Open dialog box is on the screen, doubleclicking on a module icon has the same effect as selecting it and then clicking the *New* button. The same trick works in the small dialog box that appears in response to the *New* command in the File menu.

shortcut

⚫ Works' special pointers

Sometimes, you'll notice two unusual pointer shapes— a hollow arrow and an I-beam with a circle in its center.

The first most often shows up in the spreadsheet module and the second when you're working with large word processing documents.

These special pointers mean that Works is thinking—recalculating in the spreadsheet, for example, or repaginating in the word processor. Unlike the wristwatch, these pointers don't prevent you from continuing to work, but they let you know that what's currently on the screen may be subject to change.

● *window zoom*

shortcut

Works gives you five ways to make a window fill the screen or zoom back down to the size, shape and position you set up:

- click on the zoom box
- doubleclick on the title bar
- doubleclick in the size box
- press ⌘ W
- choose the *Small Window/Full Window* command (on the Window menu)

● *window cycling*

shortcut

You can cycle through opened windows from the keyboard. ⌘ , brings the window listed at the bottom of the Windows menu to the top of the pile, and also moves its title to the top of the list. Repeated uses of ⌘ , will cycle you through all the available windows.

● *ampersand commands*

The ampersand (&) is used to give formatting commands in headers and footers. To issue the command, just type it in the text box for the header or footer. The following commands are available:

&B	make bold	*&C*	center
&D	insert date	*&I*	make italic
&L	align left	*&P*	insert page number
&R	align right	*&T*	insert time
&F	insert name of file (document)		

(You don't need to use caps for the commands—in other words, *&b* works the same as *&B*).

If you want an ampersand itself to appear in a header or footer, precede it with another ampersand: *&&*. Only one will be printed.

✎ *current date and time*

When you use *&D* or *&T* to insert the current date or time into a header or footer, *current* is the operative word. The time and date you *print* a document is what will appear in the printout, not the time or date you created or saved it.

important warning

✎ *style, size and font in headers and footers*

When creating headers and footers in the Page Setup dialog box, you can make text for bold or italic (or both) by using *&B* and *&I* (see the entry above called *ampersand commands* for more details).

These commands affect only the text that follows them in that particular text box; to change the style (and/or size) of all the text in both the header and footer, use the Style menu. (You can also change the font of both the header and footer in the Font menu.)

✎ *exporting text*

The *Export* check box in the Save As dialog box saves only the text of your document. You can then import it into another module in Works or into any Mac application that accepts text files.

✎ *importing files*

To make the *Import* check box in Works' Open dialog box available, you have to first click on one of the module icons; when the *All Works* icon is selected, the Import check box is dimmed.

esp. for beginners

Once the *Import* check box is active and you've put an X in it by clicking on it, you'll see a list of not only Works documents but of all other documents that can be imported into the module you've selected (e.g., Word files for the word processor, Excel documents for the spreadsheet, and text files for all modules).

⚜ sharing information between modules

You can share information between Works' modules in two ways: you can simply cut, copy and paste between them, or you can save a document from one module as an export (text) file and then import it to another module.

very hot tip

Sometimes the export/import method beats the simpler copy/paste. For instance, importing data into the database module that was originally created in the spreadsheet module automatically creates a database with the right number of fields (equivalent to the spreadsheet columns) and records (equivalent to the spreadsheet rows). If you simply paste the data in and don't have enough fields to hold it, rows of information will be lost.

⚜ tabs, columns and fields

As you move information from one module to another in Works, keep in mind that *tabs = columns = fields.* So several columns in the spreadsheet can be transferred to the word processor (where the columns will be separated by tabs) or into the database (where each column will be a field). The same principle applies when going from the word processor into the database and spreadsheet, or from the database into the spreadsheet and word processor.

⚜ alphabetizing lists

very hot tip

If you need to alphabetize a list in the word processor, paste it into a new spreadsheet, sort it there and then paste it back into the word processor.

⚜ columns in word processing documents

very hot tip

Use a spreadsheet whenever you have to make a columnar table in the word processor—even if it's all words and no numbers. Columns are easier to manipulate in a spreadsheet, and you can paste the whole table into the word processor when you're done.

⚫ *selected form letters*

You don't have to send form letters to everyone in a database when you're using the word processor's merge-print function *(Prepare to Merge* on the Edit menu). If you do a selection in the database (with the *Record Selection* command) before you merge-print, form letters will be generated for only the selected records.

⚫ *incremental fields*

To get incremental number fields in your database (1, 2, 3, say, or 100, 200, 300) without having to type in all the numbers, use a formula in the spreadsheet that says add 1 (or 100) to the cell above. Copy it down a column as far as you need to, copy the column and paste it into the database in the appropriate field.

very
hot
tip

⚫ *spreadsheet reports*

The Report function in the database can't handle anything beyond totals and subtotals across records. If you need more sophisticated reports that show averages, say, or use statistical functions, paste the database information into the spreadsheet and create the formulas there. You can paste it into the word processor for formatting before you print it.

⚫ *the macro recorder*

Works' macro utility only lets you use ⌷Option⌶ as a modifier key, which severely restricts the collection of keyboard commands you can create. I recommend that you ignore it and use a different one—even Apple's MacroMaker, which has the added advantage of being free.

very bad
feature

But if you do use Works' macro recorder, ignore the Playback window when choosing a macro. Just press ⌷Option⌶ along with whatever key you assigned to the macro.

♦ constraining movement with ⟨Shift⟩

bug

Having trouble using ⟨Shift⟩ to keep dragged objects in the Draw layer moving either vertically or horizontally? That's because, unlike every other Mac program I can think of, Works requires that you press ⟨Shift⟩ *after* you press the mouse button.

This only applies to dragging. When you're using the rectangle or oval tools, you can press ⟨Shift⟩ before the mouse button and still get squares and circles. (But you can also press ⟨Shift⟩ after you've started drawing with these tools.)

♦ text object into column

In Works, a text object is just a box with text in it. A column is a box with text in it that's linked to another box with text in it. To turn a text object into a column, you have to link it to another text object or column.

To link a text object, select it and then doubleclick on a column or other text object. (Depending on the link order you want, you can also select the column and then doubleclick on the text object.)

♦ unlinking columns

To unlink a column, edit its header so that it says *NONE* after *Link*. To edit the header, first click in the body of the column with the text tool to select it. (Clicking on it with the selection arrow doesn't display the header.) Then click in the header with the I-beam pointer and edit it.

♦ naming columns

Works names its draw-layer columns numerically as you create them. You can rename the columns by editing the column header, as long as you keep the word *Col* at the beginning of the name. This lets you give columns a name that better helps you set up and keep track of links and so on (e.g., *Col Front Page Article*).

♦ *centering pasted objects*

When you're in the Draw mode, choosing *Paste* while an object's selected will center the new object in or around the selected object (depending on whether it's smaller or bigger). This makes it easy to put a frame around something, for example.

very
hot
tip

You can also use this feature to align graphic elements. In Draw mode, cut an object to the Clipboard, select another object and paste. Then hold down Shift and drag one of the objects away from the other in either a vertical or horizontal direction.

Chapter 19

Where to find good information and inexpensive software

Magazines and newsletters

✦ Mac magazines (AN)

Since there are a lot of good Mac magazines, the only sensible approach is to buy an issue or two of any that interest you and check them out. For an investment of less than $10, you'll know more than we could ever tell you in a review.

In the case of "controlled-circulation" (i.e., free) magazines, you don't even have to spend any money—you just fill out their questionnaires. (Since you buy an average of ten Macintosh systems a month, you'll qualify for a free subscription without any problem.) But don't stop there— the others are also worth considering. (As always, addresses and phone numbers are in Appendix B.)

✦ MacWEEK (AN)

MacWEEK is free to qualified people (that is, to the people their advertisers want to reach—see the previous entry for details on qualifying for a subscription). Dale Coleman, whose contributions you'll find throughout this book, works at *MacWEEK*, as do the estimable Daniel Farber and Carolyn Said.

MacWEEK has a lot of very current news and is generally well-written. I find *MacWEEK* an interesting read, particularly the anonymous gossip column called *Mac the Knife*. (I know who writes it, but wild horses couldn't drag that information from me. Still, send me your offer—you never know.)

✦ MacUser

The two main Mac monthlies are *MacUser* and *Macworld*. (I was a contributing editor at *MacUser*, and wrote briefly for *Macworld* before that.) I used to prefer *MacUser* by far, but in the last couple of years, it's concentrated much more on business users and has just about forgotten about beginners. I now like the two magazines about the same.

MacUser's regular sections on important topics—networks, for instance—are packed with useful information. It also often runs large-scale comparison articles on things like hard drives or multiuser databases that really help you decide which products suit you best. (But I miss the touch of some of the original editors who have since gone on to other things—Louise Kohl and Steve Bobker, in particular.)

Macworld *(AN)*

Macworld is one of the slickest-looking magazines you're ever likely to see (unless you're a fan of European design magazines). It's particularly strong on articles about broad trends in the market and comparisons of all (or all the major) products available in a certain category, which I think is a very useful approach.

Always a pleasure to read, *Macworld* has sometimes failed to be hard-hitting enough. But this seems to be changing. They ran a great article by Paul Brodeur on the health effects of computer radiation. And Deborah Branscum's *Conspicuous Consumer* column almost single-handedly shamed Apple into extending its inadequate 90-day warranty to a year.

MacGuide

Like the phoenix, *MacGuide* keeps rising from its own ashes. Now called *MacGuide Report,* it's a 460-page compendium of product information—descriptions (from the vendors themselves), prices and references to reviews in major magazines.

MacGuide Report is published twice a year, with monthly updates. You can also order products listed through *MacGuide*—their 800 number is at the bottom of every page. $40 buys you a single issue and the five monthly updates that follow it. For $60, you get a year's subscription—two books and all the updates.

🍎 *Macintosh Buyer's Guide* (AN)

bargain

This quarterly survey of Macintosh products, published by Redgate Communications, has been around for several years. Like *MacGuide*, its listings are close to exhaustive, but there are some categories it leaves out. I find it a really valuable resource, and used it extensively to prepare Appendix B. At just $14 a year, it's a bargain too.

🍎 *desktop publishing and CAD magazines* (AN/SZA)

If you're involved in any sort of desktop publishing or computer-aided design, there are some magazines you should know about. (Most cover both Mac and PC systems, but you'll find plenty of useful information in spite of that.)

Personal Publishing is a monthly out of Chicago that does a good job of covering the field; *Publish!* is another monthly packed with terrific information. *Verbum* is a slick quarterly that bills itself as a *Journal of Personal Computer Aesthetics;* it's the most arty of the magazines described here. *Macintosh-Aided Design* is subtitled *The Magazine for Design and Engineering Professionals;* it provides a lot of good, useful, practical information.

Electronic Publishing and Printing is the newest of the crop. It's not a monthly, though—it's…well, you figure it out (here's what they say): *published monthly except bimonthly Jan/Feb, June/July, Aug/Sept and an extra issue in July.* (Jeez, Sharon, it's obvious—it's a quasidemi-hebdomensual…with a twist.) The one issue Sharon had a chance to see looked good.

🍎 *newsletters* (SZA/AN)

Newsletters don't take advertising, so their subscribers have to bear the full cost of production—plus, of course, some sort of income for the writer/publisher. While many newsletters are quite good, much of the information in them is also available elsewhere. Newsletter subscriptions can run well into three figures, and with that kind of price tag, we find it hard to wholeheartedly recommend them, no matter how good they are. Still, a single piece of information can be worth a fortune, and it doesn't cost anything to check a newsletter out, by requesting a free sample copy.

The Weigand Report has recently undergone both a design and a subtitle change: it's now *Essential Information for Communicators, Desktop Publishers and Small Business Users.* Since it's written by Mac Bible contributor C.J. Weigand, it comes as no surprise that it's well done, and that it squeezes a lot of good information into its four pages. Only four? Yes, but you get 20 issues a year. A subscription costs $128.

The Page is a monthly newsletter from Chicago that's full of useful, practical tips on desktop publishing (particularly PageMaker) you often don't find elsewhere. *Step-by-Step Electronic Design* is a beautifully designed, full-color newsletter that covers page layout and graphics. It's packed with great info and tips—and is a real bargain at $48 a year.

Bove & Rhodes Inside Report On Desktop Publishing and MultiMedia is written by Tony Bove and Cheryl Rhodes, two of the most knowledgeable people in the field. Published monthly, it gives you a level of in-depth analysis that's hard to find elsewhere. It's more technical than *The Page, Step-by-Step Electronic Design* or the desktop publishing magazines mentioned above, and is aimed at more sophisticated readers. It's also more expensive (about $200/ year).

MacArtist uses pretty large type, so you don't get quite as much information in an issue as you might expect. What is there is good, though, and is attractively presented in two colors. It costs $68/year.

🍎 *a monthly newsletter on videotape* (AN)

I usually find it tedious to get information from video-tapes, because—typically—the narration is oversimple, the narrator's voice patronizing, the music annoying and the pace at which information is presented glacial (and inter-larded with nauseating cutesy-isms). Of course, most books and magazines aren't much better, but it's much easier to browse and skip ahead in print.

Given all that, I was pleasantly surprised by *Macintosh Video News*. It's a monthly videotape magazine that mim-ics a television news show (but without the commercials). Although the announcers (newscasters?) occasionally veer towards happy talk, I found them generally quite easy to listen to, and the information they presented was well-or-ganized, insightful and interesting.

very good feature

Because most of what they cover is software, videotape has some real advantages. I found that a few minutes of watching the announcers demo a program gave me a much better idea of what it does and how it works than reading about it in print.

(You should know that *Macintosh Video News* gave *The Macintosh Bible* a good review on one of their tapes. But I would have recommended them if they'd never mentioned us. Although I didn't look forward to having to view even part of the tape, I found myself enjoying it and watched the whole hour. I even reran some parts. For someone as easily bored as me, I consider that quite a recommendation.)

You can get your first copy of *Macintosh Video News* for $7.50. If you subscribe for another five issues, they cost $17.50 per tape, or $15 if you subscribe for another eleven issues (all prices include shipping). There's a 20-day money-back guarantee.

Books

Some of these books described below would have been better reviewed in earlier chapters, but when you write a thousand+-page book, some things fall through the cracks (you try it some time). Here are our comments on some books we liked when we finally got a chance to look at them.

⬤ *The Macintosh Small Business Companion* (AN)

Longtime Mac guru Cynthia Harriman has put together a slew of creative and practical suggestions for making the most out of Macs in a small business. Interspersed between chapters that focus on specific areas like *Letters, Labels and Envelopes* and *Phone dialers, E-mail and On-line Services* are short essays (or monologues, it might be more accurate to call them) in which sixteen people tell how they use Macs in their own small businesses.

very good feature

Harriman has a relaxed, readable style and knows the Mac backwards. What's more, she understands the needs of small business users. That's a rare combination of qualities, and makes for a very useful book.

⬤ *Macintosh Repair and Upgrade Secrets* (Rich Wolfson)

Macintosh Repair and Upgrade Secrets by Mac Bible contributor Larry Pina ($33) is a book I've waited a long time for. Other books have tried to provide this information, but this is the first that provides it clearly and concisely for both the novice and the experienced Mac troubleshooter.

very good feature

The section on upgrading power supplies in classic Macs and Pluses is worth the price of the book alone—particularly when it describes the heavy-duty analog board upgrade. (In my experience, once you install that, the power supply never fails again.) There's also a very useful section on repairing the pre-ADB mouse and keyboard.

The only problem with this book is that it only covers the 128K Mac through the SE—and there isn't a lot of info on the SE. *[Larry is planning a sequel called* Mac II Repair and Upgrade Secrets.*—AN]* The disk that accompanies the book has test-pattern generators labelled 128 and 512, but they also test other monochrome and even color screens.

Until Apple comes out with a full set of schematics and repair information, this volume is a must for anyone with an older Mac—especially people, like me, who are responsible for a number of them.

✎ *Canned Art*

Canned Art: Clip Art for the Macintosh, by Erfert Fenton and Christine Morrissett, is a fairly massive roundup of bit-mapped and EPS clip art for the Mac. (Erfert also wrote *The Macintosh Font Book,* reviewed in Chapter 7.) After some brief introductory material covering Mac graphics formats and utilities, *Canned Art* devotes the rest of its million or so pages to miniature images of the contents of several clip-art packages.

Canned Art costs $30 (from Peachpit Press), but has $1000 worth of discount coupons from clip-art companies (not that you'll use them all, but you only have to use $30 worth to make the book free.). If you have a lot of clip art already, this book's index can help you find what you need (look up *pencil,* for example, and it tells you what disks you'll find pictures of pencils on).

Here's an important note, something that Gail Giaimo of 3G Graphics asked me to point out. Commercial clip art (the sort covered in this book) is *not* public-domain; when you buy a disk, you buy the right to use it yourself, but not to resell it or give it away.

important warning

✎ *two little books*

Robin Williams (no, not Mork—she's a graphic-design instructor at a small college in northern California) has written two small books for the Mac. *The Little Mac Book* ($13, from Peachpit Press) is a quick-reference guide for beginners or occasional users; its 100 pages cover just enough of what you to know to get started and keep moving for a while.

The Mac Is Not a Typewriter ($10, also from Peachpit) is a 70-page roundup of word-processing versus typewriting rules (no double spaces after periods, don't use spaces to align things, etc.). I agree with every one of them, but I'm not sure they're worth their own book.

Word 4 Companion

The Cobb Group publishes many excellent books, among them *The Word 4 Companion* ($23). It covers everything from copying the program to your hard disk to embedding PostScript commands in your Word documents.

INITInfo *(AN)*

very good feature

bargain

This guide to inits is put together by Gary Ouellet and Glenn Brown and is published by Artext in Ottawa. It functions as a clearing house on bugs, conflicts and other known problems, and summarizes them in useful charts. It's frequently updated (the one I'm looking at is version 4.1.1) and you can download the latest version from CompuServe (Gary's address is 73277,2757; Glenn's is 73777,1142), MacNET (glennbrown) or several Canadian BBS's (613/233-1474, 819/684-0120, 613/729-2763, 613/233-6262). All in all, this is a much-needed and quite useful little booklet (and service).

User groups

what user groups are *(AN)*

esp. for beginners

very good feature

User groups are clubs made up of people who are interested in computers in general, a particular kind of computer, a particular kind of software or even an individual program. They're typically nonprofit and independent of any manufacturer or publisher.

User groups are an excellent source of good information—which isn't surprising, since sharing information is their main purpose. Nowhere else are you likely to find so many dedicated people anxious to help you solve your problems, none of whom would dream of charging you a nickel for it.

User group meetings are usually open to the public and free. Joining the group normally costs somewhere between $20 and $60 a year and gives you access to the group's library of public-domain software and shareware. Large groups often feature guest speakers from the computer industry who describe new products at their meetings, and also have subgroups (called *special interest groups* or *SIGs)* for members with particular interests or needs: beginners, developers, musicians, graphic artists, desktop publishers and so on.

Here's a description of what a typical large user group meeting is like. Before the meeting starts, people line up to buy disks and other items like modems that the group sells to members, usually at very low prices. The meetings begin with an open session where people can ask any question they have about any aspect of the Mac, and usually get a definitive answer from someone in the room. When the question-and-answer session is over, one or two guest speakers describe their products (using a Mac that projects onto a giant screen).

I vividly remember the night the ebullient Andy Hertzfeld (who wrote much of the code in the Finder and in MultiFinder, as well as the software that runs on Radius monitors) debuted a program of his called Switcher at a local user group (Switcher is what MultiFinder was based on). When the display on the big screen shot from the application in the first partition to the one in the second, the audience leapt to its feet and cheered. (No lie.)

Unless you live in a very remote area, finding a local user group shouldn't be hard—especially if there's a college or university nearby. One fast way to find one is to check with an Apple dealer. Any good dealer will know all the local user groups. If you can't find a group in your community, get together with some other Mac users and start one of your own.

♦ *BCS* (AN)

There are more than forty SIGs in the country's largest user group, the Boston Computer Society, and each of them publishes a newsletter (in addition to BCS's own slick magazine). When you join BCS, you get to choose two SIGs to belong to (more than that cost extra). BCS's Mac SIG has more than 10,000 members and its newsletter, *The Active Window,* is excellent.

♦ *BMUG* (AN)

BMUG was originally called the *Berkeley Macintosh Users Group,* and *BMUG* was just its nickname. But the IRS considers a single-product or single-brand user group a promotional activity of the company, so to preserve the group's tax-exempt status, the name had to be changed to simply *BMUG.*

Membership in BMUG costs $60 a year (as of this writing); included in the price is a semiannual "newsletter" that runs to hundreds of $8\frac{1}{2}$ x 11 pages. The group maintains an extensive public-domain and shareware library and also publishes, on CD ROM, a comprehensive catalog of public-domain software.

♦ *NABVICU* (DC)

The National Association of Blind and Visually Impaired Computer Users is at Box 1352, Roseville CA 95661, Their phone numbers are 916/ 783-0364 (voice) and 916/ 786-3923 (modem).

The Macintosh Bible Software Disks (Third Edition) (AN)

bargain

This is our collection of the best public-domain software, shareware, templates, fonts and art. It costs $20 and comes with a 30-day, money-back guarantee. You get more than 1.5 megs of stuff, on two disks—one for the left brain and one for the right brain. Here's what they contain:

The Left Brain disk

Address Book 2.5 is a handy little database program specifically designed for storing names, addresses and telephone numbers. If you have a modem, the program will also dial any phone number in its files at a click of the mouse. The disk also includes a desk accessory version.

Calendar 2.1 is an elegant desk accessory for planning and scheduling.

Dictionary Helper is a 1313-word file you add to your spelling checker dictionary to greatly reduce the number of "false alarms"—words that get flagged even though they're actually correct.

DiskKeeper 1.2.2 helps you manage disks that are cluttered with multiple copies of files, have files buried several folders deep, or that just have too many files.

FreeTerm 3.0 is a simple terminal application you use with your modem to connect to BBS's (bulletin board systems) or commercial information services like CompuServe.

RamDisk+ 2.21 sets aside part of your Mac's memory (or *RAM)* and makes it act like a very fast disk drive.

Set Clock 2.0 uses your modem to accurately set your Mac's internal clock. (by making a ten-second long-distance call to an atomic clock in Virginia).

SmartKeys 1.0 is a control panel device (cdev) designed to help you conform to the standards of typesetting as you type.

SuperClock! 3.9 puts a small clock on the right side of your menu bar.

To Do! 1.0 is a DA that helps you keep track of things you need to do.

Viewer 1.05 is used to display the on-disk documentation for the files in this collection.

The Right Brain disk

Art by Esther Travis contains three gorgeous MacPaint drawings by a master Mac artist (some of which are used as incidental illustrations in this book).

Artisto+ 2.02 is a desk accessory that lets you open paint files (created with *MacPaint, FullPaint* or other Mac paint programs) and cut or copy all or any portion of them.

Blackout 1.21 is a cdev screen saver.

Chinese Menu is an outline font (for PostScript printers) that approximates the brushstroke style often found on menus in Chinese restaurants.

Clarity 1.0 is a little DA that takes bitmapped images you place on the Clipboard and reduces them to match the resolution of laser or dot-matrix printers.

The **font template** makes it easy to print out every character a font can produce, as well as samples of the sixteen possible type styles in that font.

Glider+ 3.0 is a simple, arcade style game with the objective of piloting a paper airplane through 15 rooms while avoiding crashing into obstacles.

Klondike 4.0 is a computer version of the popular solitaire game of the same name.

Layout 1.9 customizes the way the Finder displays files and folders on the desktop.

Santa Monica is an unusual but elegant bit-mapped font.

Sound Mover lets you move sounds around.

StartupSndInit lets you customize the sound the Mac makes when you start it up.

Tidy It Up! organizes cluttered system folders by categorizing each file and by positioning related icons together.

If you're interested in taking a look at The Macintosh Bible Software Disks, Third Edition, use the order from inside the back cover, or send $20 + $4 for shipping, handling and tax (if any) to Goldstein & Blair, Box 7635, Berkeley CA 94707. If you don't like the disks, just return them with your receipt within 30 days, by UPS or parcel post, and we'll send you your money back.

Copyright © 1988 by Esther Travis. All rights reserved.

Appendix A

Glossary of basic Mac terms

These definitions only apply to the Mac. They may not be accurate if you try to apply them to other computers or—heaven forfend!—to the world outside computers. Very basic terms (like mouse *and* keyboard) *are omitted.*

When a term that's defined in this glossary occurs in the definition of another term, I usually put it in italics—so you know you can look it up if you don't know what it means (but I don't do that for the most common terms.) Italics are also used for sentences that show how the word is used (see algorithm *for an example).*

Words are alphabetized as if spaces and hyphens didn't exist; thus copying *comes before* copy protection *and* E-mail *comes between* em *and* em dash.

Although I had help on some of the definitions here (particularly from Sharon), I wrote almost all them myself, and heavily edited the ones I didn't write. So if you run across the word I *below, that's me.—AN*

accelerator board

A *board* containing a faster CPU chip and/or more memory and/or other electronic wizardry to speed up the operation of a computer.

active window

The currently selected window, where the next action will take place (unless the next action is to select another window). The active window is always on top of all other windows, its *title bar* is highlighted—that is, there are six horizontal lines on either side of the title—and its *scroll bars* are gray (when all its contents won't fit).

ADB *(pronounced as separate letters—needless to say)*

A standard for connecting peripheral devices like keyboards and mice to SE's and Mac II's (as well as to the Apple IIGS). The connections are different from those on the Plus and earlier Macs.

AI *(pronounced as separate letters)*

Short for *artificial intelligence,* this term is applied to computer programs that can learn from experience.

Alarm Clock

A standard Apple-supplied *desk accessory* that lets you sound an alarm at a given time. (If the Mac is off at that time, you find out about the alarm when you turn the Mac back on.) You can also use it to set the Mac's system time.

alert box

A *box* that appears unbidden on the screen, announced by one or more beeps, to give you information. Alert boxes don't require any information back from you. A *bomb* is one example. Also called a *message box*, although *alert box* is the correct name. Some people call them simply *alerts*.

algorithm

The precise sequence of steps required to do something. The first step in programming is figuring out the algorithm. *Both programs produce the same result, but because they use different algorithms, the second one is much faster.*

Algorithmically derived type styles are ones where the computer calculates the degree of slant (for oblique type styles) or the amount of thickening (for boldface type styles), rather than a human being designing a *cutting*.

alphanumeric

Letters and numbers. Punctuation and symbols are not alphanumeric characters.

alpha tester

A person, employed by the company developing a product, who tries to discover bugs in it. Compare *beta tester*.

alpha testing

Early debugging of a product within the company developing it. It's followed by *beta testing* (unless the alpha testing is really disastrous).

alpha version

A version of a program at the point at which it's in alpha test. There are usually several alpha versions. Compare *beta version* and *release version*.

menu

The Apple menu, which is available on the *desktop* (that is, in the Finder) and from within most applications; its title is an which appears at the extreme left end of the menu bar. The menu gives you access to *desk accessories* and information about the current application. It's one of the Mac's three *standard menus*.

AppleTalk

The Mac's built-in networking software, and the *protocols* it uses. Networks using those protocols are also called *AppleTalk*. Originally, *AppleTalk* referred to the cabling as well, which is now called *LocalTalk*.

application *(or* application program*)*

Software that does relatively complex tasks and that lets you create and modify documents. Some common types of applications are word processors, spreadsheets, databases, graphics programs, page layout software and communications programs. On the Mac, all programs are called *applications*, but on other computers, a distinction is made between applications and utility programs, system software, games, etc.

arrow keys

On the standard *ADB keyboard*, four keys (indicated by ⬆ , ⬅ , ➡ and ⬇ in this book) that move the *insertion point*, move you through *list boxes* and the like.

arrow pointer

The basic shape the *pointer* takes—a left-leaning arrow that looks like this: ▶ .

ascender

The part of lowercase letters like *b, d,* and *l* that extends above the *x-height.* Compare *descender.*

ASCII *(ASK-ee)*

The *American standard code for information interchange,* a system for referring to letters, numbers and common symbols by code numbers. Since the ASCII standard is widely used, virtually any computer can understand an ASCII file. On the Mac, ASCII files are usually referred to as *text files.*

[Backspace]

What the [Delete] key is called on some older keyboards. (Both keys do exactly the same things.)

backup

A copy of a program or document that you can use if the original is destroyed. To *back up* is to make a copy.

baseline

The imaginary line on which the upper- and lowercase letters of a font sit (only *descenders* extend below it).

BASIC

A popular *high-level* (close to English) computer language that's relatively easy to learn but is also relatively lacking in power and sophistication. The name is short for *beginner's all-purpose symbolic instruction set.*

batch mode

When a spelling checker (or any other kind of program) processes an entire document (or some part of it) when you're done inputting data, instead of checking you as you input the data. Compare *interactive mode.*

baud rate

The number of bits per second. Baud rates are most commonly used as a measure of how fast data is transmitted—by a modem, for example. (In some circumstances, there's a difference between bits per second and the baud rate, but for all practical purposes you can consider them to be the same.) The term comes from the name of a communications pioneer, Baudot.

The most common baud rates are 300, 1200, 2400 and 9600. Which one you use can mean the difference between sanity and three weeks in Bellevue. If you can stand to watch text come on the screen at 300 baud, you either have no central nervous system or you're the Buddha.

BBS

Short for *bulletin board system*.

benchmark

A test (or set of tests) used to compare the speed of hardware or software.

beta site

A place where *beta testing* takes place. *We're a beta site for the new version.*

beta tester

A person, not employed by the company developing a product, who tries to discover bugs in it. Beta testers are almost never paid; they do it for the fun of being in on the development of the product and/or because their work requires that they know what's going on before the product is released. Compare *alpha tester*.

beta testing

Debugging of a product using people outside the company developing the product. Beta testing comes after *alpha testing* and before the *release version* is shipped.

beta version

A version of a program at the point at which it's in beta test. Usually there are several beta versions. Compare *alpha version* and *release version*.

Bezier curves *(BEZ-yay)*

Mathematically generated lines that can display nonuniform curvatures (as opposed to curves with uniform curvature, which are called *arcs).* Named after Pierre Bezier, they're defined by four control points. It's relatively easy to make Bezier curves assume complex shapes and to join their endpoints smoothly, which makes them particularly useful for creating the shapes of letters and other complex graphics.

binary numbers

The base-2 numbering system that almost all computers are based on, as opposed to the base-10, *decimal* numbers people use. The number 1 is the same in both binary and decimal, but 2 in decimal = 10 in binary, 3 in decimal = 11 in binary, 4 in decimal = 100 in binary, and so on.

bit

The smallest possible unit of information. It can represent only one of two things: yes or no, on or off, or—as it's expressed in the *binary* numbers used in computers—0 or 1. Short for *binary* dig*it.* Also see *byte.*

bit map

An image made up of dots.

bit-mapped

Made up of dots.

bit-mapped font

A font made up of dots and designed primarily for use on dot-matrix printers. Also called an *ImageWriter font.* Compare *outline font* and *screen font.*

bit-mapped graphic

A picture or other graphic made up of dots rather than of objects, like those produced by *paint programs.* Compare *object-oriented graphic.*

board

A piece of fiberglass or pressboard on which *chips* are mounted. Also called a *circuit board.* The connections between the chips are normally printed with metallic ink—in which case it's a *printed circuit* (or *PC) board.* The main board in a computer device is called the *motherboard.* A board made to plug directly into a *slot* is called a card.

bomb

A *message box* with a picture of a bomb in it. It appears unbidden on the screen to let you know that a serious problem has occurred with the system software (in other words, that you've *crashed).* Bombs usually force you to restart the system. Compare *hang.*

booting

Starting up a computer by loading an *operating system*—in the case of the Mac, the System and either the Finder or a Finder substitute—into its memory. The more common Mac term is *starting up* or simply *starting.* (The name *boot* comes from the idea that the operating system pulls itself up by its own bootstraps—since it's a program that tells a computer how to load other programs, but loads itself.)

box

1. An enclosed area on the Mac's screen that doesn't have a *title bar* (and thus can't be dragged around). *Dialog boxes* and *alert boxes* are two examples. Certain kinds of boxes, like *list boxes* and *text boxes,* appear inside other boxes (in this case, inside dialog boxes). Compare *window.*

2. Any of various rectangular icons that control windows—like *close boxes, scroll boxes, size boxes* and *zoom boxes.*

3. A rectangular *button,* like a *checkbox.*

bridge

The most basic sort of connection between networks. Compare *gateway* and *router.*

buffer

An area of memory—or a separate memory cache—which holds information until it's needed. Buffers are used to speed up printing, redrawing the screen, etc.

bug

A mistake, or unexpected occurrence, in a piece of software (or, less commonly, a piece of hardware). Bugs are distinguished from design flaws, which are intentional (that is, the programmer *put* them there).

Most computer programs are so complex that no programmer can test out (or even conceive of) all the possible situations they can generate. Thus most bugs aren't quite errors, but are rather untested paths, unanticipated contingencies. They're discovered when a user breaks new ground—for example, by using a particular series of commands in a particular order that no one has tried before (or in a particular set of circumstances that no one has been in before).

Bug is an old electronics and phone company term. It comes from the fact that bugs eating the insulation off wires was actually a common cause of problems in early telephone systems, until they figured out how to coat wires with stuff bugs don't like the taste of.

bulletin board (or bulletin board system)

A computer dedicated to maintaining messages and software and making them available over phone lines at no charge. People *upload* (contribute) and *download* (gather) messages by calling the bulletin board from their own computers. Abbreviated *BBS.*

button

1. On the Mac's screen, an outlined area in a dialog box that you click on to choose, confirm or cancel a command. For example, when you quit from most applications, you get a dialog box that asks if you want to save the current document, and it gives you three buttons to choose from: *Yes, No* and *Cancel.*

   A button with a heavy border, which is activated when you hit Return or Enter , is called the *default button.* Also see *radio buttons.*

2. The switch on top of the mouse you use for clicking. When there's a danger of confusion with the first meaning of *button,* it's called the *mouse button.*

bye

The standard thing to type to indicate you're ending a tele-communications session.

byte

Eight *bits.* Bytes are typically used to represent characters (letters, numbers, punctuation marks and other symbols) in text.

CAD *(pronounced as a word, not separate letters)*

Computer-aided design (it can refer to both hardware and software).

CAD/CAM *(CAD-cam)*

For *CAD,* see the previous entry. The *CAM* half stands for *computer-aided manufacturing*—computers and programs that run manufacturing machinery or even entire factories. (You seldom see the word *CAM* alone; it's usually combined with *CAD.)*

Calculator

A standard Apple-supplied *desk accessory* that simulates a simple calculator. You can cut and paste to and from it.

Cancel

A *button* that appears in most *dialog boxes,* giving you the choice of cancelling the command that generated the dialog box.

⌐Caps Lock⌐

A *modifier key* that, in addition to its normal function of making any letter you type a capital, can be used as part of a keyboard equivalent.

card

A kind of *board* that plugs directly into a *slot.* Cards have connectors right on their edges, rather than at the ends of a cable.

CD ROM *(SEE-dee RAHM)*

A *compact disk read-only memory*—a kind of optical *storage* device (or medium) used on the Mac and other computers. Hyphenated when used as an adjective.

cdev *(SEE-dev)*

A utility program that, like an *init,* must be placed in the system folder to work. Unlike an init, it then displays an icon on the left side of the Control Panel, along with the General, Keyboard and Mouse icons. *Cdev* is short for Control Panel *device.*

character

The generic name for a number, letter or symbol. Included are "invisible" characters like ⌐Tab⌐ and ⌐Return⌐.

character key

Any key that generates a *character.* Compare *modifier key.*

checkboxes

A group of boxes that work as *toggles*—that is, when you click on an empty checkbox, an *X* appears inside it, turning the option on;

when you click on a checkbox with an *X* in it, the *X* disappears and the option is turned off. Unlike *radio buttons,* any or all of a group of checkboxes can be on at one time.

chip

Silicon is a chemical element found in sand, clay, glass, pottery, concrete, brick, etc. A tiny piece of silicon (or germanium), usually about the size of a baby's fingernail, is impregnated with impurities in a pattern that creates different sorts of miniaturized computer circuits. This is a *chip.*

Chips are primarily used as *CPUs* or *memory* and are normally mounted in *DIPs* or *SIMMs,* or on *boards.*

chip family

A group of related chips, each of which (except, of course, the first) evolved from an earlier one. The *CPU chips* used in Macintosh products are all members of the Motorola *68000* family.

Chooser

A *desk accessory* primarily used to tell the Mac which printer you want to use, what port it's connected to, whether background printing is turned on and whether AppleTalk is active or inactive. The Chooser can also control network zones, mounted volumes, etc.

Chooser resource file

When you place one of these inside your system folder, it displays an icon in the Chooser window. Chooser resource files normally control external devices like printers, or emulate them. Some examples are: the ImageWriter and LaserWriter drivers that come with the Mac; the ImageSaver file that comes with Desktop Express; SuperGlue, which lets you print formatted files to disk; and AppleShare, which lets you access other volumes on a local area network. *Rdev's* are one kind of Chooser resource file.

circuit board

See *board.*

clicking

Pressing and immediately releasing the mouse button. To *click on* something is to position the pointer on it and then click.

Clipboard

The area of the Mac's memory that holds what you last cut or copied. (If there's not enough room in memory for what you cut or copy, some of it is put on disk.) Pasting inserts the contents of the Clipboard into a document.

clock rate (*or* clock speed)

The operations of a computer are synchronized to a quartz crystal that pulses millions of times each second. These pulses determine things like how often the screen is redrawn and how often the *CPU* accesses RAM or a hard disk. The frequency of these pulses—how often they occur—is measured in *megahertz* (millions of cycles per second) and is called the *clock rate* or *clock speed*.

clone

A machine that's compatible with the IBM Personal Computer but that isn't made by IBM.

close box

A small box at the left end of the active window's title bar. Clicking on it closes the window. Compare *size box* and *zoom box*.

closing

On the *desktop,* closing a *window* means collapsing it back into an *icon.* Within an application, closing a *document* means terminating your work on it without exiting the application.

code

The actual statements or instructions in a program; what programmers produce. *Clean,* or *elegant,* code is well-written; *spaghetti code* is not.

Color Wheel

A segmented circle containing many colors that appears in the Color section of the Control Panel and is used to specify the color of the *desktop*, highlighted text, etc.

command

The generic name for anything you tell a computer program to do. On the Mac, commands are usually listed on menus, or are generated by holding down the ⌘ (command) key while hitting one or more other keys. To choose a command from a menu, you drag down the menu until the command you want is *highlighted*, then release the mouse button.

###

Called the *command* key, this *modifier key* is used in combination with other keys to issue commands. For example, in most Mac applications, ⌘S saves the document you're working on. (On many keyboards, the command key also has an apple on it, and thus looks something like this: ⌘ .)

commercial

Said of computer products that are sold for profit through normal distribution channels, with the purchaser paying before taking possession of the product. Compare *shareware* and *public-domain*.

communicating

Transferring data between computers, either over phone lines *(telecommunicating)* or on a *local area network*.

compiler

Software that implements a program by translating it all at once. Compare *interpreter*.

contiguous

Said of memory or storage space that's not split apart by other pieces of memory or storage used for other information. Compare *fragmented*.

control character

The combination of the Ctrl key and one or more other characters. Control characters are widely used on the IBM PC, but the Mac mostly uses the ⌘ key for this purpose (although control characters are used in some Mac communications programs).

control key

A *modifier key* on *ADB keyboards* (but not on earlier Mac keyboards). Widely used in the world of the IBM PC, Ctrl can be used on Macs as part of *keyboard equivalents* for menu commands or for *macros.*

Control Panel

A *desk accessory* that allows you to set things like how loud the beeps (and other sounds the Mac makes) are, how fast the insertion point blinks, how fast you have to click in succession for the Mac to recognize it as a doubleclick, and so on.

coprocessor

A chip that specializes in math, graphics, or some other specific kind of computation. When the *CPU* is handed the kind of job the coprocessor specializes in, it hands the job off to it. The most common coprocessor chips used in Macs so far (the 68881 and 68882) both specialize in mathematical computation.

copying

Duplicating something from a document and placing the duplicate in the Clipboard. To do that, you select what you want to copy and then choose *Copy* from the Edit menu or hit ⌘ C . Also see *cutting* and *pasting.*

copy protection

Any of many various schemes for preventing the unauthorized copying of software. They're all a pain (although to varying degrees) and are seldom used any more.

CP/M *(pronounced as separate letters—needless to say)*

An early *operating system* for personal computers on which *MS DOS* was modeled. (The name stands for *control program for microprocessors.)*

CPU *(pronounced as separate letters)*

The *central processing unit*—the central part of a computer (or other computer device). It includes the circuitry—built around the *CPU chip* and mounted on the *motherboard*—that actually performs the computer's calculations, and the box in which that circuitry is housed. (Sometimes just the CPU chip itself is called the *CPU.)*

CPU chip

The heart of a computer (or other computer device). The CPU chip is the main determinant of what software will run on that particular computer and, with the clock rate, determines how fast the computer will run. For a list of the CPU chips in various Mac models, see pp. 73–74.

crash

A noun and verb, both of which mean that your system has suddenly and unexpectedly stopped working, or is working wrong. You normally have to restart. Also see *bomb* and *hang*.

CRT *(pronounced as separate letters)*

A *cathode ray tube*—the display technology used on virtually all computer monitors and television sets. The most common alternative is *LCD*, which is used on the Mac Portable and the Sony WatchMan (as well as on most digital watches).

curly quotes *(and* **curly apostrophes***)*

Ones that look like this: " " ', rather than like this: " '.

cursor

Unlike more primitive computers, the Mac has nothing called a *cursor* (although Mac *programmers* use the term; see the next paragraph). *Cursor* comes from the prehistoric world of CP/M (an early operating system on which MS DOS was modeled); the term is sometimes incorrectly applied to either the *pointer* or the *insertion point.* (*Cursor* is a Latin word that means *runner* or *messenger.*)

Mac programmers call the pointer the *cursor*—which doesn't make any sense at all, since the insertion point, not the pointer, is the equivalent of what's called the *cursor* on other computers. But, hey, that's why you use the Mac—so that all that nerdy computerese will be invisible to you.

cutting

1. Removing something from a document by selecting it and then choosing *Cut* from the Edit menu or hitting ⌘ X . What you cut is placed in the Clipboard. Also see *copying* and *pasting.*

2. In type design, a type style (like italic or boldface) that was actually designed by a human being, rather than being derived *algorithmically* by the computer.

DA *(pronounced as separate letters)*

An abbreviation for *desk accessory.*

daughter board

A *board* that mounts on top of, and connects to, the *motherboard.* Often used for memory upgrades and the like.

debug

To search out *bugs* in a piece of software and eliminate them.

default

What you get if you don't specify something different. Often used to refer to default settings (for example, the margins in a word processing program, or Speaker Volume on the Control Panel).

default button

A *button* with a heavy border, which is activated when you hit Return or Enter .

defragmenting

The process of making *fragmented* memory, or a fragmented hard disk, capable of storing information *contiguously*.

[Delete]

This key deletes whatever you have selected, or the character to the left of the *insertion point*. On some older keyboards, [Delete] is labeled [Backspace] .

delimiter

A character that marks the boundary (or limit) of something. For example, the standard for Mac databases uses [Tab] to delimit fields and [Return] to delimit records.

descender

The part of lowercase letters like *g, y* and *q* that extends below the *baseline*. Compare *ascender*.

desk accessories

Programs that are available from the menu in the Finder and in most applications. (It's possible to link a desk accessory to a specific application, so that it won't be available from other applications, but that's a special case.) Commonly called *DAs*.

(the) desktop

Apple's official definition for this term is: *Macintosh's working environment—the menu bar and the gray area on the screen.* But in common usage, it refers only to the Finder's desktop—that is, what the Mac's screen displays when you're in the Finder.

One way to tell if you're on the desktop—that is, if you're in the Finder—is to look for the Trash in the lower right corner. (Of course, if you're in MultiFinder, the Trash will always be there, unless you've covered it with a window.)

desktop file

An invisible file that records information like the size, shape and locations of windows on a disk.

device

A piece of computer hardware.

dialog box

A box on the screen requesting information, or a decision, from you. In some dialog boxes, the only possible response is to click on the *OK* button. Since this hardly constitutes a dialog, those are more often called *message boxes* or *alert boxes*.

dimmed

When something is *dimmed* (gray) on the Mac's screen, it means that you can't currently access it. For example, commands you can't choose (in a given context) appear dimmed on the menu. When you eject a disk, its icon is dimmed, as are all windows and icons associated with it. Also called *grayed* or *disabled*.

DIP

A *dual in-line package*—the form in which many *chips* are mounted to plug into a computer.

directory

An invisible file that keeps track of where various files are stored on a disk.

disabled

Another word for *dimmed*.

disk

A round platter with a coating similar to that on recording tape, on which computer information is stored magnetically (except for optical disks, which store information optically). Although the disk itself is always circular, the case it comes in is usually rectangular. The two main types are *floppy disks* and *hard disks*.

disk drive

A device that reads information from, and writes information onto, *disks*. The two main types are *floppy disk drives* and *hard disk drives*.

disk window

The window that opens when you doubleclick on a disk's icon. Also called the *root directory*.

display

Another name for a *monitor*.

document

What you create and modify with an *application*—a collection of information, grouped together and called by one name, and saved as a *file* on a disk or treated as one in memory. Some examples are a letter, a drawing or a mailing list.

documentation

This term includes manuals, *online* tutorials and help files, reference cards, instructional audio cassettes and videotapes, and so on.

DOS *(dahss)*

Short for *PC DOS* or *MS DOS*—the *operating system* used on IBM Personal Computers and compatible machines. (The *D* stands for *disk.*)

dot

Another name for a *pixel,* or for the smallest unit that makes up a *bit-mapped* character or graphic.

dot-matrix printer

A printer that forms characters out of a pattern of dots, the way the Mac forms images on the screen. Usually each dot is made by a separate pin pushing an inked ribbon against the paper. *ImageWriter* is the name Apple gives to its line of dot-matrix printers.

dots per inch

A measure of screen or printer resolution; the number of dots in a line one inch long. Abbreviated *dpi*.

dots per square inch

A measure of screen and printer resolution; the number of dots in a solid square one inch on a side. Abbreviated *dpsi* or *dpi^2*.

doubleclicking

Positioning the pointer and then quickly pressing and releasing the mouse button twice without moving the mouse. Doubleclicking is used to open applications and documents (when the pointer is an arrow) and to select whole words (when the pointer is an I-beam).

downloading

Retrieving a file from a distant computer and storing it on your own. Opposite of *uploading*.

dpi

An abbreviation for *dots per inch*.

dpsi, dpi^2

Abbreviations for *dots per square inch*.

dragging

Placing the pointer, holding down the mouse button, moving the mouse and then releasing the button. If you place the pointer on an object, dragging moves the object. If you place the pointer where there is no object, dragging often generates the selection rectangle (in the Finder and in graphics programs, for example). If you place the pointer on a menu title, dragging moves you down the menu (and releasing the button when a command is highlighted chooses it).

DRAM *(DEE-ram)*

A *d*ynamic *RAM* (memory) chip. *Dynamic* simply means it loses its memory when you shut the computer off *(volatile RAM* would probably have been a better name). Also see *SIMM*.

draw program

A graphics program that generates *object-oriented graphics,* which are treated as units, rather than a series of dots. Compare *paint program.*

draw/paint program

A graphics program that combines the features of *draw programs* and *paint programs,* usually by putting *object-oriented graphics* and *bit-mapped graphics* on different layers. SuperPaint was the first program to do this.

driver

A piece of software that tells a computer how to run an outside device—typically a printer—or that emulates doing that (for example, it might tell the computer how to print a file to disk as if it were sending it to a printer).

Edit menu

In the Finder and in most applications, the third menu from the left on the menu bar. It typically contains commands for cutting, copying, pasting, undoing, etc. It's one of the Mac's three *standard menus.*

ellipsis

This symbol (...) after a menu item means that selecting it won't immediately execute a command; you'll either get a *dialog box* asking for more information or a *message box* telling you something.

em

A space as wide as the size of type you're using is high (so if you're using 12-point type, an em will be twelve points wide). It gets its name from the fact that it's approximately the width of a capital *M*. Compare *en*.

E-mail

*E*lectronic *mail;* messages sent from computer to computer over phone lines (or over a *local area network*).

em dash

A dash one *em* in length. It's often used instead of parentheses or commas to set off a separate thought—particularly in this book. Compare *en dash*.

en

A space half as wide as the size of type you're using is high (so if you're using 12-point type, an en will be six points wide). It gets its name from the fact that it's approximately the width of a lowercase *n*. Compare *em*.

encapsulated PostScript

See *EPS*.

encryption

Scrambling the data in a file to prevent unauthorized access.

en dash

A dash one *en* in length. It's used in ranges of numbers (1987–91) and as a minus sign. Compare *em dash*.

[Enter]

A key on the Mac's keyboard that doesn't generate a character and is used for different purposes by various applications. In *dialog boxes* and on the *desktop,* the [Enter] key usually has the same effect as the [Return] key.

EPS *(pronounced as separate letters)*

Encapsulated PostScript, a standard graphics format that consists of the PostScript code that tells the printer how to print the image and a PICT image that tells the screen how to display it. Compare *paint, PICT* and *TIFF.*

Sometimes the abbreviation **EPSF** is used (the *f* stands for *file* or *files).* Aside from the fact that the extra letter is unnecessary, it leads to barbarisms like *EPSF files (encapsulated PostScript file files).* This reminds me of people who refer to a long street south of San Francisco as *the El Camino* (which means literally *the the road).* Actually, the offices of Adobe (the developer and publisher of PostScript) aren't far from El Camino; maybe it had an influence.

Ethernet

A relatively fast *LAN* cabling system developed by Xerox. Ethernet components are also sold by other vendors.

expansion slot

See *slot.*

expertosis *(eks-per-TOE-sis)*

The tendency of experts in a field to lose sight of the needs, concerns and limitations of people who aren't experts in that field. On the Mac, expertosis most often manifests itself in unintelligible manuals, abstruse features and strange, uncommunicative names for things.

(This is my bid to insert a word into the English language, after years of envying Paul Krassner for *yippie,* Alice Kahn for *yuppie* and Jack Mingo for *couch potato.* It does, after all, describe a common phenomenon, and one that there's no other word for. You can help me in my quest by using *expertosis* whenever possible...or you can turn the page.)

expert system

A program that simulates human expertise by using "rules of thumb" to access an extensive database of facts.

false alarms

Correctly spelled words a spelling checker doesn't recognize, and therefore flags as possible errors.

FatBits

A feature, originated by MacPaint, that lets you edit graphics in a magnified view, dot by dot.

field

1. In *databases*, a specific portion of a *record*. For example, if the record is in a mailing list program, there will be—at least—a name field, an address field, a city field, a state field and field for the zip code.

2. *In the field* means anywhere but the factory where a computer— or any piece of hardware—is manufactured. *We've designed this system so just about any repair can be made in the field.*

file

A collection of information on a disk, usually either a *document* or an *application*. Although the information in a file is normally cohesive—that is, about one thing—it doesn't actually have to be; what makes it a file is simply that it's lumped together and called by one name.

File menu

On the *desktop* and in virtually all applications, the second menu from the left. Within applications it contains commands for opening, saving, printing and closing documents, quitting the application and so on. In the Finder, the File menu contains commands for opening and closing windows, duplicating icons, ejecting disks, etc. It's one of the Mac's three *standard menus.*.

file server

A computer on a *network* that everyone on the network can access and get applications and documents from.

Finder

The basic program that generates the *desktop* and lets you access and manage files and disks. Together with the System file and the Mac's ROMs, it comprises what—on other computers—is called the *operating system*. There are also Finder substitutes, which perform the same basic tasks as the Finder (and usually give you other capabilities as well).

Fkey *(EFF-kee)*

An obsolescent kind of Mac command that's invoked by pressing Shift ⌘ plus a number. They've largely been replaced by inits and cdevs. (Although their name is derived from *f*unction *keys*, Fkeys have nothing to do with the function keys on extended keyboards that are labelled F1, F2, etc.)

The standard Mac commands to eject disks (Shift ⌘ 1 and Shift ⌘ 2) and to save or print the screen (Shift ⌘ 3 and Shift ⌘ 4) are Fkeys. The other number keys—0, 5, 6, 7, 8 and 9—are available to store other Fkey commands.

flicker

Rapid pulsation of the image on a screen, visible to some people, as the result of the *refresh rate* being too slow.

floppy disk

A removable disk that's flexible (although the case in which the actual magnetic medium is housed may be hard, as it is on the 3-1/2" floppies used by the Mac). Compare *hard disk*. Also see *disk*.

floppy disk drive

A device for reading data from, and writing data to, *floppy disks*.

folder

A grouping of files and/or other folders that's represented by a folder-shaped icon on the *desktop*. The equivalent on MS-DOS machines is called a *subdirectory*.

font

A collection of letters, numbers, punctuation marks and symbols with an identifiable and consistent look; a Macintosh typeface in all its sizes and styles.

Font/DA Mover

A utility program used for installing, removing and moving *fonts* and *desk accessories.*

footer

A piece of text automatically printed at the bottom of several pages (although the text may vary from page to page—as it would if it contained page numbers, for example).

footprint

The amount of space a device takes up on the surface where it sits (and the shape of that space).

formatting

1. All the characteristics of text other than the actual characters that make it up. Formatting includes things like italics, boldfacing, type size, margins, line spacing, justification and so on.

2. Also, another term for *initializing* a disk.

The *forward-delete key,* found on some extended keyboards. Unlike the normal ⌜Delete⌟ key, it deletes the character to the *right* of the insertion point.

fragmented

Said of memory or storage space that's split apart by other pieces of memory or storage used for other information. Compare *contiguous.*

freeware

Another name for *public-domain software*.

freeze

Another term for a *hang*.

function keys

Special keys on some extended keyboards (both from Apple and other manufacturers) that are labelled F1, F2, etc. You can assign commands of your own choosing to them. Don't confuse them with *Fkeys*.

garbage

Bizarre and/or meaningless characters. When garbage appears on the screen, it means something has gone wrong somewhere.

gateway

One of the most intelligent connections between networks. Compare *bridge* and *router*.

gig

An abbreviation for *gigabyte*.

gigabyte

A measure of computer memory, disk space and the like that's equal to 1024 *megabytes* (1,073,741,824 *bytes)*, or about 179 million words. Sometimes a gigabyte is treated as an even billion bytes but, as you can see, that's almost 74 million bytes short. Sometimes abbreviated *gig* (more often in speech than in writing). Compare *K* and *megabyte*.

Get Info window

The window that appears when you choose *Get Info* from the File menu (or hit ⌘ I). It tells you the size of the selected file, folder or disk, when it was created and last modified, and where it resides. There's also a space for entering comments and, in the case of a file or a disk, a box for locking and unlocking it.

GIGO *(GUY-go)*

Garbage in, garbage out. In other words, you're not going to get good information out of your computer if you put junk information into it.

glitch

Although sometimes used as a synonym for *bug, glitch* strictly means a sudden voltage surge or electromagnetic pulse that causes a piece of hardware to malfunction. More generally, *glitch* means a design flaw in hardware, or any suddenly occurring problem or interruption. It's not usually applied to software, but when it is, it means a design flaw and not a bug. (See *bug* for more on the distinction.) *Glitch* comes from the Yiddish *glitshen,* which means *to slip.*

glossary, Glossary

1. In English, uncapitalized, a glossary is a list of definitions like this one.

2. Capitalized, in Microsoft Word (and some other applications), a Glossary is a set of abbreviations linked with longer text entries. You type ⌘ Delete , followed by the abbreviation—*wds,* say—and Word automatically inserts the longer phrase—in this case, *wine-dark sea.* (You didn't know Homer wrote *The Odyssey* on a Mac, did you?)

grayed

Another term for *dimmed.*

hacker

Someone who enjoys fooling around with computers in a technical way, programming them and/or doing sophisticated things to the hardware. See usage note at *nerd.*

handshake

What computers do when communicating, in order to establish a connection and agree on *protocols* for the transmission of data.

hang

A kind of *crash* where the Mac ignores input from the mouse and the keyboard, usually requiring you to restart the system. Also called a *freeze*. Compare *bomb*.

hard disk *(or* hard disk drive *or* hard drive*)*

A rigid, usually nonremovable *disk,* and/or the disk drive that houses it. Hard disks store much more data and access it much more quickly than *floppy disks*. Also see *disk*.

hard hyphen

A hyphen that holds the words on either side of it together when it falls at the end of a line, rather than allowing the second word to drop down to the beginning of the next line. Often generated by pressing Option - .

hard space

A space that holds the words on either side of it together when it falls at the end of a line, rather than allowing the second word to drop down to the beginning of the next line. Often generated by pressing Option Spacebar .

hardware

The physical components of a computer system. Compare *software.*

head crash

A mechanical failure of a hard disk drive, in which the *read-write head* comes in contact with the surface of the *platter* itself.

header

A piece of text automatically printed at the top of several pages (although the text may vary from page to page—as it would if it contained page numbers, for example).

hertz

One cycle, occurrence, alteration or pulse per second. The regular electrical current that comes out of a (US) wall socket is 60 Hz—that is, it alternates sixty times a second. Named after the great German physicist, Heinrich Rudolph Hertz (1857–94). Abbreviated *Hz*. Compare *megahertz*.

HFS

A multilevel method of organizing applications, documents and folders on a Mac disk, in which folders can be nested (contained) in other folders. Short for *hierarchical file system*. Compare *MFS*.

hierarchical file system

See *HFS*.

high-level

Said of programming languages that are relatively close to English, rather than to the machine language the computer understands.

highlighting

Making something stand out from its background in order to show that it's selected, chosen or active. On the Mac, highlighting is usually achieved by reversing—that is, by substituting black for white and vice versa, or by reversing colors.

hot spot

The actual part of the *pointer* that has to be positioned over an object in order for a click to select the object (or have some other effect on it). The hot spot of the arrow pointer is its tip, and the hot spot of the crosshairs pointer is its center (where the two lines cross).

human interface

Another name for *user interface*.

Hz

An abbreviation for *hertz*.

I-beam

The shape ($\underline{\mathrm{I}}$) the pointer normally takes when it's dealing with text. Also called the *text tool*.

icon

A graphic symbol, usually representing a file, folder, disk or tool.

idiot-proofing

Designing a product so that mistakes—or, to be realistic, the most *common* mistakes—made by a user will do no harm to the user or the product.

imagesetter

A digital phototypesetting machine, like a Linotronic or a Varityper, that's capable of producing graphic images as well as type. Many imagesetters are PostScript-compatible and therefore can serve as output devices for Macs.

ImageWriter

A line of dot-matrix printers sold by Apple as the standard, low-end choice for use with Macs. Also see *LaserWriters*.

ImageWriter font

Another name for a *bit-mapped font*.

incremental backup

A *backup* in which only the files changed since the previous backup are copied.

information service

A large commercial timesharing computer that gives users access to a wide variety of information. CompuServe and America Online are examples.

init *(in-IT)*

A utility program that works as follows: you put it in your system folder, and the next time you start up your Mac, the init is read into the System and alters the way things work. (If you want to see it in action right away, choose *Restart* from the Special menu.) Short for *initialization program.* Compare *cdev.*

initializing

Preparing a disk for use on the Macintosh. Initializing checks the disk to make sure the media is OK, divides it into *tracks* and *sectors* and sets up a *directory, desktop file* and the like. If a disk contains information, initializing will remove it. Disks can be initialized again and again. Also called *formatting.*

insertion point

The place in a document where the next keystroke will add or delete text. The insertion point is represented by a blinking vertical line and is placed by clicking with the *I-beam* pointer.

interactive mode

When a spelling checker (or any other kind of program) interrupts you as you make a mistake, rather than checking over the entire document (or a part of it) when you're done. Compare *batch mode.*

interCapping

Denise Caruso's wonderfully useful term for capitalizing in the middle of a word (as in product names like *SuperPaint).*

interface

See *user interface.*

interrupt button

One of the two buttons on the *programmer's switch.* It accesses debugging software. Compare *reset button.*

jaggies

If we put even *one* picture in the glossary, it would be like opening the flood gates. So I'm not going to give in to temptation. But jaggies are so *easy* to illustrate and so *hard* to define. Well, here goes: When you enlarge *bit-mapped* characters, they lose their smooth curves (or what look like smooth curves when they're small) and instead display jagged rectilinear staircasing...you know, why don't you just look at the picture on page 357?

K

A measure of computer memory, disk space and the like that's equal to 1024 characters, or about 170 words. Short for *kilobyte*. Compare *megabyte* and *gigabyte*. Also see *mini-K*.

kerning

Closing up the space between certain letter pairs—like *AV* or *To*—to make them look better. Increasing the space between the letters is usually called *letterspacing*.

keyboard command (or keyboard equivalent)

A combination of keystrokes (almost always involving ⌘ and often Shift , Option , Ctrl and/or Caps Lock as well) that executes a command without your having to go up to a menu and choose it. Also called a *key combination*. Compare *menu command*.

key-caps font

A font whose characters represent what the top of a key actually looks like—for example: ⌘ Option Shift A B C .

key combination

Another name for a *keyboard command*.

kilobyte

A measure of computer memory, disk space and the like that's equal to 1024 characters, or about 170 words. Abbreviated *K*. Compare *megabyte* and *gigabyte*. Also see *mini-K*.

LAN *(pronounced as a word, not separate letters)*

An abbreviation for *local area network.*

laser font

Another name for an *outline font.*

laser printer

A computer printer that creates images by drawing them on a metal drum with a laser. The image is then made visible by electrostatically attracting dry ink powder to it, as in a photocopying machine.

LaserWriter

A line of laser printers sold by Apple. Also see *ImageWriters.*

launching

Opening an application.

LCD

1. *Liquid crystal display*—the display technology used on most digital wristwatches and, considerably souped up, on the Mac Portable's screen. Compare *CRT.*

2. *Lowest common denominator*—Sharon's term for simple macros that virtually any macro program can play (because they're nothing more than simple watch-me recordings).

leader

A character that fills the space between the last character of text and the next tab stop. Tabs usually have no leaders—which means the space between the last character and the tab stop is blank. When tabs do have leaders, periods (dots) are most commonly used, but many programs let you choose any leader character you want.

leading *(LEHD-ing)*

The amount of space from the *baseline* of one line of type to the *baseline* of the next. Usually measured in *points.*

list box

A box with scroll bars that appears within a dialog box or other window and lists things—files, fonts or whatever. The Open and Save As dialog boxes each contain a list box, and the Font/DA Mover contains two.

local area network

A *network* of computers and related devices that's confined to a relatively small area, like one office or one building. Abbreviated *LAN*. More often simply called a *network*.

LocalTalk

Apple's cabling hardware for *AppleTalk* networks. Compare *PhoneNET*.

locking

Preventing a file or disk from being changed (until you unlock it). You can lock individual files or whole floppy disks in the Get Info window, and you can also lock a floppy disk by moving the plastic tab in the upper right corner so that you can see through the little square hole. On a disk, another name for locked is *write-protected*.

logging on

Connecting to a computer network.

LQ

Letter-quality. Said of printers.

macro

A command that incorporates two or more other commands or actions. (The name comes from the idea that macro commands incorporate "micro" commands.)

macro program

Software that creates *macros* by recording your keystrokes and mouse clicks or by giving you a sort of pseudo programming language to write them in.

magnetic media

See *media.*

marquee

The rectangle of moving dots that surrounds a selection in some programs. So called for its resemblance to a movie marquee.

MB

An abbreviation for *megabyte.*

media

The generic name for floppy disks, hard disks (the disks themselves, not the devices that record on them), tapes and any other substances that store computer data, usually magnetically.

meg

An abbreviation for *megabyte.*

megabyte

A measure of computer memory, disk space and the like that's equal to 1024K (1,048,576 characters) or about 175,000 words. Abbreviated *MB* or *meg.* Sometimes people try to make a megabyte equal to an even million characters, often for sleazy marketing purposes. I call this smaller "meg" a *minimeg.*

megahertz

A million cycles, occurrences, alterations or pulses per second. Used to describe the speed of computers' clock rates. Abbreviated *MHz.* Also see *hertz.*

memory

The retention of information electronically, on *chips.* Compare *storage.* (For more on the distinction, see pp. 133–34.) There are two main types of memory: *RAM,* which is used for the short-term retention of information (that is, until the power is turned off) and

ROM, which is used to store programs that are seldom if ever changed. Here are some examples of how memory has grown:

machine	RAM	ROM
original Mac	128K	64K
Mac Plus	1MB	128K
Mac II	1–8MB	256K
LaserWriter I	1.5MB	512K
LaserWriter II NTX	2–12MB	1MB

menu

A list of *commands.* Compare *palette.* Also see *pop-down menu, pop-up menu, submenu* and *tear-off menu.*

menu bar

The horizontal area across the top of the screen that contains the *menu titles.*

menu box

A *menu title* or a command in a drop-shadowed box that you click on to display the rest of the menu.

menu command

A command you choose from a menu with the pointer, as opposed to a *keyboard command.* (They might both do the same thing—the difference is simply in how you invoke the command.)

menu title

Both the name by which a menu is called and the way you access it. Menu titles are arranged across the top of the screen in the *menu bar;* when you point to one and hold down the mouse button, the menu pops down.

message box

A box that appears unbidden on the screen to give you some information, and which (unlike a *dialog box)* doesn't require any information back from you. A *bomb* is one example. Also called an *alert box.*

MFS

A single-level method of organizing files and folders on a Mac disk in which folders can only be nested (contained) in other folders on the desktop, not in list boxes. Originally standard on the Mac, MFS has been superseded by *HFS.* The name is short for *Macintosh file system.*

MHz

An abbreviation for *megahertz.*

mini-K

My name for "kilobytes" that are figured at an even one thousand characters instead of the standard 1024.

minimegs

My name for "megabytes" that are figured at an even one million characters instead of the standard 1,048,576 characters (1024K).

mnemonic *(nuh-MAHN-ik)*

Aiding memory. ⌘ S is a mnemonic command, since the *S* stands for *Save,* but ⌘ V (for *Paste)* isn't. Don't confuse *mnemonic* with *Naimonic (irritable, perfectionistic).*

modem *(MOE-dum)*

A device that lets computers talk to each other over phone lines (you also need a communications program). The name is short for *modulator-demodulator.*

modifier key

A key that modifies the effect of the *character key* being pressed. The standard *ADB keyboard* has five modifier keys: [Shift] , [Option] , [⌘] , [Caps Lock] and [Ctrl] .

modules

Parts of a program that are separate yet interconnected.

monitor

The screen (usually a cathode ray tube like those used in TVs) on which a computer displays things so you can read them. Also called a *display,* or simply a *screen.*

monospaced

Said of fonts where all the characters occupy the same amount of horizontal space. Two such fonts on the Mac are Courier and Monaco. Compare *proportionally spaced.*

motherboard

The main *board* in a computer (or other computer device).

mouse button

The button on top of the mouse (using the word *mouse* helps distinguish it from a *button* in a dialog box).

mouse cursor

A barbaric substitute for the perfectly adequate—and infinitely more elegant—term *pointer.* Its use can only be attributed to creeping PC-itis in the Macintosh world.

MS DOS

The original, and still the most popular, *operating system* used on IBM PCs and compatible computers. (The name stands for *Microsoft disk operating system.)* Also sometimes called *PC DOS.*

MultiFinder

An Apple program that allows several applications, including the Finder, to be open at the same time.

multitasking

Said of software or hardware that lets you do more than one thing at once.

multiuser

Said of software or hardware that supports use by more than one person at one time.

nanosecond

A billionth of a second. Used to measure the speed of memory chips, among other things. Abbreviated *NS*.

nerd

Someone who's involved in computers to the exclusion of various social and sartorial skills. The archetypical nerd wears a plastic pocket protector full of pens and is profoundly uneasy conversing with people about anything other than computers. The term is generally used affectionately and many people apply it to themselves in mild and/or humorous self-deprecation. The adjective is *nerdy*.

Usage note: *Nerd* isn't synonymous with *hacker*. Although both terms connote passionate enthusiasm about, and involvement with, computers, *hacker* focuses on the technical sophistication and power that such involvement often produces, while *nerd* focuses on the social price at which such power and sophistication are often bought. Not all nerds are hackers, and not all hackers are nerds (although, of course, many are).

network

Two or more computers (and/or other computer-related devices) connected to share information. Usually the term refers to a *local area network*. Also see *AppleTalk*.

NFNT

The *new font numbering table.* Unlike the earlier numbering system, which only provided 256 numbers, NFNT provides 16,000.

NLQ

Near-letter-quality. Said of printers.

node

Any one of the computers or other devices connected to a network.

NS

An abbreviation for *nanosecond.*

numeric keypad

A grouping of number keys (and other, associated keys) arranged in a rectangle and separate from the regular keyboard.

NumLock *(or Num. Lock)*

On keyboards with a *numeric keypad,* the setting in which the keypad inserts numbers into your document, rather than issuing commands. On most Mac keyboards, there is no key for switching between NumLock and command mode; it's handled by the software instead (although the NumLock light on Apple's extended keyboard doesn't always get triggered by the software).

object-oriented graphic

A picture or other graphic where each object, rather than being made up of separate dots (as in a *bit-mapped* graphic) is treated as a unit, as they are in *draw programs.*

So if you have a bit-mapped rectangle, you can erase a corner of it (say). But you also have to lasso (or somehow group) all the dots to select it as a unit (in order to move it, for example). An object-oriented rectangle can be selected simply by clicking on it, but you can't cut off a corner of it—it has to remain a square (or at least a four-sided polygon of some kind.)

OCR *(pronounced as separate letters)*

Optical character recognition—the ability of software and/or hardware to read text from paper. Unlike a regular scanner that reads text (and everything else) as a series of dots, OCR scanners and software recognize the characters and thus generate editable text, as if someone had typed the characters in.

OEM *(pronounced as separate letters)*

The *original equipment manufacturer*—the actual producer of the basic equipment incorporated into a product and sold under another name. For example, Control Data Corporation makes the CDC Wren hard disks that go into Magic hard drives; Control Data is the OEM.

OEM is also used as an adjective to describe products that are incorporated into products by other companies and marketed by them. So someone might say: *We're thinking of expanding out of the OEM market and selling some products under our own name.*

offline *(or **off-line**)*

Said of things done while you're not actively connected to a computer or a network. For example, you might work on a message off-line, then log onto an electronic mail system to send it. Opposite of *online*.

online *(or **on-line**)*

On, or actively connected to, a computer or computer network. For example, on-line documentation appears on the screen rather than in a manual. Opposite of *offline*.

opening

Expanding an *icon,* or a name in a list box, to a *window*—usually by doubleclicking on it. With disk icons and folders, this happens on the *desktop.* With document icons, the application that created the icon is launched first, then the document is opened within it.

operating system

The basic software that controls a computer's operation. On the Mac, it consists of the System file, the ROMs, the Finder (or a Finder substitute) and related software.

⌷Option⌷

A *modifier key* used mostly for generating special characters.

option character

The character generated by pressing the ⌷Option⌷ key and another character simultaneously.

orphan

A single line (usually the first line of a paragraph) sitting alone at the bottom of a page of text. Compare *widow.*

outline font

A font designed for use on a laser printer or imagesetter. Rather than being composed of separate dots like a *bit-mapped* font, it's made up of an outline of the shape of each letter and can be scaled to any size without degradation of quality. Sometimes also called a *laser font.* Also see *PostScript font.*

overhead

The bytes in a file that aren't taken up by the actual text or other contents, but rather by things like the size, shape and location of the window in which the document appears on the screen, the fonts used, other formatting information, etc.

paged memory management unit

See *PMMU.*

paint

A standard graphics format for low-resolution (72-dpi) bit-mapped images. Compare *EPS, PICT* and *TIFF.*

paint program

A graphics program that generates *bit-mapped graphics* (collections of dots) rather than objects. Compare *draw program.*

palette

A collection of small symbols, usually enclosed by rectangles, that represent tools available in a graphics program. When you click on a box in the palette, the *pointer* changes to that tool. Compare *menu.*

Pantone colors

See PMS.

paragraph widow

See *widow.*

parameter RAM

A small portion of the Mac's RAM that's used to store Control Panel settings and other basic, ongoing information. It's powered by a battery so the settings aren't lost when the computer is turned off (but they are lost if you pull the battery). Also called *PRAM.*

PARC

See *Xerox PARC.*

parking

Locking the *read-write head* of a disk drive securely out of the way, so that neither it nor the media will be harmed if the drive is jarred while being moved.

partition

A section of a hard drive that's treated as a separate disk by the Mac. If you divide your drive into ten partitions, you'll get ten disk icons on the *desktop.* Most hard drives come with their own partitioning software. (See the *partitioning* entry on pp. 178–79 for more details.)

pasteboard

In page layout programs, a storage and work area outside the page, the contents of which don't print out.

pasting

Inserting something into a document from the Clipboard by choosing Paste from the Edit menu or hitting ⌘ V . Also see *copying* and *cutting*.

patch

A relatively small piece of programming *code* added to an existing program to enhance performance or fix a *bug*.

pathname

A list of all the folders a file is in, from the outermost (the disk) to the innermost, and ending with the name of the file itself. Colons are placed between the elements, so pathnames look like this:

hard disk:personal stuff:letters:to family:Happy Birthday, Rita!

This pathname means that a file called *Happy Birthday, Rita!* is in a folder called *to family,* which is in a folder called *letters,* which is in a folder called *personal stuff,* which is on a hard disk called—rather unimaginatively—*hard disk.*

PC

1. Some people who are relatively new to computers (or unsophisticated about them) call *any* personal computer a *PC;* in their usage, even a *Mac* is a PC (what a thought!). But people who've been around for a while know that the term *PC* originated as a nickname for the IBM Personal Computer, which was introduced in 1981, and its various clones. They refer to other kinds of personal computers simply as—brace yourself—*computers,* or by their specific names *(Macs, Apple II's,* etc.) That's the usage followed in this book.

2. Just to complicate things, *PC* is also an abbreviation for *printed circuit.* So be aware that a *PC board* doesn't necessarily go into an IBM PC; in fact, there's one in every Mac.

PC DOS

Another name for *MS DOS.* (It's short for *(IBM) Personal Computer disk operating system.*)

PD

An abbreviation for *public-domain* or *public-domain software.*

peripheral

Any electronic device connected to a computer (e.g., a printer, hard disk, scanner, CD-ROM reader, etc.). Usually *peripheral* only refers to something that's either sold by a third party or that clearly isn't an integral part of the original system. For example, you wouldn't normally think of a keyboard sold with a machine as a peripheral, but you might consider a *third-party* keyboard a peripheral.

PhoneNet

Farallon Computing's cabling hardware for *AppleTalk* networks. Compare *LocalTalk.*

phosphor

The coating on the inside of *CRT's* (the cathode ray tubes used in most computer *monitors* and television sets). When a beam of electrons hits it, the phosphor glows, creating the image on the screen.

pica

A typesetting measure equal (for all practical purposes) to 1/6 of an inch—and exactly equal to 12 *points.*

PICT *(pronounced as a word, not separate letters)*

A standard graphics format for object-oriented graphics. (The name is an abbreviation of *pict*ure.) The original PICT only allowed for eight colors, but the current standard, PICT2, allows for full 32-bit color. You don't need to worry about which kind of PICT you're dealing with—almost everything uses PICT2 now. Compare *EPS, paint* and *TIFF.*

pixel

Any of the little dots of light that make up the picture on a computer (or TV) screen. (The name is short for *pic*ture *el*ement.) The more pixels there are in a given area—that is, the smaller and closer together they are—the higher the *resolution*. Sometimes pixels are simply called *dots*.

platter

In a *hard disk drive*, the rigid substrate to which the information-bearing magnetic coating is applied.

PMMU

The *paged memory management unit* that makes *virtual memory* possible on the Mac (along with the appropriate software, of course). Called the 68851, it's part of the 68030 chip and can be added to the 68020.

PMS

1. The *Pantone Matching System,* an international standard coding system for colors that lets you specify and match them by number.

2. *Premenstrual stress.* I only put this in so I could tell you Roberta Cairney's line about it. She says the reason men are so crazy is that they're *always* premenstrual.

point

A typesetting measure equal (for all practical purposes) to 1/72 of an inch. The size of fonts is typically measured in points. Compare *pica*.

pointer

What moves on the screen when you move the mouse. Its most common shapes are the *arrow* (▸), the *I-beam* (⌶) and the *wristwatch* (I don't have a picture of that one; sorry).

pop down

What the Mac's regular menus actually do. Compare *pull down*.

pop-down menu

The Mac's standard kind of menu (usually—but inaccurately—called a *pull-down* menu). It pops down when you click on the menu title; to keep it extended, you hold down the mouse button. Dragging down the menu highlights each command in turn (except the dimmed ones). Compare *pop-up menu*. Also see *submenu* and *tear-off menu*.

pop-up menu

A Mac menu whose title doesn't appear in the title bar and which, as its name implies, pops up (or out) rather than down. Pop-up menus appear when you click and hold the mouse button on a box that generates them (which is indicated by a drop shadow around the box). Compare *pop-down menu*. Also see *submenu* and *tear-off menu*.

port

Computerese for a *jack* where you plug in the cables that connect computers and other devices together. Most Macs have a *SCSI* port, two *serial* ports (marked for the printer and modem) and others.

PostScript

A page-description programming language developed by Adobe, specifically designed to handle text and graphics and their placement on a page. Used primarily in *laser printers* and *imagesetters*. Compare *QuickDraw*.

PostScript font

An *outline font* that works with PostScript (although PostScript does also make its own versions of *bit-mapped fonts* when you send them to a PostScript printer.)

PRAM *(pronounced PEE-ram, or as one word)*

See *parameter RAM*. Don't confuse this with *PROM*.

print buffer

A hardware device that intercepts a print file on its way to the printer and reroutes it to the buffer's own memory, where it's held until the printer is ready for it. This allows you to continue working on other things while printing. Compare *print spooler*.

printed circuit board

A *board* on which the electrical connections between the *chips* are made by printed metallic ink. Also called a *PC board*. There's one in every Mac.

printer driver

A file that tells the Mac how to send information to a particular kind of printer.

print spooler

A piece of software that intercepts a print file on its way to the printer and reroutes it to the disk, where it's held until the printer is ready for it. This allows you to continue working on other things while the printing takes place. Compare *print buffer*.

program

A group of instructions that tells a computer what to do. Also called *software* and—by members of the Department of Redundancy Department—a *software program*.

programmer

Someone who writes programs, fixes bugs in them, adds new features to them, etc. As opposed to a *user*, who simply uses programs and to whom the programming is invisible (or should be).

programmer's switch

A small piece of plastic that, when installed on a Mac, lets you restart the system (using its *reset button*) or access debugging software (using its *interrupt button*).

PROM *(pronounced as a word, not separate letters)*

A programmable *ROM;* one you can change with a special device.

prompt

On more primitive computers than the Mac, and in the Mac's built-in debugger (accessed by hitting the *interrupt button* on the programmer's switch), a symbol on the screen (often >) that indicates that the computer is waiting for you to tell it what to do.

proportionally spaced

Said of fonts whose characters occupy different amounts of horizontal space, depending on their size. Proportional spacing makes fonts much easier to read. Virtually all Macintosh fonts are proportionally spaced. Compare *monospaced.*

protocols

A set of standard procedures that control how information is transmitted between computers.

public-domain

Said of products you have the right to copy, use, give away and sell, without having to pay any money for the right. Things come into the public domain either because the copyright on them has expired or—as is the case with computer programs—because the copyright holder (usually the author) puts them there. Abbreviated *PD.* Also called *freeware.* Compare *shareware* and *commercial.*

pull down

What most people—including Apple—say the Mac's standard menus do. But it's not true—they *pop* down (or, as Sharon prefers to put it, *drop* down). For more on this earth-shattering distinction, see the rant on pp. 51–52.

QuickDraw

Bill Atkinson's brilliant programming routines that enable the Mac to display graphic elements on the screen with great speed and agility. QuickDraw is also used for outputting text and images to certain (non-PostScript) printers. Compare *PostScript.*

quitting

Leaving an application and returning to the Finder (or a Finder equivalent).

radio buttons

A group of *buttons* only one of which can be on at a time (like the presets on a car radio). If you select one radio button, any other that's selected automatically deselects. Compare *checkboxes.*

RAM *(pronounced as a word, not separate letters)*

The part of a computer's memory used for the short-term retention of information (in other words, until the power is turned off). Programs and documents are stored in RAM while you're using them. The name is short for *random-access memory*—although, actually, just about all kinds of memory are accessed randomly these days. Also see *memory, parameter RAM, contiguous RAM* and *ROM.*

RAM cache *(cash)*

An area of memory set aside to hold information recently read in from disk—so that if the information is needed again, it can be gotten from memory (which is much faster than getting it from disk). The size of the Mac's RAM cache, and whether it's turned on, is set in the Control Panel.

RAM disk

A portion of memory that's set aside to act as a temporary disk.

rdev *(AHR-dev)*

A utility program that displays an icon in the Chooser. *Printer drivers* are an example. *Rdev* is short for Chooser *dev*ice (the *c* was already taken—see *cdev*).

read/write head

The part of a disk drive mechanism that actually deposits information on (writes) and extracts information from (reads) the disk.

reboot

To *boot* again (that was easy). Same as *restart.*

record

In a database program, a collection of related *fields*. For example, in a mailing list, a record might consist of the name, address, city, state, zip code and phone number of one particular person or company.

redraw *(or refresh) rate*

How often the image on the screen is redrawn. (It looks solid, but actually it's being recreated many times a second.)

relational database

A database program that's capable of relating information in one file to that in another.

release version

The version of a program that's actually shipped to purchasers and stores. Theoretically, all the major bugs are out of it by that point. Compare *alpha version* and *beta version*.

reset button

One of the two buttons on the *programmer's switch*. It restarts the Mac. Compare *interrupt button*.

resolution

The number of *dots* (or *pixels)* per square inch (or in any given area). The more there are, the higher the resolution.

restart

To cause a computer to reload its *operating system* from disk, as if you just turned it on, but without actually turning off the power. When you restart, you lose all work that you haven't *saved.*

Restart

When capitalized, a command on the Finder's Special menu that (amazingly enough) *restarts* the Mac. Compare *Shut Down*.

⌐Return⌐

In text, the ⌐Return⌐ key causes the insertion point to move to the beginning of the next line. Elsewhere, it's often used to confirm an entry or a command.

ROM *(rahm)*

The part of a computer's memory used to store programs that are seldom or never changed. The name is short for *read-only memory,* because you can read information from it but can't write information to it the way you can with *RAM.* A *ROM* chip is often called simply *a ROM.* Also see *memory.*

ROMs *(the Mac's)*

ROMs built into every Mac that contain part of its operating system. They were originally 64K, then 128K, 256K and 512K, with each subsequent version containing more *system software.*

root directory (or root level)

The *disk window*—the window that contains all the folders and files on a disk. (So called because if you imagine the organization of folders and files on a disk as branches on a tree, this would be the root.)

router

One kind of device that connects separate networks. Compare *bridge* and *gateway.*

sans serif

Said of a font that has no *serifs (sans* being French for *without).* Optima is sans serif font.

Save As...

A standard Mac command that lets you save a document under a different name and/or in a different location (and sometimes in a different format).

saving

Transferring information—usually a document—from memory to a disk.

scanner

A device that converts images into digital form so that they can be stored and manipulated by computers.

Scrapbook

A *desk accessory* that stores material permanently and gives you easy access to it no matter what program you're in.

screen

Another name for a *monitor.*

screen blanker

Another name for a *screen saver.*

screen dump

Another name for a *screen shot.*

screen font

The *bit-mapped* version of an *outline font,* used to represent the font on the computer's screen.

screenful

The amount of text (or other data) displayed at any one time on the screen. Used when talking about scrolling—e.g., *clicking here scrolls you up one screenful.* Also called a *windowful* (as in: *it's a windowful, s'marvelous, that you should care for me).*

screen saver

A program designed to prevent the *phosphor* on a computer screen from getting exhausted. Screen savers keep track of how long it's been since you hit a key or the mouse button and automatically black out the screen (or put a moving pattern on it) after a certain amount of time has passed. Hitting any key or the mouse button brings back the image that was on the screen before. Also called a *screen blanker.*

screen shot

A picture of what's currently on the screen (or on some portion of it), sent directly to a printer or saved to disk.

script

What a *program* or *routine* you write in HyperCard is called. Some other programs, like FileMaker and MicroPhone, also use the term.

scroll arrow

The arrow at either end of the *scroll bar.* Clicking on a scroll arrow moves the window's view up or down one line. Clicking on a scroll arrow and holding the mouse button down results in relatively smooth and continuous scrolling.

scroll bar

A rectangular bar that appears on the right and/or bottom edges of a window when there's more in it than what's displayed. Clicking in the gray area of the scroll bar moves the window's view up or down one screenful. Also see *scroll arrow* and *scroll box.*

scroll box

The white box in a *scroll bar* that indicates how what's displayed in a window relates to the total contents. So, for example, if the box is at the halfway point of the scroll bar, you're looking at the middle of the document. Dragging the scroll box allows you to scroll large distances.

scrolling

Moving through the contents of a window or a list box in order to see things not currently displayed (normally done with the *scroll bar, scroll arrow* and *scroll box).* In word processing programs and list boxes, scrolling is usually vertical, but in many other places, horizontal scrolling is equally likely.

SCSI

An industry-standard interface for hard disks and other devices that allows for very fast transfer of information. It's short for *small computer system interface* and is pronounced *scuzzy* by virtually everyone (officially, you're supposed to pronounce the individual letters, but I think I'd faint if I ever heard anyone do that). SCSI ports have been standard on all Macs since the Plus.

search path

Where a computer looks for something (i.e., on what disks and in what folders).

sector

A 512-byte section of a *track*. The basic unit of storage space into which files are saved.

selecting

Telling the Mac what you want to be affected by the next command or action. If what you're selecting is in the form of discrete objects, you normally select them by clicking on them. If it's in the form of a continuum, you normally select part of it by dragging across it.

The two most important concepts for understanding the Mac are:

- Selecting—in and of itself—never alters anything.

- You always have to select something before you can do anything to it.

(the) selection

Whatever is selected (and thus will be affected by the next command or action). The insertion point is also a kind of selection, because it indicates where the next event will take place (unless you move it).

selection rectangle

On the *desktop* and in many applications, a dotted box that appears when you click on an empty spot and drag. When you release the mouse button, the box disappears (or becomes a *marquee)* and everything that fell within it is selected. (In some programs, objects must fall entirely within the selection rectangle to be selected; in others, any object touched by the selection rectangle, however slightly, is selected.)

serial port

Either of the jacks on the back of a Mac into which you can plug printers, modems, etc. *(Serial* refers to the fact that data is transmitted through these ports serially—one bit after another—rather than in parallel—several bits side by side.)

serif

A little hook, line or blob added to the basic form of a character to make a font more readable (or for decoration). *Serif* is also used as an adjective to describe a font that has serifs; the font you're reading (Benguiat) is a serif font. Compare *sans serif*.

shareware

Software that's distributed on the honor system, usually through bulletin boards, user groups, information services, etc. You're allowed to try it out and give copies to others, and you only pay the (usually nominal) registration fee if you decide you want to continue using it. Compare *commercial* and *public-domain*.

Shift

Either of two *modifier* keys on the Mac's keyboard that are used to make letters uppercase and for many other purposes (for example, see *shift-clicking*).

shift-clicking

Holding down the Shift key while clicking the mouse button. Shift-clicking allows you to select multiple objects or large amounts of text, depending on the application.

Shut Down

A command on the Finder's Special menu that prepares the Mac to be turned off (or actually turns it off, depending on which model Mac you have). Compare *Restart*.

SIG (pronounced as a word, not separate letters)

A *special interest group* that's part of a larger organization like a *user group*.

SIMM (pronounced as a word, not separate letters)

A *single in-line memory module*—a package for memory chips used in many models of the Mac.

68000 *(sixty-eight thousand)*

A *CPU chip* used in the original 128K Mac, the 512K Mac, the Mac Plus, the SE, the Portable, the original LaserWriter, the LaserWriter Plus, the LaserWriter II SC and the LaserWriter II NT.

68020 *(sixty-eight oh twenty, or sometimes simply oh twenty)*

A faster and more powerful *CPU chip* than the *68000,* used in the Mac II, the LaserWriter II NTX and in many accelerator boards.

68030 *(sixty-eight oh thirty, or sometimes simply oh thirty)*

A faster and more powerful *CPU chip* than the *68020,* which is used in the Mac IIx, cx, ci, fx and the SE/30.

68851 *(sixty-eight eight fifty-one)*

See *PMMU.*

68881 *(sixty-eight eight eighty-one)*

The math *coprocessor* chip used in the Mac II.

68882 *(sixty-eight eight eighty-two)*

The math *coprocessor* chip used in the Mac IIx, cx, ci, fx and the SE/30.

size box

An icon consisting of two overlapping boxes, found in the bottom right corner of most *windows,* that allows you to change the window's size and shape. Compare *close box* and *zoom box.*

slot

A place in a computer where you can install a *card.* Also called an *expansion slot,* since it allows you to expand the computer's capabilities.

software

The instructions that tell a computer what to do. Also called *programs* or, redundantly, *software programs.* Compare *hardware.*

Usage note: *Software* is a *stuff* word (like *butter* or *money),* not a *things* word. It's no more correct to say *two softwares* than it is say *two stuffs.*

special interest group

See *SIG.*

spooler

See *print spooler.*

spread

Two facing pages. (Technically, this is a *two-page spread,* and *three-page spreads* and more are possible. But these don't come into play much on the Mac.)

standard menus

The three menus—, File and Edit—that appear at the left end of the menu bar in virtually all applications.

startup disk

The disk that contains the *System file* and the *Finder* the Mac is currently using. You can change it, so it doesn't necessarily have to be the disk you actually started up the Mac with.

startup document

How *inits* are usually labelled if you look at them in a text view in the Finder.

stationery

A feature of many programs that lets you create various default documents, with different margins, fonts, included text, etc. Unlike a regular document, which opens with the name you've given it, stationery opens as an untitled document (or makes you choose a name for the new document before it will open).

storage

The long-term retention of information magnetically (on *disks* or tapes) or optically (on *CD ROMs*). It persists after you turn your computer off. Compare *memory*. (For more on the distinction, see pp. 133–34.)

string

Any specified sequence of characters—a word, a phrase, a number, whatever. The term is usually used in the context of searching and replacing; for example: *type in the string you want to find, hit the tab key, then type in the string you want to replace it with.*

strobe

Another name for *flicker.*

style

A variation on a font—like bold, italic, outline or shadow. In this sense, it's also called a *type style.* Compare *Style.*

Style

In Word and other programs, a Style is a grouping of formats. In this book, we capitalize this meaning of the word, to avoid confusion (as much as possible) with *style* (see the previous definition).

submenu

A menu whose title is an item on another menu, and which appears to the right of that menu when you choose its title (or to the left, if there's not enough room on the right).

suitcase file *(or simply* suitcase*)*

A file that stores *fonts* or *desk accessories,* and is identified in the Finder by its suitcase-shaped icon. You add fonts or desk accessories to a suitcase file, or remove them from it, with Font/DA Mover. You can open (activate) suitcase files (so their contents will appear on menus) with font/DA management programs like Suitcase or Font/DA Juggler Plus.

support

Help with computer problems (either hardware or software), usually in the form of verbal advice. Support can be provided either by the vendor that sells you the product or by its manufacturer or publisher.

SYLK

Microsoft's *symbolic link* format for data transfer (especially between spreadsheets and databases).

sysop *(SISS-ahp)*

The person who runs a bulletin board (short for *system operator*).

system bomb

See *bomb*.

system crash

See *crash*.

system disk

Any disk containing the *system software* the Mac needs to begin operation (i.e., the System file and either the Finder or a Finder substitute). If it contains the system software you're using to run your Mac at the moment, it's the *startup disk*.

System file *(or simply the System)*

The basic program the Mac uses to start itself and to provide certain basic information to all applications. The System file can't be launched like a regular application; instead, it launches itself when you start up the Mac and insert a disk that contains it. Together with the Finder, the System file comprises what—on other computers—is called the *operating system*.

system folder

A standard folder on Mac disks that contains the System file, the Finder and other system software.

system hang

See *hang*.

system heap

The area of memory set aside for storing system information about fonts, DAs, chooser resources, init files, etc.

system software

A catchall term for the basic programs that help computers work; it includes *operating systems*, programming languages, certain utilities and so on. Some examples of systems software on the Mac are the Finder, the System, the Chooser, the Control Panel, the Font/DA Mover and printer drivers like the ImageWriter, LaserWriter and Laser Prep files.

[Tab]

In text, the [Tab] key moves the insertion point to the next tab stop. In databases, spreadsheets, dialog boxes and the like, it often moves the insertion point to the next area where information can be inserted (in other words, to the next field, cell, text box or whatever).

tab-delimited

Said of database programs and files that follow the Mac standard of using [Tab] to separate *fields*.

tear-off menu

A menu you can remove from the *menu bar* and move around the screen like a window. It stays fully extended when detached, so you don't have to pop it down every time you want to use it. Tear-off menus always remain in front of open document windows. Compare *pop-down menu*, *pop-up menu* and *submenu*.

telecommunicating

Transferring information between computers over telephone lines.

template *(TEM-plit, not -plate)*

A document with a special format you use repeatedly. You modify it to the present use and save it with a different name.

text box *(or **text field**)*

An area, usually in a *dialog box*, where you insert text.

text file

An *ASCII* file—just characters, no formatting.

(the) **text tool**

Another name for the *I-beam pointer*.

third-party

Said of hardware or software that doesn't come from the maker of what you're using it with, and that you didn't develop yourself. A couple of examples are a non-Apple hard disk you attach to your Mac, or a spelling checker not published by the publisher of the word processing program you're using it with.

TIFF *(pronounced as a word, not separate letters)*

A standard graphics format for high-resolution (greater than 72-dpi) bit-mapped images, like those generated by most scanners. The name is an abbreviation of *tagged image file format*. Compare *EPS*, *paint* and *PICT*.

title bar

The horizontal strip at the top of a *window* that contains its name. When the window is active, it's filled with six horizontal stripes and has a *close box*. To move a window, you drag it by the title bar.

toggle

Something which turns off and on each successive time you access it. For example, the common type styles (bold, italic, etc.) are toggles, because the first time you choose them from the menu (or with a command), they turn on, and the next time they turn off.

Other kinds of toggles are *checkboxes* and menu commands that switch names (e.g., *Show Ruler, Hide Ruler*).

tracking *(or track kerning)*

Changing the letter spacing in a selected piece of text, in order to pull a word up from the line below, or to loosen up a line that's too tight (that is, one in which the words are too tightly squeezed together).

tracks

Imaginary concentric circles running around a disk, which are divided into *sectors* and are used for storing data.

transparent

Said of programs that work so smoothly and intuitively that you forget they're there. *Transparency* lets you concentrate on your work, rather than having to hassle with the software.

Trojan Horse program

A program that conceals and transports a *virus*.

Turing test

A method devised by the brilliant British mathematician and logician Alan M. Turing (1912–54) to decide, without prejudice, whether what a computer does can be called thinking. You type questions and statements into a computer that's connected to a computer in another room, and try to determine, by means of the remote computer's replies, whether it's being handled by another person or by a program.

If you think you're talking to a human when you're actually talking to a program, then (Turing's argument goes) the remote computer must be considered capable of thinking, since what it's doing is indistinguishable from what we call thinking when people do it. All computers so far would fail the Turing test (as would most newscasters)—except in limited areas, like playing chess, where computers (but not newscasters) are among the best in the world.

Undo

A standard Mac command ($\boxed{⌘}\boxed{Z}$) that undoes the last text that was typed or the last editing or formatting command that was given. Many commands can't be undone, and the ones that can vary with the application.

In any well-written Mac program, *Undo* is a *toggle*, so you can flip back and forth between two versions of something until you decide which you prefer. Ideally, there are several levels of undo, so you can go back past the last thing you did.

Unix

An operating system developed by Bell Labs for minicomputers but now also used on microcomputers like the Mac.

uploading

Sending a file to a distant computer from your own. Opposite of *downloading*.

user

Someone who simply uses programs, as opposed to a *programmer*, who writes them. It's like the difference between an automobile mechanic and a driver. Just as you don't need to know how a carburetor works to be an expert driver, you don't need to know anything about programming to be an expert Macintosh user.

user (or users) group

A club made up of people who are interested in computers in general, a particular kind of computer, a particular kind of software or even an individual program. They're typically nonprofit and independent of any computer manufacturer or publisher. Also see *SIG*.

user interface

The way a computer (or a computer program) communicates with people; what it's like to use.

utilities

Programs that perform tasks that are either relatively simple (like searching for specific files on disk) and/or that are support tasks for *applications* (like checking the spelling in a document).

vaporware

Software that was announced a while ago but still hasn't shipped.

video card

A *card* you plug into your Mac that controls an external monitor.

virtual memory

A technique that lets a computer treat part of a hard disk as if it were *RAM*.

virus

A program that functions on your computer without your consent. A benign virus may do nothing more than duplicate itself, but some are meant to destroy data.

widow

A single line (usually the last line of a paragraph) sitting alone at the top of a page of text. Compare *orphan*.

Widow is sometimes also used to refer to a single word (or a few short words) forming the last line of a paragraph. In this sense, it's sometimes called a *paragraph widow*.

wildcard

A symbol that means *any character* or *any sequence of characters* (just as a wild card in poker can stand for any card). Wildcards are useful in searches.

window

An enclosed area on the Mac's screen that has a *title bar* (which you can use to drag the window around). Disks and folders open into windows, and documents appear in windows when you're working on them. Compare *box.*

windowful

The amount of text (or other data) displayed at any one time in a window. Used when talking about scrolling (e.g., *clicking here scrolls you up one windowful*). Also called a *screenful.*

word wrap

The feature, found in virtually all computer programs that generate text, that automatically moves you down to the next line when the line you're on is full, without your having to type Return .

wristwatch

The form the pointer normally takes (and *should* take) when you have to wait for the Mac to do something. (Unfortunately, some poorly written programs don't always implement this feature, or do so less often than they need to.)

x-height

The height of lowercase letters in a font (not counting *ascenders* and *descenders*). In a font with a high x-height, lowercase letters like *x* are closer to the height of the caps than they are in a font with a low x-height. Helvetica, Bookman and Benguiat have relatively high x-heights; Times and Zapf Chancery have relatively low x-heights.

Xerox PARC *(ZEER-ahks PARK)*

Xerox Corporation's Palo Alto Research Center where most of the early work was done on what became the Mac's *user interface.* Often called simply *PARC.*

zone

A subdivision of a network.

zoom box

A small box on the right side of the title bar of most windows. Clicking on the zoom box expands the window to fill the screen; clicking again returns it to its original size and shape. (In many Microsoft products, you can do the same thing by simply doubleclicking on the title bar.) Compare *close box* and *size box*.

Appendix B

List of companies and products

There are two kinds of entries in this appendix: company listings, which give you the address, phone number(s) and products; and product listings, which refer you to the company listings. When names of products and companies are so similar that the two listings would be right next to each other (e.g., FoxBASE and Fox Software), we drop the product listing. Entries are alphabetized as if spaces and hyphens didn't exist; thus Digital Darkroom comes before Digit-Art, and AppleCare comes before Apple Computer.

We spent a fortune in phone calls and time trying to get addresses and phone numbers for every company, but we weren't able to succeed 100%. When our information is partial, we give you what we have. Please don't bother calling us up to ask us for addresses or phone numbers not listed here; if they're not here, we don't have them. See Chapter 19 for some magazines where you might be able to find them.—AN

Aask / CE Software

Acius
10351 Bubb Rd
Cupertino CA 95014
408/252-4444; fax: 408/252-0831
 4th Dimension

Acta, Acta Advantage / Symmetry

Active Window, The /
 Boston Computer Society

ADB cables / Kensington
 Microware; Monster Cable

ADB keyboards and mouse /
 Apple Computer

Addison-Wesley
Route 128, Jacob Way
Reading MA 01867
617/944-3700;
 orders: 800/447-2226
 Human Interface Guidelines
other books written by Apple

Address Book / Leitch, Jim

Address Book Plus / Power Up

Adobe Systems
1585 Charleston Rd
Box 7900
Mountain View CA 94039
415/961-4400
 Adobe Type Manager
 Font Pac (for ATM)
 Illustrator
 outline fonts
 PostScript
 Smart Art
 StreamLine
 Type Reunion

Aesthetic Engineering
175 Duane St
New York NY 10013
212/925-7049
 Music Mouse

Affinity Microsystems
1050 Walnut St, #425
Boulder CO 80302
800/367-6771; 303/442-4840
  Tempo

After Dark /
  Berkeley Systems Design

AIC (Advanced Information Concepts)
  MacBak AR
  SyQuest drives

Airborne / Silicon Beach

Aker, Sharon Zardetto
  (writer and consultant)
20 Courtland Dr
Sussex NJ 07461
AppleLink d6145 or c/o the
  NJMUG BBS, 201/388-1676

Aladdin Systems
Deerpark Center, #23A-171
Aptos CA 95003
408/685-9175
  ShortCut
  StuffIt
  StuffIt Pro

Alderman, Eric
  (HyperCard programmer)
The HyperMedia Group
5900 Hollis St, #O
Emeryville CA 94608
510/601-0900

Aldus
411 First Av S
Seattle WA 98104
206/622-5500

tech support: 206/628-2040
customer relations: 206/628-2320
  FreeHand
  PageMaker

Allen, Christopher *(software developer and consultant)*
Consensus Development
Box 2836
Union City CA 94587
415/487-9206

Alliance Peripheral Systems (APS)
2900 S 291 Hwy
Independence MO 64111
800/233-7550; 816/478-8300
  Quantum and Wren drives
  other hardware

Alsoft
22557 Aldine Westfield
Spring TX 77373
713/353-4090
  Disk Express
  Font /DA Juggler

Altsys
269 Renner Rd
Richardson TX 75080
214/680-2060; fax: 214/424-9033
  Fontastic Plus
  Fontographer

America Online
8619 Westwood Center Dr
Vienna VA 22182
800/227-6364 x5257
  information service

AntiToxin / Mainstay

Apache Strike / Silicon Beach

AppleCare *(extended service contract)* / Apple Computer

Apple Computer
20525 Mariani Av
Cupertino CA 95014
408/996-1010
    ADB cables, keyboards and
        mouse
    AppleCare (extended service
        contract)
    AppleLink
    AppleShare
    AppleTalk
    Backgrounder (print spooler)
    bit-mapped fonts
        (Chicago, Geneva, etc.)
    CD-ROM drive
    Desktop Manager
    Easy Access
    Ethernet cards
    File Exchange Software
    FindFile DA
    Home Position Switch Kit
    HyperCard
    ImageWriters
    InterPol
    Key Caps DA
    LaserWriters
    LocalTalk
    Macintalk
    Macintosh computers
    MacroMaker
    Mini System Setup Folder
    monitors
    outline fonts (Times, Helvetica,
        Courier, Symbol)
    PrintMonitor
    QuickDraw
    ResEdit
    scanner
    Scrapbook DA
    SCSI
    SuperDrive (FDHD)
    toner cartridges
    TrueType
    VirusRx

AppleLink / Apple Computer

AppleShare / Apple Computer

AppleTalk / Apple Computer

APS / see Alliance Peripheral Sys.

Arborworks
431 Virginia Av
Ann Arbor MI 48103
800/346-6980; 313/747-7087;
    fax: 313/747-8775
    SCSI Tools

ArchiCAD / Graphisoft

Arkanoid / Discovery Software

**Art & Technology of Typography,
    The** / Compugraphic

Artext Electronic Publishing
124 O'Connor St, #500
Ottawa, Ontario, Canada
    K1P 5M9
    INITinfo

Artisto+ / Taylor, Tom

Artworx
1844 Penfield Rd
Penfield NY 14526
800/828-6573; 716/385-6120
    Bridge

Asante Technologies
1050 E Duante Av, #G
Suynnyvale CA 94086
408/736-3360
    Ethernet cards

Ashton-Tate
20101 Hamilton Av
Torrance CA 90502
213/329-8000
tech support: 213/329-0086
    Full Impact
    FullPaint
    FullWrite Professional

Automation Group
340 Townsend St, #432
San Francisco CA 94107
415/777-9167
    Hypercard stack development

AutoSave / Magic Software

Avery International
Consumer Products Division
Azusa CA 91702
    labels for printers and disks

Backgrounder *(print spooler)* /
    Apple Computer

Berkeley Systems
1700 Shattuck Av
Berkeley CA 94709
510/540-5535
    Stepping Out

Bernoulli drives / Iomega

BigCaps / Dubl-Click Software

Bitstream
Athenaeum House
215 First St
Cambridge MA 02142
800/522-3668; 617/497-6222
    PostScript fonts

BIX Information Service / BYTE

BlackOut / Mark 3 Software

Blind Watchmaker, The /
    Norton, W.W.

Blue Cloud Software
    (Ken McLoud)
    Scroll Limit (freeware)

Blyth Software
1065 E Hillsdale Blvd, #300
Foster City CA 94404
800/843-8615 (CA: 800/223-
    8050); 415/571-0222
    Omnis

BMUG
1442 A Walnut St, #62
Berkeley CA 94709
help line: 510/849-HELP; BBS:
    510/549-BMUG; recording:
    510/849-9114; office: 510/
    849-9114; fax: 510/849-9026
    BMUG on HyperCard
    public-domain and shareware
    disks

Bond, Bill
12950 Walnut Way Terrace
St. Louis MO 63146
    FreeTerm

Boston Computer Society
48 Grove St
Somerville MA 02144
617/625-7080
  The Active Window
  Macintosh SIG

Bradley, Michael (technical writer)
3825 14th Av
Oakland CA 94602
510/482-2862

Bravo Technologies
Box 10078
Berkeley CA 94709
510/841-8552
  MacCalc

Bridge / Artworx

Broadcast / Lindenberg, Joachim

Brøderbund
17 Paul Dr
San Rafael CA 94903
800/521-6263; 415/492-3200
  Electronic Whole Earth Catalog
  Jam Session
  The Manhole
  TypeStyler
  Star Wars
  Where in Europe Is Carmen
    Sandiego?

Brown, Byron (page layout)
1516 Beverly Pl
Albany CA 94706
510/527-6374

Bryan, Steve
529 S 7th St, #625
Minneapolis MN 55415
  INIT & INIT Manager

Byte Magazine / BIX

Calculator Construction Set /
  Dubl-Click Software

Calendar DA / Mosaic Codes
  (David Ostler)

Cambridge North America
424 Cumberland Av
Portland ME 04101
207/761-3700
  Z88 (laptop computer)

**Canned Art: Clip Art for the
  Macintosh** / Peachpit Press

Canon USA
One Canon Plaza
Lake Success NY 11042
516/488-6700
  SX and CX marking engines

Capture / Mainstay

Carina Software
830 Williams St
San Leandro CA 94577
510/352-7328
  Voyager

Casady & Greene
Box 223779
Carmel CA 93922
ordering: 800/359-4920; 408/
    624-8716; fax: 408/624-7865
  Fluent Fonts (bit-mapped)
  Fluent Laser Fonts
  QuickDex

Cayman Systems
26 Landsdowne St
Cambridge MA 02139
617/494-1999
  Ethernet cards

CDC Wren / Control Data, APS

CE Software
1854 Fuller Rd
Des Moines IA 50265
515/224-1995
  Aask
  DialogKeys
  Disktop
  HeapFixer
  LaserStatus
  MockWrite
  QuicKeys
  QuickMail
  Vaccine
  Widgets

Century Software
2306 Cotner Av
Los Angeles CA 90064
714/829-4436
  LaserFonts
  Start-Up On & Start-Up Off

CH Products
970 Park Center Dr
Vista CA 92083
800/624-5804; 619/598-2518
  RollerMouse

CheckNet / Farallon Computing

Christenson, Steve
  SuperClock
Donations to:

Stanford Children's Hospital
520 Sand Hill Rd
Palo Alto CA 94304

Claris
5201 Patrick Henry Dr
Box 58168
Santa Clara CA 95052
US upgrades: 800/544-8554; US
  dealers: 800/334-3535; cust.
  relations: 408/727-8227; tech
  support: 408/727-9054
  Claris CAD
  FileMaker Pro
  MacDraw
  MacPaint
  MacProject
  MacWrite
  Public Folder
  Smart Forms

Clarity / Mark 3 Software

Clear Lake Research
5615 Morningside, #127
Houston TX 77005
713/523-7842
  HyperArrays

Clement, Jerry *(Macintosh artist)*
45 Creek Rd, Fairfax CA 94930
415/485-1535

ClickArt *(bitmap images)* /
  T/Maker

ClickPaste / MainStay

ClipOut / T/Maker

Clipper, The / Solutions

Coastal Associates Publishing
301 Howard St
San Francisco CA 94105
415/243-3500
  MacWeek

Cobb Group, The
Box 35160
Louisville KY 40232
800/223-8720; 502/491-1900
  Excellence
  The Word 4 Companion

Coleman, Dale
  (writer and consultant)
630 Grand View, #108
San Francisco CA 94114

Color Test Pattern Generator /
  Pina, Larry

Colour Billiards / SoftStream

Complete Delete / MicroCom

Complete Undelete / MicroCom

Compugraphic Type Division
AGFA
90 Industrial Way
Wilmington MA 01887
800/424-8973; 508/658-5600
  Art & Technology of Typography
  outline fonts

CompuNet / Trimar USA

CompuServe
5000 Arlington Centre Blvd
Columbus OH 43220
800/848-8199; 614/457-0802
  E-Mail
  Navigator

Computer Care
Ford Center, #1180
420 N 5th St
Minneapolis MN 55401
800/950-2273; 612/371-0061
  upgrade kits

Computer Cord Keeper /
  Computer Covers Unlimited

Computer Covers Unlimited
7969 Engineer Rd, #104
San Diego CA 92111
800/ PC COVERS; 619/277-0622
  Computer Cord Keeper
  screen filters
  keyboard protector
  Nycov dust covers

Comstock
30 Irving Pl
New York NY 10003
212/353-8686
  photos in TIFF format

ConcertWare Plus / Great Wave
  Software

Connect
10161 Bubb Rd
Cupertino CA 95014
800/262-2638; 408/973-0110
  MacNet

Connectix
125 Constitution Dr
Menlo Park CA 94025
800/950-5880; 415/324-0727
  Virtual 2.0

Consolidated Printers
2630 8th St
Berkeley CA 94710
510/843-8524
contact: Michelle Selby

Control Data
2992 E La Palma, #D
Anaheim CA 92806
714/693-2000
   CDC Wren hard disk
   mechanisms

CrystalPaint /
   Great Wave Software

Cultural Resources
7 Little Falls Way
Scotch Plain NJ 07076
201/232-4333
   Culture 1.0

Culture 1.0 / Cultural Resources

Curator, The / Solutions

Custom Memory Systems
826 N Hillview Dr
Milpitas CA 95035
   SyQuest drives

Dark Castle / Silicon Beach

DAtabase / Preferred Publishers

DataDesk International
9314 Eton Av
Chatsworth CA 93311
800/592-9602 (CA: 800/826-
   5398)
   HyperDialer
   MAC-101 keyboard

DataFrame hard disks /
   SuperMac

DataPak drives / Mass
   Microsystems

Dataviz
35 Corporate Dr
Trumbull CT 06611
203/268-0030
   MacLinkPlus

Dayna Communications
50 S Main St, 5th Fl
Salt Lake City UT 84144
800/531-0600; 801/531-0203;
   fax: 801/359-9135
   DaynaTalk

DaynaTalk / Dayna
   Communications

Daystar Software
5906 NW Walnut Creek Dr
Kansas City MO 64152
816/741-4310
   Fast Cache

DefaultFont / Dubl-Click
   Software

DeltaPoint
200 Heritage Harbor, #G
Monterey CA 93940
800/367-4334; 408/648-4000
   MindWrite

Deluxe Music Construction Set /
   Electronic Arts

Deneba Systems
3305 NW 74th Av
Miami FL 33122
800/622-6827; 305/594-6965
    Spelling Coach
    Spelling Coach Professional

DesignStudio / Letraset USA

DeskJet Plus / Hewlett-Packard

Desktop Express / Dow Jones

Desktop Manager/ Apple
    Computer

DeskWriter / Hewlett-Packard

DialogKeys / CE Software

Diconix printers / Eastman
    Kodak

Digital Darkroom / Silicon Beach

Digit-Art / Image Club Graphics

Dinosaur Discovery Kit /
    First Byte

Discovery Software
163 Conduit St
Annapolis MD 21401
301/268-9877
    Arkanoid

Disinfectant / Norstad, John

DisKeeper / Geagan, J.

DiskExpress / Alsoft

DiskTools / Electronic Arts

Disktop / CE Software

DMP-130 *(printer)* / Radio Shack

Double Helix / Odesta

Dove Computer
1200 N 23rd St
Wilmington NC 28405
800/622-7627; 919/763-7918
    acclerator cards
    Ethernet cards
    fax modem
    memory upgrades

Dow Jones
Box 300
Princeton NJ 08543
609/452-7040
    Desktop Express

Dubl-Click Software
9316 Deering Av
Chatsworth CA 91311
818/700-9525; fax: 818/700-9727
    Big Caps
    Calculator Construction Set
    Default Font
    Font Charter
    MenuFonts
    Utility City (font)
    WetPaint (clip art)
    World Class Fonts

Dynodex / Portfolio Systems

Eastman Kodak
Box 3527
Mission Viejo CA 92690
    Diconix printers

Easy Access / Apple Computer

Ehman Engineering
97 S Red Willow Rd
Box 2126
Evanston WY 82931
800/257-1666; 307/789-3830;
    fax: 307/789-4656
    hard disks

'88 Vote, The / Optical Data

Electronic Arts
1820 Gateway Dr
San Mateo CA 94404
800/245-4525; 415/571-7171
    Deluxe Music Construction Kit
    DiskTools
    Thunder

Electronic Publishing & Printing /
    MacLean Hunter Publishing

Electronic Whole Earth Catalog /
    Brøderbund

E-Machines
9305 SW Gemini Dr
Beaverton OR 97005
503/646-6699; fax: 503/641-0946
    monitors

Empower / Magna

Epson printers / Seiko Epson

Eradicate'Em / Platt, Dave

Ergonomic Computer Products
    (Mike Skaar)
1753 Greenwich St
San Francisco CA 94123
415/ 673-5757
    ergonomic hardware
    screen filters

Ergotron
3450 Yankee Dr, #100
Eagan MN 55121
800/888-8458; 612/452-8135;
    fax: 612/452-8346
    MacTilt
    mouse cleaning kit
    The Muzzle

EtherGate / Shiva

Ethernet cards / Apple Com-
    puter, Asante Technologies,
    Cayman Systems, Dove Com-
    puter, Excelan

Ettore, Richard
67, rue de la Limite
1970 W. Oppen
Belgium
    Sound Mover

Excel / Microsoft

Excel consultants / Sobin, Marty;
    Umlas, Robert

Excelan
2180 Fortune Dr
San Jose CA 95131
408/434-2300
    Ethernet cards

Excellence / Cobb Group, The

Exodus Software
8620 Winton Rd, #304
Cincinnati OH 45231
513/522-0011
    Retriever

Exposure / Preferred Publishers

Farallon Computing
2000 Powell St., #600
Emeryville CA 94608
510/596-9000
  CheckNet
  Liaison
  MacRecorder
  PhoneNet cables & connectors
  repeaters
  Star Controller
  Timbuktu

Fast Cache / Daystar Software

Fast Forms / Power Up

FastPath / Shiva

Ferret / Nedry, Larry

Fiems, Guy
Av. Leopold III, 77
B 1970 Wezembeek-Oppem
Belgium
  Tidy It Up!

Fifth Generation Systems
10049 N Reiger Rd
Baton Rouge LA 70809
800/873-4384; 504/291-7221
  PowerStation
  Pyro
  Suitcase

File / Microsoft

File Exchange Software /
  Apple Computer

FileMaker Pro / Claris

FindFile DA / Apple Computer

Findswell / Working Software

First Byte
3100 S Harbor Blvd, #150
Santa Ana CA 92704
713/432-1740 (outside CA: 800/
  523-8070); fax: 714/432-7057
  Dinosaur Discovery Kit

Fluent Fonts / Casady & Greene

flyback transformer parts kits /
  Soft Solutions

Font/DA Juggler / Alsoft

Font Charter / Dubl-Click Software

Font Company, The
12629 N. Tatum Blvd, #210
Phoenix AZ 85032
800/442-FONT; 602/998-9711;
  fax: 602/998-7964
  PostScript fonts

Fontastic Plus / Altsys

FontDisplay / Shulman, Jeffrey

Fontographer / Altsys

FontShare / Olduvai

FontSizer / U.S. MicroLabs

For the Record / Nolo Press

4th Dimension / Acius

Fox Software
134 W So. Boundary
Perrysburg OH 43551
419/874-0162; fax: 419/894-8678
  FoxBASE

FreeHand / Aldus

FreeTerm / Bond, Bill

Full Impact / Ashton-Tate

FullPaint / Ashton-Tate

FullWrite Professional /
   Ashton-Tate

GDT Softworks
4664 Lougheed Hwy, #188
Burnaby BC Canada V5C 6B7
800/663-6222
   JetLink Express
   PrintLink Collection

Geagan, J.
7-H Laurel Hill Rd
Greenbelt MD 20070
   DisKeeper

General Computer
580 Winter St
Waltham MA 02154
617/890-0880
   hard disks
   laser printers

GOfer / Microlytics

Goldstein & Blair
Box 7635
Berkeley CA 94707
510/524-4000; fax: 510/524-4185

Graphisoft
400 Oyster Point Blvd, #517-A
South San Francisco CA 94080
800/344-3468, 415/266-8720
   ArchiCAD

Great Gantt! / Varcon Systems

Great Wave Software
5353 Scotts Valley Dr
Scotts Valley CA 95066
408/438-1990
   ConcertWare
   CrystalPaint
   KidsTime

Hammermill Paper
1540 East Lake Rd
Erie PA 16533
814/456-8811
   paper for laser printers

Hayes Microcomputer Products
705 Westech Dr
Norcross GA 30092
404/449-8791; 404/441-1617
   InterBridge
   modems

Headmaster / Prentke Romich

HeapFixer / CE Software

Hewlett-Packard
19310 Pruneridge Av
Cupertino CA 95014
800/752-0900
   DeskJet Plus
   DeskWriter
   LaserJet cartridge

Hidden Agenda / Spinnaker
   (previously from Springboard)

Home Position Switch Kit /
   Apple Computer

Human Interface Guidelines /
Addison-Wesley

HyperArrays / Clear Lake
Research

HyperCard / Apple Computer

HyperCard stack development /
Automation Group,
HyperMedia Group

HyperDA / Symmetry

HyperDialer / DataDesk
International

HyperMedia Group
5900 Hollis St, #O
Emeryville CA 94608
510/601-0900
　HyperCard stack development

Icom Simulations
648 S Wheeling Rd
Wheeling IL 60090
800/877-ICOM; 708/520-4440
　On Cue

Icon-It! / Tactic Software

Igra, Mark
1588 Henry St, #2
Berkeley CA 94709
　QuickFolder

Illustrator / Adobe Systems

Image Club Graphics
1902-11th St SE, #5
Calgary, Alberta, Canada T2G 3G2

800/661-9410; 403/262-8008
　Digit-Art
　photos in TIFF format
　PostScript fonts

Images with Impact / 3G
　Graphics

ImageWriter / Apple Computer

Imaging Products
12696 Rockhaven Rd
Chesterland OH 44026
216/285-2813
　labels for laser printers
　paper for laser printers
　transparency film for laser
　　printers

Individual Software
125 Shoreway Rd, #3009
San Carlos CA 94070
tech support: 800/331-3313;
　415/595-8855
　101 Macros for Excel
　101 Scripts & Buttons For
　　HyperCard

Informix Software
16011 College Blvd
Lenexa KS 66219
800/438-7627; 913/599-7100
　Wingz

Infosphere
4730 SW Macadam Av
Portland OR 97201
　(now defunct)

In-House Software
170-J Brisco Rd
Arroyo Grande CA 93420
805/481-7822
In-House Accountant

INIT & INIT Manager /
Bryan, Steve

Init CDEV / Rotenstein, John

INITinfo / Artext Electronic
Publishing

INITPicker / Microseeds
Publishing

Insignia Solutions
254 San Geronimo Way
Sunnyvale CA 94086
800/848-7677; 408/522-7600
SoftPC

InterBridge / Hayes
Microcomputer Products

InterPol / Apple Computer

Intuit
Box 3014
Menlo Park CA 94026
800/624-8742; 415/322-0573
Quicken

Iomega
1821 W 4000 S
Roy UT 84067
800/456-5522; 801/778-3000
Bernoulli drives

**ITC (International Typeface
Corporation)**
2 Hammarskjold Plaza
New York NY 10017
212/371-0699
outline fonts

Jam Session / Brøderbund

Japanese clip art /
Qualitas Trading

Jasmine
1740 Army St
San Francisco CA 94124
800/347-3228; 415/282-1111
hard disks

JetLink Express / GDT Softworks

JoliWrite / Widemann, Benoit

Kensington Microware
251 Park Av S
New York NY 10010
800/535-4242; 212/475-5200
cables
floor stands
screen filters
tilt/swivel stands
trackballs
TurboMouse

keyboard protector / Computer
Covers Unlimited

Key Caps / Apple Computer

Key Tronic
Box 14687
Spokane WA 99214
800/262-6006; 509/927-5515
MacPro keyboard

KidsTime / Great Wave Software

Koala Technologies
70 N 2nd St
San Jose CA 95113
tech support: 408/287-6311;
    408/287-6278
    MacVision

Koontz, Ty (indexer)
4000 West Plantation
Tucson AZ 85741
602/744-2258

Kwikee InHouse Pal Potpourri /
    Multi-Ad Services

Labels / Avery International

LaserJet / Hewlett-Packard

LaserOneCopy / Wolfson, Rich

LaserStatus / CE Software

Learning Company, The
6493 Kaiser Dr
Fremont CA 94555
800/852-2255; 510/792-2101
    Reader Rabbit

Leitch, Jim
61 Shaughnessy Blvd
Willowdale, Ontario, Canada
    M2J 1H9
    Address Book
    Set Clock

Lester (cordless mouse) /
    Lightwave Technologies

Letraset USA
40 Eisenhower Dr
Paramus, NJ 07653
800/343-8973; 201/845-6100
    DesignStudio
    Ready,Set,Go!

LetterPerfect
6606 Soundview Dr
Gig Harbor WA 98335
206/851-5158
    PostScript fonts

Letter Writer Plus / Power Up

Levco
6181 Cornerstone Ct E, #101
San Diego CA 92121
619/457-2011; fax: 619/457-2325
    Monster Mac

Liaison / Farallon

Liberty Systems
122 Saratoga Av, #16
Santa Clara CA 95051
408/983-1127
    hard disks

Lightwave Technologies
Box 599
Mundelein IL 60060
708/362-6555; fax: 708/816-1189
    Lester (cordless mouse)

Lindenberg, Joachim
Sommerstrasse 4
7500 Karlsruhe 1, West Germany
AppleLink GER.XSE0010
    Broadcast

Linear B / Palmer, Gary

Linotronic 100 , 300, 500 /
   Linotype

Linotype
425 Oser Av
Hauppauge NY 11788
800/633-1900; 516/434-2000
   Linotronic 100, 300, 500

Little Mac Book / Peachpit Press

LocalTalk / Apple Computer

Long, William
Digital Microware
Box 3527
Mission Viejo CA 92690
   SCSI Evaluator

Looking Good in Print /
   Ventana Press

Lookup / Working Software

Lotus Development
55 Cambridge Pkwy
Cambridge MA 02142
617/577-8500
   Lotus Express

Lotus Express / Lotus
   Development

L-View Display System /
   Sigma Designs

MacArtist
Box 10072
Costa Mesa CA 93627
   MacArtist

MacBak AR / AIC

MacCable line / Monster Cable

MacCalc / Bravo Technologies

MacCalligraphy / Qualitas Trading

MacConnection
14 Mill St
Marlowe NH 03456
800/334-4444; fax: 603/4467791

MacDraw / Claris

Macgard / Systems Control

MacGuide Report
444 17th St, #200
Denver CO 80202
800/873-1454

MacinStor hard disks / Storage
   Dimensions

Macintalk / Apple Computer

MacInTax / Softview

Macintosh Buyer's Guide /
   Redgate Communications

Macintosh computers /
   Apple Computer *[If you need this
   entry, you're in serious trouble.—AN]*

Macintosh Font Book, The /
   Peachpit Press

**Macintosh Repair & Upgrade
   Secrets** / Pina, Larry

Macintosh Video News
215 Union Blvd, #401
Lakewood CO 80228
303/988-0102

MacInUse / Softview

The Mac Is Not a Typewriter /
Peachpit Press

MacLean Hunter Publishing
29 N Wacker Dr
Chicago Il 60606
312/726-2802
Electronic Publishing & Printing

MacLinkPlus / Dataviz

Mac•Man / SoftStream

MacNet / Connect

MAC-101 Keyboard /
DataDesk International

MacPaint / Claris

MacPro Keyboard / Key Tronic

MacProducts USA
8303 MoPac Expwy, #218
Austin TX 78759
800/622-3475; 512/343-9441;
fax: 512/343-6141
Magic drives

MacProject / Claris

MacRecorder / Farallon
Computing

MacroMaker/ Apple Computer

MacTable / ScanCo

MacTilt / Ergotron

Mac 286 *(NuBus card)* /
Orange Micro

MacUser / Ziff-Davis Publishing

MacVision / Koala Technologies

MacWEEK / Coastal Associates
Publishing

Macworld
502 Second St, 5th Fl
San Francisco CA 94107
415/243-0505

MacWrite / Claris

Magic drives / MacProducts USA

Magic Software
2206 Franklin St
Bellevue NE 68005
800/342-6243; 402/291-0670
AutoSave

Magna
2540 N First St, #302
San Jose CA 95131
408/433-5467
Empower

Magnum Software
21115 Devonshire St, #337
Chatsworth CA 91311
818/700-0510
McPic

Mail / Microsoft

MainStay
5311-B Derry Av
Agoura Hills CA 91301
818/991-6540
AntiToxin
Capture
ClickPaste

Maitreya Design
Box 1480
Goleta CA 93116
   miniWRITER

Makeover Book, The /
   Ventana Press

Managing Your Money /
   MECA Ventures

ManHole, The / Brøderbund

Mark 3 Software
29 Grey Rocks Rd
Wilton CT 06897
   BlackOut
   Clarity
   To Do!

Mass Microsystems
810 W Maude Av
Sunnyvale CA 94086
800/522-7979; 408/522-1200;
   fax: 408/733-5499
   DataPak drives
   SyQuest Cartridges

MCI Mail
1150 17th St NW, #800
Washington DC 20036
800/444-6245; 202/833-8484

McPic / Magnum Software

MECA Ventures
327 Riverside Av, Bldg D
Westport CT 06880
203/226-2400
   Managing Your Money

MECC
3490 Lexington Av N
St Paul MN 55126-8097
800/228-3504; 612/481-3500
   Number Munchers
   Word Munchers

MegaGraphics
439 Calle San Pablo
Camarillo CA 93012
800/ITS-MEGA; 805/484-3799;
   fax: 805/484-5870
   monitors

MenuFonts / Dubl-Click Software

MicroCOM Software Division
Box 51816
Durham NC 27717
919/490-1277
   Complete Delete
   Complete Undelete

Microlytics
2 Tobey Village Office Pk
Pittsford NY 14534
800/828-6293; 716/248-9150
   GOfer
   Word Finder

MicroPhone / Software Ventures

Microseeds
7030 B West Hillsborough Av
Tampa FL 33634
813/882-8635
   INITPicker
   Redux
   Screen Gems

MicroSoft
1 Microsoft Way
Redmond WA 98052
800/426-9400; 206/882-8080, -
     8088
   Excel
   File
   Mail
   QuickBASIC
   Word
   Works
   Write

MicroTech
158 Commerce St
East Haven CT 06512
800/626-4276; 203/468-6223
   Ricoh removable hard disk
     drives
   SyQuest removable hard disk
     drives

Microworld
1514 University Av
Berkeley CA 94703
510/845-2000
   Z88 (laptop computer)

MindWrite / DeltaPoint

Mini System Setup Folder /
   Apple Computer

MiniWRITER / Maitreya Design

Mobius Technologies
5835 Doyle St
Emeryville CA 94608
800/669-0556; 510/654-0556;
     fax: 510/654-2834
   monitors
   SE Silencer (fan)

MockWrite / CE Software

Molé, Chris *(page layout)*
510/284-4255

Moniterm
5740 Green Circle Dr
Minnetonka MN 55343
612/935-4151
   Viking monitors

Monster Cable
274 Wallis Way
San Francisco CA 94080
415/871-6000
   cables

Monster Mac / Levco

More / Symantec

Mosaic Codes (David Oster)
2140 Shattuck, #2036
Berkeley CA 94704
510/540-8077
   Calendar DA

mouse cleaning kit / Ergotron

MouseEase / Teclind Design

Multi-Ad Services
1720 W Detweiller Dr
Peoria IL 61615
309/692-1530
   Kwikee InHouse Pal Potpourri
   ProArt

MultiFinder / Apple Computer

Music Mouse / Aesthetic
   Engineering

Muzzle, The / Ergotron

NABVICU
Box 1352
Roseville CA 95661
voice: 916/783-0364
modem: 916/786-3923

National Tele-Press
Box 79
Mendocino CA 95460
800/448-0988; 707/937-2848
  SuperMOM

Navigator / Compuserve

NetBridge / Shiva

NetModem / Shiva

NetSerial / Shiva

New Horizons Software
206 Wild Basin Rd
Austin TX 78746
512/328-6650
  WordMaker

Nisus / Paragon Concepts

Nolo Press
950 Parker St
Berkeley CA 94710
510/549-1976
  For the Record
  WillMaker

NoRad
1549 11th St
Santa Monica CA 90401
213/395-0800

Norstad, John
Academic Computing and
  Network Service
Northwestern University
2129 Sheridan Rd
Evanston IL 60208
  Disinfectant

Norton, W.W.
500 Fifth Av
New York NY 10110
  The Blind Watchmaker

Number Munchers / MECC

NuvoTech
2015 Bridgeway, #204
Sausalito CA 94965
800/232-9922; 415/331-7815
  TurboStar

Nycov covers / Computer Covers
  Unlimited

Odesta
4084 Commercial Av
Northbrook IL 60062
800/323-5423; 708/498-5615
  Double Helix

Olduvai
7520 Red Rd, #A
South Miami FL 33143
800/822-0772; 305/665-4665
  FontShare

Omnis / Blyth Software

On Cue / Icom Simulations

101 Macros for Excel / Individual
  Software

101 Scripts & Buttons for Hyper-Card / Individual Software

Optical Data
30 Technology Dr
Warren NJ 07059
800/524-2481; 908/668-0022
  The '88 Vote

Orange Micro
1400 N Lakeview Av
Anaheim CA 92807
714/779-2772; fax: 714/779-
  9332, -9978
  Mac 286 NuBus card

Page Studio Graphics
3175 N Price Rd, #1050
Chandler AZ 85224
602/839-2763
  PIXymbols Fonts

PageMaker / Aldus

Page Works
Box 14493
Chicago Il 60614
312/348-1200; fax: 312/404-0717
  The Page

Palmer, Gary
Center for Computing Applications
Humanities Dept
University of Nevada
Las Vegas NV 89154
702/739-3011
  Linear B

Panorama / ProVUE

Paragon Concepts
990 Highland Dr, #312
Solana Beach CA 92075
619/481-1477
  Nisus

Peachpit Press
1085 Keith Av
Berkeley CA 94708
800/283-9444; 510/527-8555
  Canned Art:
  The Little Mac Book
  The Macintosh Font Book
  The Mac Is Not a Typewriter

Peripheral Land
47421 Bayside Pkwy
Fremont CA 94538
800/288-8754; 800/657-2211
  Syquest removable hard drives

Personal Laser Printer /
  General Computer

Personal Press /
  Silicon Beach Software

Personal Publishing
25W550 Geneva Rd
(that's not a typo: 25W550)
Wheaton IL 60188
708/665-1000
  Personal Publishing

PhoneNET cables & connectors /
  Farallon Computing

Pina, Larry (author and consultant)
47 Meadow Rd
Westport MA 02790
  Color Test Pattern Generator
  Macintosh Repair & Upgrade
    Secrets

Pivot monitor / Radius

PIXymbols fonts / Page Studio
  Graphics

Platt, Dave
  Eradicate'Em

Playroom, The / Prolog Software

PMMU Chip / Connectix

Polic, Robert
  SCSI Probe

Portfolio Systems
158 Flushing Av
Brooklyn NY 11205
800/729-3966; 718/935-9501
  Dynodex

PowerStation / Fifth Generation
  Systems

Power Up
2929 Campus Dr
Box 7600
San Mateo CA 94403
415/345-5900
  Address Book Plus
  Fast Forms
  Letter Writer Plus

Preferred Publishers
1770 Moriah Woods Blvd, #14
Memphis TN 38117
800/829-3383 (sales only)
901/683-3383
  DAtabase
  Exposure

PrintLink Collection / GDT
  Softworks

PrintMonitor / Apple Computer

Prodigy Services
445 Hamilton Av
White Plains NY 10601
800/222-6922 x205
  information service

Prograph / TGS Systems

Prolog Software
Box 1446
Henderson TX 75653
214/657-7394
  The Playroom

ProVUE
15180 Transistor Ln
Huntington Beach CA 92649
714/892-8199; fax: 714/893-4899
  Panorama

Public Folder / Claris

Publish It! / Timeworks

Pyro / Fifth Generation Systems

Qualitas Trading *(Enzan-Hoshigumi)*
6907 Norfolk Rd
Berkeley CA 94705
510/848-8080
    Japanese clip art
    MacCalligraphy

Quark
300 S Jackson, #100
Denver CO 80209
800/356-9363; 303/934-2211, -0784
    QuarkXpress

QuickBASIC / Microsoft

QuickDex / Casady & Greene

QuickDraw/ Apple Computer

Quicken / Intuit

QuicKeys / CE Software

QuickFolder / Igra, Mark

QuickMail / CE Software

Quote Init / Stein, Lincoln D.

Radio Shack
Box 1052
Ft. Worth TX 76101
817/390-3011
    DMP-130 printer

Radius
1710 Fortune Dr
San Jose CA 95131
408/434-1010; fax: 408/434-0127
    accelerator boards
    monitors

Rae Productions International
Box 647
Gales Ferry CT 06335
    The Weigand Report

RasterOps
2500 Walsh Av
Santa Clara CA 95051
800/468-7600; 408/562-4200
    monitors

Reader Rabbit / The Learning Co.

Ready,Set,Go! / Letraset USA

Redgate Communications
660 Beachland Blvd
Vero Beach FL 32963
407/231-6904
    Macintosh Buyer's Guide

Redux / Microseeds Publishing

removable hard disks / Syquest

repeaters / Farallon Computing,
    TOPS/Sitka

ResEdit / Apple Computer

Retriever / Exodus Software

Return to Dark Castle /
    Silicon Beach

**Ricoh removable hard disk
    drives** / MicroTech

Rodime
851 Broken Sound Pkwy
Boca Raton FL 33487
407/994-5585
    hard disk drive mechanisms

RollerMouse / CH Products

Rotenstein, John
Box 165
Double Bay, NSW, 2028 Australia
    Init CDEV

R-Server / Solana Electronics

SAM / Symantec

ScanCo (Scandinavian Computer Furniture Company)
Box 3217
Redmond WA 98073
800/722-6263; 206/481-5434
    MacTable

Schwartz, Steven
    (writer and consultant)
876 Paso
Lake Havasu City AZ 86403
602/453-1921

Scrapbook / Apple Computer

Screen Gems / Microseeds

screen filters / Computer Covers
    Unlimited, Ergonomic
    Computer Products,
    Kensington Microware

Scroll Limit / Blue Cloud
    Software

SCSI Evaluator / Long, William

SCSI Probe / Polic, Robert

SCSI Tools / Arborworks

Seiko Epson /Epson America
2780 Lomita Blvd
Torrance CA 90505
213/534-4234
marketing: 213/539-9140
    Epson printers
    Seikosha SP-1000AP

Seikosha SP-1000AP / Epson
    America

Selby, Michelle /
    see Consolidated Printers

SE silencer / Mobius Technologies

Set Clock / Leitch, Jim

SetPaths / Snively, Paul

SF Scroll Init / Hertzfeld, Andy

Shiva
One Cambridge Center
Cambridge MA 02141
617/864-8500
    EtherGate
    FastPath
    NetBridge
    NetModem
    NetSerial

ShopKeeper Software
Box 38160
Tallahassee Fl 32315
904/222-8808
    ShopKeeper-4

ShortCut / Aladdin Systems

Shulman, Jeffrey
Box 1218
Morgantown WV 26504-1218
304/598-2090
  FontDisplay
  Virus Detective

Sigma Designs
46501 Landing Pkwy
Fremont CA 94538
510/770-0100
  L-View Display System

Silicon Beach Software
9770 Carrol Center Rd, #J
San Diego CA 92126
619/695-6956; fax: 619/695-7902
  Airborne
  Apache Strike
  Dark Castle
  Digital Darkroom
  Personal Press
  Return to Dark Castle
  SuperCard
  SuperPaint

SmartArt / Adobe Systems

Smart Forms / Claris

SmartKey / Volaski, Maurice

SmartScrap / Solutions

Snively, Paul
1035 Aster Av, #2174-H
Sunnyvale CA 94086
  SetPaths

Sobin, Marty *(Excel consultant)*
91 Fox Hollow Road
Sparta NJ 07871
201/729-9492

SoftPC / Insignia Solutions

Soft Solutions
907 River Rd, #98
Eugene OR 97404
503/461-1136; fax: 503/461-2005
  flyback-transformer parts kit

SoftStream
19 White Chapel Dr
Mt Laurel NJ 08054
800/262-6610; 609/866-1187
  Colour Billiards
  Mac Man

Softview
1721 Pacific Av, #100
Oxnard CA 93033
800/622-6829; 805/388-5000
  MacInTax
  MacInUse

Software Ventures
2907 Claremont Av, #220
Berkeley CA 94705
510/644-3232, -9275
CA: 800/336-3478
  MicroPhone

Solana Electronics
4907 Morena Blvd
San Diego CA 92117
619/573-0800
  R-Server

Solutions
Box 783
Williston VT 05495
802/865-9220
  The Clipper
  The Curator
  Smart Scrap

Sound Master / Tomlin, Bruce

Sound Mover / Ettore, Richard

Spectrum HoloByte
2061 Challenger Dr
Alameda CA 94501
510/522-1164
 Tetris

Spelling Coach Professional /
 Deneba Systems

Spellswell / Working Software

Spinnaker Software
201 Broadway
Cambridge MA 02139
617/494-1200
800/826-0706
 Hidden Agenda
 (formerly from Springboard)
 Springboard Publisher

Springboard Publisher /
 Spinnaker Software

Star Controller / Farallon
 Computing

Start-up On & Start-up Off /
 Century Software

Star Wars / Brøderbund

Stein, Lincoln D.
44 Boynton St, #2
Jamaica Plain MA 02130
 Quote Init

Stepping Out / Berkeley Systems

Storage Dimensions
2145 Hamilton Av
San Jose CA 95125
408/879-0300
 MacinStor hard disks

StreamLine / Adobe Systems

StuffIt and StuffIt Pro / Aladdin

Suitcase / Fifth Generation

SUM / Symantec

Sun Microsystems
950 Marina Village Pkwy
Alameda CA 94501
800/445-8677; 510/769-8700
 TOPS

SuperCard / Silicon Beach

SuperClock / Christenson, Steve

SuperDrive (FDHD) /
 Apple Computer

SuperLaserSpool / SuperMac

SuperMac Technologies
485 Potrero Av
Sunnyvale CA 94086
408/245-2202
 DataFrame hard disks
 SuperLaserSpool

SuperMOM / National Tele-Press

SuperPaint / Silicon Beach

Symantec
10201 Torre Av
Cupertino CA 95014
408/253-9600
CA: 800/626-8847
US: 800/441-7234
More
SAM
SUM

SyQuest
47923 Warm Springs Blvd
Fremont CA 94539
510/490-7511
removable hard disk cartridges
(supplied OEM to the
following manufacturers,
who build hard disk drives
around them: AIC, Custom
Memory Systems, Mass
Microsystems, MicroTech,
Peripheral Land)

Systems Control
Box 788-M
North US #2
Iron Mountain MI 49801
800/451-6866; fax: 906/779-4219
MacGard

Tactic Software
11925 SW 128th St
Miami FL 33186
305/378-4110
ArtClips
ArtFonts
FontShare
Icon-It!

Taylor, Tom
3707 Poinciana Dr, #137
Santa Clara CA 95051
Aristo+

Teclind Design
250 Cowper St
Palo Alto CA 94301
MouseEase

Tempo / Affinity Microsystems

Tetris / Spectrum HoloByte

TGS Systems
1127 Barrington St, #19
Halifax, Nova Scotia, Canada
B3H 2P8
800/565-1978; 902/429-5642
Prograph

3G Graphics
#6155-R, 11410 NE 124th St
Kirkland WA 98034
800/456-0234; 206/823-8198
EPS clip art

3M
Bldg 225-35-05, 3M Center
St. Paul MN 55144
612/733-1110
product info: 612/733-5454
Vacuum

Thunder / Electronic Arts

ThunderScan / Thunderware

Thunderware
21 Orinda Way
Orinda CA 94563
510/254-6581; fax: 510/254-3047
ThunderScan

Tidy It Up! / Fiems, Guy

Timbuktu / Farallon Computing

Timeworks
444 Lake Cook Rd
Deerfield IL 60015
708/948-9200
  Publish It!

T/Maker
1390 Villa St
Mountain View CA 94041
415/962-0195
  ClickArt
  WriteNow

To Do! / Mark 3 Software

Tomlin, Bruce
15801 Chase Hill, #109
San Antonio TX 78256
  Sound Master

TOPS / Sun Microsystems

TOPS /Sitka
950 Marina Village Pkwy
Alameda CA 94501
800/445-TOPS; 510/769-9669
  repeaters

Torii, Connie *(page layout)*
510/548-5976

Trackballs / Kensington

TrafficWatch / LanRanger

Travis, Esther *(Macintosh artist)*
2728 Yale St
Vancouver BC V5K1C3 Canada
604/255-4109

Trimar USA
236 W 15th St
New York NY 10011
800/872-4454; 212/645-7008
  CompuNet

TrueType / Apple Computer

TurboMouse / Kensington

TurboStar / NuvoTech

Type Manager / Adobe

Type Reunion / Adobe

TypeStyler / Brøderbund

Umlas, Robert *(Excel consultant)*
424 White Oak Rd
Palisades NY 10964
914/359-2150

U.S. MicroLabs
1611 Headway Cr, Bldg #3
Austin TX 78754
512/339-0001
  FontSizer

UtilityCityLaser *(font)* /
  Dubl-Click Software

Vaccine / CE Software

Vacuum / 3M

Varcon Systems
10509 San Diego Mission Rd
San Diego CA 92108
619/563-6700
  Great Gantt!

Varityper
11 Mt. Pleasant Av
East Hanover NJ 07936
201/887-8000
  Varityper

Ventana Press
Box 2468
Chapel Hill NC 27515
919/942-0220
  Looking Good in Print

Verbum
Box 15439
San Diego CA 92115
619/233-9977; fax: 619/233-9976

Viking monitors / Moniterm

Virtual 2.0 / Connectix

Virus Detective / Shulman,
  Jeffrey

VirusRx / Apple Computer

Volaski, Maurice
173 Princeton Av, #2
Amherst NY 14226-5006
716/838-6663
  SmartKeys

Voyager / Carina Software

Weigand Report, The / Rae
  Productions International

Weigand, C.J. (writer &consultant)
Box 647
Gales Ferry CT 06335

WetPaint / Dubl-Click Software

**Where in Europe Is Carmen
  Sandiego?** / Brøderbund

Widemann, Benoit
68, avenue d'Italie
Paris, France 75013
  JoliWrite

Widgets / CE Software

WillMaker / Nolo Press

Wingz / Informix Software

Wire mesh filters / NoRad

Wolfson, Rich
Montclair State College
Department of Technology
Montclair NJ 07043
201/893-4163
  LaserOneCopy

Women's Empowerment Project
415/439-0629
  data entry and checking

Word / Microsoft

Word Finder / Microlytics

Word 4 Companion / Cobb Group

WordMaker / New Horizons

Word Munchers / MECC

WordPerfect Corp.
1555 N Technology Way
Orem UT 84057
800/451-5151; 801/225-5000
  Findswell

Working Software
Box 1844
Santa Cruz CA 95061
800/229-9675; 408/423-5696
  Findswell
  Lookup
  Spellswell

Works / Microsoft

World Class Fonts / Dubl-Click
  Software

Wren *(hard disk mechanisms)* /
  Control Data, APS

Write / Microsoft

WriteNow / T/Maker

Z88 (laptop computer) /
  Cambridge North America;
  Microworld

Ziff-Davis Publishing
950 Tower Ln, 18th Fl
Foster City CA 94404
415/378-5600
  MacUser

From the WetPaint clip art collection.
Copyright © 1988–89 by
Dubl-Click Software Inc.
All rights reserved.

Lesson 3 D. Street Scene   G CLEMENT

Index

Tips for, and features of, specific programs are indexed only under the program name. Only the most common Mac-standard commands (⌘X for Cut, for example) are listed under the keystrokes that generate them. Other commands are simply indexed under their names (as are icons and symbols). Entries for margin icons are subdivided by chapters (and by sections, where necessary).

Entries are only capitalized to indicate proper names (or other words which are always capitalized).They're alphabetized as if spaces and hyphens didn't exist; thus copying comes before copy protection and E-mail comes before em dashes. Numbers are alphabetized as if spelled out, according to the most common pronunciation (for example, 68020 is alphabetized as if written sixty-eight oh twenty).

Page numbers **in boldface** *indicate extended or important discussions (including whole sections and chapters on the subjects cited). With a few exceptions, items in Appendix A (the glossary), Appendix B (the list of companies and products) and the Acknowledgments aren't in-dexed.—Ty Koontz/AN*

C

F

O

W

X

Y

Z

From the WetPaint clip-art collection.
Copyright © 1988–89 by Dubl-Click Software Inc.
All rights reserved.

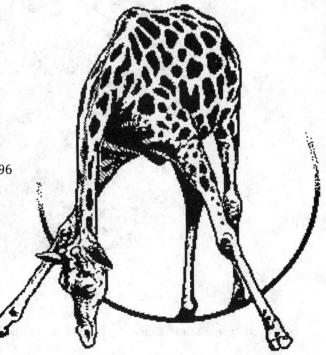

Lesson 3 E. Morning Light · © CLEMENT

The most useful book I have ever purchased.
ROBERT BARON, NORTHRIDGE CA

By far the most useful and interesting how-to book I've ever seen—on any topic.... A remarkable achievement.
ELLIOT ARONSON, SANTA CRUZ CA

Exceedingly well done. I've acquired just about every help book published for the Mac and yours is the best.
FRED J. KEENE, GREENVILLE ME

The single most useful book in my extensive computer library.
FRANK STOBBE, CARLSBAD CA

Everyone in our office is competing for it.
GEORGE D. HERMANN, PORTOLA VALLEY CA

Great book! I have to keep track of who uses it so it won't disappear.
ELLEN TOWNSEND, DUBLIN CA

I've spent the last three months searching for such a book.
JACK COREY, SANTA CLARA CA

Apple should include this with every Mac.
MICHAEL A. SHOEMAKER, LONG BEACH CA

I didn't expect so much humor in a reference book. It's great!
GRETCHEN S. SMITH, REDWOOD CITY CA

Your "Bible" is indispensible. Rarely do you find such a combination of knowledge, common sense and enthusiasm...Congratulations!
JOANNE M. YATES, ST. HELENA CA

Wonderful! It's like having a private teacher.
LEE EVAN BELFIGLIO, BELLEVUE WA

Don't know what I'd do without it.
SUSAN WESEL, WOODLAND HILLS CA

I couldn't manage without it.
SHARYN STILLMAN, LOS ANGELES

Several lifetimes' worth of hints.
ROBERT M. COTE, SANTA MONICA CA

Saved my *** often! Thanks.
KATHY FLETCHER, SAN JOSE CA

**Within five minutes of opening it,
I had a solution to a problem.**
KIERNAN BURKE, BOSTON MA

A tremendous timesaver!
MICHAEL LA BROOY, BRITISH COLUMBIA, CANADA

Paid for itself in one evening's use.
FRED MATICA, PORTLAND OR

Worth $100.
DON CHESTERS, ROSEVILLE MI

Worth a million.
CHRIS D'ANGELO, WAGONTOWN PA

**Although you state that it's not intended to be read
cover to cover...I have read it cover to cover—twice!**
JUDIE CRUMMEL, SAN FRANCISCO

As good as curling up with a favorite novel.
SUZANNE SLADE, SAN FRANCISCO

Once you start reading it, you can't put it down!
BRAD HOLIFIELD, ANCHORAGE

Addictive reading.
STEVEN MINTA, DAVIS CA

I use it constantly and read it over and over. Thanks!
SYLVIA WILSON, LOS ANGELES

I couldn't put it down.
MARSHA PATO, MILLBRAE CA

My constant companion.
J.T. DOCKING, BRIGHTON, SOUTH AUSTRALIA

A true Bible.
MARY AGAN, PHOENIX AZ

A Godsend. Thanks for writing it.
VALARIE A. SHEPPARD, AKRON OH

**I keep it by my bedside—which is more than I can
say for the King James version!**
LAUREN M. GEE, NEW YORK CITY

Now I can tell my mother I read the Bible every day.
RANDY PREUSS, BURNSVILLE MN

**Very useful! A lot easier to follow
than the instruction manuals.**
KAREN CANTOR, LONGWOOD FL

Written for normal, nontech minds.
GASPAR P. CHACON, SANTA FE NM

**I'm a new Mac user and your Bible made a huge
difference in my getting comfortable and
feeling confident. Thanks!**
STANLEY SELIB, SHARON MA

I wish I'd had this book when I first bought my Mac.
RICHARD D. VETTER, AIEA HI

I love the book!
PATRICIA ARNOLD, BAY HARBOR ISLANDS FL
LORI B. BROOKS, SAN FRANCISCO
TOM JAYCOX, REDMOND WA
JACQUES LEVY, NEW YORK CITY
MARK LUHDORFF, SACRAMENTO CA
GEORGE VENETIS, CHICAGO

Great job! Terrific value! Congratulations.
DYKES CORDELL, AUSTIN TX

Super book!
KELLY J. ALIG, EVANSVILLE IN
RICHARD MATHERS, LIVERMORE CA

Very good!
RICHARD M. GILLESPIE, ANAHEIM CA
L.P. HARDING, SANTA CLARA CA
C.G. MILLINGER, STOCKHOLM, SWEDEN
MICHEAL SEBALLOZ, HASTINGS NB
CHARLES EDWARD YOST, REPUBLIC WA

Very, very, very, very, very, very, very, very, very, very good!
DAVID BIANCO, ST. LOUIS

The best!
JOHN FONG, SAN FRANCISCO
MARK A. KATONA, COLUMBUS OH
KEVIN KINE, SIOUX FALLS SD
JANET LEVY, INDIANAPOLIS
CHRISTOPHER C. MASTEN, MONROVIA CA
KATHY PARKER, TOLEDO OH

Very helpful!
SUE FISCALINI, SAN LUIS OBISPO CA
MARILYN JENAI, SARASOTA FL
KAREN LOVINS, BALTIMORE MD
PHILIP PETTY, VISALIA CA
J.P. SAHEURS, ONTARIO, CANADA
KAREN ROUNDS, GRANDVIEW WA

Very useful!
ALLAN CUMMING, DUNEDIN, NEW ZEALAND
GEORGE W. DERUM, PACIFICA CA
M.H. MCCONEGHY, PROVIDENCE RI
BRUCE RYNDFLEISZ, LONG BEACH CA

Extremely helpful!
JOE BAUER, GRAND RAPIDS MI
JUDI JONES. TAMPA FL
BILL SHANAHAN, BLOOMINGDALE IL

Tremendously useful!
JOHN SAITO, HONOLULU

Great!

MITCHELL AIDELBAUM, ATHENS OH
EDWARD AMBINDER, M.D., NEW YORK CITY
COL. S.E. ARMISTEAD, FORT KNOX KY
RICHARD S. ARNOLD, STUDIO CITY CA
RICHARD D. BENNETT, PHOENIX
BOB BERRY, VAN NUYS CA
JERRY BLAIR, WALNUT CREEK CA
GAUDENZ BON, AARAU, SWITZERLAND
DAVID J. BROWN, KNOXVILLE TN
DIANE S. BRUCE, CUT OFF LA
NANCY BRUNSON, BLUE LAKE CA
MIMI CHAN, GLENVIEW IL
LAUREN E. CHEDA, REDDING CA
DOUGLAS R. CHEZEM, FAIRFAX VA
NARES CHOOBUA, WEST LOS ANGELES
JOE COHEN, SANTA FE NM
WAYNE COOLEY, VENTURA CA
JACK COREY, SANTA CLARA CA
KRIS. A. CUELLO, SIERRA VISTA AZ
JACK CUTTER, ORINDA CA
DAVID M. DELOACH, HONOLULU HI
NICHOLAS DEPAUL, PALO ALTO CA
P.H. DEWEY, GOODYEAR AZ
MARTIN D. DILL, PORTLAND OR
STEPHEN S. DILTS, SAN FRANCISO
DAVID L. DODD, HOUSTON
PETER R. DUFFY, VICTORIA, AUSTRALIA
JAMES M. EARLY, PALO ALTO CA
CHRIS R. EATON, SAN JOSE CA
MICHAEL A. EFFINGER, UPPER DARBY PA
PETER H. ELLZEY, SANTA FE NM
MARTHA J. ERDMANN, FARGO ND
RON C. ESTLER, DURANGO CO
DAVE FELL, CHICAGO
DR. EDWARD BERNARD GLICK, BROOMALL PA
ELAINE GOLDSTEIN, NEW ORLEANS
LARRY GOTTLIEB, WALNUT CREEK CA
MIKE GREER, CULVER CITY CA
KATHERINE A. GRIFFING, SOUTH NORWALK CT
E.J. GROTH, SCOTTSDALE AZ
NEALE HALL, QUEENSLAND, AUSTRALIA
DEAN HEINBUCH, OKOLONA MS
LORETTA HARRISON, CORVALLIS OR

JEFFREY HERMAN, CUPERTINO CA
MERRILL F. HIGHAM, BELMONT CA
KEITH HOLZMAN, LOS ANGELES
ALLEN S. HORWITZ, CANOGA PARK CA
DEBRA A. JARVENSIVU, ONTARIO, CANADA
RAYMOND JONES, BERKELEY CA
WADE T. JORDAN, M.D., CORSICANA TX
MARY ELLEN KELLY, POCATELLO ID
WALTER M. KELTING JR., SCOTTSDALE AZ
DOROTHY KETTNER, FERGUS FALLS MN
MICHAEL R. KRAINAS, EVERGREEN PARK IL
MORT LANKASKY, SAN LORENZO CA
SHELTON LANKFORD, HOLLIS NH
RICHARD S. LEE, OAKLAND CA
MARIANNE LINS, SAN DIEGO
DANIEL LYNE, NANTUCKET MA
JASPER L. MATHIS, ACTON MA
NEIL M. MCBRIDE, SAN JOSE CA
ZACHARY MILLER, SANTA BARBARA CA
JOHN MURPHY, WOODLAND HILLS CA
MARTHA OELMAN, CHICAGO
LESLIE R. PEAKE, MILWAUKIE OR
CLARE A. POE, FAIR OAKS CA
JEFFREY RENS, LA JOLLA CA
ELAINE ROSENBERG, RADNOR PA
RUDY SCHOLLÉE, TORRANCE CA
DAVID S. SECREST, REDWOOD CITY CA
KURT E. SEEL, ALBERTA, CANADA
ROBERT C. SHEPARDSON, SANTA CRUZ CA
JOAN SHERMAN, CRANBURY NJ
LARRY SILBER, NEW YORK CITY
STEVEN SILVER, SOUTHFIELD MI
RONALD SNEIDER, RANCHO MIRAGE CA
WILLIAM P. SORENSEN, GRAND TERRACE CA
GLEN SPENCE, SAN FRANCISCO
PRISCILLA TREACY, BOSTON
BURTON E. VAUGHAN, RICHLAND WA
DR. M. HILDEGARD WALTER, INNSBRUCK, AUSTRIA
LARRY WELLS, KENNEWICK WA
BRAD WEST, EL SOBRANTE CA
J. LARRY YARBOROUGH, FRANKLIN TN

Assolutamente indispensabile!
GIANCARLO GENTILE, GREAT NECK NY

Incredibly valuable!
HISASHI IZUMI, SOMERVILLE MA

Excellent!
J. ALBRECHT, MINNETONKA MN
DAVID K. ANDERSON, MONTROSE CA
KATHERINE E. BELMER, GRANITE CITY IL
SUGIMAN BINSAR, SAN FRANCISCO
ANDREAS BURNIER, SAN FRANCISCO
DAVID J. FISHMAN, NEW YORK CITY
JAMES A. FLYNN, FOND DU LAC WI
VALMORE FOURNIER, SOMERSWORTH NH
GARY L. GALEK, ROCK HILL SC
J.F. HILL, GARDEN GROVE CA
GEORGE GILDAY, AUKLAND, NEW ZEALAND
SCOTT I. HENDRICKSON, SAN DIEGO
BILL HUCKABEE, DELAWARE OH
THOMAS W. JOHNSON, CHICO CA
H. E. JONES, TUCSON AZ
MICHAEL J. KAUFMAN, VALDESE NC
HERB KLINE, MCLEAN VA
ROBERT R. REH, ALTO LOMA CA
KENT J. SHEETS, ANN ARBOR
SUZANNE SLADE, SAN FRANCISCO
DAVID STENZ, DATIL NM
HANK SZERLAG, GROSSE POINTE WOODS MI
LEO W. TAYLOR, SAN ANTONIO
PAUL S. TRUESDELL, GLENDALE AZ
ROBERT VALE, LAS VEGAS
DAVE VAUGHAN, MÜNCHEN, W.GERMANY
PATRICA A. WAITE, WESTCHESTER IL
RICHARD E. WASSERMAN, SCARSDALE NY
STEPHEN R. YOUNG, BELLINGHAM WA

Outstanding!
THOMAS E. HOEG, CANTON MI
JULES LAVNER, UPPER MONTCLAIR NJ

Fabulous!
FREDERIC SWAN, OCEANSIDE CA

Superb!
DR. IRENE M. SKULAS, TOLEDO OH
ROBERT S. RICHMOND, ASHEVILLE NC

Wonderful!

BILL ARNONE, SANTA ROSA CA
FRED BENEDETTI, SAN DIEGO
LINDA M. BUIVID, REVERE MA
LISA ANNE NEIL, TROY NY
GENE M. SCHAEFFER, PHOENIX
PAM SALATICH, CINCINNATI

Fantastic!

JOHN DIAL, HOUSTON TX
MARK J. GUERETTE, WALNUT CREEK CA
MICHAEL LAMBERT, EULESS TX
IRIS M. SCHMIDT, OROFINO ID

Marvelous!

J.H. CHANG, NEWTOWN SQUARE PA
FRANCISCO PICART, PONCE PR

Invaluable!

HOWARD I. ARONSON, CHICAGO
MARK HASKELL, OAK PARK MI

Terrific!

LEE C. BALLANCE, BERKELEY
JAMES D. BAZIN, SUDBURY MA
CHRIS BOYCE, LOS ANGELES
MARGE DELNY, MIDLAND TX
DEE ANN ESPITIA, S. SAN GABRIEL CA
IRIS ETZ, SAN ANTONIO
KATHRINE L.V. ROBINSON, SAN FRANCISCO
DAVID N. SHERRELL, FOUNTAIN VALLEY CA
JAMES R. SOLOMON, HAYWARD CA

Almost as good as sex.

ANTHONY TUSLER, ROHNERT PARK, CA

As good as sex.

MARK F. JOSEFF, NEWPORT BEACH CA

Better than sex.

RUTH LEVITSKY, QUINCY MA

Perhaps it will replace sex (I said, "perhaps").

FRED G. GARDNER, PITTSFIELD MA

Macintosh® Bible products

 The Mac Bible, Third Edition. It's the best-selling Mac book ever, with 591,000 copies in print (including six foreign translations). The Third Edition has **1,115 pages**, with a 90-page index and a 68-page glossary. At 2½¢ a page for the best—and most clearly written—Mac information available, how can you go wrong? **$28.**

 The Mac Bible Guide to FileMaker Pro. "A must for every FileMaker Pro user," as Dennis Marshall, Claris's FileMaker Pro product manager put it, this is the first comprehensive guide to the Mac's leading database program. With dozens of step-by-step procedures, shortcuts and troubleshooting tips, it will save hours of your time. **$18.**

 The Mac Bible Guide to System 7. System 7 represents the most dramatic changes ever made to the Mac's basic system software, and sets the stage for all future system improvements. Our crystal-clear, accessible and affordable guide, by veteran Mac author Charles Rubin, gets you up to speed with System 7 in no time. **$12.**

 The Mac Bible Software Disks, Third Edition. This companion to *The Mac Bible* is full of great public-domain software, shareware, templates, fonts and art. Painstakingly gleaned from literally thousands of programs, these disks offer you *la crème de la crème*. Over 1.5 megabytes of software on two 800K disks. **$20.**

 The Mac Bible "What Do I Do Now?" Book, Second Edition. Completely updated through System 7, this bestseller covers just about every sort of basic problem a Mac user can encounter—from the wrong fonts appearing in a printout to the mouse not responding. Easy to understand, it's an essential resource for beginners and experienced users alike. **$15.**

 The Dead Mac Scrolls. Now any Mac owner—from the novice to the expert—can keep repair costs down. In this unique and encyclopedic guide, Macintosh guru Larry Pina diagnoses hundreds of hardware problems, shows you the simplest and cheapest way to fix them, and tells you how much the repairs should cost. **$32.**

System 7 package. Save $5 when you buy *The Mac Bible* and our *Guide to System 7* together. **$35.**
Bible/software combo. Save $10 when you buy *The Mac Bible* and the *Bible* disks together. **$38.**
Super combo. Save $13 by buying *The Mac Bible*, the *Bible* disks and *"What Do I Do Now?" Book*. **$50.**
Ultra combo. Save $15 by buying *The Mac Bible* with the *Bible* disks, the *"What Do I Do Now?" Book* and the *Guide to System 7*. **$60.**

 The Macintosh Bible T-shirt. Our T-shirts are striking—bright magenta lettering on your choice of black or white. Here's a little picture of the front. The back says: **Easy is hard** *(The second commandment from The Macintosh Bible)*. These are high-quality, preshrunk, 100% cotton shirts; they're thick, well-made and run large. **$9.**

To order any of these products, just fill out the form on the next page and send it with your payment to **Goldstein & Blair, Box 7635, Berkeley CA 94707.** You can also order by phone with Visa or MasterCard. Call us at 510/524-4000 between 10 and 5, Pacific Time, Mon–Fri (or leave your phone number on our answering machine). If you order three or more products (except the T-shirts), we'll give you the same quantity deal as the stores we sell to—call for details.

All our products have a 30-day money-back guarantee. If you're not *completely satisfied*, just return your order within 30 days, with your receipt, in resellable condition (i.e. not damaged) and get all your money back, including what we charged to ship your order and what you spent to return it (by UPS ground or parcel post).

Order form for Macintosh® Bible products

Please send me:

_____ copies of *The Macintosh Bible, 3 ed.*	@ $28 =	$_____
_____ copies of *The Macintosh Bible Guide to FileMaker Pro*	@ $18 =	$_____
_____ copies of *The Macintosh Bible Guide to System 7*	@ $12 =	$_____
_____ copies of *The Macintosh Bible Software Disks, 3 ed.*	@ $20 =	$_____
_____ copies of *The Macintosh Bible "What Do I Do Now?" Book, 2 ed.*	@ $15 =	$_____
_____ copies of *The Dead Mac Scrolls*	@ $32 =	$_____
_____ copies of the System 7 package	@ $35 =	$_____
_____ copies of the *Bible*/software combination	@ $38 =	$_____
_____ copies of the super combo	@ $50 =	$_____
_____ copies of the ultra combo	@ $60 =	$_____
_____ *Macintosh Bible* T-shirts	@ $ 9 =	$_____

(in black:___S ___M ___L ___XL; in white:___S ___M ___L ___XL)

shipping, handling and tax (if any): $_____
[$4 total per order in the US; see following page for other rates]

TOTAL: $_____

☐ I'm enclosing a check for the total shown above. *(Customers outside the US: checks must be in US funds and payable through a US bank. You can also pay with an international postal money order, but not a Eurocheque. It's easiest if you pay by credit card.)*

☐ Please charge my charge card for the total amount shown above:

VISA/MasterCard # _____ exp. date _____

cardholder signature _____

Ship this order to: *(PLEASE PRINT CLEARLY)*

_____

name

_____

address (please give us a street address so we can ship via UPS)

_____

city, state, zip (or city, postal code, country)

_____

daytime phone number (with area code)

Enclose this order form with your payment in an envelope and send it to:
Goldstein & Blair, Box 7635, Berkeley CA 94707
Thanks.

MB3

Shipping Information

Anywhere in the US:

Shipping and handling costs $4 for up to three items, and that includes tax (if any). Each combo counts as one item. If you're buying three or more of our products, call us at 510/524-4000 to get shipping costs and find out about our quantity discounts.

Outside the US:

These prices cover *airmail* to Canada and Mexico and *surface* to everywhere else. (Surface and air rates to Canada and Mexico are nearly identical, so we automatically ship by air.)

$7 per copy of *The Macintosh Bible* or *Dead Mac Scolls;* $3 per set of software disks or the T-shirt (T-shirts are shipped free when ordered with other products); $5 per copy of the *Guide to FileMaker Pro* or *Guide to System 7;* $6 per *The "What Do I Do Now?" Book;* $10 per System 7 package, *Bible/*software or super combo; $12 per ultra combo.

International airmail shipping rates

These rates apply *only* to products shipped by *airmail* to countries *other than* the US, Canada & Mexico.

Colombia, Venezuela, Central America and the Caribbean:

$11 per *Macintosh Bible;* $5 per *Guide to System 7,* software disks or T-shirt; $7 per *Guide to FileMaker Pro* or *"What Do I Do Now?" Book;* $9 per *Dead Mac Scrolls;* $15 per System 7 package, *Bible/*software or super combo; $18 per ultra combo.

South America (except Colombia & Venezuela), Europe (except the USSR), Morocco, Algeria, Libya, Egypt & Tunisia:

$18 per *Macintosh Bible;* $6 per software disks or T-shirt; $8 per *Guide to System 7;* $12 per *"What Do I Do Now?" Book;* $10 per *Guide to FileMaker Pro;* $15 per *Dead Mac Scrolls;* $23 per System 7 package or *Bible/*software combo; $25 per super combo; $30 per ultra combo.

Everywhere else:

$24 per *Macintosh Bible;* $8 per software disks or T-shirt; $11 per *Guide to System 7;* $16 per *"What Do I Do Now?" Book;* $13 per *Guide to FileMaker Pro;* $20 per *Dead Mac Scrolls;* $31 per System 7 package or *Bible/*software combo; $35 per super combo; $42 per ultra combo.

Contains almost everything you've wanted to know about the Mac but didn't know who to ask.

[A] well-written...value-packed storehouse of information on the Mac and everything associated with it.

The equivalent of many user group meetings in one handy, straightforward book....Although it's designed as a reference book, I found myself reading whole sections of tips at a time.

An indispensable tool for those who want to get the most from their Mac.

The primary source of tips and tricks for Macintosh users. It's filled with little user shortcuts...the Mac manual never tells you about.

I can recommend The Macintosh Bible. [It] has everything from the basics to the most advanced.

Has almost everything I would want to tell a new user about the Mac, organized in a logical and easy-to-read format. I have recommended this book for years now.

For readers' comments, see pages 1108–1115.
For reviews, see the back cover and the front and back of the book.

IF YOU'RE LOOKING FOR THE ORDER FORM, TURN BACK THREE PAGES.

A great tool for all levels of Macintosh users. Humorous and well-illustrated.   Karen L. Duda, Core Talk

Biblical in proportion. Contains a wealth of information.   John Barry, Computer Currents

The Farmer's Almanac of Macintosh computing. One book that isn't going to gather dust on your bookshelf.

This gem is jam-packed with thousands of tips, tricks and shortcuts. Just about any Mac user will get his or her money's worth.   David Angell & Brent Heslop, Computer Currents

The Swiss Army knife of computer books. A definitive work. Extremely readable and even fun.

Written for Mac users on all levels. I recommend The Macintosh Bible to all.   Howard Greenstein, The Mac Street Journal

I quite frankly don't know how I've worked with my Mac all these years without having The Macintosh Bible sitting right next to me.

Each page is loaded with at least one or two gems of real help. This is one volume that no one—but no one—can take out of my home.   Max Rogel, Palm Beach MacBytes

No Mac user should be without this easy-to-use, comprehensive survey.   The Midwest Book Review

For readers' comments, see pages 1108–1115.
For reviews, see the back cover and the front and back of the book.